Readings in the Rise of Industrial America, 1865-1900

Leon Fink | Eileen Boris | Nelson Lichtenstein
Paul S. Boyer | Clifford E. Clark, Jr. | Karen Halttunen
Joseph F. Kett| Neal Salisbury | Harvard Sitkoff | Nancy Woloch
Regina Lee Blaszczyk | Philip B. Scranton

D1224124

CENGAGE
Learning·

Australia • Brazil • Japan • Korea • Mexico • Singapore • Spain • United Kingdom • United States

Readings in the Rise of Industrial America, 1865-1900

Senior Manager, Student Engagement:
Linda deStefano

Manager, Student Engagement:
Julie Dierig

Marketing Manager:
Rachael Kloos

Manager, Premedia:
Kim Fry

Manager, Intellectual Property Project Manager:
Brian Methe

Senior Manager, Production:
Donna M. Brown

Manager, Production:
Terri Daley

The Enduring Vision: A History of the American People, Volume II: Since 1865, 8th Edition
Paul S. Boyer | Clifford E. Clark, Jr. | Karen Halttunen | Joseph F. Kett Neal Salisbury | Harvard Sitkoff | Nancy Woloch

© 2014, 2011, 2008, 2004 Cengage Learning. All rights reserved.

Major Problems in the Gilded Age and the Progressive Era, 2nd Edition
Leon Fink

© 2001, 1993 Cengage Learning. All rights reserved.

Major Problems in the History of American Workers: Documents and Essays, 2nd Edition
Eileen Boris | Nelson Lichtenstein

© 2003, 1991 Cengage Learning. All rights reserved.

Major Problems in American Business History: Documents and Essays, 1st Edition
Regina Lee Blaszczyk | Philip B. Scranton

© 2006 Cengage Learning. All rights reserved.

For product information and technology assistance, contact us at
Cengage Learning Customer & Sales Support, 1-800-354-9706

For permission to use material from this text or product,
submit all requests online at **cengage.com/permissions**
Further permissions questions can be emailed to
permissionrequest@cengage.com

This book contains select works from existing Cengage Learning resources and was produced by Cengage Learning Custom Solutions for collegiate use. As such, those adopting and/or contributing to this work are responsible for editorial content accuracy, continuity and completeness.

Compilation © 2014 Cengage Learning

ISBN: 978-1-305-31131-2

WCN: 01-100-101

Cengage Learning
20 Channel Center Street
Boston, MA 02210
USA

Cengage Learning is a leading provider of customized learning solutions with office locations around the globe, including Singapore, the United Kingdom, Australia, Mexico, Brazil, and Japan. Locate your local office at:
international.cengage.com/region.

Cengage Learning products are represented in Canada by Nelson Education, Ltd.
For your lifelong learning solutions, visit **www.cengage.com/custom.**
Visit our corporate website at **www.cengage.com.**

The Rise of Industrial America, 1865–1900

This text has been constructed by bringing together materials from several different texts; their Table of Contents have been included here so that you can see the page numbers to use in your citations. As you will see in your syllabus and weekly assignments folders, the materials herein are divided into 1) your weekly assigned reading and 2) within each week, the primary ("documents") and secondary ("essays") sources you are expected to use in each weekly essay after week one. The first item in this volume is a chapter from a survey text that covers the general period under study in this course; it was included here as a reference for you.

EIGHTH EDITION

THE ENDURING VISION

A History of the American People

Paul S. Boyer
University of Wisconsin

Clifford E. Clark, Jr.
Carleton College

Karen Halttunen
University of Southern California

Joseph F. Kett
University of Virginia

Neal Salisbury
Smith College

Harvard Sitkoff
University of New Hampshire

Nancy Woloch
Barnard College

CENGAGE
Learning

Australia • Brazil • Japan • Korea • Mexico • Singapore • Spain • United Kingdom • United States

BRIEF CONTENTS

CONTENTS

Major Problems in the History of American Workers

DOCUMENTS AND ESSAYS

SECOND EDITION

EDITED BY

EILEEN BORIS

UNIVERSITY OF CALIFORNIA, SANTA BARBARA

NELSON LICHTENSTEIN

UNIVERSITY OF CALIFORNIA, SANTA BARBARA

Australia • Brazil • Japan • Korea • Mexico • Singapore • Spain • United Kingdom • United States

Contents

CHAPTER 4
Slavery and the Transition to Free Labor
Page 90

CHAPTER 5
The Age of Industrial Conflict
Page 124

CHAPTER 8
Labor in the Progressive Era
Page 248

Major Problems in American Business History

DOCUMENTS AND ESSAYS

EDITED BY

REGINA LEE BLASZCZYK

UNIVERSITY OF PENNSYLVANIA

PHILIP B. SCRANTON

RUTGERS UNIVERSITY

Contents

CHAPTER 6
Inventing American Industry, 1810–1890

CHAPTER 7

Technology in the Age of Big Business, 1870–1920

Page 208

CHAPTER 8

The Age of the Octopus: Business and the Reform Impulse, 1876–1920

Page 240

CHAPTER 9
The Many Faces of Entrepreneurship, 1840–1930
Page 272

Major Problems in the Gilded Age and the Progressive Era

DOCUMENTS AND ESSAYS

SECOND EDITION

EDITED BY

LEON FINK

UNIVERSITY OF ILLINOIS AT CHICAGO

CENGAGE
Learning·

Australia • Brazil • Japan • Korea • Mexico • Singapore • Spain • United Kingdom • United States

Contents

CHAPTER 8
Professionalism and the Uses of New Knowledge
Page 225

1

8

ISABELLE GARLAND, 1880 *(University of Southern California Libraries)*

ON OCTOBER 21, 1892, before an enormous crowd of onlookers, presidential candidate Grover Cleveland proudly opened the World's Columbian Exposition in Chicago. Grasping a small electric key connected to a two-thousand-horsepower engine, he proclaimed, "As by a touch the machinery that gives life to this vast Exposition is now set in motion, so in the same instant let our hopes and aspirations awaken forces which in all time to come shall influence the welfare, the dignity, and the freedom of mankind." A moment later, electric fountains shot streams of water high into the air, officially marking the exposition's start.

The Chicago world's fair represented the triumph of fifty years of industrial development. The country's largest corporations displayed their newest products: Westinghouse Company's dynamos mysteriously lit a tower of incandescent light bulbs; American Bell Telephone offered the first long-distance telephone calls to the East Coast; and inventor Thomas A. Edison exhibited his latest phonograph. The fair dazzled its more than 25 million visitors. But Isabelle Garland, mother of writer Hamlin Garland, who visited the fair from a small midwestern farm community, was simply stunned. "[M]y mother sat in her chair, visioning it all yet comprehending little of its meaning," Garland later observed. "Her life had been spent among homely small things, and these gorgeous scenes dazzled her, ... letting in upon her in one mighty flood a thousand stupefying suggestions of art and history and poetry of the world. ... At last utterly overcome, she leaned her head against my arm, closed her eyes and said, 'Take me home, I can't stand any more of it.'"

Isabelle Garland's emotional reaction captured the ambivalence of many late-nineteenth-century Americans who found themselves both unsettled and exhilarated as the nation was transformed by industrialization. At midcentury, the United States had played a minor role in the world economy. Five decades later, innovations in management, technology, production, and transportation, together with the settlement of the trans-Mississippi West and the exploitation of its natural resources, had expanded manufacturing output fivefold. The United States now produced 35 percent of the world's manufactured goods—more than England, Germany, and France combined. It had become one of the world's greatest industrial powers.

Driving this prodigious growth was the rise of giant corporations that mass-produced oil, steel, and a variety of consumer products. Business leaders and inventors

COURT OF HONOR, WORLD'S COLUMBIAN EXPOSITION, 1893 The Chicago World's Fair was seen as "the most significant and grandest spectacle of modern times." The monumental neoclassical buildings announced that the United States, like Greece and Rome before it, had become one of the world's most powerful economies. *(Granger Collection)*

> "The sufferings of the working classes are daily increasing, Famine has broken into the home of many of us, and is at the door of all."

in countless small industries also introduced new technologies and innovative advertising campaigns to swell production and increase sales. By 1900, new enterprises both large and small, supported by investment bankers and using a nationwide railroad distribution system, offered a vast array of goods for national and international markets.

This stunning industrial growth came at a high cost. New manufacturing processes transformed the nature of work, undercut skilled labor, and created mind-numbing, assembly-line routines. Large-scale manufacturing companies often polluted the environment, spewing noxious smoke into the air and dumping toxic waste into nearby rivers. The challenges of new business practices made the American economy difficult to control. Rather than smoothly rolling forward, it lurched between booms and busts in business cycles that produced labor unrest and crippling depressions in 1873–1879 and 1893–1897.

FOCUS Questions

- What innovations in technology and business drove increases in industrial production after 1865, and what was their social and environmental impact?
- How did Carnegie, Rockefeller, and other corporate leaders consolidate control over their industries?
- Why did the South's experience with industrialization differ from that of the North and the Midwest?
- How did the changing nature of work affect factory workers' lives, and how did they respond?
- How did corporations undercut labor's bargaining power in the 1890s?

The Rise of Corporate America

In the early nineteenth century, the corporate form of business organization had been used to raise large amounts of start-up capital for transportation enterprises such as turnpikes and canals. By selling stocks and bonds to raise money, the corporation separated the company's managers, who guided its day-to-day operation, from its owners. After the Civil War, American business leaders pioneered new forms of corporate organization that combined innovative technologies, creative management structures, and limited liability should the enterprise fail. The rise of the giant corporation is a story of risk-taking and innovation as well as of conspiracy and corruption.

The Character of Industrial Change

Six features dominated the world of large-scale manufacturing after the Civil War: (1) the exploitation of immense coal deposits as a source of cheap energy; (2) the rapid spread of technological innovation in transportation, communication, and factory systems; (3) the demand for workers who could be driven and controlled; (4) the constant pressure on firms to compete tooth-and-nail by cutting costs, eliminating rivals, and creating monopolies; (5) the relentless drop in prices (a stark contrast to the inflation of other eras); and (6) the failure of the money supply to keep pace with productivity, a development that drove up interest rates and restricted the availability of credit.

All six factors were closely related. The great coal deposits in Pennsylvania, West Virginia, and Kentucky provided cheap energy to fuel railroad and factory growth. New technologies stimulated productivity and catalyzed breathtaking industrial expansion. Technological innovation enabled manufacturers to cut costs and hire unskilled labor. Cost cutting enabled firms to undersell one another, destroy weaker competitors, and consolidate themselves into more efficient and more ruthless firms. At least until the mid-1890s, cheap energy, immigrant labor, new technology, and fierce competition forced down overall price levels.

But almost everyone struggled terribly during the depression years, when the government did nothing to relieve distress. "The sufferings of the working classes are daily increasing," wrote a Philadelphia worker in 1874. "Famine has broken into the home of many of us, and is at the door of all." Above all, business leaders' unflagging drive to reduce costs both created colossal fortunes at the top of the economic ladder and forced millions of wage earners to live near the subsistence level.

Out of the new industrial system poured clouds of haze and soot, as well as the first tantalizing trickle of what would become an avalanche of consumer goods. In turn, mounting demands for consumer

CHRONOLOGY 1865–1900

1859	First oil well drilled in Titusville, Pennsylvania.
1866	National Labor Union founded.
1869	Transcontinental railroad completed.
	Knights of Labor organized.
1870	John D. Rockefeller establishes Standard Oil Company.
1873	Panic of 1873 triggers a depression lasting until 1879.
1876	Alexander Graham Bell patents the telephone.
1877	Edison invents phonograph.
	Railway workers stage first nationwide strike.
1879	Henry George, *Progress and Poverty*.
	Edison perfects incandescent lamp.
1882	Standard Oil Trust established.
	Edison opens first electric power station in New York City.
	Chinese Exclusion Act.
1883	William Graham Sumner, *What Social Classes Owe to Each Other*.
	Lester Frank Ward, *Dynamic Sociology*.

1886	American Federation of Labor (AFL) formed.
	Haymarket riot in Chicago.
1887	Interstate Commerce Act establishes Interstate Commerce Commission.
1888	Edward Bellamy, *Looking Backward*.
1889	Andrew Carnegie, "The Gospel of Wealth."
1890	Sherman Anti-Trust Act.
	United Mine Workers formed.
1892	Standard Oil of New Jersey and General Electric formed.
	Homestead Strike.
	Columbian Exposition in Chicago.
	Miners strike at Coeur d'Alene, Idaho.
1893	Panic of 1893 triggers a depression lasting until 1897.
1894	Pullman Palace Car workers strike.
1901	J. Pierpont Morgan organizes United States Steel.

goods stimulated heavy industry's production of capital goods—machines to boost farm and factory output even further. Together with the railroads, the corporations that manufactured capital goods, refined petroleum, and made steel became driving forces in the nation's economic growth (see Figure 18.1).

Railroad Innovations

Competition among the capitalists who headed American heavy industry was most intense among the nation's railroads. By 1900, 193,000 miles of railroad track crisscrossed the United States—more than in all of Europe including Russia. Taking

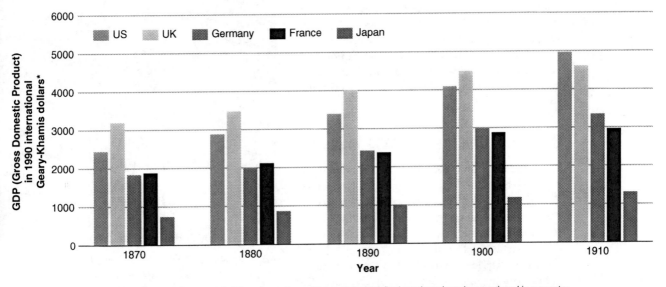

* 1990 international Geary-Khamis dollars represent the monetary values of the output of the final goods and services produced in a country in one year converted into 1990 dollars at the exchange rate which would pertain if the goods and services had the same prices in all countries (purchasing power parity). See the statistical definition at the UN site: http://unstats.un.org/unsd/methods/icp/ipc7_htm.htm.

FIGURE 18.1 LATE NINETEENTH-CENTURY ECONOMIC GROWTH IN GLOBAL PERSPECTIVE © Cengage Learning. All rights reserved. No distribution allowed without express authorization.

advantage of enormous government land subsidies, these rail lines connected every state in the Union, opened up an immense new internal market, and pioneered new forms of large-scale corporate enterprise. They created national distribution systems, and perfected new management structures.

Railroad entrepreneurs such as Collis P. Huntington of the Central Pacific Railroad, **Jay Gould** of the Union Pacific, and James J. Hill of the Northern Pacific faced enormous financial and organizational problems. To raise the staggering sums necessary for laying track and building engines, railroads obtained generous land and loan subsidies from federal, state, and local governments (see Chapter 17). At the same time, they borrowed heavily by selling stocks and bonds to the public. Bond holders earned a fixed rate of interest; stockholders received dividends only when the company earned a profit. By 1900, the yearly interest repayments required by the combined debt of all U.S. railroads (which stood at an astounding $5.1 billion—nearly five times that of the federal government) cut heavily into their earnings.

In addition to raising substantial capital, the railroads created new systems for collecting and using information. To coordinate the complex flow of cars across the country, they relied on the magnetic telegraph, invented in 1837. To improve efficiency, they set up clearly defined, hierarchical organizational structures and divided their lines into separate divisions, each with its own superintendent. Elaborate accounting systems documented the cost of every operation for each division, from coal consumption to the repair of engines and cars. Using these reports, railroad officials could set rates and accurately predict profits as early as the 1860s, a time when most businesses had no idea of their total profit until they closed their books at year's end. Railroad management innovations thus became a model for many other businesses seeking a national market.

Consolidating the Railroad Industry

The expansion and consolidation of railroading reflected both the ingenuity and the dishonesty flourishing on the corporate management scene. Despite their organizational innovations, the industry remained chaotic in the 1870s. Hundreds of small companies used different standards for track width and engine size. Financed by large eastern and British banks, Huntington, Gould, and others devoured these smaller lines to create large, integrated track networks. In the Northeast, four major trunk lines were completed. West of the Mississippi, five great companies controlled most of the track by 1893.

Huntington, Gould, and the other corporate leaders who reorganized and expanded the railroad industry in the 1870s and 1880s often were depicted by their contemporaries as villains and robber barons who manipulated stock markets to line their own pockets. Newspaper publisher Joseph Pulitzer called Jay Gould, the short, secretive president of the Union Pacific, "one of the most sinister figures that have ever flitted batlike across the vision of the American people." Historians agree that many were indeed corrupt pirates, but note that others were shrewd innovators. Indeed, some of their ideas were startling in their originality and inventiveness.

ABUSIVE MONOPOLY POWER This *Puck* cartoon depicts financiers Jay Gould (left) and Cornelius Vanderbilt (right) and suggests that their manipulation of markets and their ownership of railroads, telegraph companies, and newspapers is powerful enough to strangle Uncle Sam. (*Frank Wood Historical Collections*)

The massive railroad systems created by these entrepreneurs became the largest business enterprises in the world. As they consolidated small railroads into a few interlocking systems, these masterminds standardized all basic equipment and facilities, from engines and cars to automatic couplers, air brakes, and signal systems. In 1883, independently of the federal government, the railroads corrected scheduling problems by dividing the country into four time zones (see Map 17.3). In May 1886, all railroads shifted simultaneously to the new standard 4'8½" gauge track. Finally, cooperative billing arrangements enabled the railroads to ship cars from other roads at uniform rates nationwide.

But the systemization and consolidation of the railroads had its costs. Heavy indebtedness, overextended systems, and crooked business practices forced the railroads to compete recklessly with each other for traffic. They cut rates for large shippers, showered free passes on politicians, and granted substantial rebates and kickbacks to favored clients while ignoring worker safety. None of these tactics, however, shored up the railroads' precarious financial position. Ruthless competition and fraudulent business practices drove some overbuilt lines into bankruptcy.

Stung by exorbitant rates and secret kickbacks, farmers and small business owners turned to state governments for help. In the 1870s, midwestern state legislatures responded by outlawing rate discrimination. Initially upheld by the Supreme Court, these and other decisions were negated in the 1880s when the Court ruled that states could not regulate interstate commerce. In response in 1887, Congress passed the **Interstate Commerce Act.** A five-member Interstate Commerce Commission (ICC) was established to oversee the practices of interstate railroads. The law banned monopolistic activity like pooling, rebates, and discriminatory short-distance rates.

The railroads challenged the commission's rulings in the federal courts. Of the sixteen cases brought to the Supreme Court before 1905, the justices found in favor of the railroads in all but one, essentially nullifying the ICC's regulatory clout. The Hepburn Act (covered in Chapter 21), passed in 1906, strengthened the ICC by finally empowering it to set rates.

The railroads' vicious competition weakened in 1893 when a national depression forced a number of roads into the hands of **J. Pierpont Morgan** and other investment bankers. Morgan, a massively built man with piercing eyes and a commanding presence, took over the weakened systems, reorganized their administration, refinanced their debts, and built intersystem alliances. By 1906, under the bankers' centralized management, seven giant networks controlled two-thirds of the nation's rail mileage.

Applying the Lessons of the Railroads to Steel

The close connections between railroad expansion, which absorbed millions of tons of steel for tracks, and the growth of corporate organization and management are well illustrated in the career of **Andrew Carnegie.** Born in Scotland, Carnegie immigrated to America in 1848 at the age of twelve. His first job as a bobbin boy in a Pittsburgh textile mill paid only $1.20 a week. The following year, Carnegie became a Western Union messenger boy. Taking over when the telegraph operators wanted a break, he soon became the city's fastest telegraph operator and gained an insider's view of the operations of every major Pittsburgh business.

Carnegie's big break came in 1852 when Tom Scott, superintendent of the Pennsylvania Railroad's western division, hired him as his secretary and personal telegrapher. Later promoted to division chief, Carnegie cut costs while more than doubling the road's mileage. Having invested his earnings in the railroads, by 1868 Carnegie was earning more than $56,000 a year from his investments, a substantial fortune in that era.

In the early 1870s, Carnegie built his own steel mill to produce high-grade steel rails using a new technology named after its English inventor, Henry Bessemer, which shot a blast of air through an enormous crucible of molten iron to burn off carbon and impurities. Combining this new technology with the cost-analysis approach learned from his railroad experience, Carnegie became the first steelmaker to know the actual production cost of each ton of steel.

Carnegie's philosophy was deceptively simple: "Watch the costs, and the profits will take care of themselves." Using rigorous cost accounting and limiting wage increases to his workers, he lowered his production costs and prices below those of his competitors. When these tactics did not drive them out of business, he asked for favors from his railroad-president friends and gave "commissions" to railroad purchasing agents to win business.

As output climbed, Carnegie discovered the benefits of **vertical integration,** that is, controlling all aspects of manufacturing from the mining and smelting of ore to the selling of steel rails. Carnegie Steel thus became the classic example of how sophisticated new technology could be combined with innovative management (and brutally low wages) to create a mass-production system

> "So much oil is produced that it is impossible to care for it, and thousands of barrels are running into the creek; the surface of the river is covered with oil for miles."

that could dramatically increase production and slash consumer prices (see Figure 18.2).

The management of daily operations by his close associates left Carnegie free to pursue philanthropic activities. While still in his early thirties, Carnegie donated money to charitable projects. In his lifetime, he gave more than $300 million to libraries, universities, and international-peace causes. By 1900, Carnegie Steel, employing twenty thousand people, had become the world's largest industrial corporation. Carnegie's competitors, worried

about his domination of the market, decided to buy him out. In 1901, J. Pierpont Morgan purchased Carnegie's companies and set up the United States Steel Corporation, the first business capitalized at more than $1 billion. The corporation, made up of two hundred member companies employing 168,000 people, marked a new scale in industrial enterprise.

A systematic self-publicist, Carnegie portrayed his success as the result of self-discipline and hard

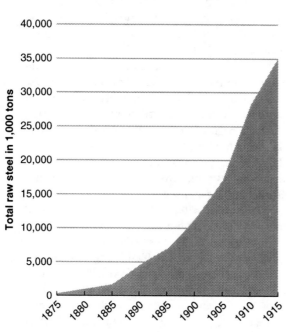

FIGURE 18.2 IRON AND STEEL PRODUCTION, 1875–1915
New technologies, improved plant organization, economies of scale, and the vertical integration of production brought a dramatic spurt in iron and steel production. *Note*: short ton = 2,000 pounds.

Source: *Historical Statistics of the United States*

ANDREW CARNEGIE Although his contemporaries called him "the world's richest man," Andrew Carnegie was careful to deflect criticism by focusing on his philanthropic and educational activities. *(Library of Congress)*

Andrew Carnegie Sums Up the Cost Savings of Vertical Integration

The eighth wonder of the world is this: two pounds of iron-stone purchased on the shores of Lake Superior and transported to Pittsburgh;

two pounds of coal mined in Connellsville and manufactured into coke and brought to Pittsburgh;

one half pound of limestone mined east of the Alleghenies and brought to Pittsburgh;

a little manganese ore,

mined in Virginia and brought to Pittsburgh.

And these four and one half pounds of material manufactured into one pound of solid steel and sold for one cent.

That's all that need be said about the steel business.

Source: *Harold C. Livesay,* Andrew Carnegie and the Rise of Big Business *(Boston: Little, Brown, 1975), 189.*

work. The full story was more complex. Carnegie did not mention his uncanny ability to see the larger picture, his cleverness in hiring talented associates who would drive themselves (and the company's factory workers) mercilessly, his ingenuity in transferring organizational systems and cost accounting methods from railroads to steel, and his callousness in keeping wages as low as possible. To a public unaware of corporate management techniques, however, Carnegie's success gave credence to the idea that anyone might rise from rags to riches.

The Trust: Creating New Forms of Corporate Organization

Between 1870 and 1900, the same fierce competition that had stimulated consolidation in the railroad and steel industries (see Table 18.1) also swept the oil, salt, sugar, tobacco, and meat-packing industries. Like steel, these highly competitive businesses required large capital investments. Entrepreneurs in each industry therefore raced to reduce costs, lower prices, and drive their rivals out of the market.

The evolution of the oil industry illustrates the process by which new corporate structures evolved. After Edwin L. Drake drilled the first successful petroleum (or "crude-oil") well in 1859 near Titusville, Pennsylvania, competitors rushed into the business. Petroleum was distilled into oil, which soon replaced animal tallow as the major lubricant, and into kerosene, which became the leading fuel for household and public lighting.

By the 1870s, the landscape near Pittsburgh and Cleveland, the sites of the first discoveries, was littered with rickety drilling rigs, assorted collection tanks, and ramshackle refineries. Oil spills were a constant problem. "So much oil is produced," reported one Pennsylvania newspaper in 1861, "that it is impossible to care for it, and thousands of barrels are running into the creek; the surface of the river is covered with oil for miles."

TABLE 18.1 Industrial Consolidation: Iron and Steel Firms, 1870 and 1900

	1870	1900
Number of firms	808	669
Number of employees	78,000	272,000
Output (tons)	3,200,000	29,500,000
Capital invested	$121,000,000	$590,000,000

Source: Robert L. Heilbroner and Aaron Singer, *The Economic Transformation of America: 1600 to Present, 2nd ed. (San Diego: Harcourt Brace Jovanovich, 1984), 92.*

In this rush for riches, **John D. Rockefeller,** a young Cleveland merchant, gradually achieved dominance. Like Andrew Carnegie, the solemn Rockefeller had a passion for cost cutting and efficiency. In one case, he insisted a manager find 750 missing barrel stoppers. He realized that in a mass-production enterprise, small changes could save thousands of dollars.

Rockefeller resembled Carnegie, too, in his ability to understand the inner workings of an entire industry and the benefits of vertical integration. The firm that controlled the shipment of oil between the well and the refinery and between the refinery and the retailers, he realized, could dominate the industry. In 1872, he purchased his own tanker cars and obtained not only a 10 percent rebate from the railroads for hauling his oil but also a kickback on his competitors' shipments. When new pipeline technology became available, Rockefeller set up his own massive interregional pipeline network.

Like Carnegie, Rockefeller aggressively forced out his competitors. If local refineries rejected his offers to buy them out, he priced his products below cost and strangled their businesses. When rival firms teamed up against him, Rockefeller set up a pool—an agreement among several companies—that established production quotas and fixed prices. By 1879, Rockefeller had seized control of 90 percent of the country's oil-refining capacity.

In 1882, Rockefeller decided to eliminate competition by establishing a new form of corporate organization, the **Standard Oil Trust.** In place of the "pool" or verbal agreement among companies to control prices and markets, which lacked legal status, the trust created an umbrella corporation that ran them all. To implement his trust, Rockefeller and his associates persuaded the stockholders of forty companies to exchange their stock for trust certificates. Under this arrangement, stockholders retained their share of the trust's profits while enabling the trust to control production. Within three years, the Standard Oil Trust had consolidated crude-oil buying throughout its member firms and slashed the number of refineries in half. In this way, Rockefeller integrated the petroleum industry both vertically, by controlling every function from production to local retailing, and horizontally, by merging the competing oil companies into one giant system.

While Standard Oil justified its trust organization by pointing to the public usefulness of inexpensive heating and cooking fuels, other monopolies did not provide such benefits. James B. "Buck" Duke's American Tobacco trust, for example, targeted youths with trading cards and prizes to persuade them to smoke cigarettes. For addictive products such as cigarettes, targeting children became a means for ensuring continuous use. To gain access to even bigger markets, Duke purchased controlling interests in tobacco companies in England and Japan.

Taking a leaf from Duke and Rockefeller's book, companies in the copper, sugar, whiskey, lead, and other industries established their own trust arrangements. By limiting the number of competitors, the trusts created an *oligopoly*, the market condition that exists when a small number of sellers can greatly influence prices. But their unscrupulous tactics, semimonopolistic control, and sky-high earnings provoked a public outcry. Both major political parties denounced them in the presidential election of 1888.

Fearful that the trusts would stamp out all competition, Congress, under the leadership of Senator John Sherman of Ohio, passed the **Sherman Anti-Trust Act** in 1890. The Sherman Act outlawed trusts and any other monopolies that fixed prices in restraint of trade and slapped violators with fines of up to $5,000 and a year in jail. But the act failed to define clearly either *trust* or *restraint of trade*. The government prosecuted only eighteen antitrust suits between 1890 and 1904. When Standard Oil's structure was challenged in 1892, its lawyers simply reorganized the trust as an enormous holding company. Unlike a trust, which literally owned other businesses, a holding company simply owned a controlling share of the stock of one or more firms. The new board of directors for Standard Oil (New Jersey), the new holding company, made more money than ever.

The Supreme Court further hamstrung congressional antitrust efforts by interpreting the Sherman Act in ways sympathetic to big business. In 1895, for example, the federal government brought suit against the sugar trust in *United States* v. *E.C. Knight Company*, arguing that by controlling more than 90 percent of all U.S. sugar refining, it operated in illegal restraint of trade. Asserting that manufacturing was not interstate commerce and ignoring the company's vast distribution network that enabled it to dominate the market, the Court threw out the suit. Thus vindicated, corporate mergers and consolidations surged ahead at the turn of the century. By 1900, these mammoth firms accounted for nearly two-fifths of the capital invested in the nation's manufacturing sector.

Stimulating Economic Growth

Large-scale corporate enterprise did not alone account for the colossal growth of the U.S. economy in the late nineteenth-century. Other factors proved equally important, including new inventions, specialty production, and innovations in advertising and marketing. In fact, the resourcefulness of small enterprises, which combined innovative technology with new methods of advertising and merchandising, enabled many sectors of the economy to grow dramatically by adapting quickly to changing fashions and consumer preferences.

BASEBALL TRADING CARD To encourage boys and young men to smoke cigarettes, the American Tobacco Company included in the cigarette package collectable cards with pictures of baseball heroes such as Ty Cobb. *(Library of Congress)*

The Triumph of Technology

New inventions not only streamlined the manufacture of traditional products but also stimulated consumer demand by creating entirely new product lines. The development of a safe, practical way to generate electricity, for example, made possible a vast number of electrical motors, household appliances, and lighting systems.

Many of the major inventions that stimulated industrial output and underlay mass production in these years were largely hidden from public view. Few Americans had heard of the improved technologies that facilitated bottle making and glassmaking, canning, flour milling, match production, and petroleum refining. Fewer still knew much about the refrigerated railcars that enabled Gustavus Swift's company to slaughter beef in Chicago and ship it east.

The inventions people did see were the ones that changed the patterns of everyday life: the sewing machine, mass-produced by the Singer Sewing Machine Company beginning in the 1860s; the telephone, developed by Alexander Graham Bell in 1876; and the light bulb, perfected by **Thomas A. Edison** in 1879.

These new inventions eased household drudgery and reshaped social interactions. The sewing machine, which relieved the tedium of sewing apparel by hand, expanded personal wardrobes. The spread of telephones—by 1900, the Bell Telephone Company had installed almost eight hundred thousand in the United States—not only transformed communication but also undermined social conventions for polite behavior that had been premised on face-to-face or written exchanges. The light bulb, by freeing people from dependence on daylight, made it possible to shop after work.

In the eyes of many, Thomas A. Edison epitomized the inventive impulse and the capacity for creating new consumer products. Born in 1847 in Milan, Ohio, Edison, like Andrew Carnegie, had little formal education and worked in the telegraphic industry. A born salesman and self-promoter, Edison shared Carnegie's vision of a large, interconnected industrial system resting on a foundation of technological innovation (see Technology and Culture).

Edison's first major invention, a stock-quotation printer, in 1868 earned enough money to finance Edison's first "invention factory" in Newark, New Jersey, a research facility he moved to nearby Menlo Park in 1876. Assembling a staff that included university-trained scientists, Edison boastfully predicted "a minor invention every ten days, and a big one every six months."

Buoyed by the success and popularity of his invention in 1877 of a phonograph, or "sound writer" (*phono*: "sound"; *graph*: "writer"), Edison set out to develop a new filament for incandescent light

THOMAS EDISON'S LABORATORIES IN MENLO PARK, NEW JERSEY, CA. 1881 Always a self-promoter, Edison used this depiction of his "invention factory" to suggest that his development of a durable light bulb in 1879 would have an impact on life around the globe. *(U.S. Department of the Interior, National Park Service, Edison National Historic Site)*

Electricity

Of all the technological achievements of the nineteenth century, none seemed more inspiring or mysterious than the ability to generate electricity. Using Alessandro Volta's discovery that chemical reactions in batteries produced a weak electric current, Samuel F.B. Morse had used batteries to power his telegraph in 1837. Alexander Graham Bell followed suit with his telephone in 1876. But higher voltages were needed to run lighting systems and motors. Michael Faraday in England and Joseph Henry in America discovered in 1831 that a rotating magnet surrounded by a conducting wire would produce a continuous flow of electric current. After the Civil War, American inventors used this discovery to develop powerful generators to run incandescent lights (1879), to power motors to run trolley cars (1888), and to drive machines in factories. For many Americans, the ability to harness electricity marked the subjugation of nature and indicated the progress of American civilization.

Nowhere did the knowledge of electricity seem more impressive than its promise to reveal the secrets of the human body. X-rays, discovered in 1895 by the German physicist Wilhelm Roentgen and developed into a practical hospital machine a year later by Thomas Edison, enabled doctors to see inside the body. Physicians discovered that the workings of the nervous system and the brain itself depended on electrical impulses. It was no accident that Edison was known as the "wizard of Menlo Park," where his research laboratory was located.

The spread of electric lighting illustrates how technological advances pushed innovation. Thomas Edison's vision went far beyond the development of a practical light bulb. He conceived of an interrelated system of power plants, transmission lines, and light fixtures, all to be produced by companies he had established. Edison's system of direct current lighting (DC—which flowed in only one direction in the wires) required that users be located near power plants. But in 1886, George Westinghouse set up a competing company that used the Italian inventor Nikola Tesla's discovery that alternating current (AC—which cycled back and forth within the wires) could send high voltage electricity efficiently over long distances. Competition between the two systems was finally resolved in 1896 when Edison's successor company, General Electric, agreed to share its patents with the Westinghouse Company. With electric current now standardized as 110 volts AC at

CREATION OF THE EDISON SYSTEM, MENLO PARK *Frank Leslie's Weekly* in 1880 illustrated Thomas Edison's process of making electric light bulbs using glass-blowers and vacuum machines in his Menlo Park laboratory. *(Library of Congress)*

60 Hertz (60 cycles per second), dozens of other inventors developed electric motors, spotlights, electric signs, water pumps, elevators, and household appliances—all drawing power from the same power grid. Only twenty years after the first power station had been built, electrification had started to transform everyday life.

By 1898, when the city of London had sixty-two different utilities that produced thirty-two different voltage levels, American companies had created a unified national electrical system with standardized voltages, and the United States had established itself as a world leader in electrical technology. The remarkable achievements of the American electrical industry resulted from a combination of factors. Skilled inventors such as Edison, Westinghouse, and Frank Sprague, who developed electric motors for trolley and subway cars, were critical. But the efforts might never have made it out of the laboratories without financiers, such as J.P. Morgan and Henry Villard, who funded the enormous investment in electric generators, power plants, and transmission lines. A third factor was the independence of large corporations like General Electric and Westinghouse, which were able to operate nationally and avoid conflicting state regulations.

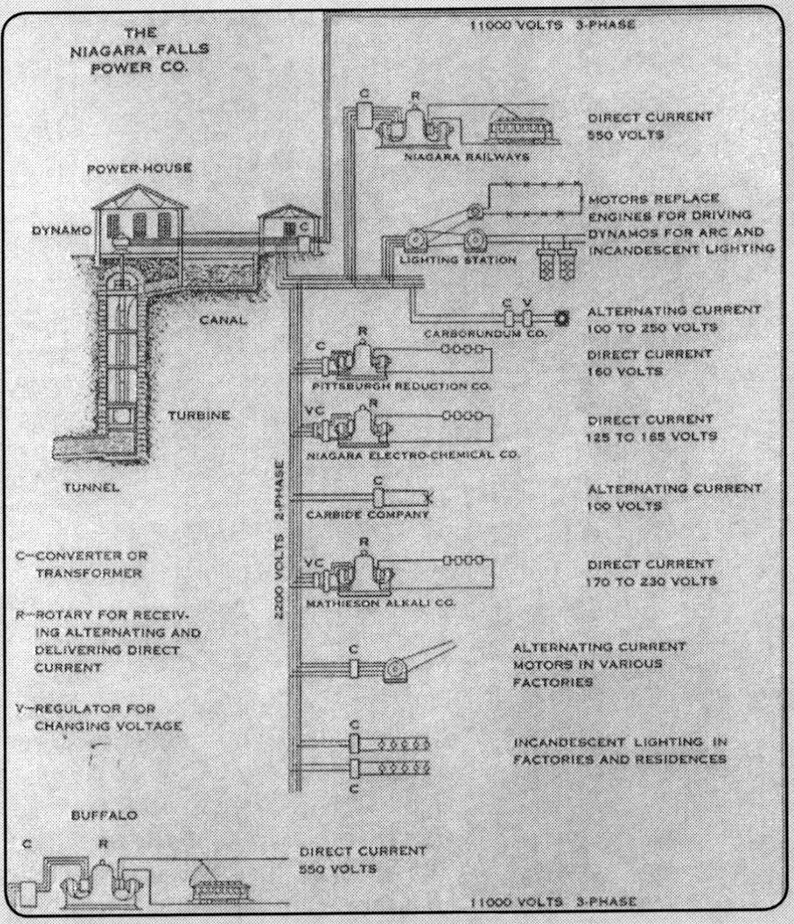
THE NIAGARA FALLS POWER CO.
11000 VOLTS 3-PHASE
DIRECT CURRENT 550 VOLTS
NIAGARA RAILWAYS
POWER-HOUSE
MOTORS REPLACE ENGINES FOR DRIVING DYNAMOS FOR ARC AND INCANDESCENT LIGHTING
DYNAMO
LIGHTING STATION
ALTERNATING CURRENT 100 TO 250 VOLTS
CANAL
CARBORUNDUM CO.
DIRECT CURRENT 160 VOLTS
PITTSBURGH REDUCTION CO.
TURBINE
DIRECT CURRENT 125 TO 165 VOLTS
NIAGARA ELECTRO-CHEMICAL CO.
TUNNEL
ALTERNATING CURRENT 100 VOLTS
CARBIDE COMPANY
2200 VOLTS 2-PHASE
C—CONVERTER OR TRANSFORMER
DIRECT CURRENT 170 TO 230 VOLTS
MATHIESON ALKALI CO.
R—ROTARY FOR RECEIVING ALTERNATING AND DELIVERING DIRECT CURRENT
ALTERNATING CURRENT MOTORS IN VARIOUS FACTORIES
V—REGULATOR FOR CHANGING VOLTAGE
INCANDESCENT LIGHTING IN FACTORIES AND RESIDENCES
BUFFALO
DIRECT CURRENT 550 VOLTS
11000 VOLTS 3-PHASE

THE NIAGARA FALLS POWER COMPANY As this diagram of the power station at Niagara Falls reveals, the early transmission of electric power was closely tied to large manufacturers who had the funds to support large investments in generating equipment and power lines. *(From Adams, Niagara Power)*

Operating as regional monopolies, these corporations standardized voltage, alternating current, and electrical fixtures nationwide. Finally, the pooling of patents was crucial. The American patent system, by granting inventors property rights in their inventions and by publicly identifying how the discoveries worked, stimulated technological innovation in general.

At first, electricity was very expensive, and the general public could not afford the cost of wiring homes. Still, even confined to the public sphere, the establishment of a national electrical system was one of the greatest technological innovations of the century. Electric streetcars and subways, public lighting systems, and electric elevators transformed urban America, allowing the construction of skyscrapers and the quick transportation of millions of people. The electrification of factories extended the workday into the night and made work safer. In the following decades, electrification made possible the invention of lighting systems, fans, washing machines, and a host of other devices to ease the drudgery of everyday life.

In the twentieth century, some shortcomings in Americans' love affair with electricity became obvious. In the early years, urban electrification accentuated the differences between city and country life. After World War II, massive power failures showed that the centralization of power distribution systems, first constructed as private monopolies between 1880 and 1932, made them vulnerable to failure when a subsystem problem cascaded throughout the network. The private ownership of power companies, now called utility companies, has enabled them at times to inflate energy prices for their own profit. Most electrical power in the United States today is produced from coal, a nonrenewable resource that also produces acid rain and air pollution. Nevertheless, the creation of a national system of electrical power generation paved the way for remarkable innovations—from lighting to televisions and computers—that remain today closely tied to America's sense of progress and material advancement.

QUESTIONS FOR ANALYSIS

- Why did the early electrical inventions seem to mark the subjugation of nature?
- What technological breakthroughs paved the way for the widespread use of electricity for street lighting and transportation?
- Why did the standardization and consolidation of the electric industry take place more quickly in the United States than in England?

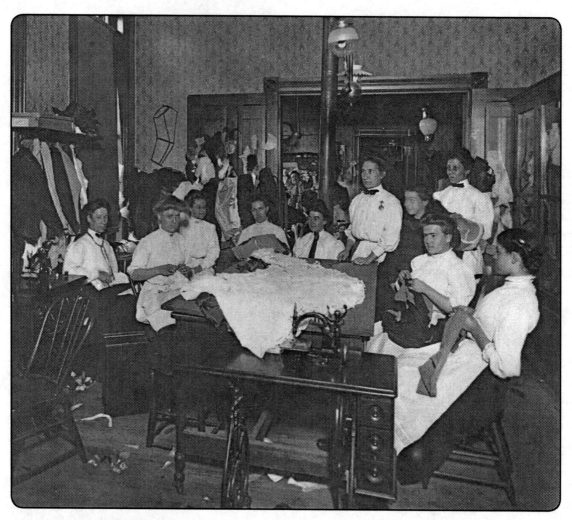

SKILLED WOMEN DRESSMAKERS, 1890 As these dressmakers in Mary Malloy's shop in St. Paul, Minnesota, indicate, industrialization did not displace all skilled workers. In this case, handwork and machine work continued together. Women's dressmaking persisted as a skilled occupation into the 1890s and gave women entrepreneurs an opportunity to run their own businesses. *(© Minnesota Historical Society/Corbis)*

bulbs. Characteristically, he announced his plans for an electricity-generation process before he perfected his inventions and then worked feverishly, testing hundreds of materials before he found a carbon filament that would glow dependably in a vacuum.

Edison realized that practical electrical lighting had to be part of a complete system containing generators, voltage regulators, electric meters, and insulated wiring and that the system needed to be easy to install and repair. It also had to be cheaper and more convenient than kerosene or natural gas lighting, its main competitors. In 1882, having built this system with the support of banker J. Pierpont Morgan, the Edison Illuminating Company opened a power plant in the heart of New York City's financial district, furnishing lighting for eighty-five buildings.

In the following years, Edison and his researchers pumped out invention after invention, including the mimeograph machine, the microphone, the motion picture camera and film, and the storage battery. By the time of his death in 1931, he had patented 1,093 inventions and amassed an estate worth more than $6 million. Yet Edison's greatest achievement remained his laboratory at Menlo Park. A model for the industrial research labs later established by Kodak, General Electric, and Du Pont, Edison's laboratory demonstrated that the systematic use of science in support of industrial technology paid large dividends. Invention had become big business.

Specialized Production

Along with inventors, manufacturers of custom and specialized products such as machinery, jewelry, furniture, and women's clothes dramatically expanded economic output. Using skilled labor, these companies crafted one-of-a-kind or small batches of articles that ranged in size from large steam engines and machine tools to silverware, furniture, and custom-made dresses. Keenly attuned to innovations in technology and design, they constantly created new products tailored to the needs of individual buyers.

Small dressmaking shops run by women were typical of flexible specialization displayed by small batch processors. Until the turn of the twentieth century, when ready-to-wear clothes came to dominate the market, most women's apparel was custom produced in small shops run by female proprietors. Unlike the tenement sweatshops that produced men's shirts and pants, dressmakers and milliners (a term derived from fancy goods vendors in sixteenth-and seventeenth-century Milan, Italy) paid good wages to highly skilled seamstresses. The small size of the shops together with the skill of the workers enabled them to shift styles quickly to follow the latest fashions.

Thus, alongside of the increasingly rationalized and bureaucratic big businesses like steel and oil in the late nineteenth century, American productivity was also stimulated by small producers who provided a variety of goods that supplemented the bulk-manufactured staples of everyday life.

Advertising and Marketing

As small and large factories alike spewed out an amazing array of new products, business leaders often discovered that their output exceeded what the market could absorb. This was particularly true for mass-produced consumer goods such as matches, flour, soap, and canned foods. Not surprisingly, these industries were trailblazers in developing advertising and marketing techniques. Strategies for whetting consumer demand and for differentiating one product from another represented a critical component of industrial expansion in the post–Civil War era.

Through the use of brand names, trademarks, guarantees, slogans, endorsements, and other gimmicks, manufacturers built demand for their products and won enduring consumer loyalty. Americans bought Ivory Soap, first made in 1879 by Procter and Gamble of Cincinnati, because of the absurdly precise but impressive pledge that it was "99 and 44/100ths percent pure."

Other manufacturers won consumer loyalty through the development of unique products. In the 1880s, George Eastman developed a paper-based photographic film as an alternative to the fragile glass plates then in use and sold this film loaded into an inexpensive camera. Consumers returned the

HEINZ KETCHUP ADVERTISEMENT, CA. 1900 To sell its products in a mass market, H J Heinz company in Pittsburgh developed the brand name "57 Varieties" for its ketchup, pickles, and other condiments. The "girl with the white cap" was meant to symbolize the purity of its food processing. *(Library & Archives Division, Historical Society of Western Pennsylvania, Pittsburgh, PA)*

camera to his Rochester factory where, for a charge of ten dollars, the film was developed and printed, the camera reloaded, and everything shipped back. In marketing a new technology, Eastman had revolutionized an industry and democratized a visual medium previously confined to a few.

Social and Environmental Costs and Benefits

By 1900, the chaos of early industrial competition, when thousands of companies had struggled to enter a national market, had given way to the most productive economy in the world, supported by a legion of small, specialized companies and dominated by a few enormous ones. An industrial transformation that had originated in railroading and expanded to steel and petroleum had spread to every nook and cranny of American business and raised the United States to a position of world leadership.

The vast expansion of economic output brought social benefits in the form of labor-saving products, lower prices, and advances in transportation and communications. The benefits and liabilities sometimes seemed inextricably interconnected. The sewing machine, for example, created thousands of new factory jobs, made available a wider variety of clothing, and eased the lives of millions of house-wives. At the same time, it encouraged avaricious entrepreneurs to operate sweatshops in which the immigrant poor—often vulnerable young women—toiled long hours for pitifully low wages (discussed further in Chapter 21).

For those who fell by the wayside in this era of spectacular economic growth, the cost could be measured in bankrupted companies and shattered dreams. John D. Rockefeller put things with characteristic bluntness when he said he wanted "only the big ones, only those who have already proved they can do a big business" in the Standard Oil Trust. "As for the others, unfortunately they will have to die."

The cost was high, too, for millions of American workers, immigrant and native-born alike. The vast expansion of new products was built on the backs of an army of laborers who were paid subsistence wages and who could be fired on a moment's notice when hard times or new technologies made them expendable.

Industrial growth often devastated the environment as well. Rivers fouled by oil or chemical waste, skies filled with clouds of soot, and a landscape littered with reeking garbage and toxic materials bore mute witness to the relentless drive for efficiency and profit.

> Rockefeller said he wanted "only the big ones, only those who have already proved they can do a big business. As for the others, unfortunately they will have to die."

Whatever the final balance sheet of social gains and costs, one thing was clear: the United States had muscled its way onto the world stage as an industrial titan. The ambition and drive of countless inventors, financiers, managerial innovators, and marketing wizards had combined to lay the groundwork for a new social and economic order in the twentieth century.

INDUSTRIAL POLLUTION Although some Americans celebrated factory smoke as a sign of industrial growth, those who lived downwind, such as the longshoreman in this Thomas Nast cartoon, often suffered from respiratory diseases and other ailments. For him as well as for other Americans, the price of industrial progress often was pollution. *(© Bettmann/Corbis)*

of southern towns and cities, lack of capital, illiteracy, northern control of financial markets and patents, and a low rate of technological innovation crippled efforts by southern business leaders to promote industrialization. Economic progress was also impeded by the myth of the Lost Cause, which, through its nostalgic portrayal of pre–Civil War society, perpetuated an image of the South as traditional and unchanging. As a result, southern industrialization inched forward haltingly and was shaped in distinctive ways.

The New South

The South entered the industrial era far more slowly than the Northeast. As late as 1900, total southern cotton-mill output, for example, remained little more than half that of the mills within a thirty-mile radius of Providence, Rhode Island. Moreover, the South's $509 average per capita income was less than half that of northerners.

The reasons for the South's late economic blossoming are not hard to discern. The Civil War's physical devastation, racism, the scarcity

Obstacles to Economic Development

Much of the South's difficulty in industrializing arose from its lack of capital and the devastation of the Civil War. So many southern banks failed during the Civil War that by 1865 the South, with more than a quarter of the nation's population, possessed just 2 percent of its banks. The federal government policies added to the banking problem by requiring anyone wishing to start a bank to have $50,000 in capital. Few southerners could meet this standard.

With banks in short supply, country merchants and storekeepers became bankers by default, lending supplies rather than cash to local farmers in return for a lien, or mortgage, on their crops (see Chapter 16). The burden of paying these liens trapped farmers on their own land and created a shortage of the labor needed for industrial expansion.

The shift from planting corn to specializing in either cotton or tobacco made small southern farmers particularly vulnerable to the fluctuations of commercial agriculture. When the price of cotton tumbled in national and international markets from eleven cents per pound in 1875 to less than five cents in 1894, well under the cost of production, many southern farmers grew desperate.

The South's chronic shortage of funds affected the economy in indirect ways as well, by limiting the resources available for education. During Reconstruction, northern philanthropists together with the Freedmen's Bureau, the American Missionary Association, and other relief agencies had begun a modest expansion of public schooling for both blacks and whites. But Georgia and many other southern states operated segregated schools and refused to tax property for school support until 1889. As a result, school attendance remained low, severely limiting the number of educated people able to staff technical and managerial positions in business and industry.

Southern states, like those in the North, often contributed the modest funds they had to war veterans' pensions. In this way, southern state governments built a white patronage system for Confederate veterans and helped reinforce southerners' idealization of the old Confederacy—the South's Lost Cause. As late as 1911, veterans' pensions in Georgia ate up 22 percent of the state's entire budget, leaving little for economic or educational development.

The New South Creed and Southern Industrialization

Despite these obstacles, energetic southern newspaper editors such as **Henry W. Grady** of the *Atlanta Constitution* and Henry Watterson of the *Louisville Courier Journal* championed the doctrine that became known as the New South creed. The South's rich coal and timber resources and cheap labor, they proclaimed in their papers, made it a natural site for industrial development.

The movement to industrialize the South gained momentum in the 1880s. To attract northern capital, southern states offered tax exemptions for new businesses, set up industrial and agricultural expositions, and leased prison convicts to serve as cheap labor. Florida, Texas, and other states gave huge tracts of lands to railroads, whose expansion in turn stimulated the birth of new towns and villages. Other states sold forest and mineral rights on nearly 6 million acres of federal lands to speculators, mostly from the North, who significantly expanded the production of iron, sulfur, coal, and lumber.

Following the lead of their northern counterparts, the southern iron and steel industries expanded as well. Birmingham, Alabama, founded in 1871 in a region blessed with rich deposits of coal, limestone, and iron ore, grew in less than three decades to a bustling city with noisy railroad yards and roaring blast furnaces. By 1900, it was the nation's largest pig-iron shipper. In these same years, Chattanooga, Tennessee, housed nine furnaces, seventeen foundries, and numerous machine shops.

As large-scale recruiters of black workers, the southern iron and steel mills contributed to the migration of blacks to the cities. By 1900, 20 percent of the southern black population was urban. Many urban blacks toiled as domestics or in similar menial capacities, but others entered the industrial work force. Southern industry reflected the patterns of racial segregation in southern life. Tobacco companies used black workers, particularly women, to clean the tobacco leaves while white women, at a different location, ran the machines that made cigarettes. The burgeoning textile mills were lily-white. In the iron and steel industry, blacks, who comprised 60 percent of the unskilled work force by 1900, had practically no chance of advancement. Nevertheless, in a rare reversal of the usual pattern, southern blacks in the iron and steel industry had a higher skill level and on average earned more than did southern white textile workers.

Black miners were also recruited by the West Virginia coal industry that lured them with free transportation, high wages, and company housing. The coal boom at first forced companies to pay similar wages to blacks and whites, and they initially joined biracial labor unions. But the depression of 1893 weakened the unions and workers became increasingly confined to separate jobs.

Southern segregation, while restricting black employment in many ways, opened up new opportunities for black barbers, doctors, and businessmen to work with black customers. Nevertheless, economic opportunities for blacks remained severely limited. In lumbering, which was the South's largest industry, large numbers of blacks worked in the turpentine industry, collecting sap from trees. In good times, wages could be better than those offered to farm laborers, but during economic downturns workers were laid off or confined to work camps by vagrancy laws and armed guards.

The Southern Mill Economy

Unlike the urban-based southern iron and steel industry, the textile mills that mushroomed in the southern countryside in the 1880s often became catalysts for the formation of new towns and villages. In these mill towns, country ways and values suffused the new industrial workplace.

The cotton-mill economy grew largely in the Piedmont, the highland country stretching from central Virginia to northern Georgia and Alabama. The Piedmont had long been the South's backcountry, a land of subsistence farming and limited roads. But postwar railroad construction sparked a period of intense town building and textile-mill expansion. By 1920, the South was the nation's leading textile-mill center. Augusta, Georgia, with 2,800 mill workers, became known as the Lowell of the South, named after the mill town in Massachusetts where industrialization had flourished earlier. The expansion of the textile industry nurtured promoters' visions of a new, more prosperous, industrialized South.

Sharecroppers and tenant farmers at first hailed the new cotton mills as a way out of rural poverty. But appearances were deceptive. The chief cotton-mill promoters were drawn from the same ranks of merchants, lawyers, doctors, and bankers who had profited from the commercialization of southern agriculture (and from the misfortunes of poor black and white tenant farmers and sharecroppers trapped in the new system). Cotton-mill entrepreneurs shamelessly exploited their workers, paying just seven to eleven cents an hour, 30 percent to 50 percent less than what comparable mill workers in New England were paid.

The mills dominated most Piedmont textile communities. The mill operator not only built and owned the workers' housing and the company store but also supported the village church, financed the local elementary school, and pried into the morals and behavior of the mill hands. To prevent workers from moving from one mill to another, the mill owner usually paid them just once a month, often in scrip—a certificate redeemable only in goods from the company store. Since few families had enough money to get through a month, they often overspent and fell behind in their payments. The charges were deducted from workers' wages the following month. In this way, the mill drew workers and their families into a cycle of indebtedness very much like that faced by sharecroppers and tenant farmers.

> To prevent workers from moving from one mill to another, the mill owner usually paid them just once a month, often in scrip—a certificate redeemable only in goods from the company store.

To help make ends meet, mill workers kept their own garden patches and raised chickens, cows, and pigs. Southern mill hands thus brought communal farm values, long associated with large farm families and nurtured through cooperative planting and harvesting, into the mills themselves. Although they had to adapt to machine-paced work and received barely enough pay to live on, the working poor in the mill districts, like their prewar counterparts in the North, eased the shift from rural to village-industrial life by embracing a cooperative country ethic.

As northern cotton mills did before the Civil War, southern textile companies exploited the cheap rural labor around them, settling transplanted farm people in paternalistic company-run villages. Using these tactics, the industry underwent a period of steady growth.

The Southern Industrial Lag

Industrialization progressed at a slower rate in the South than in the North and depended on outside financing, technology, and expertise. The late-nineteenth-century southern economy remained essentially in a colonial status, dominated by northern industries and financial syndicates. U.S. Steel, for example, controlled the Birmingham foundries and in 1900 priced Birmingham steel according to the "Pittsburgh plus" formula based on the price of Pittsburgh steel, plus the freight costs of shipping from Pittsburgh. As a result, southerners paid higher prices for steel than northerners, despite cheaper production costs.

An array of factors thus combined to retard industrialization in the South. Banking regulations requiring large reserves, scarce capital, wartime debts, lack of industrial experience, a segregated labor force, discrimination against blacks, and control by profit-hungry northern enterprises all hampered the region's economic development. Dragged down by a poorly educated white population and by a largely unskilled black population, southern industry languished. Not until after the turn of the century did southern industry undergo the restructuring and consolidation that had occurred in northern business enterprise two decades earlier.

As in the North, industrialization brought significant environmental damage, including polluted rivers and streams, decimated forests, grimy coal-mining towns, and soot-infested steel-making cities. Although Henry Grady's vision of a New South may have inspired many southerners to work toward industrialization, economic growth in the South, limited as it was by outside forces, progressed in its own distinctly regional way.

Factories and the Work Force

Industrialization proceeded unevenly nationwide, and most late-nineteenth-century Americans still worked in small shops. But as the century unfolded, large factories with armies of workers sprang onto the industrial scene. The pattern of change was evident. Between 1860 and 1900, the number of industrial workers jumped from 885,000 to 3.2 million, and the trend toward large-scale production became unmistakable.

From Workshop to Factory

The transition to a factory economy came not as an earthquake but rather as a series of seismic jolts varying in strength and duration. Whether they occurred quickly or slowly, however, the changes in factory production had a profound impact on artisans and unskilled laborers alike, because they involved a fundamental restructuring of work habits and a new emphasis on workplace discipline. The impact of these changes can be seen by examining the boot and shoe industry. As late as the 1840s, most shoes were custom-made by skilled artisans who worked in small, independent shops. Shoemakers were aristocrats in the world of labor. Taught in an apprentice system, they took pride in their work and controlled the quality of their products.

A distinctive working-class culture subdivided along ethnic lines evolved among these shoemakers. Foreign-born English, German, and Irish workers set up ethnic trade organizations and joined affiliated benevolent associations. Bound together by religious and ethnic ties, they observed weddings and funerals according to old-country traditions, relaxed together at the local saloon after work, and helped one another weather accidents or sicknesses.

As early as the 1850s, even before the widespread use of machinery, changes in the ready-made shoe trade had eroded the status of skilled labor. The manufacturing process was broken down into a sequence of repetitive, easily mastered tasks. Thus, instead of crafting a pair of shoes from start to finish, each team member specialized in only one part of the process, such as attaching the heel or polishing the leather.

In the 1880s, shoe factories became larger and more mechanized, and traditional skills largely vanished. Shoe companies replaced skilled operatives with lower-paid, less-skilled women and children. By 1890, women made up more than 35 percent of the work force. Like the laborer whose machine nailed heels on forty-eight hundred shoes a day, even "skilled" workers in the new factories found themselves performing numbingly repetitive tasks.

The Hardships of Industrial Labor

The expansion of the factory system spawned an unprecedented demand for unskilled labor. By the 1880s, nearly one-third of the 750,000 workers employed in the railroad and steel industries, for example, were common laborers.

In the construction trades and the garment-making industries, unskilled laborers were hired under the so-called contract system by a subcontractor who took responsibility for employee relations. These common workers were seasonal help, hired in times of need and laid off in slack periods. The steel industry employed them to shovel ore in the yards and to move ingots inside the mills. The foremen drove the gangs hard; in the Pittsburgh area, the workers called the foremen "pushers."

Notoriously transient, unskilled laborers drifted from city to city and from industry to industry. In the late 1870s, unskilled laborers earned $1.30 a day, while bricklayers and blacksmiths earned more than $3. Only unskilled southern mill workers, whose wages averaged a meager eighty-four cents a day, earned less.

Unskilled and skilled workers alike worked up to twelve-hour shifts and faced grave hazards to their health and safety. Children were the most vulnerable. In the coal mines and cotton mills, child laborers typically entered the work force at age eight or nine. In the cotton mills, children could be injured by the unprotected pulley belts that powered the machines or develop brown lung disease, a crippling illness caused by breathing in cotton dust. In the coal industry, where children were commonly employed to remove pieces of slate from the conveyor belts, the cloud of coal dust that swirled around them gave them black lung disease—a disorder that leads to emphysema and heart failure.

In addition to facing these workplace hazards, working children often fell behind in their schooling. Pressured by families that needed additional

> "Wherever the heat is most insupportable, the flames most scorching, the smoke and soot most choking, there we are certain to find compatriots bent and wasted in toil."

income and by the desire to have some spending money of their own, many children forged work permits and their birth certificates to avoid the compulsory schooling laws (see Chapter 19) to enter the mills and the mines. This lack of education, plus the physical trauma to their bodies, would often exclude them from better-paying jobs as adults.

For adult workers, the railroad industry was one of the most perilous. In 1889, the first year the Interstate Commerce Commission compiled reliable statistics, almost two thousand rail workers were killed on the job and more than twenty thousand injured.

Those who were maimed and disfigured by industrial accidents were further ostracized when San Francisco, Chicago, and other cities passed ordinances in the 1880s that removed "unsightly beggars" from the streets. The overall effect of these laws was to make those handicapped by industrial accidents invisible to the general population at large and to hamstring efforts to force companies to adopt more effective safety regulations.

Disabled workers and widows received minimal financial aid from employers. Until the 1890s, the courts considered employer negligence one of the normal risks borne by employees. Railroad and factory owners fought the adoption of state safety and health standards on the grounds that the cost would be excessive. For sickness and accident benefits, workers joined fraternal organizations and ethnic clubs, part of whose monthly dues benefited those in need. But in most cases, the amounts set aside were too low to be of much help. When a worker was killed or maimed in an accident, the family had to rely on relatives or friends for support.

Immigrant Labor

As we shall see in more detail in Chapter 19, factory owners turned to unskilled immigrants for the muscle they needed in dangerous and undesirable jobs. Poverty-stricken French Canadians filled the most menial positions in northeastern textile mills. On the West Coast, Chinese immigrants performed the dirtiest and most physically demanding jobs in mining, canning, and railroad construction.

Writing home in the 1890s, eastern European immigrants described the hazardous and draining work in the steel mills. "Wherever the heat is most insupportable, the flames most scorching, the smoke and soot most choking, there we are certain to find compatriots bent and wasted in toil," reported one Hungarian. Yet those immigrants disposed to live frugally in a boardinghouse and to

work an eighty-four-hour week could save fifteen dollars a month, far more than they could have earned in their homeland.

Although most immigrants worked hard, few adjusted easily to the fast pace of the factory. Factory operations were relentless, dictated by the unvarying speed of the machines. A brochure used by the International Harvester Corporation to teach English to its Polish workers promoted the "proper" values. Lesson I read:

I hear the whistle. I must hurry.
I hear the five minute whistle.
It is time to go into the shop.
I take my check from the gate board and hang it on the department board.
I change my clothes and get ready to work.
The starting whistle blows.
I eat my lunch.
It is forbidden to eat until then.
The whistle blows at five minutes of starting time.
I get ready to go to work.
I work until the whistle blows to quit.
I leave my place nice and clean.
I put all my clothes in the locker.
I must go home.

As this "lesson" reveals, factory work tied the immigrants to a rigid timetable very different from the pace of farm life.

When immigrant workers resisted the tempo of factory work, drank on the job, or took unexcused absences, employers used a variety of tactics to enforce discipline. Some sponsored temperance societies and Sunday schools to teach punctuality and sobriety. Others cut wages and put workers on the piecework system, paying them only for the items produced. Employers sometimes also provided low-cost housing to gain leverage against work stoppages; if workers went on strike, the boss could simply evict them.

In the case of immigrants from southern Europe whose skin colors were often darker than northern Europeans', employers asserted that the workers were nonwhite and thus did not deserve the same compensation as native-born Americans. Because the concept of "whiteness" in the United States bestowed a sense of privilege and the automatic extension of the rights of citizenship, Irish, Greek, Italian, Jewish, and a host of other immigrants, although of the Caucasian race, were also considered nonwhite. Rather than a fixed category based on biological differences, the concept of race was thus used to justify the harsh treatment of foreign-born labor.

TEXTILE WORKERS Young children like this one often were used in the textile mills because their small fingers could tie together broken threads more easily than those of adults. *(Library of Congress)*

Women and Work in Industrial America

Women's work experiences, like those of men, were shaped by marital status, social class, and race. Upper-class white married women widely accepted an ideology of "separate spheres" (as discussed in Chapter 19) and remained at home, raised children, and looked after the household. The well-to-do hired maids and cooks to ease their burdens.

Working-class married women, in contrast, often had to contribute to the financial support of the family. In fact, working for wages at home by sewing, button-making, taking in boarders, or doing laundry had predated industrialization. In the late nineteenth century, unscrupulous urban entrepreneurs exploited this captive work force.

In the clothing industry, manufacturers hired out finishing tasks to lower-class married women and their children, who labored long hours in crowded apartments.

Young, working-class single women often viewed factory work as an opportunity. In 1870, 13 percent of all women worked outside the home, the majority as cooks, maids, cleaning ladies, and laundresses. But most working women intensely disliked the long hours, low pay, and social stigma of being a "servant." When jobs in industry expanded in the last quarter of the century, growing numbers of single white women abandoned domestic employment for better-paying work in the textile, food-processing, and garment industries. Discrimination barred black working women from following this path. Between 1870 and 1900, the number of women of

PENNSYLVANIA CHILD SLATE PICKERS Child slate pickers risked having fingers torn off, developing black lung disease, and falling into the machinery where they could be crushed to death. *(Library of Congress)*

all races working outside the home nearly tripled. By the turn of the century, women made up 17 percent of the country's labor force.

A variety of factors propelled the rise in the employment of single women. Changes in agriculture prompted many young farmwomen to seek employment in the industrial sector (discussed further in Chapter 19), and immigrant parents often sent their daughters to the factories to supplement meager family incomes. Plant managers welcomed young immigrant women as a ready source of inexpensive unskilled labor. But factory owners treated them as temporary help and kept their wages low. In 1890, young women operating sewing machines earned as little as four dollars for seventy hours of work while their male counterparts made eight.

Despite their paltry wages, long hours, and often unpleasant working conditions, many young women relished earning their own income and joined the work force in increasing numbers. Although the financial support these working women contributed to their families was significant, few working women were paid enough to provide homes for themselves. Rather than fostering their independence, industrial work tied them more deeply to a family economy that depended on their earnings.

When the typewriter and the telephone came into general use in the 1890s, office work provided new employment opportunities, and women with high school educations moved into clerical and secretarial jobs earlier filled by men. They were attracted by the clean, safe working conditions and relatively good pay. First-rate typists could earn six to eight dollars a

> "I live in a tenement house, three stories up, where the water comes in through the roof, and I cannot better myself."

week, which compared favorably with factory wages. Office work carried higher prestige and generally was steadier than work in the factory or shop.

Despite the growing number of women workers, the late-nineteenth-century popular press portrayed women's work outside the home as temporary. Few people even considered the possibility that a woman could attain local or even national prominence in the emerging corporate order.

Hard Work and the Gospel of Success

Although women were generally excluded from the equation, influential opinion molders in these years preached that any man could achieve success in the new industrial era. In *Ragged Dick* (1867) and scores of later tales, **Horatio Alger,** a Unitarian minister turned dime novelist, recounted the adventures of

WOMEN IN THE WORKPLACE The women in this photograph are testing their typing skills at a civil service exam in Chicago in the 1890s. The expansion of banking, insurance, and a variety of other businesses opened up new career opportunities for women as secretaries, stenographers, and typists. *(Chicago Historical Society)*

poor but honest lads who rose through initiative and self-discipline.

Some critics did not accept this belief. In an 1871 essay, Mark Twain chided the public for its naïveté and suggested that business success was more likely to come to those who lied and cheated. In testimony given in 1883 before a Senate committee investigating labor conditions, a New Yorker named Thomas B. McGuire dolefully recounted how he had been forced out of the horse-cart business by larger, better financed concerns. Declared McGuire, "I live in a tenement house, three stories up, where the water comes in through the roof, and I cannot better myself. … Why? Simply because this present system … is all for the privileged classes, nothing for the man who produces the wealth." Only with starting capital of $10,000—then a large sum—said McGuire, could the independent entrepreneur hope to compete with the large companies.

What are the facts? Studies of nearly two hundred of the largest corporations reveal that few workers rose from poverty to colossal wealth. Ninety-five percent of the industrial leaders came from middle- and upper-class backgrounds. The best chance for native-born working-class Americans to get ahead was to master a skill and to rise to the top in a small company. Although only a few reaped immense fortunes, many improved their standard of living.

The different fates of immigrant workers in San Francisco show the possibilities and perils of moving up within the working class. In the 1860s, the Irish-born Donahue brothers grew wealthy from the Union Iron Works they had founded, where six hundred men built heavy equipment for the mining industry. In contrast, the nearly fifteen thousand Chinese workers who returned to the city after the Central Pacific's rail line was completed in 1869 were consigned by prejudice to work in cigar, textile, and other light-industry factories. Even successful Chinese entrepreneurs faced discrimination. When a Chinese merchant, Mr. Yung, refused to sell out to the wealthy Charles Crocker, a dry-goods merchant turned railroad entrepreneur who was building a mansion on Nob Hill, Crocker built a thirty-foot-high "spite fence" around Yung's house so that it would be completely sealed from view.

Thus, while some skilled workers became owners of their own companies, the opportunities

SHOEWORKERS Shoeworkers pose near their machines in Haverhill, Massachusetts, ca. 1880. For them as well as for others, work became increasingly repetitive and routinized. *(Courtesy of the Trustees of the Haverhill Public Library, Special Collections Department)*

for advancement for unskilled immigrant workers were considerably more limited. Some did move to semiskilled or skilled positions. Yet most immigrants, particularly the Irish, Italians, and Chinese, moved far more slowly than the sons of middle- and upper-class Americans who began with greater educational advantages and family financial backing. The upward mobility possible for such unskilled workers was generally mobility within the working class. Immigrants who got ahead in the late nineteenth century went from rags to respectability, not rags to riches.

One positive economic trend in these years was the rise in real wages, representing gains in actual buying power. Average real wages climbed 31 percent for unskilled workers and 74 percent for skilled workers between 1860 and 1900. Overall gains in purchasing power, however, often were undercut by injuries and unemployment during slack times or economic slumps. The position of unskilled immigrant laborers was particularly shaky. Even during a prosperous year like 1890, one out of every five nonagricultural workers was unemployed at least one month of the year. During the depressions of the 1870s and 1890s, wage cuts, extended layoffs, and irregular employment pushed those at the bottom of the industrial work force to the brink of starvation.

Thus, the overall picture of late-nineteenth-century economic mobility is complex. At the top of the scale, a mere 10 percent of American families owned 73 percent of the nation's wealth in 1890, while less than half of industrial laborers earned more than the five-hundred dollar poverty line annually. In between the very rich and the very poor, skilled immigrants and small shopkeepers improved their economic position significantly. So although the standard of living for millions of Americans rose, the gap between the poor and the well-off remained a yawning abyss.

Labor Unions and Industrial Conflict

Aware that the growth of large corporations gave industrial leaders unprecedented power to control the workplace, labor leaders searched for ways to create broad-based, national organizations that could protect their members. But this drive to create a nationwide labor movement faced many problems. Employers deliberately accentuated ethnic and racial divisions within the work force to hamper unionizing efforts. Skilled crafts workers, moreover, felt little kinship with low-paid common laborers. Divided into different trades, they often saw little reason to work together. Thus, unionization efforts moved forward slowly and experienced setbacks.

Two groups, the National Labor Union and the Knights of Labor, struggled to build a mass labor movement that would unite skilled and unskilled workers regardless of their specialties. After impressive initial growth, however, both efforts collapsed. Far more effective was the American Federation of Labor (AFL), which represented skilled workers in powerful independent craft unions. The AFL survived and grew, but it represented only a small portion of the total labor force.

With unions weak, labor unrest during economic downturns reached crisis proportions. When pay rates were cut or working conditions became intolerable, laborers walked off the job without union authorization. These actions, called **wildcat strikes** often exploded into violence. The labor crisis of the 1890s, with its strikes and bloodshed, would reshape the legal environment, increase the demand for state regulation, and eventually contribute to a movement for progressive reform.

Organizing Workers

From the eighteenth century on, skilled workers had organized local trade unions to fight wage reductions and provide benefits for their members in times of illness or accident. But the effectiveness of these organizations was limited. The challenge that labor leaders faced in the postwar period was how to boost the unions' clout. Some believed this goal could be achieved by forming one big association that would transcend craft lines and pull in the mass of unskilled workers.

Inspired by this vision of a nationwide labor association, William H. Sylvis, president of the Iron Molders' International Union, an organization of iron-foundry workers, in 1866 called a convention in Baltimore to form a new organization, the **National Labor Union** (NLU). Reflecting the pre–Civil War idealism, the NLU endorsed the eight-hour-day movement, which insisted that labor deserved eight hours for work, eight hours for sleep, and eight hours for personal affairs. Leaders also called for an end to convict labor, for the establishment of a federal department of labor, and for currency and banking reform. To push wage scales higher, they endorsed immigration restriction, especially of Chinese migrants, whom native-born workers blamed for undercutting prevailing wage levels. The NLU under Sylvis's leadership supported the cause of working women and elected a woman as one of its national officers. It urged black workers to organize as well, though in racially separate unions.

Chinese Labor

Despite the protests of white workers who believed that Chinese laborers undercut their wages, business leaders in the 1870s like Charles Crocker, president of the Central Pacific Railroad, argued that the Chinese should be imported to work in the U.S. Although he supported Chinese immigration, Crocker tried to evict a Chinese man who lived near his mansion in San Francisco. The following testimony by Crocker about his Chinese workers was published in an 1881 book by the former U.S. ambassador to China in opposition to the Chinese Exclusion Act that passed the following year.

Q. Do you or do you not believe that Chinese immigration to this country has the same tendency to degrade free white labor as that of Negro slavery in the South?

A. No, sir; because it is not servile labor.

Q. It is not?

A. It is not; it is free labor; just as free as yours or mine. You cannot control a Chinaman unless you pay him for it. You cannot make a contract with him, or his friend, or supposed master, and get his labor unless you pay for it, and pay him for it. ...

Q. When you employed Chinamen, did you employ the individual Chinaman, or did you employ some man to furnish you with a certain number of Chinamen?

A. On any road where we employed them for labor, we always procured them through the house of Sisson, Wallace & Co., here. That house furnished us with Chinamen. They gathered them, one at a time, two, three, four of them in a place, and got them together to make what is called a gang, and each gang is numbered.

Q. Just like mules?

A. Well, sir, we cannot distinguish Chinamen by names very well.

Q. Like mules?

A. Not like mules, but like men. We have treated them like men, and they have treated us like men, and they are men, good and true men. ... We have a foreman, and he keeps the account with the gang, and credits them. ... When the pay day comes, the gang is paid for all the labor of the gang, and then they divide it among themselves.

Q. Does the same thing obtain with the white men?

A. No, sir; we get the individual names of the white men.

Q. You do not pay the individual Chinaman when he works for you?

A. We pay the head-man of the gang.

Q. Some head-man?

A. He is a laborer among them.

Q. You do not pay them in the same manner that you pay white men?

A. In the same manner, except that we cannot keep the names of the Chinamen; it is impossible. We should not know Ah Sin, Ah You, Kong Won, and all such names. We cannot keep their names in the same way, because it is a difficult language. You understand the difficulty. It is not done in that way because they are slaves.

Q. Is it not a kind of servile labor?

A. Not a bit. I give you my word of honor, under oath here, that I do not believe there is a Chinese slave in this State, except it may be a prostitute. I hear of that, but I do not know anything about it. It will be seen from this evidence that the Central Pacific Railroad Company have not imported, through the six companies, or through a wealthy Chinese, or through any one else, any contract-laborers to work on the railroad in question, or on any of the roads controlled by them.

Source: *George F. Seward, Chinese Immigration in its Social and Economical Aspects (New York, Charles Scribners Sons, 1881), pp. 140–142.*

QUESTIONS

1. Why does the questioner link Chinese workers to slaves or mules?
2. Why does he focus on how they were paid?
3. What kinds of bias do the questions display?

When Sylvis's own union failed to win a strike in 1867 to improve wages, Sylvis turned to national political reform. He invited a number of reformers to the 1868 NLU convention, including woman suffrage advocates Susan B. Anthony and Elizabeth Cady Stanton, who, according to a reporter, made "no mean impression on the bearded delegates." But when Sylvis suddenly died in 1869, the NLU faded quickly. After a brief incarnation in 1872 as the National Labor Reform party, it vanished from the scene.

The dream of a labor movement that combined skilled and unskilled workers lived on in a new organization, the Noble and Holy Order of the **Knights of Labor,** founded in 1869. Led by Uriah H. Stephens, head of the Garment Cutters of Philadelphia, the Knights welcomed all wage earners. The Knights demanded equal pay for women, an end to child labor and convict labor, and the cooperative employer–employee ownership of factories, mines, and other businesses. At a time when no federal income tax existed, they called for a progressive tax on all earnings, graduated so that higher-income earners would pay more.

The Knights grew slowly at first. But membership rocketed in the 1880s after the eloquent Terence V. Powderly replaced Stephens as the organization's head. In the early 1880s, the Knights of Labor reflected both its idealistic origins and Powderly's collaborative vision. Powderly opposed strikes, which he considered "a relic of barbarism," and organized producer and consumer cooperatives. A teetotaler, he also urged temperance upon the membership. Powderly advocated the admission of blacks into local Knights of Labor assemblies, although he recognized the strength of racism and allowed southern local assemblies to be segregated. Under his leadership, the Knights welcomed women members; by 1886, women organizers had recruited thousands of workers, and women made up an estimated 10 percent of the union's membership.

> "The Wabash victory is with the Knights, no such victory has ever before been secured in this or any other country."

Powderly supported restrictions on immigration and a total ban on Chinese immigration. In 1877, San Francisco workers demonstrating for an eight-hour workday, destroyed twenty-five Chinese-run laundries and terrorized the local Chinese population. In 1880, both major party platforms included anti-Chinese immigration plans. Two years later, Congress passed the Chinese Exclusion Act, placing a ten-year moratorium on Chinese immigration. The ban was extended in 1902 and not repealed until 1943.

Powderly's greatest triumph came in 1885. In that year, when Jay Gould tried to get rid of the Knights of Labor on his Wabash railroad by firing active union members, Powderly and his executive board instructed all Knights on the Wabash line to walk off the job. This action crippled the Wabash's operations. To the nation's amazement, Gould met with Powderly and canceled his campaign against the Knights of Labor. "The Wabash victory is with the Knights," declared a St. Louis newspaper; "no such victory has ever before been secured in this or any other country."

Membership in the Knights of Labor soared. By 1886, more than seven hundred thousand workers were organized in nearly six thousand locals. Turning to political action that fall, the Knights mounted campaigns in nearly two hundred towns and cities nationwide, electing several mayors and judges (Powderly himself had served as mayor of Scranton since 1878). They secured passage of state laws banning convict labor and federal laws against the importation of foreign contract labor. Business executives warned that the Knights could cripple the economy and take over the country if they chose.

But the organization's strength soon waned. Workers became disillusioned when a series of unauthorized strikes failed in 1886. By the late 1880s, the Knights of Labor was a shadow of its former self.

As the Knights of Labor declined, another national labor organization, pursuing more immediate and practical goals, was gaining strength. The skilled craft unions had long been uncomfortable with labor organizations like the Knights that welcomed skilled and unskilled alike. They were also concerned that the Knights' broad reform goals would undercut their own commitment to better wages and protecting the interests of their particular crafts. The break came in May 1886 when the craft unions left the Knights of Labor to form the **American Federation of Labor** (AFL).

The AFL replaced the Knights' grand visions with practical tactics aimed at bread-and-butter issues. **Samuel Gompers,** the immigrant cigar maker who became head of the AFL in 1886 and led it until his death in 1924, believed in "trade unionism, pure and simple." For Gompers, higher wages were the necessary base to enable working class families to live decently, with respect and dignity. The stocky, mustachioed labor leader argued that labor, to stand up to the corporations, would have to harness the bargaining power of skilled workers, whom employers could not easily replace, and concentrate on the practical goals of raising wages and reducing hours.

THE FIRST LABOR DAY PARADE, 1882 Thousands of workers, led by the Knights of Labor, marched in the first Labor Day Parade in New York. As the numerous American flags in this contemporary illustration suggest, the workers believed that labor deserved substantial credit for building the American nation. *(Granger Collection)*

A master tactician, Gompers believed the trend toward large-scale industrial organization necessitated a comparable degree of organization by labor. He also recognized, however, that the skilled craft unions that made up the AFL retained a strong sense of independence. To persuade crafts workers from the various trades to join forces without violating their sense of craft autonomy, Gompers organized the AFL as a federation of trade unions, each retaining control of its own members but all linked by an executive council that coordinated strategy during boycotts and strike actions. "We want to make the trade union movement under the AFL as distinct as the billows, yet one as the sea," he told a national convention.

Focusing the federation's efforts on short-term improvements in wages and hours, Gompers at first sidestepped divisive political issues. The new organization's platform did, however, demand an eight-hour workday, employers' liability for workers' injuries, and mine safety laws. Although women participated in many craft unions, the AFL did little to recruit women workers after 1894 because Gompers and others believed that women workers undercut men's wages. By 1904, under Gompers's careful tutelage, the AFL had grown to more than 1.6 million strong.

Although the unions held up an ideal toward which many might strive, labor organizations before 1900 remained weak. Less than 5 percent of the work force joined union ranks. Split between skilled artisans and common laborers, separated along ethnic and religious lines, and divided over tactics, the unions battled with only occasional effectiveness against the growing power of corporate enterprise. Lacking financial resources, they typically watched from the sidelines when unorganized workers launched wildcat strikes that sometimes turned violent.

Strikes and Labor Unrest

Americans lived with a high level of violence from the nation's beginnings, and the nineteenth century—with its international and civil wars, urban riots, and Indian-white conflict—was no exception. Terrible labor clashes toward the end of the century were part of this continuing pattern, but they nevertheless shocked and dismayed contemporaries. From 1881 to 1905, close to thirty-seven thousand strikes erupted, in which nearly 7 million workers participated.

The first major wave of strikes began in 1873 when a Wall Street crash triggered a stock-market

ETHNIC AND RACIAL HATRED Conservative business owners used racist advertising such as this trade card stigmatizing Chinese laundry workers to promote their own products and to associate their company with patriotism. *(Library of Congress)*

PINKERTONS SURRENDER AT THE HOMESTEAD STEEL STRIKE, 1892 After a gun battle, Pinkerton security forces surrender to strikers at the Homestead, Pennsylvania, steel works. Companies cited worker violence such as this as justification for government suppression of labor unrest. *(Granger Collection)*

panic and a major depression. Six thousand businesses closed the following year, and many more cut wages and laid off workers. Striking Pennsylvania coal miners were fired and evicted from their homes. The tension turned deadly in 1877 during a wildcat railroad strike. Ignited by wage reductions on the Baltimore and Ohio Railroad in July, the strike exploded up and down the railroad lines, spreading to New York, Pittsburgh, St. Louis, Kansas City, Chicago, and San Francisco. Rioters in Pittsburgh torched Union Depot. By the time newly installed president Rutherford B. Hayes had called out the troops and quelled the strike two weeks later, nearly one hundred people had died, and two-thirds of the nation's railroads stood idle.

> "If the club of the policeman, knocking out the brains of the rioter, will answer, then well and good, [but if not] then bullets and bayonets … constitute the one remedy."

The railroad strike stunned middle-class America. The religious press responded hysterically. "If the club of the policeman, knocking out the brains of the rioter, will answer, then well and good," declared one Congregationalist journal, "[but if not] then bullets and bayonets … constitute the one remedy." The same middle-class Americans who worried about Jay Gould and the corporate abuse of power grew terrified of mob violence.

Employers capitalized on the public hysteria to crack down on labor. Many required their workers to sign "yellow dog" contracts in which they promised not to strike or join a union. Some hired Pinkerton agents, a private police force, to defend their factories and, when necessary, turned to the federal government and the U.S. army to suppress labor unrest.

Although the economy recovered, more strikes and violence followed in the 1880s. On May 1, 1886, 340,000 workers walked off their jobs in support of the campaign for an eight-hour workday.

Three days later, Chicago police shot and killed four strikers at the McCormick Harvester plant. At a protest rally the next evening in the city's Haymarket Square, someone threw a bomb, killing or fatally wounding seven policemen. In response, the police fired wildly into the crowd and killed four demonstrators.

Public reaction was immediate. Business leaders and middle-class citizens lashed out at labor activists and particularly at the sponsors of the Haymarket meeting, most of whom were associated with a German-language anarchist newspaper that advocated the violent overthrow of capitalism. Eight men were arrested. Although no evidence connected them directly to the bomb throwing, all were convicted of murder, and four were executed. One committed suicide in prison. In Haymarket's aftermath, still more Americans became convinced that the nation was in the grip of a deadly foreign conspiracy, and animosity toward labor unions intensified.

Confrontations between capital and labor became particularly violent in the West. When the Mine Owners' Protective Association cut wages at work sites along Idaho's Coeur d'Alene River in 1892, the miners, who were skilled dynamiters, blew up a mill and captured the guards sent to defend it. Mine owners responded by mustering the Idaho National Guard to round up the men and cripple their union.

Back east that same year, armed conflict broke out during the **Homestead Strike** at the Carnegie Steel Company plant in Homestead, Pennsylvania. To destroy the union, managers had cut wages and locked out the workers. When workers fired on the armed men from the Pinkerton Detective Agency who came to protect the plant, a battle broke out. Seven union members and three Pinkertons died. A week later the governor sent National Guardsmen to restore order. The union crushed, the mills resumed full operation a month later.

The most systematic use of troops to smash union power came in 1894 during a strike against the Pullman Palace Car Company. In 1880 George Pullman, a manufacturer of elegant dining and sleeping cars for the nation's railroads, had constructed a factory and town, called Pullman, ten miles south of Chicago. The carefully planned community provided solid brick houses for the workers, beautiful parks and playgrounds, and even its own sewage-treatment plant. Pullman also closely policed workers' activities, outlawed saloons, and insisted that his properties turn a profit.

When the depression of 1893 hit, Pullman slashed workers' wages without reducing their rents. In reaction, thousands of workers joined the newly formed American Railway Union and went on strike. They were led by a fiery young organizer, **Eugene V. Debs,** who vowed "to strip the mask of hypocrisy from the pretended philanthropist and show him to the world as an oppressor of labor." Union members working for the nation's largest railroads refused to switch Pullman cars, paralyzing rail traffic in and out of Chicago, one of the nation's premier rail hubs.

In response, the General Managers' Association, an organization of top railroad executives, set out to break the union. The General Managers imported strikebreakers from among jobless easterners and asked U.S. attorney general Richard Olney, who sat on the board of directors of three major railroad networks, for a federal injunction (court order) against the strikers for allegedly refusing to move railroad cars carrying U.S. mail.

In fact, union members had volunteered to switch mail cars onto any trains that did not carry Pullman cars, and it was the railroads' managers who were delaying the mail by refusing to send their trains without the full complement of cars. Nevertheless, Olney, supported by President Grover Cleveland and citing the Sherman Anti-Trust Act, secured an injunction against the leaders of the American Railway Union for restraint of commerce. When the union refused to order its members back to work, Debs was arrested, and federal troops poured in. During the ensuing riot, workers burned seven hundred freight cars, thirteen people died, and fifty-three were wounded. By July 18, the strike had been crushed.

By playing upon a popular identification of strikers with anarchism and violence, crafty corporate leaders persuaded state and federal officials to cripple organized labor's ability to bargain with business. When the Supreme Court (in the 1895 case *In re Debs*) upheld Debs's prison sentence and legalized the use of injunctions against labor unions, the judicial system gave business a potent new weapon with which to restrain labor organizers.

Yet organizers persisted. In 1897, the feisty Irish-born Mary Harris Jones, known as **Mother Jones,** persuaded coal miners in Pennsylvania to join the United Mine Workers of America, a union founded seven years earlier. She staged parades of children, invited workers' wives to stockpile food, and dramatized the importance of militant mothers fighting for their families. Her efforts were successful. Wage reductions were restored because no large companies dominated the industry and the owners needed to restore production.

Despite the achievements of the United Mine Workers, whose members had climbed to three hundred thousand by 1900, the successive attempts

MOTHER JONES Tough, fearless Mary Harris Jones, better known as "Mother Jones," supported coal mine strikes in West Virginia and Pennsylvania. At one strike, she led a group of fifty-seven little girls carrying placards that read: "Our Papas Aren't Scared." *(Library of Congress)*

> "If the United States, like the countries of the Old World, are also to grow vast crops of poor, desperate, dissatisfied, nomadic, miserably-waged populations, ... then our republican experiment, notwithstanding all its surface-successes, is at heart an unhealthy failure."

of working-class poverty. In 1879, after observing three men rummaging through garbage to find food, the poet and journalist Walt Whitman wrote, "If the United States, like the countries of the Old World, are also to grow vast crops of poor, desperate, dissatisfied, nomadic, miserably-waged populations, such as we see looming upon us of late years ... then our republican experiment, notwithstanding all its surface-successes, is at heart an unhealthy failure." Whitman's bleak speculation was part of a general public debate over the social meaning of the new industrial order. At stake was a larger issue: should government become the mechanism for helping the poor and regulating big business?

Defenders of capitalism preached the laissez-faire ("hands-off") argument, insisting that government should never attempt to control business. They buttressed their case by citing Scottish economist Adam Smith, who had argued in *The Wealth of Nations* (1776) that self-interest acted as an "invisible hand" in the marketplace, automatically regulating the supply of and demand for goods and services. In "The Gospel of Wealth," an influential essay published in 1889, Andrew Carnegie justified laissez-faire by applying the evolutionary theories of British social scientist Herbert Spencer to human society. "The law of competition," Carnegie argued, "may be sometimes hard for the individual, [but] it is best for the race, because it insures the survival of the fittest in every department."

> "A drunkard in the gutter is just where he ought to be ... The law of survival of the fittest was not made by man, and it cannot be abrogated by man."

Tough-minded Yale professor **William Graham Sumner** shared Carnegie's disapproval of government interference. His combative book *What Social Classes Owe to Each Other* (1883) applied the evolutionary theories of British naturalist Charles Darwin to human society. In an early statement of what became known as **Social Darwinism,** Sumner asserted that inexorable natural laws controlled the social order: "A drunkard in the gutter is just where he ought to be ... The law of survival of the fittest was not made by man, and it cannot be abrogated by man. We can only, by interfering with it, produce the survival of the unfittest." The state, declared Sumner, owed its citizens nothing but law, order, and basic political rights.

by the National Labor Union, Knights of Labor, American Federation of Labor, and American Railway Union to build a national working class labor movement achieved only limited success. Aggressive employer associations and conservative state and local officials hamstrung their efforts. In sharp contrast to Great Britain and Germany, where state officials often mediated disputes between labor and capital, federal and state officials in the United States increasingly sided with manufacturers. Ineffective in the political arena, blocked by state officials, divided by ethnic differences, harassed by employers, and frustrated by court decisions, American unions failed to expand their base of support. Post–Civil War labor turmoil had sapped the vitality of organized labor and given it a negative public image that it would not shed until the 1930s.

Social Thinkers Probe for Alternatives

Widespread industrial violence was particularly unsettling when examined in the context

Sumner's argument did not go unchallenged. In *Dynamic Sociology* (1883), Lester Frank Ward, a geologist, argued that contrary to Sumner's claim, the supposed "laws" of nature could be circumvented by human will. Just as scientists had applied their knowledge to breeding superior livestock, government experts could use the power of the state to regulate big business, protect society's weaker members, and prevent the heedless exploitation of natural resources.

Other social theorists offered more utopian solutions to the problems of poverty and social unrest. Henry George, a self-taught San Francisco newspaper editor and economic theorist, proposed to solve the nation's uneven distribution of wealth through what he called the single tax. In *Progress and Poverty* (1879), he noted that speculators reaped huge profits from the rising price of land that they neither developed nor improved. By taxing this "unearned increment," the government could obtain the funds necessary to ameliorate the misery caused by industrialization. The result would bring the benefits of socialism—a state controlled economic system that distributed resources according to need—without socialism's great disadvantage, the stifling of individual initiative. George's program was so popular that he lectured around the country and only narrowly missed being elected mayor of New York in 1886.

The vision of a harmonious industrialized society was vividly expressed in the utopian novel *Looking Backward* (1888) by Massachusetts newspaper editor Edward Bellamy. Cast as a glimpse into the future, Bellamy's novel tells of Julian West, who falls asleep in 1888 and awakens in the year 2000 to find a nation without poverty or strife. In this future world, West learns, a completely centralized, state-run economy and a new religion of solidarity have combined to create a society in which everyone works for the common welfare. Bellamy's vision of a conflict-free society where all share equally in industrialization's benefits so inspired middle-class Americans fearful of corporate power and working-class violence that nearly five hundred local Bellamyite organizations, called Nationalist clubs, sprang up to try to turn his dream into reality.

Ward, George, and Bellamy did not deny the benefits of the existing industrial order; they simply sought to humanize it. These utopian reformers envisioned a harmonious society whose members all worked together.

Marxist socialists advanced a different view. Elaborated by German philosopher and radical agitator Karl Marx (1818–1883) in *Das Kapital* (1867) and other works, **Marxism** rested on the labor theory of value: a proposition (which Adam Smith had also accepted) that the labor required to produce a commodity was the only true measure of that commodity's value. Any profit made by the capitalist employer was "surplus value" appropriated from the exploited workers. As competition among capitalists increased, Marx predicted, wages would decline to starvation levels, and more and more capitalists would be driven out of business. Society would be divided between a shrinking bourgeoisie (capitalists, merchants, and middle-class professionals) and an impoverished proletariat (the workers). The proletariat would then revolt and seize control of the state and of the economy. Although Marx viewed class struggle as the essence of modern history, his eyes were also fixed on the shining vision of the communist millennium that the revolution would eventually usher in—a classless utopia in which the state would "wither away" and all exploitation would cease. To lead the working class in its showdown with capitalism, Marx and his collaborator Friedrich Engels helped found socialist parties in Europe, whose strength grew steadily, beginning in the 1870s.

Despite Marx's keen interest in the United States, Marxism proved to have little appeal in late-nineteenth-century America other than for a tiny group of primarily German-born immigrants. The Marxist-oriented Socialist Labor Party (1877) had attracted only about fifteen hundred members by 1890. More alarming to the public at large was the handful of anarchists, again mostly immigrants, who rejected Marxist discipline and preached the destruction of capitalism, the violent overthrow of the state, and the immediate introduction of a stateless utopia. In 1892, Alexander Berkman, a Russian immigrant anarchist, attempted to assassinate Henry Clay Frick, the manager of Andrew Carnegie's Homestead Steel Works. Entering Frick's office with a pistol, Berkman shot him in the neck and then tried to stab him. A carpenter working in Frick's office overpowered the assailant. Rather than igniting a workers' insurrection that would usher in a new social order as he had hoped, Berkman came away with a long prison sentence. His act confirmed the business stereotype of "labor agitators" as lawless and violent.

CONCLUSION

By 1900, industrialization had propelled the United States into the forefront of the world's major powers, lowered the cost of goods through mass production, generated thousands of jobs, and produced a wide range of new consumer products. Using accounting systems first developed by the railroads and sophisticated new technologies, national corporations had pioneered innovative systems for distributing and marketing their goods. In the steel and oil industries, Andrew Carnegie and John D. Rockefeller had vertically integrated their companies, controlling production from the raw materials to the finished product. Through systematic cost cutting and ruthless underselling of their competitors, they had gained control of most of their industry and lowered prices.

Despite these advantages, most Americans recognized that industrialization's cost was high. The rise of the giant corporations had been achieved through savage competition, exploited workers, shady business practices, polluted factory sites, and the collapse of an economic order built on craft skills. In the South in particular, the devastation of the Civil War and the control of banking and raw materials by northern capitalists encouraged industrialists to adopt a paternalistic, family-oriented approach in the cotton mills and to pay exceedingly low wages.

Outbursts of labor violence, the growth of urban slums, and grinding poverty showed starkly that all was not well in industrial America. Although the Knights of Labor and the American Federation of Labor attempted to organize workers nationally, the labor movement could not control spontaneous wildcat strikes and violence. In response, company owners appealed to government authorities to arrest strikers, obtain court injunctions against union actions, and cripple the ability of labor leaders to expand their organizations.

As a result, Americans remained profoundly ambivalent about the new industrial order. Caught between their desire for the higher standard of living that industrialization made possible and their fears of capitalist power and social chaos, Americans of the 1880s and 1890s sought strategies that would preserve the benefits while eliminating corruption. Efforts to regulate railroads at the state level and such national measures as the Interstate Commerce Act and the Sherman Anti-Trust Act, as well as the fervor with which the ideas of a utopian theorist like Edward Bellamy were embraced, represented early manifestations of this impulse. In the Progressive Era of the early twentieth century, Americans would redouble their efforts to formulate political and social responses to the nation's economic transformation after the Civil War.

KEY TERMS

Jay Gould   (p. 538)

Interstate Commerce Act   (p. 539)

J. Pierpont Morgan   (p. 539)

Andrew Carnegie   (p. 539)

vertical integration   (p. 539)

John D. Rockefeller   (p. 541)

Standard Oil Trust   (p. 541)

Sherman Anti-Trust Act   (p. 542)

Thomas A. Edison   (p. 543)

Henry W. Grady   (p. 549)

Horatio Alger   (p. 554)

wildcat strikes   (p. 556)

National Labor Union   (p. 556)

Knights of Labor   (p. 558)

American Federation of Labor
   (p. 558)

Samuel Gompers   (p. 558)

Homestead Strike   (p. 561)

Eugene V. Debs   (p. 561)

Mother Jones   (p. 561)

William Graham Sumner   (p. 562)

Social Darwinism   (p. 562)

Marxism   (p. 563)

FOR FURTHER REFERENCE

Edward L. Ayers, *The Promise of the New South: Life After Reconstruction* (1992). A comprehensive overview of economic and social change in the post–Civil War South.

Alice Kessler-Harris, *Gendering Labor* (2007). Thoughtful essays on women's roles in labor history.

James D. Schmidt, *Industrial Violence and the Legal Origins of Child Labor* (2010). An important study of the complex forces that opposed child labor laws.

Richard Schneirov, Shelton Stromquist, and Nick Salvatore, eds., *The Pullman Strike and the Crisis of the 1890s: Essays on Labor and Politics* (1999). Surveys the impact of the Pullman strike on politics, the role of the state, and the public controversy over governmental regulation of corporate activity.

Susan M. Schweik, *The Ugly Laws: Disability in Public* (2009). An important study of discriminatory laws directed at people with physical handicaps.

Philip Scranton, *Endless Novelty: Specialty Production and American Industrialization, 1865–1925* (1997). A useful corrective to the argument that large corporations alone account for American economic growth in the post–Civil War era.

T.J. Stiles, *The First Tycoon: The Epic Life of Cornelius Vanderbilt* (2009). An innovative reconstruction of Vanderbilt's secretive life through the use of court records.

Joel A. Tarr, *The Search for the Ultimate Sink: Urban Pollution in Historical Perspective* (1996). An important study of the environmental problems created by industrialization.

Kim Voss, *The Making of American Exceptionalism: The Knights of Labor and Class Formation in the Nineteenth Century* (1993). A comparative analysis of American labor's attempts to mobilize workers in the face of business opposition.

Richard White, *Railroaded: The Transcontinentals and the Making of Modern America* (2011). Argues that the transcontinental railroads' achievements were not worth the corruption and social costs they entailed.

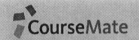

WEEK 1

Industrial Spring: America in the Gilded Age

SEAN DENNIS CASHMAN

The assassin who ended the life of Abraham Lincoln extinguished the light of the Republic. On April 14, 1865, after the president argued in the cabinet for generous treatment of the South, vanquished in the war between the states, he went to the theater. It was Good Friday and there was a conspiracy afoot to kill him. During the third act of the play at Ford's Theatre in Washington, actor John Wilkes Booth, a fanatical partisan of the southern cause, stole into his box and shot him in the head at close range. Lincoln never regained consciousness and died early the next day. Until his death Lincoln had been a most controversial president—yet his secretary of war, Edwin Stanton, could justly claim, "Now he belongs to the ages." The transfiguration of the murdered president cast a long shadow over American history from 1865 to 1901. In political terms, the period that begins with the assassination of one president ends with the assassination of another, William McKinley, in 1901.

These were formative years. The Industrial Revolution and the development of commercial monopolies, Reconstruction and the New South, the settlement of the West and closing of the frontier—all brought to the fore of politics a cast of characters that was very different from the statesmen, soldiers, and slaves of the Civil War. This was the heyday of the robber barons. Perhaps the most damaging accusation against Lincoln after his assassination was that to win the war he had been ready to sacrifice the ideals of the Republican party to spoilsmen and profiteers. Progressive journalist Lincoln Steffens observed that in England politics was a sport, in Germany it was a profession, but in the United States it was a business— and a corrupt one at that. Yet, in the absence of strong executive leadership during a prolonged period of social, industrial, and economic growth, Lincoln's reputation soared ever higher. At the end of the century New England intellectuals criticized the cult of idolizing Lincoln in an anecdote about an American traveler to England who visited Oxford University. Confused by the architectural similarity between two of the colleges in Turl Street—Jesus and Lincoln—he exclaimed, "I can't tell the difference between Lincoln and Jesus!" A passing student remarked that it was the same with all Americans. The allusion and the confusion were understandable. Lincoln had, after all, saved the Union in war, whereas his successors came close to losing the peace.

Sean Dennis Cashman, *America in the Gilded Age: From the Death of Lincoln to the Rise of Theodore Roosevelt*, 3d ed. (New York: New York University Press, 1984), 1–35. Reprinted by permission of New York University Press.

The West was settled at a fatal cost to Native Americans. The South was tied back to the Union at a humiliating cost to African-Americans. There were two depressions, in 1873 and 1893, each with devastating effects on the economy. The amazing industrial expansion of the United States was accomplished with considerable exploitation of factory artisans. The splendors of the new cities rose amid the squalor of industrial slums. The most damning indictment of this postwar American society was attributed to the future French prime minister Georges Clemenceau, who lived for a time in New York and New England. Noting its undoubted problems, he could claim the United States had gone from a stage of barbarism to one of decadence without achieving any civilization between the two.

Mark Twain paid a different but no less censorious tribute to the aspirations, autocracy, and affluence of the new American plutocracy of industrialists, financiers, and politicians in his utopian satire, *The Gilded Age* (1873). The title takes its cue from Shakespeare. King John is dissuaded from a second, superfluous coronation with the argument, "To gild refined gold, to paint the lily,/. . . Is wasteful and ridiculous excess." And Lady Macbeth implicates King Duncan's sleeping attendants in his murder by daubing them with blood from the dagger Macbeth has used to do the deed. "I'll gild the faces of the grooms withal," she says, "For it must seem their guilt." Mark Twain took this grotesque pun of gold and crime a stage further. His title was to become a triple pun. To gilt and guilt were added guilds in the sense of interest groups, labor unions, and monopolies. Twain's epithet, approved by his collaborator, Charles Dudley Warner, has survived as the most apt description of the period.

If the Gilded Age had a motto it might well have been, "The ayes have it," not only for the celebrated interest in voting stock, but also for the eyes that rejoiced in the glitter of gold, and the I's that define many of the pervasive social themes. Society was obsessed with invention, industrialization, incorporation, immigration, and, later, imperialism. It was indulgent of commercial speculation, social ostentation, and political prevarication but was indifferent to the special needs of immigrants and Indians and intolerant of African-Americans, labor unions, and political dissidents.

Whereas the Gilded Age had no predecessors, we may discern in three subsequent periods some of its features—notwithstanding the considerable differences between them. The first is the 1920s; the second, the period from 1945 to 1960; the third, the 1970s and 1980s. These were periods of predominantly (but not exclusively) Republican administrations. The government, as a whole, in each period was conservative. Accusations of nefarious links between politicians and businessmen and of widespread corruption in public life were rife. The presidency of Ulysses S. Grant in the 1870s is usually represented as a nadir of political probity. But the excesses of so-called carpetbaggers as well as of Congress and the administration in the 1870s pale in comparison with those of the Watergate burglars and White House staff during the presidency of Richard M. Nixon in the early 1970s. Yet the profligacy of the Ohio gang in the 1920s and the Republican chant of K^1C^2 (Korea, communism, and corruption) against the Democrats in 1952 have also remained a notorious part of the legend of the periodic corruption of public life in America.

Each period benefited from a boom in transportation—after 1865, the railroad; in the 1920s, the mass production of the automobile; from the late 1940s on, widespread commercial use of the airplane. Each enjoyed a revolution in communications— in the Gilded Age, telegraph and telephone; in the 1920s, motion pictures and radio; in the 1950s, long-playing vinyl phonograph records and television; in the 1980s, personal computers and compact discs. Innovations in transportation and communications together worked for a more homogeneous culture and a more informed citizenry, as well as having undisputed industrial and commercial significance in their own right.

Each period followed a war that left many Americans disillusioned, bitter, and confused: the Civil War, World War I, World War II, and the war in Vietnam. Their hostility to changed circumstances and the residue of hate engendered by the war but not yet expended partly account for the founding of the racist Ku Klux Klan after the Civil War and for its startling revival during the 1920s. This hostility was also vented against suspect ideologies. In the 1870s and 1880s labor unions were tainted by presumed association with anarchists, and the Haymarket anarchists of 1886 were tried without justice. The Great Red Scare of 1917–1921 against radicals expressed genuine if exaggerated anxiety about the dangers of a communist revolt, which was confirmed in the 1920s by the prejudicial treatment of the anarchists Sacco and Vanzetti. In 1950 Senator Joseph McCarthy lent his name to another wave of anticommunist hysteria that had been growing with the cold war.

The unsuccessful Second Indochina War of 1961–75 left bitter scars on American society. In their anguished protests against its conduct, liberals and radicals hurled accusations of indifference and injustice against the political establishment concerning its attitude toward African-Americans and other ethnic minorities, as well as toward women and the poor. The 1970s and 1980s also revealed society's recurrent obsession with intolerance and indulgence. In the 1970s the Republican party was tarnished by the burglary of the Democratic headquarters in the Watergate complex in 1972 and the stew of self-perpetuating politics by an oligarchy in the Nixon White House. Also tainted were such government agencies as the FBI and the CIA when congressional disclosures mounted about their illegal harassment of American citizens whose political views did not accord with those of the leadership of the two political parties. All this was most disturbing to a people reared in the belief that it was only the rulers of totalitarian regimes who prevented full freedom of expression. Moreover, allegations about overgenerous campaign contributions by big business to Republican coffers, sometimes laundered through Mexican banks, once again roused cries of anger about the overly close relationship between government and business.

In 1986 exposure of the Iran-Contra affair, in which the United States had supplied Iran with guns and munitions in exchange for the release of American hostages as well as for funds that were subsequently diverted to counterrevolutionaries in Nicaragua against the wishes of Congress—all arranged by Republican politicians and military personnel—once again suggested how insidious connections could develop between government, business, and military.

There was also considerable public anxiety expressed by revelations about insider trading on Wall Street, in an escapade in which Ivan Boesky became the principal culprit. A Wall Street crash in 1987 triggered a depression that had been incipient for many years, given the problems of American industry and manufacturing and the increasing debtor status of the United States. The depression deepened in the early 1990s. President George Bush's (1989–93) initial statements about the depression amounted to a doctrine of nonrecognition, and government remedial policies were nowhere in sight. It was like the restoration of an old-world picture of the Republicans as described in the 1930s by Herbert Hoover and in the 1890s by the nominally Democratic Grover Cleveland. The depression of the 1990s occurred in a period when the problems of acute social dislocation for the truly disadvantaged in the inner cities continued to upset liberal confidence in social progress. Meanwhile, the religious right, including southern ultraconservatives and fundamentalists, warned America about liberalism in religion and politics as a subversive threat to the very fabric of society.

In short, some political and cultural attitudes of the Gilded Age long survived the close of the nineteenth century when the period itself had ended.

Industrial Progress

. . . The commemorative Centennial Exhibition, which opened on the banks of the Schuylkill River outside Philadelphia for five months beginning on May 10, 1876, was conceived in a very different spirit from the celebrations for the bicentennial in 1976. Instead of political achievement, it emphasized America's mastery in the application of science. As such, it constituted an industrial revelation of America to the rest of the world.

Memorial Hall in Philadelphia was built in modern Renaissance style to exhibit American arts and culture. But nearby was Machinery Hall, a more austere yet more inviting building. It was guarded by a huge breech-loading cannon, the symbol of war, and by the Corliss steam engine. This enormous 1,400-horsepower machine, designed to furnish power to all the exhibits inside Machinery Hall astonished the 9,910,966 visitors that summer. It weighed nearly 1.7 million pounds and yet ran without vibration or noise. Here was a new symbol of peace and progress. Inside the hall inventions in the fields of agriculture, transportation, and machinery were given special prominence. By its display of drills, mowers, and reapers, of lumber wagons and Pullman sleeping cars, of sewing machines and typewriters, of planes, lathes, and looms, the United States demonstrated its preeminence in mechanics. As the *Times* of London reported on August 22, 1878, "the American mechanizes as an old Greek sculpted, as the Venetian painted." Novelist William Dean Howells gave his verdict to the *Atlantic Monthly* of July 1876. It was in engineering, rather than in art, that "the national genius most freely speaks: by and by the inspired marbles, the breathing canvases . . . [F]or the present America is voluble in the strong metals and their infinite uses. America's destiny lay in industrial development.

Between 1865 and 1901 the American Industrial Revolution transformed the United States from a country of small and isolated communities scattered across 3 million square miles of continental territory into a compact economic and industrial unit. Thus, the rural Republic of Lincoln and Lee became the industrial empire of Roosevelt and Bryan. The United States already had the prerequisites for such a transformation. It was fabulously rich in minerals, possessing about two-thirds of the world's coal; immense deposits of high-quality iron ore; great resources of petroleum; and, in the West, a natural treasury of gold, silver, and copper.

Although in 1860 the United States was still a second-rate industrial power, by 1890 it led Britain, France, and Germany. The value of its manufactured goods almost equaled the total of the others. The accompanying table, adapted from *Historical Statistics of the United States* (1975), shows increases in the production of raw materials between 1860 and 1900. It was precisely because the base of industry before the Civil War was so narrow that its advance seemed so spectacular later on.

There were five keys to America's astonishing industrial success: a superabundant supply of land and precious natural resources; excellent natural and manmade systems of transportation; a growing supply of labor caused by natural growth of population and massive immigration; special facility in invention and technology; and superb industrial organization. Thus what brought the American Industrial Revolution to fruition was human initiative, ingenuity, and physical energy.

The Agricultural Revolution hastened the Industrial Revolution in various ways. An increase in production per farmer allowed a transfer of labor from agriculture to industry without reducing the country's food supply. Moreover, such expanding agriculture did not need the transfer of limited capital from industry to agriculture. Indeed, the profits derived from agriculture could be used for buying manufactured goods, thereby further stimulating industry and manufacturing. There were two manufacturing belts across the nation. One stretched along the Atlantic coast from Maine in the North to Virginia in the South. The other was west of the Allegheny Mountains and north of the Ohio River, extending from Pittsburgh and Buffalo in the East to St. Louis and Milwaukee in the West.

From the middle of the century to the 1890s the railroads were the basis of the new industrial economy. They made possible the development of new areas of commerce as well as that of steel, iron, coal, and other industries. But in the 1890s it was the complex, varied urban market with its demand for a wider range of refined materials and manufactured goods that replaced the railroads as the principal stimulus of the economy as a whole. In the 1890s American cities were modernized, and steel was the essential medium used for building bridges, piping water and sewage, transmitting gas and electricity, and constructing ever higher buildings.

Iron replaced wood; steel replaced iron; and electricity and steam replaced horsepower. In 1870 agricultural production surpassed industrial production by about $500 million. Both were increasing year by year. But by 1900 manufacturing had increased by more than four times. Thus, industrial production now exceeded agricultural production by $13 billion to $4.7 billion. In every decade the levels of production increased in the oil refineries of Ohio and Pennsylvania; the iron and steel mills of Michigan, Illinois, and Pennsylvania; the meatpacking plants of Cincinnati and Chicago; the clothing and shoe factories of New England; and the breweries of Chicago, St. Louis, and Milwaukee. The number of people engaged in manufacturing was 2¼ times as great in 1890 as in 1870; in mining 2½ times as great; in transportation and public utilities 2½ times; in construction 2 times.

Industrial growth and westward expansion were assured by the revolution in transportation and the revolution in communications. There was a spectacular

Table   Industrial Production, 1860 and 1900

COMMODITY	1860 (MILLIONS)	1900 (MILLIONS)	INCREASE (%)
Anthracite coal (short tons)	10.9	57.3	525
Bituminous coal (short tons)	9.0	212.3	2,358
Crude Petroleum (barrels)	.5	45.8	9,160
Pig iron (long tons)	.8	13.7	1,713
Crude steel (short tons)	.01	11.2	11,227
Wheat (bushels)	173.1	599.0	339
Wheat exported (bushels)	4.0	102.0	2,550
Corn (bushels)	838.8	2,662.0	301
Cotton (bales)	3.8	10.1	261

growth in population, from 35,701,0000 in 1865 to 77,584,000 in 1901. Yet these widely dispersed people felt part of a unified whole. A transcontinental railroad network brought farm and factory, country and town closer together. Telegraph and telephone, electricity and press increased public knowledge, business efficiency, and political debate.

By their aptitude for invention and their ability to harness the inventions of others to their own purposes, Americans acquired a facility for turning raw materials into finished industrial products. Between 1860 and 1890 as many as 440,000 patents were issued for new inventions. During the Gilded Age the most significant American inventions, whether new or improved, were those that could hasten and secure *settlement:* the *s*team boilers of Babcock and Wilcox; the *e*lectric lamp of Thomas Alva Edison; the *t*elephone of Alexander Graham Bell; the *t*elegraph stock ticker of E. A. Callahan; *l*inoleum; the *e*levator of Elisha G. Otis; *m*achine tools of Pratt and Whitney; the *e*lixirs of John Wyeth; the *n*ewspaper linotype compositor of Ottmar Mergenthaler; and the *t*ypewriter of Christopher Shoes. The fundamental principles behind many of these and other inventions had long been understood. But not until technology could fashion tools of great delicacy could they be put into practice. Thus, the inventions depended on improved technology and they in turn transformed that technology, making possible ever more inventions of still greater refinement.

One reason why American technology in general became so advanced was the relatively high cost of labor in America that encouraged industrialists to invest in mechanizing. Moreover, the large domestic market allowed for great economies of scale. In addition, Americans in general were far less bound than Europeans by tradition and thus far more willing to try out new methods. Contemporary editor Mark Sullivan traces this facility to a natural ingenuity and determination in the people: "Intellectual freedom and curiosity about the new, the instinct of the American mind to look into, examine, and experiment—this led to, among other things, a willingness to 'scrap' not only old machinery but old formulas, old ideas; and brought about, among other results, the condition expressed in the saying that 'American mechanical progress could be measured by the size of its scrapheaps.'"

New York Business Elites and the Civil War

SVEN BECKERT

Paying for and equipping the war effort increased the dependence of the state on New York's bourgeoisie and the bourgeoisie's dependence on the state. Their important material role and their assumption of governmental functions during the first months of the crisis strengthened their relationship to the federal government; the relatively weak American state became, to a large extent, dependent on the material support of those who controlled capital. At the crux of the modern American state thus stood upper-class northerners, particularly those of New York City. As a result, private investment decisions became more and more entangled with the fate of the nation, and the defeat of the South became a question of economic survival. "[W]e uphold the Government in order that the institutes of commerce may be sustained," explained Abiel Abbot Low to the members of the Chamber of Commerce. Financial support for the government, confirmed the *American Railroad Journal,* was "dictated by a wise regard to their own interests, [because the] first condition of property is a stable government."

The mutual dependence of state and economic elite enabled "a vast realignment of forces in the national economy." The war presented the federal government with an opportunity to forge a new and different kind of political economy, including

Sven Beckert, *The Monied Metropolis: New York City and the Consolidation of the American Bourgeoisie, 1850–1896* (New York: Cambridge University Press, 2003), pp. 119–125. Reprinted by permission of Cambridge University Press.

strengthened forms of state intervention—from tariffs to immigration laws, from land grants to banking regulations. Though the federal government needed to bargain with all segments of New York City's upper class to gain access to the resources necessary to equip huge armies, the influence of these different segments varied widely. The power of the merchants who invested in trade with southern agricultural commodities and in the import of manufactured goods from Europe declined vis-à-vis the central state because their most important political allies, the southern slaveholders, had disappeared from the halls of power in Washington. Industrialists and some bankers, however, strengthened by a political coalition with western farmers, gained considerable influence to help shape the newly emerging political economy. If the war provided the federal government with new opportunities to intervene in existing economic arrangements, it also gave important segments of the upper class substantial bargaining power to influence this political economy.

Manufacturers in particular benefited tremendously from the mobilization for war, while at the same time, the government's new economic policy linked them solidly to the state. Demands for military equipment led many manufacturers, in particular makers of iron, textiles, and boots, to produce at capacity. At the same time, the newly enacted Morrill Tariff Act of 1861, as well as subsequent tariff increases (which by 1864 had doubled the 1857 duties on a wide range of goods), protected American industrialists from foreign competition. Homestead laws and land grants to railroads, moreover, benefited commercial agriculture in the West and increased demands for agricultural implements produced by domestic industries. Joseph Seligman, mindful of these connections, concluded in September of 1864 that if the Republicans would win the November elections, "I would be in favor of investing in manufacturing as in that case the tariff would hardly be lowered during nearly 5 years." The *American Railroad Journal* went even further, and predicted that the government's need for revenue would keep the tariff in place for at least twenty years.

Industrialists, indeed, saw the war early on as a decisive and irreversible break with the antebellum political economy. The war "has released us from the bondage to cotton," opined the *American Railroad Journal,* "which for generations has hung over us like a spell, destroying all freedom of commercial or political action, and rendering us slaves to the most absurd delusions." With "the old channels of business" gone, trade with the West, in combination with high tariffs and the provision of an abundant labor supply through immigration, spelled a bright "future of our manufacturing interests." And these new arrangements, forged by war, were to last, since "[t]emporary war measures," such as higher tariffs, have "brought into existence business interests largely dependent on the continuance of" them. Many industrialists were clearly aware that the war had the potential for revolutionizing not only the South but also the political economy of the North, and they welcomed this revolution.

Bankers, however, saw the new political economy emerging in the war years with considerably more ambivalence. Their business activities had traditionally focused on financing trade as well as the transfer of foreign capital to the United States, and both these activities were now disrupted by the conflict. Moreover, their tight economic and social links to the city's merchant community made it difficult for them to embrace wholeheartedly the newly arising economic policy of the federal government, which impeded the developmental trajectory of Atlantic trade. As if this was not enough, the war also endangered the delicate balance of state regulation and self-policing that had given a semblance of stability to the nation's monetary and banking system. Indeed, the war years decisively recast the nation's banking system, and New York's bankers could not help but feel ambivalent about such rapid change.

Ambivalence about change, however, did not equal unforgiving hostility to the newly emerging political economy. For bankers, winning the war and forcefully re-uniting the nation was of tantamount importance, since the stability of the nation's monetary and banking systems, and therefore, the stability of their enterprises, rested on subjugating the South. More immediately, the federal government owed huge and ever-growing amounts of money to them, and its ability to serve on principal and interest depended on victory in the war. Because their business interests, in effect, depended on capturing the Confederacy, they provided the government with ever more resources, making a victory in war ever more urgent. The federal government, in turn, desperately sought the resources of New York's banks, giving the bankers enormous influence over central areas of government policy.

The federal government hence depended on New York City's bankers, and vice versa. It was a dependence fraught with tensions. At their core was the question of how to restructure the nation's monetary and banking systems. The rapid mobilization for war put the old institutional framework under such tremendous strains that it effectively broke down. As early as December 1861, New York banks had suspended specie payment because of high demand for gold from the government and specu-lators. In obvious ways, the old system was not capable of sustaining the necessary war mobilizations.

Open conflict surfaced as early as February 1862, when Congress responded to the banks' suspension of specie payment by issuing legal tender notes worth $150 million. Many, but not all, of the city's bankers opposed this bold new assertion of federal powers. George S. Coe of the American Exchange Bank, Jacob D. Vermilye of the Merchants' Bank, David R. Martin of the Ocean Bank, and James Gallatin of the National Bank all spoke out against the bill. As creditors and old-fashioned mer-chant bankers, they feared the inflationary impact of such a move. Other bankers, however, supported the measure, among them Moses H. Grinnell, Moses Taylor of City Bank, and the president of the Bank of Commerce, John A. Stevens. Their move was certainly politically motivated, as both Stevens and Grinnell were leading Re-publicans in New York, but they also expressed willingness to experiment with new forms of monetary policy to advance the Union's military position.

The split in the city's banking community on monetary politics allowed Lincoln and Congress to proceed with the planned issuance of greenbacks. However, when New York's bankers stood as a phalanx against reform, the federal government lacked the power to effect change. This effective veto power of New York's bankers came into sharp focus in the winter of 1862/63 when [U.S. Treasury Secretary Salmon P.] Chase pushed for the creation of national banks, which, regulated by the federal government, would create a secure market for federal bonds and inte-grate the new greenbacks into the financial system. The measure promised to revo-lutionize the United States banking system, creating the position of Comptroller of the Currency, who could charter "national" banks. In return, these banks would receive national bank notes in the amount of 90 percent of the market value of the bonds. These national banks would have to keep reserves of greenbacks and specie of at least 25 percent of their outstanding notes and deposits.

New York's bankers opposed this reform unequivocally. Distrusting federal regulation, they feared that the reserve requirements would keep a larger share of very profitable funds away from New York City banks. This would effectively strengthen non–New York banks. As a result, by November 1863, only three national banks had organized in New York City. Yet without national banks organizing in sufficient numbers in New York, national banks in other states could not keep some of their reserves as bankers' balances in the city, thus undercutting the viability of the system as a whole. In fact, New York's bankers opposed the new law to such a degree that they collectively decided to resist its implementation. In September 1863, banker Augustus Ely Silliman went as far as to call upon members of the New York City Clearing House to refuse cooperation with the federal government.

The pressure of the city's bankers, undercutting the aims of the banking bill, was so powerful that by November, Comptroller of the Currency Hugh McCulloch proposed changing the law in order to accommodate the protesting banks. The new banking act reduced reserve requirements from 25 percent, as legislated in the first bill, to 15 percent, of which three-fifths could be kept as bankers' balances in eighteen designated redemption cities, including New York. Banks in these eighteen cities were then required "to redeem their notes in New York; in return, these banks were permitted to keep one-half of their twenty-five percent required reserves on deposit in New York City banks." The upshot of these complicated regulations was that the city's banks would be able to draw the very profitable bankers' balances into their vaults. Moreover, a special provision in the act was made solely for Stevens's Bank of Commerce, exempting it from the double liability rule, thus inducing a political friend of the Republican administration to convert to the national system. According to Charles Russell, who at that time was a director of the Bank of Commerce, "the administration and the leaders of the majority in Congress were anxious to meet the wishes of the Bank of Commerce."

The revised act was now successful; by October 12, 1864, twelve national banks were doing business in New York City, and by mid-November, the important Bank of Commerce had become a national bank. Through their determined struggle, New York City's bankers had influenced the nation's new banking structure and succeeded in concentrating ever more financial resources in the city. Most remarkably, even in times of war, the United States had opted against creating a central bank, and though for the next forty years conflicts over monetary politics would focus on the relative importance of the state vis-à-vis the market, it was the latter that remained dominant.

As a further result of this twisted path toward reform, the war catapulted bankers into the center of the newly emerging political economy. Bankers had pledged a good deal of their future on the survival of the Union, and they eventually agreed to a strong role for the federal government in financial policy making. They also agreed to and paid for a vast expansion of the state apparatus. These attachments to the nation would bring them into close contact with the federal government and its particular developmental vision for many decades to come. The institutionalization of national bank regulations, and the issue of a national currency, in particular, linked the city's bankers to the state to a degree before unknown, while simultaneously emancipating them as a group from the tight grip of the traders in southern agricultural commodities. By virtue of their importance to the war, their eventual openness to change, and their ability to shape financial policy, bankers were among the greatest beneficiaries of the conflict.

The emancipation of many of the city's bankers from the city's merchant community and its developmental vision was made all the easier because of the ever more prominent role played by a generation of bankers who only came into their own during the Civil War. It was the Morgans and Seligmans, linked to the national government and the newly emerging industries, not the Belmonts and Wards, who became the most powerful bankers of the postbellum United States. Indeed, some bankers got their start only as a result of the war. George F. Baker, as we have seen, was one of them, and Levi Parson Morton another. The Seligmans also began their career in finance during the Civil War when they sold treasury bonds in the European market, eventually giving up their clothing business and turning themselves into important international bankers. By 1865, as a result, the makeup of New York's banking community, its links to the state, and its developmental vision had all changed dramatically.

Even more ambiguous than the position of the bankers was the relationship of the city's merchants to the war. Although they profited from the conflict, their position was weakened relative to other segments of New York's upper class. Many of their trade links were disrupted, and attacks by the Confederate navy on 150 Union merchant vessels during the first three years of the war alone damaged the United States shipping industry severely, as insurance premiums skyrocketed. Rising tariffs, a cornerstone of Republican economic policy, further threatened to undermine the merchants' foreign trade. Although the Chamber of Commerce opposed the passage of new tariff laws, it did so largely without success, drawing into stark relief the merchants' weakened political power.

A minority of merchants, however, began to adjust themselves to the dynamics of the new age, and it was these who blossomed most during the war. Their trade and other business activities moved them away from dependence on the South. Republican William E. Dodge, for example, with his investments in railroads and metals rooting him firmly in the country's newly emerging political economy, ran successfully for Congress in 1864, mostly with the help of his constituents in the wealthy Murray Hill section of Manhattan. Seeing himself as the representative of the "commercial interests of the city," he still embraced the high tariffs of his Republican colleagues, envisioning a political economy in which merchants would flourish, "promoted by the prosperity of the agricultural and manufacturing interests, and by the ability of the country, which alone can come from that prosperity, to buy and pay for the vast amounts of import."

Like merchants, builders and contractors showed ambivalence about the effects of the war on the nation's political economy. Because they did not forge strong links to the federal government, and because they depended on local political connections for public construction projects, they remained sensitive to the concerns of working-class voters and politicians who fought for local autonomy, an allegiance which would come into sharp focus during the conflict over conscription in 1863.

Still, for these local capitalists, as for the merchants, bankers, and manufacturers, the importance of the federal government increased tremendously, not least because it was only through a strong state that the Union could be reunited. Never before in United States history had the federal government played such an important role in domestic economic life, and never before had upper-class Americans been so thoroughly linked to this government. As a result, the economic elites' stakes in the war increased as the fighting continued. By 1863, the Chamber of Commerce had added to its reasons to "unite in putting the rebellion down" the "vast pecuniary obligation" that the war itself had created.

WEEK 2

DOCUMENTS

4. A Northern Unionist Lectures Ex-Slaves on the Work Ethic, 1865

To the Freed People of Orangeburg District.

You have heard many stories about your condition as freemen. You do not know what to believe: you are talking too much; waiting too much; asking for too much. If you can find out the truth about this matter, you will settle down quietly to your work. Listen, then, and try to understand just how you are situated.

You are not free, but you must know that the only difference you can feel yet, between slavery and freedom, is that neither you nor your children can be bought or sold. You may have a harder time this year than you have ever had before; it will be the price you pay for your freedom. You will have to work hard, and get very little to eat, and very few clothes to wear. If you get through this year alive and well, you should be thankful. Do not expect to save up anything, or to have much corn or provisions ahead at the end of the year. You must not ask for more pay than free people get at the North. There, a field hand is paid in money, but has to spend all his pay every week, in buying food and clothes for his family and in paying rent

_____

From "Notions on the Management of Negroes," *Farmer's Register* 4 (December 1836): 495.

From Captain Charles Soule to General Oliver Otis Howard, Freedman's Bureau, June 12, 1865, in S-17, 1865, Letters Received (Series 15), Washington Headquarters, Records of the Bureau of Refugees, Freedmen & Abandoned Lands, Record Group 105, National Archives.

for his house. You cannot be paid in money,—for there is no good money in the District,—nothing but Confederate paper. Then, what can you be paid with? Why, with food, with clothes, with the free use of your little houses and lots. You do not own a cent's worth except yourselves. The plantation you live on is not yours, nor the houses, nor the cattle, mules and horses; the seed you planted with was not yours, and the ploughs and hoes do not belong to you. Now you must get something to eat and something to wear, and houses to live in. How can you get these things? By hard work—and nothing else, and it will be a good thing for you if you get them until next year, for yourselves and for your families. You must remember that your children, your old people, and the cripples, belong to you to support now, and all that is given to them is so much pay to you for your work. If you ask for anything more; if you ask for a half of the crop, or even a third, you ask too much; you wish to get more than you could get if you had been free all your lives. Do not ask for Saturday either: free people everywhere else work Saturday, and you have no more right to the day than they have. If your employer is willing to give you part of the day, or to set a task that you can finish early, be thankful for the kindness, but do not think it is something you must have. When you work, work hard. Begin early at sunrise, and do not take more than two hours at noon. Do not think, because you are free you can choose your own kind of work. Every man must work under orders. The soldiers, who are free, work under officers, the officers under the general, and the general under the president. There must be a head man everywhere, and on a plantation the head man, who gives all the orders, is the owner of the place. Whatever he tells you to do you must do at once, and cheerfully. Never give him a cross word or an impudent answer. If the work is hard, do not stop to talk about it, but do it first and rest afterwards. If you are told to go into the field and hoe, see who can go first and lead the row. If you are told to build a fence, build it better than any fence you know of. If you are told to drive the carriage Sunday, or to mind the cattle, do it, for necessary work must be done even on the Sabbath. Whatever the order is, try and obey it without a word.

Captain Charles Soule

5. "We Demand Land": Petition by Southern Freedmen, 1865

Edisto Island S. C. Oct 28th, 1865.

To the President of these United States. We the freedmen of Edisto Island South Carolina have learned From you through Major General O O Howard commissioner of the Freedman's Bureau. with deep sorrow and Painful hearts of the possibility of government restoring These lands to the former owners. We are well aware Of the

---

From Freedman of Edisto Island to General Howard and to President Johnson, October 28, 1865, in Henry Bram et al. to Major General O. O. Howard [October 28, 1865], and Henry Bram et al. to the President of the United States, October 28, 1865, B-53, 1865 and P-27, 1865, Letters Received (Series 15), Washington Headquarters, Records of the Bureau of Refugees, Freedmen & Abandoned Lands, National Archives.

many perplexing and trying questions that burden Your mind. and do therefore pray to god (the preserver of all. and who has through our Late and beloved President [Lincoln] proclamation and the war made Us A free people) that he may guide you in making Your decisions. and give you that wisdom that Cometh from above to settle these great and Important Questions for the best interests of the country and the Colored race: Here is where secession was born and Nurtured Here is were we have toiled nearly all Our lives as slaves and were treated like dumb Driven cattle. This is our home, we have made These lands what they are. we were the only true and Loyal people that were found in possession of these Lands. we have been always ready to strike for Liberty and humanity yea to fight if needs be To preserve this glorious union. Shall not we who Are freedman and have been always true to this Union have the same rights as are enjoyed by Others? Have we broken any Law of these United States? have we forfeited our rights of property in Land?— If not then! are not our rights as A free people and good citizens of these United States To be considered before the rights of those who were Found in rebellion against this good and just Government (and now being conquered) come (as they Seem) with penitent hearts and beg forgiveness For past offences and also ask if their lands Cannot be restored to them are these rebellious Spirits to be reinstated in their *possessions* And we who have been abused and oppressed For many long years not to be allowed the Privilige of purchasing land But be subject To the will of these large Land owners? God forbid. Land monopoly is injurious to the advancement of the course of freedom, and if Government Does not make some provision by which we as Freedmen can obtain A Homestead, we have Not bettered our condition.

We have been encouraged by Government to take Up these lands in small tracts, receiving Certificates of the same—we have thus far Taken Sixteen thousand (16000) acres of Land here on This Island. We are ready to pay for this land When Government calls for it. and now after What has been done will the good and just government take from us all this right and make us Subject to the will of those who have cheated and Oppressed us for many years God Forbid!

We the freedmen of this Island and of the State of South Carolina—Do therefore petition to you as the President of these United States, that some provisions be made by which Every colored man can purchase land. and Hold it as his own. We wish to have A home if It be but A few acres. without some provision is Made our future is sad to look upon. yess our Situation is dangerous. we therefore look to you In this trying hour as A true friend of the poor and Neglected race. for protection and Equal Rights. with the privilege of purchasing A Homestead— A Homestead right here in the Heart of South Carolina.

We pray that God will direct your heart in Making such provision for us as freedmen which Will tend to united these states together stronger Than ever before—May God bless you in the Administration of your duties as the President Of these United States is the humble prayer Of us all.–

In behalf of the Freedmen
Henry Bram
Committee   Ishmael. Moultrie.
yates. Sampson

6. African-American Washerwomen Demand Higher Wages, 1866

Mayor Barrows

Jackson, Mississippi, June 20, 1866

Dear Sir:

At a meeting of the colored Washerwomen of this city, on the evening of the 18th of June, the subject of raising the wages was considered, and the following preamble and resolution were unanimously adopted:

Whereas, under the influence of the present high prices of all the necessaries of life, and the attendant high rates of rent, we, the washerwomen of the city of Jackson, State of Mississippi, thinking it impossible to live uprightly and honestly in laboring for the present daily and monthly recompense, and hoping to meet with the support of all good citizens, join in adopting unanimously the following resolution:

Be it resolved by the washerwomen of this city and county, That on and after the foregoing date, we join in charging a uniform rate for our labor, and any one belonging to the class of washerwomen, violating this, shall be liable to a fine regulated by the class. We do not wish in the least to charge exorbitant prices, but desire to be able to live comfortably if possible from the fruits of our labor. We present the matter to your Honor, and hope you will not reject it. The prices charged are:

$1.50 per day for washing

$15.00 per month for family washing

$10.00 per month for single individuals

We ask you to consider the matter in our behalf, and should you deem it just and right, your sanction of the movement will be gratefully received.

Yours, very truly,
THE WASHERWOMEN OF JACKSON

7. "Colored" vs. Chinese in Galveston, 1877

Monday night colored women, emboldened by the liberties allowed their fathers, husbands and brothers decided to have a public hurrah of their own, and as the men had demanded two dollars for a day's labor they would ask $1.50 or $9 per week. As women are generally considered cleansers of dirty linen, their first move was against the steam laundry, corner of Avenue A and Tenth Street, owned by J. N. Harding.

About 6:30 A.M. colored women began collecting around his house, until they numbered about twenty-five. The laundry women were soon seen coming to work. When met and told that they should not work for less than $1.50 per day, four turned back; but, one, a Miss Murphy went into the house and began working. Seeing this,

From *Jackson Daily Clarion,* June 24, 1866.
From *Galveston News,* August 1, 1877.

the women rushed in, caught her and carried her into the street, and by threats forced her to leave.

This success emboldened the women to further demonstrations. The cry was raised, "Let's lock them out for good; here's nails I brought especially." An axe lying in the wood pile was grabbed, and the laundry house doors and windows secured. Then off they started for the heathen Chinese, who "washed Mellican man clothes so cheapee." Down Market street they went, led by a portly colored lady, whose avoir-dupois is not less than 250.

Each California laundry was visited in turn, beginning at Slam Sing's and ending at Wau Loong's corner of Bath Avenue and Post-office Street. At these laundries all the women talked at once, telling Slam Sing, Wau Loong and the rest that "they must close up and leave this city within fifteen days or they would be driven away," each Chinaman responding "Yees, yees," "Me go, yees," and closed their shops. The women scattered after avowing they would meet again at 4 o'clock and visit each place where women are fired, and if they receive less than $1.50 per day or $9 per week they would force them to quit.

8. Sharecropper Nate Shaw Makes His Crop, 1913

I've made a crop more or less every year, come too much rain or too much sun. I've had my cotton grow so fast as to grow to a weed. I've picked from many a stalk of cotton that growed so high until it was just a stalk, not many bolls I'd get for it. On the other hand, when the seasons just hit right, I've had stalks of cotton weren't no more than three foot high, just laying down with bolls. It don't take the tallest cotton to make a big crop.

In the year 1912, second crop I ever made on Miss Hattie Lu Reeve's place, good God it come a snap—and my cotton should have been thinned out, by right, but I weren't done chopin it out. And it come a cold day and and it sleeted on my crop. Done that again the next year, sleeted on that cotton in May, 1912, and 1913, too. And that cotton turned yellow as a fox and shedded off every leaf on it, but left the buds. I examined it and it looked terrible—in a day or two when the weather moderated, I examined my little old cotton and seed it was still alive, and them buds, after the sun hit em good, turnin hot after the snap of weather, little old cotton buds just kept livin and commenced a puttin out, flourishin. I just chopped it regular when I seed all that. And when I laid that cotton by, plowed it and put the dirt to it, it still looked weak and yellow. But it wouldn't die, it just kept a comin, kept a comin until it come out and made me that year eight good bales of cotton—1913. That was a high production for a one-horse farm. In them days people didn't make a bale to the acre. I had about eleven or twelve acres under cultivation and it weren't no first class land. But it was smooth land, easy to work. . . .

We hand-picked that cotton, all of it. Five years old, that's big enough to pick many a little handful, and my daddy had me out in the field pickin cotton before that. And I picked until I picked many a hundred pounds for my boy Vernon, for

From Theodore Rosengarten, *All God's Dangers: The Life of Nate Shaw,* copyright © 1974 by Theodore Rosengarten. (New York: Alfred A. Knopf, 1975), pp. 182–190. Used by permission by Alfred A. Knopf, a division of Random House, Inc.

four years after I quit foolin with it myself. When I quit off pickin for Vernon I was able to pick as much as a hundred pounds a day—that was a little help to him. Pickin regular on my own farm, to pick up to three hundred pounds a day. The Bible says, once a man and twice a child—well, it's that way pickin cotton. I picked at the end of my cotton pickin days how much I picked at the start. . . .

Gathered that cotton from when it first opened up, around the latter part of August or the first week in September, and right through till it was all gathered. White man get out there and raise a big crop of cotton—when I was a boy and after I was grown, every little Negro chap in the whole country around, as far as he had time to go get em, go get em and put em in his field pickin cotton. And his little crowd, maybe, if he had any chaps, they'd be pickin some on off-hours of school. Come home and go to pickin cotton. But mainly it was nigger children gathered the white man's crop when I come along. And if a chap had in mind that he didn't want to pick this man's cotton—chaps knowed whose cotton it was—mama and papa was sufficient to make him pick it. Carry that child out, some of em, in a white man's field, they'd work his little butt off with a switch if he didn't gather that cotton. You'd find some industrious white people that would work like colored; they was poor people, they'd get out there and pick. But ones that didn't care so much about stoopin down and pickin cotton, their cotton got ready—the little nigger chaps wasn't goin to school; scoop em up like flies and put em in the field.

Picked cotton in a sack—that's how we done it in this country, and other cotton countries I've heard spoke of. Put a sack on, long sack, sometimes the sack would be draggin behind you far enough that a little chap could walk up on the end of it. You'd have a strap to that sack, cross your chest and over your shoulder, resemblin to a harness, and the mouth of that sack right under your arm; you'd pick cotton and just drop it in there. That sack'd hold a full hundred pounds.

Take that sack and empty it in a big basket, cotton basket. White man would set it in his field, or a Negro, if it was his field and he had baskets. I used my own baskets, I made cotton baskets. Didn't pick my crops no other way but empty the cotton out of the sack and into the basket, and that relieved my sack, the weight of it on me, that would take it off, any amount of cotton I had picked in my sack.

I'd take my wagon to the field after me and my children done picked several baskets of cotton, stand it there and go the emptyin that cotton in the wagon. Set them baskets out there to keep a gatherin. I could nicely weigh my cotton in a basket then throw it on the wagon. Weighed my cotton right there, as I loaded it. My wife had good book learnin, she'd take the figures to the house—I could make figures but I didn't know enough to add em up: give her the book with the cotton figures on it, she'd add it up and tell me when I got a bale. That wagon had to move out of the field then. . . .

From my first startin off farmin after I married, even workin on halves, I had to carry my cotton to the gin. And when I got to where I rented, I'd gin at any gin I wanted to. I had mules able to do it; hitch them mules to my wagon, take em to the field; take em from the field to the barn; pull out from the barn to the gin. Drive up under a suction pipe; that suction would pull that lint cotton off the wagon and into them gins and the gins would gin it out—separate the lint from the seed and the seed would fall in a box. Another pipe carried the seed overhead from that box to a seed house out yonder. Didn't have nothin to do but go out there and open up that seed-house box and catch all my seed. Cotton went from the gin machines to a press—all them seeds and whatever trash was picked with that cotton done been ginned out. And a man at the press would work a lever and the press would press the cotton down into a box the shape of a bale so he could bale it off. He'd already have a underbaggin under it and he'd pull the top baggin down and wrap that cotton up, faster them hooks, and bale it. . . .

Right there and then, and aint aimin to sell that cotton, you take that cotton back home and dump it off your wagon. It's used, startin at home—my mother, after the cotton come back from the gin, seed removed and leave the pure lint. I've seen her take a pair of cards, two cards each about as wide as my four fingers, and its made in the resemblance and in the manner and in the style of a mule brush. And she'd take one in one hand and lay a handful of that cotton on it, take the other card and comb it—that's called cardin batts—then change cards and comb it the other way until she got a nice clear batt of cotton in them brushes. And she'd have a quilt linin stretched out in the house and she'd take that batt of cotton, nice wad of cotton, and lay them batts all over that quilt; she could lay em as thick or thin as she wanted, then spread the next layer of cloth over it and sew the top layer and the bottom layer together around the edge—sewin that cotton in there and pullin it just tight enough to make it flat like she wanted a quilt. And when she sewed as far as she could reach, then she'd roll that quilt, take it loose from the corners of her frames, pull out them nails or small spikes and roll that quilt under, roll it under, just get it far enough, close enough, far as she could reach with her hand sewin. She'd do all around that quilt thataway, from one corner to the other. Had a bed quilt then, warm quilt, plied through with cotton. . . .

. . . If you want to sell your cotton at once, you take it to the market, carry it to the Apafalya cotton market and they'll sample it. Cotton buyin man cuts a slug in the side of your bale, reaches in there and pulls the first of it out the way and get him a handful, just clawin in there. He'll look over that sample, grade that cotton—that's his job. What kind of grade do it make? You don't know until he tells you. If it's short staple, the devil, your price is cut on that cotton. Color matters too, and the way it was ginned—some gins cuts up the cotton, ruins the staple. . . .

And so, I'd have my cotton weighed and I'd go up and down the street with my sample. Meet a white man, farmin man like myself, on the street; he'd see what I been offered for my sample—the buyer's marks would be on the wrapper—or I'd tell him. And he'd take that sample, unwrap it, look at it; he'd say, "Nate, I can beat you with your own cotton, I can get more for it than that."

Aint that enough to put your boots on! The same sample. He'd say, "Let me take your sample and go around in your place. I can beat what they offered you."

Take that cotton and go right to the man that had his bid on it and he'd raise it; right behind where I was, had been, and get a better bid on it. I've gived a white man my sample right there on the streets of Apafalya; he'd go off and come back. Sometimes he'd say, "Well, Nate, I helped you a little on it but I couldn't help you much."

And sometime he'd get a good raise on it with another fellow out yonder. He'd bring my sample back to me with a bid on it. "Well, Nate, I knowed I could help you on that cotton."

That was happenin all through my farmin years: from the time I stayed on the Curtis place, and when I moved to the Ames place, and when I lived with Mr. Reeve, and when I moved down on Sitimachas Creek with Mr. Tucker, and when I lived up there at Two Forks on the Stark place, and when I moved down on the Pollard place and stayed there nine years. Colored man's cotton weren't worth as much as white man's cotton less'n it come to the buyer in the white man's hands. But the colored man's labor—that was worth more to the white man than the labor of his own color because it cost him less and he got just as much for his money.

ESSAYS

⚜ *E S S A Y S*

The Plantation Work Ethic

EUGENE GENOVESE

The slaveholders presided over a plantation system that constituted a halfway house between peasant and factory cultures. The tobacco and cotton plantations, which dominated the slave economy in the United States, ranged closer to the peasant than the factory model, in contradistinction to the great sugar plantations of the Caribbean, which in some respects resembled factories in the field; but even the small holders pushed their laborers toward modern work discipline. The planter's problem came to this: How could they themselves preserve as much as possible of that older way of life to which they aspired and yet convince their slaves to repudiate it? How could they instill factorylike discipline into a working population engaged in a rural system that, for all its tendencies toward modern discipline, remained bound to the rhythms of nature and to traditional ideas of work, time, and leisure?

They succeeded in overcoming this contradiction only to the extent that they got enough work out of their slaves to make the system pay at a level necessary to their survival as a slaveholding class in a capitalist world market. But they failed in deeper ways that cast a shadow over the long-range prospects for that very survival and over the future of both blacks and whites in American society. Too often they fell back on the whip and thereby taught and learned little. When they went to other incentives, as fortunately most tried to do, they did get satisfactory economic results, but at the same time they reinforced traditional attitudes and values instead of replacing them with more advanced ones.

The black work ethic grew up within a wider Protestant Euro-American community with a work ethic of its own. The black ethic represented at once a defense against an enforced system of economic exploitation and an autonomous assertion of values generally associated with preindustrial peoples. As such, if formed part of a more general southern work ethic, which developed in antagonism to that of the wider American society. A Euro-American, basically Anglo-Saxon work ethic helped shape that of southerners in general and slaves in particular and yet, simultaneously, generated a profound antithesis.

In the medieval Catholic formulation the necessity to work both derived from the Fall of Man and served as an expression of humility and submission. . . . To this stern doctrine of work as duty the slave opposed a religion of joy in life that echoed traditional Africa and, surprising as it may seem, even more firmly echoed the spirit of the plantation community itself. To speak of a "calling" or vocation for slaves would be absurd; but more to the point, worldly asceticism neither corresponded to the sensibilities shaped by the historical development from Africa to the New World nor could take root among a people who had no material stake in its flowering. . . .

The slaves' attitude toward time and work arose primarily from their own experience on the plantations of the South. Comparisons with Africa suggest some important cultural continuities. Traditional African time-reckoning focuses on present and past, not future. Time, being two-dimensional, moves, as it were, backward into a long past; the future, not having been experienced, appears senseless. This idea of time, which inhibited the appearance of an indigenous millennialism prior to Islamic and Christian penetrations, encouraged economic attitudes not readily assimilable to early bourgeois demands for saving, thrift, and accumulation. But, however, strong the specifically African influence, even more important are those tendencies which characterize preindustrial agricultural peoples in general, for whom the Africans provided a variant or, rather, a series of variants. . . .

Traditional society measured its time by calendars based on agricultural and seasonal patterns, which themselves formed part of an integrated religious worldview. The year proceeded according to a certain rhythm, not according to equal units of time; appropriate festivals and rites broke its continuity and marked the points at which the human spirit celebrated the rhythm of the natural order. Not pure quantities of time obtained, but such flexible units as the beginning of planting and of the harvest. Time became subordinated to the natural order of work and leisure, as their servant rather than their master.

Whereas in peasant farming the work tasks and such natural conditions as the amount of daylight determine the length of the workday, the acceptable number and duration of breaks, and the amount and type of leisure, in factory work "the arbitrarily fixed time schedule determines the beginning and the end of the work periods." In peasant societies work tasks such as planting and harvesting, which appear to conform to the demands of nature, have oriented the notation of time. E. P. Thompson argues convincingly that this "task orientation" has rendered work more humanly comprehensible: "The peasant or labourer appears to attend upon what is an observed necessity." For the preindustrial English community as a whole the distinction between "work" and "life" was much less clear than it was to become; the working day itself lengthened and contracted according to necessary tasks, and no great conflict appeared between the demands of work and those of leisure. One need not idealize the undoubtedly harsh physical conditions of preindustrial rural life to appreciate the force of Thompson's argument, especially since those who passed under industrial work discipline probably were themselves the ones who came most to idealize their previous existence and, thereby to heighten either their resistance or their despair. . . .

The advent of clock time represented more than a marking of regular work units—of minutes and hours—and of arbitrary schedules, for it supported the increasing division of labor and transformed that division of labor into a division of time itself. Capitalism production had to be measured in units of labor-time, and those units themselves took on the mysterious and apparently self-determining properties of commodities. When Benjamin Franklin said that time is money, he said much more than is generally understood. E. P. Thompson comments: "In a mature capitalist society all time must be consumed, marketed, put to *use;* it is offensive for the labour force merely to pass the time." Natural rhythms of work and leisure gave place to arbitrary schedules, which were, however, arbitrary only from the point of view of the laborers. The capitalists and those ideologues who were developing a new idea of rationality based on the demands of a rapidly developing economy saw the matter differently. The process of cultural transformation had to rest on economic and extra-economic compulsion and ultimately on violence. It served as the industrial equivalent of that which the West Indian slaveholders, with fewer inhibitions, called "seasoning." . . .

The slaves could not reckon time either according to preindustrial peasant models or according to industrial factory models. The plantations, especially the sugar plantations, that dominated most of the slaveholding regions of the New World, although not of the United States, did resemble factories in the field, but even if we take them as our norm we cannot escape the implications of their preindustrial side. However much their economic organization required and tried to compel quasi-industrial discipline, they also threw up countervailing pressures and embodied inescapable internal contradictions.

The setting remained rural, and the rhythm of work followed seasonal fluctuations. Nature remained the temporal reference point for the slaves. However much the slaveholders might have wished to transform their slaves into clock-punchers, they could not, for in a variety of sense both literal and metaphoric, there were no clocks to punch. The planters, especially the resident planters of the United States and Brazil but even the typical West Indian agents of absentee owners, hardly lived in a factory world themselves and at best could only preach what the most docile or stupid slave knew very well they did not and could not practice. Since the plantation economy required extraordinary exertion at critical points of the year, notably the harvest, it required measures to capitalize on the slaves' willingness to work in spurts rather than steadily. The slaveholders turned the inclinations of the slaves to their own advantage, but simultaneously they made far greater concessions to the value system and collective sensibility of the quarters than they intended.

The slaveholders, as usual, had their way but paid a price. The slaves, as usual, fell victim to the demands of their exploiters but had some success in pressing their own advantage. Thus, the plantation system served as a halfway house for Africans between their agricultural past and their imposed industrial future. But, it froze them into a position that allowed for their exploitation on the margins of industrial society. The advantage of this compromise, from the black point of view, lay in the protection it provided for their rich community life and its cultural consolidation. The disadvantage lay in its encouragement of a way of life that, however admirable intrinsically, ill prepared black people to compete in the economic world into which they would be catapulted by emancipation. . . .

The black view of time, conditioned by the plantation slave experience, has provided a great source of strength for a people at bay, as one of Bishop A. G. Dunston's sermons makes clear:

> You know, that's the way God does it. Same as you can't hurry God—so why don't you wait, just wait. Everybody's ripping and racing and rushing. And God is taking his time. Because he knows that it isn't hurtin' nearly so bad as you and I think it's hurtin'—and that is the way he wants us to go. But by and by he brings relief. . . .

Black people, in short, learned to take the blow and to parry it as best they could. They found themselves shut out by white racism from part of the dominant culture's value system, and they simultaneously resisted that system both by historically developed sensibility and by necessity. Accordingly, they developed their own values as a force for community cohesion and survival, but in so doing they widened the cultural gap and exposed themselves to even harder blows from a white nation that could neither understand their behavior nor respect its moral foundations.

. . . The African tradition, like the European peasant tradition, stressed hard work and condemned and derided laziness in any form. Not hard work but steady, routinized work as moral duty was discounted. In this attitude African agriculturalists resembled preindustrial peoples in general, including urban peoples. The familiar assertion that certain people would work only long enough to earn the money they needed to live was leveled not only against day laborers but against the finest and most prestigious artisans in early modern Europe. . . .

The slaves' willingness to work extraordinarily hard and yet to resist the discipline of regularity accompanied certain desires and expectations. During Reconstruction the blacks sought their own land; worked it conscientiously when they could get it; resisted being forced back into anything resembling gang labor for the white man; and had to be terrorized, swindled, and murdered to prevent their working for themselves. This story was prefigured in antebellum times when slaves were often allowed garden plots for their families and willingly worked them late at night or on Sundays in order to provide extra food or clothing. The men did not generally let their families subsist on the usual allotments of pork and corn. In addition to working with their wives in the gardens, they fished and hunted and trapped animals. In these and other ways they demonstrated considerable concern for the welfare of their families and a strong desire to take care of them. But in such instances they were working for themselves and at their own pace. Less frequently, slaves received permission to hire out their own time after having completed the week's assigned tasks. They were lured, not by some internal pressure to work steadily, but by the opportunity to work for themselves and their families in their own way.

Many slaves voluntarily worked for their masters on Sundays or holidays in return for money or goods. This arrangement demonstrated how far the notion of the slaves' "right" to a certain amount of time had been accepted by the masters; how readily the slaves would work for themselves; and how far the notion of reciprocity had entered the thinking of both masters and slaves.

The slaves responded to moral as well as economic incentives. They often took pride in their work, but not necessarily in the ways most important to their masters. Solomon Northup designed a better way to transport lumber only to find himself ridiculed by the overseer. In this case it was in the master's interest to intervene, and he did. He praised Northup and adopted the plan. Northup comments: "I was not insensible to the praise bestowed upon me, and enjoyed especially, my triumph over Taydem [the overseer], whose half-malicious ridicule had stung my pride."

From colonial days onward plantation slaves, as well as those in industry, mining, and town services, received payments in money and goods as part of a wider system of social control. These payments served either as incentive bonuses designated to stimulate productivity, or more frequently, as a return for work done during the time recognized as the slaves' own. Many planters, including those who most clearly got the best results, used such incentives. Bennett H. Barrow of Louisiana provides a noteworthy illustration, for he was not a man to spare the whip. Yet his system of rewards included frequent holidays and dinners, as well as cash bonuses and presents for outstanding work. In Hinds County, Mississippi, Thomas Dabney gave small cash prizes—a few cents, really—to his best pickers and then smaller prizes to others who worked diligently even if they could not match the output of the leaders. In Perry County, Alabama, Hugh Davis divided his workers into rival teams and had them compete for prizes. He supplemented this collective competition with individual contests. In North Carolina at the end of the eighteenth century Charles Pettigrew, like many others before and after him, paid slaves for superior or extra work.

The amounts sometimes reached substantial proportions. Captain Frederick Marryat complained that in Lexington, Kentucky, during the late 1830s a gentleman could not rent a carriage on Sundays because slaves with ready money invariably rented them first for their own pleasure. Occasionally, plantation records reported surprising figures. One slave in Georgia earned fifty to sixty dollars per year by attending to pine trees in his off hours. Others earned money by applying particular skills or by doing jobs that had to be done individually and carefully without supervision. Amounts in the tens and even hundreds of dollars, although not common, caused no astonishment.

The more significant feature of these practices, for the society as a whole if not for the economy in particular, was the regularity—almost the institutionalization—of payments for work on Sundays or holidays. Apart from occasional assignments of Sunday or holiday work as punishment and apart from self-defeating greed, not to say stupidity, which led a few masters to violate the social norm, Sunday was the slaves' day by custom as well as law. The collective agreement of the slaveholders on these measures had its origin in a concern for social peace and reflected a sensible attitude toward economic efficiency. But once the practice took root, with or without legal sanction, the slaves transformed it into a "right." So successfully did they do so that the Supreme Court of Louisiana ruled in 1836: "According to . . . law, slaves are entitled to the produce of their labor on Sunday; even the master is bound to remunerate them, if he employs them." Here again the slaves turned the paternalist doctrine of reciprocity to advantage while demonstrating the extent to which that doctrine dominated the lives of both masters and slaves. . . .

Underlying black resistance to prevailing white values, then, has been a set of particular ideas concerning individual and community responsibility. It is often asserted that blacks spend rather than save as someone else thinks they should. But the considerable evidence for this assertion must be qualified by the no less considerable evidence of the heartbreaking scraping together of nickels and dimes to pay for such things as the education of the children, which will generally draw Anglo-Saxon applause, and the provision of elaborate funerals, which generally will not but which for many peoples besides blacks constitutes a necessary measure of respect for the living as well as the dead.

The slaves could, when they chose, astonish the whites by their work-time élan and expenditure of energy. The demands of corn shucking, hog killing, logrolling, cotton picking, and especially sugar grinding confronted the slaves with particularly heavy burdens and yet drew from them particularly positive responses.

With the exception of the Christmas holiday—and not always that—former slaves recalled having looked forward to corn shucking most of all. . . .

Certainly, the slaves had some material incentives. The best shuckers would get a dollar or a suit of clothes, as might those who found a red ear. But these incentives do not look impressive and do not loom large in the testimony. Those plantations on which the prize for finding a red ear consisted of a dollar do not seem to have done any better than those on which the prize consisted of an extra swig of whiskey or a chance to kiss the prettiest girl. The shucking was generally night work—overtime, as it were—and one might have expected the slaves to resent it and to consider the modest material incentives, which came to a special dinner and dance and a lot of whiskey, to be inadequate.

The most important feature of these occasions and the most important incentive to these long hours of work was the community life they called forth. They were gala affairs. The jug passed freely, although drunkenness was discouraged; the work went on amidst singing and dancing; friends and acquaintances congregated from several plantations and farms; the house slaves joined the field slaves in common labor; and the work was followed by an all-night dinner and ball at which inhibitions, especially those of class and race, were lowered as far as anyone dared.

Slavery, a particularly savage system of oppression and exploitation, made its slaves victims. But the human beings it made victims did not consent to be just that; they struggled to make life bearable and to find as much joy in it as they could. Up to a point even the harshest of masters had to help them do so. The logic of slavery pushed the masters to try to break their slaves' spirit and to reconstruct it as an unthinking and unfeeling extension of their own will, but the slaves' own resistance to dehumanization compelled the masters to compromise in order to get an adequate level of work out of them.

The combination of festive spirit and joint effort appears to have engaged the attention of the slaves more than anything else. Gus Brown, an ex-slave from Alabama, said simply, "On those occasions as we all got together and had a regular good time." The heightened sense of fellowship with their masters also drew much comment. Even big slaveholders would join in the work, as well as in the festivities and the drinking albeit not without the customary patriarchal qualifications. They would demand that the slaves sing, and the slaves would respond boisterously. Visitors expressed wonder at the spontaneity and improvisation the slaves displayed. The songs, often made up on the spot, bristled with sharp wit, both malicious and gentle. The slaves sang of their courtships and their lovers' quarrels; sometimes the songs got bawdy, and the children had to be hustled off to bed. . . .

But the songs also turned to satire. White participation in these festivals was always condescending and self-serving, and the slaves' acceptance of it displayed something other than childlike gratitude for small favors. They turned their wit and incredible talent for improvisation into social criticism. Occasionally they risked a direct, if muted, thrust in their "corn songs," as they came to be called.

> Massa in the great house, counting out his money,
> Massa in the great house, counting out his money,
> Oh, shuck that corn and throw it in the barn.
> Mistis in the parlor, eating bread and honey,
> Oh, shuck that corn and throw it in the barn.

More often, they used a simpler and safer technique. Ole Massa was always God's gift to humanity, the salt of the earth, de bestest massa in de whole wide worl'. But somehow, one or more of his neighbors was might bad buckra. . . . Blacks—any blacks—were not supposed to sass whites—any whites; slaves—any slaves—were not supposed to sit in judgment on masters—any masters. By the device of a little flattery and by talking advantage of the looseness of the occasion, they asserted their personalities and made their judgments.

A curious sexual division of labor marked the corn shuckings. Only occasionally did women participate in the shucking. The reason for the exclusion is by no means clear. Field women matched the men in hard work, not only in picking cotton but in rolling logs, chopping wood, and plowing. Yet at corn shuckings they divided their time between preparing an elaborate spread for the dinner and taking part in quilting bees and the like. As a result, the corn shuckings took on a peculiarly male tone, replete with raucous songs and jokes not normally told in front of women, as well as those manifestations of boyish prancing associated with what is called—as if by some delightful Freudian slip—a "man's man."

The vigor with which the men worked and the insistence on a rigid sexual separation raise the central question of the slaves' attitude toward work in its relationship to their sense of family and community. The sense of community established by bringing together house and field slaves and especially slaves from several plantations undoubtedly underlay much of the slaves' positive response, and recalled the festivities, ceremonials, and rituals of traditional societies in a way no office

Christmas party in an industrial firm has ever done. And corn shucking, like hog killing, had a special meaning, for at these times the slaves were literally working for themselves. The corn and pork fed them and their families; completion of these tasks carried a special satisfaction.

From this point of view the sexual division of labor, whatever its origin, takes on new meaning. In a limited way it strengthened that role of direct provider to which the men laid claim by hunting and fishing to supplement the family diet. Even the less attractive features of the evening in effect reinforced this male self-image. Nor did the women show signs of resentment. On the contrary, they seem to have grasped the opportunity to underscore a division of labor and authority in the family and to support the pretensions of their men. Slavery represented a terrible onslaught on the personalities and spirit of the slaves, and whatever unfairness manifested itself in this sexual bias, the efforts of male and female slaves to create and support their separate roles provided a weapon for joint resistance to dehumanization. . . .

The evidence from the sugar plantations is especially instructive. Louisiana's sugar planters reputedly drove their slaves harder than any others in the slave states. Such reputations are by no means to be accepted at face value, but they certainly drove them hard during the grinding season. Yet, slaves took to the woods as limited and local runaways more often during the spring and summer months than during the autumn grinding season, when the work reached a peak of intensity and when the time for rest and sleep contracted sharply. Once again, the small material incentives cannot account for the slaves' behavior.

The slaves brought to their labor a gaiety and élan that perplexed observers, who saw them work at night with hardly a moment to catch their breath. Many, perhaps most, found themselves with special tasks to perform and special demands upon them; by all accounts they strained to rise to the occasion. The planters, knowing that the season lasted too long to sustain a fever pitch of effort, tried to break it up with parties and barbecues and at the very least promised and delivered a gala dinner and ball at the end. Ellen Betts, an ex-slave from Texas, recalled: "Massa sho' good to dem gals and bucks what cuttin' de cane. When dey git done makin' sugar, he give a drink called 'Peach 'n' Honey' to de women folk and whiskey and brandy to de men." Another ex-slave, William Stone of Alabama, said that the slaves were "happy" to work during the sugar harvest "'cause we knowed it mean us have plenty 'lasses in winter."

Still, the demands of the sugar crop meant the sacrifice of some Sundays and even the Christmas holiday. The slaves showed no resentment at the postponement of the holiday. It would come in due time, usually in mid-January, and the greater their sacrifices, the longer and fuller the holiday would likely be. For the slaves on the sugar plantations Christmas did not mean December 25; it meant the great holiday that honored the Lord's birth, brought joy to His children, and properly fell at the end of the productive seasons.

Cotton picking was another matter. One ex-slave recalled cotton-picking parties along with corn-shucking parties but added, "Dere wasn't so much foolishness at cotton pickin' time." The slaves missed, in particular, the fellowship of slaves from other plantations. An exchange of labor forces on a crash basis sometimes occurred, and ex-slaves remembered precisely those times warmly. The planters had to have their cotton picked at about the same time and could not easily exchange labor forces. But the neighborly tradition was too strong to be denied entirely, and when a planter fell dangerously behind, others would come to his aid. Unable to take time away from their own work unless well ahead of schedule, friendly planters had to send their slaves after hours to pick by moonlight. The slaves, instead of becoming indignant over the imposition, responded with enthusiasm and extra effort. Many of them later recalled this grueling all-night work as "big times," for they were helping their own friends and combining the work with festivity. Bonuses, parties, and relaxed discipline rewarded their cooperation. Scattered evidence suggests less whipping and harsh driving during the cotton-picking season on some plantations but the opposite on others.

Some planters congratulated themselves on their succession in getting a good response during the critical cotton harvest. Virginia Clay visited Governor Hammond's noteworthy plantation in South Carolina and enthusiastically reported on the magnificent singing and general spirit of the slaves, and Kate Stone was sure that "the Negroes really seemed to like the cotton picking best of all." Henry William Ravenel, in his private journal, made an interesting observation that provides a better clue to the slaves' attitude. Writing in 1865, immediately after their emancipation, he declared that the slaves had always disliked planting and cultivating cotton and would now prefer almost any alternative labor. The picking season must have struck the slaves as a mixed affair. It meant hard and distasteful work and sometimes punishment for failure to meet quotas, but also the end of a tough season, prizes for good performances, and the prelude to relaxation and a big celebration. Yet, the special spirit of the season was not strong enough to carry the slaves through the rigors of labor; the whip remained the indispensable spur. . . .

Whatever the origins of the slaves' strong preference for collective work, it drew the attention of their masters, who knew that they would have to come to terms with it. Edmund Ruffin, the South's great soil chemist and authority on plantation agriculture, complained that the pinewoods of North Carolina were set afire every spring by inconsiderate poor whites who cared nothing for the damage they did in order to provide grazing land for their few cows. He added that the slaves also set many fires because they intensely disliked collecting turpentine from the trees. This work was light and easy in Ruffin's estimation, but the slaves resisted it anyway because it had to be performed in isolation. "A negro," Ruffin explained from long experience, "cannot abide being along and will prefer work of much exposure and severe toil, in company, to any lighter work, without any company." . . .

The powerful community spirit and preference for collective patterns of working and living had their antithesis in an equally powerful individualism, manifested most attractively during and after Reconstruction in an attempt to transform themselves into peasant proprietors. This particular kind of individualism has also had less attractive manifestations, from the creation of the ghetto hustler and the devil-take-the-hindmost predator to the creation of a set attitudes that many blacks hold responsible for a chronic lack of political unity. Certainly, the old collective spirit remains powerful, as the very notion of a black "brotherhood" demonstrates, but it does rest on a contradictory historical base. The work ethic of the slaves provided a firm defense against the excesses of an oppressive labor system, but like the religious tradition on which it rested, it did not easily lend itself to counterattack. Once the worst features of the old regime fell away, the ethic itself began to dissolve into its component parts. Even today we witness the depressing effects of this dissolution in a futile and pathetic caricature of bourgeois individualism, manifested both in the frustrated aspirations so angrily depicted in E. Franklin Frazier's *Black Bourgeoisie* and in violent, antisocial nihilism. But we also witness the continued power of a collective sensibility regarded by some as "race pride" and by others as a developing black national consciousness.

Emancipation and the Reconstruction of Southern Labor

ERIC FONER

Of the many questions raised by emancipation, none was more crucial for the future of both blacks and whites in Southern society than the organization of the region's economy. Slavery had been first and foremost a system of labor. And while all Republicans agreed that "free labor" must replace slavery, few were certain how the transition should be accomplished. "If the [Emancipation] Proclamation makes the slaves actually free," declared the *New York Times* in January 1863, "there will come the further duty of making them work. . . . All this opens a vast and most difficult subject." . . .

. . . Beginning in 1865, and for years thereafter, Southern whites throughout the South complained of the difficulty of obtaining female field laborers. Planters, Freedmen's Bureau officials, and Northern visitors all ridiculed the black "female aristocracy" for "acting the *lady*" or mimicking the family patterns of middle-class whites. White employers also resented their inability to force black children to labor in the fields, especially after the spread of schools in rural areas. Contemporaries appeared uncertain whether black women, black men, or both were responsible for the withdrawal of females from agricultural labor. There is no question that many black men considered it manly to have their wives work at home and believed that, as head of the family, the male should decide how its labor was organized. But many black women desired to devote more time than under slavery to caring for their children and to domestic responsibilities like cooking, sewing, and laundering.

The shift of black female labor from the fields to the home proved a temporary phenomenon. The rise of renting and sharecropping, which made each family responsible for its own plot of land, placed a premium on the labor of all family members. The dire poverty of many black families, deepened by the depression of the 1870s, made it essential for both women and men to contribute to the family's income. Throughout this period, a far higher percentage of black than white women and children worked for wages outside their homes. Where women continued to concentrate on domestic tasks, and children attended school, they frequently engaged in seasonal field labor. Thus, emancipation did not eliminate labor outside the home by black women and children, but it fundamentally altered control over their labor. Now blacks themselves, rather than a white owner or overseer, decided where and when black women and children worked. . . .

Nowhere were blacks' efforts to define their freedom more explosive for the entire society than in the economy. Freedmen brought out of slavery a conception of themselves as a "Working Class of People" who had been unjustly deprived of the fruits of their labor. To white predictions that they would not work, blacks responded that if any class could be characterized as lazy, it was the planters, who had "lived in idleness all their lives on stolen labor." It is certainly true that many blacks expected to labor less as free men and women than they had as slaves, an understandable aim considering the conditions they had previously known. "Whence comes the assertion that the 'nigger won't work'?" asked an Alabama freedman. "It comes from this fact: . . . the freedman refuses to be driven out into the field two hours before a day, and work until 9 or 10 o'clock in the night, as was the case in the days of slavery."

Yet freedom meant more than shorter hours and payment of wages. Freedmen sought to control the conditions under which they labored, end their subordination to white authority, and carve out the greatest measure of economic autonomy. These aims led them to prefer tenancy to wage labor, and leasing land for a fixed rent to sharecropping. Above all, they inspired the quest for land. Owning land, the freedmen believed, would "complete their independence."

To those familiar with the experience of other postemancipation societies, blacks' "mania for owning a small piece of land" did not appear surprising. Freedmen in Haiti, the British and Spanish Caribbean, and Brazil all saw ownership of land as crucial to economic independence, and everywhere former slaves sought to avoid returning to plantation labor. Unlike freedmen in other countries, however, American blacks emerged from slavery convinced that the federal government had committed itself to land distribution. Belief in an imminent division of land was most pervasive in the South Carolina and Georgia lowcountry, but the idea was shared in other parts of the South as well, including counties that had never been occupied by federal troops. Blacks insisted that their past labor entitled them to at least a portion of their owners' estates. As an Alabama black convention put it: "The property which they hold was nearly all earned by the sweat of *our* brows."

In some parts of the South, blacks in 1865 did more than argue the merits of their case. Hundreds of freedmen refused either to sign labor contracts or to leave the plantations, insisting that the land belonged to them. On the property of a Tennessee planter, former slaves not only claimed to be "joint heirs," to the estate but, the owner complained, abandoned the slaves quarters and took up residence "in the rooms of my house." Few freedmen were able to maintain control of land seized in this manner. A small number did, however, obtain property through other means, squatting on unoccupied land in sparsely populated states like Florida and Texas, buying tiny city plots, or cooperatively purchasing farms and plantations. Most blacks, however, emerged from slavery unable to purchase land even at the depressed prices of early Reconstruction and confronted by a white community unwilling to advance credit to sell them property. Thus, they entered the world of free labor as wage or share workers on land owned by whites. The adjustment to a new social order in which their persons were removed from the market but their labor was bought and sold like any other commodity proved in many respects difficult.

For it required them to adapt to the logic of the economic market, where the impersonal laws of supply and demand and the balance of power between employer and employee determine a laborer's material circumstances.

Most freedmen welcomed the demise of the paternalism and mutual obligations of slavery and embraced many aspects of the free market. They patronized the stores that sprang up throughout the rural South, purchasing "luxuries" ranging from sardines, cheese, and sugar to new clothing. They saved money to build and support churches and educate their children. And they quickly learned to use and influence the market for their own ends. The early years of Reconstruction witnessed strikes or petitions for higher wages by black urban laborers including Richmond factory workers, Jackson washerwomen, New Orleans and Savannah stevedores, and mechanics in Columbus, Georgia. In rural areas, too, plantation freedmen sometimes bargained collectively over contract terms, organized strikes and occasionally even attempted to establish wage schedules for an entire area. Blacks exploited competition between planters and nonagricultural employers, seeking work on railroad construction crews and at turpentine mills and other enterprises offering pay far higher than on the plantations.

Slavery, however, did not produce workers fully socialized to the virtues of economic accumulation. Despite the profits possible in early postwar cotton farming, many freedmen strongly resisted growing the "slave crop." "If ole massa went to grow cotton," said one Georgia freedman, "let him plant it himself." Many freedmen preferred to concentrate on food crops and only secondarily on cotton or other staples to obtain ready cash. Rather than choose irrevocably between self-sufficiency and market farming, they hoped to avoid a complete dependence on either while taking advantage of the opportunities each could offer. . . .

Historical experience and modern scholarship suggest that acquiring small plots of land would hardly, by itself, have solved the economic plight of black families. Without control of credit and assess to markets, land reform can often be a hollow victory. And where political power rests in hostile hands, small landowners often find themselves subjected to oppressive taxation and other state policies that severely limit their economic prospects. In such circumstances, the autonomy offered by land ownership tends to be defensive, rather than the springboard for sustained economic advancement. Yet while hardly an economic panacea, land redistribution would have had profound consequences for Southern society, weakening the land-based economic and political power of the old ruling class, offering blacks a measure of choice as to whether, when, and under what circumstances to enter the labor market, and affecting the former slaves' conception of themselves.

⮞ Blacks' quest for economic independence not only threatened the foundations of the Southern political economy, it put the freedmen at odds with both former owners seeking to restore plantation labor discipline and Northerners committed to reinvigorating staple crop production. But as part of the broad quest for individual and collective autonomy, it remained central to the black community's effort to define the meaning of freedom. Indeed, the fulfillment of other aspirations, from family autonomy to the creation of schools and churches, all greatly depended on success in winning control of their working lives and gaining access to the economic resources of the South. . . .

For the majority of planters, as for their former slaves, the Confederacy's defeat and the end of slavery ushered in a difficult adjustment to new race and class relations and new ways of organizing labor. The first casualty of this transformation was the paternalist ethos of prewar planters. A sense of obligation based on mastership over an inferior, paternalism had no place in a social order in which labor relations were mediated by the impersonal market and blacks aggressively pressed claims to autonomy and equality. "The Law which freed the negro," a Southern editor wrote in 1865, "at the same time freed the master, all obligations springing out of the relations of master and slave, except those of kindness, cease mutually to exist." And kindness proved all too rare in the aftermath of war and emancipation. Numerous planters evicted from their plantations those blacks too old, or infirm to labor, and transformed "rights" enjoyed by slaves—clothing, housing, access to garden plots—into commodities for which payment was due. . . .

Carl Schurz and other Northerners who toured the South in 1865 concluded that white Southerners "do not know what free labor is." To which many planters replied that Northerners "do not understand the character of the negro." Free labor assumptions—economic rationality, internal self-discipline, responsiveness to the incentives of the market—could never, planters insisted, be applied to blacks. "They are improvident and reckless of the future," complained a Georgia newspaper. Nor was another free labor axiom, opportunity for social mobility, applicable in the South. A Natchez newspaper informed its readers: "The true station of the negro is that of a servant. The wants and state of our country demand that he should remain a servant."

The conviction that preindustrial lower classes share an aversion to regular, disciplined toil had a long history in both Europe and America. In the Reconstruction South, this ideology took a racial form, and although racism was endemic throughout nineteenth-century America, the requirements of the plantation economy shaped its specific content in the aftermath of emancipation. Charges of "indolence" were often directed not against blacks unwilling to work, but at those who preferred to labor for themselves. "Want of ambition will be the devil of the race, I think," wrote Kemp P. Battle, a North Carolina planter and political leader, in 1866. "Some of my most sensible men say they have no other desire than to cultivate their own land in grain and raise bacon." On the face of it, such an aspiration appears ambitious enough, and hardly unusual in the nineteenth-century South. But in a plantation society, a black man seeking to work his way up the agricultural ladder to the status of self-sufficient farmer seemed not an admirable example of industriousness, but a demoralized freedman unwilling to work—work, that is, under white supervision on a plantation.

The questions of land and labor were intimately related. Planters quickly concluded that their control of black labor rested upon maintaining their own privileged access to the productive land of the plantation belt. Even if relatively few freedmen established themselves as independent farmers, plantation discipline would dissolve since, as William H. Trescot explained, "it will be utterly impossible for the owner to find laborers that will work contentedly for wages alongside of these free colonies." At public meetings in 1865, and in their private correspondence, planters resolved never to rent or sell land to freedmen. In effect, they sought to impose upon blacks their own definition, of freedom, one that repudiated the former slaves' equation of liberty and autonomy. "They have an idea that a hireling is not a freedman," Mississippi planter Samuel Agnew noted in his diary. . . .

Between the planters' need for a disciplined labor force and the freedmen's quest for autonomy, conflict was inevitable. Planters attempted through written contracts to reestablish their authority over every aspect of their laborers' lives. "Let everything proceed as formerly," one advised, "the contractual relation being substituted for that of master and slave." These early contracts prescribed not only labor in gangs from sunup to sundown as in antebellum days, but complete subservience to the planter's will. One South Carolina planter required freedmen to obey the employer "and go by his direction the same as in slavery time." Many contracts not only specified modes of work and payment, but prohibited blacks from leaving plantations, entertaining visitors, or holding meetings without permission of the employer.

Such provisions proved easier to compose than to enforce. Planters quickly learned that labor contracts could not by themselves create a submissive labor force. On the aptly named Vexation plantation in Texas, blacks in September 1865 were said to be "insolent and refusing to work." The employees of Louisiana's former Confederate governor, Thomas O. Moore, set their own pace of work, refused to plow when the ground was hard, and answered his complaints in a "disrespectful and annoying" manner. Conflict was endemic on plantations throughout the South. Some blacks refused to weed cotton fields in the rain. Others would not perform the essential but hated "mud work" of a rice plantation—dredging canals and repairing dikes—forcing some rice planters "to hire Irishmen to do the ditching." House servants, too, had their own ideas of where their obligations began and ended. Butlers refused to cook or polish brass, domestics would not black the boots of plantation guests, chambermaids declared that it was not their duty to answer the front door, serving girls insisted on the right to entertain male visitors in their rooms.

Southern whites were not the only ones to encounter difficulty disciplining former slaves. During and immediately after the war, a new element joined the South's planter class: Northerners who purchased land, leased plantations, or formed partnerships with Southern planters. These newcomers were a varied, ambitious group, mostly former soldiers anxious to invest their savings in this promising new frontier and civilians lured South by press reports of "the fabulous sums of money to be made in the South in raising cotton." Joined with the quest for profit, however, was a reforming spirit, a vision of themselves as agents of sectional reconciliation and the South's "economic regeneration." As an Illinois man farming in Texas wrote: "I am going to introduce new ideas here in the farming line and show the beauties of free over slave labor."

Southern planters predicted that the newcomers would soon complain about the character of black labor, and they were not far wrong. The very "scientific" methods Northerners hoped to introduce, involving closely supervised work and changes in customary plantation routines, challenged the more irregular pace of work preferred by blacks and their desire to direct their own labor. As time passed, the Northern planters sounded and acted more and more like Southern. Some sought to restore corporal punishment, only to find that the freedmen would not stand for it. Perhaps the problem arose from the fact that, like Southern whites, most of the newcomers did not believe recently emancipated blacks capable of "self-directed labor." If the freedmen were to become productive free laborers, said the *New York Times* with unintended irony, "it must be done by giving them new masters." Blacks, however, wanted to be their own masters. And, against employers both Southern and Northern, they used whatever weapons they could find in the chaotic economic conditions of the postwar South to influence the conditions of their labor.

Blacks did, indeed, enjoy considerable bargaining power because of the "labor shortage" that followed the end of slavery. Particularly acute in sparsely populated Florida and the expanding cotton empire of the Southwest, competition for labor affected planters throughout the South. "The struggle seems to be who will get the negro at any price," lamented Texas planter Frank B. Conner. Planters, he concluded, must band together to "establish some maximum figure," stop "enticing" one another's workers, and agree that anyone, "breaking the established custom should be driven from the community."

The scarcity of labor was no mirage. Measured in hours worked per capita, the supply of black labor dropped by about one-third after the Civil War, largely because all former slaves were determined to work fewer hours than under slavery, and many women and children withdrew altogether from the fields. But the "labor shortage" was a question not only of numbers, but of power. It arose from black families' determination to use the rights resulting from emancipation to establish the conditions, rhythms, and compensation of their work. . . .

Despite the intensity of their conflict, neither former master nor former slave possessed the power to define the South's new system of labor. A third protagonist, the victorious North, also attempted to shape the transition from slavery to freedom. To the Freedmen's Bureau, more than any other institution, fell the task of assisting at the birth of a free labor society. The Bureau's commissioner was Gen. Oliver Otis Howard, whose close ties to the freedmen's aid societies had earned him the sobriquet "Christian General." Although temporary, Howard's agency was an experiment in social policy that, a modern scholar writes, "did not belong to the America of its day." Its responsibilities can only be described as daunting; they included introducing a workable system of free labor in the South, establishing schools for freedmen, providing aid to the destitute, aged, ill, and insane, adjudicating disputes among blacks and between the races, and attempting to secure for blacks and white Unionists equal justice from the state and local governments established during Presidential Reconstruction. The local Bureau agent was expected to win the confidence of blacks and whites alike in a situation where race and labor relations had been poisoned by mutual distrust and conflicting interests. Moreover, the Bureau employed, at its peak, not more than 900 agents in the entire South. Only a dozen served in Mississippi in 1866, and the largest contingent in Alabama at any time comprised twenty. "It is not . . . in your power to fulfill one tenth of the expectations of those who framed the Bureau," Gen. William T. Sherman advised Howard. "I fear you have Hercules' task."

At first glance, the Bureau's activities appear as a welter of contradictions, reflecting differences among individual agents in interpreting general policies laid down in Washington. But unifying the Bureau's activities was the endeavor to lay the foundation for a free labor society. To the extent that this meant putting freedmen back to work on plantations, the Bureau's policies coincided with the interests of the planters. To the extent that it prohibited coercive labor discipline, took up the burden of black education, sought to protect blacks against violence, and promoted the removal of legal barriers to blacks' advancement, the Bureau reinforced the freedmen's aspirations. In the end, the Bureau's career exposed the ambiguities and inadequacies of the free labor ideology itself. But simultaneously, the former slaves seized the opportunity offered by the Bureau's imperfect efforts on their behalf to bolster their own quest for self-improvement and autonomy. . . .

In the war's immediate aftermath, federal policy regarding black labor was established by the army. And the army seemed to many freedmen to have only one object in view—to compel them to return to work on the plantations. . . . [T]he assumption underpinning military policy, that the interests of all Americans would be best served by blacks' return to plantation labor, remained intact as the Freedmen's Bureau assumed command of the transition to free labor. . . .

. . . The free labor ideology rested on a theory of universal economic rationality and the conviction that all classes in a free labor society shared the same interests. In reality, former masters and former slaves inherited from slavery work habits and attitudes at odds with free labor assumptions, and both recognized, more clearly than the Bureau, the irreconcilability of their respective interests and aspirations. The free labor social order, moreover, ostensibly guaranteed the ambitious worker the opportunity for economic mobility, the ability to move from wage labor to independence through the acquisition of productive property. Yet what became of this axiom in an impoverished society where even the highest agricultural wages remained pitiably low, and whose white population was determined to employ every means at its disposal to prevent blacks from acquiring land or any other means of economic independence?

Establishing themselves in the South in the summer and fall of 1865, Bureau agents hoped to induce Southerners to "give the system a fair and honest trial." To planters' desire for a disciplined labor force governed by the lash, agents responded that "*bodily coercion* fell as an incident of slavery." To the contention that blacks would never work voluntary or respond to market incentives, they replied that the problem of economic readjustment should be viewed through the prism of labor, rather than race. . . .

The "two evils" against which the Bureau had to contend, an army officer observed in July 1865, were "cruelty on the part of the employer and shirking on the part of the negroes." Yet the Bureau, like the army, seemed to consider black reluctance to labor the greater threat to its economic mission. In some areas agents continued the military's urban pass systems and vagrancy patrols, as well as the practice of rounding up unemployed laborers for shipment to plantations. Bureau courts in Memphis dispatched improvised blacks convicted of crimes to labor for whites who would pay their fines. "What a mockery to call those 'Freedmen' who are still subjected to such things," commented a local minister.

United as to the glories of free labor, Bureau officials, like Northerners generally, differed among themselves about the ultimate social implications of the free labor ideology. Some believed the freedmen would remain a permanent plantation labor force; others insisted they should enjoy the same opportunity to make their way up the social ladder to independent proprietorship as Northern workers; still others hoped the federal government would assist at least some blacks in acquiring their own farms. Howard believed most freedmen must return to plantation labor, but under conditions that allowed them the opportunity to work their way out of the wage-earning class. At the same time, he took seriously the provision in the act establishing his agency that authorized it to settle freedmen on confiscated and abandoned lands. In 1865, Howard and a group of sympathetic Bureau officials attempted to breathe life into this alternative vision of a free-labor South.

. . . [T]he Bureau controlled over 850,000 acres of abandoned land in 1865, hardly enough to accommodate all the former slaves but sufficient to make a start toward creating a black yeomanry. Howard's subordinates included men sincerely committed to settling freedmen on farms of their own and protecting the rights of those who already occupied land. . . .

Initially, Howard himself shared the radical aims of [his subordinates]. At the end of July 1865 he issued Circular 13, which instructed Bureau agents to "set aside" forty-acre tracts for the freedmen as rapidly as possible. But [President] Andrew Johnson, who had been pardoning former Confederates, soon directed Howard to rescind his order. A new policy, drafted in the White House and issued in September as Howard's Circular 15, ordered the restoration to pardoned owners of all land except the small amount that had already been sold under a court decree. Once growing crops had been harvested, virtually all the land in Bureau hands would revert to its former owners. . . .

The restoration of land required the displacement of tens of thousands of freedmen throughout the South. The army evicted most of the 20,000 blacks settled on confiscated and abandoned property in southeastern Virginia. The 62,000 acres farmed by Louisiana blacks were restored to their former owners. . . .

Nowhere, however, was the restoration process so disruptive as in the Georgia and South Carolina lowcountry. On more than one occasion freedmen armed themselves, barricaded plantations, and drove off owners attempting to dispossess them. Black squatters told one party of Edisto Island landlords in February 1866, "you have better go back to Charleston, and go to work there, and if you can do nothing else, you can pick oysters and earn your living as the loyal people have done—by the sweat of their brows." Bureau agents, black and white, made every effort to induce lowcountry freedmen to sign contracts with their former owners, while federal troops forcibly evicted those who refused. In the end, only about 2,000 South Carolina and Georgia freedmen actually received the land they had been promised in 1865.

The events of 1865 and 1866 kindled a deep sense of betrayal among freedmen throughout the South. Land enough existed, wrote former Mississippi slave Merrimon Howard, for every "man and woman to have as much as they could work." Yet blacks had been left with

no *land*, no *house*, not so much as [a] place to lay our head. . . . Despised by the world, hated by the country that gives us birth, denied of all our writs as a people, we were friends on the march, . . . brothers on the battlefield, but in the peaceful pursuits of life it seems that we are strangers.

Thus, by 1866 the Bureau found itself with no alternative but to encourage virtually all freedmen to sign annual contracts to work on the plantations. Its hopes for long-term black advancement and Southern economic prosperity now came to focus exclusively on the labor contract itself. By voluntarily signing and adhering to contracts, both planters and freedmen would develop the habits of a free labor economy and come to understand their fundamental harmony of interests. Agents found themselves required to perform a nearly impossible balancing act. Disabusing blacks of the idea that they would soon obtain land from the government, and threatening to arrest those who refused to sign a contract or leave the plantations, agents simultaneously insisted on blacks' right to bargain freely for employment and attempted to secure more advantageous contracts than had prevailed in 1865. Some Bureau officers approved agreements in which the laborer would receive nothing at all if the crop failed and could incur fines for such vaguely defined offenses as failure to do satisfactory work or "impudent, profane or indecent language." More conscientious agents revoked contract provisions regulating blacks' day-to-day lives and insisted that laborers who left plantations before the harvest must be paid for their work up to the date of departure. And virtually all agents insisted that planters acknowledge that their power to employ physical coercion had come to an end.

The Bureau's role in supervising labor relations reached its peak in 1866 and 1867; thereafter, federal authorities intervened less and less frequently to oversee contracts or settle plantation disputes. To the extent that the contract system had been intended to promote stability in labor relations in the chaotic aftermath of war and allow commercial agriculture to resume, it could be deemed a success. But in other ways, the system failed. For the entire contract system in some ways violated the principles of free labor. Agreements, Howard announced soon after assuming office, "should be free, *bona fide* acts." Yet how voluntary were labor contracts signed by blacks when they were denied access to land, coerced by troops and Bureau agents if they refused to sign, and fined or imprisoned if they struck for higher wages? Propertyless individuals in the North, to be sure, were compelled to labor for wages, but the compulsion was supplied by necessity, not by public officials, and contracts did not prevent them from leaving work whenever they chose. Why, asked the New Orleans *Tribune* again and again, did the Bureau require blacks to sign year-long labor contracts when "laborers throughout the civilized world"—including agricultural laborers in the North—could leave their employment at any time? To which one may add that even the most sympathetic Bureau officials assumed that blacks would constitute the rural labor force, at least until the natural working of the market divided the great plantations into small farms. "Idle white men" were never required to sign labor contracts or ordered to leave Southern cities for the countryside, a fact that made a mockery of the Bureau's professed goal of equal treatment for the freedmen.

Howard always believed that the Bureau's policies, viewed as a whole, benefited the freedmen more than their employers, especially since civil authorities offered blacks no protection against violence or fraud and the courts provided no justice to those seeking legal redress. He viewed the system of annual labor contracts as a temporary expedient, which would disappear once free labor obtained a "permanent foothold" in the South "under its necessary protection of equal and just laws properly executed." Eventually, as in the North, the market would regulate employment. Yet in the early years of Reconstruction, operating within the constraints of the free labor ideology, adverse crop and market conditions, the desire to restore production of the South's staple crops, and presidential policy, Bureau decisions conceived as temporary exerted a powerful influence on the emergence of new economic and social relations, closing off some options for blacks, shifting the balance of power in favor of employers, and helping to stabilize the beleaguered planter class. . . .

In 1866 and 1867, the freedmen's demand for an improvement in their economic condition and greater independence in their working lives set in motion a train of events that fundamentally transformed the plantation labor system. Blacks' desire for greater autonomy in the day-to-day organization of work produced a trend toward the subdivision of the labor force. Gang labor for wages persisted where planters had access to outside capital and could offer high monthly wages, promptly paid. Thanks to an influx of Northern investment, this was the case on sugar plantations that managed to resume production. On many sugar plantations in 1866 and 1867, however, squads of a dozen or fewer freedmen replaced the gangs so reminiscent of slavery. Generally organized by the blacks themselves, these squads sometimes consisted entirely of members of a single family, but more often included unrelated men. By 1867 the gang system was disappearing from the cotton fields.

The final stage in the decentralization of plantation agriculture was the emergence of sharecropping. Unlike the earlier share-wage system, with which it is often confused, in sharecropping individual families (instead of large groups of freedmen) signed contracts with the landowner and became responsible for a specified piece of land (rather than working in gangs). Generally, sharecroppers retained one-third of the year's crop if the planter provided implements, fertilizer, work animals, and seed, and half if they supplied their own. The transition to sharecropping occurred at different rates on different plantations and continued well into the 1870s, but the arrangement appeared in some areas soon after the Civil War.

To blacks, sharecropping offered an escape from gang labor and day-to-day white supervision. For planters, the system provided a way to reduce the cost and difficulty of labor supervision, share risk with tenants, and circumvent the chronic shortage of cash and credit. Most important of all, it stabilized the work force, for sharecroppers utilized the labor of all members of the family and had a vested interest in remaining until the crop had been gathered. Yet whatever its economic rational, many planters resisted sharecropping as a threat to their overall authority and inefficient besides (since they believed blacks would not work without direct white supervision). A compromise not fully satisfactory to either party, the system's precise outlines remained a point of conflict. Planters insisted sharecroppers were wage laborers who must obey the orders of their employer and who possessed no property right in the crop until they received their share at the end of the year. But sharecroppers, a planter complained in 1866, considered themselves "partners in the crop," who insisted on farming according to their own dictates and would not brook white supervision. Only a system of wages, payable at the end of the year, he concluded, would allow whites to "work in accordance with our former management." But precisely because it seemed so far removed from "our former management," blacks came to prefer the sharecropping system.

If freedmen in the cotton fields rejected the gang labor associated with bondage, those in the rice swamps insisted on strengthening the familiar task system, the foundation of the partial autonomy they had enjoyed as slaves. "We want to work just as we have always worked," declared a group of freedmen in South Carolina's rice region, and to attract labor, rice planters found themselves obliged to let the blacks "work . . . as they choose without any overseer." Out of the wreck of the rice economy and blacks' insistence on autonomy emerged an unusual set of labor relations. Some planters simply rented their plantations to blacks for a share of the crop or divided the land among groups of freedmen to cultivate as they saw fit. Others agreed to a system of labor sharing in which freedmen worked for two days on the plantation in exchange for an allotment of land on which to grow their own crops.

Thus, the struggles of early Reconstruction planted the seeds of new labor systems in the rural South. The precise manner in which these seeds matured would be worked out not only on Southern farms and plantations, but also on the Reconstruction battlefields of local, state, and national politics.

Bent Backs in the Rural South

JACQUELINE JONES

Late nineteenth-century middle-class white women derived their status from that of their husbands. Unproductive in the context of a money-oriented, industrializing economy, and formally unable to take part in the nation's political process, they enjoyed financial security only insofar as their spouses were steady and reliable providers. In contrast, black working women in the South had a more equal relationship with their husbands in the sense that the two partners were not separated by extremes of economic power or political rights; black men and women lacked both. Oppression shaped these unions in another way. The overlapping of economic and domestic functions combined with the pressures imposed by a surrounding, hostile white society meant that black working women were not so dramatically dependent upon their husbands as were middle-class white wives. Within black families and communities, then, public-private, male-female distinctions were less tightly drawn than among middle-class whites. Together, black women and men participated in a rural folk culture based upon group cooperation rather than male competition and the accumulation of goods. The ways in which this culture both resembled and diverged from that of poor whites in the South helps to illuminate the interaction between class and racial factors in shaping the roles of women

Referring to the world view of Alabama sharecropper Hayes Shaw, Theodore Rosengarten (the biographer-interviewer of Shaw's son Nate) observed that "righteousness consisted in not having so much that it hurt to lose it." Nate himself remembered that his father as a young man had passed up promising opportunities to buy land because "he was blindfolded; he didn't look to the future." Ruled by "them old slavery thoughts," Hayes Shaw knew that

> whenever the colored man prospered too fast in this country under the old rulins, they worked every figure to cut you down, cut your britches off you. So, it . . . weren't no use in climbin too fast; weren't no use in climbin slow, neither, if they was going to take everything you worked for when you got too high.

Jaqueline Jones, *Labor of Love, Labor of Sorrow* (New York: Basic Books, 1985), 99–109. Reprinted by permission of Basic Books, a member of Perseus Books, LLC.

Rural black communities that abided by this philosophy sought to achieve self-determination within a limited sphere of action. In this way they insulated themselves from whites and from the disappointment that often accompanied individual self-seeking. They lived like Nate's brother Peter; he "made up his mind that he weren't goin to have anything and after that, why nothin could hurt him."

Northern scholars and journalists, as well as southern planters, charged that rural blacks valued freedom of movement, "furious religious revivals," and community holidays—"none of which brings them profit of any sort." A Georgia landowner characterized in this way the philosophy of his tenants, who tended to "dismiss further thought of economy" once they had fulfilled their financial obligations to him: "*dum vivimus vivamus*" ("while we are living let us live"). Some white observers seized upon this theme and warned of its ramifications for the future of American society. Within a growing economy based upon the production of consumer goods, black people's apparent willingness to make do with the little they had represented not so much a moral transgression as a threat to employee discipline on the one hand and incentives to buy on the other. Why should a black husband and father work hard if he was "content with a log cabin and a fireplace, and with corn, bacon, and molasses as articles of food"? How would he profit southern or national economic development if he was satisfied with "merely enough to keep soul and body together"? . . .

Black settlements in remote areas—especially those that remained relatively self-sufficient through hunting and fishing—experienced the mixed blessings of semiautonomy. These communities existed almost wholly outside the larger regional and national economic system. For example, the people of the Sea Islands who "labor only for the fulfillment of the petition, 'Give us this day our daily bread,' and literally 'take no thought for the morrow,' working only when their necessities compel them," revealed the dilemma of a premodern subculture located within an industrial nation. As independent, self-respecting farmers (a proportionately large number owned their own land), the Sea Islanders remained relatively unmolested by whites and managed to preserve African traditions and folkways to a remarkable degree. Their diet, consisting of fowl, fish, shellfish, and fresh vegetables, was nutritionally superior to that of Cotton Belt sharecroppers. Yet these people lacked proper medical care and the most basic household conveniences. (Water-toting women hailed the installation of a water pump in the early twentieth century as "a most spectacular innovation in domestic economy. . . .") Floods and other natural disasters periodically wrought havoc on their way of life, and pushed young people off the islands and into nearby cities, leaving behind primarily the elderly and the blind.

Even rural communities that lacked the almost total isolation of the Sea Islands possessed a strong commitment to corporatism and a concomitant scorn for the hoarding of private possessions. As government researcher J. Bradford Laws wrote disapprovingly of the sugar workers he studied in 1902, "They have an unfortunate notion of generosity, which enables the more worthless to borrow fuel, food, and what not on all hands from the more thrifty." It is clear that these patterns of behavior were determined as much by economic necessity as by cultural "choice." if black household members pooled their energies to make a good crop, and if communities collectively provided for their own welfare, then poverty and oppression ruled out most of the alternative strategies. Individualism was a luxury that sharecroppers simply could not afford.

Rural folk relied on one another to help celebrate the wedding of a young couple, rejoice in a preacher's fervent exhortation, mark the annual closing of the local school, minister to the ill, and bury the dead. Women participated in all these rites and communal events. In addition, they had their own gender-based activities, as well as societies that contributed to the general good of the community. On the Sea Islands, young women would "often take Saturday afternoon as a time for cleaning the yard or the parlor, for ironing their clothes, or for preparing their hair." (Their brothers gathered at a favorite meeting place or organized a "cornfield baseball game.") Quilting brought young and old women together for a daylong festival of sewing, chatting, and feasting. Supported by the modest dues of their members, female voluntary beneficial societies met vital social-welfare needs that individual families could not always afford; these groups helped their members to pay for life insurance, medical care, and burial services. Even the poorest women managed to contribute a few pennies a month and to attend weekly meetings. In turn-of-the-century Alabama, "The woman who is not a member of one of these is pitied and considered rather out of date."

The impulse for mutual solace and support among rural Afro-Americans culminated in their religious institutions and worship services. At monthly meetings women and men met to reaffirm their unique spiritual heritage, to seek comfort, and to comfort one another. Black women found a "psychological center" in religious belief, and the church provided strength for those overcome by the day-to-day business of living. For many weary sharecroppers' wives and mothers, worship services allowed for physical and spiritual release and offered a means of transcending earthly cares in the company of one's friends and family. Faith created "a private world inside the self, sustained by religious sentiment and religious symbolism . . . fashioned to contain the world without." "Spiritual mothers" served as the "main pillars" of Methodist and Baptist churches, but they also exercised religious leadership outside formal institutional boundaries; elderly women in particular commanded respect as the standard-bearers of tradition and as the younger generation's link with its ancestors.

Of course, life in "places behind God's back" was shaped as much by racial prejudice as by black solidarity, and the "ethos of mutuality" that pervaded rural communities did not preclude physical violence or overt conflict between individuals. At times a Saturday night "frolic" ended in a bloody confrontation between two men who sought courage from a whiskey bottle and self-esteem through hand-to-hand conflict. Similarly, oppression could bind a family tightly together, but it could also heighten tensions among people who had few outlets for their rage and frustration. Patterns of domestic conflict reflected both historical injustices and daily family pressures. These forces affected black women and men in different ways.

On a superficial level, the roots of domestic violence are not difficult to recognize or understand. Cramped living quarters and unexpected setbacks provoked the most even-tempered of household heads. Like their slave parents, mothers and fathers often used harsh disciplinary techniques on children, not only to prepare them for life in a white-dominated world where all blacks had to act cautiously, but also to exert rigid control over this one vital facet of domestic life. If whites attempted to cut "the britches off" black fathers and husbands, then these men would try to assert their authority over their households with even greater determination. At times that determination was manifested in violence and brutality.

Hayes Shaw epitomized the sharecropping father who lorded over his wives (he married three times) and children. More than once the Shaw children watched helplessly as their father beat their mother, and they too were "whipped . . . up scandalous" for the slightest infraction. Hayes divided his time between his "outside woman"—an unmarried laundress in the neighborhood—and his "regular" family, and he made no effort to conceal the fact. The Shaw womenfolk were hired out or sent to the fields like children, without daring to protest, while Hayes spent his days in a characteristically masculine fashion—alone, away from the house, hunting. . . .

Hayes Shaw was undoubtedly an extreme example of a domestic tyrant, but he and other husbands like him inspired white and black women community leaders, educators, and social workers to formulate a critique of Afro-American family life in the late nineteenth century. Sensitive to the economic problems confronted by black marriage partners, these observers charged that black men enjoyed certain male prerogatives without the corresponding striving and ambition that those prerogatives were meant to reward. Juxtaposed with this "irresponsible" man was his wife—no doubt a "real drudge," but certainly "the greatest sufferer from the stress and strain attendant upon the economic conditions" faced by all Afro-Americans. The chief problem seemed to stem from the fact that black women played a prominent role in supporting the family in addition to performing their domestic responsibilities. In the eyes of their critics, black men as a group were not particularly concerned about "getting ahead" in the world and thus fell short of their wives' spirit of industry and self-sacrifice.

White teacher-social workers like Rossa Cooley and Georgia Washington and black writers and educators like Anna J. Cooper, Katherine Davis Tillman, Frances Harper, and Fannie Barrier Williams focused on the domestic achievements of poor women and with varying degrees of subtlety condemned their "worthless" husbands. Their critique of black womanhood marked the emergence of the "black matriarchy thesis," for they suggested that the main problem in Afro-American family life was an "irresponsible" father who took advantage of his "faithful, hard-working womenfolks." By the mid-twentieth century sociologists had shifted public attention to the "irresponsible" father's *absence;* the relatively large number of single, working mothers in the nation's urban ghettos seemed to lend additional credence to an argument that originally purported to deal with the problems of rural women. Thus the image of the strong, overburdened black mother persisted through the years, and it was usually accompanied by the implicit assumption that women wielded authority over men and children in Afro-American families.

Yet Hayes Shaw's household was never a "matriarchy." Recent historians who have labeled the postemancipation rural black family "patriarchal" hardly help to clarify the issue. The difficulty in conceptualizing black male-female roles derives from the fact that most observers (whether writing in the nineteenth or twentieth century) have used as their basis for comparison the white middle-class model of family life. Black men headed the vast majority of southern rural families, and they self-consciously ruled their wives and children; hence the use of the term patriarchy to describe family relationships. But these households deviated from the traditional sexual division of labor in the sense that wives worked to supplement the family income, and fathers often lacked the incentive to try to earn money so that they could purchase property or goods and thus advance the family's status. These men worked hard—they had to, in order to survive the ruthlessly exploitative sharecropping system—but most realized that even harder work would not necessarily enable them to escape poverty. Those who confronted this dilemma hardly deserved the epithet "worthless manhood." Still, for the two sexes, relative equality of economic function did not imply equality of domestic authority.

Although a husband and wife each made an essential contribution to the welfare of the household, they were compensated in different ways for their labor. This reward differential reflected their contrasting household responsibilities and produced contrasting attitudes toward work and its personal and social value. As a participant in a staple-crop economy, a black father assumed responsibility for a crop that would be exchanged in the marketplace at the end of the year. He supposedly toiled for future compensation in the form of cash. However, not only did his physical exertion gain him little in the way of immediate reward, in fact he tilled the ground only to repay one debt and to ensure that he would have another in the coming year. Under such conditions, most men took pride in their farming abilities, but worked no more strenuously than was absolutely necessary to satisfy white creditors and keep their own families alive in the process.

Their wives, on the other hand, remained relatively insulated from the inevitable frustrations linked to a future-oriented, market economy. For example, women daily performed discreet tasks that yielded tangible results upon completion. Meal preparation, laundering, egg gathering—these chores had finite boundaries in the course of a day. Childcare was a special case, but it had its own special joys. It was an ongoing responsibility that began when a woman had her first baby and ended only years later when her youngest child left home. On a more mundane level, childcare was a constant preoccupation of mothers during their waking hours, and infants' needs often invaded their sleep. Yet a woman's exclusive authority in this area of domestic life earned her emotional gratification. Her husband hardly derived a similar sense of gratification from his responsibility for the cotton crop; he "earned" only what a white man was willing to pay him. Hence the distinction between work patterns simplistically labeled by some contemporary writers as male "laziness" and female "self-sacrifice" actually represented a complex phenomenon shaped by the different demands made upon black men and women and the degree of personal satisfaction resulting from the fulfillment of those demands.

Poor whites in the late nineteenth-century South were also stigmatized by charges of laziness and lethargy; together black and white sharecroppers and tenants endured a form of opprobrium traditionally directed at working people by their employers and social "betters." Like their black counterparts, propertyless whites valued self-sufficiency over cash-crop tenancy, and they too confronted new class relationships established after the war—relationships that turned on mortgages, credit, and crop liens as much as on race and kinship. By 1900 over one-third of all whites employed in agriculture were tenants, and even small landowners remained perched precariously on the brink of financial disaster, only a drought or a boll weevil plague away from indebtedness. . . . Thus all landless farmers, white and black, confronted uncertainties in a period of declining agricultural prices and general economic hardship. It seems likely then that southern poor people as a group deviated from the predominant (that is, white middle-class northern-industrial) culture, a way of life shaped by the powerful ideology of ambition and personal gain.

A comparison of the experiences of poor white and black women in the rural South suggests that to a great extent, class and gender conjoined to determine what all sharecroppers' wives did and how they did it. For example, data on black and white households in the Cotton South for 1880 and 1900 indicate some striking similarities between the family structures characteristic of the two races. For instance, both types of "average" households possessed a male head, and a male head accompanied by his spouse, in the same proportions. Black and white wives shared the same age patterns relative to their husbands. Though slightly larger, white households had a similar configuration compared to black ones and lived near at least some of their kin to the same extent. . . .

. . . Like black women, poor white farm wives bore the domestic burdens that were endemic to the economic system of southern staple-crop agriculture. They married in their late teens and had an average of six children (although large households of twelve or thirteen were not uncommon). Because the family was constantly in debt to a local merchant, family members felt glad if they broke even at the end of the year. Most women made do with very little cash in piecing together the family's subsistence. They performed all the household chores of washing, sewing, cleaning, cooking, and churning, often with the assistance of their eldest daughter, but a majority also helped out in the cotton or tobacco fields during the busy seasons. . . . These wives often added to the family income with the proceeds they earned from selling eggs, vegetables, or milk. In the Deep South, some couples experienced periodic separations when the wives went off to work temporarily in factories, or when their men folk found jobs on the levees in the off-season.

In terms of earthly comforts, life offered little more to white tenant-farm wives than it did to blacks; white women too lived in sparsely furnished two- or three-room cabins that lacked running water, and their Cotton Belt families tended to move every three years or so. Mothers were attended by a midwife during childbirth. Predictably, they knew nothing about modern contraceptive techniques, and although they took pride in their child-rearing abilities, they suffered from the consequent drain on their emotional and physical resources. Dreams and fortune-tellers explained the past and predicted the future for many of these illiterate women, but they seemed to lack the religious devotion and denominational loyalties exhibited by black wives and mothers. Undernourished and overworked, they had to remind themselves of the biblical dictate, "Be content with your lot."

In a rural society that honored a code of neighborliness and mutual cooperation, black and white women had few opportunities for interracial contact on any level. Husbands and fathers of both races and all classes observed the ritualized etiquette of southern race relations in the public arena—in town, at the post office, court house, or supply store—but their wives were largely excluded from these encounters. Middle-class white women acted out their own presumptions of racial superiority in their dealings with black servants and laundresses. Tenant-farm wives of course could not afford to employ black women for any length of time or exploit them in a direct way. A few women of the two races did come together in situations that held the promise of enhancing mutual respect and appreciation—for example, when they participated in the Southern Farmers Alliance in the 1880s and 1890s, or when black "grannies" attended white women during childbirth. Yet these opportunities were rare, and for the most part women lacked a formal voice in the politics of interracial protest.

In the end, the fact that the labor of white sharecroppers' wives was so similar to that of their black counterparts is less significant than the social environment in which that work took place. For the outcast group, the preservation of family integrity served as a political statement to the white South. To nurse a child, send a daughter to school, feed a hungry family after a long day at work in the fields, or patch a shirt by the light of a flickering fire—these simple acts of domesticity acquired special significance when performed for a people so beleaguered by human as well as natural forces. If white women also had to make soup out of scraps, at least they and their families remained secure from "bulldosers" (mobs) and Judge Lynch. Finally, and perhaps most important, women of the two races had different things to teach their children about the "southern way of life," its freedoms and its dangers.

Despite the transition in labor organization from slavery to sharecropping, the work of black women in the rural South continued to respond to the same human and seasonal rhythms over the generations. By the early twentieth century, they still structured their labor around household chores and childcare, field and wage work, and community welfare activities. Moreover, emancipation hardly lessened the demands made upon females of all ages; young girls worked alongside their mothers, and elderly women had to provide for themselves and their families as long as they were physically able. Although the specific tasks performed by women reflected constantly changing priorities (determined by the cotton-growing cycle and the size and maturity of individual households), the need for a woman to labor rarely abated in the course of a day, a year, or her lifetime.

In its functional response to unique historical circumstances, the rural black household necessarily differed from the late nineteenth-century middle-class ideal, which assumed that men would engage in individual self-aggrandizement. Furthermore, according to this ideal, women were to remain isolated at home, only indirectly sharing in the larger social values of wealth and power accumulation. In contrast, rural black women labored in harmony with the priorities of cooperation and sharing established by their own communities, even as their husbands were prevented from participating in the cash economy in a way that would answer to white-defined notions of masculinity.

Despite the hard, never-ending work performed by rural women—who, ironically, were labeled part of a "lazy" culture by contemporaries and recent historians alike—they could not entirely compensate for the loss of both a husband (through death or another form of permanent separation) and older sons or male relatives who established households on their own. The sharecropping family strove to maintain a delicate balance between its labor resources and its economic needs, and men, as both negotiators in the public sphere and as field workers, were crucial to that balance. Therefore, during the latter part of the nineteenth century, when the natural selection process endemic to commercial crop agriculture weeded out "unfit" households, it forced single mothers, widows, and unmarried daughters to look cityward. Many of them would discover that while the southern countryside continued to mirror the slave past, in the towns that past was refracted into new shapes and images.

WEEK 3

DOCUMENTS

1. Technology Enshrined at the World's Fair, 1876

Mechanism is the grand and leading science of the world. For centuries, nations, held in ignorance, were only ruled by force; the will of the ruler compelling obedience and controlling the lives and actions of the multitude. Freedom of action was denied, and freedom of conscience bound with an iron rod. Men were the machines of kings and princes. . . .

. . . But peoples were not always to be thus ruled. When the world was ready for intellectual advancement, He who governs nations raised the curtain of the earth and called man to a higher destiny. In the midst of superstition, the printing press burst upon the darkness, and the light of letters flashed out upon the bewildered world. Knowledge spread. Men compared thoughts and joined action. Ignorance was driven from her wonted haunts, while educated intelligence assumed the mastery. Letters commanded attention, and the hidden genius of the world wore a bold front, claimed its right, and forced the despots of the day to acknowledge its strength and its ability. Brains had always force, but they were never aggregated and marched in a body upon ignorance until the invention of letters.

Immediately mechanism began to develop its suppressed powers; and though its progress was slow at first, it continued to advance in its career of usefulness. The closing years of the 18th century found the scientist, philosopher, and mechanic blending ideas and preparing the grand march of the present century. And now, turn where we may, we find machinery providing for the wants of the peoples, and ruling the future of nations. The mighty powers of the forge and furnace are riveting the bonds of peace.

Men think. Machines are automatic, and almost think. Nations think, and so do armies. The advance of the last seventy years has been more than that of previous hundreds. The world is thrown forward a thousand years, and mechanism takes its place among the first sciences.

As we enter Machinery Hall, we hear the hum of thousands of machines, from the tiniest hand-power to the mighty steam-engine. The clamor interrupts conversation, but eyes are not idle. Every wheel and pulley is scrutinized. We are in the largest and grandest machine shop that the world has ever seen. All the expositions of the world heretofore, have failed to concentrate so much strength and usefulness—so much thought and intelligence. Most prominent of all are the machines made in the United States; and, taken as a whole at the present day, they can not be surpassed. The mechanics have sent here their best efforts; and being, as it were, at home, they have spared no exertions to make the Hall attractive in all its features.

. . . More than four-fifths of the space are occupied with machines of this country, and near the center of all we find the—

Corliss Engine

This engine stands as a great double-armed giant, quietly—almost noiselessly—and yet effectively throwing its exhaustless powers upon the heavy beltings, and thence to the innumerable shaftings—main and auxiliary—that speed ten thousand machines

---

Samuel J. Burr, *Memorial of the International Exhibition* (Hartford, Conn.: L. Stebbins, 1877), pp. 37–38, 43, 90–92.

from 9 A.M. to 5 P.M. daily. We can not be minute in our description of this mighty motor, but will give a few prominent features that we trust will interest our readers. The engine is placed in the transept near the center of the Hall, and where the building is 70 feet from the floor to the top of the ventilator. . . . The main belts, instead of being an eye-sore and in the way, as is too often the case, pass through the Hall in out of the way places, and are inclosed in glass apartments eight by six feet in size, so as to make a proper exhibit of the belts.

The engines are what are known as "beam engines" of the Corliss improved pattern, with all the latest improvements, and nominally of 700 horse-power each, or 1,400 horse-power in both, though this can be increased even to 2,500 horse-power should occasion require. The cylinders are forty inches in diameter, with ten feet stroke. The engines are provided with air-pumps and condensing apparatus, and are intended to work with from fifteen to eighty pounds of steam, according to the requirements of the exhibition.

The gear fly-wheel is thirty feet in diameter, two feet across the face, and has 216 teeth, the wheel makes thirty-six revolutions per minute, and the periphery moves at the rate of about thirty-eight miles an hour. . . .

The large gear with which the gear fly-wheel connects is ten feet in diameter, and is a solid casting of 17,000 pounds. The height of the engine from the floor is thirty-nine feet, and every part is accessible by means of iron staircases and balconies, which add much to the artistic beauty of the design. The weight of the engine and its appurtenances amounts to 1,383,264 pounds, making sixty-one car loads of 22,676 pounds each. . . .

It has now been running for five months, and shows not the least imperfection, and without the slightest interruption. It is the design and construction of Geo. H. Corliss, engineer; and is his individual property, furnished by him free of all expenses and generously run at his individual cost. When the exhibition closes, he will take it back to Rhode Island and hold it until an improved condition of manufacturing business shall create a demand for such a power. . . .

The extent and capacity of the Corliss Steam-Engine Works can be best appreciated by considering the fact, that the Centennial engine was constructed from the crude materials—transported—set up, and put in operation in the short space of nine months and twenty-six days. . . .

Sewing Machines

The sewing machine is, comparatively, a recent invention; and can hardly be said to have reached perfection. There are many very excellent devices; and great ingenuity, deep thought, and mints of money have been expended in order to render them complete. The contest still rages, and every year we encounter improvements more and more valuable. . . .

HOWE'S SEWING MACHINE CO., New York; Factories, Bridgeport, Conn.; Peru, Ind., and Glasgow, Scot.—The exhibit embraces many machines, and several cases containing elegantly dressed dolls, the work, embroidery, and braiding having been done on the Howe machine. One case has a lady's saddle beautifully adorned on this machine, showing its adaptability to piercing heavy leather as well as fine fabrics.

After devoting years of thought to the perfecting of a sewing machine, Mr. Howe conceived the idea of placing the eye near the point of the needle—a plan that is now used in all machines; and which eventually made a fortune for the inventor. The following year he sewed the first seam ever made by machinery. The machine is now on exhibition at the pavilion of the Howe company in Machinery Hall. . . . His patent was issued September 10, 1846. The model accompanying the application for this patent may now be seen in the Government Building, Centennial Grounds. His brother, Amasa, was sent to England the same year; and sold the English right to Wm. Thomas for $1,000; and he (Thomas) realized therefrom over $1,000,000. Mr. Howe went to England in 1847, and after various trials, returned to the United States in 1849, penniless. To secure passage home, he was obliged to pawn his first machine and also his letters patent. Again he was compelled to pursue his trade as a machinist in order to obtain a living.

Many began to infringe upon his patent; suits were commenced; and to prosecute these, his father mortgaged a valuable farm. It was not until 1854 that a decision was obtained in his favor. In pronouncing the opinion of the Court, Judge Sprague, of Massachusetts, used the following emphatic language:—"There is no evidence in this case that leaves a shadow of doubt that for all the benefits conferred by the introduction of sewing machines, the public are indebted to Elias Howe, Jr." Upon the rendition of this opinion, the various manufacturers formed a combination to protect each other against infringements, and all agreed to pay Mr. Howe a royalty upon every machine made. In 1869 Mr. Howe exhibited his machine at the Paris Exposition, where he was awarded a gold medal, the highest premium; and was decorated by the Emperor with the Cross of the Legion of Honor. Shortly after his return home he died.

A bronze statue of Mr. Howe has been erected on the border of the lake in the park, opposite the main entrance of Machinery Hall. It is of heroic size, nine feet six inches in height. It was designed by Robert Wood & Co., at a cost of $20,000; and at the close of the present exhibition, is to be placed in Central Park, New York. We give the particulars of the trial of this remarkable man for the encouragement of young inventors, to whom we say never be discouraged by difficulties in introducing new inventions. Trials always await genius, and the moment of success may be the hour of the greatest peril. It was so with him, but his determined will overcame all, and placed him eventually upon the pinnacle of fortune. No less than thirty-two companies have been formed, with an aggregate capital of $30,000,000, and producing 400,000 machines annually. More than 12,000 men are engaged in the various factories, and nearly an equal number in the sales and agencies.

The exhibit of this company has cost $38,000; $12,000 of which have been expended for pamphlets and catalogues. The [Howe] factories give employment to 3,500 people, and cover a space of over twelve acres.

2. Duplicating Before Xerox: The Rapid Roller Copier, 1897

THE RAPID ✦ ✦ ✦ ROLLER COPIER ❀ ❀ ❀ ❀

Instantaneous damp-leaf copies of any writing can be secured by merely turning a crank. This Copier is invaluable, not only in mercantile and public offices, but also in banks, insurance and real estate agencies, and in hotels for the convenience of commercial patrons.

THE ONLY PERFECT COPYING MACHINE.
SAVES TIME AND MONEY.

IT IS TWENTY-FIVE YEARS IN ADVANCE
OF THE SCREW LETTER-PRESS.

NO DELAY. NO INCONVENIENCE. ALWAYS RELIABLE.

The SHANNON FILING CABINET and RAPID ROLLER COPIER when used together afford the most perfect system of filing correspondence. Copies can be filed with the letters to which they are answers and the entire correspondence of an individual thus kept together.

Office Specialty Manufacturing Company (Rochester, N.Y.: Office Specialty Manufacturing Company, 1897), n.p. Trade catalog collection, Hagley Museum and Library, Wilmington, Del. Courtesy Hagley Museum and Library.

3. An Office Supply Company Advertises the Globe Routing System, 1897

For many years the serious problem to manufacturers, jobbers, in fact to all commercial houses has been to systematically keep track of their traveling salesmen, agents, inquiries, exclusive territory, reports, mortgages, etc. The old system of hanging maps on the wall and using different colored pencils, strings, pin tags, etc., for indicators, whenever a change was necessary, scratching or erasing the old mark and adding the new, caused these maps at the end of a very short time not only to have the appearance of a "Chinese puzzle," but to be discarded as utterly worthless.

The Globe Company offers to the commercial world its "Globe Routing System" for keeping track of their traveling salesmen, agencies, exclusive territory, etc. . . .

A Brief Description Of How The Routing System Can Be Used

The plan which is embodied in The Globe Routing System employs maps mounted in drawers and built in cabinets of sizes to suit any class or size of business. The whole, or any part of the country, can be included in the system, as the requirements of the business may determine. The drawers contain maps 21 × 28 inches in size, with certain smaller States combined, making single maps of 21 × 14 inches, and properly labeled. The maps themselves vary, for a single map may cover any territory desired—for example, the whole United States, or a single State, or a single county, or even a single city. This feature demonstrates the elasticity of the system. To cover the entire United States and Canada, using a single drawer for each of the larger states, a 44 drawer cabinet is employed.

Different colored silk headed tacks are employed as indicators. In some cases these indicators are numbered from 1 to 12, and designate the different months. For example, if a traveling man visits a city in February, and his color is yellow, a yellow tack numbered 2, is used, indicating that the city was last visited in February. Similar variations and combinations are used in the matter of mortgages and collections, indicating the month due, and, in some cases, the man in charge of that particular piece of business.

We will first consider its application in managing traveling men. In laying out the route for a traveling salesman named Jones, we select some color for him, we will say green. Using the green indicators, we stick one on the map at every city to be visited. After Jones has started on his trip, we follow the route with a white indicator, thus showing at all times the city in which Jones is at the present time. Or, we may vary the plan by replacing the green indicators with numbered ones, showing the month the city was visited, the last numbered indicator showing the city in which Jones is at the present time.

Let us next consider the system in the matter of agents. We would select a number of colors among the indicators to be known as agent's indicators. Or, we may choose a single color, but with different numbers for different values. Upon the latter

Office Appliances (New York: Globe Company, 1897), pp. 38, 40. Trade catalog collection, Hagley Museum and Library, Wilmington, Del.

plan we will take yellow as the agents' indicator. Number 1 of the yellow is to indicate exclusive territory; number 2 to indicate that the house is represented in that territory, but no exclusive rights have been given. Number 3 would be still another variation in these particulars, and so on. By placing these indicators over the territory, there is at once revealed to the managing man who glances at the map the exact condition at any given point.

Still another colored indicator may refer to collections, for example, denoting bad debts or slow accounts. Wherever a debt of this kind exists, one of these indicators is placed. When in making up the route of traveling men, glancing at the map for information, these indicators call attention to the fact that an account at a certain place is to be collected or looked up. Still other variations and adaptations are possible, for the system is sufficiently elastic to meet every requirement made in the conduct of business. A key is, of course, necessary in order to maintain proper system in the use of the indicators. In a corner of the drawer, as shown in cut of drawer, a key can be placed, showing what the different indicators represent, as for example, travelers: Jones, green; Hopkins, blue; Smith, black and Kelly, red. Collections may be indicated by orange, agents by yellow, and so on. Instead of writing the names of the colors on the key slip it is best to put after the heading an indicator of the color used, thus appealing to the eye by means of color and form, as well as to the brain by name.

In this account only a few uses of the system have been given, for as previously indicated, the users find new adaptations constantly, and the utility grows as familiarity is acquired. Any record of a geographical nature can be kept by this system, and the records read at a glance, thereby doing away with memorandas, tedious reference to correspondence, and taxing the memory with details that are hard to retain. The Routing System may be very properly supplemented by an adaptation of a Card System, so that one becomes the key to the other. The cards may be arranged alphabetically by state and city, or by salesmen's routes. Changes and alterations are made without interfering with the index arrangement.

The advantages of a system of this kind to the progressive business house of the present day when every point must be counted, are obvious.

4. A Vice President at the New York Central Railroad Describes Railroad Management as a Manly Profession, 1903

The avenues open to the young man contemplating entering railroading are many—all leading to the common goal, the presidency of the company. The principal grand divisions are engineering, motive power and rolling-stock, transportation, traffic, law, finance and accounting. Each of these in turn splits up into many specialties. The selection among these departments depends entirely on the natural bent and tastes of the young man.

William J. Wilgus, "Making a Choice of a Profession, VIII—Railroading," *Cosmopolitan* 35 (1903): 462–464.

Engineering embraces the duties of constructing and maintaining the fixed or stationary property of the company, as distinguished from the movable motive power or rolling-stock. The results attained by this department determine the degree of safety and economy with which the railroad can be operated. Therefore, it will be realized that the engineering officer bears a heavy responsibility. His mistakes, when made, are not of a temporary character, buried and soon forgotten, but they stand out so that all can see them, irremediable except at great expense. The successful engineer has not only a technical training in his own profession, but also a suitable knowledge of the details of the other departments, in order properly to design, construct and maintain for their needs. In other words, the modern railway engineer must be a broad-gauge man of the strictest integrity and common sense.

The construction side of engineering has jurisdiction over new work of magnitude, such as the reconnoissance, location, and construction of new lines of railway, double-tracking, new bridges, tunnels and important buildings, signals, terminals, grade-reductions, heat-, light- and power-plants, water-supply, the elimination of grade-crossings, electrification of traffic; and also of the real estate of the company, and of standard plans and specifications. Construction engineering usually calls for men with a technical education, studious tendencies and a taste for scheming, planning, designing and executing new work.

Maintenance of way comprises what may be termed the executive branch of engineering. It includes all forces engaged in the maintenance of the company's existing physical property in accordance with standards fixed by the chief engineer of the construction department. Supervisors or roadmasters, trackmen, signalmen, wreckers, carpenters, masons, bridgemen and other mechanics and laborers report to this department, and on the larger systems aggregate from ten to twenty thousand men. This large force is subdivided and organized so as to maintain the property in a safe condition for operation under all conditions of weather. The direction of such forces requires men possessing executive ability of the first quality, physical strength and practical experience. An engineering training, either technical or acquired, is a great aid to success. Storms, washouts, wrecks, and emergencies of all kinds call for constant watchfulness day and night, frequent long-continued exposure to the elements, with little sleep, and require the ability to anticipate and prevent trouble. The experience in this department is an excellent education for entrance into the transportation department, with its opportunities for continued advancement.

The motive-power and rolling-stock department has jurisdiction over the building and maintenance of locomotives, cars and other rolling-stock. The forces include the foremen and mechanics in the shops and engine-houses, and in some instances the enginemen and firemen. Usually, however, the motive-power department is responsible only for the mechanical fitness of the latter two classes of employees, and the transportation department passes on their knowledge and observance of operating rules. The department of motive-power and rolling-stock appeals to mechanically inclined men who are either educated in technical schools or who have learned the trade. Such men should have inventive skill, careful habits, physical endurance and keen intelligence.

Transportation claims the most numerous and varied class of employees in the service, and is the closest in contact with the general public. It uses the facilities given by the engineering and motive-power departments to transport the freight and passengers delivered to it by the traffic department. The proper administration of this department is of the first importance to the company. Trains must run safely and on time; freight must be promptly handled without friction with shippers; ingenuity and resourcefulness are always demanded to meet unexpected conditions, such as moving business despite blockades, accidents, washouts and snow-storms; and the maximum tonnage must be moved with a minimum of cost. The men in the transportation department are, above all others, expected to render faithful, loyal service. Enginemen and firemen, conductors, baggagemen and trainmen carry the safety and comfort of the train service in their hands; agents, clerks, telegraphers and their assistants serve the public in stations and depots; signal-operators man the towers; flagmen guard the highway-crossings; yardmasters and switchmen operate the terminals, which are the digestive organs of a railroad; the medical staff renders aid to the injured; and the superintendents, car-accountants, trainmasters and despatchers oversee and direct the movements of the entire transportation machine.

Traffic covers the securing of passenger and freight business, and its success is vital to the prosperity of the company. In competitive territory where many railroads are striving for business the traffic official is required to have the highest grade of tact and diplomacy to hold and increase the shipments over his line.

The passenger traffic officer taxes his ingenuity to attract the attention of the public to his line by unique advertisements, timetables, maps and notices.

Law commands an important place in railroading, as it is the bulwark against which all kinds of claimants, of varying degrees of honesty, surge to mulct the company. The railroad lawyer is required to have a keen knowledge of human nature, ready wit, and the mental characteristics of the judge, in order to distinguish between the just and the unjust claim. On one hand, he can save the company from unnecessary lawsuits, and deserving claimants from injustice; and, on the other hand, he protects his client from extortion and robbery. All contracts, deeds, bonds and mortgages pass under his scrutiny, and must have his approval. Legislative acts require his watchfulness to see that laws that would be unjust to the company as well as to the general public do not pass surreptitiously.

Finance comprises supervision over the receipts and expenditures of the railroad. The payments of interest on the securities of the company, the issuance and recording of new securities, pay-rolls, vouchers, and all matters affecting the financial obligations are handled by this department.

Accounting watches and checks the results of operation, and feels the pulse of business to quickly detect variations in the financial health of the company. The comptroller or auditor is the first to know what the railroad is earning from month to month. All vouchers for expenditures approved by heads of departments are first compared with formal contracts or authorities, and must have the endorsement of the comptroller or auditor before payment by the treasurer. All bills for collection of revenue, and all receipts from passenger and freight traffic are checked by this department. Monthly statistics that illustrate the operative efficiency of the various departments, the total receipts and expenditures and the net revenue, are issued monthly or oftener for the information of the president, the general officers, and of the investing public. A mass of data is tabulated that enables the executive to know exactly what each department is doing, and, if necessary, institute changes or reforms before the interests of the company might suffer.

Thus it will be seen that the young man considering the choice of a profession has a wide range of selection in railroading. His decision should be guided, not by the immediate gain that one branch may offer over the others, but rather by the class of work that best suits his talents, and that can hold enthusiastic and undivided affection. Promotion step by step widens the knowledge until, upon reaching the top of the ladder of one of the specialties, without effort the climber passes over to the next ladder, mounting higher, and this, repeated, gradually leads to the climax.

5. Male and Female Telegraph Operators Go on Strike, 1907

The main office of a telegraph company impresses the uninitiated observer but does not enlighten him. All that electricity implies of the miraculous seems expressed in the keys of the Morse instruments and in the wizardry of control that connects the operator at the board with his co-worker a thousand miles away. You see men and women, row back of row, receiving, sending, writing messages. You hear the intermittent click of the telegraph keys, the banging of typewriters, and you are conscious of a steady undercurrent of haste, concentration, quick efficiency.

The main and branch offices of the two telegraph companies in Pittsburgh employ 90 women and 198 men. Men and women do the same kind of work, which they learn for the most part through apprenticeship as floor messengers and gradual promotion to manipulation of the keys. If there is a difference in the grade of work assigned, it is that the women are employed more generally at branch offices and at the lighter wires.

Yet although the work done by men and by women in telegraph offices is apparently the same, conditions growing out of the employment of women proved to be the pivot about which swung the strike of the summer of 1907 against one of the Pittsburgh companies. . . .

In Pittsburgh 38 women and about 150 men were in the union, together making up 75 per cent of the operating force. When the strike was ordered, the union asked that typewriters be furnished by the company, that the sliding scale of wages be abolished, and that a shorter working day be arranged. The typewriter is part of the operator's equipment. When it was first introduced, a special bonus was offered to employes who would learn to use it, and as its use became general, it proved as valuable to the employes as to the company. Many whose handwriting was poor, and who on this account had been classed below first-class, were able to draw higher pay. Operators, however, are required to buy and to keep in repair their own machines, which is a heavy initial expense.

The demand for a shorter working day grew out of the fact that the telegraph service is continuous through the twenty-four hours. Shifts and relays have to be arranged for among the operating force. The schedule provided for a nine-hour day with overtime service to fill the places of absentees or in cases of emergency, and

Elizabeth Beardsley Butler, *Women and the Trades: Pittsburgh, 1907–1908.* The Pittsburgh Survey, ed. Paul Underwood Kellogg (New York: Charities Publication Committee, 1909), pp. 292–294.

different turns were assigned to the operators in rotation. The night work schedule was shorter, seven hours and a half; and the "split trick," planned to accommodate the period of heaviest traffic, was eight hours,—ten to two, and five to nine. Once at the key-board, relief was granted for no cause, without specific permission from the traffic chief; and operators complained that at times they would have to stay at their posts all day without being relieved, and when relieved would frequently be allowed only twenty minutes at noon. Sunday work was assigned to different members of the force as extra work with pay based on seven hours as a full day.

But important as these points were, abolition of the sliding scale was the cardinal demand. The grievance referred to as the "sliding scale" was the outcome of alleged differences in the work done by men and by women, and of resultant unfair discrimination. Managers and operators as a rule agree that the lesser physical strength of women tells against them after several years of light wrist and finger motions; that because of this lesser strength, women have neither the speed nor the accuracy of men; and that they get "glass arm," a nervous inability to work, more frequently. On the other hand, both managers and operators agree that although women work for the most part on light wires, the quantity of work done by given operators is fairly well equalized, and that the difference between a light and a heavy wire is less than would be supposed. Whereas an operator on a heavy wire does sending only, or receiving only, the operator on a light wire does both sending and receiving, or else works by a system of "floats" whereby three wires are handled by two operators. Yet the potential ability of men operators to do heavier work than women is reflected in the differences in wages. One company paid $30, $35, and $44 a month to women in branch offices, and $62 to women in the main office. The other company paid two-thirds of its women employes $30 to $55 a month, and one-third of its women employes from $55 to $75 a month. It was charged that the former company paid its salaries on the basis of individual bargaining, and not on the basis of kind or quantity of work done; that a man who had earned $82.50 on a heavy wire would be superseded by a woman at $75; and that a man who had been receiving $75 would be superseded by a woman at $62. By this system, the rates of payment for given wires were being lowered. Although the work might tell on women sooner than on men, and although they might in some cases be less efficient than men, they were yet sufficiently capable to supersede men at a lower rate of pay. They were lending themselves to a scheme for cutting wages.

The strike was broken in the fall, in part through the agency of unorganized women. Most of the women went out when the men went out, but a few of them stayed in, and others who had formerly been in the employ of the company were impressed for the occasion. In one point, however, the strike was not without effect. Conditions in the company against which the strike was chiefly directed remained unchanged, but the other company granted a 10 per cent increase in wages by which some of the women operators are now earning as much as the men can earn at the heavy wires. Two-thirds of the women employes of this company now earn from $33 to $60.50 a month; and one-third of the women earn from $60.50 to $82.50 a month. This scale would seem to show that this company does not discriminate against women nor force competition between women and men, but pays equally for equal work.

6. AT&T President Theodore N. Vail Celebrates the Bell System, 1909

The Bell system is one system telephonically interconnected, intercommunicating and interdependent. This is such a system that any one of over 4,000,000 subscribers can talk with any other one within carrying power of the voice over wires, the only exception being that the Pacific Coast and the Middle Rocky Mountain region are not yet connected.

This system was built up under this policy and its continuance as a system depends on the continuance of the policy.

In the telephone business development is continuous. As conditions enlarge and change, new methods develop. The whole business suggests changes and stimulates inventions, and opportunities for improvements are frequent.

If each separate exchange or group of exchanges had not been assisted and directed in the development and introduction of these new ideas, methods and inventions, there would now be as many systems, as many methods of operating as there are separate companies. This would have made impossible the organization which now gives the Bell system that universality and preponderance on account of which no matter how many other systems may exist, every one of any commercial or social importance must have connection with the Bell system.

The same generalization runs through many departments. The companies are so organized, or fast becoming so, that every department continues through the local administration to the central administration of the American Telephone and Telegraph Company.

The American Telephone and Telegraph Company owns and maintains all telephones. It also owns either directly or through the Western Electric Company all patents.

It has a department which was organized at the very beginning of the business and has continued since, where is to be found practically everything known about inventions pertaining to the telephone or kindred subjects. Every new idea is there examined, and its value determined so far as the patent features are concerned.

The Engineering Department takes all new ideas, suggestions and inventions, and studies, develops, and passes upon them.

It has under continuous observation and study all traffic methods and troubles, improving or remedying them.

It studies all construction, present and future development or extension schemes, makes plans and specifications for the same, and gives when desired general supervision and advice. It has a corps of experts which, in addition to the above work, is at all times at the service of any or all of the separate companies.

When it is considered that some of these questions involve the permanency, duration and usefulness of a telephone plant costing millions of dollars, and changes

---

Theodore N. Vail, "American Telephone and Telegraph Company's Relations to Associated Companies," *Annual Report of the American Telephone and Telegraph Company*, March 1909, in *Views on Public Questions: A Collection of Papers and Addresses of Theodore Newton Vail, 1907–1917* (New York: Privately Printed, 1917), pp. 13–18.

costing hundreds of thousands, some idea of its importance can be formed. To give an illustration: One group of patents covering inventions which seemed likely to be useful and economical in the service was purchased by the company. These inventions were developed into operating apparatus and put into use. While this cost hundreds of thousands of dollars, placing it beyond the scope of one operating company, the saving already accomplished to the associated companies runs into the millions.

A large staff has been and is continuously engaged in the consideration of disturbances arising from transmission and other lines carrying heavy currents, and in many cases that any telephone system can even exist in the vicinity of such lines is due to the constant and continued attention given this subject.

Every new trouble, and there are many, comes before this department. When settled there, it is settled for all. This has established a commercial, operating and plant practice not only for our own associated companies, but for others of high standing throughout the world.

All devices or inventions submitted receive the most thorough and painstaking investigation, and it [is] safe to say that there has as yet been no instance where any invention, system or method, rejected by the Patent and Engineering Departments of the American Telephone and Telegraph Company has ever had any permanent success when used elsewhere.

The Manufacturing Department creates and builds the equipment and apparatus which have been adopted. In this way throughout the whole grand system will be found standardization and uniformity. This is not any handicap on improvement or development of the art, for, on the contrary, every suggestion or idea, and there are many, has abundant opportunity to be tested, which would not be possible otherwise. No one of the companies could by itself maintain such an organization, and it would be fatal to any service to introduce or try out undeveloped ideas in actual service.

In the Legal Department all the big and general questions are looked after. It forms a clearing house in all legal matters for all the legal departments of the separate companies to which assistance and advice are given on all questions of general scope.

In the administration all questions which affect all companies, all questions between the associated companies, and the general policy and the general conduct of the business, are considered and close touch and relationship maintained with all parts of the system. Experts on every subject connected with this business are continually at work on old or new subjects and ready at call to go to the assistance of any of the companies. In short, the great work and substantially all the expense of the American Telephone and Telegraph Company are involved in this "Centralized General Administration," taking care of all those matters which are common to all companies, or which if taken care of by each company would mean multiplication of work, effort, expense without corresponding advantage or efficiency.

To sum up, quoting the words of the representative of a large stockholding interest in one of the associated companies: "The contract relation with the American Telephone and Telegraph Company is the biggest asset this company has."

In submitting this report, we wish to call your attention to two things which indicate the stability of the company and property.

One is the wide dispersion and small average holding of the shares—including the shareholders in the associated and connected companies, there are over 70,000 shareholders in the Bell system. From January 1 to March 2, the date of bond conversion, the shareholders increased about one hundred per week.

Another is the stability of the business, year after year shows an increase, no matter what the prevailing business conditions. There has, it is true, been a slight decline in the rate of increase in exchange earnings, and the toll line business has given some indication that conditions were not normal, but even in that there was an increase in earnings.

This stability and the position that the Bell system holds is due very largely to the policy and conditions under which it was developed, not alone to the telephone.

A telephone—without a connection at the other end of the line—is not even a toy or a scientific instrument. It is one of the most useless things in the world. Its value depends on the connection with the other telephone—and increases with the number of connections.

The Bell system under an intelligent control and broad policy has developed until it has assimilated itself into and in fact become the nervous system of the business and social organization of the country.

This is the result of the centralized general control exercised by the company, the combination of all local systems into one combined system developed as a whole.

Nor could the development have been made in any other way. If the business had been developed by different organizations—each absolutely independent of and unrelated to the others—each little system would have been independent and self-contained without benefit to any other. No one has use for two telephone connections if he can reach all with whom he desires connection through one. Through the development of the Bell system, the relation and benefit as a whole have been considered. The policy has been to bring together all units which contribute to the value of the whole. The demand for facilities is seldom found waiting in these days for the facilities to come. The demand is created by the existence of the facilities. This is particularly true of the telephone service. It took courage to build the first toll line—short as it was—and it took more to build the first long-distance line to Chicago. . . .

There are no other countries where the telephone service occupies the same relation to the public. Elsewhere narrow control and a policy of restriction have prevented its full development. Whatever is good in those systems has been adopted from the practice in this country. . . .

Promptness and certainty therefore mean that each message, connection or other unit of actual service availed of must bear the expense of a number of unused possible units not availed of. If, instead of the immediate or prompt service of this country, the service as it exists in most other countries were in vogue, the cost would be reduced, but to a much greater extent would the value be reduced. Delayed service—service which keeps a line of customers waiting, so that there need be no loss of units of service, would reduce to a minimum the number of operators and given facilities, and all that creates cost.

Instead of waiting and idle operators and facilities, there would be waiting, idle and patient, customers.

We do not think the American public desires this kind of service.

ESSAYS

✣ E S S A Y S

In the first essay, Yale University historian David Montgomery describes the rich, potent work culture of skilled, male industrial workers. He unveils a late-nineteenth-century world in which their unique knowledge of the labor process and their proud, "manly" values gave these autonomous craftsman substantial control of their workplace. Setting work rules, first informally and then through their unions, these machinists, iron molders, coal miners, and other skilled and semiskilled men developed an ethos of mutuality grounded in a self-confident masculine identity. Strikes, especially those undertaken to support other crafts, testified to their willingness to defend working-class institutions and values against employer encroachment.

Work Rules and Manliness in the World
of the Nineteen-Century Craftsman

DAVID MONTGOMERY

"In an industrial establishment which employs say from 500 to 1000 workmen, there will be found in many cases at least twenty to thirty different trades," wrote Frederick Winslow Taylor in his famous critique of the practices of industrial management which were then in vogue.

> The workmen in each of these trades have had their knowledge handed down to them by word of mouth. . . . This mass of rule-of-thumb or traditional knowledge may be said to be the principle asset or possession of every tradesman. . . . [The] foremen and superintendents . . . recognize the task before them as that of inducing each workman to use his best endeavors, his hardest work, all his traditional knowledge, his skill, his ingenuity, and his good-will—in a word, his "initiative," so as to yield the largest possible return to his employer."

Big Bill Haywood put the same point somewhat more pungently, when he declared: "The manager's brains are under the workman's cap."

Both Taylor and Haywood were describing the power which certain groups of workers exercised over the direction of production processes at the end of the nineteenth century, a power which the scientific management movement strove to abolish, and which the Industrial Workers of the World wished to enlarge and extend to all workers. It is important to note that both men found the basis of workers' power in the superiority of their knowledge over that of the factory owners. It is even more important to note that they were referring not to "pre-industrial" work practices, but to the factory itself. . . .

My concern here [is] with the patterns of behavior which took shape in the second and third generations of industrial experience, largely among workers whose world had been fashioned from their youngest days by smoky mills, congested streets, recreation as a week-end affair and toil at the times and the pace dictated by the clock (except when a more or less lengthy layoff meant no work at all). It as such workers, the veterans, if you will, of industrial life, with whom Taylor was

David Montgomery, "Workers' Control of Machine Production in the Nineteenth Century," *Labor History*, 17 (Fall 1976): pp. 485–509. Reprinted by permission of Taylor & Francis, Ltd., http://www.tandf.co.uk/journals.

preoccupied. They had internalized the industrial sense of time, they were highly disciplined in both individual and collective behavior, and they regarded both an extensive division of labor and machine production as their natural environments. But they had often fashioned from these attributes neither the docile obedience of automatons, nor the individualism of the "upwardly mobile," but a form of control of productive processes which became increasingly collective, deliberate and aggressive, until American employers launched a partially successful counterattack under the banners of scientific management and the open shop drive.

Workers' control of production, however, was not a condition or state of affairs which existed at any point in time, but a struggle, a chronic battle in industrial life which assumed a variety of forms. Those forms may be treated as successive stages in a pattern of historical evolution, though one must always remember that the stages overlapped each other chronologically in different industries, or even at different localities within the same industry, and that each successive stage incorporated the previous one, rather than replacing it. The three levels of development which appeared in the second half of the nineteenth century were those characterized by (1) the functional autonomy of the craftsman, (2) the union work rule, and (3) mutual support of diverse trades in rule enforcement and sympathetic strikes. Each of these levels will be examined here in turn, then in conclusion some observations will be made on the impact of scientific management and the open shop drive on the patterns of behavior which they represented.

The functional autonomy of craftsmen rested on both their superior knowledge, which made them self-directing at their tasks, and the supervision which they gave to one or more helpers. Iron molders, glass blowers, coopers, paper machine tenders, locomotive engineers, mule spinners, boiler makers, pipe fitters, typographers, jiggermen in potteries, coal miners, iron rollers, puddlers and heaters, the operators of McKay or Goodyear stitching machines in shoe factories, and, in many instances, journeymen machinists and fitters in metal works exercised broad discretion in the direction of their own work and that of their helpers. They often hired and fired their own helpers and paid the latter some fixed portion of their own earnings.

James J. Davis, who was to end up as Warren Harding's Secretary of Labor, learned the trade of puddling iron by working as his father's helper in Sharon, Pennsylvania. "None of us ever went to school and learned the chemistry of it from books," he recalled. "We learned the trick by doing it, standing with our faces in the scorching heat while our hands puddled the metal in its glaring bath." His first job, in fact, had come at the age of twelve, when an aged puddler devised a scheme to enable him to continue the physically arduous exertion of the trade by taking on a boy (twelve-year old Davis) to relieve the helper of mundane tasks like stoking the furnace, so that the helper in turn could assume a larger share of the taxing work of stirring the iron as it "came to nature." By the time Davis felt he had learned enough to master his own furnace, he had to leave Sharon, because furnaces passed from father to son, and Davis' father was not yet ready to step down. As late as 1900, when Davis was living at home while attending business college after having been elected to public office, he took over his father's furnace every afternoon, through an arrangement the two had worked out between themselves.

The iron rollers of the Columbus Iron Works, in Ohio, have left us a clear record of how they managed their trade in the minute books of their local union from 1873 to 1876. The three twelve-man rolling teams, which constituted the union, negotiated a single tonnage rate with the company for each specific rolling job the company undertook. The workers then decided collectively, among themselves, what portion of that rate should go to each of them (and the shares were far from equal, ranging from 19¼ cents, out of the negotiated $1.13 a ton, for the roller, to 5 cents for the runout hooker), how work should be allocated among them, how many rounds on the rolls should be undertaken per day, what special arrangements should be made for the fiercely hot labors of the hookers during the summer, and how members should be hired and progress through the various ranks of the gang. To put it another way, all the boss did was to buy the equipment and raw materials and sell the finished product. . . .

Three aspects of the moral code, in which the craftsmen's autonomy was protectively enmeshed, deserve close attention. First, on most jobs there was a stint, an output quota fixed by the workers themselves. As the laments of scientific management's apostles about workers "soldiering" and the remarkable 1904 survey by the Commissioner of Labor, *Regulation and Restriction of Output,* made clear, stints flourished as widely without unions as with them. Abram Hewitt testified in 1867 that his puddlers in New Jersey, who were not unionized, worked 11 turns per week (5½ days), made three heats per turn, and put 450 pounds of iron in each charge, all by arrangement among themselves. Thirty-five years later a stint still governed the trade, though a dramatic improvement in puddling furnaces was reflected in union rules which specified 11 turns with five heats per turn and 550 pounds per charge (a 104% improvement in productivity), while some nonunion mill workers followed the same routine but boiled bigger charges.

Stints were always under pressure from the employers, and were often stretched over the course of time by the combined force of competition among employers and improving technology. In this instance, productivity under union rules expanded more than three per cent annually over three and half decades. But workers clung doggedly to the practice, and used their superior knowledge both to determine how much they should do and to outwit employers' efforts to wring more production out of them. In a farm equipment factory studied in 1902, for example, the machine shop, polishing department, fitting department and blacksmith shop all had fixed stints, which made each group of workers average very similar earnings despite the fact that all departments were on piecework. . . . Similarly, Taylor's colleague Carl Barth discovered a planer operator who avoided exceeding the stint while always looking busy, by simply removing the cutting tool from his machine from time to time, while letting it run merrily on.

"There is in every workroom a fashion, a habit of work," wrote efficiency consultant Henry Gantt, "and the new workers follows that fashion, for it isn't respectable not to." A quiver full of epithets awaited the deviant: 'hog,' 'hogger-in,' 'leader,' 'rooter,' 'chaser,' 'rusher,' 'runner,' 'swift,' 'boss's pet,' to mention some politer versions. And when a whole factory gained a reputation for feverish work, disdainful craftsmen would describe its occupants, as one did of the Gisholt turret lathe works, as comprised half "of farmers, and the other half, with few exceptions, of horse thieves." On the other hand, those who held fast to the carefully measured stint, despite the curses of their employers and the lure of higher earnings, depicted themselves as sober and trustworthy masters of their trades. Unlimited output led to slashed piece rates, irregular employment, drink and debaucher, they argued. Rationally restricted output, however, reflected "unselfish brotherhood," personal dignity, and "cultivation of the mind."

Second, as this language vividly suggests, the craftsmen's ethical code demanded a "manly" bearing toward the boss. Few words enjoyed more popularity in the nineteenth century than this honorific, with all its connotations of dignity, respectability, defiant egalitarianism, and patriarchal male supremacy. The worker who merited it refused to cower before the foreman's glares—in fact, often would not work at all when a boss was watching. . . .

Finally, "manliness" toward one's fellow workers was an important as it was toward the owners. "Undermining or conniving" at a brother's job was a form of hoggish behavior as objectional as running more than one machine, or otherwise doing the work that belonged to two men. Union rules commanded the expulsion of members who performed such "dirty work," in order to secure employment or advancement for themselves. When the members of the Iron Heaters and Rollers Union at a Philadelphia mill learned in 1875 that one of their brothers had been fired "for dissatisfaction in regard to his management of the mill," and that another member had "undermined" the first with the superintendent and been promised his rolls, the delinquent was expelled from the lodge, along with a lodge member who defended him, and everyone went on strike to demand the immediate discharge of both excommunicates by the firm.

In short, a simple technological explanation for the control exercised by nineteenth-century craftsmen will not suffice. Technical knowledge acquired on the job was embedded in a mutualistic ethical code, also acquired on the job, and together these attributes provided skilled workers with considerable autonomy at their work and powers of resistance to the wishes of their employers. On the other hand, it was technologically possible for the worker's autonomy to be used in individualistic ways, which might promote his own mobility and identify his interests with those of the owner. The ubiquitous practice of subcontracting encouraged this tendency. In the needle trades, the long established custom of a tailor's taking work home to his family was transformed by his employment of other piece workers into the iniquitous "sweat shop" system. Among iron molders, the "berkshire" system expanded rapidly after 1850, as individual molders hired whole teams of helpers to assist them in producing a multitude of castings. Carpenters and bricklayers were lured into piece work systems of petty exploitations, and other forms of subcontracting flourished in stone quarrying, iron mining, anthracite mining, and even in railroad locomotive works, where entire units of an engine's construction were let out to the machinist who filed the lowest bid, and who then hired a crew to assist him in making and fitting the parts.

Subcontracting practices readily undermined both stints and the mutualistic ethic (though contractors were known to fix stints for their own protection in both garment and locomotive works), and they tended to flood many trades with trained, or semi-trained, workers who undercut wages and work standards. Their spread encouraged many craftsmen to move beyond reliance on their functional autonomy to the next higher level of craft control, the enactment and enforcement of union work rules. In one respect, union rules simply codified the autonomy I have already described. In fact, because they were often written down and enforced by joint action, union rules have a visibility to historians, which has made me resort to them already for evidence in the discussion of autonomy per se. But this intimate historical relationship between customary workers' autonomy and the union rule should not blind us to the fact that the latter represents a significant new stage of development.

The work rules of unions were referred to by their members as "legislation." The phrase denotes a shift from spontaneous to deliberate collective action, from a group ethical code to formal rules and sanctions, and from resistance to employers' pretentions to control over them. In some unions the rules were rather simple. The International Association of Machinists, for example, like its predecessors the Machinists and Blacksmiths' International Union and the many machinists' local assemblies of the Knights of Labor, simply specified a fixed term of apprenticeship for any prospective journeyman, established a standard wage for the trade, prohibited helpers of handymen from performing journeymen's work, and forbade any member from running more than one machine at a time or accepting any form of piece work payment.

Other unions had much detailed and complex rules. There were, for example, sixty-six "Rules for Working" in the by-laws of the window-glass workers' Local Assembly 300 of the Knights of Labor. They specified that full crews had to be present "at each pot setting," that skimming could be done only at the beginning of blowing and at meal time, that blowers and gatherers should not "work faster than at the rate of nine rollers per hour," and that the "standard size of single strength rollers" should "be 40 × 58 to cut 38 × 56." No work was to be performed on Thanksgiving Day, Christmas, Decoration Day or Washington's Birthday, and no blower, gatherer or cutter could work between June 15 and September 15. In other words, during the summer months the union ruled that the fires were to be out. In 1884 the local assembly waged a long and successful strike to preserve its limit of 48 boxes of glass a week, a rule which its members considered the key to the dignity and welfare of the trade.

Nineteenth-century work rules were not ordinarily negotiated with employers or embodied in a contract. From the 1860s onward it became increasingly common for standard *wages* to be negotiated with employers or their associations, rather than fixed unilaterally as unions had tried earlier, but working rules changed more slowly. They were usually adopted unilaterally by local unions, or by the delegates to a national convention, and enforced by the refusal of the individual member to obey any command from an employer which violated them. Hopefully, the worker's refusal would be supported by the joint action of his shop mates, but if it was not, he was honor bound to pack his tool box and walk out alone, rather than break the union's laws. . . .

On the other hand, the autonomy of craftsmen which was codified in union rules was clearly not individualistic. Craftsmen were unmistakably and consciously group-made men, who sought to pull themselves upward by their collective boot straps. As unions waxed stronger after 1886, the number of strikes to enforce union rules grew steadily. It was, however, in union legislation against subcontracting that both the practical and ideological aspects of the conflict between group solidarity and upwardly mobile individualism became most evident, for these rules sought to regulate in the first instance not the employers' behavior, but that of the workers themselves. Thus the Iron Molders Union attacked the "berkshire" system by rules forbidding any of its members to employ a helper for any other purpose than "to skim, shake out and to cut sand," or to pay a helper out of his own earnings. In 1867, when 8,615 out of some 10,400 known molders in the country were union members, the national union legislated further that no member was allowed to go to work earlier than seven o'clock in the morning. During the 1880s the Brick Layers' Union checked subcontracting by banning its members from working for any contractor who could not raise enough capital to buy his own bricks. All building trades' unions instructed their members not to permit contractors to work with tools along side with them. . . . All such regulations secured the group welfare of the workers involved by sharply rejecting society's enticements to become petty entrepreneurs, clarifying and intensifying the division of labor at the work place, and sharpening the line between employer and employee.

Where a trade was well unionized, a committee in each shop supervised the enforcement in that plant of the rules and standard wage which the union had adopted for the trade as a whole. The craft union and the craft local assembly of the Knights of Labor were forms of organization well adapted to such regulatory activities. The members were legislating, on matters on which they were unchallenged experts, rules which only their courage and solidarity could enforce. On one hand, the craft form of organization linked their personal interests to those of the trade, rather than those of the company in which they worked, while, on the other hand, their efforts to enforce the same rules on all of their employers, where they were successful, created at least a few islands of order in the nineteenth-century's economic ocean of anarchic competition.

Labor organizations of the late nineteenth century struggled persistently to transform worker's struggles to manage their own work from spontaneous to deliberate actions, just as they tried to subject wage strikes and efforts to shorten the working day to their conscious regulation. "The trade union movement is one of reason, one of deliberation, depending entirely upon the voluntary and sovereign actions of its members," declared the executive Council of the AFL. Only through "thorough organization," to use a favorite phrase of the day, was it possible to enforce a trade's work rules throughout a factory, mine, or construction site. Despite the growing number of strikes over union rules and union recognition in the late 1880s, the enforcement of workers' standards of control spread more often through the daily self-assertion of craftsmen on the job than through large and dramatic strikes.

Conversely, strikes over wage reductions at times involved thinly disguised attacks by employers on craftsmen's job controls. Fall River's textile manufacturers in 1870 and the Hocking Valley coal operators in 1884, to cite only two examples, deliberately foisted severe wage reductions on their highly unionized workers in order to provoke strikes. The owners' hope was that in time hunger would force their employees to abandon union membership, and thus free the companies' hands to change production methods. As the treasurer of one Fall River mill testified in 1870: "I think the question with the spinners was not wages, but whether they or the manufacturers should rule. For the last six or eight years they have ruled Fall River." Defeat in a strike temporarily broke the union's control, which had grown through steady recruiting and rule enforcement during years which were largely free of work stoppages.

The third level of control struggles emerged when different trades lent each other support in their battles to enforce union rules and recognition. An examination of the strike statistics gathered by the U.S. Commissioner of Labor for the period 1881–1905 reveals the basis patterns of this development. Although there had been a steady increase in both the number and size of strikes between 1881 and 1886, the following 12 years saw a reversal of that growth, as stoppages became both smaller and increasingly confined to skilled crafts (except in 1894). With that change came three important and interrelated trends. First, the proportion of strikes called by unions rose sharply in comparison to spontaneous strikes. Nearly half of all strikes between 1881 and 1886 had occurred without union sanction or aid. In the seven years beginning with 1887 more than two-thirds of each year's strikes were deliberately called by a union, and in 1891 almost 75 per cent of the strikes were official.

Secondly, as strikes became more deliberate and unionized, the proportion of strikes which dealt mainly with wages fell abruptly. Strikes to enforce union rules, enforce recognition of the union, and protect its members grew from 10 per cent of the total or less before 1885 to the level of 19–20 per cent between 1891 and 1893. Spontaneous strikes and strikes of laborers and factory operatives had almost invariably been aimed at increasing wages or preventing wage reductions, with the partial exception of 1886 when 20 per cent of all strikes had been over hours. The more highly craftsmen became organized, however, the more often they struck and were locked out over work rules.

Third, unionization of workers grew on the whole faster than strike participation. The ratio of strike participants to membership in labor organizations fell almost smoothly from 109 in 1881 to 24 in 1888, rose abruptly in 1890 and 1891 (to 71 and 86, respectively), then resumed its downward trend to 36 in 1898, interrupted, or course, by a leap to 182 in 1894. In a word, calculation and organization were the dominant tendencies in strike activity, just as they were in the evolution of work rules during the nineteenth century. But the assertion of deliberate control through formal organization was sustained not only by high levels of militancy (a persistently high propensity to strike), but also by remarkably aggressive mutual support, which sometimes took the form of the unionization of all grades of workers within a single industry, but more often appeared in the form of sympathetic strikes involving members of different trade unions.

Joint organization of all grades of workers seemed most likely to flourish where no single craft clearly dominated the life of the workplace, in the way iron molders, brick layers, or iron puddlers did where they worked. It was also most likely to appear at the crest of the waves of strike activity among unskilled workers and operatives, as is hardly surprising, and to offer evidence of the organizational impulse in their ranks. In Philadelphia's shoe industry between 1884 and 1887, for example, the Knights of Labor successfully organized eleven local assemblies, ranging in size from 55 to 1000 members, each of which represented a different craft or cluster of related occupations, and formulated wage demands and work rules for its own members. Each assembly sent three delegates to District Assembly 70, the highest governing body of the Knights for the industry, which in turn selected seven representatives to meet in a city-wide arbitration committee with an equal number of employers' representatives. Within each factory a "shop union" elected by the workers in that plant handled grievances and enforced the rules of the local assemblies, aided by one male and one female "statistician," who kept track of the complex piece rates.

There is no evidence that local assemblies of unskilled workers or of semi-skilled operatives ever attempted to regulate production processes themselves in the way assemblies of glass blowers and other craftsmen did. They did try to restrict hiring to members of the Knights and sometimes regulated layoffs by seniority clauses. For the most part, however, assemblies of operatives and laborers confined their attention to wages and to protection of their members against arbitrary treatment by supervisors. On the other hand, the mere fact that such workers had been organized made it difficult for employees to grant concessions to their craftsmen at the expense of helpers and laborers. Consequently, the owners were faced simultaneously with higher wage bills and a reduction of their control in a domain where they had been accustomed to exercise unlimited authority.

Moreover, workers who directed important production processes were themselves at times reluctant to see their own underlings organized, and frequently sought to dominate the larger organization to which their helpers belonged. A case in point was offered by the experience of the Knights of Labor in the garment industry, where contractors were organized into local assemblies of their own, supposedly to cooperate with those of cutters, pressers, tailors, and sewing machine operators. Contractors were often charged with disrupting the unionization of their own employees, in order to promote their personal competitive advantages. Above all, they tried to discourage women from joining the operators' assemblies. As the secretary of a St. Louis tailors' local assembly revealed, contractors who were his fellow Knights were telling the parents of operators that "no dissent [sic] girl belong to an assembly."

On the other hand, the experience of the Knights in both the shoe and garment industries suggests that effective unionization of women operatives was likely to have a remarkably radicalizing impact on the organization. It closed the door decisively both on employers who wished to compensate for higher wages paid to craftsmen by exacting more from the unskilled, and on craftsmen who were tempted to advance themselves by sweating others. In Philadelphia, Toronto, Cincinnati, Beverly, and Lynn both the resistance of the manufacturers to unionism and the level of mutuality exhibited by the workers leapt upward noticeably when the women shoe workers organized along with the men. Furthermore, the sense of total organization made all shoe workers more exacting in their demands and less patient with the protracted arbitration procedures employed by the Knights. Quickie strikes became increasingly frequent as more and more shoe workers enrolled in the Order. Conversely, the shoe manufacturers banded tightly together to destroy the Knights of Labor.

In short, the organization of all grades of workers in any industry propelled craftsmen's collective rule making into a more aggressive relationship with the employers, even where it left existing styles of work substantially unchanged. The other form of joint action, sympathetic strikes, most often involved the unionized skilled crafts themselves, and consequently was more directly related to questions of control of production processes. When Fred S. Hall wrote in 1898 that sympathetic strikes had "come so much in vogue during the last few years," he was looking back on a period during which organized workers had shown a greater tendency to walk out in support of the struggles of other groups of workers than was the case in any other period in the history of recorded strike data. Only the years between 1901 and 1904 and those between 1917 and 1921 were to see the absolute number of sympathetic strikes approach even *one-half* the levels of 1890 and 1891. . . .

Eugene V. Debs was to extoll this extreme manifestation of mutuality as the "Christ-like virtue of sympathy," and to depict his own Pullman boycott, the epoch's most massive sympathetic action, as an open confrontation between that working-class virtue and a social order which sanctified selfishness. It is true that the mutualistic ethic which supported craftsmen's control was displayed in its highest form by sympathetic strikes. It is equally true, however, that the element of calculation, which was increasingly dominating all strike activity, was particularly evident here. As Fred S. Hall pointed out, sympathetic strikes of this epoch differed sharply from "contagious" strikes, which spread spontaneously like those of 1877, in two respects. First, the sympathetic strikes were called by the workers involved, through formal union procedures. Although figures comparing officials with unofficial strikes are not available, two contrasting statistics illustrate Hall's point. The construction industry was always the leading center of sympathetic strikes. In New York more than 70 per cent of the establishments shut by sympathetic action between 1890 and 1892 were involved in building construction. On the other hand, over the entire period of federal data (1881–1905) no less than 98.03 per cent of the strikes in that industry were called by unions.

Second, as Hall observed, the tendency toward sympathetic strikes was "least in those cases where the dispute concerns conditions of employment such as wages and hours, and [was] greatest in regard to disputes which involve questions of unionism—the employment of only union men, the recognition of the union, etc." The rise of sympathetic strikes, like the rise of strikes over rules and recognition, was part of the struggle for craftsmen's control—its most aggressive and far-reaching manifestation. . . .

. . . As craftsmen unionized, they not only made their struggles for control increasingly collective and deliberate, but also manifested a *growing* consciousness of the dependence of their efforts on those of workers in other crafts. They drew strength in this struggle from their functional autonomy, which was derived from their superior knowledge, exercised through self-direction and their direction of others at work, and both nurtured and in turn was nurtured by a mutualistic ethic, which repudiated important elements of acquisitive individualism. As time passed this autonomy was increasingly often codified in union rules, which were collectively "legislated" and upheld through the commitment of the individual craftsmen and through a swelling number of strikes to enforce them. Organized efforts reached the most aggressive and inclusive level of all in joint action among the various crafts for mutual support. When such actions enlisted all workers in an industry (as happened when women unionized in shoe manufacturing), and when they produced a strong propensity of unionized craftsmen to strike in support of each other's claims, they sharply separated the aggressive from the conservative consequences of craftsmen's autonomy and simultaneously provoked an intense, concerted response from the business community.

In an important sense, the last years of the depression represented only a lull in the battle. With the return of prosperity in 1898, both strikes and union organizing quickly resumed their upward spiral, work rules again seized the center of the stage, and sympathetic strikes became increasingly numerous and bitterly fought. Manufacturers' organizations leapt into the fray with the open shop drive, while their spokesmen cited new government surveys to support their denunciations of workers "restriction of output."

On the other hand, important new developments distinguished the first decade of the twentieth century from what had gone before. Trade union officials, who increasingly served long terms in full-time salaried positions, sought to negotiate the terms of work with employers, rather than letting their members "legislate" them. The anxiety of AFL leaders to secure trade agreements and to ally with "friendly employers," like those affiliated with the National Civic Federation, against the open shop drive, prompted them to repudiate the use of sympathetic strikes. The many such strikes which took place were increasingly lacking in union sanction and in any event never reached the level of the early 1890s.

Most important of all, new methods of industrial management undermined the very foundation of craftsmen's functional autonomy. Job analysis through time and motion study allowed management to learn, then to systematize the way the work itself was done. Coupled with systematic supervision and new forms of incentive payment it permitted what Frederick Winslow Taylor called "*enforced* standardization of methods, *enforced* adoption of the best implements and working conditions, and *enforced* cooperation of all the employees under management's detailed direction." Scientific management, in fact, fundamentally disrupted the craftsmen's styles of work, their union rules and standards rates, and their mutualistic ethic, as it transformed American industrial practice between 1900 and 1930. Its basic effect, as Roethlisberger and Dickson discovered in their experiments at Western Electric's Hawthorne Works, was to place the worker "at the bottom level of a highly stratified organization," leaving his "established routines of work, his cultural traditions of craftsmanship, [and] his personal interrelations" all "at the mercy of technical specialists."

Two important attributes of the scientific management movement become evident only against the background of the struggles of nineteenth-century craftsmen to direct their own work in their own collective way. First, the appeal of the new managerial techniques to manufacturers involved more than simply a response to new technology and a new scale of business organization. It also implied a conscious endeavor to uproot those work practices which had been the taproot of whatever strength organized labor enjoyed in the late nineteenth century. A purely technological explanation of the spread of Taylorism is every bit as inadequate as a purely technological explanation of craftsmen's autonomy.

Second, the apostles of scientific management needed not only to abolish older industrial work practices, but also to discredit them in the public eye. Thus Taylor roundly denied that even "the high class mechanic" could "ever thoroughly understand the science of doing his work," and pasted the contemptuous label of "soldiering" over all craft rules, formal and informal alike. Progressive intellectuals seconded his arguments. Louis Brandeis hailed scientific management for "reliev[ing] labor of responsibilities not its own." And John R. Commons considered it "immoral to hold up to this miscellaneous labor, as a class, the hope that it can ever manage industry." If some workers do "shoulder responsibility," he explained, "it is because certain *individuals* succeed, and then those individuals immediately close the doors, and labor, as a class, remains where it was."

It was in this setting that the phrase "workers' control" first entered the vocabulary of the American labor movement. It appeared to express a radical, if often amorphous, set of demands which welled up around the end of World War I among workers in the metal trades, railroading, coal mining, and garment industries. Although those demands represented very new styles of struggle in a unique industrial and political environment, many of the workers who expressed them could remember the recent day when in fact, the manager's brains had been under the workman's cap.

Mastering Technology, Channeling Change:
The Testing Laboratory at the Pennsylvania Railroad

STEVEN W. USSELMAN

Over the course of the late nineteenth century, railroad managers . . . developed a powerful set of tools for evaluating technology and monitoring the course of innovation in their industry. By establishing testing facilities and creating staffs of technical advisors linked by a technical press, trade associations, and engineering societies, railroads mobilized a large community of highly trained technical experts who had no responsibilities other than assessing the condition of railroad technology. At a time when rapid growth made traditional methods of personal exchange difficult to

"Fashioning Political Identities: Cultural Studies and the Historical Construction of Political Subjects," *American Quarterly*, Vol. 50, No. 4 (December 1998), pp. 745–782. © 1998 American Studies. Reprinted by permission of The Johns Hopkins University Press.

Steven W. Usselman, *Regulating Railroad Innovation: Business, Technology, and Politics in America, 1840–1920* (New York: Cambridge University Press, 2002), pp. 211–213, 199, 201–210, 213–214. Reprinted by permission of Cambridge University Press.

sustain even at individual lines, the language and analytical methods of engineering lifted discussions of technology to a more abstract plane, free from the peculiarities of particular devices and locales. Managers could readily exchange information about techniques gathered from across their industry, and they could implement desired changes in technology quickly throughout their sprawling enterprises. "The professionalization of the railroad manager increased the productivity of the American transportation system," states esteemed business historian Alfred Chandler [in *The Visible Hand*] unequivocally after pointing out the increasing prominence of engineers in railroad management. "Repeated discussions by the salaried managers of both organizational and technological innovations permitted their quick development and rapid adoption by American railroads."

These benefits resulted not so much from a vast effort aimed at generating and promoting technical novelty but from attempts to focus technical efforts on a few areas of particular importance. Managers charged with responsibility for operating highly developed systems of great complexity had little interest in revolutionary change that might seriously disrupt established operations. They sought to gain small economies by incorporating minor innovations and refinements as smoothly and as fully as possible. This desire to optimize performance in the context of a fixed system and established practices drew railroads readily into alliance with the growing body of academically trained scientists and engineers and with the educational institutions that trained them. Engineers and scientists possessed just the sort of knowledge and orientation to problems that railroads needed. Their novel methods of analysis sought not to generate significant departures in technology but to evaluate existing practices and materials and to establish standards of performance. Laboratory facilities and testing equipment subjected materials to routine evaluation along well-established criteria. . . . To the extent high-level managers perceived the laboratories as centers of experiment and novelty, they deemed them suspect. Faced with a particularly acute financial crisis during the early 1890s, Charles Perkins [of the Chicago, Quincy, and Burlington Railroad based in Illinois] advised a subordinate who proposed a test that "we cannot be experimenting" and suggested that "our policy is to let our richer neighbors in the East point the way for us." Even at progressive lines such as the Pennsylvania [Railroad], laboratories rarely assumed new responsibilities outside their established realm of standards-setting. No railroad turned to research and testing of new products as a possible avenue of escape from the woes of the depression. . . .

New testing equipment . . . figured prominently in perhaps the most significant development in railroad research: the founding of formal laboratories for physical and chemical analysis staffed by professionally trained experts. The Pennsylvania initiated this movement in the early 1870s when it consolidated its study of mechanical engineering problems in a new bureau of experiments located at its Altoona shops. The company replaced the bureau in 1874 with a Department of Physical Tests, which though located at Altoona fell directly under the authority of Superintendent of Motive Power Theodore N. Ely. Soon Ely bypassed the master mechanic at Altoona entirely and placed this facility under John W. Cloud, a formally trained mechanical engineer who assumed the title "mechanical engineer." . . . In November of the following year, Charles B. Dudley joined the small staff in the testing department. A

Ph.D. chemist recently graduated from Yale's Sheffield Scientific School, Dudley organized a chemical laboratory to supplement the new mechanical engineering facility.

Ely, who by all accounts originated the idea, apparently launched these ventures with no clear idea of what they would accomplish. Looking back years later, he characterized the decision to create the test department as an "experiment" and stressed that the company had authorized "an engineering laboratory in its broadest sense." The choice of Dudley—a general experimentalist fresh out of college with no direct experience in railroad affairs—reflected the unspecified character of the new testing facility. . . .

While undeniably modest and perhaps lacking a clear sense of purpose, these pioneering laboratories did not take shape out of thin air. In several respects, they fit squarely within emergent trends that garnered considerable attention in American industry at the time. The U.S. Government Testing Board, which had responsibility for assessing materials purchased by the navy and other federal agencies, had with the cooperation of Robert Thurston of Stevens Institute of Technology just opened a laboratory containing machines designed by Thurston and a few other engineers. Ely appeared to mimic this widely publicized venture when outfitting his lab. . . .

. . . The foundry at Altoona had begun casting steel car wheels shortly before Cloud arrived, and he devoted a great deal of his time to testing samples of the material that went into them. Gradually, Cloud came to perform similar bending and breaking tests on metals used in items such as boilers, springs, axles, brake chains, and crank pins. Such analyses rapidly became the bread-and-butter activity of the physical laboratory. . . .

Dudley took a bit longer to establish a niche for his chemical laboratory but ultimately traced a similar course toward routine analysis of purchased materials and supplies. During his first few years at the Pennsylvania, Dudley acted something like an in-house consultant, bringing his techniques of chemical analysis to bear upon a number of technical problems that arose in the course of running the railroad. He spent much of his first eighteen months, for instance, attempting to determine why the valves on locomotive boilers clogged so frequently. Toward the end of the 1870s, . . . he undertook a study intended to reveal why some steel rails wore more rapidly than others. Trained in the basic methods of scientific experiment, Dudley collected random samples of any materials that might contribute to these problems and performed chemical analyses of them, then correlated his findings to the observed performance. When seeking an answer to the problems with clogged boiler valves, for instance, he analyzed the mineral content of water from various sources used in the boilers and also determined the amounts of impurities in the tallows used to lubricate the valves. In the case of rails, he looked for possible variations between the chemical constituents of rails that wore more or less rapidly. In similar fashion, Dudley analyzed the contents of oils the Pennsylvania used in its lamps, searching for clues to why some burned cleaner than others.

The sort of knowledge Dudley accumulated through these early studies soon drew him into alliance with the purchasing agent, whose authority the Pennsylvania bolstered in late 1878. In another example of the intensified drive for uniformity that pervaded the railroad at the time, this officer would coordinate all purchasing activities of the various departments and geographical divisions of the entire system. Dudley's work dovetailed readily with this mission. In several cases, his investigations revealed that supplies such as lubricants and lighting oil contained adulterants that lay at the roots of the problems. By prescribing a preferred formula and analyzing samples from purchased lots, the Pennsylvania could identify such potential sources of difficulty in advance. As this practice grew routine, the purchasing agent began publishing the formulae as official specifications and letting suppliers know that the railroad would reject any lots that deviated from the stipulated amounts.

In addition to providing a check against unscrupulous suppliers, such specifications provided the purchasing agent with an important tool in his struggle to impose uniformity throughout the Pennsylvania system. Under the old, decentralized system of purchasing, individual managers had grown accustomed to selecting supplies and products based largely on their personal preferences. Dudley and his chemical analyses, like the apparatus for testing metals in the physical laboratory, in effect functioned as a neutral arbiter. They provided the purchasing agent with independent and impersonal assessments he could easily invoke when managers disagreed with his choice of material for a certain purpose. . . . [T]he goal was not to produce the most accurate analyses possible, but to provide consistent assessments from one time to the next.

During the remaining years of the 1880s—his most productive period—Dudley set out to extend the practice of purchasing according to specifications to as many products as possible. Though operational problems generally still first drew him to a topic, Dudley consistently expanded his inquiries into exhaustive studies covering all varieties of materials that might have contributed to the problem. He would then suggest detailed guidelines for an entire line of products, and the purchasing agent would issue specifications based on his advice. When shock-absorbing springs on railroad cars began to break with alarming frequency, for example, Dudley analyzed the steel used in the springs and recommended a certain type of steel for that application. This work, which flowed in part out of Dudley's investigations of steel rails, in turn prompted him to devise specifications for all steel and cast-iron products purchased by the railroad. . . .

By proceeding in this fashion, Dudley had by 1889 secured a well-defined role for the chemical laboratory in the management of the Pennsylvania Railroad. The established character of the lab emerged clearly in a series of articles Dudley and his assistant, F. N. Pease, wrote for the *Railroad and Engineering Journal*. Naming their series "Chemistry Applied to Railroads," Dudley and Pease described in detail the work done in their laboratory at the Pennsylvania. They portrayed the facility as an established institution built firmly on the foundation of making and enforcing specifications. By 1889, they reported, the Pennsylvania regularly purchased twenty-five products according to chemical specifications drawn up by Dudley in collaboration with the purchasing agent. To enforce these specifications the company maintained an expanded laboratory facility and employed several additional personnel. Under Dudley's supervision this staff performed over 25,000 chemical analyses each year, making it perhaps the largest analytical chemistry laboratory in the country.

Informed observers had long since detected the benefits of the facilities at the Pennsylvania and begun to emulate them. An 1880 article in the *Railroad Gazette* described activities at the test department in glowing terms, and another published two years later concluded that the laboratory "proves that science, as a method of investigation, is fully recognized as having a place in railroad affairs." Such facilities, its author confidently declared, would soon become standard in the railroad industry. The Burlington, in characteristic fashion, followed the Pennsylvania nearly from the start. In October 1876 it hired a mechanical engineer and a chemist and set up laboratory facilities for both in its main shops at Aurora, Illinois. . . . By 1883, the practice of purchasing materials based on specifications had become so established that the Burlington extended the work of Higginson and the laboratory to cover purchases by its branch lines. Several more railroads followed suit during the 1880s, as assistants trained in the laboratories of the two pioneers moved on to set up testing facilities and laboratories at other companies. . . .

While routine analyses performed in connection with purchasing materials rapidly became the raison d'etre of most railroad laboratories, the chemists and mechanical engineers also contributed to the developing tradition of testing when they assisted in occasional tests of new technology. By the mid-1880s, Dudley had established ongoing programs for examining products such as storage batteries, fire extinguishers, paints, greases, and a variety of lighting systems used to illuminate cars, tracks, and buildings. . . .

Executives at the Pennsylvania and many other lines identified the laboratories and testing departments as important drawing cards in the recruitment of young scientists and engineers. As early as 1880, *Railroad Gazette* noted that the experimental department usually "becomes a training school for subordinate officers." New graduates of scientific and technical schools were offered jobs as "special apprentices" in the labs, where they would find a familiar environment and perhaps work on the same problems and with the same equipment they had used in college laboratories. Applicants requested these positions even though they paid little. "There is now such a large and increasing class of educated young men, many of whom can afford to spend from one to five years in practical training with little or no compensation," observed the *Gazette*, "that the salaries of assistants in such a department are a very small item."

Over time, railroads came to view the laboratories as ideal entry points on the path to careers in management. New graduates refined their drafting and analytical techniques in the laboratories and test facilities while beginning to familiarize themselves with all aspects of railroading. Within months of arriving at the railroad, the young recruits would move from the lab to some mechanical or even commercial department. Both the Pennsylvania and the Burlington relied heavily on such men for their managerial talent. By the 1890s, most Pennsylvania division superintendents and master mechanics had served as special apprentices, and many executives not directly involved with machinery had spent time in the testing facilities and laboratory as well. The laboratory became so important to recruitment and training at the Burlington that when an economizing Perkins threatened to cut back the facility during the depression of the 1890s, Superintendent of Motive Power Godfrey Rhodes objected on the grounds that it would harm the Burlington's technical reputation and undermine efforts in these areas. "The CBQ RR would never hold its present position in motive power matters among railroads were it not for the information it has gathered through its laboratory," Rhodes wrote. "It would be better to abandon the practice of starting young men in the mechanical department if they are to be discharged at every falling off in business."

While testing facilities at several lines came under similar scrutiny from economizing executives during the financial crises of the 1890s, they generally survived the cutbacks and came back stronger than ever. Though Perkins in reviewing possible areas to make cuts had inquired "whether we might not cut off entirely or materially curtail the laboratory at Aurora," Rhodes and Higginson managed to nurse the facility through the crisis until the tide turned in 1896. The Burlington then expanded its standards-setting activities, adding a physical laboratory to its chemical facility. Testing activities at the Pennsylvania slumped a bit with the onset of depression, but in 1896 the line completed improvements that tripled the size of its chemical laboratory. Dudley and Pease curtailed their experimental work slightly but continued to develop new standard analytical techniques for use in connection with specifications. By 1903, the Pennsylvania employed a laboratory staff of approximately twenty-five people and enforced forty-seven sets of chemical specifications. Top executives at the Reading, besieged by a second bankruptcy, repeatedly turned down requests from the chemist for a higher salary and an expanded facility but did not eliminate them altogether. Other companies, accepting specifications as a routine component of railroad operations, built their first separate laboratory facilities during the decade. . . .

While the turn toward engineering methods shifted analysis of railroad technology onto terms that transcended conditions at particular firms and in many respects depersonalized choices regarding technology, the institutional and organizational changes worked in some ways to centralize technical decision-making and to concentrate it in the hands of a few individuals. Matthias Forney, through his dual position as editor of *Railroad Gazette* and secretary of the Master Car Builders Association, exerted a strong influence over the flow of information and attitudes pertaining to innovation. The Pennsylvania Railroad and, in particular, General Superintendent of Motive Power Theodore N. Ely, assumed a position as the foremost expert in technical matters. Burlington President Charles Perkins described Ely as "the highest authority," and the CB&Q, along with nearly every other railroad, kept an eye turned to practices deployed by the Pennsylvania. The Burlington itself became the leader in technical matters among the many Chicago roads. By cooperating freely and allowing this informal hierarchy of expertise to develop, railroads avoided unnecessary duplication of research and kept the costs of evaluating and selecting techniques low. Railroads obtained similar benefits by concentrating their purchases of equipment and supplies in a handful of manufacturers. Executives looking for novel technology no longer scoured a diffuse market, but instead entrusted established firms such as Baldwin and Westinghouse with the task of finding and marketing the best available devices. In entering into such established relationships, railroads looked for reliability more than novelty. Producers and consumers of railroad technology engaged in sustained collaboration that encouraged ongoing refinement but perhaps placed less emphasis on radical departures from routine.

. . . [T]hese policies may have led managers to overlook innovations that would have been tried and used widely in an earlier era. Relying on the judgment of experts at a few railroads and suppliers was a cheap and efficient way to evaluate innovation across a narrow spectrum; it was not a policy designed to ensure that the best ideas came to fruition. Rather than many inventions being tried and some ultimately surviving and becoming common, most inventions never received a trial. But in the competitive conditions of the late nineteenth century, managers were willing to risk missing the benefits of a dramatic innovation if they could incorporate minor changes without difficulty while maintaining efficient operations.

Switchboard Operators or Girl-Free Automation?
Gender Stereotypes and Managerial Choice
in the Bell Telephone System

KENNETH J. LIPARTITO

Before the invention of automatic equipment, female operators carried out the crucial task of connecting telephone subscribers. In simplest form, the work of the operator involved receiving verbal requests for connections and physically plugging one line into another at the switchboard. But the rudiments of the work belied a complex labor process built on a number of related factors: the economics of networks, the strategies of telephone firms, evolving switchboard hardware, and the culture of the workers.

Early in the history of telephony, managers had recognized the importance of the operator's task. At large urban telephone exchanges, managers quickly perceived switching to be a potentially serious bottleneck. As telephone networks grew, the number of possible calls to be switched increased geometrically. Mathematics indicated that at some point demand for switching might exceed capacity. The problem was not a purely technical one. It related to the strategy of the Bell Telephone Company, a sprawling monopoly composed of dozens of regional firms that dominated telephony in America from 1880 until 1894. Bell had built its strategy around the promotion of urban telecommunications. Its prime concern was cultivating telephone use in big city markets, rather than in less densely populated rural areas. Urban telephone networks quickly reached the size at which switching became a problem. Managers avoided a breakdown in the networks by organizing a techno-labor system that employed human operators carefully selected by class, race, and sex. A complex of women and machines solved the critical problem of switching.

Multiple switchboards were the crucial hardware of this techno-labor system. To overcome capacity constraints in cities such as New York, telephone engineers designed a three-panel board containing jacks for every subscriber line—up to 10,000 lines. Operators sat before one panel but, by stretching to the right or left, were able to reach all the other subscriber jacks in the exchange. Each operator was responsible for only a small number of incoming lines but could complete her calls to any other line in the exchange. Multiplying this triptych arrangement, firms engaged dozens of operators working together to handle the heavy load of large central offices.

Manual switching had a gender, and here we can see how cultural categories combined with strategy and technology to form a labor process. The social construction of telephone technology created an entirely new group of skilled workers—telephone operators. Since the 1880s, the telephone companies had employed women almost exclusively in this position, a practice also followed in other nations. The origins of this sexual division of labor remain obscure, but two things stand out. Women, male telephone managers believed, possessed the inherent qualities needed in a manual system; and they were available in large numbers.

Kenneth J. Lipartito, "When Women Were Switches: Technology, Work, and Gender in the Telephone Industry, 1890–1920," *American Historical Review* 99, no. 4 (October 1994): 1074–1111 (excerpt, pp. 1081–1082, 1084–1085, 1087–1088, 1091, 1093, 1095–1097, 1099–1110). Reprinted by permission of American Historical Association and the author.

Many historians have speculated about the link between the feminization of occupations such as telephone operator and management's drive to cut costs and control its labor force. Here we have to distinguish carefully between entrepreneurial strategies aimed at reaching new markets and labor strategies designed to increase worker effort and compliance. The nature of the operator's task reflected telephone managers' entrepreneurial strategy for differentiating telephone service from rival forms of communications such as the telegraph. Telegraph firms employed male operators, who received and transmitted coded information but who did not speak with customers. The job required mastery of Morse code, facility with the telegraph key, and a quick and neat pen. But telegraphy was not a switched form of communications, as was telephony. Telephone companies stressed the interactive quality of their service, which allowed users to speak directly with each other. Fast, accurate switching was vital to this more complex method of communications. Switching required new specialized forms of labor utilizing different skills.

Since manual technology required operators to speak with subscribers, if only briefly, telephone firms wanted employees who would project a comfortable and genteel image to their customers. Applicants for the job were expected to have at least a grammar school education. Policy in both the North and South was "whites only," and companies sought native-born workers, rejecting those with strong ethnic accents. By hiring employees of "good character," telephone firms were seeking workers who could deal with customers "on an equal plane," as one manager put it. Telephones in the early twentieth century remained a luxury even for the middle class. A prime category of user—who made expensive and profitable long distance calls—was the businessman.

The job requirements quickly took on a gender, for telephone managers believed that women possessed the qualities they sought. Respectable deportment, accuracy, attention to detail, good hearing, and good speech were commonly held to be female more than male traits. They characterized traditional female occupations such as teaching and women's jobs in such industries as textiles and paper making. Astute companies were not above exploiting male solicitude for the weaker sex, reminding subscribers that operators were "entitled to the same consideration and courtesy that is extended to women in our everyday business and social activities and that we expect for our wives, sisters or daughters." When dealing with cranky and irritable customers, women's purportedly more patient nature—formed, no doubt, from their maternal instincts—was seen to be especially valuable. Early trials with male operators did not pan out because young men had neither the discipline nor deportment desired. By 1900, over 80 percent of operators were single, white, native-born females. . . .

Telecommunications provides an extreme example of how technology and innovation could contribute to the construction of new female occupations while at the same time confirming old ideas about female work. Women's contributions were crucial to the success of the complex technology of manual switching. While scanning ten thousand tiny jacks, keeping an eye open for lights indicating new calls, and sweeping the board of old connections, operators had to complete several hundred calls per hour during peak times. Months of practice were required before they mastered the "overlaps," or the knack of performing multiple tasks simultaneously. Managers recognized that "the attainment of service standards necessarily involves a good grade of well-trained operator." The good operator, however, became the female operator, a definition that carried with it many old assumptions about women's work. Operators were expected to be young and unmarried. They were restricted to repetitive tasks that could be monitored and controlled by male engineers. And they were not allowed to advance outside their own separate employment track. . . .

Unlike other women workers in the age of mechanization, telephone operators were engaged with the latest technology of a complex technological system. Companies improved the switching process by incremental adjustments that substantially raised operator productivity. They invested in worker training and accommodations, although, of course, they also profited from the discrimination that limited women's job options. Telephone operating, however, was a new source of employment for women. By bringing together technology and women, telephone companies created a highly successful techno-labor system. . . . Redesigning the labor process proved far more difficult than simple models of technological change would suppose. By turning to issues beyond cost and control, we can understand why this process was so stable and what caused it to change.

By the mid-1880s, Bell was well on its way to building telephone systems in the nation's major urban centers. Secure with a virtual monopoly, the corporation embarked on another path that it would follow for more than half a century—construction of a national long distance network. . . .

Although the new strategy followed in the footsteps of the old, it placed even more pressure on the switching bottleneck. The larger the total system, the more calls that flowed through a given point. Building an interconnected network, moreover, demanded a high degree of standardization, since each part interacted with the others. Accordingly, Bell centralized research, development, and manufacturing. It limited the range of options available to consumers, keeping research on a narrow path. Innovation focused on incremental rather than radical improvements in individual components such as switching.

Fixed firmly on its course, Bell ran into some heavy seas after 1894. The firm's telephone patents expired, and numerous new competitors entered the industry. No longer able to maintain monopoly prices, Bell saw its revenues plummet. As prices fell, telephones became more widely available. Even more people gained telephones for the first time when so-called independent firms rushed to serve towns and cities neglected during the monopoly years. Flourishing between 1898 and 1907, they took almost half the market from the senior firm.

Competition altered the mode of innovation in the industry. Upstart firms experimented with different combinations of equipment to produce novel services for new markets. . . . One new contribution was the automatic switch. In 1891, a Kansas City undertaker named Almon Strowger patented a device that switched telephone calls mechanically. . . . In a society that had long believed labor-saving technology meant progress, many predicted that the day of the human operator was over. But events did not unfold so predictably. Invention was only the start of a long course of change.

Strowger was neither a capitalist faced with an intractable work force nor a rational engineer carefully weighing the price of labor and capital. . . . Invention, the creation of the first model of a new technology, remains a mysterious and poorly understood practice, and Strowger's story does little to clear up the picture. Exactly why he devoted himself to making a telephone switch is unknown, although one legend suggests a motivation related to labor problems. Apparently, Strowger believed that the local telephone operators were sending calls intended for his undertaking business to rivals. This dissatisfied consumer of telephone services made a dramatic and unexpected contribution to the art. . . .

Transforming this raw invention into a component of a giant technological system fell to the many telephone firms now competing sharply for business. An outsider to the industry, Strowger was ill equipped for the task. The newly competitive market, however, seemed to promise a great opportunity to promote his infant invention. But the largest firm of the industry, American Bell, greeted it with suspicion. Bell patent expert Thomas Lockwood asserted that "both experience and observation have united to show us that an operation so complex as that of uniting two telephone subscribers' lines . . . can never efficiently or satisfactorily be performed by automatic apparatus, dependent on the volition and intelligent action of the subscriber." "The telephone girl has come to stay," predicted another observer, more succinctly. The Bell corporation declined to either purchase or license Strowger's breakthrough. . . .

Conceiving of technology as a system helps to explain why Bell resisted automation despite . . . potential savings. After invention of the Strowger switch, telephone companies had a choice: either invest in the new technology or continue to improve their existing techno-labor methods. Although costs and benefits are clear in hindsight, the alteration of a complex technical system to make room for a radical new device involves much uncertainty about whether the change will yield sufficient returns to justify its expense. . . . Savings offered by mechanization also had to be weighed against the advantages of human operators. They served as a point of personal contact between subscribers and telephone companies, helped to locate trouble, and assisted users with an unfamiliar technology.

For a corporation dedicated to a competitive strategy that emphasized long distance service, standardization of components, and vertical and horizontal integration, the uncertainty of the new technology made it especially risky. Bell engineers and managers had long focused their attention on the "critical problems" that threatened to block system growth. Manual technology embodied this substantial experience and expertise. Automatic switching, however, introduced an entirely new set of considerations. It served only for local telephone calls, offering no means of switching long distance calls. At the very least, Bell engineers observed, more work was needed on the link between manual long distance and automatic local switching. Modifying the device to fit the firm's strategy became more difficult, however, when Strowger sold his patent to a new manufacturing concern, the Automatic Electric Company. Bell firms would have to purchase or license the switches from a competing organization if they wanted to use them. Either move ran counter to the corporation's pursuit of vertical control and standardization of technology.

Given the risks of radical change, it seemed more expedient to continue investing in manual switching. . . . Centralized power . . . permitted new features at the switchboard. Lights now signaled operators to answer or disconnect calls, replacing noisy and confusing mechanical drops, which had to be reset by hand. Switchboards were also wired for "automatic ringing," so that merely plugging the connecting line into the jack rang the telephone of the called party.

These and other improvements allowed the female labor force to handle the growth in telephone calls between 1900 and 1910. Company engineers modified and redesigned the switching process to take full advantage of its new potential for raising labor productivity. . . . [S]witching capacity expanded without resort to automation. . . .

. . . Only by increasing switching capacity could the corporation achieve its goal of expanding telephone service nationally. Incremental improvements in existing technology seemed a less risky means of doing so than investing in a radical new mechanism. At the time, competition was driving down profits, which created financial pressures on the company to reduce all unnecessary capital expenditures.

The position of top management on these matters was summed up concisely by Chief Engineer J. J. Carty in 1910. The system, he maintained, not any one component, should be the focus of concern. Improved switching, Carty went on, depended more on the overall design of the switching process than on any one machine. Not explicitly addressed to issues of labor, the statement nonetheless had implications for how AT&T should handle labor conflict. So long as it did not substantially interfere with the operational requirements of the system, it could be dealt with by incremental adjustments. Worker culture and resistance could be important issues, as we shall see. But unless managers perceived labor conflict as a critical problem of system growth or as a challenge to their basic strategy, they did not replace workers with machines. . . .

With the industry's largest player content with manual switching methods, it fell to others to promote automation. Non-Bell firms turned to the Strowger switch as a means of challenging their corporate rival for control of the telephone market. Some of them saw it as a means of reducing costs and bringing service to new areas. To new entrants without preexisting commitments to technology, savings that the incumbent could afford to ignore mattered greatly. Even among these firms, however, labor costs did not wholly determine behavior. These companies tended to operate in smaller towns and cities, where switching capacity and labor conflict were not great problems. Market share was their prime concern, and automatic switching proved an effective marketing tool. Heartened by an impression that customers liked dialing, independents appealed to the belief that the mechanical was modern and efficient, the human quaint and slightly out-of-date. Advertisements explained that machines kept their secrets and "never gossiped." They did not require customers to speak with operators, who could be "surly" or "saucy" (and who often received the blame when calls went awry). As one sales brochure exclaimed, the day of the "cussless, waitless, out-of-orderless, girlless telephone" was now at hand. . . .

Despite creative campaigns, the independents made only limited headway with automation. By 1915, only about 4 percent of the market was served by mechanical switches. Some urban telephone concerns had prospered through automation—Los Angeles had the largest system, with 60,000 subscribers. Many independents, however, served places too small to reap substantial savings by eliminating workers. Others had customers to whom "girlless" telephones were a mixed blessing. Though often decried as the town gossip, the telephone operator was also appreciated as a source of information. She located missing parties, took messages, provided wake-up calls, and gave out the correct time. With automatic switching, it was impossible to provide such services.

The failure of automation to catch on was less a result of its technical and economic shortcomings than of structural weaknesses in markets and organizations. These institutional factors hampered the spread of this technology. Almost all the independent telephone enterprises were beset by organizational problems. Equipment manufacturers such as Automatic Electric were not integrated into the operating end of the business. Independent operating companies themselves remained largely separate and either uninterested in or incapable of effective cooperation. Unlike the vertically integrated Bell System, manufacturers and operating companies of the independent sector lacked the means to coordinate research, production, and operations. It was difficult for them to adjust technology to customers' needs or to upgrade local facilities so that they were compatible with new equipment.

Most significant, independents did not achieve the integration needed to provide a telephone service competitive with AT&T's long distance network. Without this competitive asset, they were largely unable to penetrate the big city market, where the advantages of automatic switches were greatest. . . . Their market share shrank steadily, and Bell was able to recapture its dominant position. With market dominance came the ability to shape telecommunications technology. The fate of automatic switching rested largely in the hands of one giant corporation.

When AT&T regained control of the telephone market in 1913, it still showed little interest in automatic switching. Yet, within a few years, the corporation reversed course and was deploying the machines in its exchanges. This change of heart reflected the intersection of technology, business strategy, and politics with new labor issues. After 1913, a series of developments threw automatic technology into a more favorable light. Years of speculation, experimentation, and field trials finally convinced skeptics that there were indeed places where automation saved money. In the conjectural realm of innovation, such knowledge was important. Nonetheless, like a big ship in the water, the corporation was turning slowly. It was still unclear precisely where and when to automate, how fast and how far to go. Strong internal dissension was still brewing over the technology. Crucial to erasing these doubts and determining policy was a growing perception that the manual techno-labor process was nearing a maximum. When the existing system seemed to be in crisis, the will to change was forthcoming. . . .

[First,] system growth, the cornerstone of the Bell strategy, was falling victim to its own success. Bell companies were forced to continually build new exchanges as old ones reached the limit of manual switchboards. By 1920, New York City had nearly two hundred exchanges. Ninety percent of all calls in Manhattan terminated at an exchange other than the one of the calling party. Requiring many more steps to complete, these trunk calls lowered switching speed and efficiency. . . .

Even though virtually a monopolist, AT&T could not afford to meet this crisis by either allowing service to deteriorate or raising prices. Politics limited its room to maneuver. Under the threat of an antitrust suit, company president Theodore Vail had compromised with the remaining independent firms in 1913. Bell would serve as the senior partner and "manager" of the nation's telecommunications network, dominating the large urban areas and long distance transmission but allowing non-Bell firms to operate on the periphery as "sub-licensees" and permitting them access to its toll lines. To seal the bargain, Vail launched a massive public relations campaign, portraying his firm as progressive and socially responsible. He emphasized the speed, quality, and availability of Bell service. He pronounced monopoly superior to competition in building the telephone network that the nation needed. After such statements, for the company to appear technologically backward was to invite government intervention. . . .

. . . [Second,] changes taking place in the labor market suddenly increased the power of the formerly docile female operator corps. . . . During World War I, . . . labor problems arose that threatened manual switching and pushed AT&T to embrace automation more rapidly and more thoroughly than it otherwise would have. Between 1917 and 1920, a sudden jump in government demand for female clerks, plus generally high levels of employment, cut into the supply of operators. The decrease in operators coincided with the increase in telephone demand brought on by system growth and led to rapid wage escalation. Wages as a percentage of total costs in the Bell System reached a high of 58 percent in 1920, when top operators in large cities were earning up to $900 per year.

Despite higher wages, telephone operators were lured away by opportunities in the military and in booming wartime industries. . . . "The greater demand for women in the trades," one Bell executive wrote, "is making it difficult to secure enough operators." By 1920, yearly operator turnover averaged 93 percent nationwide, rising to as much as 120 percent in some cities. . . . Lack of experienced personnel placed additional burdens on those who remained, particularly in the vulnerable urban exchanges. Problems pyramided, and absenteeism more than doubled. . . .

The war years also brought to the surface some deeper labor issues. The strata of society that AT&T managers believed made the best operators constituted only about 5 percent of the population, less when those of "questionable character" were eliminated. "In most parts of the country," one manager noted, "we are requiring a larger and larger proportion of the available female labor." In the nation's fifty-eight largest cities, about 8 percent of the female labor force was already employed as operators. In some places, it was as high as 20 percent. Even when the war ended, the group of women on which telephone companies traditionally drew was likely to have more and more options for employment, while the need for skilled operators to meet the requirements of a growing, increasingly complex telephone system continued to rise.

In the tightening labor market, power shifted in favor of workers. Bell System employees grew restive and militant, ready to organize their own unions rather than take hand-outs from management. . . . Operator strikes swept through towns and cities in New England, the Pacific Coast, and the Southwest between 1917 and 1919. . . .

The sudden expression of independence among the operators unsettled Bell management. As one member of the corporation observed, unions instilled in operators a "lack of respect for authority" and resulted in "independence of action by the individual." . . . [T]he same order and purpose that made for efficient switching could be turned against the company. Because manual switching required machine-like discipline, independence of mind endangered the entire telephone network. Strikes, stoppages, and slowdowns resulted in "a continual fight to maintain orderliness and efficiency of service." Service was the watchword of the re-monopolized industry. President Vail remarked, "The service which [the Bell System] furnishes is of the first importance in the business and family life of the nation . . . [it] must be prompt, reliable and accessible." In providing such service, Vail continued, "the importance of having an intelligent, interested, satisfied and loyal body of employees cannot be overestimated." . . .

. . . [T]he experience between 1918 and 1919 had revealed some of the other weaknesses of the manual switching system. AT&T was particularly concerned about its shrinking pool of "appropriate" women. Having defined the job as women's work, the corporation did not believe it would be appealing to men, and it refused to recruit from the lower end of the socioeconomic scale. AT&T hired some immigrants, notably Irish women, whose accents, it felt, were not offensive to middle-class subscribers. But it did not employ working-class men, black women, or other immigrants. . . . AT&T had configured manual switching to rely on the skills, deportment, and dedication of a certain group of women, whose numbers were dwindling. Changing the hardware of the techno-labor process—something management could fully control—proved easier than changing the gender and culture of the work force, which it could only partially influence.

The system nature of technology . . . means that even capitalists who are ever on the search for profits engage in a complex series of decisions before they determine to substitute capital for labor. One cannot assume that the effects of technology—skill-destroying or labor-saving—also explain its origins and path of development. In telecommunications, firms could choose from several methods to deal with labor. Different firms made different choices at different times. Some took the plunge into automatic switching without experiencing any labor problems; others, such as AT&T, continued to invest in manual switching. Only the convergence of a number of factors—strategic managerial objectives, system bottlenecks, government telecommunications policy, and shifts in the labor market—led to the automation of telephone operating.

Technology and the Treadmill of Urban Progress

MAURY KLEIN AND HARVEY A. KANTOR

To the modern urbanite the industrial city seems a quaint, almost primitive place. Its sights and smells bear a strong flavor of nostalgia: streets lit by gas lamps and filled with carriages, drays, and streetcars; sidewalks bustling with gentlemen in tall hats or derbies, wearing high, starched collars; ladies in long dresses with parasols resting on their shoulders; workmen dressed in cheap drab shirts and pants, brightened by gaudy bandanas tied about their neck or head; messenger boys dashing from one office building to another; deliverymen straining beneath their blocks of ice, kegs of beer, or racks of clothing; sidestreets filled with peddlers' carts loaded with wares of every kind, their cries intermingling in a cacophony of confusion; sidewalk markets bulging with fresh fruit and produce, tiers of fish or slabs of meat, all picked over by swarms of shoppers; strolling policemen with bright brass buttons and fat nightsticks; and ragged newsboys trumpeting the day's headlines above the din of the street traffic.

The wishful flavor of this scene is deceptive. While its pace and tumult may appear tame to people in a high-speed, computerized, automated society, contemporaries regarded the city as an engine of progress in which everything seemed constantly on the move. In this feeling, that generation was no less correct than our own; the difference lay largely in the level of technology achieved by each era. To an amazing degree advances in technology shaped the growth, appearance, and pace of the industrial city. Then as now, cities could expand only by discovering new techniques for moving people, goods, and information. New machines, materials, and designs revamped the city's face and accelerated its inner rhythms. Urban growth was therefore both a function of technology and a reflection of its pervasive influence.

Yet technology, even in its most imaginative forms, did not solve problems so much as recast them. Rapid growth strained the city's ability to perform such elementary functions as transporting, feeding, and housing people, protecting them from fire and crime, educating their children, and providing a healthy, attractive environment in which to live. It complicated every aspect of urban life and fragmented urban society. Almost every industrial city endured a phase of madcap expansion during which its distended social system threatened to collapse beneath the weight of increased demands for services and accumulated social tensions.

To solve the physical problems created by rapid growth, most cities resorted to sophisticated technology and techniques. But every "solution" unmasked a tangle of new problems which in turn called for still more sophisticated hardware. Thus the electric trolley and elevated railway moved more people at greater speed than the omnibus, but both presented problems unforeseen in the heyday of the horse and buggy. The result was a vicious circle, a kind of "Catch-22" in which every new stage of technological advance proved less a gateway into some new golden age than a harbinger of fresh difficulties.

Nor was this all. The vicious circle traced by the interaction between technology and growth uncovered a deeper contradiction in the American notion of progress. Americans had always tended to equate progress with growth. During the industrial era, progress came increasingly to be defined in material and mechanical terms. This faith in the notion that "bigger is better" assumed that quantitative growth would improve the quality of life. Since technology was a primary instrument in quantitative growth, Americans logically turned to it as a means for resolving the perplexities of industrial society.

Urban growth especially fed upon advances in technology. In quantitative terms, that growth proceeded at breakneck pace and reached gigantic proportions. But the industrial city turned out to be something less than the promised land. For all the splendors of its swelling statistics, it never became a pleasant or even decent place in which to live for a majority of its inhabitants. Too late city-dwellers discovered that their faith in technology had been misplaced; that mere quantitative growth did not automatically bring qualitative improvement. In their quest for a better life, urbanites had created not a road to utopia but a treadmill which they labeled "progress."

Just as the railroad affected the locations and functions of cities on a national scale, the street railway shaped their internal growth. From its crude beginnings with horse-drawn omnibuses to steam-power trolleys and later the electrified lines, mass transit moved urbanites faster and more efficiently. Every advance in transportation technology quickly outmoded its predecessor only to create new problems in construction, congestion, and pollution.

The most important effect of mass transit was its expanding the physical limits of the city. The street railway destroyed the compact "walking city" of colonial and preindustrial towns. Prior to about 1850 most towns were still intimate locales where street congestion involved nothing more than people on foot, on horseback, or in carriages. Most people lived near their place of work and could reach nearly any spot in the city in a thirty-minute walk. Few towns extended farther than two miles from their core, which usually nestled against some waterway.

During the 1820s the omnibus emerged as the first urban passenger carrier. Initially little more than enlarged hackney coaches, these wagons later resembled boxes on wheels with two lengthwise seats holding twelve to twenty people. They appeared first in the larger cities—New York, Boston, Philadelphia, New Orleans, Washington. . . .

. . . Even though the fare was too steep for the masses, omnibuses drew heavy patronage from small businessmen and clerks, many of whom still went home for lunch. By the 1840s Boston had eighteen omnibus lines, of which twelve extended to outlying suburban communities. Despite its limitations, the omnibus speeded up the tempo of life, regularized transportation patterns, and launched the outward migration of wealthier people from the center of the city to the suburbs.

The era of the omnibus lasted scarcely a generation before the horse railway surpassed it in the 1850s. The horse railway, too, resembled a stagecoach, but utilized flanged wheels operating on iron tracks. . . . By the 1850s [New York,] Boston, Philadelphia, Chicago, Baltimore, St. Louis, Cincinnati, Newark, and Pittsburgh all had laid horsecar tracks and were extending their boundaries. Iron rails allowed horsecars to reach speeds of six to eight miles per hour, about one-third more than the omnibus could muster. Reduced friction did more than add speed. It provided a smoother ride and increased the number of passengers that could be hauled.

Iron rails also increased costs. Inevitably the horsecar companies required a greater capital investment than the omnibus lines. As expenses mounted, financing became more feasible through incorporation rather than individual ownership. . . . Ownership of transit facilities fell increasingly into the hands of outside entrepreneurs who neither knew the local scene nor cared about how cities developed. Each phase of technological innovation made urban transportation a bigger business than it had been. By the end of the nineteenth century, transit or "traction" enterprises held the nexus of political and economic power in most major cities. . . .

The horsecar had another unsavory effect upon the urban landscape: it added to the piles of horse manure littering the streets. Lest we forget that pollution comes in many forms, it is well to heed Joel Tarr's reminder that the automobile was once hailed as the savior of the city from animal waste. "In a city like Milwaukee in 1907," he wrote, ". . . with a human population of 350,000 and a horse population of 12,500, this meant 133 tons of manure a day, for a daily average of nearly three-quarters of a pound of manure for each resident." For New York and Brooklyn in the 1880s, with a total horse population of around 150,000, the problem was much worse. Carcasses of dead horses sprawled in the streets added to the sanitation nightmare.

This contemporary image of mass transit as a crowded, unsafe, unpleasant, and polluting form of transportation sounds hauntingly familiar to the modern ear. Moreover, the horsecar had inherent limitations as a form of transportation: it could go no faster than the horse pulling it and could not increase its passenger load without adding more horses, which posed other difficulties. To growing cities, these became intolerable drawbacks. The obvious solution was to devise a transit system that utilized mechanical rather than muscle power. By the 1860s the search for alternatives was well underway. Louis Ransom of Akron, Ohio, advocated adopting his Ransom Steamer to iron rails. George Clark of Cincinnati promoted a system of compressed-air cars, while a New Orleans firm experimented with a car propelled by ammonia gas. . . .

No innovation in urban mass transit rivaled the application of electircal power. Oddly enough, the pioneer projects developed in the least urbanized area of the nation. James A. Gaboury, the owner of an animal traction line in Montgomery, Alabama, witnessed a demonstration of an electrical car at the Toronto Agricultural Fair in 1885 and determined to adopt the method to his system. In 1886 Montgomery's Court Street line became the first in the country to offer a citywide system of electric transportation. Several years later, Frank J. Sprague, a naval engineer who had worked for Thomas Edison, formed his own company and secured a contract to build a line in Richmond, Virginia. The success of his project spurred the construction of electrical transit lines elsewhere.

The electric cars moved along iron tracks in the streets, drawing current from a central power source passed to the trains through overhead wires. The effect of a wire leading a car resembled that of a "troller"; soon the corruption of the word became universal and the new vehicles were dubbed "trolleys." Trolleys displaced horses so rapidly that by 1900 only 2 percent of the lines were horse-drawn, compared to 70 percent a decade earlier. By 1895, 850 lines embraced over 10,000 miles of electrified track. The new trolleys speeded up travel service to about twelve miles per hour and more in less congested areas. Their overhead wires cluttered the streetscapes of American cities and wreaked havoc during high winds and storms.

Frank Sprague made a second major contribution to transportation systems. He designed an electrical multiple-unit control system which allowed each car to be independently powered, lighted, heated, and braked. These cars did not require a locomotive since they possessed their own power source; yet they could be controlled by a master switch located in any one of them. At one stroke Sprague removed the major obstacles to constructing underground railways. Automated electric cars could operate without the accumulation of smoke, gas, and dirt discharged by steam-powered cars. Between 1895 and 1897 Boston built a mile-and-a-half subway at a cost of $4,000,000. Immediately after the turn of the century, New York constructed a route from downtown City Hall to 145th Street. . . . The popularity of the subway, coupled with the city's extreme congestion, led New York to take the lead in the underground transportation. Moreover, its hard-rock geological formation could support the construction of tall buildings above ground and tunnels below.

All these achievements in the technology of transportation affected the physical growth of cities. The rural ideal retained its hold upon Americans even in the city, where its influence drove people toward the suburbs. Prior to the advent of mass transit lines, however, only the wealthy could maintain houses on the outskirts of the city. Once the pedestrian confines were broken in the 1850s, an outward migration commenced. [Samuel Bass] Warner has painstakingly traced the development of Roxbury, West Roxbury, and Dorchester as bedroom satellites of Boston. Every stage of suburban development expanded the physical limits of Boston to house wealthy, middle-class, and lower middle-class expatriates from the city. Since all of the transit lines were privately built, the new suburbs alongside their tracks were the product of individual decision-making rather than coordinated social policy. . . .

Traction entrepreneurs enthusiastically promoted the flight to the suburbs. They found support among those who regarded the exodus as a boon for relieving congestion in the city's inner core. Adna Weber, the leading student of American cities in the nineteenth century, stated flatly, "it is clear that we are now in the sight of a solution of the problem of concentration of population." Weber advocated the extension of electrified transit lines and cheap fares because he saw in the rise of the suburbs "the solid basis of a hope that the evils of city life, so far as they result from overcrowding, may be in large part removed."

Unhappily, things did not work out that way. While upper- and middle-class urbanites left for greener pastures, the poor remained packed together in the central city, where they shared space with businesses and industries. Mass transit promoted this pattern of segregation within the city. More than any other factor, it transformed the diversified walking city into a central urban core of poor people and businesses surrounded by successive rings of suburban neighborhoods.

In fact, mass transit failed even to relieve population congestion. Transit lines did not scatter people about so much as cluster them in dense communities wherever transportation was available. New housing developments pursued every new construction or extension and quickly overflowed its service. As one alert observer wrote in an 1896 *Harper's Weekly*, "the trolleys seem to have created a new patronage of their own. Travel has been stimulated rather than diverted." Instead of thinning out settlement, mass transit created corridors of dense groupings alongside their lines. This magnetic pull pleased the traction promoters immensely. It was great for business; its effect upon the city's already strained social structure was quite another matter.

Technology extended the city's boundaries in another important way. Innovations in bridge-building made it possible for the first time to span the widest rivers. The implications of this breakthrough for urban growth were enormous: waterways ceased to be an obstacle to physical expansion. More important, it allowed traffic to flow in and out of the city with ease. Just as railroads dissolved limitations upon land travel, so the new bridges banished the fickle vagaries of waterways. Small wonder that to many Americans the Brooklyn Bridge and other mighty spans became the supreme symbol of American civilization. . . .

As mass transit and great bridges expanded the city's outer limits, innovations in building forms lifted its inner face. Like bridge-building, the new age of construction dawned with the shift from wood to iron and steel. Preindustrial cities were filled with two- or three-story buildings, shops, warehouses, and row houses made of timber. Government buildings, merchant exchanges, and athenaeums comprised the major public buildings; the church spire still dominated the skyline.

The industrial city presented a radically different scene. Multi-story buildings filled with corporate and professional offices stretched high into the sky. Cast-iron and sash-steel factories housed long ranks of machines whose operators lived in tall brick tenements. New kinds of buildings—railroad terminals, department stores, theaters, apartments—ornamented the urban landscape. The transition from church spire to skyscraper signified a revolution in construction techniques and in the way city-dwellers identified with their surroundings.

Great movements often hinge upon small details. In construction it was the lowly nail that boomed residential building and urban expansion. Prior to the 1820s home-building in America copied the English method of using heavy beams shaped at the ends to fit into slots in adjoining beams. If there was tension on the two beams, a hole was augured and a wooden peg fitted into place to hold the stress. This mortise-and-tenon method required skilled craftsmen. Houses built in this manner were sturdy but expensive.

The mass production of iron nails in the 1820s liberated builders from the English method. With these inexpensive joining devices, houses could be built in the skeleton form still common today. The "balloon frame," as it was called, consisted of thin plates and studs (usually 2" x 4") "nailed together in such a way that every strain went in the direction of the wood (i.e., against the grain)." The first balloon-frame building appeared in Chicago, where in 1833 a carpenter named Augustine Deodat Taylor built the city's first Catholic church in three months at a cost of only $400.

With that simple edifice, Chicago commenced its long career as a pioneer in urban design. Balloon-frame structures sprang up all over the city, and the popularity of skeleton construction survived even the Great Fire of 1871. Other young western towns like San Francisco, Denver, and Seattle adopted the balloon-frame form, as did the more established cities of the East. Although attacked by contemporaries as shoddy and tasteless, the balloon frame proved irresistible to the urban market with its insatiable appetite for cheap housing. Once transit lines made commuting feasible, developers and speculators bought large tracts of farmland adjacent to the city, carved them into lots, and threw up whole neighborhoods of houses modeled upon a common design.

Like another simple innovation, Eli Whitney's cotton gin, the balloon frame energized an entire industry. It put single-unit dwellings within the reach of many people once unable to afford such a luxury. Home construction soared in every major industrial city and fueled the exodus to the suburbs. Once this pattern of settlement emerged, most cities hastened to annex the new subdivisions that dotted their perimeters. Urban boundaries marched steadily into the surrounding countryside in random fashion, and new towns sprang up everywhere. As Carl W. Condit noted, "Within a generation the balloon frame dominated the West. . . . Without it the towns of the prairies could never have been built in the short time that saw the establishment of rural and urban society in the region."

Commercial buildings underwent no less drastic changes in design and construction techniques. Preindustrial cities utilized wood or bulky masonry for all their buildings. In downtown areas, where buildings were packed closely together, the inhabitants lived in constant fear of fire. The search for stronger, less inflammable materials began as early as the 1820s when two American architects—John Haviland and William Strickland—experimented with iron supports on some of their buildings. . . .

[In the 1850s] James Bogardus, an imaginative mechanic and inventor, . . . constructed the first wholly cast-iron building in New York at the corner of Centre and Duane Streets. The cast-iron design . . . eliminated the thick, space-consuming masonry columns in the interiors, thereby offering more room to economy-minded occupants. Iron buildings went up quickly and could be disassembled quickly if the need arose. For two decades cast iron dominated the construction of warehouses, department stores, and office buildings in American cities. . . . The ability of cast iron to reproduce elaborate details as decorations at low cost gave five- or six-story buildings a unique flavor of elegance in the 1850s and 1860s.

Yet cast iron's primacy lasted only two decades before steel replaced it as the leading construction material. Steel was more durable and stronger for both tension and compression and, unlike cast iron, did not melt when fire reached it. It allowed architects and engineers to raise their structures higher, a compelling feature at a time when downtown land values were soaring. By the 1890s steel framing had converted most major architects through its ability to provide added height and more flexible interior space. The mass production of plate glass gave architects a material for large windows strong enough to withstand wind and stress at high altitudes. This combination of steel framing and plate glass laid the foundation for skyscraper construction in the twentieth century. . . .

The skyscraper mania was not without its detractors. In 1896 the New York Chamber of Commerce declared that tall buildings were "not consistent with public health and that the interests of the majority of our citizens require that the height should be limited." That same year *The New York Times* warned that "the time is evidently near when it will be necessary to proceed in the public interest against the excess of selfishness." The major complaints were that the tall buildings exacerbated the already crowded conditions of most downtown areas, cut off sunlight to adjacent structures and sidewalks, and were basically unsafe. Completion of the Woolworth Building sparked the drive to limit building heights. In 1916 New York City adopted its comprehensive zoning law which included a restriction on height. But architects deftly circumvented the provision by utilizing the "wedding cake" design and skyscrapers continued their upward spiral.* . . .

The physical strain wrought by urban growth involved more than land and buildings. Expanding populations required not only housing but water, gas, electricity, and sewer lines. Better and wider streets were needed to handle the city's heavier traffic. Small cities suddenly grown large found themselves called upon to provide more utilities and services than ever before. Once again municipalities sought refuge in new technology and techniques, and once again every solution gave rise to new problems. As with mass transit, "progress" brought fewer benefits to the public than to the corporate interests that owned the utilities and charged exorbitant rates for their services. Utility franchises, paving contracts, street cleaning, garbage hauling, and maintenance work all reaped financial windfalls for the contractors and politicians in charge of dispensing contracts or fulfilling them.

The importance of streets to urban growth and commerce is so obvious that it needs no elaboration. Yet the history of their construction and care is a dismal chapter in the conflict between public and private interest. Streets in most American cities took a terrific pounding and most were in wretched condition. Any city-dweller who ventured beyond his front door understood that fact only too well. When civic-minded individuals complained about the scandalous condition of their town's thoroughfares, the lament usually fell upon deaf ears. A first-rate street system required a large capital investment, which meant higher taxes. Many other services were also clamoring for more funds even while urbanites protested against more taxes. The result was a pattern of benign neglect in which streets got a relatively low priority in the municipal budget. On one hand, few cities allocated sufficient funds for street construction and care; on the other, graft, inefficiency, and lack of planning sapped the effectiveness of the funds that were allocated.

When it came to paving, for example, most city governments agreed to it only as a last resort, and then tried to do the job as cheaply as possible. Streets were extended long before money was available to pave them. When they were finally paved, the contractor concentrated on the surface rather than the foundation. As a result, few streets enjoyed a long or happy life. Repair were frequent and recurring. . . . But if this "pound-foolish" economy did not serve the public well, it proved a boon to politicians and their friends who discovered that paving contracts were lucrative plums for "friendly" contractors. . . .

---

*The "wedding cake" design involved setting each five or ten stories back from those beneath it. The effect resembled the layers of a wedding cake. . . .

The erratic surfaces of most American streets provoked much consternation as traffic increased. In the 1880s Washington, Buffalo, and Philadelphia adopted the European practice of paving with asphalt. Although it refracted the heat and tended to be slippery, asphalt did provide a quiet surface. Usually it was laid in the suburbs and new sections of town. For the central business district, which required a stronger material, bricks became common in the 1880s, particularly in cities like Philadelphia, Des Moines, Columbus, and Cleveland, which manufactured them.

But American streets did not improve appreciably until builders got beneath the surface of the problem. A substantial and well-drained foundation reduced the amount of surface material used and provided a longer-lasting road. Once cities and their contractors took the trouble to prepare the roadbed, macadam soared in popularity. Cheap stones crushed and mixed with oil, then placed in a well-laid foundation, became the standard paving practice in many cities during the 1880s and 1890s. . . .

Most cities in the 1870s and 1880s constructed major waterworks but the inability to keep up with spiraling demand caused many places to experience "water famines." And the water that did come was virtually untreated. In 1870 no city had a filtration system, and by 1900 only 6 percent of the urban population received filtered water. Pittsburgh, which deposited its industrial waste into and drew its drinking water from the Allegheny River, waited until its death rate from typhoid fever reached four times the national average before constructing a filter system. Between 1908 and 1914, the city installed pumping stations along the Allegheny to filter the water through sediment, whereupon the death rate promptly dropped. Yet even after the improvements, the city's typhoid death rate, although only about half the American average, remained twice that of major European centers.

By 1920 a majority of large American cities possessed filtration and treatment plants. Jersey City pioneered in chemical treatment with a plant built in 1908. But everywhere the surge of population growth pressed hard upon the ingenuity of engineers and resources of municipal governments. The passing decades have brought no solution to the water dilemma; on the contrary, it has reached crisis proportions in many modern cities. Even a century ago it often seemed that in the complex urban environment the most basic needs were the hardest to fulfill satisfactorily.

Technology had another curious effect upon the urban environment: it transformed innovations into necessities of life. The advent of electric energy illustrates the process by which technological breakthroughs generate on a colossal scale demands which had never before existed. Electricity touched every aspect of the city's life—it powered machinery, ran trains, lifted elevators, and lighted streets and homes. To some extent, electricity merely replaced other sources of power and performed old functions in a new way. But once its versatility was recognized, new inventions utilized it for an incredible variety of purposes which urbanites by 1920 accepted as indispensable to their life-style. No one grasped the impact of the dynamo, the means for converting mechanical energy into electric energy, more surely than Henry Adams. "Among the thousand symbols of ultimate energy," he concluded, "the dynamo was not so human as some, but it was the most expressive.". . . .

Even more than gas lamps, electric lighting transformed the city into a twenty-four-hour place. The pace of urban activities livened as nightlife entertainment was extended, people were able to get around more freely and safely, and the evening hours began to attract rather than discourage walkers. Merchants extended their hours, and some industrialists kept their factories running longer. New lighting inspired aesthetic adornments for the city like well-designed lampposts and illuminated monuments, statues, and fountains. The whole atmosphere of city streets seemed cleaner and whiter, a bit like the "Great White City" of the Chicago Fair which had impressed visitors so deeply. It was as if someone, by turning on these electric wonders, had caused urbanites to take a closer look at their cities, and to extract from the shadows a new sense of the degree to which the magic of technology had altered their lives.

As new inventions changed the outward appearance of the industrial city, so did they improve its inner efficiency. . . .

Edison's mimeograph machine (1876), along with the cash register (1876), the stenotype (1876), the adding machine (1888), and the spring-weighing scale (1895), combined with the telephone and typewriter to indicate how far business operations had come from the quill pen, letter book, musty ledger, messenger boy, and hand copyist of an earlier era. Yet none of these equaled another instrument as the supreme symbol of the industrial order: the mass-produced watch.

The hand watch embodied both the genius of American inventiveness and the spirit of the age of mechanization. Fittingly enough, machine watchmaking developed during the 1850s, the same decade in which the preindustrial walking city was giving way to the industrial city. Aaron Dennison's factory in Roxbury, Massachusetts, was the first to manufacture a watch with interchangeable parts in large quantities. Dennison removed his factory to Waltham, Massachusetts, and with Edward Howard formed the American Watch Company which anticipated Henry Ford's assembly line production by fifty years.

Waltham quickly emerged as the center of America's watchmaking industry. By 1900 the factories there averaged 250 watches a year per worker, while Swiss watchmakers could manage only 40. . . . By the late 1870s watchmakers in Waterbury, Connecticut, were producing timepieces at a price the masses could afford. In 1900 a mass-produced watch, complete with a year's guarantee, sold for a dollar. The dollar watch offered tangible benefits and some intangible liabilities. On one hand, the workingman owned a fine timepiece to slide in and out of his pocket; on the other hand, he could no longer plead ignorance or poverty as an excuse for being late to work. . . .

. . . The clock vastly transcended its immediate function of telling time. It symbolized the concerted attempt to harness the raw material of labor to the iron regimen of American work habits. Workmen predictably resisted the efforts as best they could, but the odds turned against them. As immigration swelled the labor force, it created a surplus which heightened the competition for jobs, especially in hard times. However distasteful the factory routine, it was preferable—even inviting—when starvation seemed the only alternative. [Herbert] Gutman cites a verse by Yiddish poet Morris Rosenfeld which vividly portrays the clock as oppressor:

> The Clock in the workshop,—it rests not a moment;
> It points on, and ticks on: eternity—time;
> Once someone told me the clock had a meaning,—
> In pointing and ticking had reason and rhyme. . . .
> At times, when I listen, I hear the clock plainly;—

The reason of old—the old meaning—is gone!
The maddening pendulum urges me forward
To labor and still labor on.
The tick of the clock is the boss in his anger.
The face of the clock has the eyes of the foe.
The clock—I shudder—Dost hear how it draws me?
It calls me "Machine" and it cries [to] me "Sew"!

As urban man grew more apart from his rural cousin with every passing year, nothing separated them more than the clock. While the farmer measured his life by the organic rhythms of seasonal change, of sunrise and sunset, the urbanite chained himself to the "tyranny of time." Trains ran on schedule and were expected to be "on time"; work proceeded with "clockwork efficiency"; mechanical processes were geared "according to the clock"; novels gave way to "periodicals"; and when electricity was mated with the clock in plants, workers had to "clock in." . . .

Technology powered the city, expanded it upward and outward, provided its water, lighted it, carried its wastes, and organized its work patterns. It did much of this crudely, inefficiently, and at great human sacrifice, but Americans had always been slow to reckon the social cost of "progress." More important, it fixed the destiny of the industrial city. Future change or improvement would center upon more sophisticated technology, more prudently applied. No amount of daydreaming or wishful thinking could banish or reverse the technological presence.

The industrial revolution changed the physical city into a larger, more congested, more polluted place. But it had done so under man's guidance. Blind faith in mechanical progress as human progress and the unfettered power of the profit system left little room for pondering the larger ramifications of success. By World War I the industrial city was the dominant urban form which the legacy of unbridled technology willed to the twentieth century.

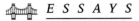 *E S S A Y S*

The Machine as Deity and Demon

ALAN TRACHTENBERG

I

Even before the Civil War, the westward trails were destined to be lined with tracks; the pony express and the covered wagon, like the mounted Plains Indian, would yield to the Iron Horse. For if the West of "myth and symbol" . . . provided one perspective by which Americans might view their society, the machine provided another. The two images fused into a single picture of a progressive civilization fulfilling a providential mission. . . . Many Americans before the Civil War had believed that industrial technology and the factory system would serve as historic instruments of republican values, diffusing civic virtue and enlightenment along with material wealth. Factories, railroads, and telegraph wires seemed the very engines of a democratic future. Ritual celebrations of machinery and fervently optimistic prophecies of abundance continued throughout the Gilded Age, notably at the two great international expositions, in Philadelphia in 1876, and in Chicago in 1893.

The image of the machine, like the image of the West, proved to be a complex symbol, increasingly charged with contradictory meanings and implications. If the machine seemed the prime cause of the abundance of new products changing the character of daily life, it also seemed responsible for newly visible poverty, slums, and an unexpected wretchedness of industrial conditions. While it inspired confidence in some quarters, it also provoked dismay, often arousing hope and gloom in the same minds. For, accompanying the mechanization of industry, of transportation, and of daily existence, were the most severe contrasts yet visible in American society, contrasts between "progress and poverty" (in Henry George's words), which seemed to many a mockery of the republican dream, a haunting paradox. Each act of national celebration seemed to evoke its opposite. The 1877 railroad strike, the first instance of machine smashing and class violence on a national scale, followed the 1876 Centennial Exposition, and the even fiercer Pullman strike of 1894 came fast on the heels of the World's Columbian Exposition of 1893.

It is no wonder that closer examination of popular celebrations discloses bewilderment and fear. . . . In the language of literature, a machine (railroad or steamship) bursting on a peaceful natural setting represented a symbolic version of the trauma inflicted on American society by unexpectedly rapid mechanization. The popular mode of celebration covered over all signs of trauma with expressions of confidence and fulsome praise. But confidence proved difficult to sustain in the face of the evidence.

Current events instilled doubt at the very site of celebration. A period of great economic growth, of steadily rising per capita wealth, and new urban markets feeding an expanding industrial plant, the Gilded Age was also wracked with persisting crises. An international "great depression" from 1873 to 1896 afflicted all industrial nations with chronic overproduction and dramatically falling prices, averaging onethird on all commodities. . . . A perilously uneven business cycle continued for more than twenty years, affecting all sections of the economy: constant market uncertainties and stiffening competition at home and abroad for business; inexplicable surpluses and declining world prices, together with tightening credit for farmers; wage cuts, extended layoffs and irregular employment and worsening conditions, even starvation, for industrial workers. . . . Thus, even in the shadow of glorious new machines displayed at the fairs, the public sense of crisis deepened.

No wonder modern machinery struck observers, especially those associated with the business community, as in Charles Francis Adams, Jr.'s words, "an incalculable force." The tempo of crisis accelerated in the 1870's. Farmers agitated through Granger clubs and the Greenback Party against the government's policy of supporting business through deflationary hard money and the gold standard. Industrial unrest reached a climax and a momentary catharsis in July 1877, when fears of a new civil war spread across the country during the great railroad strike. Provoked by a 10 percent wage cut announced without warning by the Baltimore and Ohio line, a measure to halt a declining rate of profit, the strike spread like wildfire to other lines, reaching from Baltimore to Pittsburgh, Chicago, St. Louis, Kansas City, and San Francisco. The apparently spontaneous work stoppages met with approval and support from local merchants, farmers, clergy, and politicians, tapping reserves of anger and wrath against the railroad companies. Workers in other industries joined the walkout, and for a short spell it seemed that the United States faced a mass rebellion, a recurrence of the Paris Commune of 1871 on an even vaster scale. In some communities (St. Louis, for example) committees of strikers briefly assumed control of government and railroad services.

The strike turned bloody and destructive, arousing a vehemence of response from big business and the national government even surpassing the wrath vented by strikers against railroad yards and equipment. . . . The newly inaugurated President, Rutherford Hayes, invoked his powers of military intervention and called out federal troops to protect "by force" (as he noted in his diary) the property of the railroad companies, among whose leaders he counted many of his closest friends and supporters. In the end, the strike left more than a hundred dead, millions of dollars of property destroyed, and a toughened company and government stand against unions. Strikers were very often fired and blacklisted, their leaders fined and jailed. The War Department issued a pamphlet on "riot duty" and constructed for the first time a system of armories in major cities to house a standing "national guard." Industrialization of the state's military force seemed a necessary adjunct to the mechanization of production.

The very extremes of effect lent to the machine an aura of supreme power, as if it were an autonomous force that held human society in its grip. In *The First Century of the Republic,* a book of essays published by *Harper's* magazine in celebration of the nation's centennial in 1876, the economist David Wells observed that "like one of our mighty rivers," mechanization was "beyond control." And indeed the display in Machinery Hall in Philadelphia that summer gave credence to the image of a flood, though without Wells's ominous note. Here, in an exposition of machines removed from their working location, a profusion of mechanisms seduced the eye: power looms, lathes, sewing machines, presses, pumps, toolmaking machines, axles, shafts, wire cables, and locomotives. . . . Alexander Graham Bell here gave the world first notice of the greatest wonder of electrical communication: the telephone. For sheer grandeur and sublimity, however, the mechanisms of communication could not compete with the two most imposing structures in the Hall: the thirty-foot-high Corliss Double Walking-Beam Steam Engine, which powered the entire ensemble from a single source, and its counterpart, a 7,000-pound electrical pendulum clock which governed, to the second, twenty-six lesser "slave" clocks around the building. Unstinted but channeled power, and precisely regulated time: that combination seemed to hold the secret of progress. . . .

II

The idea of an autonomous and omnipotent machine, brooking no resistance against its untold and ineluctable powers, became an article of faith. The image implied a popular social theory: the machine as a "human benefactor," a "great emancipator of man from the bondage of labor." Modern technology was mankind's "civilizing force," driving out superstition, poverty, ignorance. "Better morals, better sanitary conditions, better health, better wages," wrote Carroll D. Wright, chief of the Massachusetts Bureau of Statistics of Labor, in 1882; "these are the practical results of the factory system, as compared with what preceded it, and the results of all these have been a keener intelligence." Wright's paper, originally given as an address before the American Social Science Association, bore the title "The Factory System as an Element in Civilization."

The events of the 1870's and 1880's however, also elicited less sanguine accounts of what the factory system had wrought. . . . Not surprisingly, a growing number of Americans openly questioned whether industrialization was in fact, in Henry George's words, "an unmixed good." As if in pointed rebuke of Wright's arguments and images, George observed the following year, in *Social Problems* (1883), that so-called labor-saving inventions, the "greater employment of machinery," and "greater division of labor," result in "positive evils" for the working masses, "degrading men into the position of mere feeders of machines." Machines employed in production under the present system are "absolutely injurious," "rendering the workman more dependent; depriving him of skill and of opportunities to acquire it; lessening his control over his own condition and his hope of improving it; cramping his mind, and in many cases distorting and enervating his body." . . . George plainly perceived the process of degradation in factory labor as strictly mechanical, experienced as an *effect* of machinery.

. . . George, a native Philadelphian of middle-class birth who had wandered to California in the late 1850's, working as a seaman, printer, newspaperman, failing as a Democratic candidate for office and as the owner of an independent newspaper, wished to arouse the nation to its plight, urging the adoption of a "single tax" against land rents as the solution to the paradox whereby "laborsaving machinery everywhere fails to benefit laborers." His *Progress and Poverty,* written in the wake of the destruction, violence, and frustration of the summer of 1877, fuses evangelical fervor with simplified Ricardian economic theory; its simplicity of analysis and solution, its jeremiad rhetoric of righteousness and exhortation, helped the book find a remarkably wide audience. It reached more than 2 million readers by the end of the century. Appealing to a range of political sentiments and economic interests, George evoked a vision of older republican and entrepreneurial values restored through the "single tax" in the new corporate industrial world. . . .

George's picture of the failures of the machine and of its potential promise corresponded to the perceptions of a significant section of the society, particularly since he promised a change fundamentally within the existing order, the existing relations of capital and labor. Among representatives of older ruling groups, the picture held less promise. "It is useless for men to stand in the way of steam-engines," wrote Charles Francis Adams, Jr., in 1868. Adams, from one of the oldest Eastern families of property and former political status, would soon join forces with the engine as corporate executive of railroad and other enterprises. His less sanguine brother, Henry Adams, wrote later in *The Education of Henry Adams* (1907), regarding his own "failure," that "the whole mechanical consolidation of force ruthlessly stamped out the life of the class into which Adams was born." Devising a theory of history based on "forces," Adams crystallized the technological determinism implicit in both the popular and academic thought of his time. . . .

. . . The familiarization of American society with machinery represents one of the major cultural processes of these years, even in such simple matters as riding in streetcars and elevators, getting used to packaged processed foods and the style of machine-made clothing, let alone growing accustomed to new harsh sounds and noxious odors near factories and railroad terminals. The proliferation of new machines and machine-made tools for industrial and agricultural production marked an even more drastic upheaval in the forms, rhythms, and patterns of physical labor.

Perhaps more expressive of changing cultural perceptions because of its greater diffusion than serious or "high" literature, popular fiction and folklore in these years represented machinery especially in its sheer power and exemption from human vulnerability. In regional folktales and ballads, such figures as the lumberjack Paul Bunyan, the railroad worker John Henry, the locomotive engineer Casey Jones pit their strength and skill and daring against the machine.

Dime-novel Western adventures depict orgies of shootings and killings with every variety of automatic repeating weapons, each named precisely. A magical machine, endowing its owner with ultimate powers of "civilization" against "savagery," the gun not only won the West in such fictions (as it did in fact) but helped make the notion of repeatability, of automation, familiar. Indeed, as recent scholars have remarked, the interchangeability of plots and characters in dime novels parallels the standardization of machine production that became a central feature of factory life in the 1880's. Dime novels also provided a field for technological fantasy; beginning with *The Huge Hunter,* or *The Steam Man of the Prairies* in 1865, these novels included inventors (often boys) as standard fare, along with robots (like the ten-foot steam man), armored flying vessels, electrified wire, and remote-control weapons. The fiction provided vicarious mechanical thrills along with fantasies of control and power. Machines are imagined as exotic instruments of destruction, only obliquely linked to the means of production revolutionizing the industrial system.

The fictive imagination of terror, of technological cataclysm, served as a form of familiarization. The implications of a technologized world and its potential for explosion were not lost on more troubled observers, who felt themselves on a precarious bridge between an earlier America and the present. . . .

. . . Nervousness provoked by modern mechanical life provided the theme of the widely read medical treatise by George M. Beard in 1884. A pioneering work in the study of neurasthenia, *American Nervousness* builds its case through an elaborate mechanical metaphor: the nervous system is like a machine presently under strain in response to the pressures of the machinery of civilized life. Like Thomas Edison's central electric-light generator, wrote Beard (a friend of the inventor), "the nervous system of man is the centre of the nerve-force supplying all the organs of the body." "Modern nervousness," he explains, "is the cry of the system struggling with its environment," with all the pressures exerted on striving Americans by the telegraph and railroad and printing press. Simply to be on time, Beard argues, exacts a toll from the human system. . . .

. . . [Beard] also discloses another source of severe anxiety prevalent among middle- and upper-class Americans, that of impending chaos, the rule of accident, exigency, and rampant city mobs. . . .

The fear of cataclysm implicit here is not so much technological as social: a fear manifest throughout the popular media after 1877 of uprisings and insurrection, of a smoldering volcano under the streets. For David Wells, writing in 1885, such popular disturbances as the agitation for an eight-hour day and talk of socialism "seem full of menace of a mustering of the barbarians from within rather than as of old from without, for an attack on the whole present organization of society, and even the permanency of civilization itself." Henry George, too, concluded *Progress and Poverty* with a picture of potential collapse, of "carnivals of destruction." "Whence shall come the new barbarians," he asked. "Go through the squalid quarters of great cities, and you may see, even now, their gathering hordes! How shall learning perish? Men will cease to read, and books will kindle fires and be turned into cartridges!" The association of social unrest with the imagery of technological violence, of new city crowds with ignorance and contempt for culture (or regression to "savagery"), fired the imagination with a nightmarish narrative of impending apocalypse. . . .

III

. . . Association of machines with violence suggest profound tensions among Americans who . . . otherwise saluted modern technology as a boon to republican ideals. Metaphors of wreckage and self-destruction seem to express unresolved cultural dilemmas, conflicting value systems such as those described by Leo Marx as "machine" and "garden," the values of mechanical progress and those of pastoral harmony in a peaceful landscape. But the coexistence of figures of destruction, of "dark Satanic mills," with those of unbounded Promethean production, also points in the direction of the Promethean effort itself, toward the character of the mechanization process. Subtle interweavings of destruction and creation formed the inner logic of the industrial capitalist system, a logic less conspicuous but nonetheless compelling in its consequences than the more dramatic versions of contradiction evoked by Henry George. . . . As analysts here and in Europe had begun to discover, that system possessed a baffling unconscious energy which resulted in recurrent cycles of expansion and contraction, inflation and deflation, confidence and depression. Such aberrations seemed to follow from precisely those increases in productive power which marked the industrial world in these years.

If Americans seemed especially intense in their response to mechanization, especially obsessed with alternating images of mechanical plentitude and devastation, an explanation lies in the special circumstances of native industrialization, its speed, its scale, its thoroughness within a brief period. Suffering fewer social barriers, possessing the largest domestic region convertible to a national market without internal restriction, by the end of the century American industry rapidly surpassed its chief European rivals, England and Germany. Figures of absolute increase signified the triumph: the production of raw steel rising from 13 tons in 1860 to near 5,000 in 1890, and of steel rails multiplying ten times in the same years; total agricultural output tripling between 1870 and 1900. Agriculture showed the most dramatic and immediate evidence. A single mechanized farmer in 1896 was able to reap more wheat than eighteen men working with horses and hand equipment sixty years earlier. . . .

[The American] propensity [for mechanical improvement] characterized the entire industrial world, but it had been a special mark of American manufacturing since its beginnings. With a scarcity of skilled labor, of craftsmen and artisans with accumulated experience in nascent industrial processes such as spinning, weaving, and milling, American circumstances placed a premium on mechanical invention and improvement. Scarcity of skills together with cheapness of land had maintained a relatively high cost of labor in the young United States. . . . Without an inherited aristocratic social order, the new country held out more hope to entrepreneurs for social acceptance as well as material rewards. Many early industrial entrepreneurs had begun their working lives as craftsmen, mechanics with a knack for invention, and had risen to wealth and status as a result of their mechanical skill and entrepreneurial expertise. . . . By the 1850's the practical Yankee inventor-entrepreneur, the tinkerer with an eye on profit, had come to seem an American type, proof of the republican principle that self-taught men of skill and ingenuity might rise to wealth and social position. . . .

Technological determinism implied that machines demanded their own improvement, that they controlled the forms of production and drove their owners and workers. Americans were taught to view their machines as independent agencies of power, causes of "progress." Machines seemed fixed in shape, definite self-propelled objects in space. In fact, however, machinery underwent constant change in appearance, in function, in design. Machines were working parts of a dynamic system. And the motives for change, the source of industrial dynamism, lay not in the inanimate machine but in the economic necessities perceived by its owners. Higher rates of productivity through economies of scale and velocity, through greater exploitation of machinery and reorganization of both factory labor and corporate structures, were deliberate goals chosen by business leaders out of economic need. . . .

. . . The American fascination with the machine . . . tended to divert attention from the countless small innovations at the work place, changes both in machinery and the design of work. . . . The belief that viewed "progress" as a relation between new machines and old, a matter of replacing the outmoded by the novel, obscured the transformations of labor, of the human relation to production, each mechanical improvement represented. Technological change in these years consisted of a vast interrelated pattern of novelty, developments in metallurgy, mining, chemistry, hydraulics, electricity feeding back into each other. . . . With steam power prevailing in the 1870's, machines grew bigger and faster, and factories resembled jungles of shafts, belts, axles, and gears to transmit power from immense prime movers. . . . Electricity offered new possibilities of conversion of power into heat, light, and motion, and permitted new efficiencies and economics in the design of factories, including decentralization, dispersion of work areas, and assembly lines. In both the transformative (textiles, chemicals, food processing, glass making) and assembling (construction, clothing, shoe, machine making) industries, electricity worked major alterations in the forms of labor. . . .

. . . Unsettled economic conditions made manufacturers obsessed with efficiency, with the breaking of bottlenecks, the logistics of work flow, the standardization of parts, measurements, and human effort. . . . As a result, human effort fell more and more into mechanical categories, as if the laborer might also be conceived as an interchangeable part. Furious efforts to cut labor costs led to the announcement of severe work rules, the replacement of traditional craftsmen by unskilled or semiskilled labor: the effort, that is, to lower the cost of wages by increasing investment in the fixed capital of new machinery. Such developments, . . . set the stage for several of the fiercest labor struggles of the 1880's and 1890's. The process of continual refinement and rationalization of machinery, leading to twentieth-century automation, represented to industrial workers a steady erosion of their autonomy, their control, and their crafts.

In the record, then, of mechanical change lay an intermingling of production and destruction, the scrapping of old machines, old processes, and old human skills. An inevitable wreckage accompanied the "progress in manufacturing" David Wells had described as a "mighty river." That image hinted at unconscious meanings, the figure of speech disclosing more than Wells himself recognized. "Like one of our mighty rivers," he wrote in 1876 about manufacturing, "its movement is beyond control." . . .

IV

. . . In the quest for greater productivity, for more efficient machines, more output per unit of cost, calculation of several kinds played an increasingly significant role. With the enlarged role of the accounting office in decisions relevant to materials and labor, transportation, advertising, and sales, mathematical considerations entered the business world in a major way. . . .

As if called forth by this prime economic motive, Frederick W. Taylor, a foreman at the Midvale Steel Company in Pennsylvania, inaugurated in the 1880's his famous "time-study" experiments, aimed at elimination of waste, inefficiency, and what he called "soldiering" on the part of workers. With his stopwatch—a further encroachment of time on physical movement—Taylor proposed to systematize exactly that process Wells had described as production through destruction: the absolute subordination of "living labor" to the machine. He envisioned a complete renovation of the production process, with standardization of tools and equipment, replanning of factories for greater efficiency, and a "piece-rate" method of payment as incentive for workers. In *The Principles of Scientific Management* (1911), Taylor made explicit the heart of his program: to take possession for management of the "mass of traditional knowledge" once possessed by the workers themselves, "knowledge handed down to them by word of mouth, through the many years in which their trade has been developed from the primitive condition." For Taylor the stopwatch and flowchart were basic instruments whereby management might reduce that knowledge to measurable motions, eradicating their workers' autonomy at one stroke while enhancing their productivity.

Thus, the social distribution of knowledge begins a major shift, a transference (as far as technology and technique are concerned) from bottom to top, in these years of extensive and intensive mechanization. Just as important, and as a symbol of the process, *thought* now appears often in the dumb, mystifying shapes of machines, of standing and moving mechanical objects as incapable of explaining themselves to the unknowing eye as the standing stones of ancient peoples. The momentous event of mechanization, of science and technology coming to perform the labor most significant to the productivity of the system, reproduced itself in ambivalent cultural images of machines and inventors, and in displacements running like waves of shock through the social order.

Class Consciousness American-Style

LEON FINK

Two well-traveled routes into the Gilded Age are likely to leave the present-day visitor with the same puzzled and unsatisfied feeling. One itinerary pursuing the political history of the era begins in 1876 with the official end of Reconstruction and winds through the election of William McKinley in 1896. The other route, this one taking a social prospectus, departs with the great railroad strikes of 1877 and picks its way through the drama and debris of an industrializing society. The problem is that the two paths never seem to meet. Compartmentalization of subject matter in most textbooks into "politics," "economic change," "social movements," and so on, only papers over the obvious unanswered question—what impact did an industrial revolution of unprecedented magnitude have on the world's most democratic nation?

Leon Fink, *In Search of the Working Class: Essays in American Labor History and Political Culture* (Urbana: University of Illinois Press, 1994), 15–29. Used by permission.

The question, of course, permits no simple answer. By most accounts the
political era inaugurated in 1876 appears, except for the Populist outburst of the
mid-1890s, as a conservative, comparatively uneventful time sandwiched between
the end of Radical Reconstruction and the new complexities of the twentieth century. With the Civil War's financial and social settlement out of the way, a society
desperately wanting to believe that it had removed its last barriers to social harmony by and large lapsed into a period of ideological torpor and narrow-minded
partisanship. Political contests, while still the national pastime (national elections
regularly drew 80 percent, state and local elections 60–80 percent of eligible voters,
1876–96), seem to have dwelt less on major social issues than on simple party
fealty. Fierce rivalries engendered by the sectional, ethnocultural, and economic interest group divisions among the American people increasingly were presided over
and manipulated by party professionals. To be sure, genuine policy differences—
e.g., over how best to encourage both industry and trade, the degree of danger
posed by the saloon, honesty in government—fueled a venomous political rhetoric.
As echoed by both national parties from the late 1870s through the early 1890s,
however, a complacent political consensus had emerged, stressing individual
opportunity, rights in property, and economic freedom from constraints. The welfare of the American Dream, in the minds of both Democrats and Republicans,
required no significant governmental tinkering or popular mobilization. Acknowledging the parties' avoidance of changing social and economic realities, a most
compelling recent commentary on the late nineteenth-century polity suggests that
the "distinct, social need" of the time was in part filled by heightened partisanship
and the act of political participation itself.

In contrast to the ritualistic quality of politics, the contemporary social world
seems positively explosive. Consolidation of America's industrial revolution
touched off an era of unexampled change and turmoil. As work shifted decisively
away from agriculture between 1870 and 1890, the manufacturing sector, with
a spectacular increase in the amount of capital invested, the monetary value of
product, and the number employed, sparked a great economic leap forward. By
1880 Carroll D. Wright, U.S. commissioner of labor statistics, found that the application of steam and water power to production had so expanded that "at least four-
fifths" of the "nearly 3 millions of people employed in the mechanical industries of
this country" were working under the factory system. It was not just the places of
production but the people working within them that represented a dramatic departure from preindustrial America. While only 13 percent of the total population was
classified as foreign-born in 1880, 42 percent of those engaged in manufacturing
and extractive industries were immigrants. If one adds to this figure workers of
foreign parentage and of Afro-American descent, the resulting nonnative/nonwhite
population clearly encompassed the great majority of America's industrial work
force. Not only, therefore, had the industrial revolution turned a small minority in
America's towns and cities into the direct employers of their fellow citizens, but
the owners of industry also differed from their employees in national and cultural
background. This sudden transformation of American communities, accompanied
as it was by a period of intense price competition and unregulated swings in the
business cycle, provided plentiful ingredients for social unrest, first manifest on a
national scale in the railroad strike of 1877.

The quintessential expression of the labor movement in the Gilded Age was the Noble and Holy Order of the Knights of Labor, the first mass organization of the North American working class. Launched as one of several secret societies among Philadelphia artisans in the late 1860s, the Knights grew in spurts by the accretion of miners (1874–79) and skilled urban tradesmen (1879–85). While the movement formally concentrated on moral and political education, cooperative enterprise, and land settlement, members found it a convenient vehicle for trade union action, particularly in the auspicious economic climate following the depression of the 1870s. Beginning in 1883, local skirmishes escalated into highly publicized confrontations with the railroad financier Jay Gould, a national symbol of new corporate power. Strikes by Knights of Labor telegraphers and railroad shop craft workers touched off an unprecedented wave of strikes and boycotts that carried on into the renewed depression in 1884–85 and spread to thousands of previously unorganized semi-skilled and unskilled laborers, both urban and rural. The Southwest Strike on Gould's Missouri and Texas-Pacific railroad lines, together with massive urban eight-hour campaigns in 1886, swelled a tide of unrest that has become known as the "Great Upheaval." The turbulence aided the efforts of organized labor, and the Knights exploded in size, reaching more than three-quarters of a million members. Although membership dropped off drastically in the late 1880s, the Knights remained a powerful force in many areas through the mid-1890s. Not until the Congress of Industrial Organizations' revival of the 1930s would the organized labor movement again lay claim to such influence within the working population.

At its zenith the movement around the Knights helped to sustain a national debate over the social implications of industrial capitalism. Newspaper editors, lecturers, and clergymen everywhere addressed the Social Question. John Swinton, the leading labor journalist of the day, counted Karl Marx, Hawaii's king Kalakaua, and the Republican party's chief orator, Robert G. Ingersoll, among the enlightened commentators on the subject. Even the U.S. Senate in 1883 formally investigated "Relations between Labor and Capital." Nor was the debate conducted only from on high. In laboring communities across the nation the local press as well as private correspondence bore witness to no shortage of eloquence from the so-called inarticulate. One of the busiest terminals of communications was the Philadelphia office of Terence Vincent Powderly, general master workman of the Knights of Labor. Unsolicited personal letters expressing the private hopes and desperations of ordinary American citizens daily poured in upon the labor leader: an indigent southern mother prayed that her four young girls would grow up to find an honorable living: an unemployed New York cakemaker applied for a charter as an organizer; a Cheyenne chief sought protection for his people's land; an inventor offered to share a new idea for the cotton gin on condition that it be used cooperatively.

Amid spreading agitation, massed strength, and growing public awareness, the labor issues ultimately took tangible political form. Wherever the Knights of Labor had organized by the mid-1880s, it seemed, contests over power and rights at the workplace evolved into a community-wide fissure over control of public policy as well. Indeed, in some 200 towns and cities from 1885 to 1888 the labor movement actively fielded its own political slates. Adopting "Workingmen's," "United Labor," "Union Labor" "People's party," and Independent" labels for their tickets, or alternatively taking over one of the standing two-party organizations in town, those local political efforts revealed deep divisions within the contemporary political culture and evoked sharp reactions from traditional centers of power. Even as manufacturers' associations met labor's challenge at the industrial level, business response at the political level was felt in the dissolution of party structures, creation of antilabor citizens' coalitions, new restrictive legislation, and extralegal law and order leagues. In their ensemble, therefore, the political confrontations of the 1880s offer a most dramatic point of convergence between the world leading out of 1876 and that stretching from 1877. As a phenomenon simultaneously entwined in the political and industrial history of the Gilded Age, the subject offers an opportunity to redefine the main issues of the period.

The labor movement of the Gilded Age . . . spoke a "language of class" that was "as much political as economic." In important ways an eighteenth-century republican political inheritance still provided the basic vocabulary. The emphasis within the movement on equal rights, on the identity of work and self-worth, and on secure, family-centered households had informed American political radicalism for decades. A republican outlook lay at the heart of the protests of journeymen-mechanics and women millworkers during the Jacksonian period; it likewise inspired abolitionists and the woman suffrage and temperance movements and even contributed to the common-school crusade. . . .

Working-class radicalism in the Gilded Age derived its principles—as grouped around economic, national-political, and cultural themes—from the period of the early revolutionary-democratic bourgeoisie. Implicitly, labor radicals embraced a unifying conception of work and culture that Norman Birnbaum has labeled the *Homo faber* ideal: "an artisanal conception of activity, a visible, limited, and directed relationship to nature." The *Homo faber* ethic found its political embodiment in Enlightenment liberalism. "From that source," notes Trygve R. Tholfson in a commentary on mid-Victorian English labor radicalism, "came a trenchant rationalism, a vision of human emancipation, the expectation of progress based on reason, and an inclination to take the action necessary to bring society into conformity with rationally demonstrable principles." In the late nineteenth century, Enlightenment liberalism was harnessed to a historical understanding of American nationalism, confirmed by both the American Revolution and the Civil War. Together these political, economic, and moral conceptions coalesced around a twin commitment to the citizen-as-producer and the producer-as-citizen. For nearly a century Americans had been proud that their country, more than anywhere else in the world, made republican principles real. In this respect the bloody war over slavery served only to confirm the ultimate power of the ideal.

Certain tendencies of the Gilded Age, however, heralded for some an alarming social regression. The permanency of wage labor, the physical and mental exhaustion inflicted by the factory system, and the arrogant exercise of power by the owners of capital threatened the rational and progressive march of history. "Republican institutions," the preamble to the constitution of the Knights of Labor declared simply, "are not safe under such conditions." "We have openly arrayed against us," a Chicago radical despaired in 1883, "the powers of the world, most of the intelligence, all the wealth, and even law itself." The lament of a Connecticut man that "factoryism, bankism, collegism, capitalism, insuranceism and the presence of such lump-headed malignants as Professor William Graham Sumner" were stultifying "the native genius of this state" framed the evil in more homespun terms. In 1883 the cigar-makers' leader Samuel Gompers, not yet accepting the inevitability of capitalist industry, bemoaned the passing of the day of "partners at the work bench" that had given way to "the tendency . . . which makes man, the worker, a part of the machine." The British-born journalist Richard J. Hinton, an old Chartist who had commanded black troops during the Civil War, also reflected on the sudden darkening of the social horizon. The "average, middle-class American," he complained, simply could not appreciate the contemporary position of American workers: "They all look back to the days when they were born in some little American village. . . . They have seen their time and opportunity of getting on in the world, and they think that is the condition of society today, when it is totally a different condition."

In response the labor movement in the Gilded Age turned the plowshares of a consensual political past into a sword of class conflict. "We declare," went the Knights' manifesto, "an inevitable and irresistible conflict between the wage-system of labor and republican system of government." To some extent older demons seemed simply to have reappeared in new garb, and, as such, older struggles beckoned with renewed urgency. A Greenback* editor in Rochester, New Hampshire, thus proclaimed that "patriots" who overturn the "lords of labor" would be remembered next to "the immortal heroes of the revolution and emancipation."

To many outside observers in the 1880s, the American working class—in terms of organization, militancy, and collective self-consciousness—appeared more advanced than its European counterparts. . . . Eleanor Marx and Edward Aveling returned from an 1886 American tour with a glowing assessment of the workers' mood. Friedrich Engels, too, in the aftermath of the eight-hour strikes and the Henry George campaign, attached a special preface to the 1887 American edition of *The Condition of the Working Class in England in 1844:*

> In European countries, it took the working class years and years before they fully realized the fact that they formed a distinct and, under the existing social conditions, a permanent class of modern society; and it took years again until this class-consciousness led them to form themselves into a distinct political party, independent of, and opposed to, all the old political parties, formed by the various sections of the ruling classes. On the more favored soil of America, where no medieval ruins bar the way, where history begins with the elements of the modern bourgeois society as evolved in the seventeenth century, the working class passed through these two stages of its development within ten months.

Nor was it only in the eyes of eager well-wishers that the developments of the 1880s seemed to take on a larger significance. Surveying the map of labor upheaval, the conservative Richmond *Whig* wrote in 1886 of "socialistic and agrarian elements" threatening "the genius of our free institutions." The Chicago *Times* went so far in its fear of impending revolution as to counsel the use of hand grenades against strikers.

---

*The Greenback-Labor Party (1875–1878) called for an inflated money supply, based on the retention of Civil War greenback dollars and the coinage of silver, to benefit workers and debtor farmers.

Revolutionary anticipations, pro or con, proved premature. That was true at least partly because both the movement's distant boosters as well as its domestic detractors sometimes misrepresented its intentions. Gilded Age labor radicals did not self-consciously place themselves in opposition to a prevailing economic system but displayed a sincere ideological ambivalence toward the capitalist marketplace. On the one hand, they frequently invoked a call for the "abolition of the wage system." On the other hand, like the classical economists, they sometimes spoke of the operation of "natural law" in the marketplace, acknowledged the need for a "fair return" on invested capital, and did not oppose profit per se. . . . The Knights thus modified an earlier radical interpretation of the labor-cost theory of value, wherein labor, being the source of all wealth, should individually be vested with the value of its product, and demanded for workers only an intentionally vague "proper share of the wealth they create." In so doing they were able to shift the weight of the analysis . . . to the general, collective plight of the laboring classes. In their eyes aggregation of capital together with cutthroat price competition had destroyed any semblance of marketplace balance between employer and employee. Under the prevailing economic calculus, labor had been demoted into just another factor of production whose remuneration was determined not by custom or human character but by market price. In such a situation they concluded, as Samuel Walker has noted, that "the contract was not and could not be entered into freely. . . . The process of wage determination was a moral affront because it degraded the personal dignity of the workingman." This subservient position to the iron law of the market constituted "wage slavery," and like other forms of involuntary servitude it had to be "abolished."

Labor's emancipation did not, ipso facto, imply the overthrow of capitalism, a system of productive relations that the Knights in any case never defined. To escape wage slavery workers needed the strength to redefine the social balance of power with employers and their allies—and the will and intelligence to use that strength. One after another the Knights harnessed the various means at their disposal—education, organization, cooperation, economic sanction, and political influence—to this broad end: "To secure to the workers the full enjoyment [note, not the full return] of the wealth they create, sufficient leisure in which to develop their intellectual, moral and social faculties, all of the benefits of recreation, and pleasures of association; in a word to enable them to share in the gains and honors of advancing civilization."

A wide range of strategic options was represented within the counsels of the labor movement. One tendency sought to check the rampant concentration of wealth and power with specific correctives on the operation of the free market. Radical Greenbackism (with roots in Kelloggism and related monetary theories), Henry George's single tax, and land nationalization, each of which commanded considerable influence among the Knights of Labor, fit this category. Another important tendency, cooperation, offered a more self-reliant strategy of alternative institution building, or, as one advocate put it, "the organization of production without the intervention of the capitalist." Socialism, generally understood at the time as a system of state as opposed to private ownership of production, offered a third alternative to wage slavery. Except for a few influential worker-intellectuals and strong pockets of support among German-Americans, however, socialism carried comparatively little influence in the 1880s. . . .

If Gilded Age labor representatives tended to stop short of a frontal rejection of the political-economic order, there was nevertheless no mistaking their philosophic radicalism. Notwithstanding differences in emphasis, the labor movement's political sentiments encompassed both a sharp critique of social inequality and a broad-based prescription for a more humane future. Indeed, the labor representative who shrugged off larger philosophical and political commitments in favor of a narrow incrementalism was likely to meet with incredulity. One of the first, and most classic, enunciations of business unionism, for example, received just this response from the Senate Committee on Labor and Capital in 1883. After taking testimony from workers and labor reformers across the country for six months, the committee, chaired by New Hampshire senator Henry Blair, interviewed Adolph Strasser, president of the cigarmakers' union. Following a disquisition on the stimulating impact of shorter working hours on workers' consumption patterns, Strasser was asked if he did not contemplate a future beyond the contemporary exigencies of panic and over-production, "some time [when] every man is to be an intelligent man and an enlightened man?" When Strasser did not reply, Senator Blair interceded to elaborate the question. Still Strasser rebuffed the queries: "Well, our organization does not consist of idealists. . . . we do [not] control the production of the world. That is controlled by employers, and that is a matter for them." Senator Blair was take aback.

> *Blair.* I was only asking you in regard to your ultimate ends.
> *Witness.* We have no ultimate ends. We are going on from day to day. We are fighting only for immediate objects—objects that can be realized in a few years. . . .
> *Blair.* I see that you are a little sensitive lest it should be thought that you are a mere theorizer. I do not look upon you in that light at all.
> *Witness.* Well, we say in our constitution that we are opposed to theorists, and I have to represent the organization here. We are all practical men.
> *Blair.* Have you not a theory upon which you have organized?
> *Witness.* Yes, sir: our theory is the experience of the past in the United States and in Great Britain. That is our theory, based upon actual facts. . . .
> *Blair.* In other words you have arrived at the theory which you are trying to apply?
> *Witness.* We have arrived at a practical result.
> *Blair.* But a practical result is the application of a theory is it not?

On a cultural level, labor's critique of American society bore the same relation to Victorian respectability that its political radicalism bore to contemporary liberalism. In both cases the middle-class and working-class radical variants derived from a set of common assumptions but drew from them quite different, even opposing, implications. No contemporary, for example, took more seriously than the Knights of Labor the cultural imperatives toward productive work, civic responsibility, education, a wholesome family life, temperance, and self-improvement. The intellectual and moral development of the individual, they would have agreed with almost every early nineteenth-century lyceum lecturer, was a precondition for the advancement of democratic civilization. In the day of Benjamin Franklin such values may well have knit together master craftsmen, journeymen, and apprentices. In the age of the factory system, however, the gulf between employer and employee had so widened that the lived meanings of the words were no longer the same.

For the Knights the concept of the producing classes indicated an ultimate social division that they perceived in the world around them. Only those associated with idleness (bankers, speculators), corruption (lawyers, liquor dealers, gamblers), or social parasitism (all of the above) were categorically excluded from membership in the Order. Other social strata such as local merchants and manufacturers were judged by their individual acts, not by any inherent structural antagonism to the workers' movement. Those who showed respect for the dignity of labor (i.e., who sold union-made goods or employed union workers at union conditions) were welcomed into the Order. Those who denigrated the laborer or his product laid themselves open to the righteous wrath of the boycott or strike. Powderly characteristically chastised one ruthless West Virginia coal owner: "Don't die, even if you do smell bad. We'll need you in a few years as a sample to show how *mean* men used to be." This rather elastic notion of class boundaries on the part of the labor movement was reciprocated in the not inconsequential number of shopkeepers and small manufacturers who expressed sympathy and support for the labor movement.

Idealization of hearth and home, a mainstay of familial sentimentality in the Gilded Age, also enjoyed special status within the labor movement. For here, as clearly as anywhere in the radicals' worldview, conventional assumptions had a critical, albeit ambivalent, edge in the context of changing social circumstances. Defense of an idealized family life as both moral and material mainstay of society served as one basis of criticism of capitalist industry. The machinist John Morrison argued before the Senate investigating committee that the insecurities of the unskilled labor market were so threatening family life as to make the house "more like a dull prison instead of a home." A self-educated Scottish-born leader of the type-founders, Edward King, associated trade union morality with the domestic "sentiments of sympathy and humanity" against the "business principles" of the age. Almost unanimously, the vision of the good life for labor radicals included the home.

The importance of the domestic moral order to the late nineteeth-century radical vision also translated into an unparalleled opening of the labor movement to women. As Susan Levine has documented, the Knights of Labor beckoned to wage-earning women and workingmen's wives to join in construction of a "cooperative commonwealth," which, without disavowing the Victorian ideal of a separate female sphere of morality and domestic virtue, sought to make that sphere the center of an active community life.

The Knights' self-improving and domestic commitments both converged in the working-class radicals' antipathy to excessive drinking. The oath of temperance, which became known as "the Powderly pledge," appealed in turn to intellectual development and protection of the family as well as to the collective interests of the labor movement. Like monopoly, the bottle lay waiting to fasten a new form of slavery upon the free worker. In another sense, as David Brundage has suggested, the growing capitalization of saloons together with expansion of saloon-linked variety theater directly threatened a family-based producers' community. While most radicals stopped short of prohibition, exhortations in behalf of temperance were commonplace. . . .

In general, then, the labor movement of the late nineteenth century provided a distinct arena of articulation and practice for values that crossed class lines. Two aspects of this use of inherited values for radical ends merit reemphasis. First, to the extent that labor radicalism shared in the nineteenth century's cult of individualism, it established a social and moral framework for individual achievement. The culture of the labor movement stressed the development of individual capacity but not competition with other individuals; while striving to elevate humanity, it ignored what S. G. Boritt has identified as the essence of the Lincoln-sanctified American Dream—the individual's "right to rise." The necessary reliance by the labor movement upon collective strength and community sanction militated against the possessive individualism that anchored the world of the workers' better-off neighbors. By its very nature, the labor movement set limits to the individual accumulation of wealth extracted from others' efforts and represented, in Edward King's words, "the graduated elimination of the personal selfishness of man."

Second, in an age of evolutionary, sometimes even revolutionary, faith in progress and the future (a faith generally shared by labor radicals), the movement made striking use of the past. Without renouncing the potential of industrialism for both human liberty and material progress, radicals dipped selectively into a popular storehouse of memory and myth to capture alternative images of human possibility. The choice of the name "Knights of Labor" itself presented images of chivalry and nobility fighting the unfeeling capitalist marketplace. Appeals to the "nobility of toil" and to the worker's "independence" conjured up the proud village smithy—not the degradation of labor in the factory system. Finally, celebrations of historic moments of human liberation and political advancement challenged a political-economic orthodoxy beholden to notions of unchanging, universal laws of development. Indeed, so conspicuously sentimental were the celebrations of Independence Day and Memorial Day that Powderly had to defend the Order from taunts of "spreadeagleism" and "Yankee doodleism."

This sketch of working-class radicalism in the Gilded Age raises one final question. Whose movement—and culture—was it? In a country as diverse as the United States, with a labor force and labor movement drawn from a heterogeneous mass of trades, races, and nationalities, any group portrait runs the risk of oversimplification. The articulate leadership of the Knights of Labor and the political movement that sprang from it included brainworkers (especially the editors of the labor press), skilled craft workers, and shopkeepers who looked to the labor movement as a source of order in a disorderly age. The self-conception of the radical labor leadership as a middle social stratum, balanced between the very rich and very poor, was evident in Powderly's 1885 characterization of his own ancestors—"they did not move in court circles; nor did they figure in police courts."

This dominant stream within the labor movement included people who had enjoyed considerable control over their jobs, if not also economic autonomy, men who often retained claim to the tools as well as the knowledge of their trade. They had taken seriously the ideal of a republic of producers in which hard work would contribute not only to the individual's improved economic standing but also to the welfare of the community. So long as they could rely on their own strength as well as their neighbors' support, this skilled stratum organized in an array of craft unions showed economic and political resilience. But the spreading confrontations with national corporate power, beginning in the 1870s, indicated just how much erosion had occurred in the position of those who relied on custom, skill, and moral censure as ultimate weapons. Industrial dilution of craft skills and a direct economic and political attack on union practices provided decisive proof to these culturally conservative workingmen of both the illegitimacy and ruthlessness of the growing power of capital. It was they, according to every recent study of late nineteenth-century laboring communities, who formed the backbone of local labor movements. The Knights were, therefore, first of all a coalition of reactivating, or already organized, trade unions.

For reasons of their own, masses of workers who had not lost full and equal citizenship—for they had never possessed it—joined the skilled workers within the Knights. Wherever the Order achieved political successes, it did so by linking semiskilled and unskilled industrial workers, including blacks and new immigrants, to its base of skilled workers and leaders. Although lacking the vote, the presence of women in the Order also undoubtedly strengthened its broader community orientation. The special strength of the Knights, noted the Boston *Labor Leader* astutely, lay "in the fact that the whole life of the community is drawn into it, that people of all kinds are together . . . , and that they all get directly the sense of each others' needs."

Politically, the Knights of Labor envisioned a kind of producer democracy. The organized power of labor was capable of revitalizing democratic citizenship and safeguarding the public good within a regulated marketplace economy. Through vigilant shop committees and demands such as the eight-hour day, organized workers—both men and women—would ensure minimal standards of safety and health at the industrial workplace, even as they surrounded the dominant corporate organizational model of business with cooperative models of their own. A pride in honest and useful work, rational education, and personal virtue would be nurtured through a rich associational life spread out from the workplace to meeting hall to the hearth and home. Finally, the integrity of public institutions would be vouchsafed by the workingmen in politics. Purifying government of party parasitism and corruption, cutting off the access to power that allowed antilabor employers to bring the state apparatus to their side in industrial disputes, improving and widening the scope of vital public services, and even contemplating the takeover of economic enterprises that had passed irreversibly into monopoly hands—by these means worker-citizens would lay active claim to a republican heritage.

The dream was not to be. At the workplace management seized the initiative toward the future design and control of work. A managerial revolution overcoming the tenacious defenses of the craft unions transferred autonomy over such matters as productivity and skill from custom and negotiation to the realm of corporate planning. Except for the garment trades and the mines, the national trade unions had generally retreated from the country's industrial heartland by 1920. In the local community as well, the differences, even antagonisms, among workers often stood out more than did the similarities. Segmentation of labor markets, urban ethnic and socioeconomic residential segregation, cultural as well as a protectionist economic disdain for the new immigrants, and the depoliticization of leisure time (i.e., the decline of associational life sponsored by labor organizations) all contributed toward a process of social fragmentation. In such circumstances working-class political cooperation proved impossible. The Socialist party and the Progressive slates could make little more than a dent in the hold of the two increasingly conservative national parties over the electorate. Only with the repolarization of political life beginning in 1928 and culminating in the New Deal was the relation of labor and the party system again transformed. By the late 1930s and 1940s a revived labor movement was beginning, with mixed success, to play the role of a leading interest group and reform conscience within the Democratic party.

This impressionistic overview permits one further observation of a quite general nature. One of the favorite tasks of American historians has been to explain why the United States, alone among the nations of the Western world, passed through the industrial revolution without the establishment of a class consciousness and an independent working-class political movement. Cheap land, the cult of individualism, a heterogeneous labor force, social mobility, and the federal separation of powers comprise several of the numerous explanations that have been offered. While not directly denying the importance of any of the factors listed above, this study implicitly suggests a different approach to the problem of American exceptionalism.

The answer appears to lie less in a permanent structural determinism—whether the analytic brace be political, economic, or ideological—than in a dynamic and indeed somewhat fortuitous convergence of events. To understand the vicissitudes of urban politics, we have had to keep in mind the action on at least three levels: the level of working-class social organization (i.e., the nature and strength of the labor movement), the level of business response, and the level of governmental response. During the Gilded Age each of these areas took an incendiary turn, but only briefly and irregularly and most rarely at the same moment. The 1880s, as R. Laurence Moore has reiterated, were the international seed time for the strong European working-class parties of the twentieth century. In America, too, the momentum in the 1880s was great. Indeed, examined at the levels of working-class organization and industrial militancy, a European visitor might understandably have expected the most to happen here first. At the political level, as well, American workers were in certain respects relatively advanced. In the 1870s and in the 1880s they established independently organized local labor regimes well before the famous French Roubaix or English West Ham labor-Socialist town councils of the 1890s. Then, a combination of forces in the United States shifted radically away from the possibilities outlined in the 1880s. The labor movement fragmented, business reorganized, and the political parties helped to pick up the pieces. The initiatives from without directed at the American working class from the mid-1890s through the mid-1920s—part repression, part reform, part assimilation, and part recruitment of a new labor force—at an internationally critical period in the gestation of working-class movements may mark the most telling exceptionalism about American developments.

It would in any case be years before the necessary conditions again converged and labor rose from the discredited icons of pre-Depression America with a new and powerful political message. Workplace, community, and ballot box would all once again be harnessed to a great social movement. But no two actors are ever in quite the same space at the same time. The choices open to the CIO, it is fair to say, were undoubtedly influenced by both the achievement and failure of their counterparts a half-century earlier.*

FURTHER READING

Paul Avrich, *The Haymarket Tragedy* (1984)
Stuart W. Bruchey, *Enterprise: The Dynamic Economy of a Free People* (1990)
Sean Cashman, *America in the Gilded Age* (1984)
Alfred D. Chandler, Jr., *The Visible Hand: The Managerial Revolution in American Business* (1977)
Melvyn Dubofsky, *Industrialism and the American Worker, 1865–1920* (1975)
Leon Fink, *Workingmen's Democracy: The Knights of Labor and American Politics* (1983)
———, *In Search of the Working Class: Essays in American Labor History and Political Culture* (1994)
Herbert G. Gutman, *Work, Culture, and Society in Industrializing America* (1976)
Naomi R. Lamoreaux, *The Great Merger Movement in American Business, 1895–1904* (1985)
Christopher Lasch, *The True and Only Heaven: Progress and Its Critics* (1991)
Bruce Laurie, *Artisans Into Workers: Labor in Nineteenth-Century America* (1989)
Susan Levine, *Labor's True Woman* (1984)
Harold C. Livesay, *Andrew Carnegie and the Rise of Big Business* (1975)
J. Anthony Lukas, *Big Trouble* (1997)
David Montgomery, *The Fall of the House of Labor* (1987)
Richard J. Oestreicher, *Solidarity and Fragmentation: Working People and Class Consciousness in Detroit, 1875–1900* (1986)
C. Joseph Pusateri, *A History of American Business* (1988)
John L. Thomas, *Alternative America: Henry George, Edward Bellamy, Henry Demarest Lloyd and the Adversary Tradition* (1983)

---

*The CIO (Congress of Industrial Organizations), a breakaway from the AFL (American Federation of Labor) in the 1930s, enrolled masses of workers from America's basic industries.

 E S S A Y S

Why Did Some American Businesses
Get So Big?

COLLEEN A. DUNLAVY

Why did big business in the United States become so big that in the late nineteenth century Americans came to demand antitrust legislation? Historians, by and large, have agreed that pure economic forces brought on concentration. But in taking this view they have neglected a strikingly different explanation that was widely propounded at the time it was all happening. This alternative view saw the bigness of some American business as the result of government policies—in particular, protectionism in the form of high tariffs. Because they believed that protective tariffs had encouraged excessive concentration, a number of them viewed free trade as one of the best remedies against the trusts.

Colleen A. Dunlavy, "Why Did American Business Get So Big?" *Audacity, The Magazine of Business Experience* 2 (Spring 1994): 43, 45–47, 49. Reprinted by permission of American Heritage.

The accepted view among business historians, strongly influenced by the work of Alfred D. Chandler, Jr., is that the extraordinary bigness of American business grew naturally from the workings of the market and the demands of modern, capital-intensive technology. The United States, already world-renowned for giant enterprise by the turn of the century, possessed both the world's largest domestic market and entrepreneurs capable of perceiving, exploiting, and expanding that market. In doing so, some built mass production enterprises of impressive proportions and then went on to integrate forward and backward, producing even larger firms, while others joined forces with their competitors, combining horizontally during the great merger movement (1895–1904). The two paths often intertwined, but the result in every case was enterprises of truly enormous proportions. U.S. Steel, formed in 1901, epitomized the process of concentration.

In 1898 Congress created the United States Industrial Commission. It immediately began investigating the trusts, and from April 1899 through early January 1900 it heard testimony from a broad array of public figures. Among the witnesses was the New York attorney John R. Dos Passos.

In testimony that filled nearly forty pages, Dos Passos defended economic concentration as a natural development that legislation should not—and could not—inhibit. History makes abundantly clear, he declared, the futility of legislation to block combinations, whether of manufacturers, distributors, or labor. "And the simple reason," he maintained, "is that the laws of trade, the natural laws of commercial relations, defy human legislation; and that is all there is in it. Wherever the two clash the statute law must go down before the operations of those natural laws."

John D. Rockefeller, the head of what was popularly termed the Standard Oil Trust, echoed this view in a written response to the commission in 1899. "It is too late to argue about advantages of industrial combinations," he flatly asserted. "They are a necessity."

Halfway across the country, Chicago's Civic Federation convened the Chicago Conference on Trusts in September 1899. "Some months since," the federation president, Franklin H. Head, explained, "no topic seemed so widely discussed as what was designated by the general title of 'Trusts,'—and . . . upon no current topic was there so widespread and general an ignorance and confusion of ideas." So the federation invited hundreds of men to Chicago for "a conference in search of truth and light." They included governors, attorneys general, state delegates, academics, congressmen, state and federal officials, representatives of chambers of commerce and boards of trade, and delegates from a large number of associations that represented agricultural, labor, and other interests.

Many speakers at the Chicago conference also concurred with the economic view. "Consolidations are the outgrowth and the symptom of the advancing civilization of to-day, and the inevitable tendency of its complex trade conditions," maintained a Pennsylvania lawyer, A. Leo Weil. David Ross of the Illinois Bureau of Labor Statistics observed, "Men talk of destroying such combinations by legal enactment, on the supposition, presumably, that it is possible and desirable to return to the simpler systems of the past." But it would do no good, he thought: "Our development as an industrial state is the result of trade conditions and opportunities which no legislative power could anticipate or control." Even the labor leader Samuel Gompers adhered to the economic view. "For our part, we are convinced," he explained, "that the state is not capable of preventing the legitimate development or natural concentration of industry." Instead Gompers merely wanted the right for his men to organize on a scale comparable to the level of organization achieved in industry.

Two years later a Chicago lawyer and the author of a two-volume tract on the law of combinations put the economic view succinctly. The legal world had not yet come to grips with combinations, Arthur J. Eddy observed; "the lack of harmony is only too apparent." But eventually the law would be brought in line: "Combination as an economic factor in the industrial and commercial world is a fact with which courts and legislatures may struggle, and struggle in vain, until they frankly recognize that, like all other conditions, it is a result of evolution to be conserved, regulated and made use of, but not suppressed."

The economic interpretation of the concentration movement then under way thrived in business circles in the ensuing years. "The business world generally," Francis Walker reported in 1912, "regards great combinations . . . as the natural and necessary development of trade, and declares in picturesque metaphor that 'natural laws can not be repealed by statute.'"

This is the view that has come down to us as a consensus, but it was nothing of the kind. On the contrary, out of the diversity of views expressed before the Industrial Commission, at the Chicago Conference on Trusts, and in print, a broadly opposing view emerged, one that saw dangerous economic concentration as a political phenomenon. The Industrial Commission recognized this broad dichotomy of views on the trust problem, and it concluded its hearings with testimony from both camps. Two men were called to speak on "general aspects" of the problem. One was Dos Passos; the other was the St. Louis lawyer Charles Claflin Allen, whose testimony filled another thirty pages and who took issue with Dos Passos on nearly every point.

Allen did not deny that *some* consolidations in the merger movement then under way "followed a natural normal tendency under economic laws," as the economic view maintained, but like others who endorsed a political view of trusts, he saw the bigness of American business as a product of the nation's industrial policy.

We usually associate the term *industrial policy* with direct intervention or "industrial targeting" of specific industries. But Chalmers Johnson, much acclaimed for his 1982 study of Japan's Ministry of International Trade and Industry (MITI) and Japanese policy, sees this as only one kind of industrial policy—what he terms *microindustrial policy*. More broadly, he argues, "industrial policy" also encompasses "all government measures [that] . . . have a significant impact on the well-being or ill-health of whole sectors, industries, and enterprises in a market economy." Thus what he terms *macroindustrial policy* comprises the array of policies (e.g., fiscal, monetary, trade, or labor policies) that subtly shape the broad environment in which business operates. Macroindustrial policies, in effect, create what Germans call the *Wirtschaftsordnung* (economic order).

Adherents of the political view of big business did not like the direction in which the American economic order was moving at the turn of the century, but it would be wrong to assume (as their contemporaries often did and as historians frequently do) that these critics opposed economic development or did not understand the value of large-scale enterprise. Their quarrel was with the form that economic change was taking. Those who saw economic change as fundamentally political in origin, as the historian Victoria Hattam suggests in *Labor, Visions, and State Power,* preferred a decentralized pattern of growth that would be devoid of concentrations of power. Seeing government policies at the root of the problem, they sought to revamp those policies to promote economic development along more decentralized lines. Therefore, they drew special attention to two aspects of late-nineteenth-century industrial policy: tariffs and railroad-rate regulation.

"The mother of all trusts is the customs tariff bill," Henry O. Havemeyer, the president of the American Sugar Refining Company, declared before the Industrial Commission in June 1899. Since he headed what was popularly known as the Sugar Trust, Havemeyer's statement generated a good deal of excitement. The potential benefits of horizontal combination, he argued, "bear a very insignificant proportion to the advantages granted in the way of protection under the customs tariff." He at first testified that tariff protection had helped the leaders of the iron and steel industries; but under questioning he admitted that his own sugar industry was affected too, conceding, as the commission's summary of evidence noted, "that had it not been for the high protective tariff existing at the time the original Sugar Trust was formed he would probably not have taken the risk of putting his refineries into the trust."

At the Chicago Conference on Trusts three months later, Havemeyer's opinions stirred considerable interest. Byron W. Holt, of the New England Free Trade League, applauded his comments. Havemeyer's views had "startled the country," Holt reported, but they ought not to have: "That the tariff, by shielding our manufacturers from foreign competition, makes it easy for them to combine, to restrict production, and to fix prices—up to the tariff limit—ought to be evident to every intelligent man." Among protected industries, he named "glass, furniture, leather, iron and steel, paper, coal, woolen goods, and silk goods"—not to mention Havemeyer's refined sugar—and he singled out for lengthy discussion the tinplate industry. "The heart of the trust problem is in our tariff system of plunder," Holt concluded. "The quickest and most certain way of reaching the evils of trusts is not by direct legislation against them, or by constitutional amendment, but by the abolition of tariff duties."

In *The Tariff and the Trusts,* a book published in 1907, the New York lawyer Franklin Pierce also laid the problem at the feet of Congress: "Our protective tariff is the genesis of the trust. The trust comes out of it as naturally as fruit from blossom. Obviously the control of a market by a combination or trust is facilitated where the field of competition is artificially limited to one country since it is easier to combine the producers of one country than those of all countries, and to that extent all must concede that the tariff encourages trusts."

The McKinley tariff of 1890 had raised rates to levels not seen since the Civil War, and the Dingley tariff of 1897 had pushed them even higher. Events in the business world since then, Pierce maintained, left little doubt about how the process worked.

But in one sense Pierce endorsed the economic view of American "bigness." He too saw the nation's large domestic market as essential to the rise of the trusts: "When the trust is established the very largeness of our country results in the largeness and success of the trust." But only market size and tariff protection working in tandem produced giant enterprise: "So vast a field secured to them from outside competition is tempting enough to invoke the energies of immense capital for its exploitation, and as a result gigantic trusts protected by the tariff come into existence with a power for evil in trade and politics which would be impossible in a small country, however high might be the tariff sheltering them from competition."

Although pessimistic, Pierce knew what should be done: "The true remedy against our trusts is to seek out the cause of a trust and remove that cause." He meant lower tariff levels: "Throw down the tariff wall which encircles every trust . . . and let the trust contend with the full stream of international commerce. If it continues to exist, it will be because it sells its products at home for cheaper prices than the cost of the imported foreign product."

But the necessary political action, Pierce thought, would demand "a rebirth of patriotism." His words sound oddly contemporary to the late-twentieth-century ear: "Let the people come together, not as Republicans nor as Democrats but as Americans loving their country and ready to join battle against the interests which corruptly rule it. There is no other question of importance before the country. It is simply a fight at close quarters between the people and this mighty system of wrong and corruption." In the late twentieth century his words would have rallied support for NAFTA—provided, of course, that *it* would not be surrounded by a new wall of protection.

Turn-of-the-century proponents of the political view also perceived another kind of tacit industrial policy promoting combination: railroad rate regulation, or more precisely the failure of regulation to eliminate discriminatory rates. "Numerous witnesses," according to the Industrial Commission's summary of evidence, "attribute the growth of combinations primarily to discriminating rates or other advantages given by railways."

Independent oil producers, for example, argued before the Commission that Standard Oil's market control depended on the special low rail rates that it enjoyed, even after creation of the Interstate Commerce Commission. M. L. Lockwood, the president of the American Anti-Trust League and an oil producer in Pennsylvania since 1865, maintained that the roots of the problem extended back to his first years in business: "Away back in the latter part of the sixties some of the refinery men in the oil regions who did not have the ear of the railway managers were unable to get a freight rate over the railroads that would enable them to sell their oil in New York and the export cities at a profit. They were obliged to sell the refined oil to the men who afterwards helped to create the Standard Oil Company, for these men even at that early date seemed to have an advantage in freight rates that enabled them to market oil at a profit when no one else could." He wanted it understood that his testimony was directed not at the Standard Oil men themselves but "against an accursed system of railway discriminations which has made this great curse, the Standard Oil Trust monopoly, a possibility. . . ."

Lockwood proposed three measures to combat monopoly: government ownership of the railroads, a policy of equal rates, and "a law forcing the great trusts and monopolistic combinations to fix a price upon their goods which, freights considered, will be the same in every township and hamlet of the land." Lockwood, like others at the time, saw capital-intensive industry in a class with natural monopolies and wanted to see pro rata principles applied to the mass production industries as well as to the railroads. A committee member interrupted to clarify Lockwood's views: Did he consider rate discrimination "the mother of all the great trusts of this country?"

Lockwood replied: "I do, largely, yes; that is really the foundation; a trust must be protected in some way; the brains of the country are not in the heads of a few men. The protection which has created the Standard Oil Company, the Big Four Beef Combine, and trusts and monopolies of that class, is that of discrimination in freights."

In these views Lockwood had the support not only of other independent oil producers but also of men outside the industry. Charles Claflin Allen concurred with and elaborated on Lockwood's views. "It is in the railroad companies that the greatest danger lies," he declared, for their discriminatory rates, contrary to law, formed the basis on which "the large trusts or combinations" accumulated "their wealth and power." At the Chicago conference testimony ran along similar lines, although with interesting variations. S. H. Greeley, of the National Grain Growers' Association, viewed railroads as "the very mainspring of many of the combinations and trusts, which are now crushing out the middle class in the United States." The "skillfully managed combinations" that controlled the grain trade of the Mississippi Valley, he said, had been "created by secret rates and special privileges, granted them by railroads." His solution was government ownership of the railroads.

Others at the Chicago conference went further, however, stressing the interplay of tariffs and discriminatory railroad rates. J. G. Schonfarber, a member of the Executive Committee of the Knights of Labor, neatly tied trusts to railroads [and] to tariffs, and he advocated political action to cut the knots that bound them: "Corporate ownership of railroads is the backbone of the trust and a protective tariff its right arm. It is within the limit of possibilities for the government, by the right of eminent domain, to come into the ownership and control of the railroad, and also to repeal the tariff tax upon every article controlled by a trust. Do both these things, and it is scarcely probable that trusts could exist at all." Implicitly, his words denied that concentration was a natural economic process. In his view, a trust problem created by government policy could be cured by government policy.

But not all those who adhered to the political view of big business agreed. The Democratic presidential candidate William Jennings Bryan also spoke to the Chicago conference, creating a great stir among the public. Although Bryan maintained "that the primary cause of monopoly is the love of money and the desire to secure the fruits of monopoly," he also allowed that high tariffs and discriminatory rates were contributing factors. "No question about it," he said of rate discrimination. But he did not think that lowering tariffs and equalizing rates would suffice. "The great trouble has been," he noted, "that, while our platforms denounce corporations, corporations control the elections and place the men who are elected to enforce the law under obligations to them." Thus he proposed that antitrust law be made uniform at the state and national levels and that it be made "a penal offense for any corporation to contribute to the campaign fund of any political party."

Such differences in strategy aside, these men clearly brought to bear a broader analysis than business historians and economists have employed in understanding how American business became so big. Viewing the world through the lens of a different political economy, they saw a de facto industrial policy at the root of the trust problem—and at least a partial remedy in free trade.

WEEK 4

DOCUMENTS

1. Sharecroppers' Contracts, 1876–1886

STATE OF NORTH CAROLINA, Wake County

Articles of Agreement, Between *Alonzo T. Mial* of said County and State, of the first part, and *A. Robert Medlin* of the County and State aforesaid, of the second part, to secure an Agricultural Lien according to an Act of General Assembly of North Carolina, entitled "An Act to secure advances for Agricultural purposes":

Whereas, the said *A. R. Medlin* being engaged in the cultivation of the soil, and being without the necessary means to cultivate his crop, *The Said A. T. Mial* has agreed to furnish goods and supplies to the said *A. R. Medlin* to an amount not to exceed *One Hundred and fifty* Dollars, to enable him to cultivate and harvest his crops for the year 1876.

And in consideration thereof, the said *A. R. Medlin* doth hereby give and convey to the said *A. T. Mial* a LIEN upon all of his crops grown in said County in said year, on the lands described as follows: *The land of A. R. Medlin adjoining the lands of Nelson D. Pain Samuel Bunch & others.*

And further, in Consideration thereof, the said *A. R. Medlin* for One Dollar in hand paid, the receipt of which is hereby acknowledged, have bargained and sold, and by these presents do bargain, sell and convey unto the said *A. T. Mial his* heirs and assigns forever, the following described Real and Personal Property to-wit: *All of his Stock horses, Cattle Sheep and Hogs — Carts and Wagons House hold and kitchen furnishings.* To Have and to Hold the above described premises, together with the appurtenances thereof, and the above described personal property, to the said *A. T. Mial his* heirs and assigns.

The above to be null and void should the amount found to be due on account of said advancements be discharged on or before the *1st* day of *November* 1876: otherwise the said *A. T. Mial his* executors, administrators or assigns, are hereby

---

"Sharecroppers' Contract, 1876–1886," found in the Alonzo T. Millard Mial Papers, North Carolina Division of Archives and History. As edited in Carolyn Merchant, ed., *Major Problems in American Environmental History: Documents and Essays* (Lexingon, Mass.: D. C. Heath, 1993), 218–219. Reprinted by permission of Houghton Mifflin Company.

authorized and empowered to seize the crops and Personal Property aforesaid, and sell the same, together with the above Real Estate, for cash, after first advertising the same for fifteen days, and the proceeds thereof apply to the discharge of this Lien, together with the cost and expenses of making such sale, and the surplus to be paid to the said *A. R. Medlin,* or his legal representatives.

IN WITNESS WHEREOF, The said parties have hereunto set their hands and seals this *29th* day of *February,* 1876.

his

A. Robert × *Medlin,* [seal]

mark

Witness: *L. D. Goodloe* [signed]   *A. T. Mial* [signed], [seal]

This contract made and entered into between A. T. Mial of one part and Fenner Powell of the other part both of the County of Wake and State of North Carolina—

Witnesseth—That the Said Fenner Powell hath barganed and agreed with the Said Mial to work as a cropper for the year 1886 on Said Mial's land on the land now occupied by Said Powell on the west Side of Poplar Creek and a point on the east Side of Said Creek and both South and North of the Mial road, leading to Raleigh, That the Said Fenner Powell agrees to work faithfully and dilligently without any unnecessary loss of time, to do all manner of work on Said farm as may be directed by Said Mial, And to be respectful in manners and deportment to Said Mial. And the Said Mial agrees on his part to furnish mule and feed for the same and all plantation tools and Seed to plant the crop free of charge, and to give the Said Powell One half of all crops raised and housed by Said Powell on Said land except the cotton seed. The Said Mial agrees to advance as provisions to Said Powell fifty pound of bacon and two sacks of meal pr month and occationally Some flour to be paid out of his the Said Powell's part of the crop or from any other advance that may be made to Said Powell by Said Mial. As witness our hands and seals this the 16th day of January A.D 1886

A. T. Mial [signed] [Seal]

his

Witness

Fenner × *Powell* [Seal]

mark

W. S. Mial [signed]

"The New South," speech delivered before New England Society of New York City, Dec. 21, 1886, in Edna Henry Lee Turpin, ed., *The North, South, and Other Addresses by Henry Woodfin Grady* (New York: Charles Merill, 1904), 23–42.

4. Labor Organizer Mother Jones Compares Southern Mill Life to Serfdom, 1901

The Rope Factory

I visited the factory in Tuscaloosa, Ala., at 10 o'clock at night. The superintendent, not knowing my mission, gave me the entire freedom of the factory and I made good use of it. Standing by a siding that contained 155 spindles were two little girls. I asked a man standing near if the children were his, and he replied that they were. "How old are they?" I asked. "This one is 9, the other 10," he replied. "How many hours do they work?" "Twelve," was the answer. "How much do they get a night?" "We all three together get 60 cents. They get 10 cents each and I 40."

I watched them as they left their slave-pen in the morning and saw them gather their rags around their frail forms to hide them from the wintry blast. Half-fed, half-cbthed, half-housed, they toil on, while the poodle dogs of their masters are petted and coddled and sleep on pillows of down, and the capitalistic judges jail the agitators that would dare to help these helpless ones to better their condition.

Gibson is another of those little sections of hell with which the South is covered. The weaving of gingham is the principal work. The town is owned by a banker who possesses both people and mills. One of his slaves told me she had received one dollar for her labor for one year. Every weekly pay day her employer gave her a dollar. On Monday she deposited that dollar in the "pluck-me" store to secure food enough to last until the next pay day, and so on week after week.

There was once a law on the statute books of Alabama prohibiting the employment of children under twelve years of age more than eight hours each day. The Gadston Company would not build their mill until they were promised that this law should be repealed.

When the repeal came up for the final reading I find by an examination of the records of the House that there were sixty members present. Of these fifty-seven voted for the repeal and but three against. . . .

I asked one member of the House why he voted to murder the children, and he replied that he did not think they could earn enough to support themselves if they only worked eight hours. These are the kind of tools the intelligent workingmen put in office. . . .

Almost every one of my shop-mates in these mills was a victim of some disease or other. All are worked to the limit of existence. The weavers are expected to weave so many yards of cloth each working day. To come short of this estimate jeopardizes their job. The factory operator loses all energy either of body or of mind. The brain is so crushed as to be incapable of thinking, and one who mingles with these people soon discovers that their minds like their bodies are wrecked. Loss of sleep and loss of rest gives rise to abnormal appetites, indigestion, shrinkage of stature, bent backs and aching hearts.

Such a factory system is one of torture and murder as dreadful as a long-drawn-out Turkish massacre, and is a disgrace to any race or age. As the picture rises before me I shudder for the future of a nation that is building up a moneyed aristocracy out of the life-blood of the children of the proletariat. It seems as if our flag is a funeral bandage splotched with blood. The whole picture is one of the most horrible avarice, selfishness and cruelty and is fraught with present horror and promise of future degeneration. The mother over-worked and under-fed, gives birth to tired and worn-out human beings.

Mother Jones, "Civilization in Southern Mills," *International Socialist Review,* I (March 1901) 539–541.

5. *Atlantic Monthly* Visits Pittsburg, the Workshop of the West, 1868

It is chiefly at Pittsburg that the products of the Pennsylvania hills and mountains are converted into wealth and distributed over the world. The wonder is, not that Pittsburg is an assemblage of flourishing towns of 230,000 inhabitants, but that, placed at such a commanding point, it is not the *most* flourishing and the *most* populous city in America. . . .

Pittsburg announces its peculiar character from afar off. Those who approach it in the night see before them, first of all, a black hill, in the side of which are six round flaming fires, in a row, like six fiery eyes. Then other black hills loom dimly up, with other rows of fires half-way up their sides; and there are similar fiery dots in the gloom as far as the eye can reach. This is wonderfully picturesque, and excites the curiosity of the traveller to the highest point. He thinks that Pittsburg must be at work behind those fires, naked to the waist, with hairy chest and brawny arms, doing tremendous things with molten iron, or forging huge masses white-hot, amid showers of sparks. No such thing. These rows of fires, of which scores can be counted from a favorable point, are merely the chimneys of coke-ovens, quietly doing their duty during the night, unattended. That duty is to convert the waste coal-dust at the mouths of the mines, where it has been accumulating for a century, into serviceable coke. These are almost the only fires about Pittsburg that are always burning, night and day, Sundays and holidays. . . .

There is one evening scene in Pittsburg which no visitor should miss. Owing to the abruptness of the hill behind the town, there is a street along the edge of a bluff, from which you can look directly down upon all that part of the city which lies low, near the level of the rivers. On the evening of this dark day, we were conducted to the edge of the abyss, and looked over the iron railing upon the most striking spectacle we ever beheld. The entire space lying between the hills was filled with blackest smoke, from out of which the hidden chimneys sent forth tongues of flame, while from the depths of the abyss came up the noise of hundreds of steam-hammers. There would be moments when no flames were visible; but soon the wind would force the smoky curtains aside, and the whole black expanse would be dimly lighted with dull wreaths of fire. It is an unprofitable business, view-hunting; but if any one would enjoy a spectacle as striking as Niagara, he may do so by simply walking up a long hill to Cliff Street in Pittsburg, and looking over into—hell with the lid taken off.

Such is the kind of day of which Pittsburg boasts. The first feeling of the stranger is one of compassion for the people who are compelled to live in such an atmosphere. . . . It is interesting to hear a Pittsburgher discourse on this subject; and it much relieves the mind of a visitor to be told, and to have the assertion proved, that the smoke, so far from being an evil, is a blessing. The really pernicious atmospheres, say the Pittsburg philosophers, convey to man no intimation of the poison with which they are laden, and we inhale death while enjoying every breath we draw;

James Parton, "Pittsburg," *Atlantic Monthly* 21 (January 1868): 17–18, 21–22, 25–26, 28, 30–32, 34–35. Another edited version of this document can be found in Roy Lubove, ed., *Pittsburgh* (New York: New Viewpoints, 1976), pp. 8–16. The nineteenth-century spelling of Pittsburg has been preserved in this document.

but this smoke is an evil only to the imagination, and it destroys every property of the atmosphere which is hostile to life. In proof of which the traveller is referred to the tables of mortality, which show that Pittsburg is the most favorable city in the world to longevity. . . .

The "great fact" of Pittsburg is coal. Iron and copper can better afford to come to coal to be melted, than send for coal to come and melt them. All those hills that frown down upon Pittsburg, and those that rise from the rivers back of Pittsburg, have a stratum of coal in them from four to twelve feet thick. . . . The mere quantity of coal in this region is sufficiently staggering. All the foundries and iron-works on earth could find ample room in this region, at the edge of a navigable stream, and have a coal mine at their back doors. . . . [T]here are fifteen thousand square miles of "this sort of thing." The "great Pittsburg coal seam," as it is called, which consists of bituminous coal only, is put down in the books as covering eight and a half millions of acres. . . .

. . . There are in the congregation of towns which the outside world knows only by the name of Pittsburg, five hundred manufactories and "works." Fifty of these are glass-works, in which one half of all our glass-ware is made, and which employ three thousand persons. . . .

Oil Creek is a branch of the Alleghany River, and empties into it one hundred miles above Pittsburg. Pittsburg is, consequently, the great petroleum mart of the world. It is but five years ago that this material became important; and yet there were received at Pittsburg during the year 1866 more than sixteen hundred thousand barrels of it. The Alleghany River is one of the swiftest of navigable streams; but there is never a moment when its surface at Pittsburg is not streaked with petroleum. It would not require remarkable talent in an inhabitant of this place to "set the river on fire." The crude oil is floated down this impetuous river in the slightest-built barges . . . into which the oil is poured as into an enormous trough. . . . It needs but a slight accident to knock a hole in one of these thin barges. When such an accident has occurred, . . . the petroleum lies all spread out upon the swift river, making its way toward Pittsburg, while the barge is filled with water and sunk. . . .

Down by the swift and turbid Alleghany, close to the river, as all the great foundries are, we discovered with difficulty, on a very dark morning, the celebrated Fort Pitt Foundry, where twenty-five hundred of the great guns were cast that blew the late "So-Called" out of water. In this establishment may be seen the sublime of the mechanic arts. Only here, on the continent of America, have there ever been cast those monsters of artillery which are called by the ridiculous diminutive of "the twenty-inch gun." . . .

From seeing one of these enormous guns cast, the visitor at Pittsburg may go, if he chooses, to an establishment where they make tacks so minute that it takes a thousand of them to weigh an ounce. We went thither, having long had an imbecile curiosity to know how nails and tacks are made. How startling the contrast between the slow movements, and tranquil, gloomy vastness of the cannon foundry, and the animation of the great rattling, roaring, crowded nail-works of Chess, Smyth, & Co., all glaring and flashing with light, with many tall chimneys pouring out black smoke and red blaze into the December evening! Noise? There is only one place in this world as noisy as a large nail-factory in full operation, and that is under the sheet at Niagara Falls. How should it be otherwise, when the factory is making many thousand nails a minute, and when every single nail, spike, brad, and tack is *cut* from a strip of cold iron, and headed by a blow upon cold iron? We saw one machine there pouring out shoemakers' brads at the rate of three thousand a minute, and it required the attendance of only one boy. They came rattling down a tin gutter as fast as meal comes from a mill. But to see this wonderful machine astonishes the stranger less than to see a girl in the packing-room who *weighs* and packs two thousand papers of tacks in nine hours. . . .

The crowning glory of Pittsburg is the "American Iron-Works" of Messrs. Jones and Laughlins. This establishment, which employs twenty-five hundred men, which has a coal mine at its back door and an iron mine on Lake Superior, which makes almost every large and difficult iron thing the country requires, which usually has "on hand" seven hundred thousand dollars' worth of finished work, is such a world of wonder that this whole magazine would not contain an adequate account of it. Here are machines ponderous and exact; here are a thousand ingenuities; here is the net result of all that man has done in iron masses during the whole period of his residence upon earth. What should there be here, too, but a specimen of what man can *undo* in iron, in the form of a great heap of rusty twisted rails from Georgia, so completely spoiled by General Sherman's troops that there was nothing to be done with them but sell them for old iron! . . .

We cannot linger among these wondrous "works" of the strong men of Pittsburg. The men themselves have claims upon our notice.

The masters of Pittsburg are mostly of the Scotch-Irish race, Presbyterians, keen and steady in the prosecution of their affairs, indifferent to pleasure, singularly devoid of the usual vanities and ostentations, proud to possess a solid and spacious factory, and to live in an insignificant house. There are no men of leisure in the town. Mr. George H. Thurston, President of the Pacific and Atlantic Telegraph Company, . . . assured us positively that there were not, in all the region which we call Pittsburg, three persons out of business who were physically capable of conducting business. The old men never think of "retiring," nor is there anything for them to retire to. The family tie being powerful in this race, the great firms are usually composed of near relatives, and generally survive the generation that founded them. Thus, the Fort Pitt Foundry, founded in 1803, has cast cannon for every war in which the United States has been engaged, and is now conducted by the worthy and talented nephews of the Charles Knap who made the establishment what it is. In the American Iron-Works, we find six partners, namely, the two chiefs, Messrs. Jones and Laughlin, two sons of one of these chiefs, and two brothers of the other,—a nice family party. Hence, there are few hired clerks in Pittsburg. These mighty "works" are managed with the minimum of expense. The visitor generally finds "the old man" bustling about the "works" in his cap and fustian jacket; while perhaps his eldest son is keeping the books, a son-in-law or nephew is making up the wages accounts, and a younger son is in the warehouse.

The conservative elements here are powerful, as they are in all communities in which families *endure*. Until very recently, in Pittsburg, it would have boded ill for a man to build a handsome house a few miles out of the smoke; and to this day it is said that a Pittsburg man of business who should publish a poem would find his "paper" doubted at the bank. "A good man, sir, but not practical." These excellent and strenuous men accuse themselves vehemently of a want of public spirit, and it is evident the charge is just. For the last few years, business has rushed in upon them like a torrent; and all their force having been expended in doing this business, they now awake to the fact, that a GREAT CITY is upon their hands, to be consolidated, organized, paved, policed, parked, purified, and adorned. They now feel that some of those iron kings, those great men of glass, oil, coal, salt, and clay, must leave business to their sons and nephews, and take hold of Pittsburg. . . .

Nothing in the life of Pittsburg is more striking to a visitor than the completeness of the cessation from labor at the close of the week. The Scotch-Irish race are strict Sabbatarians, and nothing goes on in Pittsburg on Sundays which it is possible to stop. Of all those five hundred tall chimneys, there will not usually be more than two that smoke on Sundays. During the week the town gets under such a headway of industry, that it takes all Saturday afternoon for it to come to a stand. The regular work ceases at noon, but the afternoon is spent in paying wages, grinding tools, cleaning up, making repairs, and getting ready for a fair start on Monday morning. By seven in the evening, the principal streets of Pittsburg are densely filled with washed men. They stroll about; they stand conversing in groups; they gather, in thick semicircles, about every shop-window that has a picture in it, or any bright or curious object; especially do they haunt the news-stands, which provide a free picture-gallery for them of Illustrated News, Comic Monthlies, and Funny Fellows. The men are so numerous, that the whole width of some of the streets is filled with them; and there is not a woman to be seen! Not a single petticoat among thousands of other coats! Yet no crowd could be more orderly and quiet. These men, after a week of intense monotony,—gazing at dull objects and doing the same dull act ten hours a day,—how hungry they seemed for some brightness to flash into their lives! How we longed to usher them all into some gorgeous scene, and give them a banquet of splendors! Mere brilliancy of color and light is transport, we should suppose, to a man who has been making nails or digging coal from Monday morning until Saturday noon.

7. Andrew Carnegie, How Young Men Can Succeed, 1885

It is well that young men should begin at the beginning and occupy the most subordinate positions. Many of the leading businessmen of Pittsburg had a serious responsibility thrust upon them at the very threshold of their career. They were introduced to the broom, and spent the first hours of their business lives sweeping out the office. I notice we have janitors and janitresses now in offices, and our young men unfortunately miss that salutary branch of a business education. But if by chance the professional sweeper is absent any morning the boy who has the genius of the future partner in him will not hesitate to try his hand at the broom. . . . I was one of those sweepers myself, and who do you suppose were my fellow sweepers? David McCargo, now superintendent of the Alleghany Valley Railroad; Robert Pitcairn, Superintendent of the Pennsylvania Railroad, and Mr. Moreland, City Attorney. We all took turns, two each morning did the sweeping; and now I remember Davie

Andrew Carnegie, "The Road to Business Success: A Talk to Young Men," address at Curry Commercial College, Pittsburgh, Pa., June 23, 1885, in Joseph Frazier Wall, ed., *The Andrew Carnegie Reader* (Pittsburgh: University of Pittsburgh Press, 1992), pp. 42–50. The nineteenth-century spelling of Pittsburg has been preserved in this document.

was so proud of his clean white shirt bosom that he used to spread over it an old silk bandana handkerchief which he kept for the purpose, and we other boys thought he was putting on airs. So he was. None of us had a silk handkerchief.

Assuming that you have all obtained employment and are fairly started, my advice to you is "aim high." I would not give a fig for the young man who does not already see himself the partner or the head of an important firm. Do not rest content for a moment in your thoughts as head clerk, or foreman, or general manager in any concern, no matter how extensive. Say each to yourself, "My place is at the top." *Be king in your dreams.* . . .

Let me indicate two or three conditions essential to success. Do not be afraid that I am going to moralize, or inflict a homily upon you. I speak upon the subject only from the view of a man of the world, desirous of aiding you to become successful businessmen. You all know that there is no genuine, praiseworthy success in life if you are not honest, truthful, fair-dealing. . . . I hope you will not take it amiss if I warn you against three of the gravest dangers which will beset you in your upward path.

The first and most seductive, and the destroyer of most young men, is the drinking of liquor. I am no temperance lecturer in disguise, but a man who knows and tells you what observation has proved to him; and I say to you that you are more likely to fail in your career from acquiring the habit of drinking liquor than from any, or all, the other temptations likely to assail you. . . .

The next greatest danger to a young business man in this community I believe to be that of speculation. When I was a telegraph operator here we had no Exchanges in the City, but the men or firms who speculated upon the Eastern Exchanges were necessarily known to the operators. They could be counted on the fingers of one hand. These men were not our citizens of first repute: they were regarded with suspicion. I have lived to see all of these speculators irreparably ruined men, bankrupt in money and bankrupt in character. There is scarcely an instance of a man who has made a fortune by speculation and kept it. Gamesters die poor, and there is certainly not an instance of a speculator who has lived a life creditable to himself, or advantageous to the community. . . .

The third and last danger against which I shall warn you is one which has wrecked many a fair craft which started well and gave promise of a prosperous voyage. It is the perilous habit of indorsing—all the more dangerous, inasmuch as it assails one generally in the garb of friendship. . . . You will as businessmen now and then probably become security for friends. Now, here is the line at which regard for the success of friends should cease and regard for your own honour begin. . . .

Assuming you are safe in regard to these your gravest dangers, the question now is how to rise from the subordinate position we have imagined you in, through the successive grades to the position for which you are, in my opinion, and, I trust, in your own, evidently intended. I can give you the secret. It lies mainly in this. Instead of the question, "What must I do for my employer?" substitute "What can I do?" Faithful and conscientious discharge of the duties assigned you is all very well, but the verdict in such cases generally is that you perform your present duties so well that you had better continue performing them. Now, young gentlemen, this will not do. It will not do for the coming partners. There must be something beyond this. We make Clerks, Bookkeepers, Treasurers, Bank Tellers of this class, and there they remain to the end of the chapter. The rising man must do something exceptional, and beyond the range of his special department. HE MUST ATTRACT ATTENTION. A shipping clerk, he may do so by discovering in an invoice an error with which he has nothing to do, and which has escaped the attention of the proper party. If a weighing clerk, he may save for the firm by doubting the adjustment of the scales and having them corrected, even if this be the province of the master mechanic. If a messenger boy, even he can lay the seed of promotion by going beyond the letter of his instructions in order to secure the desired reply. . . . Such an employee must perforce be thought of, and thought of kindly and well. It will not be long before his advice is asked in his special branch, and if the advice given be sound, it will soon be asked and taken upon questions of broader bearing. This means partnership; if not with present employers then with others. Your foot, in such a case, is upon the ladder; the amount of climbing done depends entirely upon yourself. . . .

There is one sure mark of the coming partner, the future millionnaire; his revenues always exceed his expenditures. He begins to save early, almost as soon as he begins to earn. No matter how little it may be possible to save, save that little. Invest it securely, not necessarily in bonds, but in anything which you have good reason to believe will be profitable, but no gambling with it, remember. A rare chance will soon present itself for investment. The little you have saved will prove the basis for an amount of credit utterly surprising to you. Capitalists trust the saving young man. . . .

You may grow important, or become discouraged when year by year you float on in subordinate positions. There is no doubt that it is becoming harder and harder as business gravitates more and more to immense concerns, for a young man without capital to get a start for himself, and in this city especially, where large capital is essential, it is unusually difficult. Still, let me tell you for your encouragement that there is no country in the world where able and energetic young men can so readily rise as this, nor any city where there is more room at the top. It has been impossible to meet the demand for capable, first-class bookkeepers (mark the adjectives), the supply has *never* been equal to the demand. . . .

And here is the prime condition of success, the great secret: concentrate your energy, thought, and capital exclusively upon the business in which you are engaged. Having begun in one line, resolve to fight it out on that line, to lead in it; adopt every improvement, have the best machinery, and know the most about it.

The concerns which fail are those which have scattered their capital, which means that they have scattered their brains also. They have investments in this, or that, or the other, here, there and everywhere. "Don't put all your eggs in one basket" is all wrong. I tell you "put all your eggs in one basket, and then watch that basket." Look round you and take notice; men who do that do not often fail. It is easy to watch and carry the one basket. It is trying to carry too many baskets that breaks most eggs in this country. He who carries three baskets must put one on his head, which is apt to tumble and trip him up. One fault of the American businessman is lack of concentration.

To summarize what I have said: Aim for the highest; never enter a barroom; do not touch liquor, or if at all only at meals; never speculate; never indorse beyond your surplus cash fund; make the firm's interest yours; break orders always to save owners; concentrate; put all your eggs in one basket, and watch that basket; expenditure always within revenue; lastly, be not impatient, for, as Emerson says, "no one can cheat you out of ultimate success but yourselves."

1. Andrew Carnegie Hails the Triumph of America, 1885

The old nations of the earth creep on at a snail's pace; the Republic thunders past with the rush of the express. The United States, the growth of a single century, has already reached the foremost rank among nations, and is destined soon to outdistance all others in the race. In population, in wealth, in annual savings, and in public credit; in freedom from debt, in agriculture, and in manufactures, America already leads the civilized world. . . .

Into the distant future of this giant nation we need not seek to peer; but if we cast a glance forward, as we have done backward, for only fifty years, and assume that in that short interval no serious change will occur, the astounding fact startles us that in 1935, fifty years from now, when many in manhood will still be living, one hundred and eighty millions of English-speaking republicans will exist under one flag and possess more than two hundred and fifty thousand millions of dollars, or fifty thousand millions sterling of national wealth. Eighty years ago the whole of America and Europe did not contain so many people; and, if Europe and America continue their normal growth, it will be little more than another eighty years ere the mighty Republic may boast as many loyal citizens as all the rulers of Europe combined, for before the year 1980 Europe and America will each have a population of about six hundred millions.

The causes which have led to the rapid growth and aggrandizement of this latest addition to the family of nations constitute one of the most interesting problems in the social history of mankind. What has brought about such stupendous results—so unparalleled a development of a nation within so brief a period! The most important factors in this problem are three: the ethnic character of the people, the topographical and climatic conditions under which they developed, and the influence of political institutions founded upon the equality of the citizen.

Certain writers in the past have maintained that the ethnic type of a people has less influence upon its growth as a nation than the conditions of life under which it is developing. The modern ethnologist knows better. We have only to imagine what America would be to-day if she had fallen in the beginning, into the hands of any other people than the colonizing British, to see how vitally important is this question of race. America was indeed fortunate in the seed planted upon her soil. With the exception of a few Dutch and French it was wholly British; and . . . the American of to-day remains true to this noble strain and is four-fifths British.

Andrew Carnegie, "The Upward March of Labor," in *Problems of Today: Wealth, Labor, Socialism* (Garden City, N.J.: Doubleday, 1933 [1908]), 43–46.

The special aptitude of this race for colonization, its vigor and enterprise, and its capacity for governing, although brilliantly manifested in all parts of the world, have never been shown to such advantage as in America. Freed here from the pressure of feudal institutions no longer fitted to their present development, and freed also from the dominion of the upper classes, which have kept the people at home from effective management of affairs and sacrificed the nation's interest for their own, as is the nature of classes, these masses of the lower ranks of Britons, called upon to found a new state, have proved themselves possessors of a positive genius for political administration.

The second, and perhaps equally important factor in the problem of the rapid advancement of this branch of the British race, is the superiority of the conditions under which it has developed. The home which has fallen to its lot, a domain more magnificent than has cradled any other race in the history of the world, presents no obstructions to unity—to the thorough amalgamation of its dwellers, North, South, East, and West, into one homogeneous mass—for the conformation of the American continent differs in important respects from that of every other great division of the globe. In Europe the Alps occupy a central position, forming on each side watersheds of rivers which flow into opposite seas. In Asia the Himalaya, the Hindu Kush, and the Altai Mountains divide the continent, rolling from their sides many great rivers which pour their floods into widely separated oceans. But in North America the mountains rise up on each coast, and from them the land slopes gradually into great central plains, forming an immense basin where the rivers flow together in one valley, offering to commerce many thousand miles of navigable streams. The map thus proclaims the unity of North America, for in this great central basin, three million square miles in extent, free from impassable rivers or mountain barriers great enough to hinder free intercourse, political integration is a necessity and consolidation a certainty. . . .

The unity of the American people is further powerfully promoted by the foundation upon which the political structure rests, the equality of the citizen. There is not one shred of privilege to be met with anywhere in all the laws. One man's right is every man's right. The flag is the guarantor and symbol of equality. The people are not emasculated by being made to feel that their own country decrees their inferiority, and holds them unworthy of privileges accorded to others. No ranks, no titles, no hereditary dignities, and therefore no classes. Suffrage is universal, and votes are of equal weight. Representatives are paid, and political life and usefulness thereby thrown open to all. Thus there is brought about a community of interests and aims which a Briton, accustomed to monarchical and aristocratic institutions, dividing the people into classes with separate interests, aims, thoughts, and feelings, can only with difficulty understand.

The free common school system of the land is probably, after all, the greatest single power in the unifying process which is producing the new American race. Through the crucible of a good common English education, furnished free by the State, pass the various racial elements—children of Irishmen, Germans, Italians, Spaniards, and Swedes, side by side with the native American, all to be fused into one, in language, in thought, in feeling, and in patriotism. The Irish boy loses his brogue, and the German child learns English. The sympathies suited to the feudal systems of Europe, which they inherit from their fathers, pass off as dross, leaving behind the pure gold of the only noble political creed: "All men are created free and equal." Taught now to live and work for the common weal, and not for the maintenance of a royal family or an overbearing aristocracy, not for the continuance of a social system which ranks them beneath an arrogant class of drones, children of Russian and German serfs, of Irish evicted tenants, Scotch crofters, and other victims of feudal tyranny, are transmuted into republican Americans, and are made one in love for a country which provides equal rights and privileges for all her children. There is no class so intensely patriotic, so wildly devoted to the Republic as the naturalized citizen and his child, for little does the native-born citizen know of the values of rights which have never been denied. Only the man born abroad, like myself, under institutions which insult him at his birth, can know the full meaning of Republicanism. . . .

It is these causes which render possible the growth of a great homogeneous nation, alike in race, language, literature, interest, patriotism—an empire of such overwhelming power and proportions as to require neither army nor navy to ensure its safety, and a people so educated and advanced as to value the victories of peace.

The student of American affairs to-day sees no influences at work save those which make for closer and closer union. The Republic has solved the problem of governing large areas by adopting the federal, or home-rule system, and has proved to the world that the freest self-government of the parts produces the strongest government of the whole.

2. Henry George Dissects the Paradox of Capitalist Growth, 1879

The present century has been marked by a prodigious increase in wealth-producing power. The utilization of steam and electricity, the introduction of improved processes and labor-saving machinery, the greater subdivision and grander scale of production, the wonderful facilitation of exchanges, have multiplied enormously the effectiveness of labor.

At the beginning of this marvelous era it was natural to expect, and it was expected, that labor-saving inventions would lighten the toil and improve the condition of the laborer; that the enormous increase in the power of producing wealth would make real poverty a thing of the past. Could a man of the last century— a Franklin or a Priestley—have seen, in a vision of the future, the steamship taking the place of the sailing vessel, the railroad train of the wagon, the reaping machine of the scythe, the threshing machine of the flail; could he have heard the throb of the engines that in obedience to human will, and for the satisfaction of human desire, exert a power greater than that of all the men and all the beasts of burden of the earth combined; could he have seen the forest tree transformed into finished lumber—into doors, sashes, blinds, boxes or barrels, with hardly the touch of a human hand; the great workshops where boots and shoes are turned out by the case with less labor than the old-fashioned cobbler could have put on a sole; the factories where, under the eye of a girl, cotton becomes cloth faster than hundreds of

Henry George, *Progress and Poverty* in *Works,* Vol. I (New York: Doubleday, 1904), 3–8, 10–13.

stalwart weavers could have turned it out with their handlooms; could he have seen steam hammers shaping mammoth shafts and mighty anchors, and delicate machinery making tiny watches; the diamond drill cutting through the heart of the rocks, and coal oil sparing the whale; could he have realized the enormous saving of labor resulting from improved facilities of exchange and communication—sheep killed in Australia eaten fresh in England, and the order given by the London banker in the afternoon executed in San Francisco in the morning of the same day; could he have conceived of the hundred thousand improvements which these only suggest, what would he have inferred as to the social condition of mankind? . . .

. . . Out of these bounteous material conditions he would have seen arising, as necessary sequences, moral conditions realizing the golden age of which mankind has always dreamed. Youth no longer stunted and starved; age no longer harried by avarice; the child at play with the tiger; the man with the muck-rake drinking in the glory of the stars. Foul things fled, fierce things tame; discord turned to harmony! For how could there be greed where all had enough? How could the vice, the crime, the ignorance, the brutality, that spring from poverty and the fear of poverty, exist where poverty had vanished? Who should crouch where all were freemen; who oppress where all were peers? . . .

Now, however, we are coming into collision with facts which there can be no mistaking. From all parts of the civilized world come complaints of industrial depression; of labor condemned to involuntary idleness; of capital massed and wasting; of pecuniary distress among business men; of want and suffering and anxiety among the working classes. All the dull, deadening pain, all the keen, maddening anguish, that to great masses of men are involved in the words "hard times," afflict the world to-day. This state of things, common to communities differing so widely in situation, in political institutions, in fiscal and financial systems, in density of population and in social organization, can hardly be accounted for by local causes. . . .

That there is a common cause, and that it is either what we call material progress or something closely connected with material progress, becomes more than an inference when it is noted that the phenomena we class together and speak of as industrial depression are but intensifications of phenomena which always accompany material progress, and which show themselves more clearly and strongly as material progress goes on.

Just as . . . a community realizes the conditions which all civilized communities are striving for, and advances in the scale of material progress—just as closer settlement and a more intimate connection with the rest of the world, and greater utilization of labor-saving machinery, make possible greater economies in production and exchange, and wealth in consequence increases, not merely in the aggregate, but in proportion to population—so does poverty take a darker aspect. Some get an infinitely better and easier living, but others find it hard to get a living at all. The "tramp" comes with the locomotive, and almshouses and prisons are as surely the marks of "material progress" as are costly dwellings, rich warehouses, and magnificent churches. Upon streets lighted with gas and patrolled by uniformed policemen, beggars wait for the passer-by, and in the shadow of college, and library, and museum, are gathering the more hideous Huns and fiercer Vandals of whom Macaulay prophesied.

This fact—the great fact that poverty and all its concomitants show themselves in communities just as they develop into the conditions toward which material progress tends—proves that the social difficulties existing wherever a certain stage of progress has been reached, do not arise from local circumstances, but are, in some way or another, engendered by progress itself.

And, unpleasant as it may be to admit it, it is at last becoming evident that the enormous increase in productive power which has marked the present century and is still going on with accelerating ratio, has no tendency to extirpate poverty or to lighten the burdens of those compelled to toil. It simply widens the gulf between Dives and Lazarus, and makes the struggle for existence more intense. The march of invention has clothed mankind with powers of which a century ago the boldest imagination could not have dreamed. But in factories where labor-saving machinery has reached its most wonderful development, little children are at work; wherever the new forces are anything like fully utilized, large classes are maintained by charity or live on the verge of recourse to it; amid the greatest accumulations of wealth, men die of starvation, and puny infants suckle dry breasts; while everywhere the greed of gain, the worship of wealth, shows the force of the fear of want. The promised land flies before us like the mirage. The fruits of the tree of knowledge turn as we grasp them to apples of Sodom that crumble at the touch.

It is true that wealth has been greatly increased, and that the average of comfort, leisure, and refinement has been raised; but these gains are not general. In them the lowest class do not share. I do not mean that the condition of the lowest class has nowhere nor in anything been improved; but that there is nowhere any improvement which can be credited to increase productive power. I mean that the tendency of what we call material progress is in nowise to improve the condition of the lowest class in the essentials of healthy, happy human life. Nay, more, that it is still further to depress the condition of the lowest class. The new forces, elevating in their nature though they be, do not act upon the social fabric from underneath, as was for a long time hoped and believed, but strike it at a point intermediate between top and bottom. It is as though an immense wedge were being forced, not underneath society, but through society. Those who are above the point of separation are elevated, but those who are below are crushed down. . . .

This association of poverty with progress is the great enigma of our times. It is the central fact from which spring industrial, social, and political difficulties that perplex the world, and with which statesmanship and philanthropy and education grapple in vain. From it come the clouds that overhand the future of the most progressive and self-reliant nations. It is the riddle which the Sphinx of Fate puts to our civilization, and which not to answer is to be destroyed. So long as all the increased wealth which modern progress brings goes but to build up great fortunes, to increase luxury and make sharper the contrast between the House of Have and the House of Want, progress is not real and cannot be permanent. The reaction must come. The tower leans from its foundations, and every new story but hastens the final catastrophe. To educate men who must be condemned to poverty, is but to make them restive; to base on a state of most glaring social inequality political institutions under which men are theoretically equal, is to stand a pyramid on its apex.

3. The Reverend Alexander Lewis Offers an Ode to Upward Mobility, 1902

There is always a way to rise, my boy,
Always a way to advance;
Yet the road that leads to Mount Success
Does not pass by the way of Chance,
But goes through the stations of Work and
    Strive,
through the valley of Persevere;
And the man that succeeds while others fail,
Must be willing to pay most dear.

For there's always a way to fall my boy,
Always a way to slide,
And the men you find at the foot of the hill
All sought for an easy ride.
So on and up, though the road be rough,
And the storms come thick and fast;
There is room at the top for the man who tries,
And victory comes at last.

4. Mark Twain Satirizes the Great American Myth, 1879

Poor Little Stephen Girard

The man lived in Philadelphia who, when young and poor, entered a bank, and says he: "Please, sir, don't you want a boy?" And the stately personage said: "No, little boy, I don't want a little boy." The little boy, whose heart was too full for utterance, chewing a piece of licorice stick he had bought with a cent stolen from his good and pious aunt, with sobs plainly audible, and with great globules of water rolling down his cheeks, glided silently down the marble steps of the bank. Bending his noble form, the bank man dodged behind a door, for he thought the little boy was going to shy a stone at him. But the little boy picked up something, and stuck it in his poor but ragged jacket. "Come here, little boy," and the little boy did come here; and the bank man said: "Lo, what pickest thou up?" And he answered and replied: "A pin." And the bank man said: "Little boy, are you good?" and he said he was. And the bank man said: "How do you vote?—excuse me, do you go to Sunday school?" and he said he did. Then the bank man took down a pen made of pure gold, and flowing with pure ink, and he wrote on a piece of paper, "St. Peter;" and he asked the little boy what it stood for, and he said "Salt Peter," Then the bank man said it meant "Saint Peter." The little boy said; "Oh!"

Reverend Alexander Lewis, *Manhood Making, Studies in the Elemental Principles of Success* (Boston: Pilgrim Press, 1902).

Mark Twain, "Poor Little Stephen Girard," in Anna Randall-Diehl, ed., *Carleton's Popular Readings* (New York, 1879), 183–184.

Then the bank man took the little boy to his bosom, and the little boy said, "Oh!" again, for he squeezed him. Then the bank man took the little boy into partnership, and gave him half the profits and all the capital, and he married the bank man's daughter, and now all he has is all his, and all his own too.

My uncle told me this story, and I spent six weeks in picking up pins in front of a bank. I expected the bank man would call me in and say: "Little boy, are you good?" and I was going to say "Yes"; and when he asked me what "St. John" stood for, I was going to say "Salt John." But the bank man wasn't anxious to have a partner, and I guess the daughter was a son, for one day says he to me: "Little boy, what's that you're picking up?" Says I, awful meekly, "Pins." Says he: "Let's see 'em." And he took 'em, and I took off my cap, all ready to go in the bank, and become a partner, and marry his daughter. But I didn't get an invitation. He said: "Those pins belong to the bank, and if I catch you hanging around here any more I'll set the dog on you!" Then I left, and the mean old fellow kept the pins. Such is life as I find it.

5. The Purposes and Program of the Knights of Labor, 1878

The recent alarming development and aggression of aggregated wealth, which, unless checked, will inevitably lead to the pauperization and hopeless degradation of the toiling masses, render it imperative, if we desire to enjoy the blessings of life, that a check should be placed upon its power and upon unjust accumulation, and a system adopted which will secure to the laborer the fruits of his toil; and as this much-desired object can only be accomplished by the thorough unification of labor, and the united efforts of those who obey the divine injunction that "in the sweat of thy brow shalt thou eat bread," we have formed the [*name of local assembly*] with a view to securing the organization and direction, by co-operative effort, of the power of the industrial classes; and we submit to the world the objects sought to be accomplished by our organization, calling upon all who believe in securing "the greatest good to the greatest number" to aid and assist us.

Objectives

I. To bring within the folds of organization every department of productive industry, making knowledge a standpoint for action, and industrial, moral worth, not wealth, the true standard of individual and national greatness.

II. To secure to the toilers a proper share of the wealth that they create; more of the leisure that rightfully belongs to them; more [social] advantages, more of the benefits, privileges, and emoluments of the world; in a word, all those rights and privileges necessary to make them capable of enjoying, appreciating, defending, and perpetuating the blessings of good government.

III. To arrive at the true condition of the producing masses in their educational, moral, and financial condition, by demanding from the various governments the establishment of bureaus of Labor Statistics.

T. V. Powderly, *Thirty Years of Labor* (Columbus, Ohio: Excelssor Publishing House, 1890), 243–246.

IV. The establishment of co-operative institutions, productive and distributive.

V. The reserving of the public lands—the heritage of the people—for the actual settler. Not another acre [is to be allocated] for railroads or speculators.

VI. The abrogation of all laws that do not bear equally upon capital and labor, the removal of unjust technicalities, delays, and discriminations in the administration of justice, and the adopting of measures providing for the health and safety of those engaged in mining, manufacturing, or building pursuits.

VII. The enactment of laws to compel chartered corporations to pay their employees weekly, in full, for labor performed during the preceding week, in the lawful money of the country.

VIII. The enactment of laws giving mechanics and laborers a first lien on their work for their full wages.

IX. The abolishment of the contract system on national, state, and municipal work.

X. The substitution of arbitration for strikes, whenever and wherever employers and employees are willing to meet on equitable grounds.

XI. The prohibition of the employment of children in workshops, mines and factories before attaining their fourteenth year.

XII. To abolish the system of letting out by contract the labor of convicts in our prisons and reformatory institutions.

XIII. To secure for both sexes equal pay for equal work.

XIV. The reduction of the hours of labor to eight per day, so that the laborers may have more time for social enjoyment and intellectual improvement, and be enabled to reap the advantages conferred by the labor-saving machinery which their brains have created.

XV. To prevail upon governments to establish a purely national circulating medium, based upon the faith and resources of the nation, and issued directly to the people, without the intervention of any system of banking corporations, which money shall be a legal tender in payment of all debts, public or private.

6. A Trade Union Official Enunciates a Restrictive AFL Policy Toward Women Workers, 1897

The invasion of the crafts by women has been developing for years amid irritation and injury to the workman. The right of the woman to win honest bread is accorded on all sides, but with craftsmen it is an open question whether this manifestation is of a healthy social growth or not.

The rapid displacement of men by women in the factory and workshop has to be met sooner or later, and the question is forcing itself upon the leaders and thinkers among the labor organizations of the land.

Edward O'Donnell, "Women as Bread Winners—the Error of the Age," *American Federationist* 4, No. 8 (October 1897). As edited in Eileen Boris and Nelson Lichtenstein, eds., *Major Problems in the History of American Workers: Documents and Essays* (Lexington, Mass.: D. C. Heath, 1991), 232–234. Reprinted by permission of Houghton Mifflin Company.

Is it a pleasing indication of progress to see the father, the brother and the son displaced as the bread winner by the mother, sister and daughter?

Is not this evolutionary backslide, which certainly modernizes the present wage system in vogue, a menace to prosperity—a foe to our civilized pretensions? . . .

The growing demand for female labor is not founded upon philanthropy, as those who encourage it would have sentimentalists believe; it does not spring from the milk of human kindness. It is an insidious assault upon the home; it is the knife of the assassin, aimed at the family circle—the divine injunction. It debars the man through financial embarrassment from family responsibility, and physically, mentally and socially excludes the woman equally from nature's dearest impulse. Is this the demand of civilized progress; is it the desire of Christian dogma? . . .

Capital thrives not upon the peaceful, united, contented family circle; rather are its palaces, pleasures and vices fostered and increased upon the disruption, ruin or abolition of the home, because with its decay and ever glaring privation, manhood loses its dignity, its backbone, its aspirations. . . .

To combat these impertinent inclinations, dangerous to the few, the old and well-tried policy of divide and conquer is invoked, and to our own shame, it must be said, one too often renders blind aid to capital in its warfare upon us. The employer in the magnanimity of his generosity will give employment to the daughter, while her two brothers are weary because of their daily tramp in quest of work. The father, who has a fair, steady job, sees not the infamous policy back of the flattering propositions. Somebody else's daughter is called in in the same manner, by and by, and very soon the shop or factory are full of women, while their fathers have the option of working for the same wages or a few cents more, or take their places in the large army of unemployed. . . .

College professors and graduates tell us that this is the natural sequence of industrial development, an integral part of economic claim.

Never was a greater fallacy uttered of more poisonous import. It is false and wholly illogical. The great demand for women and their preference over men does not spring from a desire to elevate humanity; at any rate that is not its trend.

The wholesale employment of women in the various handicrafts must gradually unsex them, as it most assuredly is demoralizing them, or stripping them of that modest demeanor that lends a charm to their kind, while it numerically strengthens the multitudinous army of loafers, paupers, tramps and policemen, for no man who desires honest employment, and can secure it, cares to throw his life away upon such a wretched occupation as the latter.

The employment of women in the mechanical departments is encouraged because of its cheapness and easy manipulation, regardless of the consequent perils; and for no other reason. The generous sentiment enveloping this inducement is of criminal design, since it comes from a thirst to build riches upon the dismemberment of the family or the hearthstone cruelly dishonored. . . .

But somebody will say, would you have women pursue lives of shame rather than work? Certainly not; it is to the alarming introduction of women into the mechanical industries, hitherto enjoyed by the sterner sex, at a wage uncommandable by them, that leads so many into that deplorable pursuit.

ESSAYS

Work Rules and Manliness in the World
of the Nineteen-Century Craftsman

DAVID MONTGOMERY

"In an industrial establishment which employs say from 500 to 1000 workmen, there will be found in many cases at least twenty to thirty different trades," wrote Frederick Winslow Taylor in his famous critique of the practices of industrial management which were then in vogue.

> The workmen in each of these trades have had their knowledge handed down to them by word of mouth. . . . This mass of rule-of-thumb or traditional knowledge may be said to be the principle asset or possession of every tradesman. . . . [The] foremen and superintendents . . . recognize the task before them as that of inducing each workman to use his best endeavors, his hardest work, all his traditional knowledge, his skill, his ingenuity, and his good-will—in a word, his "initiative," so as to yield the largest possible return to his employer."

Big Bill Haywood put the same point somewhat more pungently, when he declared: "The manager's brains are under the workman's cap."

Both Taylor and Haywood were describing the power which certain groups of workers exercised over the direction of production processes at the end of the nineteenth century, a power which the scientific management movement strove to abolish, and which the Industrial Workers of the World wished to enlarge and extend to all workers. It is important to note that both men found the basis of workers' power in the superiority of their knowledge over that of the factory owners. It is even more important to note that they were referring not to "pre-industrial" work practices, but to the factory itself. . . .

My concern here [is] with the patterns of behavior which took shape in the second and third generations of industrial experience, largely among workers whose world had been fashioned from their youngest days by smoky mills, congested streets, recreation as a week-end affair and toil at the times and the pace dictated by the clock (except when a more or less lengthy layoff meant no work at all). It as such workers, the veterans, if you will, of industrial life, with whom Taylor was

---

David Montgomery, "Workers' Control of Machine Production in the Nineteenth Century," *Labor History,* 17 (Fall 1976): pp. 485–509. Reprinted by permission of Taylor & Francis, Ltd., http://www.tandf.co.uk/journals.

preoccupied. They had internalized the industrial sense of time, they were highly disciplined in both individual and collective behavior, and they regarded both an extensive division of labor and machine production as their natural environments. But they had often fashioned from these attributes neither the docile obedience of automatons, nor the individualism of the "upwardly mobile," but a form of control of productive processes which became increasingly collective, deliberate and aggressive, until American employers launched a partially successful counterattack under the banners of scientific management and the open shop drive.

Workers' control of production, however, was not a condition or state of affairs which existed at any point in time, but a struggle, a chronic battle in industrial life which assumed a variety of forms. Those forms may be treated as successive stages in a pattern of historical evolution, though one must always remember that the stages overlapped each other chronologically in different industries, or even at different localities within the same industry, and that each successive stage incorporated the previous one, rather than replacing it. The three levels of development which appeared in the second half of the nineteenth century were those characterized by (1) the functional autonomy of the craftsman, (2) the union work rule, and (3) mutual support of diverse trades in rule enforcement and sympathetic strikes. Each of these levels will be examined here in turn, then in conclusion some observations will be made on the impact of scientific management and the open shop drive on the patterns of behavior which they represented.

The functional autonomy of craftsmen rested on both their superior knowledge, which made them self-directing at their tasks, and the supervision which they gave to one or more helpers. Iron molders, glass blowers, coopers, paper machine tenders, locomotive engineers, mule spinners, boiler makers, pipe fitters, typographers, jiggermen in potteries, coal miners, iron rollers, puddlers and heaters, the operators of McKay or Goodyear stitching machines in shoe factories, and, in many instances, journeymen machinists and fitters in metal works exercised broad discretion in the direction of their own work and that of their helpers. They often hired and fired their own helpers and paid the latter some fixed portion of their own earnings.

James J. Davis, who was to end up as Warren Harding's Secretary of Labor, learned the trade of puddling iron by working as his father's helper in Sharon, Pennsylvania. "None of us ever went to school and learned the chemistry of it from books," he recalled. "We learned the trick by doing it, standing with our faces in the scorching heat while our hands puddled the metal in its glaring bath." His first job, in fact, had come at the age of twelve, when an aged puddler devised a scheme to enable him to continue the physically arduous exertion of the trade by taking on a boy (twelve-year old Davis) to relieve the helper of mundane tasks like stoking the furnace, so that the helper in turn could assume a larger share of the taxing work of stirring the iron as it "came to nature." By the time Davis felt he had learned enough to master his own furnace, he had to leave Sharon, because furnaces passed from father to son, and Davis' father was not yet ready to step down. As late as 1900, when Davis was living at home while attending business college after having been elected to public office, he took over his father's furnace every afternoon, through an arrangement the two had worked out between themselves.

The iron rollers of the Columbus Iron Works, in Ohio, have left us a clear record of how they managed their trade in the minute books of their local union from 1873 to 1876. The three twelve-man rolling teams, which constituted the union, negotiated a single tonnage rate with the company for each specific rolling job the company undertook. The workers then decided collectively, among themselves, what portion of that rate should go to each of them (and the shares were far from equal, ranging from 19¼ cents, out of the negotiated $1.13 a ton, for the roller, to 5 cents for the runout hooker), how work should be allocated among them, how many rounds on the rolls should be undertaken per day, what special arrangements should be made for the fiercely hot labors of the hookers during the summer, and how members should be hired and progress through the various ranks of the gang. To put it another way, all the boss did was to buy the equipment and raw materials and sell the finished product. . . .

Three aspects of the moral code, in which the craftsmen's autonomy was protectively enmeshed, deserve close attention. First, on most jobs there was a stint, an output quota fixed by the workers themselves. As the laments of scientific management's apostles about workers "soldiering" and the remarkable 1904 survey by the Commissioner of Labor, *Regulation and Restriction of Output*, made clear, stints flourished as widely without unions as with them. Abram Hewitt testified in 1867 that his puddlers in New Jersey, who were not unionized, worked 11 turns per week (5½ days), made three heats per turn, and put 450 pounds of iron in each charge, all by arrangement among themselves. Thirty-five years later a stint still governed the trade, though a dramatic improvement in puddling furnaces was reflected in union rules which specified 11 turns with five heats per turn and 550 pounds per charge (a 104% improvement in productivity), while some nonunion mill workers followed the same routine but boiled bigger charges.

Stints were always under pressure from the employers, and were often stretched over the course of time by the combined force of competition among employers and improving technology. In this instance, productivity under union rules expanded more than three per cent annually over three and half decades. But workers clung doggedly to the practice, and used their superior knowledge both to determine how much they should do and to outwit employers' efforts to wring more production out of them. In a farm equipment factory studied in 1902, for example, the machine shop, polishing department, fitting department and blacksmith shop all had fixed stints, which made each group of workers average very similar earnings despite the fact that all departments were on piecework. . . . Similarly, Taylor's colleague Carl Barth discovered a planer operator who avoided exceeding the stint while always looking busy, by simply removing the cutting tool from his machine from time to time, while letting it run merrily on.

"There is in every workroom a fashion, a habit of work," wrote efficiency consultant Henry Gantt, "and the new workers follows that fashion, for it isn't respectable not to." A quiver full of epithets awaited the deviant: 'hog,' 'hogger-in,' 'leader,' 'rooter,' 'chaser,' 'rusher,' 'runner,' 'swift,' 'boss's pet,' to mention some politer versions. And when a whole factory gained a reputation for feverish work, disdainful craftsmen would describe its occupants, as one did of the Gisholt turret lathe works, as comprised half "of farmers, and the other half, with few exceptions, of horse thieves." On the other hand, those who held fast to the carefully measured stint, despite the curses of their employers and the lure of higher earnings, depicted themselves as sober and trustworthy masters of their trades. Unlimited output led to slashed piece rates, irregular employment, drink and debaucher, they argued. Rationally restricted output, however, reflected "unselfish brotherhood," personal dignity, and "cultivation of the mind."

Second, as this language vividly suggests, the craftsmen's ethical code demanded a "manly" bearing toward the boss. Few words enjoyed more popularity in the nineteenth century than this honorific, with all its connotations of dignity, respectability, defiant egalitarianism, and patriarchal male supremacy. The worker who merited it refused to cower before the foreman's glares—in fact, often would not work at all when a boss was watching. . . .

Finally, "manliness" toward one's fellow workers was an important as it was toward the owners. "Undermining or conniving" at a brother's job was a form of hoggish behavior as objectional as running more than one machine, or otherwise doing the work that belonged to two men. Union rules commanded the expulsion of members who performed such "dirty work," in order to secure employment or advancement for themselves. When the members of the Iron Heaters and Rollers Union at a Philadelphia mill learned in 1875 that one of their brothers had been fired "for dissatisfaction in regard to his management of the mill," and that another member had "undermined" the first with the superintendent and been promised his rolls, the delinquent was expelled from the lodge, along with a lodge member who defended him, and everyone went on strike to demand the immediate discharge of both excommunicates by the firm.

In short, a simple technological explanation for the control exercised by nineteenth-century craftsmen will not suffice. Technical knowledge acquired on the job was embedded in a mutualistic ethical code, also acquired on the job, and together these attributes provided skilled workers with considerable autonomy at their work and powers of resistance to the wishes of their employers. On the other hand, it was technologically possible for the worker's autonomy to be used in individualistic ways, which might promote his own mobility and identify his interests with those of the owner. The ubiquitous practice of subcontracting encouraged this tendency. In the needle trades, the long established custom of a tailor's taking work home to his family was transformed by his employment of other piece workers into the iniquitous "sweat shop" system. Among iron molders, the "berkshire" system expanded rapidly after 1850, as individual molders hired whole teams of helpers to assist them in producing a multitude of castings. Carpenters and bricklayers were lured into piece work systems of petty exploitations, and other forms of subcontracting flourished in stone quarrying, iron mining, anthracite mining, and even in railroad locomotive works, where entire units of an engine's construction were let out to the machinist who filed the lowest bid, and who then hired a crew to assist him in making and fitting the parts.

Subcontracting practices readily undermined both stints and the mutualistic ethic (though contractors were known to fix stints for their own protection in both garment and locomotive works), and they tended to flood many trades with trained, or semi-trained, workers who undercut wages and work standards. Their spread encouraged many craftsmen to move beyond reliance on their functional autonomy to the next higher level of craft control, the enactment and enforcement of union work rules. In one respect, union rules simply codified the autonomy I have already described. In fact, because they were often written down and enforced by joint action, union rules have a visibility to historians, which has made me resort to them already for evidence in the discussion of autonomy per se. But this intimate historical relationship between customary workers' autonomy and the union rule should not blind us to the fact that the latter represents a significant new stage of development.

The work rules of unions were referred to by their members as "legislation." The phrase denotes a shift from spontaneous to deliberate collective action, from a group ethical code to formal rules and sanctions, and from resistance to employers' pretentions to control over them. In some unions the rules were rather simple. The International Association of Machinists, for example, like its predecessors the Machinists and Blacksmiths' International Union and the many machinists' local assemblies of the Knights of Labor, simply specified a fixed term of apprenticeship for any prospective journeyman, established a standard wage for the trade, prohibited helpers of handymen from performing journeymen's work, and forbade any member from running more than one machine at a time or accepting any form of piece work payment.

Other unions had much detailed and complex rules. There were, for example, sixty-six "Rules for Working" in the by-laws of the window-glass workers' Local Assembly 300 of the Knights of Labor. They specified that full crews had to be present "at each pot setting," that skimming could be done only at the beginning of blowing and at meal time, that blowers and gatherers should not "work faster than at the rate of nine rollers per hour," and that the "standard size of single strength rollers" should "be 40 × 58 to cut 38 × 56." No work was to be performed on Thanksgiving Day, Christmas, Decoration Day or Washington's Birthday, and no blower, gatherer or cutter could work between June 15 and September 15. In other words, during the summer months the union ruled that the fires were to be out. In 1884 the local assembly waged a long and successful strike to preserve its limit of 48 boxes of glass a week, a rule which its members considered the key to the dignity and welfare of the trade.

Nineteenth-century work rules were not ordinarily negotiated with employers or embodied in a contract. From the 1860s onward it became increasingly common for standard *wages* to be negotiated with employers or their associations, rather than fixed unilaterally as unions had tried earlier, but working rules changed more slowly. They were usually adopted unilaterally by local unions, or by the delegates to a national convention, and enforced by the refusal of the individual member to obey any command from an employer which violated them. Hopefully, the worker's refusal would be supported by the joint action of his shop mates, but if it was not, he was honor bound to pack his tool box and walk out alone, rather than break the union's laws. . . .

On the other hand, the autonomy of craftsmen which was codified in union rules was clearly not individualistic. Craftsmen were unmistakably and consciously group-made men, who sought to pull themselves upward by their collective boot straps. As unions waxed stronger after 1886, the number of strikes to enforce union rules grew steadily. It was, however, in union legislation against subcontracting that both the practical and ideological aspects of the conflict between group solidarity and upwardly mobile individualism became most evident, for these rules sought to regulate in the first instance not the employers' behavior, but that of the workers themselves. Thus the Iron Molders Union attacked the "berkshire" system by rules forbidding any of its members to employ a helper for any other purpose than "to skim, shake out and to cut sand," or to pay a helper out of his own earnings. In 1867, when 8,615 out of some 10,400 known molders in the country were union members, the national union legislated further that no member was allowed to go to work earlier than seven o'clock in the morning. During the 1880s the Brick Layers' Union checked subcontracting by banning its members from working for any contractor who could not raise enough capital to buy his own bricks. All building trades' unions instructed their members not to permit contractors to work with tools along side with them. . . . All such regulations secured the group welfare of the workers involved by sharply rejecting society's enticements to become petty entrepreneurs, clarifying and intensifying the division of labor at the work place, and sharpening the line between employer and employee.

Where a trade was well unionized, a committee in each shop supervised the enforcement in that plant of the rules and standard wage which the union had adopted for the trade as a whole. The craft union and the craft local assembly of the Knights of Labor were forms of organization well adapted to such regulatory activities. The members were legislating, on matters on which they were unchallenged experts, rules which only their courage and solidarity could enforce. On one hand, the craft form of organization linked their personal interests to those of the trade, rather than those of the company in which they worked, while, on the other hand, their efforts to enforce the same rules on all of their employers, where they were successful, created at least a few islands of order in the nineteenth-century's economic ocean of anarchic competition.

Labor organizations of the late nineteenth century struggled persistently to transform worker's struggles to manage their own work from spontaneous to deliberate actions, just as they tried to subject wage strikes and efforts to shorten the working day to their conscious regulation. "The trade union movement is one of reason, one of deliberation, depending entirely upon the voluntary and sovereign actions of its members," declared the executive Council of the AFL. Only through "thorough organization," to use a favorite phrase of the day, was it possible to enforce a trade's work rules throughout a factory, mine, or construction site. Despite the growing number of strikes over union rules and union recognition in the late 1880s, the enforcement of workers' standards of control spread more often through the daily self-assertion of craftsmen on the job than through large and dramatic strikes.

Conversely, strikes over wage reductions at times involved thinly disguised attacks by employers on craftsmen's job controls. Fall River's textile manufacturers in 1870 and the Hocking Valley coal operators in 1884, to cite only two examples, deliberately foisted severe wage reductions on their highly unionized workers in order to provoke strikes. The owners' hope was that in time hunger would force their employees to abandon union membership, and thus free the companies' hands to change production methods. As the treasurer of one Fall River mill testified in 1870: "I think the question with the spinners was not wages, but whether they or the manufacturers should rule. For the last six or eight years they have ruled Fall River." Defeat in a strike temporarily broke the union's control, which had grown through steady recruiting and rule enforcement during years which were largely free of work stoppages.

The third level of control struggles emerged when different trades lent each other support in their battles to enforce union rules and recognition. An examination of the strike statistics gathered by the U.S. Commissioner of Labor for the period 1881–1905 reveals the basis patterns of this development. Although there had been a steady increase in both the number and size of strikes between 1881 and 1886, the following 12 years saw a reversal of that growth, as stoppages became both smaller and increasingly confined to skilled crafts (except in 1894). With that change came three important and interrelated trends. First, the proportion of strikes called by unions rose sharply in comparison to spontaneous strikes. Nearly half of all strikes between 1881 and 1886 had occurred without union sanction or aid. In the seven years beginning with 1887 more than two-thirds of each year's strikes were deliberately called by a union, and in 1891 almost 75 per cent of the strikes were official.

Secondly, as strikes became more deliberate and unionized, the proportion of strikes which dealt mainly with wages fell abruptly. Strikes to enforce union rules, enforce recognition of the union, and protect its members grew from 10 per cent of the total or less before 1885 to the level of 19–20 per cent between 1891 and 1893. Spontaneous strikes and strikes of laborers and factory operatives had almost invariably been aimed at increasing wages or preventing wage reductions, with the partial exception of 1886 when 20 per cent of all strikes had been over hours. The more highly craftsmen became organized, however, the more often they struck and were locked out over work rules.

Third, unionization of workers grew on the whole faster than strike participation. The ratio of strike participants to membership in labor organizations fell almost smoothly from 109 in 1881 to 24 in 1888, rose abruptly in 1890 and 1891 (to 71 and 86, respectively), then resumed its downward trend to 36 in 1898, interrupted, or course, by a leap to 182 in 1894. In a word, calculation and organization were the dominant tendencies in strike activity, just as they were in the evolution of work rules during the nineteenth century. But the assertion of deliberate control through formal organization was sustained not only by high levels of militancy (a persistently high propensity to strike), but also by remarkably aggressive mutual support, which sometimes took the form of the unionization of all grades of workers within a single industry, but more often appeared in the form of sympathetic strikes involving members of different trade unions.

Joint organization of all grades of workers seemed most likely to flourish where no single craft clearly dominated the life of the workplace, in the way iron molders, brick layers, or iron puddlers did where they worked. It was also most likely to appear at the crest of the waves of strike activity among unskilled workers and operatives, as is hardly surprising, and to offer evidence of the organizational impulse in their ranks. In Philadelphia's shoe industry between 1884 and 1887, for example, the Knights of Labor successfully organized eleven local assemblies, ranging in size from 55 to 1000 members, each of which represented a different craft or cluster of related occupations, and formulated wage demands and work rules for its own members. Each assembly sent three delegates to District Assembly 70, the highest governing body of the Knights for the industry, which in turn selected seven representatives to meet in a city-wide arbitration committee with an equal number of employers' representatives. Within each factory a "shop union" elected by the workers in that plant handled grievances and enforced the rules of the local assemblies, aided by one male and one female "statistician," who kept track of the complex piece rates.

There is no evidence that local assemblies of unskilled workers or of semi-skilled operatives ever attempted to regulate production processes themselves in the way assemblies of glass blowers and other craftsmen did. They did try to restrict hiring to members of the Knights and sometimes regulated layoffs by seniority clauses. For the most part, however, assemblies of operatives and laborers confined their attention to wages and to protection of their members against arbitrary treatment by supervisors. On the other hand, the mere fact that such workers had been organized made it difficult for employees to grant concessions to their craftsmen at the expense of helpers and laborers. Consequently, the owners were faced simultaneously with higher wage bills and a reduction of their control in a domain where they had been accustomed to exercise unlimited authority.

Moreover, workers who directed important production processes were themselves at times reluctant to see their own underlings organized, and frequently sought to dominate the larger organization to which their helpers belonged. A case in point was offered by the experience of the Knights of Labor in the garment industry, where contractors were organized into local assemblies of their own, supposedly to cooperate with those of cutters, pressers, tailors, and sewing machine operators. Contractors were often charged with disrupting the unionization of their own employees, in order to promote their personal competitive advantages. Above all, they tried to discourage women from joining the operators' assemblies. As the secretary of a St. Louis tailors' local assembly revealed, contractors who were his fellow Knights were telling the parents of operators that "no dissent [sic] girl belong to an assembly."

On the other hand, the experience of the Knights in both the shoe and garment industries suggests that effective unionization of women operatives was likely to have a remarkably radicalizing impact on the organization. It closed the door decisively both on employers who wished to compensate for higher wages paid to craftsmen by exacting more from the unskilled, and on craftsmen who were tempted to advance themselves by sweating others. In Philadelphia, Toronto, Cincinnati, Beverly, and Lynn both the resistance of the manufacturers to unionism and the level of mutuality exhibited by the workers leapt upward noticeably when the women shoe workers organized along with the men. Furthermore, the sense of total organization made all shoe workers more exacting in their demands and less patient with the protracted arbitration procedures employed by the Knights. Quickie strikes became increasingly frequent as more and more shoe workers enrolled in the Order. Conversely, the shoe manufacturers banded tightly together to destroy the Knights of Labor.

In short, the organization of all grades of workers in any industry propelled craftsmen's collective rule making into a more aggressive relationship with the employers, even where it left existing styles of work substantially unchanged. The other form of joint action, sympathetic strikes, most often involved the unionized skilled crafts themselves, and consequently was more directly related to questions of control of production processes. When Fred S. Hall wrote in 1898 that sympathetic strikes had "come so much in vogue during the last few years," he was looking back on a period during which organized workers had shown a greater tendency to walk out in support of the struggles of other groups of workers than was the case in any other period in the history of recorded strike data. Only the years between 1901 and 1904 and those between 1917 and 1921 were to see the absolute number of sympathetic strikes approach even *one-half* the levels of 1890 and 1891. . . .

Eugene V. Debs was to extoll this extreme manifestation of mutuality as the "Christ-like virtue of sympathy," and to depict his own Pullman boycott, the epoch's most massive sympathetic action, as an open confrontation between that working-class virtue and a social order which sanctified selfishness. It is true that the mutualistic ethic which supported craftsmen's control was displayed in its highest form by sympathetic strikes. It is equally true, however, that the element of calculation, which was increasingly dominating all strike activity, was particularly evident here. As Fred S. Hall pointed out, sympathetic strikes of this epoch differed sharply from "contagious" strikes, which spread spontaneously like those of 1877, in two respects. First, the sympathetic strikes were called by the workers involved, through formal union procedures. Although figures comparing officials with unofficial strikes are not available, two contrasting statistics illustrate Hall's point. The construction industry was always the leading center of sympathetic strikes. In New York more than 70 per cent of the establishments shut by sympathetic action between 1890 and 1892 were involved in building construction. On the other hand, over the entire period of federal data (1881–1905) no less than 98.03 per cent of the strikes in that industry were called by unions.

Second, as Hall observed, the tendency toward sympathetic strikes was "least in those cases where the dispute concerns conditions of employment such as wages and hours, and [was] greatest in regard to disputes which involve questions of unionism—the employment of only union men, the recognition of the union, etc." The rise of sympathetic strikes, like the rise of strikes over rules and recognition, was part of the struggle for craftsmen's control—its most aggressive and far-reaching manifestation. . . .

. . . As craftsmen unionized, they not only made their struggles for control increasingly collective and deliberate, but also manifested a *growing* consciousness of the dependence of their efforts on those of workers in other crafts. They drew strength in this struggle from their functional autonomy, which was derived from their superior knowledge, exercised through self-direction and their direction of others at work, and both nurtured and in turn was nurtured by a mutualistic ethic, which repudiated important elements of acquisitive individualism. As time passed this autonomy was increasingly often codified in union rules, which were collectively "legislated" and upheld through the commitment of the individual craftsmen and through a swelling number of strikes to enforce them. Organized efforts reached the most aggressive and inclusive level of all in joint action among the various crafts for mutual support. When such actions enlisted all workers in an industry (as happened when women unionized in shoe manufacturing), and when they produced a strong propensity of unionized craftsmen to strike in support of each other's claims, they sharply separated the aggressive from the conservative consequences of craftsmen's autonomy and simultaneously provoked an intense, concerted response from the business community.

In an important sense, the last years of the depression represented only a lull in the battle. With the return of prosperity in 1898, both strikes and union organizing quickly resumed their upward spiral, work rules again seized the center of the stage, and sympathetic strikes became increasingly numerous and bitterly fought. Manufacturers' organizations leapt into the fray with the open shop drive, while their spokesmen cited new government surveys to support their denunciations of workers "restriction of output."

On the other hand, important new developments distinguished the first decade of the twentieth century from what had gone before. Trade union officials, who increasingly served long terms in full-time salaried positions, sought to negotiate the terms of work with employers, rather than letting their members "legislate" them. The anxiety of AFL leaders to secure trade agreements and to ally with "friendly employers," like those affiliated with the National Civic Federation, against the open shop drive, prompted them to repudiate the use of sympathetic strikes. The many such strikes which took place were increasingly lacking in union sanction and in any event never reached the level of the early 1890s.

Most important of all, new methods of industrial management undermined the very foundation of craftsmen's functional autonomy. Job analysis through time and motion study allowed management to learn, then to systematize the way the work itself was done. Coupled with systematic supervision and new forms of incentive payment it permitted what Frederick Winslow Taylor called "*enforced* standardization of methods, *enforced* adoption of the best implements and working conditions, and *enforced* cooperation of all the employees under management's detailed direction." Scientific management, in fact, fundamentally disrupted the craftsmen's styles of work, their union rules and standards rates, and their mutualistic ethic, as it transformed American industrial practice between 1900 and 1930. Its basic effect, as Roethlisberger and Dickson discovered in their experiments at Western Electric's Hawthorne Works, was to place the worker "at the bottom level of a highly stratified organization," leaving his "established routines of work, his cultural traditions of craftsmanship, [and] his personal interrelations" all "at the mercy of technical specialists."

Two important attributes of the scientific management movement become evident only against the background of the struggles of nineteenth-century craftsmen to direct their own work in their own collective way. First, the appeal of the new managerial techniques to manufacturers involved more than simply a response to new technology and a new scale of business organization. It also implied a conscious endeavor to uproot those work practices which had been the taproot of whatever strength organized labor enjoyed in the late nineteenth century. A purely technological explanation of the spread of Taylorism is every bit as inadequate as a purely technological explanation of craftsmen's autonomy.

Second, the apostles of scientific management needed not only to abolish older industrial work practices, but also to discredit them in the public eye. Thus Taylor roundly denied that even "the high class mechanic" could "ever thoroughly understand the science of doing his work," and pasted the contemptuous label of "soldiering" over all craft rules, formal and informal alike. Progressive intellectuals seconded his arguments. Louis Brandeis hailed scientific management for "reliev[ing] labor of responsibilities not its own." And John R. Commons considered it "immoral to hold up to this miscellaneous labor, as a class, the hope that it can ever manage industry." If some workers do "shoulder responsibility," he explained, "it is because certain *individuals* succeed, and then those individuals immediately close the doors, and labor, as a class, remains where it was."

It was in this setting that the phrase "workers' control" first entered the vocabulary of the American labor movement. It appeared to express a radical, if often amorphous, set of demands which welled up around the end of World War I among workers in the metal trades, railroading, coal mining, and garment industries. Although those demands represented very new styles of struggle in a unique industrial and political environment, many of the workers who expressed them could remember the recent day when in fact, the manager's brains had been under the workman's cap.

"Fashioning Political Identities: Cultural Studies and the Historical Construction of Political Subjects," *American Quarterly,* Vol. 50, No. 4 (December 1998), pp. 745–782. © 1998 American Studies. Reprinted by permission of The Johns Hopkins University Press.

The Cultures of First-Generation
Industrial Workers

HERBERT GUTMAN

Common work habits rooted in diverse premodern cultures (different in many ways but nevertheless all ill fitted to the regular routines demanded by machine-centered factory processes) existed among distinctive first-generation factory workers all through American history. We focus on two quite different time periods: the years before 1843 when the factory and machine were still new to America and the years between 1893 and 1917 when the country had become the world's industrial colossus. In both periods workers new to factory production brought strange and seemingly useless work habits to the factory gate. The irregular and undisciplined work patterns of factory hands before 1843 frustrated cost-conscious manufacturers and caused frequent complaint among them. Textile factory work rules often were designed to tame such rude customs. A New Hampshire cotton factory that hired mostly women and children forbade "spiritous liquor, smoking, nor any kind of amusement . . . in the workshops, yards, or factories" and promised the "immediate and disgraceful dismissal" of employees found gambling, drinking, or committing "any other debaucheries." . . . Manufacturers elsewhere worried about the example "idle" men set for women and children. Massachusetts family heads who rented "a piece of land on shares" to grow corn and potatoes while their wives and children labored in factories worried one manufacturer. "I would prefer giving constant employment at some sacrifice," he said, "to having a man of the village seen in the streets on a rainy day at leisure." Men who worked in Massachusetts woolen mills upset expected work routines in other ways. "The wool business requires more man labour," said a manufacturer, "and this we study to avoid. Women are much more ready to follow good regulations, are not captious, and do not clan as the men do against the overseers." Male factory workers posed other difficulties, too. In 1817 a shipbuilder in Medford, Massachusetts, refused his men grog privileges. They quit work, but he managed to finish a ship without using further spirits, "a remarkable achievement." . . .

Employers responded differently to such behavior by first-generation factory hands. "Moral reform" as well as . . . carrot-and-stick policies meant to tame or to transform such work habits. Fining was common. . . . Special material rewards encouraged steady work. A Hopewell Village blacksmith contracted for nineteen dollars a month, and "if he does his work well we are to give him a pair of coarse boots." In these and later years manufacturers in Fall River and Paterson institutionalized traditional customs and arranged for festivals and parades to celebrate with their workers a new mill, a retiring superintendent, or a finished locomotive. . . . Where factory work could be learned easily, new hands replaced irregular ones. A factory worker in New England remembered that years before the Civil War her employer had hired "all American girls" but later shifted to immigrant laborers because "not coming from country homes, but living as the Irish do, in the town, they take no

From *Work, Culture, and Society in Industrializing America* by Herbert G. Gutman, Vintage, 1977, pp. 19–32, 63–75. Copyright © 1973 by Herbert G. Gutman. Used by permission of Alfred A. Knopf, Inc., a division of Random House, Inc.

vacations, and can be relied on at the mill all year round." Not all such devices worked to the satisfaction of workers or their employers. Sometime in the late 1830s merchant capitalists sent a skilled British silk weaver to manage a new mill in Nantucket that would employ the wives and children of local whalers and fishermen. Machinery was installed, and in the first days women and children besieged the mill for work. After a month had passed, they started dropping off in small groups. Soon nearly all had returned "to their shore gazing and to their seats by the sea." The Nantucket mill shut down, its hollow frame an empty monument to the unwillingness of resident women and children to conform to the regularities demanded by rising manufacturers.

First-generation factory workers were not unique to premodern America. And the work habits common to such workers plagued American manufacturers in later generations when manufacturers and most native urban whites scarcely remembered that native Americans had once been hesitant first-generation factory workers. To shift forward in time to East and South European immigrants new to steam, machinery, and electricity and new to the United States itself is to find much that seems the same. American society, of course, had changed greatly, but in some ways it is as if a film—run at a much faster speed—is being viewed for the second time: primitive work rules for unskilled labor, fines, gang labor, and subcontracting were commonplace. In 1910 two-thirds of the workers in twenty-one major manufacturing and mining industries came from Eastern and Southern Europe or were native American blacks, and studies of these "new immigrants" record much evidence of preindustrial work habits among the men and women new to American industry. . . . [S]killed immigrant Jews carried to New York City town and village employment patterns, such as the *landsmannschaft* economy and a preference for small shops as opposed to larger factories, that sparked frequent disorders but hindered stable trade unions until 1910. Specialization spurred anxiety: in Chicago Jewish glovemakers resisted the subdivision of labor even though it promised better wages. . . . American work rules also conflicted with religious imperatives. On the eighth day after the birth of a son, Orthodox Jews in Eastern Europe held a festival, "an occasion of much rejoicing." But the American work week had a different logic, and if the day fell during the week the celebration occurred the following Sunday. "The host . . . and his guests," David Blaustein remarked, "know it is not the right day," and "they fall to mourning over the conditions that will not permit them to observe the old custom." The occasion became "one for secret sadness rather than rejoicing." Radical Yiddish poets, like Morris Rosenfeld, the presser of men's clothing, measured in verse the psychic and social costs exacted by American industrial work rules:

> The Clock in the workshop,—it rests not a moment;
> It points on, and ticks on: eternity—time;
> Once someone told me the clock had a meaning,—
> In pointing and ticking had reason and rhyme. . . .
> At times, when I listen, I hear the clock plainly;—
> The reason of old—the old meaning—is gone!
> The maddening pendulum urges me forward
> To labor and still labor on.
> The tick of the clock is the boss in his anger.
> The face of the clock has the eyes of the foe.

The clock—I shudder—Dost hear how it draws me?
It calls me "Machine"—and it cries [to] me "Sew"!

Slavic and Italian immigrants carried with them to industrial America subcultures quite different from that of village Jews, but their work habits were just as alien to the modern factory. Rudolph Vecoli has reconstructed Chicago's South Italian community to show that adult male seasonal construction gangs as contrasted to factory labor were one of many traditional customs adapted to the new environment, and in her study of South Italian peasant immigrants Phyllis H. Williams found among them men who never adjusted to factory labor. After "years" of "excellent" factory work, some "began . . . to have minor accidents" and others "suddenly give up and are found in their homes complaining of a vague indisposition with no apparent physical basis." Such labor worried early twentieth-century efficiency experts, and so did Slavic festivals, church holidays, and "prolonged merriment." "Man," Adam Smith wisely observed, "is, of all sorts of luggage, the most difficult to be transported." That was just as true for these Slavic immigrants as for the early nineteenth-century native American factory workers. A Polish wedding in a Pennsylvania mining or mill town lasted between three and five days. Greek and Roman Catholics shared the same jobs but had different holy days, "an annoyance to many employers." The Greek Church had "more than eighty festivals in the year," and "the Slav religiously observes the days on which the saints are commemorated and invariably takes a holiday." A celebration of the American Day of Independence in Mahanoy City, Pennsylvania, caught the eye of a hostile observer. Men parading the streets drew a handcart with a barrel of lager in it. Over the barrel "stood a comrade, goblet in hand and crowned with a garland of laurel, singing some jargon." Another sat and played an accordion. At intervals, the men stopped to "drink the good beverage they celebrated in song." The witness called the entertainment "an imitation of the honor paid Bacchus which was one of the most joyous festivals of ancient Rome" and felt it proof of "a lower type of civilization." Great Lakes dock workers "believed that a vessel could not be unloaded unless they had from four to five kegs of beer." (And in the early irregular strikes among male Jewish garment workers, employers negotiated with them out of doors and after each settlement "would roll out a keg of beer for their entertainment of the workers." Contemporary betters could not comprehend such behavior. . . .

More than irregular work habits bound together the behavior of first-generation factory workers separated from one another by time and by the larger structure of the society they first encountered. Few distinctive American working-class populations differed in so many essentials (their sex, their religion, their nativity, and their prior rural and village cultures) as the Lowell mill girls and women of the Era of Good Feelings and the South and East European steelworkers of the Progressive Era. To describe similarities in their expectations of factory labor is not to blur these important differences but to suggest that otherwise quite distinctive men and women interpreted such work in similar ways. . . .

Historians of the Lowell mill girls find little evidence before 1840 of organized protest among them and attribute their collective passivity to corporation policing policies, the frequent turnover in the labor force, the irregular pace of work (after it was rationalized in the 1840s, it provoked collective protest), the freedom the mill girls enjoyed away from rural family dominance, and their relatively decent earnings. The women managed the transition to mill life because they did not expect to remain factory workers too long. Nevertheless frequent inner tension revealed itself among the mobile mill women. In an early year, a single mill discharged twenty-eight women for such reasons as "misconduct," "captiousness," "disobedience," "impudence," "levity," and even "mutiny." . . .

Aspirations and expectations interpret experience and thereby help shape behavior. Some Lowell mill girls revealed dissatisfactions, and others made a difficult transition from rural New England to that model factory town, but that so few planned to remain mill workers eased that transition and hampered collective protest. Men as well as women, who expect to spend only a few years as factory workers have little incentive to join unions. That was just as true of the immigrant male common laborers in the steel mills of the late nineteenth and early twentieth centuries (when multiplant oligopoly characterized the nation's most important manufacturing industry) as in the Lowell cotton mills nearly a century earlier. . . . In those years, the steel companies successfully divorced wages from productivity to allow the market to shape them. Between 1890 and 1910, efficiencies in plant organization cut labor costs by about a third. The great Carnegie Pittsburg plants employed 14,359 common laborers, 11,694 of them South and East Europeans. Most, peasant in origin, earned less than $12.50 a week (a family needed fifteen dollars for subsistence). A staggering accident rate damaged these and other men: nearly 25 percent of the recent immigrants employed at the Carnegie South Works were injured or killed each year between 1907 and 1910, 3,723 in all. But like the Lowell mill women, these men rarely protested in collective ways, and for good reason. They did not plan to stay in the steel mills long. Most had come to the United States as single men (or married men who had left their families behind) to work briefly in the mills, save some money, return home, and purchase farmland. Their private letters to European relatives indicated a realistic awareness of their working life that paralleled some of the Lowell fiction: "if I don't earn $1.50 a day, it would not be worth thinking about America"; "a golden land so long as there is work"; "here in America one must work for three horses"; "let him not risk coming, for he is too young"; "too weak for America." Men who wrote such letters and avoided injury often saved small amounts of money, and a significant number fulfilled their expectations and quit the factory and even the country. Forty-four South and East Europeans left the United States for every one hundred that arrived between 1908 and 1910. . . . Immigrant expectations coincided for a time with the fiscal needs of industrial manufacturers. The Pittsburgh steel magnates had as much good fortune as the Boston Associates. But the stability and passivity they counted on among their unskilled workers depended upon steady work and the opportunity to escape the mills. When frequent recessions caused recurrent unemployment, immigrant expectations and behavior changed. . . .[P]easant "group consciousness" and "communal loyalty" sustained bitter wildcat strikes after employment picked up. The tenacity of these immigrant strikers for higher wages amazed contemporaries, and brutal suppression often accompanied them (Cleveland, 1899; East Chicago, 1905; McKees Rock, 1909; Bethlehem, 1910; and Youngstown in 1915 where, after a policeman shot into a peaceful parade, a riot caused an estimated one million dollars in damages). The First World War and its aftermath blocked the traditional route of overseas outward mobility, and the consciousness of immigrant steelworkers changed. They sparked the 1919 steel strike. The steel mill had become a way of life for them and was no longer the means by which to reaffirm and even strengthen older peasant and village life-styles. . . .

Even though American society itself underwent radical structural changes between 1815 and the First World War, the shifting composition of its wage-earning population meant that traditional customs, rituals, and beliefs repeatedly helped shape the behavior of its diverse working-class groups. The street battle in 1843 that followed Irish efforts to prevent New York City authorities from stopping pigs from running loose in the streets is but one example of the force of old styles of behavior. Both the form and the content of much expressive working-class behavior, including labor disputes, often revealed the powerful role of secular and religious rituals. In 1857 the New York City unemployed kidnapped a musical band to give legitimacy to its parade for public works. After the Civil War, a Fall River cotton manufacturer boasted that the arrival of fresh Lancashire operatives meant the coming of "a lot of greenhorns here," but an overseer advised him, "Yes, but you'll find they have brought their horns with them." A few years later, the Pittsburgh courts prevented three women married to coal miners from "tin-horning" nonstrikers. The women, however, purchased mouth organs. ("Tinhorning," of course, was not merely an imported institution. In Franklin, Virginia, in 1867, for example, a Northern white clergyman who started a school for former slave children had two nighttime "tin horn serenade[s]" from hostile whites.) Recurrent street demonstrations in Paterson accompanying frequent strikes and lockouts nearly always involved horns, whistles, and even Irish "banshee" calls. These had a deeply symbolic meaning, and, rooted in a shared culture, they sustained disputes. A Paterson manufacturer said of nonstrikers: "They cannot go anywhere without being molested or insulted, and no matter what they do they are met and blackguarded and taunted in a way that no one can stand . . . which is a great deal worse than actual assaults." . . .

But the manufacturers could not convince the town's mayor (himself a British immigrant and an artisan who had become a small manufacturer) to ban street demonstrations. The manufacturers even financed their own private militia to manage further disorders, but the street demonstrations continued with varying effectiveness until 1901 when a court injunction essentially defined the streets as private space by banning talking and singing banshee (or death) wails in them during industrial disputes. In part, the frequent recourse to the courts and to the state militia after the Civil War during industrial disputes was the consequence of working-class rituals that helped sustain long and protracted conflicts.

Symbolic secular and, especially, religious rituals and beliefs differed among Catholic and Jewish workers fresh to industrial America between 1894 and the First World War, but their function remained the same. Striking Jewish vestmakers finished a formal complaint by quoting the Law of Moses to prove that "our bosses who rob us and don't pay us regularly commit a sin and that the cause of our union is a just one." ("What do we come to America for?" these same men asked. "To bathe in tears and to see our wives and children rot in poverty?") An old Jewish ritual oath helped spark the shirtwaist strike of women workers in 1909 that laid the basis for the International Ladies Garment Workers Union. A strike vote resulted in the plea, "Do you mean faith? Will you take the old Jewish oath?" The audience responded in Yiddish: "If I turn traitor to the cause, I now pledge, may this hand wither and drop off at the wrist from the arm I now raise." . . . Immigrant Catholic workers shared similar experiences with these immigrant Jews. A reporter noticed in 1910 at a meeting of striking Slavic steelworkers in Hammond, Indiana: "The lights of the hall were extinguished. A candle stuck into a bottle was placed on a platform. One by one the men came and kissed the ivory image on the cross, kneeling before it. They swore not to scab." Not all rituals were that pacific. That same year, Slavic miners in Avelia, Pennsylvania, a tiny patch on the West Virginia border, crucified George Rabish, a mine boss and an alleged labor spy. . . . That event was certainly unusual, but it was commonplace for time-honored religious symbols as well as American flags to be carried in the frequent parades of American workers. Western Pennsylvania Slavic and Italian coal miners in a bitter strike just east of Pittsburg (eighteen of twenty thousand miners quit work for seventeen months when denied the right to join the United Mine Workers of America) in 1910 and 1911 carried such symbols. "These rural marches," said Paul Kellogg [*Survey* editor], "were in a way reminiscent of the old time agrarian uprisings which have marked English history." But theirs was the behavior of peasant and village Slavs and Italians fresh to modern industrial America, and it was just such tenacious peasant-worker protests that caused the head of the Pennsylvania State Police to say that he modeled his force on the Royal Irish Constabulary, not, he insisted, "as an anti-labor measure" but because "conditions in Pennsylvania resembled those in strife-torn Ireland." Peasant parades and rituals, religious oaths and food riots, and much else in the culture and behavior of early twentieth-century immigrant American factory workers were cultural anachronisms to this man and to others, including Theodore Roosevelt, William Jennings Bryan, Elbert Gary, and even Samuel Gompers, but participants found them natural and effective forms of self-assertion and self-protection.

The perspective emphasized in these pages tells about more than the behavior of diverse groups of American working men and women. It also suggests how larger, well-studied aspects of American society have been affected by a historical process that has "industrialized" different peoples over protracted periods of time. . . . Contact and conflict between diverse preindustrial cultures and a changing and increasingly bureaucratized industrial society also affected the larger society in ways that await systematic examination. Contemporaries realized this fact. Concerned in 1886 about the South's "dead"—that is, unproductive—population, the Richmond *Whig* felt the "true remedy" to be "educating the industrial morale of the people." The *Whig* emphasized socializing institutions primarily outside of the working class itself. "In the work of inculcating industrial ideas and impulses," said the *Whig,* "all proper agencies should be enlisted—family discipline, public school education, pulpit instruction, business standards and requirements, and the power and influence of the workingmen's associations." What the *Whig* worried over in 1886 concerned other Americans before and after that time. And the resultant tension shaped society in important ways. . . .

The same process also affected the shaping and reshaping of American police and domestic military institutions. We need only realize that the burning of a Boston convent in 1834 by a crowd of Charlestown truckmen and New Hampshire Scotch-Irish brickmakers caused the first revision of the Massachusetts Riot Act since Shays' Rebellion, and that three years later interference by native firemen in a Sunday Irish funeral procession led to a two-hour riot involving upward of fifteen thousand persons (more than a sixth of Boston's population), brought militia to that city for the first time, and caused the first of many reorganizations of the Boston police force. The regular contact between alien work cultures and a larger industrializing or industrial society had other consequences. It often worried industrialists, causing C. E. Perkins, the president of the Chicago, Burlington, and Quincy Railroad to confide in a friend in the late nineteenth century. "If I were able, I would found a school for the study of political economy in order to harden men's hearts." It affected the popular culture. A guidebook for immigrant Jews in the 1890s advised how to make it in the New World: "Hold fast, this is most necessary in America. Forget your past, your customs, and your ideals. . . . A bit of advice to you: do not take a moment's rest. Run, do, work, and keep your own good in mind." Cultures and customs, however, are not that easily discarded. So it may be that America's extraordinary technological supremacy—its talent before the Second World War for developing labor-saving machinery and simplifying complex mechanical processes—depended less on "Yankee know-how" than on the continued infusion of prefactory peoples into an increasingly industrialized society. The same process, moreover, may also explain why movements to legislate morality and to alter habits have lasted much longer in the United States than in most other industrial countries, extending from the temperance crusades of the 1820s and the 1830s to the violent opposition among Germans to such rules in the 1850s and the 1860s and finally to formal prohibition earlier in this century. Important relationships also exist between this process and the elite and popular nativist and racist social movements that have ebbed and flowed regularly from the 1840s until our own time, as well as between this process and elite political "reform" movements between 1850 and the First World War.

The sweeping social process had yet another important consequence: it reinforced the biases that otherwise distort the ways in which elite observers perceive the world below them. When in 1902 *The New York Times* cast scorn upon and urged that force be used against the Jewish women food rioters, it conformed to a fairly settled elite tradition. Immigrant groups and the working population had changed in composition over time, but the rhetoric of influential nineteenth- and early twentieth-century elite observers remained constant. Disorders among the Jersey City Irish seeking wages due them from the Erie Railroad in 1859 led the Jersey City *American Standard* to call them "imported *beggars*" and "*animals,*" "a mongrel mass of ignorance and crime and superstition, as utterly unfit for its duties, as they are for the common courtesies and decencies of civilized life." . . .

Although the Civil War ended slavery, it did not abolish these distorted perceptions and fears of new American workers. In 1869 *Scientific American* welcomed the "ruder" laborers of Europe but urged them to "assimilate" quickly or face "a quiet but sure extermination." Those who retained their alien ways, it insisted, "will share the fate of the native Indian." Elite nativism neither died out during the Civil War nor awaited a rebirth under the auspices of the American Protective Association and the Immigration Restriction League. In the mid-1870s, for example, the Chicago *Tribune* called striking immigrant brickmakers men but "not reasoning creatures," and the Chicago *Post-Mail* described that city's Bohemian residents as "depraved beasts, harpies, decayed physically and spiritually, mentally and morally, thievish and licentious." The Democratic Chicago *Times* cast an even wider net in complaining that the country had become "the cess-pool of Europe under the pretense that it is the asylum of the poor." Most Chicago inhabitants in the Gilded Age were foreign-born or the children of the foreign-born, and most English-language Chicago news-papers scorned them. . . . Here, as in the Jersey City *American Standard* (1859) and *The New York Times* (1902), much more was involved than mere ethnic distaste or "nativism." In quite a different connection and in a relatively homogeneous country, the Italian Antonio Gramsci concluded of such evidence that "for a social elite the features of subordinate groups always display something barbaric and pathologi-cal." The changing composition of the American working class may make so severe a dictum more pertinent to the United States than to Italy. Class and ethnic fears and biases combined together to worry elite observers about the diverse worlds below them to distort gravely their perceptions of these worlds. . . .

These pages have fractured historical time, ranging forward and backward, to make comparisons for several reasons. One has been to suggest how much remains to be learned about the transition of native and foreign-born American men and women to industrial society, and how that transition affected such persons and the society into which they entered. "Much of what gets into American literature," Ralph Ellison has shrewdly observed "gets there because so much is left out." That has also been the case in the writing of American working-class history, and the framework and methods suggested here merely hint at what will be known about American workers and American society when the many transitions are studied in detail. Such studies, however, need to focus on the particularities of both the groups involved and the society into which they enter. Transitions differ and de-pend upon the interaction between the two at specific historical moments. But at all times there is a resultant tension. [E. P.] Thompson writes:

> There has never been any single type of "the transition." The stress of the transition falls upon the whole culture: resistance to change and assent to change arise from the whole culture. And this culture includes the systems of power, property-relations, religious in-stitutions, etc., inattention to which merely flattens phenomena and trivializes analysis.

Enough has been savored in these pages to suggest the particular importance of these transitions in American social history. And their recurrence in different pe-riods of time indicates why there has been so much discontinuity in American labor and social history. The changing composition of the working population, the continued entry into the United States of nonindustrial people with distinctive cul-tures, and the changing structure of American society have combined together to produce common modes of thought and patterns of behavior. But these have been experiences disconnected in time and shared by quite distinctive first-generation native and immigrant industrial Americans. It was not possible for the grand-children of the Lowell mill girls to understand that their Massachusetts literary ancestors shared a great deal with their contemporaries, the peasant Slavs in the Pennsylvania steel mills and coals fields. And the grandchildren of New York City Jewish garment workers see little connection between black ghetto unrest in the 1960s and the kosher meat riots seventy years ago. A half-century has passed since Robert Park and Herbert Miller published W. I. Thomas's *Old World Traits Transplanted,* a study which worried that the function of Americanization was the "destruction of memories."

Clash of the Titans: Andrew Carnegie and Pittsburgh's Old Iron Masters

JOHN N. INGHAM

If Pittsburgh's mercantile aristocracy was confronted by a sizable challenge with the emergence of the iron industry during the antebellum years, it faced an unbelievably awesome encounter with the rise of Andrew Carnegie and the Bessemer steel industry in the years after the war. The stable, contented, almost smug Presbyterian local elite watched massive steel mills rise from dusty fields and observed the emergence of new men who commanded these enterprises—men who were sometimes from divergent social, economic, and cultural origins but who also brought radically new ideas about the way business should be conducted in the city. This new group, most dramatically presented in the person of Andrew Carnegie, bid fair to be a plutocracy in the young industrial city, one that would supplant the older mercantile and small industry iron and steel elite. Within this context, then, a class war of enormous proportions ensued during the last years of the nineteenth century.

That class war had its origins in Braddock's Field, about twelve miles from downtown Pittsburgh on the Monongahela River. There, in 1875, Andrew Carnegie was building a massive Bessemer steel complex, one larger, more integrated, and more complete than existed anywhere in the world. Since the nation was caught in the grip of its first modern depression, most sensible businessmen were cutting back, waiting out the hard times before expanding their operations. Not the impetuous Carnegie. Like Henry Clay Frick, his future partner, Carnegie viewed hard times as ideal for expansion, since costs were so much lower. Nonetheless, the depression caused him much trouble, as several of his business associates were bankrupted and Carnegie's own resources were stretched to the limit. All of this was characteristic of the man and his technique. It was a method that would frustrate, awe, and alienate many members of the older Pittsburgh aristocracy.

But what a wonder Carnegie constructed at Braddock's Field! Soon to be known as the Edgar Thomson Works (significantly and not coincidentally named for the president of the Pennsylvania Railroad), it was a technological and organizational marvel of the modern world. Located at the junction of three railroads (the Pennsylvania, the Baltimore & Ohio, and the Pittsburgh & Lake Erie), it was a sprawling series of buildings, switchyards, engines, sheds, and smokestacks. The crowning glory of the mill was a wonder of the industrial world: a screaming, belching series

John N. Ingham, *Making Iron and Steel: Independent Mills in Pittsburgh, 1820–1920* (Columbus: Ohio State University Press, 1991), pp. 47–49, 74–75, 77–80, 84, 94–95. Reprinted by permission of Ohio State University Press.

of Bessemer converters, capable of making steel in vast quantities. This new company was a model of modern integration. . . .

When the Edgar Thomson Works reached its production peak later in the century, it was capable of producing three thousand tons of steel rails daily, as much as a typical Pittsburgh puddling mill of the 1830s could produce in an entire year. This greatly increased velocity of flow through the works placed increased demands on the managers. As a result, Carnegie hired William P. Shinn, formerly a railroad accountant, to install railroad accounting techniques in his new steel plant. . . . Shinn and Carnegie revolutionized manufacturing practice and the traditions of accountability in American business. Carnegie's dictum had always been "Watch the costs, and the profits will take care of themselves," and his accounting system, a revolutionary change from traditional lump accounting techniques in the iron industry, allowed him to fulfill his ideals. Carnegie used Shinn's cost sheets to give him control over the entire operation, even from New York City, where he had already moved by this time. All of this was an enormous departure from the hovering, personal, idiosyncratic rule-of-thumb methods practiced by most Pittsburgh iron masters.

As a result, Carnegie and his massive steel complexes have naturally dominated our view of the late nineteenth-century iron and steel industry. He was, after all, the most dynamic element on the Pittsburgh industrial scene. And his techniques of mass production, high throughput, accountability, control, and professional bureaucratic management came to characterize large-scale American industries increasingly in the twentieth century. Carnegie was a harbinger of what Chandler has called "the managerial revolution in American business." Yet, the unspoken assumption seems to be that the rest of the iron and steel industry, especially in Pittsburgh, the very cockpit of America's industrial transformation, either followed suit or, more likely, was bludgeoned to death by the massively efficient Carnegie mills. Nothing could be further from the truth. . . .

Most of Pittsburgh's independent iron and steel makers never directly challenged Carnegie or became involved in the large-batch rail market. And even those who did quickly learned their lesson, a deceptively simple one that has resurfaced in recent years as a maxim for businessmen: "Stick to your knitting." In this case, sticking to their knitting often meant staying with familiar markets and technologies. If they did branch out into new markets and technologies, these old-line steel men made sure these endeavors suited their temperaments and abilities. As a result, the independent iron and steel manufacturers at the turn of the century in Pittsburgh engaged in a quest that has become the hallmark of small business, the search for a specialized market niche in which they could survive and prosper and, at the same time, be shielded from the economies of scale and cost efficiencies of large-scale operators like Andrew Carnegie.

It is difficult to make broad general statements about specialized niche marketing. It is, after all, by its very nature rather small, unique, and resistant to generalization. It was precisely those characteristics that made it difficult for the large-scale producers to enter these markets. If the markets had been amenable to generalization, products and market strategies could have been standardized and large-scale producers would have conquered them. Nonetheless, it is possible to isolate certain essential features of the market strategies and technological responses employed by Pittsburgh's independent iron and steel manufacturers during these years. . . .

. . . In 1894, . . . Pittsburgh was still in many respects Iron City. Of the sixty-three iron and steel plants in Pittsburgh and the surrounding area, thirty (48 percent) made wrought iron. At a time when the number of puddling furnaces had declined to 4,700 nationally, there were still 1,050 single puddling furnaces in Pittsburgh, representing 22 percent of the national total. These furnaces produced about 808,000 tons of wrought iron annually. At the same time, there were just eight Bessemer plants in the city, eighteen open hearth plants, and ten crucible operations. Wrought iron was still king in Pittsburgh in the mid-1890s, even though the output of the Carnegie works alone exceeded that of all thirty-one iron mills combined.

By 1901, the number of plants producing wrought iron in the Pittsburgh area had dwindled significantly. In that year, there were just nineteen such plants, containing 573 puddling furnaces with a capacity for about 605,000 tons of wrought iron. Of these, only a dozen remained independent entities, with production capacity of 363,000 tons. At this time, there were sixty-three steel plants and rolling mills in Pittsburgh and Allegheny County, seven producing Bessemer steel, twenty-two making open hearth steel, ten producing crucible, and four making blister steel. Pittsburgh was no longer Iron City, but wrought iron production was not quite dead, and, in fact, manufacturers still found lucrative markets for its products. We shall examine a few of those firms and their market strategies, better to understand the complex operation of the iron and steel industry at the turn of the century.

Most of the iron firms that managed to operate successfully in the late nineteenth century were not exciting or spectacular. As a result, there has been a tendency to dismiss them as unimportant. That is a mistake, because although they were certainly less dramatic than the Carnegie operations, they were far more typical of the iron and steel industry in Pittsburgh, and of American manufacturing generally, at the turn of the century. One such firm was the Sable Rolling Mill. One of the oldest and most conservative merchant iron firms in the city, it was run by Christopher Zug and his son Charles. The plant had been built in 1845 in partnership with the Graff family. When the Graffs erected their blast furnace in Pittsburgh in 1859, it gave the Zug and Graff iron firm an informally integrated structure. During the Civil War, the Sable mill emerged as one of the strongest and wealthiest in the city; by 1874 it had thirty-four puddling furnaces with an annual capacity of fifteen thousand tons of merchant iron, along with a nail factory in the city's Ninth Ward. . . . [I]t was worth $1 million by this time.

The Sable mill was crippled by a combination of factors in the mid-1870s. Partly, it was caused by the depression of the time, but even more by a dispute between Charles H. Zug and his sisters over the distribution of their father's estate. The result was that the firm, with assets of between $800,000 and $900,000 and liabilities of only $400,000 to $600,000, was forced to file for bankruptcy. It is quite clear that on the business side, Sable was still doing well, but the family feud over inheritance rights caused great problems. The firm was reorganized in 1877, with Charles Zug and his son still running it, but with a number of new partners who brought in additional capital. By 1880, Sable mill was in good financial condition, and the company continued to prosper despite the vicissitudes of the 1880s and 1890s. By the turn of the century, Sable Iron was a small- to moderate-size iron mill (they made no steel) with an annual capacity for 22,500 tons of merchant bar iron. Their one concession to finding new markets and new products was the erection of a sheet mill, which produced 14,000 tons of sheet per year. Like many other small Pittsburgh iron firms, the Sable mill marketed its products with its own sales force, seldom relying on the services of metals or hardware brokers. It was a business that depended on a reputation for high-quality products and personal service. Sable mill, as one of the old-line iron firms in the city, was steeped in reputation and rectitude, and this fact was of great benefit to the company in terms of its economic survival at the turn of the century. The quiet, conservative Sable Rolling Mill continued to be run profitably and successfully by the Zug family until it was dismantled around the time of World War I. Like many other Pittsburgh iron families, the Zugs found a safe and profitable market niche in the late 1870s and 1880s and never tried to produce steel or to challenge any of the larger firms in areas where their economies of scale gave them an advantage. Quiet, cautious Sable Iron and the Zug family did not make headlines and were seldom noticed. All they did was survive and make money.

Vesuvius Iron was similar to Sable Iron in many respects. Built in 1846, it was run for years by the Lewis, Dalzell, O'Hara, and Bailey families. By 1868, . . . it was worth between $500,000 and $600,000. Six years later, it had twenty-four single puddling furnaces and produced twelve thousand tons of bar and sheet iron, rods, hoops, and nails. As it was for Sable Iron, the depression of the 1870s was hard on Vesuvius, and the plant sat idle for two years, until it was taken over by John Moorhead, Jr., member of another wealthy pre–Civil War . . . upper-class iron family.

Moorhead, who had just graduated from Yale, ran Vesuvius for nearly fifty years until his death in 1927. During these years, although Vesuvius increased its output slightly, it never changed its basic structure of operation. In 1884, the plant had twenty-eight single puddling furnaces and could produce 12,000 tons of iron, along with 105,000 kegs of cut nails. By 1894, it produced 22,500 tons of iron annually and no longer made cut nails, which had been rendered largely obsolete by wire nails. In 1901, still only puddling wrought iron, Vesuvius had forty single puddling furnaces with an annual capacity for 100,000 tons. No steel of any kind was ever produced in the works. Like Sable and other independent iron and steel firms, Moorhead marketed Vesuvius's products in traditional markets, using his own contacts and in-house sales force to pursue them. There was nothing fancy or innovative here, just old-line basic business enterprise, a business system inherited from the nineteenth century that lasted well into the twentieth.

The A. M. Byers Pipe Works was perhaps the most successful of the old Pittsburgh iron firms that stuck to their knitting. Taking as its motto "Wrought iron pipe or bust," Byers Pipe profitably pursued rather traditional technologies and markets until the 1960s. Much of the market for Byers's product came from the burgeoning oil and gas industry during the first half of the twentieth century. Its pipe was also used for irrigation systems and hydraulic mining. It was a market that the Byers family executives began exploiting when the oil and gas industry was located in western Pennsylvania, and when the industry began migrating west and south, they used their contacts with industry executives, especially the Mellon-and-Guffey-owned Gulf Oil, to enhance their network of personal contacts.

Just as it is inaccurate to assume that Pittsburgh's wrought iron firms were all dying out at the turn of the century, it is wrong to conclude that all of them were able to find the elusive secret of success. A stark example of failure was the Pittsburgh Iron Mill, one of the oldest and most prestigious merchant iron firms in the city. Owned by the Painter family, it was worth over $1 million in the mid-1870s and as late as 1879 was the second-largest iron mill in the city, producing twenty-seven thousand tons annually. But although Pittsburgh iron underwent some linear expansion, it did not move successfully into profitable market areas. As a result, the Painters sold the plant to American Steel & Wire in 1898, turning their attention to the lucrative banking field. If Pittsburgh Iron did not survive, the Painters did, simply transferring their wealth and social connections to banking. Other old iron mills, such as Sligo Iron, Pennsylvania Iron, Kensington Iron, and Keystone Rolling Mill, had varied experiences during the later years of the nineteenth century. Sligo, like Sable, continued running profitably until it was sold in 1903, but Kensington Iron, Pennsylvania Iron, and Keystone Rolling Mill were dismantled in the late 1890s. . . .

Andrew Carnegie was the least typical of all of Pittsburgh's iron and steel manufacturers; rather it was men and firms like the Zugs at Sable Iron and John Moorhead at Vesuvius who constituted the archetype. Normally cautious and conservative, they were successful in finding profitable markets and adopting the proper technologies. Attaining great wealth and esteemed social status, few were willing to risk them. . . . These men were determined to run their mills, and to run them in their own way, so they chose a quieter and safer path of survival.

For most Pittsburgh iron and steel manufacturers in the late nineteenth century, the route to survival and profitability lay neither with breathtaking expansion and innovation nor with steadfast refusal to produce anything but wrought iron. . . . They continually sought out new markets, markets of a more specialized nature that could be serviced by small production runs of specialty iron and steel. A majority of the older Pittsburgh iron and steel men followed this path. . . .

. . . [T]he independent iron and steel makers in Pittsburgh were hardly an aberration. If literature on the American scene has tended to glorify the large and the dynamic, to thrust forward images of Andrew Carnegie and the large-scale integrated organization with its armies of professional managers and bureaucrats, it is useful to recall that all of the world was not America. Not even all of America was America, or at least the standard textbook version of the country. America, despite the Carnegies and Rockefellers, was still largely dominated by small business at the turn of the century.

The same was true of the iron and steel industry, of which Pittsburgh was the largest and most important center in the country. Long before Carnegie made his first Bessemer steel at the Edgar Thomson Works in 1875, Pittsburgh's mills dominated the industrial scene in the city, state, and nation. The dazzling brilliance of the Carnegie works obscured their role and accomplishments in the last quarter of the nineteenth century. But they did not fail, or even cease to grow and change. They continued as a strong backbone of more traditional segments of the wrought iron and crucible steel production. . . . With their more traditional methods on the shop floor and in the office, these iron and steel masters were not simply a forgotten remnant of the past. They continued to grow and prosper until at least the outbreak of World War II and represented an American equivalent to the smaller, traditional family-dominated iron and steel firms in Britain and France.

Progress and the Double Meaning of Industry

PAMELA WALKER LAIRD

The fiercest battles in the West's perpetual war between spiritual and material values may well have been fought in nineteenth-century America, and they very much colored the popular culture, including the advertisements, of that period. Never before had such material opportunities presented themselves to so many, and never since has outspoken religious morality had such a hold on those same people. The tensions between these two powerful attractions pulled at everyone. The decisions about how to balance the opposing attractions dominated some people's public lives, pushing them to take strong positions—a few ascetics at one extreme and the most ostentatious of the robber barons and their families at the other. Most people who had the option found a more even balance comfortable, and their compromise contributed to the formation of the Victorian-era American middle class and its bourgeois cultural style. . . .

Businesspeople often operate in the center of the battle between materialism and moralism, the targets of proselytizing from all sides, receiving both praise and criticism. Nineteenth-century entrepreneurs experienced the lures of materialism in part because money measured their business success, yet they also carried the still-strong traces of a deeply rooted tradition of wrestling with materialism. . . . In this context, those who took on the task of advising people with ambitions in business always addressed the problem of balancing the tensions between materialism and moralism. For instance, in Haines's *Worth and Wealth: Or the Art of Getting, Saving and Using Money,* the chapter on "Money-Getting" began with the assertion that "Money-getting is the aim, the paramount end, of business." The 1884 tome described in tantalizing detail the merits of money and "its secret charm" for meeting practical and social needs, despite the "intonation of contempt [with which] the word is sometimes uttered." But then the author joined ranks with thousands of others in print and pulpit who warned the ambitious of the difficulties of seeking both money and salvation, for "Money is king; and here lies the danger. . . . For money is hardening to the heart. . . . [Every] true business man . . . [must] feel . . . that while he is laboring for the increase and distribution of wealth, he is working for the elevation and civilization of the masses." If men followed the commandments "to be diligent in business, to be active, to contrive, to invent, to waken up intellect, to render the material world tributary and subservient, and to accumulate the products of art and nature," then they would be able "to accumulate money to enhance their own and others' happiness." . . .

Most nineteenth-century writers offering this kind of advice identified their own balances as "success." Thousands of missives, including trade journals, proclaimed the Victorian compromise that exalted character as the sure road to success. *One Hundred Lessons in Business,* 1887, preached typically, "Let a young man *fear God, be industrious, know his business, spend a little less than he earns,* and success is sure." The popularity of the Victorian compromise did not reside only in print. In 1867, Horace Greeley spoke to thousands of young men on at least two occasions at the behest of S. S. Packard, the president of Bryant & Stratton Business College in New York. Indeed, people were turned away for lack of space when Greeley gave his "Address on Success in Business." Inspired by the opportunities for success in an America that was destined "to bound forward on a career of prosperous activity such as the world has not known," Greeley extolled his audiences to "believe that success in life is within the reach of every one who will truly and nobly seek it." Reciting the usual list of characteristics that ensured success, Greeley emphasized "that thrift, within reasonable limits, is the moral obligation of every man; that he should endeavor and aspire to be a little better off at the close of each year."

Yet wealth alone could not serve as the measurement of success for Victorian businesspeople in the United States. An 1891 trade journal article with advice to young men began: "Being an American, you are ambitious. If that ambition is of the right kind, you are striving for two things: first of all, reputation, and second, money. Success in these two things will make you an example of what is every American young man's ideal—'The successful business man.'" Moral character, in turn, determined the success or failure of a person's business career. Thus, young people were extolled to piety, industry, honesty, frugality, punctuality, and like virtues—the standards of middle-class respectability—plus the virtues of masculine, middle-class heroics, such as initiative and competitiveness, all entirely within the range of any young man's potential. By this logic, success implied that a person must have followed the path of rectitude. . . .

Linking Business and Personal Industry

The intimate association between owner-managers and their businesses linked the industrialists' sense of personal worth with that of their firms. The owner-manager represented more than the typical mode of operating the American firm before 1890: the owner-manager also exemplified the ideal of the businessperson for the century. Owning and managing well one's own business was everywhere cited as how one could elevate oneself above anonymity without artistic or literary genius, but with the steadfast application of good character. Within this context that so prized self-employment, one's business and its reputation became an extension of one's self and personal reputation. . . . Andrew Carnegie declared that for business men, "Your firm is your monument." Similarly, Cyrus Hall McCormick frequently made it known that he was, according to his biographer William Hutchinson, "proud of his industry, and to have his name synonymous with harvesting machinery the world over was the chief ambition of his life." McCormick's grandson accorded the inventor the accolade that "the reaper was his life." . . .

The ethos of work pervaded popular literature of that century, and the businesspeople of whom we have direct reports seem to have gloried in their never-ending labors. Particularly the materially successful employers of others, or those who sought their patronage, praised the virtues of discipline and work in a marketplace allegedly teeming with opportunities for the diligent. The multitudinous nineteenth-century declarations on the virtues of work include *Triumphant Democracy*, throughout which Carnegie proclaims that work is the mark of the Republic. Of all the character traits that the advice literature of the period expounded upon to guide ambitious young people, willingness to work was the most central. The messages typically followed this pattern: "Accordingly, labor has ever been the indispensable condition of success in any and all departments of life. We are now pointing out to you, reader, an imperial highway to fortune, but we do most earnestly assure you that this highway can never be built without the most unremitting and indefatigable exertion on your part. . . . Industry is the price of excellence in everything." A firm's success, therefore, indicated the hard-working, good character of its owner-manager.

Embedded within this ethos of work was the importance of productiveness, as both an extension of the Protestant ethos of calling and as a major component of the traditional middle-class critique of nonproductive elements in society, both upper- and lower-class. The impulse to measure success in some way that transcended wealth derived in part from industrialists' desire to distinguish themselves from the traditional elites, the mercantile, financial, or idle rich. . . . [A]fter the Civil War "the title of 'producer' had taken on the lustre formerly inherent in the word 'merchant.'" Increasing employment and the stocks of available goods, in addition to lowering costs, were grand accomplishments for innovative producers. Under the title of "The Greatest Wealth Producers," the lead editorial in an 1893 issue of the *Iron Age* praised those whose work created more wealth than they consumed. . . . The double meanings of *industry*—more widely applied then than now—as a production activity and as diligence in personal character, also indicates these linkages. . . .

Progress as the Measure of Legitimacy

The productivity on which the nineteenth-century industrialists prided themselves required not only their own diligent labors but also their employment of the period's newest technologies of production, transportation, and communication. The larger cultural context within which manufacturers operated was a century of phenomenally dramatic changes in people's material and cultural experiences. . . .

Once American industrialization was under way, debates abounded about what sort of changes might best move society closer to perfection, but only the hopeless and rare skeptics did not adopt some version of progress. Even working-class people generally hoped that their children would someday share in the abundance that their exploited labor produced. The artisans whose shops were outmoded by mechanization tended to displace their distress, blaming immigrants or other minorities, including women factory workers. . . . Although some scientists and philosophers held more sophisticated interpretations of progress, many shared the popular views that "the growth of free-enterprise commercialism as the driving force of progress paved the way for a social evolutionism in which the attainment of middle-class values was the last step in the ascent of a linear hierarchy of developmental stages." At the core of this process was "the individual's effort to conquer his environment through the exploitation of better technology." . . .

Virtually every writer in the late nineteenth century who addressed contemporary issues included references to achieved progress, hopes for more, programs to ensure it, or concerns for its inequities. In fact, the concept was so ubiquitous that it is almost meaningless to refer to a separate literature of progress. Rather, the themes of improvement on personal, national, and world levels pervaded the century's writing and iconography. In particular, the vast majority of writers favorably associated technological developments with positive change and, hence, progress. Horace Greeley wrote in 1872 that industrial growth "is in the line of progress, in the direction of securing to each individual the largest liberty for his personal endeavors, and for society at large the greatest amount of material for its collective comfort and well-being." Even those who criticized the destructive and exploitative aspects of American development generally believed that industrialization itself was not the source of problems. Both Henry George in *Poverty and Progress* and Edward Bellamy in *Looking Backward* firmly believed that a positive progress through the advances of technology and industry could be had, although it required significant redirection of the nation's patterns of power and distribution. Most writers did not debate the merits of contemporary progress as generally defined, but simply accepted the changes as natural and appropriate. For example, a reference manual of "facts and figures" on American development was entitled *The National Hand-Book of American Progress,* expressing the connection between quantitative development and the author's notions of progress.

The industrialist class was prominent among the many Americans "convinced" . . . of both the reality and the merits of progress, as they experienced it. Indeed, as important actors in the material developments of their era, industrialists . . . helped to define progress by their enterprise both in production and in marketing. Their industries made available new and increasingly abundant material goods; their messages to the public about the desirability of those goods helped to set the direction and pace of America's sense of progress. Yet they also experienced great anxieties about their status as a new class as well as tensions when their materialism challenged their traditional values. They were, therefore, of all Americans, particularly likely to find attractive the notions of industrialization as progress. For them, participation in the developments of the era became an important indication of success because it combined control over technological power and acquiring wealth from it with a transcendent value, namely, the betterment of humankind. Such notions of progress resolved their internal tensions between spiritual and worldly ambitions; they gave industrialists a measure of their successes and thereby legitimated their agency in the century's transformations. Of the various transcendent values that industrialists could have adapted to project their successful enterprises, such as piety, charity, family devotion, and so on, progress offered the most powerful explanation and legitimation for the revolution in which they participated.

Yet material progress was not an unmixed blessing, then any more than now. The transformations entailed enormous costs, and some of those costs have been accounted extensively. From our vantage point, we are recently sensitive to the environmental costs. Other costs included the greatest mass dislocation—still ongoing—in history, as wave after wave of rural and village peoples subjected themselves to industry's regimentation of time and behavior. City living eliminated cheap, fresh food from most people's diets, even during harvest season, as it also did away with traditional communities and quiet. The exploitation and degradation of the laboring classes have been well documented, as have myriad other tragic consequences.

Such lists of the costs of the industrial, urban transformation typically focus on the people who suffered most obviously and who had the least control over the conditions under which they struggled. Other Americans seemed to have gained more than they had lost in the transformation. The Victorian bourgeois, for example, and those close enough to aspire to join that dominant stratum, were generally reckoned the successes of the era. Certainly in terms of material goods, they had opportunities to partake of the new profusion of goods from industry and world trade that marked material progress. Yet there were costs for these successful people, too. Indeed, the dislocations and stresses of "modern" living generated new ailments for Victorian women and men, such as neurasthenia and varieties of depression and anxiety. Furthermore, explosive urbanization and industrialization threatened and often destroyed the spaces people had known and trusted. Confrontations with the new technological systems, living conditions, and multicultural melange that were intrinsic parts of the changes at every level created tensions even as they fascinated and challenged people, individually and collectively. . . .

Why, then, did Victorian Americans subject themselves to such stresses and dislocations? Unlike the laboring classes, who mainly sought modest improvements in their meager standards of living through their decisions, the middle and upper classes had to have been driven by ambitions beyond subsistence. To a great extent, a desire to keep up with the processes of industrial, urban transformation propelled many people; they did not want to be left behind by either their peers or the abstract standards of success that signified participation in the progress of the time. Their cultural inheritance also attributed spiritual as well as worldly value to work as the means to success and progress. In 1883, *The Golden Gems of Life* typified how the Victorian compromise tied together the work ethos with success and progress. "Labor may be a burden and a chastisement, but it is also an honor and a glory. Without it nothing can be accomplished. All that to man is great and precious is acquired only through labor. . . . It is by labor that mankind have risen from a state of barbarism to the light of the present. It is only by labor that progression can continue. Labor [is] the grand measure of progress." In a complex and powerfully motivating spiral, the very people whose access to the means of production made them the prime actors in the era's transformations, themselves felt a compelling need to keep step with the processes that they and their peers drove forward. . . .

This ideology of progress linked material and social improvements. Its power to justify and to motivate enterprise helps explain why industrialization and urbanization dominated the American nineteenth century despite their disruptions and costs. Although these processes have appeared so vast and profound that both contemporary and later observers have been inclined to declare them inevitable, even deterministic processes, they were not. Like any other historical process, they resulted from countless decisions by countless individuals driven by their personal needs, ambitions, and expectations. There were, of course, different orders of self-determination in people's decision making; investors generally had more freedom of choice than did unskilled laborers, for example. Whatever their circumstances, people generally tried—as they do now—to weigh as well as possible the consequences of alternative decisions. The sum total of infinite numbers of individual decisions determined the nature of the industrial and urban transformations the nation experienced. In this context, Victorian beliefs about progress dominated a worldview that could explain what people experienced, while motivating them and providing some direction for their efforts. Attributing changes to progress, with its positive connotations, legitimized, even glorified, both the changes and their consequences, however unfortunate or disruptive they appeared in the short run. As Lewis Mumford has written of the American nineteenth century, "Life was judged by the extent to which it ministered to progress, progress was not judged by the extent to which it ministered to life." Successful participation in the new order could also validate an individual's activities and values by placing them into the perspective of this grand historical sweep. Since the products of material progress themselves defined the rewards of participating in modern times, producing as well as acquiring and using modern manufactured and marketed goods became a primary measure of one's successes, and hence one's worth in the new order.

Competition and Progress

Besides self-justification, why might nineteenth-century industrialists try to project a public image of themselves as progressive producers? Without question, a fiercely competitive experience dominated businesspeople's activities and thoughts. In a collection of biographies, *Men of Business,* written for Scribner's Men of Achievement series in 1893, William O. Stoddard compared business with the "ancient idea that war is the normal condition of the human race." In the "warlike rivalry" of business, "there is perpetual conflict. Business men of all occupations still speak of the season before them as 'the campaign.' In it they expect to meet with competition, and . . . enemies in the field." Accounts and trade were, and are still, *won* in the business world. Some commentators even attributed the intensification of competition to the very technological developments also responsible for material progress. "With the introduction of such forces as steam, machinery and electricity, the laws which prevailed fifty years ago no longer avail. This is aptly shown in the remark of the French economist, who said: 'In ancient days, when fortunes were made by war, war was a business; in these later days, when fortunes are made by business, business is war.'" Exacerbating this sense of competition were business owners' very realistic fears for the survival of their firms and the personal finances and commitments tied up in them. [The historian Edward Chase] Kirkland indicates that "contemporary observers were prone to assert that ninety-five per cent of all capitalists, 'men carrying on business,' failed." As a result, fears and anxieties about "hazardous" and "perilous" businesses and times filled their letters and conversations, including those of highly successful figures such as Andrew Carnegie and John D. Rockefeller. Furthermore, entrepreneurs ever "tend to seek novel ventures in the context of an environment of uncertainty" and to operate during rapidly changing times, and these conditions also add to their sense of insecurity. In light of the industrialists' perceptions of the world as dominated by risky competition, imperiling business survival, Social Darwinism gained adherents much more as a reflection than a cause of their worldviews, including racism. It provided a discourse to explain and communicate their experiences in terms of "the survival of the fittest" and a "struggle for success." It also allowed the successful to discount the suffering of others whose failures allegedly evinced their inferiority. Participation in progress could validate their efforts and investments, and demonstrating that participation to others argued for the merits of their activities as well as their wares.

Industrialists of this period also experienced competition outside of the marketplace. . . . An intense competition for cultural authority determined whose ideas and whose values would direct the nation's course in the throes of unprecedented change. Writers and speakers of innumerable persuasions proselytized avidly and prolifically, competing to influence the populace or portions thereof. The American industrialists figured as important actors in the dominant changes that some people praised, some questioned, and yet others decried. As a prospering and highly visible new class, the industrialists often felt uneasy about their status and identity relative to the ambient value systems. Even the Boston patricians who founded and profited from the Merrimack River's industrialization experienced this source of concern in the first half of the nineteenth century, when factories were a new and alien phenomenon in the United States. As a study of later American business attitudes theorized, "the content of the business ideology can best be explained in terms of the *strains* to which men in the business role are almost inevitably subject." They respond to "the emotional conflicts, the anxieties, and the doubts engendered by [their] actions" and the "conflicting demands of other social roles which they must play in family and community." Within the constraints of their cultural contexts, businesspeople shape their ideology "to resolve these conflicts, alleviate these anxieties, overcome these doubts." In the nineteenth-century competition for cultural hegemony, the industrialists had investments of time and financial resources, family security and status, and personal reputation to enhance as well as to protect. The ideologies of the American Victorian compromise and progress through increased productivity served these functions in their time.

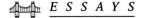 *E S S A Y S*

Mill and Mine

EDWARD L. AYERS

To many people, Southern industry seemed more of a charade than an actuality. After enduring twenty years of exaggerated claims in the *Manufacturer's Record*, even a Southern trade paper could stand the puffery no longer: "If all the saw mills, cotton mills, tobacco factories, new towns, and other enterprises and undertakings which it has heralded to its advertisers and 'subscribers' as having been started up in the various states of the South, had really been erected and put into operation," the *Southern Lumberman* sneered in 1908, "there wouldn't be surface room for them to stand on, water enough under the earth to supply their boilers, nor room enough in the sky for the smoke from their chimneys." Reality looked nothing like this.

Federal banking policy, railroad freight rates, absentee ownership, reliance on outside expertise, high interest rates, cautious state governments, lack of industrial experience—all these hindered the growth of Southern industry. New Southern enterprises had to compete with long-established Northern counterparts for capital, a share of the market, and skilled technicians. In these ways, much of the broad economic development that industrial growth brought to the North in the nineteenth century did not occur in the South.

Southerners recognized their disadvantages. "The shops north owe their success largely to the mechanics in their employ," a businessman complained, but "down here anybody who can pull a monkey wrench and pound his machine with a hammer and cuss the builder for making such a machine is called a mechanic." Industrial experience on the part of management was in short supply as well. Because "every city, town, and village wanted a cotton mill," a prominent mill owner recalled, it was often impossible to find an experienced textile executive and so "recourse was had to 'leading citizens' to head ventures. Sometimes a 'leading' citizen was a banker, a lawyer, a doctor, or a business man who had demonstrated that he could make a success of his private business. In most instances, however, they possessed no knowledge of manufacturing." This commentator built his own chain of mills by buying such enterprises, which had soon floundered and become available at a fraction of their worth.

Southern critics of the new order were not difficult to find, especially as the passing years bore witness to its hidden costs. The Southerner "performs the labor, gets the tuberculosis, reaps the desolation and hardships, while the Northern or Eastern capitalist gets the profits, and returns the same with a philanthropic strut in an occasion donation to a negro school or maybe a library building," Corra Harris, a white novelist, fumed. "And the blame of this arrangement rests no less upon the devilishly enterprising capitalists than it does upon the shiftless, short-visioned Southerners who not only permit but seek this method of destroying themselves." The capitalists might be "ethical rogues trained in the conscienceless school of finance," but the Southerners were "merely simple-hearted fools with an avarice for nickels instead of dollars."

Southern manufacturing did not fit what we recognize as the general pattern of industrial development that transformed other Western countries in the nineteenth century. While the cigarette, furniture, and textile industries made impressive strides in the New South, most Southern industrial workers labored in forests and mines rather than in factories. Those extractive industries became increasingly dominant throughout the New South era, outstripping the growth of more heavily mechanized enterprises. Southern industry created relatively few salaried clerks and other officials and failed to fuel the widespread economic development of the sort experienced in the Midwest at the same time.

Given these very real limitations, many contemporaries and subsequent scholars have seen the Southern economy as essentially "colonial," producing new products for distant markets where the profitable finishing and use of the products took place. Some have ascribed the South's colonial position to the actions of the federal government, to the unfair policies of major corporations, to the selling-out of the region by its own political and business leaders, to the machinations of Northern capitalists, to the resistance of powerful planters. These critics stress, with good reason, the conscious decisions that shaped the industrial experience of the South and look for those to blame for the region's lack of long-term development.

It is misleading, though, to stop there. Whether or not Southern industry in the aggregate measured up to standards achieved elsewhere under more favorable circumstances, it touched the lives of a million people. Whether or not Southern industry measured up to the claims of the region's boosters—and it did not—it shaped the histories of hundreds of counties. The impact of industry in the New South needs to be measured in people's experience, not merely in numbers, not merely by debunking inflated rhetoric. . . .

The New South had more than enough stories of great expectations followed by great disappointment, stories of boom and bust, stories of simple stagnation. One of these stories involved what must have seemed like a sure bet: the mining of phosphates on the coast of South Carolina, only a short distance by rail from the major market for such fertilizers, the older plantation districts of the Southeast. "Almost the whole country adjacent to the railroads in the South Atlantic States, is pervaded by the pungent fragrance of phosphates and other fertilizers," a reporter for the *Atlantic Monthly* wrote in 1882. "Travelers in the Pullman night coaches say they know when they are approaching a station by the potent odors which they encounter. Whole freight trains are laden with these substances, and hundreds of tons in sacks fill the freight platforms at all the stations."

The mining of phosphates began in the coastal areas around Charleston in the 1860s, flourished through the depression of the 1870s, and by the early 1880s was paying large dividends to the investors in the city. The amount of capital invested in the district's phosphate mining rose from $3.5 million in 1880 to $5.5 million in 1892, while the number of employees grew from 3,155 to 5,242. Nevertheless, those workers, almost all black men, performed distinctly old-fashioned back-breaking labor. For one kind of rock, they used a pick and shovel to dig pits from which the phosphate was extracted; for another, they simply waded into the rivers and used crowbars, picks, or oyster tongs to pry the phosphate loose; others dove for the rock in deeper water.

The black men in the phosphate mines, like others along the Carolina coast, refused to work in gangs. They insisted, instead, on working by the task, on getting paid for performing a certain amount of labor rather than for a set amount of time: they were more interested in controlling the pace of work and their daily wage than in making the maximum amount of money. Such preferences had characterized the Afro-American population of the coastal region for generations and had been the way they worked on the rice plantations before the phosphate boom began. The employers had to permit this labor arrangement if they were to get workers at all, for most of the laborers apparently preferred to work as independent farmers. Only steady wages, housing provided by the mine owners, health care, and credit (with its attendant indebtedness) could keep a labor force in the phosphate mines. When the industry went into decline in the 1890s, the black workers resumed the ways of making a living they had pursued before the mines opened.

Just as the labor force sought to conserve the ways of the past, so did the investors. The planters, cotton factors, and merchants who ran the mines used them mainly as a source of revenue to help maintain their accustomed way of life, not to create a New South. Charleston continued to pride itself on its conservatism, its aversion to the allure of progress. As a result of the city's resistance to new men and new money, in fact, businessmen and their capital fled Charleston. "The flower of Charleston's youth" left the city for the better chances of the textile mills in the up-country or the stores and factories of Birmingham or Atlanta. When the phosphate magnates died, their wills showed that their money had not remained in their ancestral city with them. Iron foundries in Alabama, street cars in newer cities, mills in raw textile villages—those were the distant beneficiaries of the phosphate profits.

South Carolina's phosphate boom proved short-lived. A series of terrible storms wrecked the Carolina industry in the early 1890s, just when strong competition from Florida began. "Compare that little speck in South Carolina with the broad flowing band that sweeps through Florida—and then think of the millions of tons—yes probably billions of tons—of phosphate that has been mined and shipped in Charleston," a Tallahassee paper exulted soon after the discovery of phosphate in Florida in 1890. "Think of the millions of money it's brought into South Carolina and your knees will grow weak in attempting to calculate how many trillions of money the Florida phosphate beds will bring into our beloved and flower decked state."

Whereas the older Carolina mines had operated in an environment where generations of blacks and whites had evolved traditional ways of doing things and where men with capital remained quite conservative, the phosphate boom of Florida unleashed the far more typical New South feeding frenzy. "Trains were filled with prospecting parties armed with spades, chemicals, and camping apparatus, Thousands came by horseback, by wagon, and on foot," the industry's historian has written. "The open woods were tracked everywhere by buggy wheels and punctured like a sieve" by the twenty-foot-long steel sounding rods that prospectors used to locate phosphate beds. The few nearby hotels filled to overflowing, and livery stables raked in money renting out horses by the day. "Companies were formed hourly," one observer noted, and "gilt-edged stock" flooded the state.

All through the early 1890s, even through the depression, the boom continued. By 1891, two counties alone could claim eighteen mining companies worth $5 million; within another year, the state saw more than 215 companies in operation; by 1896 over 400 companies had arisen. A familiar pattern set in, though: harder times caused the smaller operations to fail, and larger companies consolidated or replaced them. By 1900, only 50 companies mined phosphate in Florida. The big companies brought in centrifugal pumps, driven by steam engines on dredge boats, that sucked the phosphate pebbles from the beds and dumped them on a revolving screen to separate them from the sand and clay. After the phosphate dried on the wood fires and was screened another time, it was ready to be sold for fertilizer. The mines used prodigious amounts of wood to dry the phosphate—often five hundred cords per day—and local whites cut cord wood by contract. The phosphate boom echoed deep into Florida, Georgia, and Alabama, as the mining companies recruited thousands of black laborers.

The promise of mineral wealth brought capitalists and workers to other places in the South. In the 1870s the transition to coke as a fuel to make pig iron allowed Chattanooga to surge ahead in the industry, and by 1885 the small Tennessee city claimed nine furnaces and seventeen foundries and machine shops. The iron industry was growing just as fast in Virginia and Alabama: the 205,000 tons of pig iron produced in the Southern mineral belt in 1880 had grown to 1,568,000 in 1892. Throughout the 1870s, Birmingham had been merely one of a host of towns between southwest Virginia and north Alabama trying to cash in on the bonanza. In the mid-1880s, though, the Tennessee Coal Iron and Railway Company threw its money and power behind Birmingham and that city rapidly left its Southern competitors behind. As the nation's and the region's cities installed miles of cast-iron pipe for their new utilities, most of it came out of Birmingham; in 1889, even Andrew Carnegie had come to believe that "the South is Pennsylvania's most formidable industrial enemy."

Indeed, Birmingham pig iron was beating Northern competition in Chicago and Cincinnati, in Philadelphia and New York, even in Britain. In one sense, Alabama succeeded too well, for the state's iron makers poured their capital and their energy into pig iron while most American iron producers converted to steel. The merchants and investors laboring to create new iron towns often held on to familiar and successful technologies rather than experimenting with expensive methods that had not yet been proven in the South.

Even the South's greatest drawing card for every industry—cheap and plentiful labor—hurt the iron and steel industry in the long run, delaying the adoption of new techniques. With plenty of black workers rushing into Birmingham to work in the mills at rates far below Northern wages, the mills had little incentive to adopt labor-saving machinery. Even when a mill superintendent invented an important machine in Birmingham in the mid-nineties, only advanced Northern mills bothered to install it; forty years passed before Southern mills adopted the advance. As a result, the South steadily fell behind in productivity.

Ironically, too, the natural attributes that so excited Alabama boosters proved to be deficient in the century of steel: the underground (rather than pit) mines, the erratic seams and topography, and the low iron and high phosphorous content of the ore made the switch to steel far more difficult in Alabama than in the North. Characteristics of the larger regional situation also worked against Alabama steel. The Southern iron industry's late start, its reliance on outside technical expertise, its need for vast sums of capital that could be acquired only outside the South, the relatively small and slowly growing Southern market for steel, and the neglect of the Southern industry by its Northern-oriented parent company, U.S. Steel—all these conspired to keep Birmingham from attaining what had seemed so close at hand in the early 1890s.

Even as iron and steel failed to live up to expectations, Southern cotton textile mills prospered. Although textiles, like iron, involved competition with mature international rivals and required sophisticated technology, they displayed important—and critical—differences from the metals industry. Textile mills could be built anywhere that there was power to run the machinery, and the Piedmont from Virginia through Alabama offered dozens of rivers and streams with an adequate flow of water. After the 1890s, when the production of the Southern coal fields made steam power feasible, textile mills could be located over a much broader area. Moreover, a textile mill required far less capitalization than an iron or steel mill, and most labor in a textile factory required little experience and little physical strength; even children would do for some jobs. Finally, the competition with other regions and countries was less harsh in textiles than in iron and steel, because mills could specialize in particular weaves or grades that other mills were not producing.

While the Southern iron and steel industry became concentrated in the Birmingham district after 1880, the Southern textile industry steadily spread over a large area. The 10,000 textile hands in the South of 1870 (the same number as in 1850 and 1860) grew to 17,000 by 1880, 36,000 by 1890, and 98,000 by 1900. In 1870, the South held only 8 percent of the nation's textile workers; by 1900, 32 percent. Although Georgia claimed twice as many textile operatives as any other Southern state in the 1870s—a continuation of its antebellum domination—in the 1880s both of the Carolinas closed the gap and in the 1890s raced ahead even as Georgia nearly doubled its own labor force. Of the nearly 100,000 people who labored in Southern mills by the turn of the century, a third worked in South Carolina, another third in North Carolina, and a fifth in Georgia; the rest were distributed throughout Alabama, Virginia, Tennessee, Mississippi, and Kentucky. Over a thousand textile workers appeared in Arkansas, Louisiana, and West Virginia, states not usually associated with the industry. The mills varied widely in size: in 1900, the average mill in South Carolina employed 377 workers, in Georgia 270, and in North Carolina 171; the regional average was 243. The larger mills tended to be located in or near cities and large towns, not in isolated enclaves.

The South's textile mills boasted the latest and most sophisticated machinery. While steam drove only 17 percent of Southern mills in 1880, the proportion increased to 47 percent in 1890 and to more than 60 percent by 1900; electricity powered a rapidly growing share of its own. By the 1890s electric lights illuminated some mills during the night shifts, and automatic sprinklers and humidifiers appeared in the more advanced factories. Southern manufacturers were among the first to adopt the latest in manufacturing equipment as well, including a new revolving card in the 1880s and an automatic loom in the 1890s. Of the 222,000 looms installed in American factories around the turn of the century, the South claimed 153,000. The most important innovation, the ring spindle—easily run and repaired, and doubling the output per spinner—operated in 90 percent of Southern mills in the 1890s but in only 70 percent of New England mills.

This rapid proliferation of up-to-date textile mills inspired much of the South's boosterism. Here was evidence, in county after county, state after state, that factories could prosper in the South. Here was an industry that used expensive and sophisticated machinery to manufacture products that could hold their own with those produced in Great Britain or Massachusetts. Here were products sought in China, India, and Latin America, for the South supplied 60 percent of all the American cloth sent abroad at the turn of the century. Here were factories that paid a profit early on and kept on paying for decades. Here were factories that tapped the South's great cotton crop at the source, that saved the expense of transporting the bulky fiber thousands of miles. Here were factories that prospered even during the depression of the 1890s, while virtually every other business in the country—including New England textile factories—suffered.

Perhaps most important for the South's perception of itself, the textile mills were built with local capital and employed local people. Until after the turn of the century, Northern capital played only a small role in building the Southern factories. The Northern capital that did arrive came through the companies that also supplied the machinery and marketing of the Southern crop—not, as in the case of Birmingham, from the owners and managers of competing firms in the North. Every property holder in and around the towns that built textile mills could reasonably expect to profit from the mill's arrival. "Impress this fact upon your merchants," an Atlanta man wrote to an associate in the small Georgia town of Ellijay trying to boost a mill, "a cotton factory means an increase in population with more money in circulation weekly, and means a high price paid farmers for the cotton, with an enlarged market for their produce. Factory operatives being unable to attend gardens buy their produce."

People caught in the excitement of mill-building spoke often of the benefits the mills' working people would enjoy. The argument took different shapes depending on the context. Sometimes the mills were healthy because they would employ "white women and children who could find no other work equally well-adapted to their strength, and producing as large a return for their labor"; sometimes the mill village seemed wholesome because it brought isolated rural folk "together in groups, where they are subject to elevating social influences, encourages them to seek education, and improves them in every conceivable respect, as future husbands and wives, sons and daughters, parents and children." The town people saw the operatives from the very beginning as people unlike themselves, as helpless women, benighted rustics, or failed farmers. For some, that perception of the workers fed a desire to minister to them, to help bring them into the fold of the progressive New South; for others, perhaps most, that sense of otherness bred only pity or contempt.

Near the turn of the century a writer for the *Outlook* visited a mill town near Augusta. He asked several mill families why they had come there. "The reasons given for leaving their rural homes were widely various: 'because we lost our "plantation"'; 'because my wife was lonely'; 'because the darkeys came in.'" The pervasive decline of Southern rural life created a sense of dissatisfaction and desperation among white farming families that made it easier for mill operators to find a work force. The demographic pressure on the land, the decline of cotton prices, the growing proportion of women to men in the older regions, the mobility of blacks, the disaffection of the young for rural life—all these dislocations made it easier to undergo the powerful dislocation of leaving home to work in a textile mill. Instead of leaving his new wife behind to seek work on a railroad or logging crew, one young east Tennessee man told his skeptical father, he would go with his new wife to a mill town. "Well, if I had to go to public works"—the phrase Southerners at the turn of the century used to describe wage labor—"why not move to them [mills] where it would be in my family?"

Some people were obviously more willing to leave than others. Widows with children found the mills a place where they could keep their families together and live without dependence on others; in 1880, early in the mill-building period, almost half of all the mill households in Augusta were headed by women, virtually all widowed. Any family with several young daughters at home might find the mills attractive, for the labor of those daughters was worth far more in a factory than in the countryside. Single young men, on the other hand, found opportunities that paid about as well as the textile mills; at least until the turn of the century, a farm hand made as much as a spinner in a mill and a hard worker could make considerably more money cutting logs or working on a railroad. Those young men who stayed on at a mill through their mid-twenties, however, often remained for the rest of their working lives and rose in the company hierarchy. Women, who moved in and out of the mill as they had children, generally stayed in the lower-paying jobs.

While some parents would do anything to keep the children out of the mills and in school, others saw nothing wrong with children learning to work early on in life, contributing to the family income and being where they could be watched. Employers differed as well; some were anxious to have the cheap labor of children, while others would have happily replaced them with other, more dependable and less controversial workers. In any case, a quarter of all male mill workers at the turn of the century were fifteen or under, and over a third of females were that young; most workers of both genders were in their late teens or early twenties.

This profile of the laboring force was unique among Southern industries, both within the Piedmont and within the South as a whole. While women represented about 15 percent of all manufacturing workers in the Piedmont, the average for the rest of the region was only 4 percent. While youths under sixteen years of age represented about 13 percent of the Piedmont's workers, the regional average was only 3 percent. The textile labor force was also unique in its racial composition. Whereas the workers in virtually every other major industry in the South were nearly balanced between the races, the machine rooms of the cotton mills rapidly became the preserve of whites only. Mill owners would not allow blacks to work alongside the white women and girls who made up the bulk of the work force. Black men were permitted to work only at outside loading and unloading and in the suffocating rooms where they opened bales for processing. Black women found no work at all. . . .

This labor force held many attractions to mill management. By employing the entire family, the employer received not only inexpensive labor but also considerable sway over that labor. Unlike a single man, a family had a difficult time leaving; while workers who moved from mill to mill during those frequent times when there was not enough labor to go around inflated turnover figures, most mills enjoyed a stable core of families. The famous "mill village" setting increased that stability, for the company provided the school, the church, the recreation, and the store as well as the work. At the turn of the century, 92 percent of Southern textile workers lived in such settlements. The villages initially arose because employers had no choice but to provide housing and services for mills located on remote streams, where most of the early mills were built. They persisted because they gave the operatives things they came to expect—houses, schools, churches, stores—and because they gave employers effective means of keeping a steady and sober labor force. Born of necessity, the mill villages quickly became a resilient tradition.

These villages exhibited a broad range of conditions and elicited a broad range of reactions. The workers' evaluation of the results of their move from the countryside varied just as widely as the reasons they had left in the first place: "Some declared they had improved their conditions; others that they had ruined what good fortunes they had had." At first, one mill owner commented, workers seemed "supremely happy and contented" as they enjoyed the water pumps and nearby churches and schools unavailable in most farm communities. Yet "by and by the novelty wears away. Things once longed for and regarded as unattainable become commonplace." As one mill worker put it, "They's more money at the mill, but a better livin' on the farm. Unless a man's mighty sorry he can raise good somethin' t'eat on the land, while he has more spendin' money in the mill—and he spends it too. All he does at either one is jus' about break even."

The typical village combined urban crowding with the kerosene lamps, hand pumps, meddlesome livestock, flies, and mud of the countryside. The factory itself, filled with choking fibers and loud machines, was little better. The typical mill looked something like the one described in a novel of the time: "a low, one-story structure of half-burnt bricks" next to "a squatty low-browed engine room" with a "black, soggy exhaust-pipe stuck out of a hole in its side."

A rare contemporary view of a mill town from a worker's point of view appeared in a letter from J. W. Mehaffry of Concord, North Carolina, to Senator Zebulon Vance. Mehaffry was furious at conditions in the mill and the town. The local cotton mill owners, J. M. Odell and Son, "work their employees, women and children from 6 A.M. to 7 P.M. with a half hour for dinner." Worse, the Odells held back the workers' pay for a month, and used the money to buy cotton for the mill. "Although the owner and his son are *zealous Methodists,*" they are "our slave drivers. J. M. Odell has built a $5000 mausoleum to entomb *his* dead, but the poor women and children can be buried in the Potters field." The workers' houses were piled next to one another, creating a terrible sewage problem and contributing to the deaths of 47 adults and children in the last six months. The letter charged that Southern politicians, despite all their rhetoric, were no help: "We curse the northern people, when to do justice *all* our cursing should be expended on home monsters like J. M. and W. R. Odell." In the 1880s and 1890s, mill owners managed their affairs with little interference from politicians or reformers.

Because not enough families or young women were willing to work in the textile factories, owners experienced recurring labor shortages, especially in the years around the turn of the century. During those times, a steady stream of transient workers flowed into and out of the mill villages, moving to find higher wages, a better house, or merely a new setting. "This mill will be o.k. if we ever get enough weavers to run everything without depending on floating 'bum' labor," a manager for a North Carolina mill wrote his mother in 1897. "Whenever I see a strong, robust country girl, I am almost on my knees in my effort to try to get her to go to the mill to learn to weave." While the mills of the 1880s and 1890s managed to get most of their workers from nearby rural areas, by 1900 mill recruiters often had to search 250 miles afield. Some ran trains into the mountains to persuade families to come to the mill villages. Other mills sent agents into their competitors' towns to entice experienced hands to move, partly by "getting them dissatisfied" with their present lot.

The mill villages, while often separated from neighboring towns by different school systems and churches, were not self-contained paternalistic enclaves. Not only did "floaters" move from village to village, but even the long-term workers seldom had a personal relationship, positive or negative, with the mill owner. The kind of men who had the money to invest in mills had no interest in living in mill villages. "I was so impressed with the uninviting surroundings, lack of educational facilities and civilized society, etc.," one South Carolina man who was considering buying a small mill remarked, "that I decided that I would not move my family down there for the whole outfit as a gift." Groups of investors owned most mills and merely paid a superintendent to keep an eye on things. Those superintendents lived in the villages themselves and sent their children to school with the operative children. Chosen for their character and the respect they held among the workers as well as for their ability to keep things in order and to turn a profit, the superintendents often found themselves caught between employer and employee. Of the worker's class and background, but acting as the agent of absentee owners, the superintendent "only demanded of the operatives what the president demanded of him," a mill pastor pointed out. In turn, "the president demanded what the directors demanded of him; the directors demanded what the stockholders demanded of them. The stockholders demanded large dividends and there is where the driving began and there is where the responsibility rests." As in so much of the South, distant forces seemed to power the machinery, while people struggled in their face-to-face encounters to make the best of hard situations.

The mill people were part of the unstable and rapidly evolving world of the New South, and we should not allow the images conjured up by the phrase "mill village" to obscure the connections between the mill operatives and the world beyond. New and larger mills appeared near towns and cities of considerable size; mill towns ringed cities such as Charlotte or Burlington. Company stores became less common as the years passed; only a third of the mill villages had such a store at the turn of the century, and that proportion declined as competing private stores grew up near the mills. Complex divisions developed among the mill workers, as those who owned their homes in a mill town distanced themselves from the more transient workers renting houses from the company.

Mill workers found it easy to visit nearby saloons or brothels as well as friends back on the farm or in town; mill families saw sons and daughters leave for work elsewhere or to establish families outside the mill village; many mill families took in boarders, kin and strangers; considerable numbers of mill workers farmed nearby, some of them owning land. Even after the mills became firmly established at the turn of the century, high cotton prices enticed enough workers back to the land to try farming again that employers complained of labor shortages. All these trends quickened with the accelerating growth of the industry in the nineties and after, although people then and ever since have tended to envision the villages as they were for a few years in the early 1880s: the embodiments of personal concern or personal domination. Instead, they were part of the much larger transformation of the South, a transformation that soon eroded any lingering paternalistic style. The mills were based on industrial work, on dependence upon friends and allies among one's own class, not a longing for a lost plantation ideal.

The workers' dependence on one another was tested in the years between 1898 and 1902, when strikes shook the Piedmont. Some workers had joined the Knights of Labor in the early 1880s, but unions made little headway in the textile mills through all the boom years. In 1898 and 1899, though, faced with wage reductions, workers quickly organized in the National Union of Textile Workers and launched dozens of strikes against the mill owners. Those most likely to join the union and strike were those who labored in the big urban mills—in Columbus, Augusta, and Atlanta—where skilled workers congregated and from where there was little chance to turn to farming for a season. The supremely confident owners locked the workers out of the mills, coordinating their efforts so that workers would have nowhere to turn. Despite help from Northern unions, the owners crushed the strikes and broke the unions in August in 1902. Organized labor did not reappear in the textile mills for more than a decade.

Jaqueline Jones, *Labor of Love, Labor of Sorrow* (New York: Basic Books, 1985), 99–109. Reprinted by permission of Basic Books, a member of Perseus Books, LLC.

WEEK 5

DOCUMENTS

2. A Credit Agency Monitors Businesses Nationwide, 1850s–1880s

James Rorke, glassware, 102 John Street, New York City

Nov. 1, 1850. An Irishman by birth, formerly in Boston, commenced there by peddling and while doing so, his sons learned the glass trade, making vials, etc. He came to NY about six years since. Commenced here in a very small way and gradually worked himself into a fair trade. Profitable business, no doubt made money. Buys a good deal for cash and has good credit with glass manufacturers. Business not extensive. Buys in his own name, no endorsers.

John Ryan, crockery, 577 Eighth Avenue, New York City

Aug. 25, 1856. Began this business some years ago, kept a small stock of crockery on the sidewalk, which he still continues. Is of steady, industrious habits and good character. Has made some money, all invested in his stock, surplus of which he keeps in this cellar. Thought honest, doing well, worth of small credit. . . . July 21, 1863. Has his stock still in the cellar, his stand on the sidewalk; failed three years ago and compromised at 30 cents on dollar; making several hundred by the operation, under very small expenses and has no occasion to ask for credit. Should buy for cash. Is miserly and estimated worth $3,000 to $4,000.

R. G. Dun & Company Collection, Baker Library, Harvard University Graduate School of Business Administration, Boston, Mass. Ledger N.Y. 191, p. 431 (James Rorke); Ledger N.Y. 191, p. 480 (John Ryan); Ledger Mass. 72, p. 294 (George Burnham); Ledger Mass. 75, p. 106 (Mrs. Emaline H. Torrey); Ledger Mass. 68, p. 460 (S. E. Kendall & Company); Ledger Ohio 33 (Columbiana County 2): 671 (Gaston & Brother).

George P. Burnham, Boston, Mass.

Aug. 7, 1855. Is author of the "hen book" [*The History of the Hen Fever: A Humorous Record* (Boston: James French and Co., 1855)]. Said to be worth $20,000 to $25,000. Owns some real estate in Melrose, uninsured. Has an interest in a stock of refreshments and books at the Fitchburg railroad station and pays $1,800 rent. Is of the "Barnum" order of men, but said to be good though an unwilling and tardy paymaster. . . . Nov. 24, 1857. Lately of Burnham, Federhen & Co. Is about 40 years of age and has a family. Lives at Melrose. Has been connected with various newspapers and held government offices. Was the chief promoter of the "hen fever" a few years ago, by which he made considerable money; has been author and publisher. . . . July 25, 1859 . . . Appointed by Gov. Banks, State Liquor Commissioner, the most lucrative office under the state administration; his income is variously estimated at from $10,000 to $30,000. He lives like a prince, giving frequent and large parties to his political and personal friends, procures his liquors in this market through one house . . . and with it is prompt in payment; not generally regarded as a scrupulous man but his interest doubtless will make him safe while holding his present position.

Mrs. Emaline H. Torrey, dry goods, South Boston, Mass.

Sept. 12, 1860. A sister of Edwin Tilden . . . and a widow, has a small property which she has put into a dry goods stock and deals in a most quiet way. An exemplary woman, who will not thoroughly go beyond her ability to respond. . . . Oct. 29, 1861. A respectable widow with no family, lives with her mother, been in business some 2 years, and sells a fair amount of goods. Pays her rent promptly. Means small, but considered a fair risk for such modest credit as she would be likely to ask. Aug. 22, 1862. No change. Does a modest business, pays in 30 days, and considered safe for her modest wants. . . . July 20, 1864. Deceased.

S. E. Kendall & Company, eating house, 8 Congress Square, Boston, Mass.

Nov. 12, 1862. Kendall failed and went through insolvency four years ago. Owed $6,000 or $7,000 and had $250 assets, paid no dividend. Has since taken in a partner, D. W. Powers, who formerly worked for him and who had $1,000 or $1,500, it is said. Do considerable in their lines and make a living but not much more. We understand they don't ask credit at all now and ought not to. A friend . . . says he would trust them $100 to $300 on 30 days if asked. . . . Jan. 14, 1865. S. E. Kendall and John W. Dearborn mortgaged furniture, etc., in restaurant, 8 Congress Square, to Merrill Frost for $2,000.

Gaston & Brother, drugs and hardware, East Liverpool, Ohio

June 1879. In business under style Gaston & Brother, $8,000 to $10,000. George and Ephriam Gaston. George owns a farm, $5,000, and a nice residence, $6,000, think clear. Ephriam owns farm worth $3,000 and the firm owns store building worth $3,000 or $4,000, think clear. Ephriam's property is well mortgaged, . . . estimated worth all told $15,000. Are close, saving men, "but not the best accountants," and sometimes slow pay more from want of ability in management than means. Ephriam is a tolerably honest fellow, but George very close and mean. Are quite responsible for the requirements of the business. It does them no harm to "Dun" them keenly as they do not appreciate the necessity of promptness. Jan. 26. 1880. Slow pay, but responsible for their debts. Not much danger of their contracting debts beyond their ability to pay. April 8, 1880. Dissolved. George Gaston taking the hardware and Ephriam taking the drugs. George is worth in real estate, $5,000, and worth all told about $10,000, but rather slow pay. May 1881. Owns farm and residence and ½ interest in store property and is estimated worth all told $10,000. Very close and mean and not pleasant in his business manners. Quite responsible but better have contracts well defined.

4. Mrs. M. L. Rayne Highlights Proper Business Ventures for Victorian Women, 1893

As a forceful illustration of the extent to which women are now invading the fields of labor which have hitherto been occupied in the main by men, we append the following list which offers an interesting study. There are a great many branches not included in this list into which women are making their way, and to which reference is made elsewhere in the book.

Bankers and brokers, clergy, teachers, lawyers, physicians and surgeons, dentists, nurses, poets, dramatists, artists, journalists, editors, reporters, printers and type-setters, proof-readers, stenographers and type-writers, telegraphers, musicians, elocutionists, piano tuners, teachers of dancing, photographers, retouchers of photographs, government clerks and officials, dressmakers, professional cooks, hotel and boarding-house keepers, restaurateurs, inventors, electricians, lecturers, pilots, bookkeepers, commercial travelers, canvassers, engravers, wood turners and carvers, carriage trimmers, bell foundry operators, brass founders, gun and locksmiths, tinners, architects, auctioneers, clockmakers, agricultural laborers, gardeners, bee-keepers, poultry raisers, stock herders and stock raisers, barbers and hair dressers, cigarmakers, brewers, fishers, distillers, curriers and tanners, weavers.

It is now almost impossible to find any business in which a woman is not engaged, if not as principal, as assistant; in which position she pays the penalty of a lack of business knowledge and experience, by receiving a lower rate of remuneration

Martha Louise Rayne, *What Can a Woman Do; or, Her Position in the Business and Literary World* (Petersburgh, N.Y.: Eagle Publishing Co., 1893), pp. 22–24.

than a man would for doing exactly the same work; but she must patiently bide her time and learn what it is that she can do best, and not be spasmodic in her work or in her business relations.

False Pride.

When a young girl selects some money-making business she will naturally aspire to one of the professions, such as teaching, because of the desirable associations which surround it. School influences are all good, and a teacher is fitted to appear in the best society, as the result of association with the cultured and refined educators of youth. But all can not be teachers, nor are they adapted to the work if they could secure situations. What then? The shop, cashiers, bookkeepers or clerks? The training for any of these positions must be such that they can compete with the male clerk who began by sweeping out the store, and not only learned to cast up accounts with accuracy and precision, but to understand and take an interest in the fundamental laws upon which business is based. The girl who was playing with dolls when her fellow-clerk began his apprenticeship expects to pick it up in a few months, and earn as much as he! She will learn in a few lessons that she is mistaken, and if she is wise will pocket her pride and go down to the bottom of things as he did, learning the science as well as the routine of what she is doing. She need not abate a particle of her dignity of character, or grow hard and commonplace through the service of life, any more than she need ape the manners or don the garb of her male co-worker. It is not necessary that she lose that essential charm of womanhood, which is her natural heritage, because she turns the pages of a ledger. The whole tendency of her being is to grow in womanly strength, not to develop into some kind of a masculine nondescript.

3. Photographer Lewis Hine Depicts Child Laborers in the New York City Tenements, 1911

Children carried garments from the factory to be sewn at home. In fieldnotes accompanying this photograph, Lewis Hine wrote, "A load of kimonos just finished. Girl very reticent. Thompson St., N.Y." (National Archives)

From the Prints and Photographs Division, Library of Congress, Tenement House Scrapbook of Lewis Hine.

Reflecting on this New York City scene, Hine noted, "Mrs. Lucy Libertine and family: Johnnie, 4 years old, Mary 6 years, Millie 9 years, picking nuts in their basement tenement, 143 Hudson St. Mary was standing on the open mouth of the bag holding the cracked nuts [to be picked], with her dirty shoes on, and using a huge, dirty jacknife." (National Archives)

4. African Americans Seek Work in the North, 1917

Memphis, Tenn., May 5, 1917.

Dear Sir: I saw your add in the Chicago Defender papa and me being a firman and a all around man I thought I would write you. perhaps You might could do me lots of good. and if you can use me any way write me and let me No. in my trade or in foundry work. all so I got a boy 19 years old he is pretty apt in Learning I would Like to get him up there and Learn him a trade and I have several others would come previding if there be an opening for them. So this is all ans. soon

Algiers, La., May 16–17.

Sir: I saw sometime ago in the Chicago Defender, that you needed me for different work, would like to state that I can bring you all the men that you need, to do anything of work, or send them, would like to Come my self Con recomend all

From "Letters Home from Black Migrants to the North, 1916–1918," Emit Scott, ed., in *Journal of Negro History* 4 (July 1919), pp. 305–306. Reprinted by permission of the Association for Study of Afro-American Life and History, Inc.

the men I bring to do any kind of work, and will give satisfaction; I have bin fore-man for 20 yrs over some of these men in different work from R. R. work to Boiler Shop machine shop Blacksmith shop Concreet finishing or putting down pipe or any work to be did. they are all hard working men and will work at any kind of work also plastering anything in the labor line, from Clerical work down, I will not bring a man that is looking for a easy time only hard working men, that want good wages for there work, let me here from you at once.

Ellisville, Miss., 5/1/17.

Kind Sir: I have been takeing the Defender 4 months I injoy reading it very much I dont think that there could be a grander paper printed for the race, then the defender. Dear Editor I am thinking of leaving for Some good place in the North or West one I dont Know just which I learn that Nebraska was a very good climate for the people of the South. I wont you to give me some ideas on it, Or Some good farming country. I have been public working for 10 year. I am tired of that, And want to get out on a good farm. I have a wife and 5 children and we all wont to get our from town a place an try to buy a good home near good Schools good Churchs. I am going to leave here as soon as I get able to work. Some are talking of a free train May 15 But I dont no anything of that. So I will go to work an then I will be sure, of my leaving Of course if it run I will go but I am not depending on it Wages here are so low can scarcely live We can buy enough to eat we only buy enough to Keep up alive I mean the greater part of the Race. Women wages are from $1.25 Some time as high as $2.50. just some time for a whole week.

Hoping Dear Editor that I will get a hearing from you through return mail, giving me Some ideas and Some Sketches on the different Climate suitable for our health.

P.S. You can place my letter in Some of the Defender Columns but done use my name in print, for it might get back down here.

5. Helen B. Sayre Praises the Progress of Negro Women in Industry, 1924

The Negro woman's sudden entrance into industry is a new adventure and a dra-matic innovation. In the urgent quest for workers to "carry on" during the World War, she saw her longed-for opportunity, saw—as she visioned it—the end of the rainbow, and she came seeking it by thousands from her sunny, quiet southern home and plantation and placid housework and was at once swallowed up in the industrial centers in northern cities. Plucked so abruptly from the narrow spheres of such service as field hands, domestics and children's nurses, it is amazing to observe the transition and transformation of this same gentle, leisurely southern woman into the high-tension industrial worker in a large factory. Labor turnover, time clocks, piece work, output, maximum and minimum production, these words were unknown in her vocabulary a few years back. But today there are thousands

From Helen B. Sayre, "Negro Women in Industry," *Opportunity* 2 (August 1924): 242–244.

of these girls and women, working tirelessly and patiently and steadily in our large industrial plants,—and *making good.*

At the close of the War and during the general depression in business which followed, many Negro girls were released and replaced with white help. It was a tragedy to the Negro girl, as she had not had time to lay aside anything for the rainy day, to gain needed experience and skill, and to overcome the impatience of the average employer and an antagonistic foreman. She was hired in a period of crisis, to fill the gap at the bottom of the scale,—the most undesirable and unskilled jobs in the factory were assigned to her. The idea seemed very general that she could not be trusted to do the skilled work in any event—usually she was not given an opportunity if white help could be secured. Wet and sloppy work, heavy and tedious, with little chance for advancement, and if she did succeed, it was by sheer grit and determination, as many have told me. She had to be able to outdo her white competitor; sometimes she failed through lack of experience, and this would cause employers to say she was not capable, when in most cases it was simply due to poor selective instinct on his part or lack of intelligence or adaptability in her particular case.

Left to the mercy of ignorant, prejudiced, intolerant foremen, what could be expected? However, the whole story is not so dark. Though her progress was retarded by the turn in events, still we know that she did retain some very worthwhile places and she has progressed in them wherever possible to semi-skilled and skilled jobs. It is worthy of note, that wherever an employer was humane and appreciative and gave his Negro help a chance to advance and a square deal in wages and working conditions, he had steady, cheerful workers—which refutes a charge so prone to be made about their being undependable. Employers have found her amiable in disposition, intelligent and more adaptable than the unskilled foreign worker for whom white social agencies are engaged in season and out to aid them to adjust themselves, develop technique and become capable, highly skilled workers. For the Negro girl there are no such agencies outside of a small work being done by the Y.W.C.A. in the City of Chicago. In my experience with both white and Negro girls, I have found no difference between them in capacity for work. . . .

The story of the Negro women employed at the Nachman Springfilled Cushion Company of Chicago, Illinois, may be of some value in understanding the whole situation. It will also show the splendid growth of a business whose enviable record for superior quality and excellence in manufactured products is the output of these same women power machine operators, who make the durable covers for the softly resilient springs.

In the beginning this company employed less than fifty persons. It was a simple matter for the heads of the firm to know each individual worker. Today there are between six and seven hundred on the pay-roll. The employment of such large numbers has tended to destroy any personal relation between employer and employees, and there is practically no contact with the workers. The making of these cushion covers was also a simple process in the beginning; they were used mostly for chair seats and a perfectly "green" girl who had never seen a power machine before could learn in a very few days to sew them. Today this firm manufactures cushions for all kinds of upholstered furniture, day-beds, mattresses, and automobile seats. Each unit-spring is enclosed in a separate pocket and these covers are made in two operations.

When I tell you we have girls who can sew from five to seven thousand pockets in a day, you will realize that they have become "peppy" and mastered the speeding-up in industry. They are put on piece work in about three weeks and we have many girls making from twenty to thirty dollars per week. An average girl can make eighteen dollars per week. This is good pay for a year round job.

There came a time when this large group of girls, with no previous factory experience and no one to encourage and reprove them or give them any personal attention whatever, were doing about as they pleased. They were very irregular in attendance,—a very serious matter to the firm, in trying to give prompt service and keep up production.

The cushion is an unfinished product and is delivered in large quantities to factories to be upholstered. The girls would say, "If we stay out we are the only losers, being on piece work." So the week would go something like this: Monday—bad; Tuesday—a little better; Wednesday—very good, being pay day; Thursday—very poor; Friday—somewhat better; Saturday—a half-day and the worst day of the week. The company was about three months behind in delivery of orders due to the fact that girls were given a chance to learn to operate the machines with pay, and many stayed just long enough to learn. Continually employing new help, of course, was responsible for poor quality of work as well as large labor turnover and financial loss. The girls were disposed to be late for work and quit anywhere from a half-hour to fifteen minutes before closing time. There was considerable lack of respect for authority when it came to the forelady and inspector, as there was more or less a division of authority; so the firm had almost decided to release all the colored help, which meant a terrible blow to future opportunities. It was at this juncture that the Chicago Urban League was appealed to and they advised putting a Negro woman as Personnel Director in charge to save the situation if possible for these hundreds of girls. The work of this Director has been very interesting and to some considerable degree satisfactory to the firm. It must be acknowledged to the credit of the firm that they have done everything possible for the Director to carry out her plans.

Her first task was to establish confidence and good-will in the hearts of the workers for herself. This was done by bringing about some very needed improvements for the physical welfare of the workers, such as individual towels, rest-room, installing a wholesome lunch service, ice-water coolers on each floor during the summer months, having the space between the rows of machines widened seventeen inches so that the girls could swing the large work more easily in sewing, installation of ventilators. There was a need to develop a spirit of respect for those in authority and this has been brought about gradually by the careful handling of individual cases needing adjustment. It was necessary to educate those in authority as to their duty and responsibility as well as to require respect from the girls toward them.

The girls soon realized that if they had just cause for complaint, they were upheld; if they were in the wrong, their Director gave them a warning the first time that a second offense would mean dismissal, and it did mean just that. Misfits were gradually released; careless and poor operators were discharged; certain factory rules were established, such as for punctuality, attendance, general conduct. This was done after heart to heart talks with the girls and they were made to realize the necessity for these adjustments.

We have without doubt today, we believe, the best disciplined group of factory employees to be found. We have an average of 97% on time; 95%–98% on the job! Our production has increased steadily from about 250,000 pockets to an average of 400,000 per day and on special occasions when we have needed an increased production they have easily speeded up to 500,000. This is the output of about 170 operators. . . . Eighteen months ago we were three months behind in filling orders; today we guarantee a twenty-four hour delivery. Posting an hourly production scale on the bulletin board stimulates interest and it is great sport to watch the figures mount. We issue from time to time a printed bulletin or news sheet containing instructions and matters of general interest and information for the workers. We encourage the girls to larger earning effort by giving each girl a new dollar bill for every five dollars increase in her pay check; we also issue stars to the girls to wear on their caps, showing their rating,—one star for fifteen dollars; two stars for twenty dollars. . . .

Until the Negro woman in industry has had a longer factory experience, until she has acquired the modern industry complex, where they are employed in large numbers, they must be guided. In a few years they will have established themselves without question as to their ability and capacity for routine factory work. Then they may be counted upon to make their contribution and become an integral part of the great industrial systems of America. Give her time, give her guidance—most of all, give her opportunity.

From Reports on the Immigration Commission, 61st Congress, 2nd Session, Senate Document 633, *Immigrants in Industries,* Part 25: Japanese and Other Immigrant Races in the Pacific Coast and Rocky Mountain States, vol. II: Agriculture (Washington, D.C.: U.S. Government Printing Office, 1911), 108–110.

1. Population Growth in Select U.S. Cities, 1870–1920

	1870	1880	1890	1900	1910	1920
New England						
Boston	250,526	362,839	448,477	560,892	670,585	748,060
Lowell	40,928	59,475	77,696	94,969	106,294	112,759
Providence	68,904	104,857	132,146	175,597	224,326	237,595
New Haven	50,840	62,882	86,045	108,027	133,605	162,537
Worcester	41,105	58,291	84,655	118,421	145,986	179,754
Middle Atlantic						
New York	942,292	1,164,673	1,441,216	3,437,202	4,766,883	5,620,048
Brooklyn	419,921	599,495	838,547	In N.Y.C.	In N.Y.C.	In N.Y.C.
Rochester	62,386	89,366	133,896	162,608	218,149	295,750
Buffalo	117,714	155,134	255,664	352,387	423,715	506,775
Newark	105,059	136,508	181,830	246,070	347,469	414,524
Jersey City	82,546	120,722	163,003	206,433	267,779	298,103
Philadelphia	674,022	847,170	1,046,964	1,293,697	1,549,008	1,823,779
Pittsburgh	139,256	235,071	343,904	451,512	533,905	588,343
South Atlantic						
Baltimore	267,354	332,313	434,439	508,957	558,485	733,826
Washington	109,199	147,293	188,932	278,718	331,069	437,571
Richmond	51,038	63,600	81,388	85,050	127,628	171,667
Durham, N.C.	—	2,041	5,485	6,679	18,241	21,719
Charlotte, N.C.	4,473	7,094	11,557	18,091	34,014	46,338
Charleston	48,956	49,984	54,955	55,807	58,833	67,957
Savannah	28,235	30,709	43,189	54,244	65,064	83,252
Atlanta	21,789	37,409	65,533	89,872	154,839	200,616

North Central					
Cincinnati	216,239	255,139	296,908	325,902	363,591	401,247
Cleveland	92,829	160,146	261,353	381,768	560,663	796,841
Detroit	79,577	116,340	205,876	285,704	465,766	993,678
Milwaukee	71,440	115,587	204,468	285,315	373,857	457,147
Chicago	298,977	503,185	1,099,850	1,698,575	2,185,283	2,701,705
St. Louis	310,864	350,518	451,770	575,238	687,029	772,897
Kansas City, Mo.	32,260	55,785	132,716	163,752	248,381	324,410
Wichita, Kans.	—	4,911	23,853	24,671	52,450	72,217
Omaha	16,083	30,518	140,452	102,555	124,096	191,601
Minneapolis	13,066	46,887	164,738	202,718	310,408	380,582
South Central					
Mobile	32,034	29,132	31,076	38,469	51,521	60,777
Birmingham	—	3,086	26,178	38,415	132,685	178,806
New Orleans	191,418	216,090	243,039	287,104	339,075	387,219
Memphis	40,226	33,592	64,495	102,320	131,105	162,351
Nashville	25,865	43,350	76,168	80,865	110,364	118,342
Louisville	100,753	123,758	161,129	204,731	223,928	234,891
Houston	9,382	16,513	27,557	44,633	78,800	138,276
Dallas	—	10,358	38,067	42,638	92,104	158,976
Mountain					
Denver	4,759	35,629	106,713	133,859	213,381	256,491
Salt Lake City	12,854	20,768	44,843	53,531	92,777	118,110
Pacific					
Los Angeles	5,728	11,183	50,395	102,479	319,198	576,673
San Francisco	149,473	233,959	298,997	342,782	416,912	506,676
Portland, Ore.	8,293	17,577	46,385	90,426	207,214	258,288
Seattle	1,107	3,533	42,837	80,671	237,194	315,312

Bayrd Still, *Urban America: A History with Documents* (Boston: Little Brown, 1974), pp. 210–211. Reprinted by permission of Little, Brown and Company.

2. Immigrant Distribution in Six Cities, 1870–1920

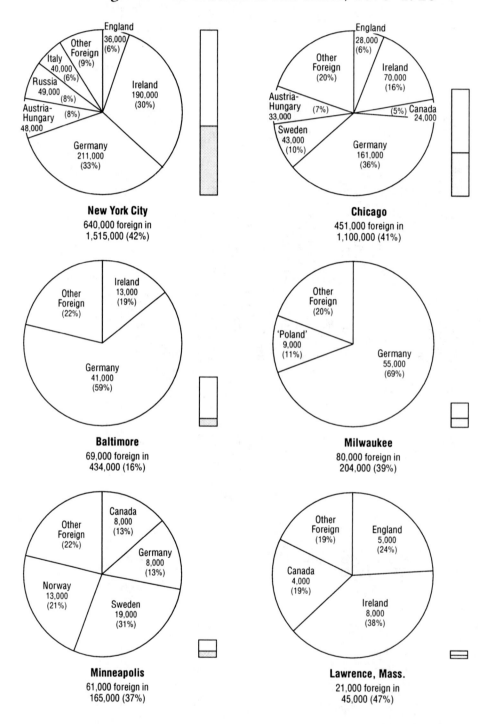

New York City
640,000 foreign in
1,515,000 (42%)

Chicago
451,000 foreign in
1,100,000 (41%)

Baltimore
69,000 foreign in
434,000 (16%)

Milwaukee
80,000 foreign in
204,000 (39%)

Minneapolis
61,000 foreign in
165,000 (37%)

Lawrence, Mass.
21,000 foreign in
45,000 (47%)

3. A Visiting Rudyard Kipling Returns, Unimpressed, from Chicago, 1899

I have struck a city,—a real city,—and they call it Chicago. The other places do not count. San Francisco was a pleasure-resort as well as a city, and Salt Lake City was a phenomenon. This place is the first American city I have encountered. It holds rather more than a million people with bodies, and stands on the same sort of soil as Calcutta. Having seen it, I urgently desire never to see it again. It is inhabited by savages. Its water is the water of the Hugli, and its air is dirt. Also it says that it is the 'boss' town of America.

I do not believe that it has anything to do with this country. They told me to go to the Palmer House, which is a gilded and mirrored rabbit-warren, and there I found a huge hall of tessellated marble, crammed with people talking about money and spitting about everywhere. Other barbarians charged in and out of this inferno with letters and telegrams in their hands, and yet others shouted at each other. A man who had drunk quite as much as was good for him told me that this was 'the finest hotel in the finest city on God Almighty's earth.' By the way, when an American wishes to indicate the next county or State he says, 'God A'mighty's earth.' This prevents discussion and flatters his vanity.

Then I went out into the streets, which are long and flat and without end. And verily it is not a good thing to live in the East for any length of time. Your ideas grow to clash with those held by every right-thinking white man. I looked down interminable vistas flanked with nine-, ten-, and fifteen-storeyed houses, and crowded with men and women, and the show impressed me with a great horror. Except in London—and I have forgotten what London is like—I had never seen so many white people together, and never such a collection of miserables. There was no colour in the street and no beauty—only a maze of wire ropes overhead and dirty stone flagging underfoot. A cab-driver volunteered to show me the glory of the town for so much an hour, and with him I wandered far. He conceived that all this turmoil and squash was a thing to be reverently admired; that it was good to huddle men together in fifteen layers, one atop of the other, and to dig holes in the ground for offices. He said that Chicago was a live town, and that all the creatures hurrying by me were engaged in business. That is to say, they were trying to make some money, that they might not die through lack of food to put into their bellies. He took me to canals, black as ink, and filled with untold abominations, and bade me watch the stream of traffic across the bridges. He then took me into a saloon, and, while I drank, made me note that the floor was covered with coins sunk into cement. A Hottentot would not have been guilty of this sort of barbarism. The coins made an effect pretty enough, but the man who put then there had no thought to beauty, and therefore he was a savage. Then my cab-driver showed me business-blocks, gay with signs and studded with fantastic and absurd advertisements of goods, and looking down the long street so adorned it was as though each vendor stood at his door howling: 'For the sake of money, employ or buy of me and me

Rudyard Kipling, "Chicago Barbarism," In *From Sea to Sea; Letters of Travel* (New York: Doubleday & McClure, 1899), II, 126–130.

only!' Have you ever seen a crowd at our famine-relief distributions? You know then how men leap into the air, stretching out their arms above the crowd in the hope of being seen; while the women dolorously slap the stomachs of their children and whimper. I had sooner watch famine-relief than the white man engaged in what he calls legitimate competition. The one I understand. The other makes me ill. And the cabman said that these things were the proof of progress; and by that I knew he had been reading his newspaper, as every intelligent American should. The papers tell their readers in language fitted to their comprehension that the snarling together of telegraph wires, the heaving up of houses, and the making of money is progress.

I spent ten hours in that huge wilderness, wandering through scores of miles of these terrible streets, and jostling some few hundred thousand of these terrible people who talked money through their noses. The cabman left me: but after a while I picked up another man who was full of figures, and into my ears he poured them as occasion required or the big blank factories suggested. Here they turned out so many hundred thousand dollars' worth of such-and-such an article; there so many million other things; this house was worth so many million dollars; that one so many million more or less. It was like listening to a child babbling of its hoard of shells. It was like watching a fool playing with buttons. But I was expected to do more than listen or watch. He demanded that I should admire; and the utmost that I could say was: 'Are these things so? Then I am very sorry for you.' That made him angry, and he said that insular envy made me unresponsive. So you see I could not make him understand.

4. Poet Carl Sandburg Extols the City of the Big Shoulders, 1916

Chicago

> Hog Butcher for the World,
> Tool Maker, Stacker of Wheat,
> Player with Railroads and the Nation's Freight Handler;
> Stormy, husky, brawling,
> City of the Big Shoulders:
>
> They tell me you are wicked and I believe them, for I
>   have seen your painted women under the gas lamps
>   luring the farm boys.
> And they tell me you are crooked and I answer: Yes, it
>   is true I have seen the gunman kill and go free to
>   kill again.
> And they tell me you are brutal and my reply is: On the
>   faces of women and children I have seen the marks
>   of wanton hunger.

"Chicago" (1916) in Carl Sandburg, *Chicago Poems* (New York: Henry Holt, 1916), 3–4.

And having answered so I turn once more to those who
   sneer at this my city, and I give them back the sneer
   and say to them:
Come and show me another city with lifted head singing
     so proud to be alive and coarse and strong and
     cunning.
Flinging magnetic curses amid the toil of piling job on
   job, here is a tall bold slugger set vivid against the
   little soft cities;
Fierce as a dog with tongue lapping for action, cunning
   as a savage pitted against the wilderness,
     Bareheaded,
     Shoveling,
     Wrecking,
     Planning,
     Building, breaking, rebuilding,
Under the smoke, dust all over his mouth, laughing with
   white teeth,
Under the terrible burden of destiny laughing as a young
   man laughs,
Laughing even as an ignorant fighter laughs who has
   never lost a battle,
Bragging and laughing that under his wrist is the pulse,
   and under his ribs the heart of the people,
     Laughing!
Laughing the stormy, husky, brawling laughter of
   Youth, half-naked, sweating, proud to be Hog
   Butcher, Tool Maker, Stacker of Wheat, Player with
   Railroads and Freight Handler to the Nation.

5. Congress Takes Aim at the "Chinese Menace," 1892

There is urgent necessity for prompt legislation on the subject of Chinese immigration. The exclusion act approved May 6, 1882, and its supplement expires by limitation of time on May 6, 1892, and after that time there will be no law to prevent
the Chinese hordes from invading our country in number so vast, as soon to out-
number the present population of our flourishing States on the Pacific slope. . . .

   ⊁ The popular demand for legislation excluding the Chinese from this country is
urgent and imperative and almost universal. Their presence here is inimical to our
institutions and is deemed injurious and a source of danger. They are a distinct
race, saving from their earnings a few hundred dollars and returning to China. This
they succeed in doing in from five to ten years by living in the most miserable manner, when in cities and towns in crowded tenement houses, surrounded by dirt,
filth, corruption, pollution and prostitution; and gambling houses and opium joints
abound. When used as cooks, farm-hands, servants, and gardeners, they are more
cleanly in habits and manners. They, as a rule, have no families here; all are men,

---

"The Chinese Menace," Congressional Report on Immigration, U.S. Congress, House of Representatives, Report No. 255, Feb. 10, 1892.

save a few women, usually prostitutes. They have no attachment to our country, its laws or its institutions, nor are they interested in its prosperity. They never assimilate with our people, our manners, tastes, religion, or ideas. With us they have nothing in common.

Living on the cheapest diet (mostly vegetable), wearing the poorest clothing, with no family to support, they enter the field of labor in competition with the American workman. In San Francisco, and in fact throughout the whole Pacific slope, we learn from the testimony heretofore alluded to, that the Chinamen have invaded almost every branch of industry; manufacturers of cigars, cigar boxes, brooms, tailors, laundrymen, cooks, servants, farmhands, fishermen, miners and all departments of manual labor, for wages and prices at which white men and women could not support themselves and those dependent upon them. Recently this was a new country, and the Chinese may have been a necessity at one time, but now our own people are fast filling up and developing this rich and highly favored land, and American citizens will not and can not afford to stand idly by and see this undesirable race carry away the fruits of the labor which justly belongs to them. A war of races would soon be inaugurated; several times it has broken out, and bloodshed was followed. The town of Tacoma, in 1887, banished some 3,000 Chinamen on twenty-four hours' notice, and no Chinaman has ever been permitted to return.

Our people are willing, however, that those now here may remain, protected by the laws which they do not appreciate or obey, provided strong provision be made that no more shall be allowed to come, and that the smuggling of Chinese across the frontiers be scrupulously guarded against, so that gradually, by voluntary departures, death by sickness, accident, or old age, this race may be eliminated from this country, and the white race fill their places without inconvenience to our own people or to the Chinese, and thus a desirable change be happily and peacefully accomplished. It was thought that the exclusion act of 1882 would bring about this result; but it now appears that although at San Francisco the departures largely exceed the arrivals, yet the business of smuggling Chinese persons across the lines from the British Possessions and Mexico has so greatly increased that the number of arrivals now exceed the departures. This must be effectually stopped.

6. Huang Zunxian Expresses the Chinese Perspective in Poetry, c. 1884

Expulsion of the Immigrants

Alas! What crime have our people committed,
That they suffer this calamity in our nation's fortunes?
Five thousand years since the Yellow Emperor,
Our country today is exceedingly weak.
Demons and ghouls are hard to fathom;

"Expulsion of the Immigrants" in R. David Arkush and Leo O. Lee, trans. and eds., *Land Without Ghosts: Chinese Impressions of America from the Mid-Nineteenth Century to the Present* (Berkeley: University of California Press, 1989), 61–65. Copyright © 1989 The Regents of the University of California. Reprinted by permission.

Even worse than the woodland and monsters.
Who can say our fellow men have not met an inhuman fate,
In the end oppressed by another race?
Within the vastness of the six directions,
Where can our people find asylum?

When the Chinese first crossed the ocean,
They were the same as pioneers.
They lived in straw hovels, cramped as snail shells;
For protecting gradually built bamboo fences.
Dressed in tatters, they cleared mountain forests;
Wilderness and waste turned into towns and villages.
Mountains of gold towered on high,
Which men could grab with their hands left and right.
Eureka! They return with a load full of gold,
And bragging this land is paradise.
They beckon and beg their families to come;
Legs in the rear file behind legs in the front.
Wearing short coats, they braid their queues;
Men carry bamboo rainhats, wear straw sandals.
Bartenders lead along cooks;
Some hold tailors' needles, others workmen's axes.
They clap with excitement, traveling overseas;
Everyone surnamed Wong creates confusion. . . .

Gradually the natives turned jealous.
Time to time spreading false rumors,
They say these Chinese paupers
Only wish to fill their money bags.
Soon as their feet touch the ground,
All the gold leaps out of the earth.
They hand ten thousand cash on their waists,
And catch the next boat back to China.
Which of them is willing to loosen his queue,
And do some hard labor for us?
Some say the Chinese are shiftless; . . .
Others say the Chinese are a bunch of hoodlums,
By nature all filthy and unclean.
Their houses are as dirty as dogs';
Their food even worse than pigs'.
All they need is a dollar a day;
Who is as scrawny as they are?
If we allow this cheap labor of theirs,
Then all of us are finished.
We see our own brothers being injured;
Who can stand these venomous vermin? . . .

From now on they set up a strict ban,
Establishing customs posts everywhere.
They have sealed all the gates tightly,
Door after door with guards beating alarms.

Chinese who leave are like magpies circling a tree,
Those staying like swallows nesting on curtains. . . .

Those who do not carry passports
Are arrested as soon as they arrive.
Anyone with a yellow-colored face
Is beaten even if guiltless.
I sadly recollect George Washington,
Who had the makings of a great ruler.
He proclaimed that in America,
There is a broad land to the west of the desert.
All kinds of foreigners and immigrants,
Are allowed to settle in these new lands.
The yellow, white, red, and black races
Are all equal with our native people.
Not even a hundred years till today,
But they are not ashamed to eat his words. . . .
The land of the red man is vast and remote;
I know you are eager to settle and open it.
The American eagle strides the heavens soaring,
With half of the globe clutched in his claw.

7. W. E. B. Du Bois Denounces Racial Prejudice in Philadelphia, 1899

Incidentally throughout this study the prejudice against the Negro has been again and again mentioned. It is time now to reduce this somewhat indefinite term to something tangible. Everybody speaks of the matter, everybody knows that it exists, but in just what form it shows itself or how influential it is few agree. In the Negro's mind, color prejudice in Philadelphia is that widespread feeling of dislike for his blood, which keeps him and his children out of decent employment, from certain public conveniences and amusements, from hiring houses in many sections, and in general, from being recognized as a man. Negroes regard this prejudice as the chief cause of their present unfortunate condition. On the other hand most white people are quite unconscious of any such powerful and vindictive feeling; they regard color prejudice as the easily explicable feeling that intimate social intercourse with a lower race is not only undesirable but impracticable if our present standards of culture are to be maintained; and although they are aware that some people feel the aversion more intensely than others, they cannot see how such a feeling has much influence on the real situation, or alters the social condition of the mass of Negroes.

As a matter of fact, color prejudice in this city is something between these two extreme views: it is not to-day responsible for all, or perhaps the greater part of the Negro problems, or of the disabilities under which the race labors; on the other

W. E. B. Du Bois, *The Philadelphia Negro* (Philadelphia: University of Pennsylvania, 1899), 322–325, 353–355.

hand it is a far more powerful social force than most Philadelphians realize. The practical results of the attitude of most of the inhabitants of Philadelphia toward persons of Negro descent are as follows:

1. As to getting work:

No matter how well trained a Negro may be, or how fitted for work of any kind, he cannot in the ordinary course of competition hope to be much more than a menial servant.

He cannot get clerical or supervisory work to do save in exceptional cases.

He cannot teach save in a few of the remaining Negro schools.

He cannot become a mechanic except for small transient jobs, and cannot join a trades union.

A Negro woman has but three careers open to her in this city: domestic service, sewing, or married life.

2. As to keeping work:

The Negro suffers in competition more severely than white men.

Change in fashion is causing him to be replaced by whites in the better paid positions of domestic service.

Whim and accident will cause him to lose a hard-earned place more quickly than the same things would affect a white man.

Being few in number compared with the whites the crime or carelessness of a few of his race is easily imputed to all, and the reputation of the good, industrious and reliable suffer thereby.

Because Negro workmen may not often work side by side with white workmen, the individual black workman is rated not by his own efficiency, but by the efficiency of a whole group of black fellow workmen which may often be low.

Because of these difficulties which virtually increase competition in his case, he is forced to take lower wages for the same work than white workmen.

3. As to entering new lines of work:

Men are used to seeing Negroes in inferior positions; when, therefore, by any chance a Negro gets in a better position, most men immediately conclude that he is not fitted for it, even before he has a chance to show his fitness.

If, therefore, he set up a store, men will not patronize him.

If he is put into public position men will complain.

If he gain a position in the commercial world, men will quietly secure his dismissal or see that a white man succeeds him.

4. As to his expenditure:

The comparative smallness of the patronage of the Negro, and the dislike of other customers makes it usual to increase the charges or difficulties in certain directions in which a Negro must spend money.

He must pay more house-rent for worse houses than most white people pay.

He is sometimes liable to insult or reluctant service in some restaurants, hotels and stores, at public resorts, theatres and places of recreation; and at nearly all barber-shops.

5. As to his children:

The Negro finds it extremely difficult to rear children in such an atmosphere and not have them either cringing or impudent: if he impresses upon them patience with their lot, they may grow up satisfied with their condition; if he inspires them with ambition to rise, they may grow to despise their own people, hate the whites and become embittered with the world.

His children are discriminated against, often in public schools.

They are advised when seeking employment to become waiters and maids.

They are liable to species of insult and temptation peculiarly trying to children.

6. As to social intercourse:

In all walks of life the Negro is liable to meet some objection to his presence or some discourteous treatment; and the ties of friendship or memory seldom are strong enough to hold across the color line.

If an invitation is issued to the public for any occasion, the Negro can never know whether he would be welcomed or not; if he goes he is liable to have his feelings hurt and get into unpleasant altercation; if he stays away, he is blamed for indifference.

If he meet a lifelong white friend on the street, he is in a dilemma; if he does not greet the friend he is put down as boorish and impolite; if he does greet the friend he is liable to be flatly snubbed.

If by chance he is introduced to a white woman or man, he expects to be ignored on the next meeting, and usually is.

White friends may call on him, but he is scarcely expected to call on them, save for strictly business matters.

If he gain the affections of a white woman and marry her he may invariably expect that slurs will be thrown on her reputation and on his, and that both his and her race will shun their company.

When he dies he cannot be buried beside white corpses.

7. The result:

Any one of these things happening now and then would not be remarkable or call for especial comment: but when one group of people suffer all these little differences of treatment and discriminations and insults continually, the result is either discouragement, or bitterness, or over-sensitiveness, or recklessness. And a people feeling thus cannot do their best.

﹨ 8. An Advice Column for Jewish Immigrants, 1906, 1907

Worthy Editor,

We are a small family who recently came to the "Golden Land." My husband, my boy and I are together, and our daughter lives in another city.

I had opened a grocery store here, but soon lost all my money. In Europe we were in business; we had people working for us and paid them well. In short, there we made a good living but here we are badly off.

My husband became a peddler. The "pleasure" of knocking on doors and ringing bells cannot be known by anyone but a peddler. If anybody does buy anything "on time," a lot of the money is lost, because there are some people who never intend to

---

Excerpt from the *Jewish Daily Forward* can be found in Isaac Metzker, *A Bintel Brief* (New York: Doubleday, 1971), 42–44, 54–55, 63–64, 101–102.

pay. In addition, my husband has trouble because he has a beard, and because of the beard he gets beaten up by the hoodlums.

Also we have problems with our boy, who throws money around. He works every day till late at night in a grocery for three dollars a week. I watch over him and give him the best because I'm sorry that he has to work so hard. But he costs me plenty and he borrows money from everybody. He has many friends and owes them all money. I get more and more worried as he takes here and borrows there. All my talking doesn't help. I am afraid to chase him away from home because he might get worse among strangers. I want to point out that he is well versed in Russian and Hebrew and he is not a child any more, but his behavior is not that of an intelligent adult.

I don't know what to do. My husband argues that he doesn't want to continue peddling. He doesn't want to shave off his beard, and it's not fitting for such a man to do so. The boy wants to go to his sister, but that's a twenty-five-dollar fare. What can I do? I beg you for a suggestion.

Your constant reader,

F.L.

Answer: Since her husband doesn't earn a living anyway, it would be advisable for all three of them to move to the city where the daughter is living. As for the beard, we feel that if the man is religious and the beard is dear to him because the Jewish law does not allow him to shave it off, it's up to him to decide. But if he is not religious, and the beard interferes with his earnings, it should be sacrificed.

Dear Editor,

For a long time I worked in a shop with a Gentile girl, and we began to go out together and fell in love. We agreed that I would remain a Jew and she a Christian. But after we had been married for a year, I realized that it would not work.

I began to notice that whenever one of my Jewish friends comes to the house, she is displeased. Worse yet, when she sees me reading a Jewish newspaper her face changes color. She says nothing, but I can see that she has changed. I feel that she is very unhappy with me, though I know she loves me. She will soon become a mother, and she is more dependent on me than ever.

She used to be quite liberal, but lately she is being drawn back to the Christian religion. She gets up early Sunday mornings, runs to church and comes home with eyes swollen from crying. When we pass a church now and then, she trembles.

Dear Editor, advise me what to do now. I could never convert, and there's no hope for me to keep her from going to church. What can we do now?

Thankfully,

A Reader

Answer: Unfortunately, we often hear of such tragedies, which stem from marriages between people of different worlds. It's possible that if this couple were to move to a Jewish neighborhood, the young man might have more influence on his wife.

Dear Editor,

I, too, want to take advantage of this opportunity to tell about my troubles, and I ask you to answer me.

Eight months ago I brought my girlfriend from Russia to the States. We had been in love for seven years and were married shortly after her arrival. We were very happy together until my wife became ill. She was pregnant and the doctors said her condition was poor. She was taken to the hospital, but after a few days was sent home. At home, she became worse, and there was no one to tend her.

You can hardly imagine our bitter lot. I had to work all day in the shop and my sick wife lay alone at home. Once as I opened the door when I came home at dinner-time, I heard my wife singing with a changed, hoarse voice. I was terror-stricken, and when I ran to her I saw she was out of her head with fever.

Imagine how I felt. My wife was so ill and I was supposed to run back to the shop because the last whistle was about to blow. Everybody was rushing back to work, but I couldn't leave. I knew that my boss would fire me. He had warned me the day before that if I came late again he wouldn't let me in. But how could I think of work now, when my wife was so ill? Yet without the job what would happen? There would not be a penny coming into the house. I stayed at my wife's bedside and didn't move till four o'clock.

Suddenly I jumped up and began to run around the room, in despair. My wife's singing and talking drove me insane. Like a madman I ran to the door and locked it. I leaped to the gas jet, opened the valve, then lay down in the bed near my wife and embraced her. In a few minutes I was nearer death than she.

Suddenly my wife cried out, "Water! water!" I dragged myself from the bed. With my last ounce of strength I crept to the door and opened it, closed the gas valve, and when I came to, gave her milk instead of water. She finished a glassful and wanted more, but there wasn't any more so I brought her some seltzer. I revived myself with water, and both of us slowly recovered.

The next morning they took my wife to the hospital, and after a stay of fourteen days she got well. Now I am happy that we are alive, but I keep thinking of what almost happened to us. Until now I never told anyone about it, but it bothers me. I have no secrets from my wife, and I want to know whether I should now tell her all, or not mention it. I beg you to answer me.

The Newborn

Answer: This letter depicting the sad life of the worker is more powerful than any protest against the inequality between rich and poor. The advice to the writer is that he should not tell his wife that he almost ended both their lives. This secret may be withheld from his beloved wife, since it is clear he keeps it from her out of love.

Worthy Editor,

I am eighteen years old and a machinist by trade. During the past year I suffered a great deal, just because I am a Jew.

It is common knowledge that my trade is run mainly by the Gentiles and, working among the Gentiles, I have seen things that cast a dark shadow on the American labor scene. Just listen:

I worked in a shop in a small town in New Jersey, with twenty Gentiles. There was one other Jew besides me, and both of us endured the greatest hardships. That we were insulted goes without saying. At times we were even beaten up. We work in an area where there are many factories, and once, when we were leaving the shop, a group of workers fell on us like hoodlums and beat us. To top it off, we and one of our attackers were arrested. The hoodlum was let out on bail, but we, beaten and bleeding, had to stay in jail. At the trial, they fined the hoodlum eight dollars and let him go free.

After that I went to work on a job in Brooklyn. As soon as they found out that I was a Jew they began to torment me so that I had to leave the place. I have already worked at many places, and I either have to leave, voluntarily, or they fire me because I am a Jew.

Till now, I was alone and didn't care. At this trade you can make good wages, and I had enough. But now I've brought my parents over, and of course I have to support them.

Lately I've been working on one job for three months and I would be satisfied, but the worm of anti-Semitism is beginning to eat at my bones again. I go to work in the morning as to Gehenna, and I run away at night as from a fire. It's impossible to talk to them because they are common boors, so-called "American sports." I have already tried in various ways, but the only way to deal with them is with a strong fist. But I am too weak and they are too many.

Perhaps you can help me in this matter. I know it is not an easy problem.

Your reader,

E.H.

Answer: In the answer, the Jewish machinist is advised to appeal to the United Hebrew Trades and ask them to intercede for him and bring up charges before the Machinists Union about this persecution. His attention is also drawn to the fact that there are Gentile factories where Jews and Gentiles work together and get along well with each other.

Finally it is noted that people will have to work long and hard before this senseless racial hatred can be completely uprooted.

ESSAYS

Families Enter America

JOHN BODNAR

Networks of Migration

Throughout the immigrants' homelands families were forced to select emigration as one possible option in confronting the new order of capitalism. But a multitude of practical problems remained once the decision to move was made. How would information of specific jobs be found? Where could living accommodations be located? How in general did individuals enter sprawling new factories and expanding cities? The answers to these pressing issues emerged not from any long and tedious thought process but largely from familiar patterns cultivated over years of dealing with the vagaries of economic systems, social relationships, and human desires. Work, shelter, and order would be secured in industrial America—as they had been in the pre-industrial and proto-industrial homeland—through an intricate web of kin and communal associations. The immigrant would not enter America

John Bodnar, *The Transplanted: A History of Immigrants in Urban America* (Bloomington: Indiana University Press, 1985), 57–66, 68–84. Reprinted by permission of Indiana University Press.

alone. The intrusion of capitalism in the premigration lands may have raised the alternative of emigration, but it had not destroyed the essential relationship between family and work that most emigrants, regardless of ethnic background, had nurtured. It was a relationship which would enjoy a rejuvenation in the mills and neighborhoods of American industrial cities.

Because families and friends were in close contact even when separated by wide oceans, immigrants seldom left their homelands without knowing exactly where they wanted to go and how to get there. Relatives and friends constantly sent information back regarding locations to live and potential places of employment. Thousands of Poles were brought from Gdansk to Polish Hill in Pittsburgh by aunts, uncles, brothers, and sisters who sent them passage money and instructions of what to bring and where to make steamship and railroad connections. By 1915, as a result of such patterns, investigators could find heavy clusters of families in city neighborhoods. About three-fourths of the Italians and one-half of the Jews who owned property in Providence, Rhode Island, lived in a building with kin at the same address. One Jewish immigrant explained that her father had bought a three-family house with his cousins. Her family lived downstairs, one cousin on the second floor, and another cousin on the top floor. An Italian working for the Scovill Company in Connecticut brought friends who were "big and strong" from Italy. Women brought their sisters or friends into domestic jobs or gave them references of where to go. Chicanos followed each other along railroad lines into Los Angeles and from there throughout southern California. In the early 1920s Chicanos like José Anquiano were arriving in the Chicago area after hearing about openings at the Inland Steel Company and then sending for friends and kin in Texas and in their home villages in Mexico. In fact, relatives and friends were often responsible for movement to second and third locations in America when employment became slack in areas of first settlement. Thus, Italians from southern Illinois moved to the Italian "hill" in St. Louis when coal mining operations were reduced in the 1920s, and Slavs from mines in western Pennsylvania and northern Michigan moved to Detroit's expanding car industry in the same decade.

It was not unheard of for "middlemen" or labor agents to direct large flows of immigrant workers to particular industries or cities in return for modest fees. Such individuals usually shared a common ancestry and language with newcomers and could effectively gather them for shipment to a waiting industry. Oriental workers were channeled in such a fashion into western railroads for a time. . . . Italian "padrones" funneled their fellow countrymen to railroads and public works projects and into labor turmoil as strike-breakers. Ethnic "bankers," such as Luigi Spizziri, advanced passage to individuals in Italy and then found them work in Chicago. . . . In nearly all instances, however, intermediaries functioned only in the early stages of a migration stream. Inevitably the continual and enduring movement of all groups into industrial America would rest on ties and links established in the old world.

Immigrants did not need middlemen in the long run because they received a steady stream of information on labor market conditions and wages from friends and relatives, which allowed them to make reasonably well-informed decisions about where to go and what types of work they could expect to find. Immigrant letters were frequently filled with information on employment prospects, wages, and even the manner in which workers were treated. . . . A Polish steelworker in

Pittsburgh wrote to his family in Poland not to keep his younger brother in school much longer; an extended education would be unnecessary for the toil required in the Pittsburgh mills.

Comparative analysis of Italians migrating to Argentina and New York City further revealed the specificity of the information immigrants used to make the decisions to move. In Argentina Italians formed a sizable portion of the economic structure and had access to numerous opportunities to own business and industrial establishments. At the turn of the century 57 percent of the owners of industrial establishments in Buenos Aires were Italian. The New York labor market offered considerably different opportunities for Italians. In the American metropolis they formed a much smaller percentage of the population and were unable to dominate any important economic sector. Because Italians were generally knowledgeable about the divergent opportunity structures in the two cities, different groups selected different destinations. Those from northern Italy, usually more literate, who intended to remain abroad permanently, went to Buenos Aires. Southern Italians, less literate and with less capital, who hoped to return to Italy, tended to move to New York, where they could easily find unskilled, temporary jobs. Indeed, some indications exist that over time, Italians in Argentina when compared to their American counterparts, invested more in business and their children's education than in housing, because they saw a greater chance for success in the future. . . .

Wages alone, however, did not attract immigrants to specific locations. They were frequently concerned about the type of work they would encounter. Italians often sought outdoor employment and were heavily represented in railroad and other forms of outdoor construction in many American cities. In Chicago they shunned meat-packing because they had heard of the intense cold of refrigerated compartments and the sweltering heat and offensive odors of the killing floors. . . . St. Paul, Minnesota, proved attractive to Irish and German women as a second stop in America because of numerous opportunities for domestic work awaiting them. . . . East European Jews moved into garment trades run by German Jews because they found them easier to work with than Gentile employers.

While immigrants clearly had preferences for work and some advance knowledge of wages and opportunities, however, they were not completely free to move into the industrial economy on an individual basis. Throughout the first century of American industrial expansion both workers and employers experimented with techniques of recruitment and job placement, and no method appeared to be as pervasive or as effective as that of informal familial and ethnic networks. The workplace of early industrial capitalism was a relatively accessible place especially during the six or seven decades after 1850, and kinship ties functioned effectively to provide labor, train new members, and effectively offer status and consolation. Poles, relying on relatives and friends, established occupational beachheads in Pittsburgh at the Jones and Laughlin steel plant. . . . As one newcomer recalled, "The only way you got a job was through somebody at work who got you in." . . . Frequently fathers and uncles taught sons and nephews the operation of industrial equipment. At the Amoskeag textile mills in New Hampshire, French-Canadians brought relatives to work, assisted in their placement in the mills, taught them specific work tasks, substituted for them when they were ill, and informally established production quotas. . . . In one New England textile plant nepotism became so widespread in securing employment that workers with familial connections within the plant were actually held in higher esteem than "unattached" employees who were presumed to be more transient.

Kinship not only facilitated the entry of immigrant males into the industrial economy but females as well. A 1930 study of 2,000 foreign-born women revealed that most had secured their initial jobs through relatives and friends. All had worked in either cigar or textile factories, and less than 10 percent had acquired relevant skills for those jobs prior to migrating. Surveys of full-fashioned, hosiery loopers discovered that the majority obtained their positions through acquaintances. . . . A 1924 investigation of Italian females in New York City reported that 75 percent acquired their first jobs through friends or relatives and that these women were "ashamed" to seek employment alone and would quit a job if friends or kin left as well. . . .

The central dynamic, which gradually allowed the industrial workplace to be filled informally by clusters of unskilled immigrants who were usually related, was the quest for greater production. Capitalism in its steady drive toward larger profits and lower costs demanded that goods be produced as quickly and as efficiently as possible. Invariably this imperative required that newer forms of production and technology replace skilled workers. This would not only allow for a faster pace of production but would diminish the influence that skilled workers had exerted over a particular workplace and put more control in the hands of managers and owners. . . .

The most striking result of the decline in skilled jobs was the growing number of immigrant clusters in the nineteenth and twentieth centuries. Nearly one-half of the Philadelphia Irish in 1850 were in unskilled labor, for instance, while 67 percent of the Germans were artisans. In Buffalo, Germans dominated crafts such as masonry, cooperage, and shoemaking while the Irish worked largely as unskilled laborers, domestics, ship carpenters, and teamsters. This early bunching resulted directly from the possession or lack of premigration skills, and newer immigrants after 1880, generally with less skills than the Germans, intensified the pattern of clustering. By 1911 a study of seven urban areas revealed that nearly one-third of all South Italians were categorized as "general laborers" in contrast to only 9 percent of the Poles and 7 percent of the Germans. Fully 65 percent of the Poles were in manufacturing and mechanical pursuits compared to only 28.8 percent of the South Italians. . . . Groups such as the Swedes, Jews, and Germans were considerably underrepresented in "unspecified labor" positions. . . .

Much of this bunching of immigrant workers could be attributed directly to the alteration of skill levels of American workers. As early as the 1840s textile mills in Lowell, Massachusetts, were attempting to improve their productive capacity by switching to spinning mules which could perform more than twice as much work as the older throstle spinners and implement the stretch-out on the assigning of additional looms or spindles to each worker at reduced piece rates. These changes eliminated the homogeneity of the workforce, which was largely native-born, and led directly to an increase in the proportion of immigrants. At one mill, for instance, the foreign-born proportion of the labor force rose from 3.7 percent in 1836 to 61.8 percent by 1860. Thousands of Irish immigrants entered the mills including many women and children who needed the wages and were willing to accept speed-ups and stretch-outs, in part because they were not familiar with an earlier, slower pace. . . .

. . . The substitution of unskilled for skilled labor proceeded rapidly during the final quarter of the nineteenth century. Employers intensified the drive to establish more efficient worker training programs by reducing skill requirements for incoming laborers. Expansion of child, female, and unskilled, foreign-born labor and the decline of apprenticeship programs and of highly skilled operatives underscored the trend. During the early decades of the twentieth century, the number of blacksmiths, machinists, and glassblowers declined substantially. Apprenticeships among brick and stone machinists fell from 39,463 in 1920 to 13,606 a decade later. . . .

The diminution of crafts and skills accelerated after 1900 and had a negative impact upon the older immigrant stocks from northern and western Europe. Germans in nineteenth-century Philadelphia predominated in skilled butchering, tailoring, and shoemaking positions. As these occupations declined, Germans were frequently dislocated and found it more difficult to transfer jobs to their sons. . . .

The blurring of skill distinctions among workers and the implementation of new efficiency schemes were accelerated during the period of the "new immigration." With proletarian protest growing in the late nineteenth century and larger concentrations of workers emerging in urban areas, industrial managers began to impose a bureaucratic structure upon the work force with hierarchical gradations of unskilled and semiskilled operations. This restructuring of work itself resulted in something of a segmentation of the labor market, . . . which created an infinite number of "entry-level" jobs and intensified the process of clustering, while making it extremely unlikely that newcomers could implement any previously acquired skills. The promise of industrial America to immigrant workers was not so much that one could rise as that one could gain access at any number of points of entry. Opportunity was not vertical but horizontal, a fact which tended to blunt any rhetoric of social mobility immediately upon arrival.

If skills were no longer crucial to obtaining work in the expanding sectors of the economy, something else would have to take their place. The alternative would be a random entry of thousands of immigrant workers into the industrial complex. But the widespread existence of clusters suggests that a sense of order in joining newcomers and occupations was operative. In even the most cursory survey of immigrant job acquisition, kinship and ethnic ties invariably emerge as the vital link. . . .

While most newcomers arrived in friendly groups, they were not allowed to function as independently as they might have thought. The industrial economy was certainly accessible but not at every particular point. Frequently, networks of families and relatives could function only where prospective employers allowed them to do so. Owners and managers had distinct impressions regarding the abilities of particular groups, a fact which encouraged group rather than individual movement, and took steps to encourage the hiring of one group at the expense of another. . . . On the Boston and Lowell Railroad in the mid-nineteenth century, only Irishmen were hired as firemen, since it was believed, unlike Yankees, they would not want further promotions. In early Milwaukee, Germans were considered "thrifty, frugal, and industrious" by employers and Poles more industrious than Italians and Greeks. . . . Jewish garment owners sometimes hired only Italians because they were felt to be less amenable to unionization than Jews. On other occasions the owners hired only fellow Jews, hoping that "fraternal instincts" with employers might keep them from unionizing. . . . Scandinavian women were strongly preferred in American homes as domestics, in part because they were Protestants while Irish girls were Catholics. This view caused Finnish women to be in heavy demand in large cities such as New York. The overall preference for western rather than eastern Europeans for better-paying jobs, it has been estimated, cost the "new immigrants" on the average of $1.07 per week in wages.

In the case of Chicanos, employer recruitment and attitude were almost solely responsible for determining where their kinship networks would function. The first significant movement of Mexican workers into the southwest was due to the agitation of agricultural, mining, and railroad companies in the southwest. Restrictions of the 1917 Immigration Law were even waived during World War I. Chicanos could not move into Santa Barbara until the 1880s after inexpensive Chinese labor had been curtailed, and even then they were confined to work in laundries, domestic work, and railroad section gangs. . . . A general assumption existed in the southwest that [Mexicans] were interested in working only a short while and then returning to Mexico, although increasing numbers were settling permanently north of the border after 1880. At El Paso, railroad recruiters considered them "docile, patient, orderly in camp, fairly intelligent under competent supervision, obedient and cheap." . . .

The Rise of a Family Economy

While it is apparent that immigrants were not free to move into the industrial economy wherever they desired, they were able to remain within the confines of small groups and networks, which assisted them tremendously. Such groups could mass around links of friends, villages, or regions but were mostly held together by ties of blood. Kinship formed the stable core of immigrant groups as they flowed into the openings available to them in particular times and places. . . .

The world the immigrant left had exhibited numerous examples of family, in one form or another, as a central focus of organizing life itself. Families were responsible for socialization patterns, the distribution of land and other resources, and even served as a forum to resolve the question of who should emigrate and why. Because they also performed valuable functions in industrial America meant they were not as much cultural baggage as they were institutions which continued to find a relevant role to play in both societies. Family economies were as much a product of industrial capitalism as they were of subsistence agriculture, for in both systems a mediating institution was necessary to stand between economy and society in order to reconcile individual and group demands.

The manner in which the immigrant family remained functional in two economies was its central and enduring attachment to the value of cooperation. Family members were continually instructed in the necessity of sharing and notions of reciprocity were constantly reinforced. Parents, children, boarders, and others who shared particular households were all assigned a series of duties and obligations. By working together, pooling limited resources, and muting individual inclinations, families attempted to assemble the resources sufficient for economic survival and, occasionally, for an improvement in their standard of living. But the

vays the most immediate: cooperate and survive. French-Canadian
England recalled how all contributed their savings to their parents.
sed in a large family claimed that it stood to reason that everyone
working and pitch in." . . .
iigrant elaborated on the reciprocal nature of immigrant life. He

k, you understand, you used to bring your pay home and give it to your
hatever they feel they want to give you, they decide. There was no dis-
it was their style. And don't you dare talk about paying board, especially
If you want to pay board you have to go somewhere else. "This is no
This is a family," my father would say. He said to us to bring our pay
ever it was, we would make do.

e era of postindustrialism after 1940, when kinship ties to the
adually weakened and success was equated with an individual
erlying system of familial cooperation would be threatened.
mily goals came to supersede individual goals, and parents and
ed vigorously to contribute to familial welfare. Immigrant parents
direct the career paths of their progeny because of the leverage
being able to provide access to industrial jobs or housing in
s and girls were frequently asked to leave school early and start
ll or in a family business. Girls were often kept at home caring
rs and sisters or performing household chores. Females who
isic were told it was more practical to stay at home and learn
nd sewing. One girl wept when forced by her father to leave
th grade because he felt a woman did not need schooling "to
ys were urged to learn a job skill or a business rather than pursue a formal education, as families responded to the nature of the economy during
the first century of American capitalism. Often they received such training on the
job from fathers or other kin. Interviews with Poles in the Lawrenceville section of
Pittsburgh revealed that during the 1920s and 1930s boys worked alongside their
fathers in neighborhood foundries and meat-packing plants.

The family economy was not a product of natural evolution, and the effort to
insure that children participated directly in the mustering of resources for familial
survival was not accomplished without turmoil and tension. . . . Siblings often
complained bitterly if one were allowed to stay in school longer than another. And
a few resisted parental attempts to send them to work early. Individual plans and
dreams were often formulated but reluctantly put aside for family need. Interviews
with immigrant children found careers in electrical engineering, bookkeeping, the
priesthood, and business relinquished at the insistence of parents. Studies conducted among Polish immigrant girls in the Chicago stockyard areas revealed that
many complained if enough of their wages were not "returned" to them by their
parents. . . . Not surprisingly, some immigrant children left home, for they saw
their parents as obstacles to happiness.

But parents endured difficult tensions as well. In one study of northern New
England textile mills, Steven Dubnoff found that Irish fathers lost some influence
in the household as their children began to earn more of their own income. . . .

It is not entirely surprising that the cooperative ideal pervaded most immigrant families. These newcomers were not coming from widely disparate sectors of their homeland social structures but from the ranks of middle-class farm owners and tradesmen and the mass of marginal farmers and landless laborers just below them. A sense of hierarchy existed within the total group but all resided somewhere in the middle of society and experienced neither the hopelessness of extreme poverty nor the self-assurance of power and wealth. Surviving together was a constant preoccupation. . . .

Steeped heavily in a tradition of household and familial cooperation as a vehicle for achieving economic stability and finding an economic system in America which frequently encouraged a good deal of group assistance, immigrants who wished to remain found it relatively easy to establish households of their own. Indeed, the decision to do so represented not only a major commitment to remain in industrial society but suggested the means by which economic and emotional stability would be achieved in new circumstances. The creation of a new family often eased the pain of severing familial ties in the premigration society, especially for women who saw motherhood as a means of adjusting to a new life. Financial considerations also prompted many men to seek a companion who would cook, clean, and care for them for no wages at all. Many immigrants were anxious to reunite with wives and children out of fear that continued separation would ultimately lead to complete family disintegration. One scholar has found that southern Italians were quicker to send for their wives than northern Italians because they were sexually jealous and less culturally prepared to establish strong social relations outside the nuclear family.

If no wife existed in the homeland, immigrant males quickly took whatever steps were necessary to find women of similar linguistic and cultural backgrounds with whom they could establish a household. Marriage patterns remained largely within the ethnic group during the first and much of the second generation. Japanese men sought "picture brides" from Japan and initiated unions which stressed the importance of duty and obligation over love and romance. About one of every four Italians who moved to San Francisco actually returned to their native village just for a marriage. Whether they returned to the homeland or found a wife in America the chances were great she would be from the same region or village, a fact which reinforced notions about the manner in which families and households should function. Thus, it is not surprising to learn that among Germans in Wisconsin 86 percent of the first generation and 80 percent of the second married other Germans. Similar high rates were exhibited by Poles and Russians in the state. . . .

But it would be erroneous to assume that the cooperative family economy grew inevitably out of premigration traditions of collective enterprise or the regional and cultural homogeneity of immigrant streams. Both of these factors . . . would have been insufficient . . . in themselves without the accompanying reality of an industrial workplace which encouraged mutual aid and especially the widespread existence of wages insufficient for even modest standards of living. American industrial wages may have looked attractive to the residents of rural regions undergoing transition, but the available information suggests that the families of most immigrants in this country could not survive on the income of one wage earner. Among Irish millhands in Lowell, Massachusetts, in the 1860s, most fathers could earn only about 54 percent of what was needed to support a family at a minimum level of subsistence. Among packinghouse workers in Chicago in the decade after 1910, the average individual wage earner could earn 38 percent of the minimum needed for a family of four; he could still earn only 48 percent in 1922. . . . Clearly, family income had to be supplemented in some way.

The economic margin of an immigrant family did not usually improve until children reached working age, about fourteen, and began to contribute to family income. In Philadelphia, to illustrate a case, the children of immigrant Irish and German families entered the labor market to a greater degree than did the children from native-born households. . . . Irish children contribut [ed] between 38 and 46 percent of total family labor. . . . The most "vulnerable" economically were those with small children who could not work and who prevented a mother from working. At Amoskeag about 38 percent of all households had members working other than the head or the wife, but for immigrant households the figure was 50 percent. In fact, textile towns, because they offered employment to teenagers, tended to attract families with children of employment age. . . . Families in Chicago's packinghouse district even sent wives and daughters into the packinghouses, a move which ironically helped to keep overall wages low. . . .

While opportunities were sought for adolescent employment, immigrant women, like other women, usually terminated toil outside the household with marriage and focused attention on the roles of wife, mother, and homemaker. By 1920 in urban America, married women accounted for only 21 percent of the female work force. It is true that the percentage of wage earners among foreign-born adult females over the age of sixteen was one-third higher than the percentage for all white women, but this could be attributed to the heavier reliance of the immigrant family on the earnings of their unmarried daughters. Even for immigrant wives the general plan was not leave home for work after marriage. . . . In Chicago in 1900 less than 2 percent of a sample of Polish, Italian, Jewish, German, and Irish wives left the household to toil, while between 52 and 74 percent of the unmarried females over the age of fifteen in these groups left each day for work.

Strong imperatives existed in many immigrant families to prevent [married] women [from leaving] their homes in search of employment. Traditional perspectives on the domestic roles of mothers and wives persisted but were insufficient to account for the pattern by themselves, especially when it was not uncommon for married women to work in the fields of the rural world. Married women also had to raise children, manage the household, and care for boarders because they really had fewer employment opportunities than adult men and adolescents. Restricted opportunity in this case was continually supported by a myriad of cultural preferences. Irish immigrants strongly believed that married women should not work at all. This view was rooted not only in the model family of Irish Catholicism but in a social belief that a working married woman diminished the status of her husband. In Ireland female subservience had reached the point in the 1840s that married women had a shorter life expectancy than fathers and sons because the males were to receive the most nutritious food. . . . Greek families actually considered it a disgrace for a wife, and sometimes a sister, to work outside the house. Whatever the reason for keeping married women at home, the pattern of working-class domesticity was established prior to its celebration by middle-class reformers in urban America. Culture did not simply flow downward from social superiors. . . .

Conclusion

The predisposition toward doing whatever was necessary to sustain a family-based household was nothing new. It had pervaded the immigrant homelands and received additional support ironically from the new system of industrial capitalism which restructured its labor market in a manner which facilitated the entry of groups of untrained toilers who were often related or at least acquainted with each other. Kin and friends were free to assist each other in entering America by providing access to jobs and homes and supplying important information of labor market conditions. New arrivals were adept at determining where they might enter a very large economy. The immigrant family economy survived and flourished among most newcomers in industrial America because new economic structures actually reinforced traditional ways of ordering life and, consequently, contributed to a supportive "external environment" for capitalism to proceed. In this system, individual inclinations were muted and the household, managed effectively by immigrant females, superseded all other goals and objectives. In the face of a sprawling and complex urban industrial structure, newcomers forged a relatively simple device for establishing order and purpose in their lives. This system would remain predominant among working-class families until the labor market was reshaped again after World War II and credentials and skills regained importance in entering new professional sectors of work. It was a system which would be challenged by outside institutions and values as the stay in America became more permanent.

Finally, it could be argued that not all immigrant families functioned alike and that significant differences existed in religion, cultural background, and particular family strategies. Certainly, this was true. But it was also true that such differences coexisted with a fundamental similarity. Families and households were the predominant form in which all immigrants entered the industrial-urban economy and ordered their lives. Members of nearly all groups received indoctrination in the need to remain loyal to the familial and household unit. The goals of individual households could differ as a result of cultural background or positioning within the economy, and these divergences would come into play over time as separate paths of education, occupation, and mobility were taken. But in the movement to a capitalist world and in the initial decades of settlement, familial and communal networks abounded.

Americanization of the Mexican Immigrant

GEORGE J. SANCHEZ

The mechanism by which Mexican immigrant women were to be reached was already in place in the infrastructure of the Commission's activities. In 1915, the California state legislature passed the Home Teacher Act, a law which allowed school districts to employ teachers "to work in the homes of the pupils, instructing children and adults in matters relating to school attendance . . . in sanitation, in the

George J. Sanchez, *Becoming Mexican-American: Ethnicity, Culture, and Identity in Chicano Los Angeles, 1900–1945* (New York: Oxford University Press, 1993), 99–107. Copyright © 1995 by George J. Sanchez. Used by permission of Oxford University Press.

English language, in household duties . . . and in the fundamental principles of the American system of government and the rights and duties of citizenship." After World War I, the home teacher program was expanded, professionalized, and located within the public school system. From 1915 to 1929, the home teacher—usually a single, middle-class, Anglo woman—was the linchpin of Americanization efforts aimed at the Mexican family.

Mexican immigrant women were targeted for a variety of reasons. First, they were assumed to be the individuals primarily responsible for the transmission of values in the home. According to reformer's strategy, if the female adopted American values, the rest of her family would follow suit. Pearl Ellis, who worked with young Mexican women in southern California throughout the 1920s, stressed the important "influence of the home" in creating an employee who is "more dependable and less revolutionary in his tendencies . . . The homekeeper creates the atmosphere, whether it be one of harmony and cooperation or of dissatisfaction and revolt."

Americanization advocates were interested in the contribution Mexican women could make in transforming their families' habits from those of a rural, pre-industrial lifestyle to a modern American one. . . . Because the Southwest lagged behind the rest of the nation in industrialization, local reformers were anxious to introduce Mexican women and men as rapidly as possible to the temperament of industrial society and inculcate Mexican families with the "Protestant work ethic." Targeting mothers was crucial to the overall strategy of Americanization.

Motherhood, in fact, was the Mexican immigrant woman's most highly valued role in Americanization schemes. By focusing on the strategic position of the mother in the Mexican family, Americanizers hoped to have an impact on the second generation, even if the immigrant generation itself turned out to be less malleable than expected. Undeniably, Americanization ideology was infused with the traditional American belief in the exalted role of the mother in shaping the citizenry of the Republic. . . .

Although Americans had debated for almost three decades the conflicts between women's private family responsibilities and their public roles as workers, Americanization programs demonstrated no such concern when addressing the ideal future of the Mexican American woman. With regard to immigrant women, Americanization advocates were readily capable of blurring the public and private spheres. Teaching the Mexican mother proper American homemaking skills was meant to solve two problems at once: a happy and efficient mother would create an environment suitable for molding workers to the industrial order, and her new-found homemaking skills could be utilized in the cheap labor market outside the home. In 1908, a U.S. Bureau of Labor inspector had regretfully noted that Mexican "immigrant women have so little conception of domestic arrangements in the United States that the task of training them would be too heavy for American housewives." However, black and European immigrant women had not migrated to southern California in large enough numbers to fill the growing demand for domestic labor. Consequently, Americanization teachers targeted Mexican women to help alleviate the shortage of housemaids, seamstresses, laundresses, and service workers in the Southwest. By the 1920s, Americanization programs were busy training Mexican women to perform these tasks.

The most potent weapon used to imbue the foreigner with American values was the English language. All social reformers cited the ability to speak English as a fundamental skill necessary for assimilation. During and after World War I, however, English instruction was intended to provide the immigrant with much more than facility with the spoken language of the United States. In 1917, California's Commission of Immigration and Housing recommended "that employers of immigrants be shown the relation between a unified working force, speaking a common language, and industrial prosperity." In 1918, Mrs. Amanda Matthews Chase, a home teacher with twelve years' experience teaching in Mexico City, was hired by the Daughters of the American Revolution and developed a primer to teach English. Home teachers were instructed to associate their lessons "with the pupils' own lives and affairs." Thus, for example, they used the following song (sung to the tune, "Tramp, Tramp, Tramp, the Boys are Marching") to instruct female pupils about women's work as they learned twenty-seven new English words:

> We are working every day,
> So our boys and girls can play.
>   We are working for our homes and country, too;
> We like to wash, to sew, to cook,
> We like to write, or read a book,
>   We are working, working, working every day.
> Work, work, work,
> We are always working,
>   Working for our boys and girls,
> Working for our boys and girls,
> For our homes and country, too—
>   We are working, working, working every day.

Yet despite the attention of reformers, Mexican women continued to lag behind men in learning the English language. A study of 1,081 Mexican families in Los Angeles conducted in 1921 found that while 55 percent of the men were unable to speak English, an overwhelming 74 percent of the women could not speak the language. Similar gaps existed in English reading and writing.

Advocates of Americanization blamed the patriarchal nature of the Mexican family for this discrepancy. "The married Mexican laborer does not allow his wife, as a rule, to attend evening classes," reported USC's Emory Bogardus. Americanization teachers consistently criticized as traditional and unprogressive the alleged limitations placed upon the Mexican wife by her husband. According to one Americanization instructor, if left in the home, the Mexican woman's "intellectual ability is stimulated only by her husband and if he be of the average peon type, the stimulation is not very great." The Mexican home, she concluded, "being a sacred institution, is guarded by all the stolid tradition of centuries." If the Mexican home remained such a fortress, Americanization specialists would not be able to accomplish their mission.

Getting the Mexican woman out of her home, therefore, became a priority for Americanization programs because reformers saw this not only as the only avenue available for her intellectual progress, but as the only method by which they could succeed in altering her values. Home teachers visited each individual Mexican family in their district to gain the trust of members and encourage the husband to allow his wife to attend classes. The scheduling of alternative sessions in the afternoon for wives and mothers facilitated this progress.

Americanization programs, however, did not mean to undermine entirely the traditional Mexican family structure. Ironically, they counted on the cohesiveness of the Mexican family to achieve their assimilationist goals. Home teachers, even when they did get Mexican women out of the house and into classes, encouraged the acquisition of traditionally feminine household skills. In the ditty, "The Day's Work," for example, home teachers utilized the following sequence of phrases both to teach the English language and to instruct women about the proper organization of the family economy in American society.

> In the morning the women get breakfast.
> Their husbands go to work.
> Their children go to school.
> Then the women get their houses in good order.
> They give the baby its bath.
> They wash, or iron, or cook.
> They get the dinner.
> After dinner they wash the dishes.
> Then they sew, or rest, or visit their friends, or go to school.

Americanization programs sought to maintain the structure of family life while transforming familial habits, especially those concerning diet and health. Reformers encouraged Mexican women to give up their penchant for fried foods, their too frequent consumption of rice and beans, and their custom of serving all members of the family—from infants to grandparents—the same meal. According to proponents of Americanization, the modern Mexican woman should replace tortillas with bread, serve lettuce instead of beans, and broil instead of fry. Malnourishment in Mexican families was not blamed on lack of food or resources, but rather on "not having the right varieties of foods containing constituents favorable to growth and development."

Women in the American reform movement were certainly conversant with the turn-of-the-century domestic science movement—a movement which associated scientific homemaking with moral regeneration. Within the rubric of Americanization efforts, food and diet management became yet another tool in a system of social control intended to construct a well-behaved, productive citizenry. In the eyes of reformers, the typical noon lunch of the Mexican child, thought to consist of "a folded tortilla with no filling," could easily be the first step to a lifetime of crime. With "no milk or fruit to whet the appetite" the child could become lazy as well as hungry and might subsequently "take food from the lunch boxes of more fortunate children. Thus, the initial step in a life of thieving is taken." Teaching immigrant women proper food values became a route to keeping the head of the family out of jail and the rest of the family off charity.

Health and cleanliness represented additional catchwords for Americanization programs. One of the primary functions of home teachers was to impress upon the minds of Mexican mothers and mothers-to-be "that a clean body and clean mind are the attributes of a good citizen." . . . Reformers blamed Mexicans' slovenliness for their poor state of health. Such labeling reinforced the stereotype of the "dirty Mexican" and expanded its usage among Anglo urban dwellers. One eminent sociologist working with Americanization programs noted that Anglo Americans objected to the presence of Mexican children in the public schools for fear that their own children would catch a contagious disease.

Pressing "American" standards of diet, health, and cleanliness upon Mexican women was not the only component essential in creating a healthy home environment. None of the potential gains made by these programs could be considered noteworthy if the Mexican female continued to bear too many children. Americanization advocates worried that unless she learned to limit family size, the Mexican mother would be unable to train adequately each individual member of her household.

Limiting the growth of the immigrant population was a long-standing concern of both Progressives and nativists. Americans first noticed that immigrant groups had a higher birthrate than native-born Americans at the end of the nineteenth century, and fears of "race suicide" had existed in the Anglo American mind ever since. When this fear rose in relation to the Mexican immigrant, both nativists and proponents of Americanization became alarmed: nativists wished to stave off an "invasion," while Americanization advocates viewed all unrestricted population growth as a vestige of Old World ways that must be abandoned in a modern industrial setting.

Americanizers held Mexican women responsible for family planning. They also saw her hampered in these efforts by a number of factors. Traditional early marriage and the "inherent sentimentality" of the Mexican female promoted, they believed, a primitive sexuality and reinforced sexual ignorance. In addition, Catholicism discouraged birth control. Despite these barriers, Americanization teachers reported that Mexican mothers were beginning to exhibit dismay with their large families, and occasionally inquired about birth control measures. Some even warned others to delay marriage on the grounds of "much work, too much children."

Americanists viewed such evidence of changing attitudes as a hopeful sign, because limited reproduction opened up new opportunities for Mexican women within and outside the home. As proper household managers, Mexican women could devote more time to raising fewer and more productive children. But family limitation also created new possibilities for female employment by freeing Mexican women from the demands of continual childrearing. Traditionally, Mexican women's family obligations had barred them from wage labor outside the home. When a Mexican immigrant woman worked, it was almost always in her late adolescent or early adult years before marriage.

As industrialization in the American southwestern economy developed, so too did demands for cheap labor performing tasks that had traditionally been performed by women inside the home. While the garment, laundering, domestic service, and food preparation industries gradually relied more on "women's work" in the marketplace, employers in the region had fewer workers because of the restrictions placed upon Asian and European immigration, and because black migration to the Southwest was still quite low. Moreover, demands of the Anglo middle class for these services increased, exacerbating further the labor supply problems. Despite all the traditional objections to Mexican women working outside the home, Americanization programs actively promoted Mexican immigrant women for entrance into these sex-segregated occupations. . . .

Given the dual role reformers envisioned that the Mexican woman would play within and outside the home, every newly learned skill supposedly benefited American society doubly. When Americanists stressed the ability to set a table and to serve food properly, they were encouraging Mexican women not only to arrange home meals by American standards but also to learn that "sloppy appearance and uncleanliness of person would not be tolerated in a waitress." In addition, the burden on a private citizen employing a Mexican woman as a domestic servant would be considerably lightened if the employee had already been adequately trained through their programs. . . .

Encouraging Mexican women to engage in hard work was also viewed as an important step toward "curing" the habits of the stereotypical "lazy Mexican." According to one Americanization teacher, "'*Quien sabe?*' (who knows?) was the philosophy of all of Mexico, and the inability of Mexicans to connect the things that are valued as worthwhile to the effort necessary to obtain them made Mexican laborers inefficient." Another felt that "the laziness of Mexicans was due to climate conditions and inherited tendencies" which only hard work could root out. Consequently, putting Mexican women to work would have the effect of promoting discipline in them, which in turn would encourage them to pass on a similar level of self-control to their children.

Eventually, as national attention increasingly turned toward restricting future immigration from Mexico, Americanization advocates found themselves caught in the middle of the controversy, with little concrete evidence to prove that their efforts had effectively resolved the "Mexican problem." One of the few quantifiable means by which to measure success or failure in Americanization was the rate of naturalization, and in this area Mexican immigrants displayed little progress. Statistics from the period simply did not suggest that Americanization had affected the rate of naturalization. In fact, among the Mexican immigrant population in California, which already had the lowest rate of naturalization of any immigrant group in the state in 1920, the ratio of naturalized citizens to the total foreign-born Mexican population declined during the 1920s. Given this trend, and the long-standing ambivalence of reformers toward the immigrant, Americanizers shifted their focus. In 1927, the Commission of Immigration and Housing sided with restrictionists, calling for an end to unlimited immigration from Mexico, and blaming immigrants for "causing an immense social problem in our charities, schools and health departments."

Moreover, the efforts to alter the immigrant generation itself were abandoned in favor of school-based programs which sought to teach American-born children a culture different from that of their immigrant parents. In the schools, socialization in American values and language skills were even more emphatically combined with the goal of social stability. The increase application of I.Q. testing, always administered in English, invariably segregated Mexican children in special classes for the mentally inferior or mentally retarded. . . . By the late 1920s, the promoters of Americanization put their hopes for the future in vocational education and classes in citizenry directed at American-born Mexican children.

The efforts directed at children, like those aimed earlier at their parents, promoted above all the habits of thrift and time discipline. In southern California, business interests ardently favored Americanization programs that advocated promptness and diligence at work. Businessmen learned to cooperate both with the

Protestant reformers interested in fostering internal controls over morality and economy and with the social feminists hoping to upgrade women's position within the Mexican family. They understood full well that despite the range of motiva- tions behind Americanization, the price of acceptance for Mexicans into American society via their programs was predicated on the abandonment of a culture they perceived as inherently inferior.

Rather than provide Mexican immigrants with an attainable picture of assimila- tion, Americanization programs could offer these immigrants only idealized versions of American values. In reality what was presented turned out to be little more than second-class citizenship. The most progressive assumptions behind Americanization programs were never fully shared by the government or business interests involved, and thus they could never be fully implemented. One Americanization teacher who spent the decade working with Mexican immigrants noted with disappointment in 1923 that the newly elected governor of California had eliminated financial provi- sions for the Americanization program in the public schools from his budget. At least one historian has concluded that the "love affair between the progressive and the businessman" in California inevitably led, in the 1920s, to a blunting of "the cut- ting edge of progressive social reform."

The halfhearted effort of administrators of Americanization programs limited available personnel and resources and ensured that the programs would never be able to cope with the volume of the Mexican migration. The barrios expanded so quickly in the 1920s that any single Americanization teacher found it impossible to keep abreast of the number of new Mexican families in her district who needed a resumption of her program from scratch. Newer areas of Mexican settlement were usually beyond the reach of established Americanization programs entirely. Fur- thermore, Mexicans experienced a high degree of geographic mobility in this period that easily wiped out whatever progress had been made by these programs in a given community. According to historian Ricardo Romo, fewer than one-third of Mexicans present in Los Angeles in 1917–18 were present in the city one decade later. Americanization teacher Amanda Chase acknowledged the extent of this problem when dealing with Mexican women: "I have had in my class record book this year the names of about half as many Mexican women as there are Mexican families in the district. But a third of them moved to other districts." Mexican im- migrants could not hope to develop allegiances to the United States when the eco- nomic condition of their families forced them to migrate consistently in search of an economic livelihood.

In the end, Americanization programs never had the time to develop suffi- ciently even to approach a solution to the problem of Mexican immigrants in the United States. With the stock market crash of 1929 and the subsequent Great Depression of the 1930s, all attempts to Americanize Mexican immigrants came to an abrupt end. Rather than search for ways to assimilate these newcomers, American society looked for methods to be rid of them altogether. About 500,000 Mexicans left the United States during the 1930s under strong pressure from the government and up to one-tenth of these individuals had resided in Los Angeles. Americanists joined in these efforts to repatriate Mexican residents; their commit- ment to improving the conditions of the Mexican had no place in an economically depressed America.

Instead, Americanization programs are an important window for looking at the assumptions made about both Mexican and American culture by progressive Californians during the 1920s. Mexican culture was seen as malleable, but required intense education in "American values" to fit into a modern, industrialized society. These efforts also made clear, however, that Mexicans were intended only to assimilate into the bottom segment of the American work force as low-paid, yet loyal, workers. As we shall see, Mexican immigrants generated their own version of Americanism without abandoning Mexican culture. What they would create would be quite a different product indeed.

FURTHER READING

Gunther Barth, *City People* (1980)

John Bodnar, *The Transplanted: A History of Immigrants in Urban America* (1985)

Charles W. Cheape, *Moving the Masses* (1980)

Elizabeth Ewen, *Immigrant Women in the Land of Dollars* (1985)

Donna R. Gabaccia, *Militants and Migrants: Rural Sicilians Become American Workers* (1988)

John Higham, *Strangers in the Land: Patterns of American Nativism, 1860–1925* (1971)

Hartmut Keil, ed., *German Workers in Industrial Chicago, 1850–1920* (1988)

Maury Klein and Harvey A. Kantor, *Prisoners of Progress: American Industrial Cities, 1850–1920* (1976)

Alan M. Kraut, *The Huddled Masses: The Immigrant in American Society, 1860–1921* (1982)

Stephen Meyer, *The Five Dollar Day: Labor Management and Social Control in the Ford Motor Company, 1908–1921* (1981)

Joanne J. Meyerowitz, *Women Adrift: Independent Wage Earners in Chicago, 1880–1930* (1988)

Raymond A. Mohl, *The New City: Urban America in the Industrial Age, 1860–1920* (1985)

Gilbert Osofsky, *Harlem* (1971)

Harold L. Platt, *The Electric City: Energy and the Growth of the Chicago Area* (1991)

George J. Sanchez, *Becoming Mexican-American: Ethnicity, Culture, and Identity in Chicano Los Angeles, 1900–1945* (1993)

Alexander P. Saxton, *The Indispensable Enemy: Labor and the Anti-Chinese Movement in California* (1971)

Judith E. Smith, *Family Connections: A History of Jewish and Italian Immigrant Lives in Providence, Rhode Island, 1900–1940* (1985)

Jon C. Teaford, *The Unheralded Triumph: City Government in America, 1870–1900* (1984)

Judy Yung, *Unbound Feet: A Social History of Chinese Women in San Francisco* (1995)

Women's Businesses, New and Old

ANGEL KWOLEK-FOLLAND

Women's engagement in various aspects of business at the turn of the century was a decisive element in creating the modern business world. Conversely, business developments were important to the lives of women. In almost no other area, besides perhaps politics, can we see so clearly the changed nature of women's lives in the early twentieth century. Understanding women's involvement in business requires a closer look at several issues. Women in general, and women in the business world particularly, heard conflicting messages about their latent chances for individual entrepreneurial success and career or job fulfillment and their capabilities for negotiating the public economy. Adjustments in divorce, inheritance, labor, and citizenship laws affected women's economic status. The ascent of big business and professionalism opened up some arenas such as the so-called women's professions even as they blocked others. New technologies diversified women's relationship to entrepreneurship, professionalism, and even housework. Finally, the federal government's response to the increased presence of women in the workforce highlighted women's role on the national economic stage. . . .

Ethnicity operated as both a bar and an opportunity for many women in the business world. Social and economic segregation of ethnic groups had long been a part of American life, but it took on renewed vigor with the end of slavery and the

Angel Kwolek-Folland, *Incorporating Women: A History of Women and Business in the United States* (New York: Twayne Publishers, 1998), pp. 87–88, 116–122, 124–129. Reproduced with permission of Palgrave Macmillan.

appearance of scientific and racial justifications for ethnic differences. For African-Americans released from slavery, economic viability quickly became a vital issue. Its importance was widely discussed, beginning with the economic demands of politicians and black leaders during Reconstruction. Booker T. Washington's articulation of a philosophy of self-help and segregation as a necessary temporary stage on the way to full assimilation merely framed in new form what many African-Americans had long known. Without meaningful economic autonomy, social and political power and "racial uplift"—the improvement of the social and economic status of all American blacks—would be impossible.

Throughout the major cities of the South, where most black Americans lived, local leaders and entrepreneurs began in the 1880s to build an economic infrastructure of African-American businesses—banks, barber shops, restaurants, and insurance companies—that would undergird autonomy. . . . The presence of black consumers, the growth of black businesses, the segregation of occupations that reserved certain types of businesses and jobs to blacks, and the traditional business niches afforded women allowed black businesswomen to operate hairdressing, confectionery, and catering establishments, as well as restaurants, laundries, and taverns. . . .

One of the most spectacular success stories of this era was that of Madame C. J. Walker, . . . who started a traditional type of women's business—beauty aids—by identifying the particular needs of African-Americans and building on the existing support networks for black businesses. She was among the first women in the United States to become a millionaire through her own efforts. . . . Walker (1867–1919) was born to former slaves. Her life began in absolute poverty and was marred by the early death of her parents and physical abuse by her brother-in-law. She was married at 14 and widowed at 16 with a two-year-old daughter to raise. She moved in with relatives in St. Louis, Missouri, and earned a precarious living doing laundry. Then, in 1904, Walker began marketing a hair-care preparation, the recipe for which she claimed to have learned in a dream. Along with her daughter, sister, and nieces, Walker bottled her home remedy, which was designed to meet the unique needs of African-American women, many of whom did not have access to running water and struggled with products designed for a different type of hair. The product found an eager public, and Walker's business expanded quickly, in large part because of her shrewd entrepreneurship.

In 1910 Walker had more than 5,000 African-American women selling on commission her hair preparation and a hot comb she had invented. By 1919 Walker agents numbered 25,000. She founded several beauty schools to teach the Walker hair-care method, developed a real estate complex in Indianapolis, built a personal mansion on the Hudson River, and contributed to numerous educational and philanthropic charities. Illiterate, she hired tutors to teach her reading and writing. . . . Madame Walker was profoundly interested in the fate of black women and consciously aimed both her products and her self-help message at them. "The girls and women of our race," she observed, "must not be afraid to take hold of business endeavors. . . . I have made it possible for many colored women to abandon the washtub for a more pleasant and profitable occupation." Like many progressive blacks of her day, Walker saw economic development and business entrepreneurship as an avenue to racial uplift. She also believed, like many reformers, in the importance of women's financial autonomy.

Ethnic businesses also embodied many of the contradictions of negotiating ethnicity in a nation that reserved its largest rewards for the assimilated. Madame Walker's hair preparations, for example, generated intense controversy because the tonics and hot combs she sold were designed to straighten and smooth African-American hair, making it appear more like that of whites. Some black newspaper editors and community leaders deplored the use of such products, arguing instead for maintaining the physical markers of ethnic identity. However, the popularity of Walker's products suggests that African-American consumers saw advantages in adopting white standards of beauty and self-presentation, advantages that probably ranged from passing for white to merely striving to emulate the mainstream white ideal. The tensions between assimilation and ethnic assertion could be found in many products that catered to ethnic groups.

Ethnicity also affected whether women went into business at all. Recent immigrants since at least the mid-nineteenth century have consistently found small businesses attractive. These entrepreneurial ventures draw on family and kin networks as well as voluntary associations and mutual aid groups and require less capitalization. The more than 2 million immigrants from southern and eastern Europe between 1870 and 1910 included a large contingent of Jews. Eastern European Jewish culture afforded women—who handled household finances and often participated actively in family businesses—importance as economic actors within the family. Consequently, urban Jewish women were among the most active entrepreneurial women in the United States at the turn of the century. Usually these businesses were small, such as corner groceries. Sometimes they could be spectacular successes. A case in point is Lena Himmelstein Bryant (1879–1951), who came to the United States in 1895 and took work in a lingerie factory until she married. When she found herself a widow with a small child in 1906, she pawned earrings her husband had given her and bought a sewing machine and went back to making lingerie. She was particularly skilled in designing clothing that hid figure flaws, and her attractive creations sold well. Her biggest marketing innovation was to address the ready-made clothing needs of women who were ignored by other companies. She designed and produced clothes that pregnant women could wear on the street, and maternity wear became the basis of the Lane Bryant Company's fortune. After World War I, Bryant began production of a line of clothing for larger women. By 1923 the company had several stores in major cities and an annual sales volume of $5 million. Lena Bryant continued to run the business until her death.

New technologies—particularly the development of film at the turn of the century—radically altered the world of popular entertainment and generally opened important business avenues to women. Moving pictures went from a curiosity at their inception in 1895 to the status of a full-fledged industry by the 1920s....

. . . The history of women's involvement in the film industry is in many ways a scenario typical of women's opportunities and limitations in any new industry. In its earliest years, making films was a seat-of-the-pants process. Most films were "written" as they were being filmed, the actors often contributing ideas, direction, and even production money. Since virtually all of the tasks involved in filmmaking were new, there was little previous gender typing with which to contend. Film's antecedent, the theater, traditionally had made room for women. . . . [T]he work culture of filmmaking—the set of behaviors and expectations generated within this community of workers—emphasized the sort of individualized, even masculinized, behavior connected with the image of the modern "new woman." These new women, like the settlement house founders, Progressive reformers, and professionals of all types, were committed to their careers and believed in the importance of economic independence for women. Finally, in its earliest years, the industry was financed mostly from internal sources, and investors were willing to take a chance on an unknown director, actor, or writer. This generally more open and unrationalized climate allowed women full participation in the growth of the industry, and women took advantage of these factors.

The most common avenue for women entering the fledgling industry before about 1920 was as screenwriters. Women made up about 50 percent of all screenwriters in the silent era. However, women could be found in every aspect of filmmaking, from props and cameras to acting, producing, and directing. In fact, acting and writing often led to producing and directing. The most famous actress of her day, Mary Pickford (1893–1979) was also the first person to make a million dollars from acting. Her on-screen image as a fragile and helpless orphan was belied by her firm control over her career and her steely business acumen. In her early career, she insisted on and got the same pay scale as comparable male stars. Unable to get the extravagant terms that she wanted from two major production companies in 1919—essentially complete control of the product—she created her own studio with her second husband, Douglas Fairbanks, and Charlie Chaplin. As studio owner, star, executive producer, and director of United Artists, Pickford gave herself the gross proceeds of her films.

The theater also provided women an avenue into filmmaking. Mae West (1893–1980), who went on to become the second-highest-salaried individual in the United States in the mid-1930s (after William Randolph Hearst), started her entertainment career in vaudeville, achieved renown as a Broadway playwright, and entered motion pictures at the relatively late age of 40 in 1933. That year, Paramount Studios asked her to convert her 1928 hit Broadway play, *Diamond Lil,* into her first motion picture, *She Done Him Wrong.* The unique ability of motion pictures to bring fame to a few recognizable faces worked to many stars' advantage, as it did for Mary Pickford and Mae West, among others. To get West and her play in 1933, Paramount had to concede to her absolute creative control over the script, casting, production values, and directorial choices.

The best-known woman director of the early twentieth century started as a typist in 1919 at Famous Players-Lasky and went on to a 24-year career in film. Dorothy Arzner (1900–1979) directed or codirected 21 attributed films and worked as first or second director on countless others. Arzner's career spanned the shake-ups brought to the industry by the advent of talking pictures and job specialization, the creation of the star system, and the corporate mergers that created the major studios after 1920. She survived, in fact, as the only woman director in the major studios by 1930. . . . She always attributed her staying power in Hollywood to her ability to bring films in on time and under budget—an efficiency expert in a risky and often decidedly inefficient business.

The film industry underwent profound changes after World War I. Various developments increased the complexity of filmmaking, and the marketing, production, distribution, and exhibition of films became more expensive. As the capitalization needs of production companies increased, it became more difficult for independent companies to compete. Larger production budgets were needed to cover the swelling costs of new technologies. The conversion to multiple-reel films after 1910 and the advent of indoor filming between 1910 and 1920 and sound after 1929 all required larger capital investment. Popular stars demanded heftier salaries, and the sheer numbers of people necessary to the complex production process swelled expenses. All of these costs led production companies to search for capital sources from banks, investment companies, and stockholders. The resulting corporatization of the film industry created a much more conservative investment atmosphere—and sometimes the intrusion of powerful outside investors into artistic decisions. In this environment actors, directors, writers, and editors became more like laborers, and even the most popular stars found themselves bound to salaries and exclusive contracts. These changes in the industry made it less open to women in positions of power, such as producers, directors, and studio heads. Not until the 1980s would women again attain the important institutional presence they had in the earliest years of the film industry.

A uniquely twentieth-century phenomenon—the celebrity—allowed some women with special talents or abilities to achieve not only fame but also a measure of financial independence. The celebrity, in effect, is a person who makes himself or herself into a business by selling an image, persona, or talent. . . . Although fame is not a modern invention, the intense public scrutiny and familiarity that fed celebrity-hood was made possible by the mass media of the twentieth century: radio, film, and sound recording. It became possible, for the first time in history, for anyone to hear and see individuals performing in their own living rooms or the corner theater.

Probably one of the best-known Americans in the early twentieth century was Amelia Earhart, the aviatrix whose flights across the Atlantic and Pacific Oceans made her a household name. "Earhart the Aviatrix" was the product. In addition, Earhart started and oversaw her own line of casual clothing for women. As was typical of women celebrities who were independent of a film studio or other institution, Earhart was "managed" by her husband. He sought out contacts and funding for her flights, handled publicity, arranged scheduling, and supervised their domestic arrangements. She flew at a time when both flying and women pilots were highly unusual and fascinating. Her widely publicized transoceanic and cross-country flights, as well as her clothing business, brought in enough money to support Earhart, some of her family members, and her husband and to allow her to continue flying. . . .

. . . [M]ost women continued to inhabit the business world in much more traditional ways, even as the environment in which those traditional forms operated changed, sometimes dramatically. New technologies in farming and agriculture, for example, influenced women's involvement in this type of business. In many ways women's farming tasks in 1930 were the same as those of 100 or 200 years earlier. They raised poultry, prepared butter, preserved food, sewed, cleaned, and cooked. By 1900, however, agriculture had changed radically. Farming had become oriented almost completely to a mass-production market. Cash crops had also become increasingly specialized. Farmers grew wheat but not rye, celery but not tomatoes. Processing companies interposed themselves between farmers and ranchers and their markets. The railroads transported crops to market, canneries processed them, and chain stores sold them. The nation's farmers and ranchers were almost completely integrated into the national market economy.

The gap between men's and women's experience within the family farming business widened. New machines and other products that could simplify both household tasks and general farm chores such as plowing, reaping, and milking became available. Among these products were washing machines, the telephone, self-feeders for animals, mechanical corn shredders, indoor plumbing and running water, modern cookstoves, and home canning equipment. But whether a farm woman had access to these new items involved a complex set of equations. Farm families made their economic decisions on much the same basis as any other business: where to place resources so that they would generate the most return. Since about the late eighteenth century, generating the most return meant putting financial and human resources back into major cash crops, the province of men, rather than into improvements that would assist or simplify women's contribution to the household economy. Many farm women were faced with continuing to operate their part of the family business in an almost preindustrial environment while men's farming tasks were mechanized and rationalized—in short, modernized. The economic decision-making process that was part of farming as a family business widened the gap between men's and women's work and thus their contribution to the household economy, which further devalued women's labor. . . .

Other traditional business venues remained for women as well. Women continued to operate family businesses and businesses in typically feminized areas such as catering, confectionery shops, hairdressing, and boardinghouses. In 1900 85 percent of all boardinghouses were owned and operated by women. About 30 percent of confectioners and 99 percent of dressmakers, seamstresses, and milliners were women. These numbers remained relatively unchanged from 1890. In Wilmington, Delaware, Edith McConnell took over the D. B. Jones catering and confectionery company in 1921 and ran it successfully until about 1957. The complexities of the catering business had increased from a similar type of business 100 years earlier. McConnell was typical of small-business owners in doing most of the work herself, including bookkeeping, dealing with a variety of vendors, hiring waiters and maids for large public functions, and—after the passage of the federal income tax amendment in 1913—paying federal as well as local and state taxes. As was also true historically, running a boardinghouse, making baked goods or liquor for neighborhood sale, and taking in laundry were often the province of widows or female-headed households with few other options. . . .

The bright prospects that seemed attainable in 1880 seemed less possible 50 years later. New types of businesses and technologies, as in motion pictures, provided new opportunities for women but also followed the familiar process of narrowed opportunities as industries matured, requiring more capital, adopting professional management, and addressing larger markets. Although early in this period women's access to professional training in areas such as medicine and the law increased, by the 1920s those opportunities had shrunk, and instead a series of "women's professions" had developed in social work, librarianship, teaching, and nursing. These professions were less well paid than related professions for men. Patterns of gender segregation first noticeable in the early nineteenth century continued on into the twentieth, even as new jobs appeared in various white-collar industries. . . .

Some fabulous success stories came out of the years between 1880 and 1930. There is no question that this 50-year period witnessed more profound growth in women's waged labor than any previous time. What is equally important, however, is the fact that traditional models of women's business role continued to hold such force for so many. Women developed a managerial role for themselves, but it was a role justified and shaped by domesticity. During the depression in the 1930s, women's business and professional opportunities would shrink even further as the economy contracted and state and federal agencies stepped in to regulate business in a variety of ways.

The Cultures of First-Generation Industrial Workers

HERBERT GUTMAN

Common work habits rooted in diverse premodern cultures (different in many ways but nevertheless all ill fitted to the regular routines demanded by machine-centered factory processes) existed among distinctive first-generation factory workers all through American history. We focus on two quite different time periods: the years before 1843 when the factory and machine were still new to America and the years between 1893 and 1917 when the country had become the world's industrial colossus. In both periods workers new to factory production brought strange and seemingly useless work habits to the factory gate. The irregular and undisciplined work patterns of factory hands before 1843 frustrated cost-conscious manufacturers and caused frequent complaint among them. Textile factory work rules often were designed to tame such rude customs. A New Hampshire cotton factory that hired mostly women and children forbade "spiritous liquor, smoking, nor any kind of amusement . . . in the workshops, yards, or factories" and promised the "immediate and disgraceful dismissal" of employees found gambling, drinking, or committing "any other debaucheries." . . . Manufacturers elsewhere worried about the example "idle" men set for women and children. Massachusetts family heads who rented "a piece of land on shares" to grow corn and potatoes while their wives and children labored in factories worried one manufacturer. "I would prefer giving constant employment at some sacrifice," he said, "to having a man of the village seen in the streets on a rainy day at leisure." Men who worked in Massachusetts woolen mills upset expected work routines in other ways. "The wool business requires more man labour," said a manufacturer, "and this we study to avoid. Women are much more ready to follow good regulations, are not captious, and do not clan as the men do against the overseers." Male factory workers posed other difficulties, too. In 1817 a shipbuilder in Medford, Massachusetts, refused his men grog privileges. They quit work, but he managed to finish a ship without using further spirits, "a remarkable achievement." . . .

Employers responded differently to such behavior by first-generation factory hands. "Moral reform" as well as . . . carrot-and-stick policies meant to tame or to transform such work habits. Fining was common. . . . Special material rewards encouraged steady work. A Hopewell Village blacksmith contracted for nineteen dollars a month, and "if he does his work well we are to give him a pair of coarse boots." In these and later years manufacturers in Fall River and Paterson institutionalized traditional customs and arranged for festivals and parades to celebrate with their workers a new mill, a retiring superintendent, or a finished locomotive. . . . Where factory work could be learned easily, new hands replaced irregular ones. A factory worker in New England remembered that years before the Civil War her employer had hired "all American girls" but later shifted to immigrant laborers because "not coming from country homes, but living as the Irish do, in the town, they take no vacations, and can be relied on at the mill all year round." Not all such devices worked to the satisfaction of workers or their employers. Sometime in the late 1830s merchant capitalists sent a skilled British silk weaver to manage a new mill in Nantucket that would employ the wives and children of local whalers and fishermen. Machinery was installed, and in the first days women and children besieged the mill for work. After a month had passed, they started dropping off in small groups. Soon nearly all had returned "to their shore gazing and to their seats by the sea." The Nantucket mill shut down, its hollow frame an empty monument to the unwillingness of resident women and children to conform to the regularities demanded by rising manufacturers.

First-generation factory workers were not unique to premodern America. And the work habits common to such workers plagued American manufacturers in later generations when manufacturers and most native urban whites scarcely remembered that native Americans had once been hesitant first-generation factory workers. To shift forward in time to East and South European immigrants new to steam, machinery, and electricity and new to the United States itself is to find much that seems the same. American society, of course, had changed greatly, but in some ways it is as if a film—run at a much faster speed—is being viewed for the second time: primitive work rules for unskilled labor, fines, gang labor, and subcontracting were commonplace. In 1910 two-thirds of the workers in twenty-one major manufacturing and mining industries came from Eastern and Southern Europe or were native American blacks, and studies of these "new immigrants" record much evidence of pre-industrial work habits among the men and women new to American industry. . . . [S]killed immigrant Jews carried to New York City town and village employment patterns, such as the *landsmannschaft* economy and a preference for small shops as opposed to larger factories, that sparked frequent disorders but hindered stable trade unions until 1910. Specialization spurred anxiety: in Chicago Jewish glovemakers resisted the subdivision of labor even though it promised better wages. . . . American work rules also conflicted with religious imperatives. On the eighth day after the birth of a son, Orthodox Jews in Eastern Europe held a festival, "an occasion of much rejoicing." But the American work week had a different logic, and if the day fell during the week the celebration occurred the following Sunday. "The host . . . and his guests," David Blaustein remarked, "know it is not the right day," and "they fall to mourning over the conditions that will not permit them to observe the old custom." The occasion became "one for secret sadness rather than rejoicing." Radical Yiddish poets, like Morris Rosenfeld, the presser of men's clothing, measured in verse the psychic and social costs exacted by American industrial work rules:

> The Clock in the workshop,—it rests not a moment;
> It points on, and ticks on: eternity—time;
> Once someone told me the clock had a meaning,—
> In pointing and ticking had reason and rhyme. . . .
> At times, when I listen, I hear the clock plainly;—
> The reason of old—the old meaning—is gone!
> The maddening pendulum urges me forward
> To labor and still labor on.
> The tick of the clock is the boss in his anger.
> The face of the clock has the eyes of the foe.

The clock—I shudder—Dost hear how it draws me?
It calls me "Machine"—and it cries [to] me "Sew"!

Slavic and Italian immigrants carried with them to industrial America subcultures quite different from that of village Jews, but their work habits were just as alien to the modern factory. Rudolph Vecoli has reconstructed Chicago's South Italian community to show that adult male seasonal construction gangs as contrasted to factory labor were one of many traditional customs adapted to the new environment, and in her study of South Italian peasant immigrants Phyllis H. Williams found among them men who never adjusted to factory labor. After "years" of "excellent" factory work, some "began . . . to have minor accidents" and others "suddenly give up and are found in their homes complaining of a vague indisposition with no apparent physical basis." Such labor worried early twentieth-century efficiency experts, and so did Slavic festivals, church holidays, and "prolonged merriment." "Man," Adam Smith wisely observed, "is, of all sorts of luggage, the most difficult to be transported." That was just as true for these Slavic immigrants as for the early nineteenth-century native American factory workers. A Polish wedding in a Pennsylvania mining or mill town lasted between three and five days. Greek and Roman Catholics shared the same jobs but had different holy days, "an annoyance to many employers." The Greek Church had "more than eighty festivals in the year," and "the Slav religiously observes the days on which the saints are commemorated and invariably takes a holiday." A celebration of the American Day of Independence in Mahanoy City, Pennsylvania, caught the eye of a hostile observer. Men parading the streets drew a handcart with a barrel of lager in it. Over the barrel "stood a comrade, goblet in hand and crowned with a garland of laurel, singing some jargon." Another sat and played an accordion. At intervals, the men stopped to "drink the good beverage they celebrated in song." The witness called the entertainment "an imitation of the honor paid Bacchus which was one of the most joyous festivals of ancient Rome" and felt it proof of "a lower type of civilization." Great Lakes dock workers "believed that a vessel could not be unloaded unless they had from four to five kegs of beer." (And in the early irregular strikes among male Jewish garment workers, employers negotiated with them out of doors and after each settlement "would roll out a keg of beer for their entertainment of the workers." Contemporary betters could not comprehend such behavior. . . .

More than irregular work habits bound together the behavior of first-generation factory workers separated from one another by time and by the larger structure of the society they first encountered. Few distinctive American working-class populations differed in so many essentials (their sex, their religion, their nativity, and their prior rural and village cultures) as the Lowell mill girls and women of the Era of Good Feelings and the South and East European steelworkers of the Progressive Era. To describe similarities in their expectations of factory labor is not to blur these important differences but to suggest that otherwise quite distinctive men and women interpreted such work in similar ways. . . .

Historians of the Lowell mill girls find little evidence before 1840 of organized protest among them and attribute their collective passivity to corporation policing policies, the frequent turnover in the labor force, the irregular pace of work (after it was rationalized in the 1840s, it provoked collective protest), the freedom the mill girls enjoyed away from rural family dominance, and their relatively decent earnings. The women managed the transition to mill life because they did not expect to remain factory workers too long. Nevertheless frequent inner tension revealed itself among the mobile mill women. In an early year, a single mill discharged twenty-eight women for such reasons as "misconduct," "captiousness," "disobedience," "impudence," "levity," and even "mutiny." . . .

Aspirations and expectations interpret experience and thereby help shape behavior. Some Lowell mill girls revealed dissatisfactions, and others made a difficult transition from rural New England to that model factory town, but that so few planned to remain mill workers eased that transition and hampered collective protest. Men as well as women, who expect to spend only a few years as factory workers have little incentive to join unions. That was just as true of the immigrant male common laborers in the steel mills of the late nineteenth and early twentieth centuries (when multiplant oligopoly characterized the nation's most important manufacturing industry) as in the Lowell cotton mills nearly a century earlier. . . . In those years, the steel companies successfully divorced wages from productivity to allow the market to shape them. Between 1890 and 1910, efficiencies in plant organization cut labor costs by about a third. The great Carnegie Pittsburg plants employed 14,359 common laborers, 11,694 of them South and East Europeans. Most, peasant in origin, earned less than $12.50 a week (a family needed fifteen dollars for subsistence). A staggering accident rate damaged these and other men: nearly 25 percent of the recent immigrants employed at the Carnegie South Works were injured or killed each year between 1907 and 1910, 3,723 in all. But like the Lowell mill women, these men rarely protested in collective ways, and for good reason. They did not plan to stay in the steel mills long. Most had come to the United States as single men (or married men who had left their families behind) to work briefly in the mills, save some money, return home, and purchase farmland. Their private letters to European relatives indicated a realistic awareness of their working life that paralleled some of the Lowell fiction: "if I don't earn $1.50 a day, it would not be worth thinking about America"; "a golden land so long as there is work"; "here in America one must work for three horses"; "let him not risk coming, for he is too young"; "too weak for America." Men who wrote such letters and avoided injury often saved small amounts of money, and a significant number fulfilled their expectations and quit the factory and even the country. Forty-four South and East Europeans left the United States for every one hundred that arrived between 1908 and 1910. . . . Immigrant expectations coincided for a time with the fiscal needs of industrial manufacturers. The Pittsburgh steel magnates had as much good fortune as the Boston Associates. But the stability and passivity they counted on among their unskilled workers depended upon steady work and the opportunity to escape the mills. When frequent recessions caused recurrent unemployment, immigrant expectations and behavior changed. . . .[P]easant "group consciousness" and "communal loyalty" sustained bitter wildcat strikes after employment picked up. The tenacity of these immigrant strikers for higher wages amazed contemporaries, and brutal suppression often accompanied them (Cleveland, 1899; East Chicago, 1905; McKees Rock, 1909; Bethlehem, 1910; and Youngstown in 1915 where, after a policeman shot into a peaceful parade, a riot caused an estimated one million dollars in damages). The First World War and its aftermath blocked the traditional route of overseas outward mobility, and the consciousness of immigrant steelworkers changed. They sparked the 1919 steel strike. The steel mill had become a way of life for them and was no longer the means by which to reaffirm and even strengthen older peasant and village life-styles. . . .

Even though American society itself underwent radical structural changes between 1815 and the First World War, the shifting composition of its wage-earning population meant that traditional customs, rituals, and beliefs repeatedly helped shape the behavior of its diverse working-class groups. The street battle in 1843 that followed Irish efforts to prevent New York City authorities from stopping pigs from running loose in the streets is but one example of the force of old styles of behavior. Both the form and the content of much expressive working-class behavior, including labor disputes, often revealed the powerful role of secular and religious rituals. In 1857 the New York City unemployed kidnapped a musical band to give legitimacy to its parade for public works. After the Civil War, a Fall River cotton manufacturer boasted that the arrival of fresh Lancashire operatives meant the coming of "a lot of greenhorns here," but an overseer advised him, "Yes, but you'll find they have brought their horns with them." A few years later, the Pittsburgh courts prevented three women married to coal miners from "tin-horning" nonstrikers. The women, however, purchased mouth organs. ("Tinhorning," of course, was not merely an imported institution. In Franklin, Virginia, in 1867, for example, a Northern white clergyman who started a school for former slave children had two nighttime "tin horn serenade[s]" from hostile whites.) Recurrent street demonstrations in Paterson accompanying frequent strikes and lockouts nearly always involved horns, whistles, and even Irish "banshee" calls. These had a deeply symbolic meaning, and, rooted in a shared culture, they sustained disputes. A Paterson manufacturer said of nonstrikers: "They cannot go anywhere without being molested or insulted, and no matter what they do they are met and blackguarded and taunted in a way that no one can stand . . . which is a great deal worse than actual assaults." . . .

But the manufacturers could not convince the town's mayor (himself a British immigrant and an artisan who had become a small manufacturer) to ban street demonstrations. The manufacturers even financed their own private militia to manage further disorders, but the street demonstrations continued with varying effectiveness until 1901 when a court injunction essentially defined the streets as private space by banning talking and singing banshee (or death) wails in them during industrial disputes. In part, the frequent recourse to the courts and to the state militia after the Civil War during industrial disputes was the consequence of working-class rituals that helped sustain long and protracted conflicts.

Symbolic secular and, especially, religious rituals and beliefs differed among Catholic and Jewish workers fresh to industrial America between 1894 and the First World War, but their function remained the same. Striking Jewish vestmakers finished a formal complaint by quoting the Law of Moses to prove that "our bosses who rob us and don't pay us regularly commit a sin and that the cause of our union is a just one." ("What do we come to America for?" these same men asked. "To bathe in tears and to see our wives and children rot in poverty?") An old Jewish ritual oath helped spark the shirtwaist strike of women workers in 1909 that laid the basis for the International Ladies Garment Workers Union. A strike vote resulted in the plea, "Do you mean faith? Will you take the old Jewish oath?" The audience responded in Yiddish: "If I turn traitor to the cause, I now pledge, may this hand wither and drop off at the wrist from the arm I now raise." . . . Immigrant Catholic workers shared similar experiences with these immigrant Jews. A reporter noticed in 1910 at a meeting of striking Slavic steelworkers in Hammond, Indiana: "The lights of the hall were extinguished. A candle stuck into a bottle was placed on a platform. One by one the men came and kissed the ivory image on the cross, kneeling before it. They swore not to scab." Not all rituals were that pacific. That same year, Slavic miners in Avelia, Pennsylvania, a tiny patch on the West Virginia border, crucified George Rabish, a mine boss and an alleged labor spy. . . . That event was certainly unusual, but it was commonplace for time-honored religious symbols as well as American flags to be carried in the frequent parades of American workers. Western Pennsylvania Slavic and Italian coal miners in a bitter strike just east of Pittsburg (eighteen of twenty thousand miners quit work for seventeen months when denied the right to join the United Mine Workers of America) in 1910 and 1911 carried such symbols. "These rural marches," said Paul Kellogg [*Survey* editor], "were in a way reminiscent of the old time agrarian uprisings which have marked English history." But theirs was the behavior of peasant and village Slavs and Italians fresh to modern industrial America, and it was just such tenacious peasant-worker protests that caused the head of the Pennsylvania State Police to say that he modeled his force on the Royal Irish Constabulary, not, he insisted, "as an anti-labor measure" but because "conditions in Pennsylvania resembled those in strife-torn Ireland." Peasant parades and rituals, religious oaths and food riots, and much else in the culture and behavior of early twentieth-century immigrant American factory workers were cultural anachronisms to this man and to others, including Theodore Roosevelt, William Jennings Bryan, Elbert Gary, and even Samuel Gompers, but participants found them natural and effective forms of self-assertion and self-protection.

The perspective emphasized in these pages tells about more than the behavior of diverse groups of American working men and women. It also suggests how larger, well-studied aspects of American society have been affected by a historical process that has "industrialized" different peoples over protracted periods of time. . . . Contact and conflict between diverse preindustrial cultures and a changing and increasingly bureaucratized industrial society also affected the larger society in ways that await systematic examination. Contemporaries realized this fact. Concerned in 1886 about the South's "dead"—that is, unproductive—population, the Richmond *Whig* felt the "true remedy" to be "educating the industrial morale of the people." The *Whig* emphasized socializing institutions primarily outside of the working class itself. "In the work of inculcating industrial ideas and impulses," said the *Whig,* "all proper agencies should be enlisted—family discipline, public school education, pulpit instruction, business standards and requirements, and the power and influence of the workingmen's associations." What the *Whig* worried over in 1886 concerned other Americans before and after that time. And the resultant tension shaped society in important ways. . . .

The same process also affected the shaping and reshaping of American police and domestic military institutions. We need only realize that the burning of a Boston convent in 1834 by a crowd of Charlestown truckmen and New Hampshire Scotch-Irish brickmakers caused the first revision of the Massachusetts Riot Act since Shays' Rebellion, and that three years later interference by native firemen in a Sunday Irish funeral procession led to a two-hour riot involving upward of fifteen thousand persons (more than a sixth of Boston's population), brought militia to that city for the first time, and caused the first of many reorganizations of the Boston police force. The regular contact between alien work cultures and a larger industrializing or industrial society had other consequences. It often worried industrialists, causing C. E. Perkins, the president of the Chicago, Burlington, and Quincy Railroad to confide in a friend in the late nineteenth century. "If I were able, I would found a school for the study of political economy in order to harden men's hearts." It affected the popular culture. A guidebook for immigrant Jews in the 1890s advised how to make it in the New World: "Hold fast, this is most necessary in America. Forget your past, your customs, and your ideals. . . . A bit of advice to you: do not take a moment's rest. Run, do, work, and keep your own good in mind." Cultures and customs, however, are not that easily discarded. So it may be that America's extraordinary technological supremacy—its talent before the Second World War for developing labor-saving machinery and simplifying complex mechanical processes—depended less on "Yankee know-how" than on the continued infusion of prefactory peoples into an increasingly industrialized society. The same process, moreover, may also explain why movements to legislate morality and to alter habits have lasted much longer in the United States than in most other industrial countries, extending from the temperance crusades of the 1820s and the 1830s to the violent opposition among Germans to such rules in the 1850s and the 1860s and finally to formal prohibition earlier in this century. Important relationships also exist between this process and the elite and popular nativist and racist social movements that have ebbed and flowed regularly from the 1840s until our own time, as well as between this process and elite political "reform" movements between 1850 and the First World War.

The sweeping social process had yet another important consequence: it reinforced the biases that otherwise distort the ways in which elite observers perceive the world below them. When in 1902 *The New York Times* cast scorn upon and urged that force be used against the Jewish women food rioters, it conformed to a fairly settled elite tradition. Immigrant groups and the working population had changed in composition over time, but the rhetoric of influential nineteenth- and early twentieth-century elite observers remained constant. Disorders among the Jersey City Irish seeking wages due them from the Erie Railroad in 1859 led the Jersey City *American Standard* to call them "imported *beggars*" and "*animals*," "a mongrel mass of ignorance and crime and superstition, as utterly unfit for its duties, as they are for the common courtesies and decencies of civilized life." . . .

Although the Civil War ended slavery, it did not abolish these distorted perceptions and fears of new American workers. In 1869 *Scientific American* welcomed the "ruder" laborers of Europe but urged them to "assimilate" quickly or face "a quiet but sure extermination." Those who retained their alien ways, it insisted, "will share the fate of the native Indian." Elite nativism neither died out during the Civil War nor awaited a rebirth under the auspices of the American Protective Association and the Immigration Restriction League. In the mid-1870s, for example, the Chicago *Tribune* called striking immigrant brickmakers men but "not reasoning creatures," and the Chicago *Post-Mail* described that city's Bohemian residents as "depraved beasts, harpies, decayed physically and spiritually, mentally and morally, thievish and licentious." The Democratic Chicago *Times* cast an even wider net in complaining that the country had become "the cess-pool of Europe under the pretense that it is the asylum of the poor." Most Chicago inhabitants in the Gilded Age were foreign-born or the children of the foreign-born, and most English-language Chicago news-papers scorned them. . . . Here, as in the Jersey City *American Standard* (1859) and *The New York Times* (1902), much more was involved than mere ethnic distaste or "nativism." In quite a different connection and in a relatively homogeneous country, the Italian Antonio Gramsci concluded of such evidence that "for a social elite the features of subordinate groups always display something barbaric and pathologi-cal." The changing composition of the American working class may make so severe a dictum more pertinent to the United States than to Italy. Class and ethnic fears and biases combined together to worry elite observers about the diverse worlds below them to distort gravely their perceptions of these worlds. . . .

These pages have fractured historical time, ranging forward and backward, to make comparisons for several reasons. One has been to suggest how much remains to be learned about the transition of native and foreign-born American men and women to industrial society, and how that transition affected such persons and the society into which they entered. "Much of what gets into American literature," Ralph Ellison has shrewdly observed "gets there because so much is left out." That has also been the case in the writing of American working-class history, and the framework and methods suggested here merely hint at what will be known about American workers and American society when the many transitions are studied in detail. Such studies, however, need to focus on the particularities of both the groups involved and the society into which they enter. Transitions differ and de-pend upon the interaction between the two at specific historical moments. But at all times there is a resultant tension. [E. P.] Thompson writes:

> There has never been any single type of "the transition." The stress of the transition falls upon the whole culture: resistance to change and assent to change arise from the whole culture. And this culture includes the systems of power, property-relations, religious in-stitutions, etc., inattention to which merely flattens phenomena and trivializes analysis.

Enough has been savored in these pages to suggest the particular importance of these transitions in American social history. And their recurrence in different pe-riods of time indicates why there has been so much discontinuity in American labor and social history. The changing composition of the working population, the continued entry into the United States of nonindustrial people with distinctive cul-tures, and the changing structure of American society have combined together to produce common modes of thought and patterns of behavior. But these have been experiences disconnected in time and shared by quite distinctive first-generation native and immigrant industrial Americans. It was not possible for the grand-children of the Lowell mill girls to understand that their Massachusetts literary ancestors shared a great deal with their contemporaries, the peasant Slavs in the Pennsylvania steel mills and coals fields. And the grandchildren of New York City Jewish garment workers see little connection between black ghetto unrest in the 1960s and the kosher meat riots seventy years ago. A half-century has passed since Robert Park and Herbert Miller published W. I. Thomas's *Old World Traits Transplanted*, a study which worried that the function of Americanization was the "destruction of memories."

WEEK 6

DOCUMENTS

1. *In Re Debs,* 1895

Mr. Lyman Trumbull, for Petitioners.

The bill states that the prisoners are officers and members of an organization known as the American Railway Union; that in May, 1894, a dispute arose between the Pullman Palace Car Company and its employés which resulted in the employés leaving the service of the company; that the prisoners, officers of the American Railway Union combining together, and with others unknown, with the purpose to compel an adjustment of the said difference and dispute between said Pullman Co. and its employés, caused it to be given out through the newspapers of Chicago, generally, that the American Railway Union would at once create a boycott against the cars manufactured by said Pullman Palace Co., and that in order to make said boycott effective, the members of the American Railway Union who were some of them employed as trainmen or switchmen, or otherwise, in the service of the railroads mentioned, which railroads or some of them are accustomed to haul the sleeping cars manufactured by the Pullman Palace Car Co., would be directed to refuse to perform their usual duties for said railroad companies and receivers in case said railroad companies thereafter attempted to haul Pullman sleeping cars.

Such is the gist of the bill. All that is subsequently alleged as to what was done by the prisoners, was for the purpose of compelling an adjustment of the difference between the Pullman Company and its employés. To accomplish this, the American Railway Union called upon its members to quit work for the companies which had persisted in hauling the Pullman cars. Was there anything unlawful in this? If not, then the prisoners and the members of the American Railway Union were engaged in no unlawful combination or conspiracy. The allegation that the prisoners, officers and directors of the American Railway Union did issue and promulgate certain orders and requests to the members of the unions in the service of certain railway companies in pursuance of said unlawful purpose or conspiracy did not make the purpose unlawful, when the facts stated in the bill show that the purpose was not unlawful. All that the prisoners are charged with threatening to do, or having done, was for the purpose, primarily, of bringing about an adjustment of the differences between the Pullman Company and its employés. It is only incidentally in pursuit of this lawful purpose that prisoners are charged with obstructing commerce.

The boycott of the Pullman sleepers was, as the bill shows, not to obstruct commerce, but for an entirely different purpose.

From *In Re Debs,* 158 US 564 (1895).

It was not unlawful for the American Railway Union to call off the members of the organization, although it might incidentally affect the operation of the railroads. Refusing to work for a railroad company is no crime, and though such action may incidentally delay the mails or interfere with interstate commerce, it being a lawful act, and not done for that purpose, is no offence. . . .

Mr. Justice Brewer, After Stating the Case, Delivered the Opinion of the Court.

The case presented by the bill is this: The United States, finding that the interstate transportation of persons and property, as well as the carriage of the mails, is forcibly obstructed, and that a combination and conspiracy exists to subject the control of such transportation to the will of the conspirators, applied to one of their courts, sitting as a court of equity, for an injunction to restrain such obstruction and prevent carrying into effect such conspiracy. Two questions of importance are presented: First. Are the relations of the general government to interstate commerce and the transportation of the mails such as authorize a direct interference to prevent a forcible obstruction thereof? Second. If authority exists, as authority in governmental affairs implies both power and duty, has a court of equity jurisdiction to issue an injunction in aid of the performance of such duty. . . .

It must be borne in mind that this bill was not simply to enjoin a mob and mob violence. It was not a bill to command a keeping of the peace; much less was its purport to restrain the defendants from abandoning whatever employment they were engaged in. The right of any laborer, or any number of laborers, to quit work was not challenged. The scope and purpose of the bill was only to restrain forcible obstructions of the highways along which interstate commerce travels and the mails are carried. And the facts set forth at length are only those facts which tended to show that the defendants were engaged in such obstructions.

A most earnest and eloquent appeal was made to us in eulogy of the heroic spirit of those who threw up their employment, and gave up their means of earning a livelihood, not in defence of their own rights, but in sympathy for and to assist others whom they believed to be wronged. We yield to none in our admiration of any act of heroism or self-sacrifice, but we may be permitted to add that it is a lesson which cannot be learned too soon or too thoroughly that under this government of and by the people the means of redress of all wrongs are through the courts and at the ballot-box, and that no wrong, real or fancied, carries with it legal warrant to invite as a means of redress the coöperation of a mob, with its accompanying acts of violence.

We have given to this case the most careful and anxious attention, for we realize that it touches closely questions of supreme importance to the people of this country. Summing up our conclusions, we hold that the government of the United States is one having jurisdiction over every foot of soil within its territory, and acting directly upon each citizen; that while it is a government of enumerated powers, it has within the limits of those powers all the attributes of sovereignty; that to it is committed power over interstate commerce and the transmission of the mail; that the powers thus conferred upon the national government are not dormant, but have been assumed and put into practical exercise by the legislation of Congress; that in the exercise of those powers it is competent for the nation to remove all obstructions upon highways, natural or artificial, to the passage of interstate commerce or the carrying of the mail; that while it may be competent for the government (through the executive branch and in the use of the entire executive power of the nation) to forcibly remove all such obstructions, it is equally within its competency to appeal to the civil courts for an inquiry and determination as to the existence and character of any alleged obstructions, and if such are found to exist, or threaten to occur, to invoke the powers of those courts to remove or restrain such obstructions; that the jurisdiction of courts to interfere in such matters by injunction is one recognized from ancient times and by indubitable authority; that such jurisdiction is not ousted by the fact that the obstructions are accompanied by or consist of acts in themselves violations of the criminal law; that the proceeding by injunction is of a civil character, and may be enforced by proceedings in contempt; that such proceedings are not in execution of the criminal laws of the land; that the penalty for a violation of injunction is no substitute for and no defence to a prosecution for any criminal offences committed in the course of such violation; that the complaint filed in this case clearly showed an existing obstruction of artificial highways for the passage of interstate commerce and the transmission of the mail—an obstruction not only temporarily existing, but threatening to continue; that under such complaint the Circuit Court had power to issue its process of injunction; that it having been issued and served on these defendants, the Circuit Court had authority to inquire whether its orders had been disobeyed, and when it found that they had been, then to proceed under section 725, Revised Statutes, which grants power "to punish, by fine or imprisonment, . . . disobedience, . . . by any party . . . or other person, to any lawful writ, process, order, rule, decree or command," and enter the order of punishment complained of; and, finally, that, the Circuit Court, having full jurisdiction in the premises, its finding of the fact of disobedience is not open to review on *habeas corpus* in this or any other court. . . .

The petition for a writ of *habeas corpus* is

Denied.

2. *Muller* v. *Oregon*, 1908

Mr. Justice Brewer Delivered the Opinion of the Court.

It is undoubtedly true, as more than once declared by this court, that the general right to contract in relation to one's business is part of the liberty of the individual, protected by the Fourteenth Amendment to the Federal Constitution; yet it equally well settled that this liberty is not absolute and extending to all contracts, and that a State may, without conflicting with the provisions of the Fourteenth Amendment, restrict in many respects the individual's power of contract. . . .

That woman's physical structure and the performance of maternal functions place her at a disadvantage in the struggle for subsistence is obvious. This is especially true when the burdens of motherhood are upon her. Even when they are not,

From *Muller* v. *Oregon*, 208 US 412 (1908).

by abundant testimony of the medical fraternity continuance for a long time on her feet at work, repeating this from day to day, tends to injurious effects upon the body, and as healthy mothers are essential to vigorous offspring, the physical well-being of woman becomes an object of public interest and care in order to preserve the strength and vigor of the race.

Still again, history discloses the fact that woman has always been dependent upon man. He established his control at the outset by superior physical strength, and this control in various forms, with diminishing intensity, has continued to the present. As minors, though not to the same extent, she has been looked upon in the courts as needing especial care that her rights may be preserved. Education was long denied her, and while now the doors of the school room are opened and her opportunities for acquiring knowledge are great, yet even with that and the consequent increase of capacity for business affairs it is still true that in the struggle for subsistence she is not an equal competitor with her brother. Though limitations upon personal and contractual rights may be removed by legislation, there is that in her disposition and habits of life which will operate against a full assertion of those rights. She will still be where some legislation to protect her seems necessary to secure a real equality of right. Doubtless there are individual exceptions, and there are many respects in which she has an advantage over him; but looking at it from the viewpoint of the effort to maintain an independent position in life, she is not upon an equality. Differentiated by these matters from the other sex, she is properly placed in a class by herself, and legislation designed for her protection may be sustained, even when like legislation is not necessary for men and could not be sustained. It is impossible to close one's eyes to the fact that she still looks to her brother and depends upon him. Even though all restrictions on political, personal and contractual rights were taken away, and she stood, so far as statutes are concerned, upon an absolutely equal plane with him, it would still be true that she is so constituted that she will rest upon and look to him for protection; that her physical structure and a proper discharge of her maternal functions—having in view not merely her own health, but the well-being of the race—justify legislation to protect her from the greed as well as the passion of man. The limitations which this statute places upon her contractual powers, upon her right to agree with her employer as to the time she shall labor, are not imposed solely for her benefit, but also largely for the benefit of all. Many words cannot make this plainer. The two sexes differ in structure of body, in the functions to be performed by each, in the amount of physical strength, in the capacity for long-continued labor, particularly when done standing, the influence of vigorous health upon the future well-being of the race, the self-reliance which enables one to assert full rights, and in the capacity to maintain the struggle for subsistence. This difference justifies a difference in legislation and upholds that which is designed to compensate for some of the burdens which rest upon her.

We have not referred in this discussion to the denial of the elective franchise in the State of Oregon, for while it may disclose a lack of political equality in all things with her brother, that is not itself decisive. The reason runs deeper, and rests in the inherent difference between the two sexes, and in the different functions in life which they perform. . . .

Affirmed.

1. Three Cartoonists Interpret the Political Scene, 1880, 1888

Thomas Nast Attacks the Democrats, 1880

AS SOLID AND DEFIANT AS EVER

In this vintage example of "waving the bloody shirt," German-born staunch Republican cartoonist Thomas Nast invokes powerful symbols of good and evil to elevate the significance of late-nineteenth-century partisanship. With what counter-imagery might the Democrats have responded?

Thomas Nast cartoon from *Harper's Weekly*, Oct. 2, 1880. Reprinted in J. Chad Vinson, *Thomas Nast: Political Cartoonist* (Athens: University of Georgia Press, 1967), illustration no. 125.

Joseph Keppler Ridicules the Third-Term Aspirations of President Grant, 1880

PUCK WANTS "A STRONG MAN AT THE HEAD OF GOVERNMENT"—BUT NOT THIS KIND.

Keppler, a less partisan but worthy successor to Nast as the nation's leading cartoonist, visually documents the influence peddling that had accompanied the first two Grant administrations. Given this record of scandal, why do you suppose Grant was even considered by party leaders for a third term?

Joseph Keppler cartoon from *Puck* (New York: Puck Publishing Company), Feb. 4, 1880.

Watson Heston Lampoons Parties and Their Corporate Patrons, 1888

How the Voting Cattle Obey the Will of the "Powers that Be."--*(Will show the "Powers That Be" in our Next.)*

Heston's critique of the two-party system reflected a common viewpoint among the economically and politically disaffected in the late 1880s and early 1890s. Who might be so alienated and why? What options did they have?

Watson Heston cartoon from *American Non-Conformist and Kansas Industrial Liberator,* March 8, 1888.

2. Free-Thinker Robert G. Ingersoll Waves the Bloody Shirt, c. 1880

Why I Am a Republican

That party has thrown every safeguard around the ballot-box in every State in the Union where any safeguard has been thrown. That party has always been in favor of registration; the Democratic party has always opposed it. That party—the Republican party—has done all it could possibly do to secure an honest expression of the great will of the people. Every man here who is in favor of an honest ballot-box ought to vote the Republican ticket; every man here in favor of free speech ought to vote the Republican ticket. Free speech is the brain of this Republic, and an honest vote is its life-blood. (Applause.) There are two reasons, then, why I am a Republican: First, I believe in free speech; secondly, I want an honest vote.

A crust that the worms had eaten before was a democrat; every man who shot down our men when they happened to step an inch beyond the dead line, every one was a Democrat; and when some poor, emaciated Union patriot, driven to insanity by famine, saw at home in his innocent dreams the face of his mother, and she seemed to beckon him to come to her, and he, following that dream, stepped one inch beyond the dead line, the wretch who put a bullet through his throbbing, loving heart was a Democrat.

We should never forget these things. (A voice, "That's so.") Every man who wept over the corpse of slavery; every man who was sorry when the chains fell from four millions of people; every man who regretted to see the shackles drop from, women and children, every one was a Democrat. In the House of Representatives and in the Senate the resolution was submitted to amend the Constitution so that every man treading the soil of the Republic should be forever free, and every man who voted against it was a Democrat. Every man who swore that greenbacks never would be worth any more than withered leaves, every man who swore that he would never pay, our bonds, every man who slandered our credit and prophesied defeat, was a Democrat. Now, recollect it. Do not forget it. And if there is any young man here who is this fall to cast his first vote, I beg of him, I beseech him, not to join that party whose history for the last twenty years has been a disgrace to this country.

3. Virginia Activist Live Pryor Seeks Help for Her Downtrodden Black Sisters, 1880

A Letter to Susan B. Anthony

[I read] Your Call for all woman of These United States to sign a petition . . . to be sent to you, from Your Mass Meeting to be sent to the Republican Presidential Convention asking them to extend to us Woman some recognition of our rights. We are your Sister though Colored still we feel in our Bosom and want of Faternal love

---

Wit, Wisdom and Eloquence of Col. R. G. Ingersoll (Chicago: Rhodes and McClure, 1894), 126–127.

Chicago Historical Society, National Woman Suffrage Association Correspondence Volume. Reprinted in Ellen Carol DuBois, ed., *Elizabeth Cady Stanton and Susan B. Anthony: Correspondence, Writings, Speeches* (New York: Schocken, 1981), 205–206.

from our White Sister of the Country. Our White men of this State of Virginia, who rule us with a rod of iron, and show themselves on every occasion the same Crule Task Master, as ever, have introduce on the Statute books right to wipp woman for any poor Discretion, that she might be guilt of. During the early part of febuary a poor weak colored Woman who was in the Extremes wants, stole a Over skirt Value fifty Cent, for which the presiding Magistrate Named J. J. Gruchfield, Did order the poor creature 72 lashes to be well laid on. 36 lashes at the time the Other 36 in a week time and the man or, brute, went himself and saw the whipping was executed. Captain Scott a Col man became indignant went to the jail to see the poor Creature, was refused admission at first but succeed at Last. O My God, what a sight he then saw. the poor Woman Breast Cut wide open by the lash, her poor back cut to pieces I call some woman together went to the Governor and stated the Case. he forbid the further lashing of the poor woman because the Dr. Beal said she could not live to receive further whipping. Yet the woman still have to remain in jail 12 months for stealing one over skirt Value fifty Cent and have since then been enable to enroll quite a number of Woman to gather form a Club. Our Object is to petition Lecture and to do all things wich shall so soffen the heart of Mankind that they will see and must grant and respect our rights. Would and pray that the Mass Meeting may endorse or demand of the Republican Convention to be Held in Chicigo the rights of Woman to put an Amendment to the Constitution a Cumpulsory Education of Every state of this Union.

Pardon me for this long letter i must i feel let my feeling go out, so to you Dear Madam have i address you on Behalf of your Down Trodden Colored Sisters of Virginia.

> Live Pryor, Richmond, Virginia
> President, Ladies Enterprise Club

If you have any papers or book that is of no use to you our society would feel grateful to receive them as we wish to form a library.

4. Elizabeth Cady Stanton Demands Suffrage as the Protection of Selfhood, 1892

The point I wished plainly to bring before you on this occasion is the individuality of each human soul—our Protestant idea, the right of individual conscience and judgment—our republican idea, individual citizenship. In discussing the rights of woman, we are to consider, first, what belongs to her as an individual, in a world of her own, the arbiter of her own destiny, an imaginary Robinson Crusoe with her woman Friday on a solitary island. Her rights under such circumstances are to use all her faculties for her own safety and happiness. . . .

The isolation of every human soul and the necessity of self-dependence must give each individual the right to choose his own surroundings. The strongest reason for giving woman all the opportunities for higher education, for the full development

The Woman's Column, Jan. 1892, pp. 2–3. This document can be found in Ellen Carol DuBois, ed., *Elizabeth Cady Stanton and Susan B. Anthony Reader* (Boston: Northeastern University Press, 1992), 247–254.

of her faculties, her forces of mind and body; for giving her the most enlarged freedom of thought and action; a complete emancipation from all forms of bondage, of custom, dependence, superstition; from all the crippling influences of fear—is the solitude and personal responsibility of her own individual life. The strongest reason why we ask for woman a voice in the government under which she lives; in the religion she is asked to believe; equality in social life, where she is the chief factor; a place in the trades and professions, where she may earn her bread, is because of her birthright to self-sovereignty; because, as an individual, she must rely on herself. . . .

To throw obstacles in the way of a complete education is like putting out the eyes; to deny the rights of property is like cutting off the hands. To refuse political equality is to rob the ostracized of all self-respect, of credit in the market place, of recompense in the world of work, of a voice in choosing those who make and administer the law, a choice in the jury before whom they are tried, and in the judge who decides their punishment. Shakespeare's play of Titus and Andronicus contains a terrible satire on woman's position in the nineteenth century—"Rude men seized the king's daughter, cut out her tongue, cut off her hands, and then bade her go call for water and wash her hands." What a picture of woman's position! Robbed of her natural rights, handicapped by law and custom at every turn, yet compelled to fight her own battles, and in the emergencies of life to fall back on herself for protection. . . .

How the little courtesies of life on the surface of society, deemed so important from man towards woman, fade into utter insignificance in view of the deeper tragedies in which she must play her part alone, where no human aid is possible! . . .

Is it, then, consistent to hold the developed woman of this day within the same narrow political limits as the dame with the spinning wheel and knitting needle occupied in the past? No, no! Machinery has taken the labors of woman as well as man on its tireless shoulders; the loom and the spinning wheel are but dreams of the past; the pen, the brush, the easel, the chisel, have taken their places, while the hopes and ambitions of women are essentially changed.

We see reason sufficient in the outer conditions of human beings for individual liberty and development, but when we consider the self-dependence of every human soul, we see the need of courage, judgment and the exercise of every faculty of mind and body, strengthened and developed by use, in woman as well as man.

ESSAYS

Law and Free Labor

ALICE KESSLER-HARRIS

Supreme Court decisions are frequently unpopular. Yet few have faced the storm of national derision that confronted the April 1923 opinion handed down in *Adkins* v. *Children's Hospital.* By a vote of 5 to 3 (Brandeis abstaining), the Court negated the constitutionality of a Washington, D.C., law that provided minimum wages for women and minors. With its act the Court also placed in jeopardy the minimum wage legislation of thirteen other states.

Newspaper editorials, public meetings, and placards denounced the decision. Mary Anderson, head of the Women's Bureau, called it "nothing short of a calamity." Samuel Gompers declared it to be a "logical next step in perfecting the doctrine that those who cannot help themselves shall not be helped." The *New York World* ran a cartoon that depicted Justice Sutherland handing the document to a woman wage earner, with the caption, "This decision, madam, affirms your constitutional right to starve." In the immediate aftermath of the decision, the National Women's Trade Union League called a conference to stave off what it feared would be "a wholesale reduction of wages for more than 1,500,000 women and girls." The "greatest wrong" in the decision, as Gompers and others pointed out, was that in describing labor as a commodity to be bought and sold Justice Sutherland had likened "the labor of a woman to the purchase of a shinbone over the counter to make soup." . . .

The response might have been louder because the decision was apparently so unexpected. Fifteen years earlier, in *Muller* v. *Oregon,* the Court had accepted the principle that women's health was a proper subject of state concern and therefore of state regulation. In the wake of that decision, most industrial states had taken it upon themselves to regulate the hours and working conditions of women and minors. These laws, quintessentially progressive in that they attempted to redress the imbalances of rapid industrial growth, had withstood many legal challenges and, just a year after Adkins, were to survive another. Though states were more cautious when it came to regulating wages, thirteen states and the District of Columbia had enacted minimum wage laws before 1923. Each was grounded in the assumption that the needs of working women for food, clothing, and shelter could be accurately determined and in the desire to maintain women's health and protect their morals by establishing wages at a level "adequate to supply the necessary cost of living."

. . . Why then had the Court so unexpectedly countered what seemed like a well-established trend?

The answer may lie in the competing paradigms embedded in the issue of minimum wages for women. Decisions about minimum wages were grounded both in legal precedents around labor and in those around women. Watching the judiciary confront these issues tells us something about the vital importance of the idea of gender differences in the progressive era. And looking at the evolution of the relationship between a doctrine grounded in changing theories of labor and one that

From Alice Kessler-Harris, *A Woman's Wage: Historical Meanings and Social Consequences* (Lexington: University of Kentucky Press, 1990), pp. 33–56. Reprinted by permission of the University of Kentucky Press.

rested on separate spheres may tell us something about the relationship of gender differences to other influential ideas in the construction of law and social policy. As we examine the roots of Adkins, we begin to understand something of how the gendered content of ideas governed an important set of political and judicial decisions and, not inadvertently, laid the groundwork for incorporating nineteenth century notions of workers' dignity and independence into the judicial system.

Minimum wage legislation derived its rationale from the gendered arguments used to gain passage of other regulatory legislation. Its purpose, as the title of the Oregon Act makes clear, was "to protect the lives and health and morals of women and minor workers . . . ," or, as the District of Columbia Act put it, "to protect women and minors from conditions detrimental to their health and morals, resulting from wages which are inadequate to maintain decent standards of living." As such, it was firmly rooted in progressive notions of women's separate sphere. . . . The widely accepted notion that women were mothers of the race provided more than adequate justification for the courts to regulate women's working lives. But although the courts in earlier decisions had accepted sex difference as a reasonable basis for restraining the freedom of women and employers to contract, and would subsequently continue to rely on sex difference, the Supreme Court rejected the idea in Adkins.

In so doing, the Court simply affirmed what had been well established by 1923, namely that an individual's freedom to contract was not subject to restraint by the state, unless the public welfare was affected. The decision was rooted in nineteenth century arguments over free labor. As Justice Sutherland noted, freedom of contract while not absolute was "the general rule, and restraint the exception." But the idea of free labor was not gender neutral. And therein lay the difficulty. For the Court, in this decision, insisted that women were individuals within the meaning of the law and thus overturned two decades of precedent that held that the requirements of gender difference superseded the right to freely contract their services. How had the two, so carefully reconciled for a generation, come into conflict?

We need to step back for a moment. Two alternative conceptions of "free labor" contested in the 1870s. The first, deriving from the early republic, had taken root in the period before the Civil War and, by the postwar period, was championed by such working class advocates as the Knights of Labor. In this view, labor was free when it had the capacity to participate independently in civic life. But that capacity inhered in the dignity and independence of the working person and therefore assumed that each person had equal rights or access to economic self-sufficiency. This doctrine of equal rights embodied at least a theoretical social equality that, workers and their representatives held, could not be sustained if workers were reduced to permanent wage-earning status. Implicit in this view was the notion that only economic independence could guarantee effective self-representation and the perpetuation of a democratic republic. The idea of free labor as it evolved in the nineteenth century thus assumed that, in order to participate effectively in the polity, workers required at least the possibility of escape from wage labor into self-directed employment.

From this conception of free labor, women as individuals were virtually excluded. They were not expected to be members of the polity in the same sense as men, nor was their wage work expected to offer access to independent judgment. In the eyes of male workers women's wage labor, while dignified and offering access to self-support, ought not to lead either to independence or to self-sufficiency. Rather, just as men's free labor was predicted on their capacity to support a family, so women's was assumed to sustain the family labor of men. As family members, women participated in the polity through their menfolk. Their wage work was encouraged only in occupational fields and at moments in the life cycle that did not violate customary conceptions of free labor. For women's wage work to threaten the male's capacity to be free was a problem just as it was a problem if women's wage work undermined the capacity of either men or women to be effective family members. . . .

But labor had rules that did not necessarily derive from families. In the late nineteenth century, a dramatic acceleration in the process of industrialization threatened possibilities for self-directed employment for men as well as for women. While the defenders of free labor confronted the challenges of a debilitating and all-encompassing wage system with such innovations as cooperative producer associations and political action, a new generation of industrialists and entrepreneurs battled them at every turn. Eager for a rapid transformation of control into their own hands and anxious to maximize the possibilities of cheap labor, entrepreneurs treated workers as individuals, each capable of negotiating and each protected by the Fourteenth Amendment's prohibitions on deprivation of property. Labor's freedom, they suggested, with the concurrence of the courts, inhered only in its right to freely contract to sell itself.

This view, commonly known as freedom of contract, challenged labor's notions of putative social equality and threatened the economic independence from which it derived. Within its perspective, equal rights were embedded in the capacity of each individual to compete freely. Workers (male and female) were free only to enter into contracts to sell their labor without restraint. In this position entrepreneurs were joined by the courts. As a matter of formal and legal principle, the courts, beginning in the 1880s, ignored the vulnerable position of workers and turned the Fourteenth Amendment's prohibition on depriving citizens of life, liberty, and property on its head. Consistently, they interpreted freedom of contract as a ban on state efforts to restrict the rights of employers to offer even the most debilitating working conditions. The courts thus effectively snuffed the political vision of free labor. . . .

The effort to limit labors' expectations by means of freedom of contract expressed the stake of a rapidly industrializing society in cheap and available labor. While theoretically, the tendency of such a system was to pull women into the labor force as individuals, there remained some questions as to whether they were "protected" by the Fourteenth Amendment as men were. For the same assault on free labor that had undermined notions of work as the locus of dignity relied upon, and perpetuated, the idea of the family as an economic unit and as the source of values by which a new generation of laborers would be raised. If, on the one hand, this provided a large pool of "cheap labor," on the other, even the most hardboiled advocates of freedom of contract could not be insensitive to the problem that women who were treated as individuals for the purpose of the workplace still needed to fulfill demanding roles as family members. Jobs that undermined the working class family by destroying women's health or fertility, or by encouraging women to compete for male jobs, could easily destroy the golden egg that produced cheap labor.

Advocates of freedom of contract differed from the champions of free labor on virtually every score. Yet both agreed to some sense of separate spheres. The content of women's roles differed for each. Labor's conception was rooted in the belief that effective civic participation demanded workplace dignity that in turn rested on an ordered and comfortable family life. Business's conception derived from the desire to preserve the family as an economic unit that could provide incentives to stable and loyal work force participation. Either way, ideas of gender difference defined women as family members whose work roles were secondary. Ideally, at least, this led to no contradiction for male workers: women, seen either as individuals who competed with them for jobs or as family members on whose household labor they relied, belonged at home. But for employers, placing women in separate spheres meant that they needed to treat women simultaneously as individuals with a sacrosanct freedom of contract and as family members in whom they and the state had a special interest. It was this contradiction that the courts were called upon to resolve in the minimum wage cases.

By 1908 they had successfully done so with regard to hours. Under pressure from coalitions of women workers, reformers, and trade unions, legislatures and courts had legitimized the now familiar device of making women "wards of the state." But what worked for hours had special consequences when applied to wages. Regulating hours, as the Court noted in Adkins, had "no necessary effect on the heart of the contract, that is, the amount of wages to be paid and received." The minimum wage, in contrast, touched its core. It was designed to defend freedom of contract by ensuring that women who could not otherwise survive did not undermine an ideology that relied on the fiction of a worker's liberty to negotiate fair terms for labor. At the same time the minimum wage threatened the idea of freedom of contract by clearly identifying some workers as lacking the appropriate liberty. Tracing the resolution of this dilemma will tell us something of how ideas of gender difference help to construct social reality. For in one of the wonderful ironies of history, judicial decisions and the legal system contributed to definitions of female difference that in the end threatened the idea of the free labor market they were meant to protect.

The progressive attempt to accommodate gender invigorated a free labor debate that had been all but lost. Arguably, it helped to alter the terms of the debate. In creating sex as a category outside the common expectation of labor and law, the courts opened the door to an evaluation of the proper relation of the state to labor as a whole. The language with which this struggle was enacted tells us something about the centrality of separate spheres in the lives of men and women and also about its competing functions. It enables us to watch how the notion of separate spheres first confronted and eventually helped to break down the pernicious idea of freedom of contract.

Let us begin with the case of Quong Wing, the Chinese laundry man who, in the winter of 1911–12, petitioned the United States Supreme Court for relief. Quong Wing, a male, had sued the treasurer of Lewis and Clark County, Montana, to return the $10 he had paid for a license to take in hand laundry. The Montana law, as cited by Justice Oliver Wendell Holmes in the Supreme Court decision, "imposed the payment upon all persons engaged in the laundry business, other than the steam laundry business, with a proviso that it should not apply to women so employed where not more than two women were employed." Because the law applied to all laundries except steam laundries, it taxed small enterprises while exempting large ones, and because it applied to all persons who worked in hand laundries except women who worked alone or in pairs, it in effect, taxed men who did what was considered women's work. There can be little doubt that the state meant to tax Chinese men, while exempting women and large operators; for, as Justice Holmes observed in his opinion for the Court, "hand laundry work is a widespread occupation of Chinamen in this country while on the other hand it is so rare to see men of our race engaged in it that many of us would be unable to say that they had ever observed a case." Yet Quong Wing did not charge racial discrimination—an issue on which Holmes thought he might well have won. Instead, he charged sexual discrimination—and lost. The Supreme Court upheld the Montana statute because, as Holmes put it,

> If the state sees fit to encourage steam laundries and discourage hand laundries that is its own affair. And if again it finds a ground of distinction in sex, that is not without precedent. . . . If Montana deems it advisable to put a lighter burden upon women than upon men with regard to an employment that our people commonly regard as more appropriate for the former, the Fourteenth Amendment does not interfere by creating a fictitious equality where there is a real difference. The particular points at which that difference shall be emphasized by legislation are largely in the power of the state.

This case is not the first to identify gender differences as a legal category. But, unlike the rationales for restricting women's working hours, on which the Court drew and which were rooted in the presumed physical disadvantages of women and the social benefits of legislation, the Court here asserted an arbitrary power to discriminate between men and women—not a new phenomenon but one that it did not even seek to justify except as a matter of legislative choice. Quong Wing thus extended Muller's standard of sex as an appropriate classification to assert a state's right to define which sex differences could be taken into account. In imposing a new standard for legislative review, the case raises many issues, among them how readily gender "difference" is deployed under circumstances that would have explicitly precluded ethnic "difference," and the content of the "distinction" or "difference" to which the Court so blithely refers and that it makes no attempt to define. But for our purposes the most interesting question is the way in which the decision illuminates the social meaning of men's and women's wages.

The decision in Quong Wing suggests that the "common regard" (or popular perceptions of women's roles) is determinative in legislative choice as to which differences shall be emphasized. But surely that is a problem. If we take seriously Justice Holmes's comment that "the particular points at which that difference shall be emphasized by legislation are largely in the power of the state," then we have little choice but to view gender difference as an idea with a political content that moves people to behave in certain kinds of ways—in short, as an ideological construct. The decision tells us quite clearly that male and female job choices, and the earnings that result, are subject to regulation to bring them into line with the "common regard." A look at the evidence suggests the ideological level at which gender entered the debate.

In 1912 the common regard held that women belonged in families. Employers freely (and largely falsely) expressed the belief that women did not need the incomes of males because they could rely on families to support them. More subtly, in the common regard, questions of masculinity entered into every decision on wages. For men the wage encompassed family support; for women it tended to incorporate only the self-support of a single person. . . . [I]t was appropriate for women to derive part of their support from families. This assumption found its way into *Adkins* where Justice Sutherland objected to the District of Columbia law because it failed to take account of "the cooperative economies of the family group, though they constitute an important consideration in estimating the cost of living, for it is obvious that the individual expense will be less in the case of a member of a family than in the case of one living alone." . . .

Because the battle was hard fought, the price of maintaining separate spheres was high. It took the form of a vicious and clearly ideological attack on women as workers that exaggerated their "natural" attachment to the home and belittled their ability to earn wages. The popular imagination conjured up pictures of wage-earning women who were helpless, dependent, weak, handicapped, ignorant, delicate, and exploitable. Portraits of wage-earning women depicted them as greedy and lazy as well. They had, it was said, a "natural longing for recreation . . . adornment" and luxury. At the same time, women lived in a world where unscrupulous employers did not hesitate to subject them to conditions "akin to slavery" and thus leave them vulnerable to peculiar dangers that threatened to lure them into vice and immorality. These conditions prevented women from living in "decency" or from enjoying "healthy and normal lives," and they inhibited the peace of a "satisfied mind" and a "wholesome existence." Worse, they threatened the "health and well-being" of future mothers and therefore held "the strength of the nation hostage." While these images expand upon those evoked to justify shorter hours for women but not for men, their consequences were not at all alike.

In the debate over the minimum wage, both sides had a stake in maintaining wage differentials, and so both resorted to this imagery. The terms of the debate thus contributed to depicting women in the extreme language of childhood and vulnerability. For example, both sides saw women as inefficient workers who lacked training. Proponents of the minimum wage argued that wage earners could be divided between those who "are earning what they receive or more" and those "whose services are worth little or nothing." Even sympathetic reformers like Florence Kelley held that too many untrained and unskilled women flooding the job market depressed women's wages. To raise wages required educating and training women to be more efficient and effective workers. That this had not happened as a natural result of the market was due to defects in women's character.

Women competed with each other. Like the notion that women workers were inefficient, the idea that female competition reduced wages pervaded the imagery. One side depicted women as "undutiful daughters" who, tempted by luxurious living, allowed their mothers to overwork themselves while they sought riches in the factory or department store. Or it imagined dissatisfied wives not content to live on their husbands' earnings. Though sympathetic to the minimum wage, the other constructed a picture of "women whose earnings are supplemented from other sources" and who are therefore a "constant drag on the wage level and offer formidable competition to the growing thousands of women dependent on their own labor for support. . . . " The circular logic of this argument appears when we place it in the form of a syllogism: Women do not earn enough, therefore they live with others, therefore they reduce the level of wages for all women, therefore women do not earn enough.

Another explanation was that women chose the wrong jobs. For example, opponents of the minimum wage suggested that women could easily save money and achieve mobility if they were willing to become domestic servants. Such jobs were widely available. But women, objecting to their endless hours, close supervision, and live-in conditions, frequently refused them. In view of their willingness to turn down these jobs, a minimum wage would only reinforce women's worst qualities, rewarding the inefficient without benefiting those who were oriented towards hard work and mobility. On the other side of this coin, a picture of women's inability to advance themselves could yield an argument for state aid as illustrated by the belief that they were in occupations not reachable in the normal course of trade union organization. "A great deal can be said for minimum wage laws and laws limiting the hours of labor for women," asserted feminist Crystal Eastman, who normally opposed special laws for women only, "on the ground that women's labor is the least adapted to organization and therefore the most easily exploited and most in need of legislative protection." Women who selected jobs that restricted their ability to bargain collectively and were, therefore, incapable of securing a fair return on their wages constituted, according to some labor leaders, "a helpless class of labor, broken in spirit." "Practically impossible to organize under existing conditions," they might be more readily organized once their "broken spirit had been reinforced by a minimum wage."

Women had weak characters. Opponents of a minimum wage suggested that legislation would increase immortality because it would give extra money to frivolous, unworthy people. Those who favored the minimum argued that weak women would succumb to vice and prostitution at the least temptation and needed higher wages to enable them to resist. Neither argument seemed to have much to do with reality. . . .

Arguments against the minimum wage were predicated heavily on the assumption that employers paid a natural wage that was the equivalent of the service rendered—that women were worth no more than what they earned. The neoclassical economic theory on which such arguments rested held the worker responsible for his or her place in the job market. In a free market, workers who could freely sell their labor earned the economic value of what they produced. Employers hired workers at different levels of wages calculated to reflect the value of the product created as well as the supply of workers willing to accept the wages offered. If women tended to work on low-value products (garments, paper flowers, boxes, textiles, shoes, for example), that was not the employer's fault but a result of women's choices. Business could not pay more than a "natural" wage without threatening the profits that enabled it to survive. If women's wages tended to be low, the logical explanation lay in a persistent assertion of a woman's "difference." A regulated minimum that forced employers to "supply individual needs . . . in excess of what the employee earns or is worth" would be disastrous. From this flowed a series of questions: Should the wage be determined not by the value of the services rendered but by the cost of supporting women? Should industry be required to cover the deficit on women's wages? Was there a constitutional question implicit in the issue of "whether an employer may be compelled to pay the cost of maintaining the employer whose full services he voluntarily uses in the conduct of an enterprise?" Since no employer would stay in business without profits, would attempts to regulate wages (as a function of the cost of supporting women as opposed to the value of the services they rendered) not drive employers out?

Circumventing the idea of freedom of contract by exacerbating women's weakness and helplessness transformed the debate. Freedom of contract rested on the notion that the wage was an abstraction—the product of agreement between employer and employee. The argument over the minimum wage, because it was gendered, exposed the social issue embodied in the wage and thus kept alive a social meaning on which defenders of free labor had insisted. The Progressives connected the wage argument to hours by suggesting that if women's wages were so low as to undermine their childbearing and rearing capacities then the state as a whole would suffer because its future citizens would be weak and without good discipline and values. Under those circumstances freedom of contract would threaten the "future of the race." For the courts to accept this argument required suspending wage theory and arguing for redistribution of income according to norms of social justice that recalled the ideals of advocates of free labor.

In focusing so heavily on separate spheres, protagonists and antagonists alike begged the question of social justice in the industrial sector, evoking fears that the extreme solutions required to compensate for women's weakness might threaten the free market. Thus, the argument over wages placed the judiciary squarely in the position of deciding whether to concede separate spheres to women in order to redistribute income sufficiently for women to maintain families (granting some credence to the older free labor ideology and enabling women to keep open possibilities for gendered action) or whether to sustain freedom of contract in the face of the apparent threat to families. The conundrum that this posed is revealed in the language and arguments used during the course of the debate.

First, it raised the issue of the appropriate relationship between male and female wages. If the natural wage was a male wage and women's wages were low because they "could not earn a wage," then attempts to create an arbitrary minimum for women and not for men would threaten the balance between male and female spheres. The alternative would be to raise male wages. But his begged the issue of whether a state that could impose a minimum wage could not also impose a maximum. Some who agreed that the public welfare was menaced by low wages for women had to agree that it was equally vulnerable to low male wages. For if higher wages were necessary to health and morality—if a law fixing wages was a health law—surely then it was desirable for both men and women. If benefits claimed for women were given to men after all, then whole families would benefit. As one commentator put it, "If . . . a minimum wage law for women is constitutional because it tends to provide the race with healthy moral mothers, so would a minimum wage law for men, because it would tend to provide the race with strong honest fathers." Once opened, that Pandora's box could only produce a case for a higher wage for all.

Closely related to the issue of health was that of morality. One of the basic arguments for minimum wages was that women with insufficient incomes were regularly tempted into amorous relationships or even into prostitution in order to make ends meet. Raising this issue involved not only questions of male morality but those of women's character as well. As Justice Sutherland put it, "It cannot be shown that well paid women safeguard their morals more carefully than those who are poorly paid." Then he added, "If women require a minimum wage to preserve their morals, men require it to preserve their honesty." . . .

If women could not earn their keep, then society, not women, would pay the cost of women's low wages. Again, women who worked were depicted as mere parasites who imposed a financial burden on the state and on other industries. Women's low wages, in this view, were nothing less than a "menace to public welfare." As Felix Frankfurter put it in the famous case of *Stettler* v. *O'Hara*, "Industries supporting male workers were being drawn upon to assist in supporting women workers engaged in other industries, which were refusing to carry their cost." Frankfurter, defending Oregon's minimum wage law, argued that the immediate effects of women's low wages were to impose financial burdens on the state, "which threatened excessive and unremunerative taxation." Women's wages, he argued, were a "community problem—a problem affecting the state in its pervasive entirety."

The degree to which arguments over women's wages threatened freedom of contract emerges most forcefully in the suggestion that depictions of women's difference that fueled a demand for the minimum wage would in the end raise false expectations as to the distribution of income and property. These expectations could not, according to some, be met under the limits of the constitution, for they required "A to give part of his property to B." Such an action would deny individual rights, destroy natural competition, and evoke the specter of social revolution. Minimum wage legislation, in the words of a June 1917 commentator, was "a new expression of the paternalistic and socialistic tendencies of the day. It savors of the division of property between those who have and those who have not, and the leveling of fortunes by division under governmental supervision. It is consistent with the orthodox socialist creed, but it is not consistent with the principles of our government which are based upon the protection of individual rights."

Champions of the minimum wage did not deny that individual rights were endangered by regulation. Rather, they argued that individual rights could not be allowed to supersede the rights of "women who must labor in order to live. It would seem," noted Justice Wendell Stafford, who had been part of the majority in the original D.C. Supreme Court decision that upheld the constitutionality of minimum wages, "that the right of this class to live on a barely decent level, and the right of the public to have them so live, should outweigh the right of those who do not need to work in order to live, and who therefore are merely asserting a right to earn money and thereby accumulate property."

The idea that weak women were at some level responsible for undermining a cherished principle of government was echoed and expanded by court decisions at all levels beginning in 1917. It finally became a key argument for invalidating the minimum wage. From 1912 to 1923, the minimum wage was more or less sustained. But by 1917 tensions provoked by the emphasis on gender difference became apparent. Writing for the District of Columbia Supreme Court in the penultimate round of *Children's Hospital* v. *Adkins,* Justice Van Orsdel declared that "legislation tending to fix the prices at which private property shall be sold, . . . places a limitation upon the distribution of wealth, and is aimed at the correction of the inequalities of fortune which are inevitable under our form of government, due to personal liberty and the private ownership of property. These principles are embodied in the Constitution itself."

Imposing a minimum wage was thus the equivalent of using the police power to "level inequalities of fortune." Van Orsdel made his own economic bias clear: "A wage based upon competitive ability is just, and leads to frugality and honest industry, and inspires an ambition to attain the highest possible efficiency, while the equal wage paralyzes ambition and promotes prodigality and indolence. It takes away the strongest incentive to human labor, thrift, and efficiency, and works injustice to employee and employer alike, thus affecting injuriously the whole social and industrial fabric." . . .

. . . Advocates of the minimum wage had couched their arguments in exaggerated assertions about the traditional roles of women. But to maintain those roles at the expense of freedom of contract would, in the view of a conservative judiciary, undermine the principle of individual rights and the economic system itself. To accommodate to the pressure would jeopardize the wages of men and of other women, the profits of industry, and the free enterprise system. Minimum wages, in short, would so alter the role of the state as to produce nothing less than the dreaded disease of sovietism.

Faced with a sharp conflict between two ideological systems, one had to give way. If women were to continue as paid workers, the courts could either deny the importance of gender difference or negate freedom of contract. In the event, the Supreme Court chose to sustain freedom of contract by declaring the minimum wage "to be wholly beyond legislative discretion." Divided 5 to 3 (with Brandeis abstaining because his daughter had been involved in preparing the brief), the Court declared that gender differences had come to the vanishing point, that there was no reason therefore to abrogate freedom of contract, and that the minimum wage was unconstitutional.

To some observers it appeared that the Court had done an "anomalous somersault." But in fact, a closer view reveals the decision to have been a logical consequence of the contradictions produced by the way in which women's differences had been incorporated into the social meaning of the wage. Speaking for the majority, Justice Sutherland evoked the underlying issues as he saw them: free enterprise was arrayed against motherhood. He concluded that free enterprise had to be preserved, even at the cost of wiping out the separate spheres. The wage, he asserted, was based on a "just equivalence of the service rendered," not on the need of the worker. No matter how pressing, the need of the worker could not avail. . . . Castigating those who did not pay attention to employers' needs and acknowledging that a women was worth little in the free labor market, he attacked the statute for failing to "require that the wage have any relation to the reasonable value of the workers' services."

Bold as the decision was, it might have been expected. It built upon what was implicit in Holmes's opinion in Quong Wing. Holmes had there asserted that the existence of sexual difference (or separate spheres) was the legitimate province of the state to define. In his view sexual difference was a legitimate classification for legislators. By 1923, in a new political environment, the Supreme Court, stymied by the tension between attributions of gender difference and an economic system that assumed freedom of contract, chose to take the opposite position. It simply defined sexual difference out of existence.

But the issue was not so simply put to rest. The rhetoric of the debate and the reality of women's lives conspired to keep it alive. In the dissents to Adkins and in the protest that ensued, a strong appeal to social justice, rooted in family and domestic life, persisted. Dissenting Chief Justice Taft, for example, thought the majority decision unwise because "it is not the function of this court to hold Congressional acts invalid simply because they are passed to carry out economic views which the Court believes to be unwise or unsound." To others it violated simple principles of social justice. "It demeans humanity," said Samuel Gompers, that "women and girl wage earners are to be bought over the counter." Confusion reigned over the Court's consistent affirmation of gender difference when it came to hours and working conditions and its equally consistent opposition to sex-based classifications when wages were at stake. Case after case came to the Supreme Court, only to be turned back. But by 1937 the Court once again reestablished an interest in women's difference as the opening wedge of a fight for social justice.

In *West Coast Hotel Co.* v. *Parrish,* the Court reversed itself. Chief Justice Hughes, speaking for the Court, rejected a freedom of contract defense against minimum wage legislation because, he said, "the Constitution does not speak of freedom of contract. It speaks of liberty. . . . But the liberty safeguarded is liberty in a social organization which requires the protection of law against the evils which menace the health, safety, morals and welfare of the people." Speaking in the language of nineteenth century advocates of free labor, he denied any "absolute" freedom of contract and argued that liberty did not imply "immunity from reasonable regulations and prohibitions imposed in the interest of the community." What were the interests of the community? They resided in protecting those parties that did not stand upon an equality and therefore in the state's interest in women.

Calling upon *Muller* v. *Oregon* and repeating the words of Quong Wing, that only a "fictitious equality" existed between men and women, the Court argued, in overturning Adkins, that women "are relatively defenseless against the denial of a living wage." Low wages were "detrimental to their health and well-being" and "cast a direct burden for their support upon the community." Echoing Holmes's insistence on the state's right to determine where difference shall be emphasized, the Court castigated selfish employers for disregarding the public interest, noted the anguish of the economic depression, and asserted that the "relative need" of women "in the presence of the evil, no less than the evil itself, is a matter for legislative judgment."

But the premonitions of Van Orsdel, Sutherland, and others had not been misplaced. For though Chief Justice Hughes used gender difference to highlight the state's interest in "the exploitation of a class of workers who are in an unequal position with respect to bargaining power and are thus relatively defenseless against the denial of a living wage," he explicitly utilized female difference as the entering wedge for judicial decisions about others in need. In so doing, he ensured that a new definition of liberty would prevail. Less than three years later, the Court relied on its decision in *West Coast Hotel* to sustain the constitutionality of the Fair Labor Standards Act which legislated minimum wages for men and women. But it abandoned sex difference as the crucial criterion for undermining freedom of contract. In *United States* v. *Darby,* the case that affirmed the FLSA and cleared the path for the social legislation of the modern period, the Court transcended gender and argued that "it is no longer open to question that the fixing of a minimum wage is within the legislative power."

How do we explain the shift? Part of the answer lies in the change in social conditions in the fourteen years between the two decisions. Sutherland, in dissent from the majority in *West Coast Hotel,* tried once again to make the case that there was no longer any reason why women "should be put in different classes in respect of their legal right to make contracts. Nor should they be denied, in effect, the right to compete with men for work paying lower wages which men may be willing to accept." This argument carried little weight in the depression climate. But much of the shift in Court opinion lies in the way that language about women and agitation around them had demonstrated the evident social purposes of such legislation. By the 1930s, when public opinion was once again ready to consider the search for social justice as part of the legitimate end of government, the idea that women constituted a separate and deserving class could and did serve to illustrate the rigidity of old doctrines of freedom of contract. Attention to gender differences had kept alive the possibility that all workers deserved state protection. As Justice Stone put it in his dissent from the Court's final attempt to preserve the sanctity of freedom of contract in *Morehead* v. *New York,* "In the years which have intervened since the Adkins case . . . we have had opportunity to perceive more clearly that a wage insufficient to support the worker does not visit its consequences upon him alone; that it may affect profoundly the entire economic structure of society and, in any case, that it casts on every taxpayer, and on government itself, the burden of solving the problems of poverty, subsistence, health and morals of large numbers in the community."

From Joseph A. McCartin, " 'An American Feeling': Workers, Managers, and the Struggle over Industrial Democracy in the World War I Era," in Nelson Lichtenstein and Howell John Harris, eds., *Industrial Democracy in America: The Ambiguous Promise* (New York: Cambridge University Press, 1996), pp. 67–86. Reprinted by permission of Cambridge University Press.

The Political Culture: Public Life and the Conduct of Politics

CHARLES W. CALHOUN

The last third of the nineteenth century is the most misunderstood and disparaged period in the political history of the United States. For the better part of the twentieth century, historians painted the era in the darkest hues imaginable, arguing that spoilsmen and corruptionists ruled its political life and that obtaining office for its own sake was the primary motivation for politicians more devoted to partisan advantage than the public good. According to this interpretation, issues and principles counted for little in political contention, and few real differences existed between the Republicans and the Democrats, who dominated elections and officeholding. Over the years scholars sought to outdo one another in censuring the Gilded Age in the most derogatory terms; it was, they said, an age of "negation," "cynicism," and "excess"—a "huge barbecue" for politicos and robber barons that excluded poor farmers and laborers. . . .

What caused traditional historians and some modern scholars to take such a dim view of Gilded Age politics? To a considerable degree, this negative assessment originated in the jaundiced observations of late nineteenth-century critics who were outside the political system. In trying to explain the period, many historians have paid closer attention to these commentators' biting criticisms than to the words and accomplishments of politicians themselves. The very name that scholars assign to the period, the Gilded Age, derives from an 1873 novel of that title by Mark Twain and Charles Dudley Warner, which satirized politics as rife with corruption and fraud committed by self-seeking politicians. Historians have also been fond of quoting Henry Adams, whose insufferable arrogance doomed his own quest for a political career. Late in life Adams used his autobiography to strike back at the system that overlooked him, charging that "one might search the whole list of Congress, Judiciary, and Executive during the twenty-five years 1870 to 1895, and find little but damaged reputation." He could have added that his own prejudiced diatribes had done much to damage the reputations of others.

One of the most influential critics was the Englishman James Bryce, whose 1880s trip to the United States, resulting in his two-volume study, *The American Commonwealth,* led some Americans to label him the Gilded Age Alexis de Tocqueville. Bryce alleged that neither the Republican nor the Democratic party "has anything definite to say on . . . issues; neither party has any principles, any distinctive tenets. . . . All has been lost, except office or the hope of it." In reaching these conclusions, however, Bryce had come under the sway of Edwin L. Godkin, editor of the Mugwump journal *The Nation,* whose disdain for his contemporaries in politics was boundless and not altogether rational. Taking their cue from Adams, Bryce, Godkin, and other hostile contemporaries, many twentieth-century historians looked back with distaste at the politics of the last three decades of the nineteenth century.

Other historical sources, such as newspapers, have contributed to slanted interpretations. Most Gilded Age dailies and weeklies were intensely loyal partisans of one party and had nothing good to say about the politicians of the other. Their "news" pages as well as their editorial columns served up mixtures of vituperation, trumped-up charges of fraud and corruption, and downright falsehoods about the opposing party. Ohio Governor Joseph B. Foraker exaggerated only somewhat when he complained in 1885 that for some newspapers it was a "common thing to call the man with whom they do not happen to agree, a liar, a thief, a villain, a scoundrel, a Yahoo, a marplot, a traitor, a beast, anything and everything they may be able to command in the way of an epithet." One study shows that a movement for "independent" journalism in the 1870s led zealous reporters to produce stories about politicians that were often scurrilous and sometimes wholly imaginary. Scholars' later reliance on these biased journals as sources contributed to their overall negative impression of politics in the period.

Investigations in Congress had a similar effect. At times the party in control of the House or the Senate used committee hearings or other legislative reports to discredit actions or doctrines of the opposing party. As an American diplomat in Paris wrote home to a senator in 1876, "The fury of 'investigation' in Washington has reached such a stage that it is something like the days of the French Revolution when it was enough to cry 'suspect' and the man was ruined." Often rooted more in partisanship than reality, these inquiries seemed to lend an official authentication to charges that, when taken together, have led historians to see the period's politics in the worst possible light.

This problem of skewed sources has been compounded by the tendency of some scholars to read back into the period modern values concerning government activism. In the words of Geoffrey Blodgett, such historians exhibit "a profound impatience with the Gilded Age for having not yet discovered the Welfare State." Today the idea that the government is responsible for the nation's economic growth and the citizens' well-being is widely accepted, but in the late nineteenth century most people clung to the traditional notion that good government meant limited government. Its main purpose was to maintain order and protect persons and property. Most citizens would have resisted the redistributive tendency of many twentieth-century economic policies as a perversion of governmental power. Moreover, allegations of corrupt purposes by government officials, whether true or not, evoked calls for retrenchment and aroused suspicion of government in general that inhibited the espousal, let alone the enactment, of positive programs. The cry of "Job!" greeted many legitimate and worthwhile proposals, particularly those involving subsidies or other expenditures of money. The resulting climate of distrust reinforced among voters a small-government notion that restrained leaders who might have taken more aggressive action but who also wished to win elections. As one congressman who lost reelection in 1868 stated, "My opponent is . . . a popular because a negative man." In 1890 the Republican majority in Congress passed an extraordinary number of important laws, with the result that the party lost overwhelmingly in the congressional elections that year. Lack of achievement is one of the principal failings that scholars have alleged about Gilded Age governance. In reality, leaders accomplished more than historians used to give them credit for, but they often did so in spite of the limitations placed on them by an essentially conservative electorate.

Divided control of the national government also slowed the formulation and adoption of policy. Between 1875 and 1897 each major party held the presidency and a clear majority in both houses of Congress for only a single two-year period, the Republicans in 1889–1891 and the Democrats in 1893–1895. During most of this era, Congress was divided, the Democrats more often than not controlling the House of Representatives and the Republicans usually holding a majority in the Senate. These divisions made the passage of legislation difficult. Each of the seven Congresses between 1875 and 1889, on the average, enacted only 317 public laws. But in the 51st Congress (1889–1891), when Republican President Benjamin Harrison worked with a Republican majority in both the House and the Senate, the number of laws passed shot up to 531, representing an unprecedented level of legislative accomplishment unequalled until Theodore Roosevelt's second term.

The balance between the parties in Congress mirrored an equilibrium between Republicans and Democrats in the national electorate. Except for Democrat Grover Cleveland's two terms, Republicans typically sat in the White House, but in four of the five presidential elections from 1876 to 1892 the Democratic nominee wound up with more popular votes than his Republican opponent. In 1880 defeated Democrat Winfield Scott Hancock trailed Republican James A. Garfield by less than half of 1 percent. A considerable portion of the Democratic votes came from former slave states which, after the end of Reconstruction, witnessed a widespread suppression of voting by African Americans, who nearly unanimously supported the Republican party. To take the two most egregious examples, in Louisiana the black population grew by 33 percent between 1870 and 1880, but from the presidential election of 1872 to that of 1880 the number of Republican votes decreased by 47 percent. In Mississippi the black population growth was 46 percent, and the Republican vote decline was 59 percent. Because of this denial of the suffrage, by 1880 the conservative, white Solid South had emerged, assuring the Democrats of a large bloc of electoral votes that year and in future presidential elections.

To counterbalance the South the Republicans could depend almost as surely on winning several states in the Northeast and the upper Midwest, but neither of these two blocs of sure states by itself held enough electoral votes to win the presidency. Hence, election results usually turned on the outcome in a half-dozen swing or "doubtful" states, the most important of which were New York and Indiana. During campaigns, party leaders and committees focused their efforts in these states, enlisting the aid of the party's best speakers and expending the largest proportion of campaign funds. In addition, the parties often chose residents from doubtful states for their national tickets. Between 1876 and 1892 the two major parties selected twenty nominees for president and vice president; eight were from New York and five from Indiana.

One of the criticisms traditional historians leveled against Gilded Age politics was that no real substantive differences divided Republicans from Democrats. Here again, the equilibrium in party strength offers some explanation. With the outcome of elections in doubt, party leaders and spokesmen saw the need to exercise caution in articulating party positions and were wary of getting too far ahead of public opinion. Taking too strong a stand, even on a minor issue, might offend just enough members of some group to bring defeat at the next election. In 1884, for instance, the Republicans lost the presidential election after trailing in pivotal New York by about one thousand votes out of one million. Contemporaries and historians alike could cite many factors, both ideological and organizational, any one of which could have tipped the balance.

When scholars charge that Gilded Age Republicans and Democrats were largely indistinguishable, they tend to apply an inappropriate standard. Historically, American political parties have not been like those of European countries, with starkly differentiated groupings of left and right. Instead, largely because victory in the electoral college requires a majority rather than a plurality, major parties in the United States seek broad consensus and try to make their appeals as wide as possible, with the result that a considerable area of agreement often exists between them. In the Gilded Age the even balance between Republicans and Democrats simply reinforced their perceived need to avoid the fringes of political assertion.

Despite this need for caution, the major parties were not like Tweedledum and Tweedledee, as some traditional historians have alleged. As several of the revisionists scholars have shown, important ideological distinctions existed between Republicans and Democrats. Certainly, each party had its internal disagreements and inconsistencies, but overall they espoused philosophies and policies that clashed in significant ways and offered voters real choices at the polls. Generally speaking, Republicans placed greater stress on government activism, especially at the national level, with the primary aim of fostering economic development. They welcomed the nation's burgeoning industrialization and believed the federal government should assist the process. In the words of Senator John P. Jones, "One of the highest duties of Government is the adoption of such economic policy as may encourage and develop every industry to which the soil and climate of the country are adapted." As the period progressed, the protective tariff emerged as the centerpiece of the Republicans' economic program. Democrats, on the other hand, tended to cling to their party's traditional belief in small government and states' rights. They criticized elements in the Republicans' program as favoring special interests. With its low-tariff wing from the agrarian, largely preindustrial South still looming large, the Democratic party continued its decades-old opposition to tariff protectionism. In pursuit of their goals Republicans read the Constitution broadly to find sanction for national government action; Democrats' interpretation viewed federal power as more restricted. In the past generation modern scholars have begun to recognize the differences between parties that Gilded Age politicians knew instinctively. As the

Maine statesman James G. Blaine put it (in a somewhat partisan fashion) in his book *Twenty Years of Congress,* late nineteenth-century Democrats and Republicans displayed the same "enduring and persistent line[s] of division between the two parties which in a generic sense have always existed in the United States;—the party of strict construction and the party of liberal construction, the party of State Rights and the party of National Supremacy, the party of stinted revenue and restricted expenditure and the party of generous income with its wise application to public improvement."

At the state and local levels Republicans again were more willing to resort to government action for what they perceived to be the good of society. They were more likely than Democrats to advocate restrictions on the consumption of alcohol, although many Republicans approached the question warily, fearful of repelling blocs of voters, such as German Americans or Irish Americans, who resented such interference in their personal lives. Similarly, Republicans were more inclined to favor measures to hasten the assimilation of immigrants, such as requiring the use of the English language in parochial schools. Again, Democrats tended to oppose such paternalism. In the past few decades several historians, using quantitative methods to measure voter reaction to such issues, have argued that ethnic and religious distinctions lay at the root of party affiliation. In this view, voters from pietistic, evangelical Protestant denominations tended to favor the moralistic stewardship associated with the Republicans, while liturgical, ritualistic sects, especially Roman Catholics, found comfort in the Democrats' defense of individuals' private lives.

Not all citizens felt well-served by either of the two major parties, and the period witnessed occasional third-party campaigns. In 1872 a group of Republicans, primarily well-educated, economically independent professionals and businessmen, bolted their party. Disenchanted with the policies and administrative style of President Ulysses S. Grant, these self-proclaimed Liberal Republicans mounted an effort to block his reelection. Their nominee, Horace Greeley, won endorsement by the Democrats, but he met the fate of most third-party candidates, a crushing defeat. The Prohibitionists, another group drawn mostly from Republican ranks, fielded presidential tickets every year starting in 1880. They reached their high-water mark in 1888 with just under 2.2 percent of the popular vote. The Greenback-Labor or National party, whose chief policy objective was the inflation of the currency, ran nominees for president from 1876 to 1884. They garnered their largest vote in 1880 with 3.36 percent of the total. They did manage to elect a few congressmen, their greatest success coming in 1878 with fifteen members of the House out of a total of 293. Occasionally these third parties were able to upset the calculations of major party leaders, especially in closely contested states. As Senator Benjamin Harrison noted in 1885, "I have little hope of making Indiana a Republican state with 4,000 Republican Prohibitionists and 8,000 Republican Greenbackers voting separate tickets." Even so, the possibility of such parties achieving power themselves remained virtually non-existent, and fringe groups, such as the Socialists, had even less chance.

The third party that came closest to moving into major party status was the People's party, or the Populists, in the 1890s. Historians disagree over the degree to which economic distress or other causes moved farmers to become Populists, but the party's rhetoric was heavily freighted with economic issues. Farmers found themselves increasingly caught up in a world market structure with volatile prices for farm commodities. A general downward trend in prices magnified the debt burden of farmers, many of whom had overextended themselves into regions of dubious agricultural productivity. Blaming their troubles on a variety of scapegoats, including railroads, manufacturing trusts, bankers, and the monetary system, many farmers were disappointed when the two-party system seemed unwilling to adopt their various proposals for relief. In 1892 the Populist presidential candidate, James B. Weaver, won over one million popular votes (out of twelve million cast) and twenty-two electoral votes. The Populists elected some members of Congress and achieved momentary success in some individual states and parts of states. In the nation as a whole, however, most voters, even in many farming regions, stuck with the two major parties.

Indeed, throughout the late nineteenth century the vast majority of voters stood by the Republicans or the Democrats, in congressional and state elections as well as in presidential contests. Moreover, whatever their motivation, party supporters went to the polls in huge numbers. In presidential election years over 75 percent of eligible voters typically cast ballots, a turnout rate far in excess of twentieth-century averages. In this sense the active political community in the Gilded Age was much broader than its modern-day counterpart. In another sense, however, the political community was narrower, for virtually everywhere women were denied the ballot, and in the South, after the end of Reconstruction, conservative white Democrats employed a variety of means to block voting by African Americans. But even with these egregious exclusions from the suffrage, politics remained a consuming interest to people throughout the nation, engaging the enthusiastic participation of millions of citizens.

What kind of leader emerged in this popular political culture? Among the most enduring stereotypes from the period is that of small-minded, grasping politicians who used public office mostly to serve their own interests, and often for their own financial gain, with little real concern for matters of policy or the public good. Recent research reveals a strikingly different portrait of the people who lead the two major parties, especially at the national level. Certainly, the idea of conflict of interest was underdeveloped and some politicians took bribes or otherwise engaged in corrupt practices, but in all likelihood no higher percentage did so than during most other times in the nation's history. Indeed, the zealous partisan quest for scandalous material about political opponents probably resulted in allegations of questionable conduct regarding behavior that in other eras might have been winked at or overlooked.

In reality many men who rose to be party leaders considered politics much more a financial burden than a boon. The pay of a congressman or cabinet member, for instance, while considerably above the wages of the average American, fell far short of what most such men could earn in private life. Moreover, the expenses that accompanied politics and government service diminished their finances still further. Typically, a congressman discovered that campaign costs ate up a year's worth of his salary. . . .

. . . The result too frequently was that only men of independent means or substantial wealth could afford or would accept such service. If, by the end of the century, Americans complained that the Senate had become a "millionaires' club," to some degree they had themselves to blame.

One compensation for congressional service was supposed to be the patronage power, the privilege of placing one's political friends and supporters in subordinate offices. Typically, senators and representatives from the party in power sent the president and other executive-branch officers recommendations of people to fill federal offices in their own states and in Washington. As a personnel program for the federal bureaucracy with its one hundred thousand-plus positions, this so-called spoils system was not without its own internal logic. With respect to governance, the system's defenders maintained that the president's policy aims would best be served by employees recruited from his own party and that he should gladly take the advice of senators and representatives who better knew the qualifications of applicants from their localities. On the political level, they argued, elections were won through the interested labor of a committed cadre of party workers, and rewarding such labor by the bestowal of appointive office was essential to the recruitment and maintenance of these cadres.

To many political leaders, however, dealing with patronage seemed more a punishment than a power. Yes, one might build a loyal core of backers from those who received appointments, but for each office, ranging from postal clerk to cabinet officer, a dozen or more applicants might press their claims, and as Senator John Sherman noted, "however wise may be the selection there will be many disappointments." Disappointing an office seeker might be politically damaging, but it could also be personally wrenching. As one Interior Department official wrote during the depression of the 1890s, "I have hungry men and women by the score coming to see me in the hope and belief that I can give them employment, and this has made my office here a burden. I cannot refuse to see them, and my inability to help them has come to be a kind of torture." On top of it all, politicians who recommended or who made appointments found themselves severely denounced by a growing civil service reform lobby that called for merit considerations over partisanship in the selection and promotion of government employees. . . .

National political leaders faced other vexations, not least of which was the sheer physical discomfort of working in Washington much of the year. "It is so terribly hot here that we can hardly live," one congressman wrote his wife in 1870. During the summer the mercury inside the House of Representatives frequently topped ninety degrees, even after sundown. In September 1888, Spooner described the poorly ventilated Senate chamber as "a box within a box." "I have been pretty nearly laid up with a headache for a week or ten days," he complained. "Hardly a man in the Senate feels well." Moreover, although committee chairmen had the use of their committee rooms as quasi-offices, most members of Congress received no office space beyond their small desks in the crowded chamber. They were thus forced to rent offices at their own expense or do most of their work in their living quarters. Similarly, a committee chairman enjoyed the assistance of the committee's clerk, but the typical member had no staff unless he hired and paid a clerk out of his own pocket.

Even with the help of a clerk, a member frequently felt overwhelmed by the work. In addition to the patronage burden, constituent correspondence was often heavy, and a member could delay answers to letters only at his political peril. Citizens expected their representative or senator to serve as their agent whenever they had business before the government, with the result that congressmen spent much time prowling the executive departments tracking down veterans' pensions, pushing claims, or otherwise advocating constituents' causes. Furthermore, with rare exceptions, members of Congress researched and wrote their own speeches, sometimes several hours in length. The work did not stop once a speech was given; a congressman who delivered a major speech or extended remarks during a day's session might stay up until two or three o'clock the next morning correcting the text for the *Congressional Record.* "It is up hill work all of it," one wrote to his wife in 1872, "and last night when I came home I could hardly draw one foot after another."

Over in the executive branch conditions were hardly better. In 1891 the second in command of the Post Office Department begged for another assistant, telling Congress, "I average at my desk—without a moment's absence from the building— more than ten hours a day, besides night work." Two months after leaving the White House, Harrison confessed, "There is nothing further from my mind or thought or wish than the resumption of public office. I was thoroughly tired and worn out." Possibilities for achievement by politicians did, of course, exist, and many posted creditable records. "But," as Senator George F. Edmunds noted, "whether their own lives have been the happier for such labor, with such inevitable trials and exposures, may be greatly doubted."

Grueling work, pay unequal to the labor, uncertainty of tenure—who would want such a job? Why would men pursue careers in national politics? Explaining the mystery of ambition lies perhaps more with the psychologist than the historian, but it seems clear that, like most successful politicians, men who attained positions of leadership in the late nineteenth century simply took immense satisfaction from being at the center of action and power. Garfield, a man of intellect with wide interests, frequently thought of leaving politics but could never quite bring himself to do it. After reading poet Ralph Waldo Emerson's book *Society and Solitude,* the Ohio congressman mused that "the calm spirit which [Emerson] breathes around him, makes me desire greatly to get up and out of the smoke and dust and noise of politics into the serene air of literature. Still," he confessed, "I suppose, if I were there, I should grow weary of the silence." In the words of Senator Spooner, "There is in public life . . . much that is burdensome and distasteful to a man of sensibility," and yet, "with it all there is a fascination about public life which I hardly know how to define but the existence of which is unmistakable." . . .

For most Gilded Age political leaders, their commitment to principle, as well as their personal ambition, was inextricably linked to devotion to party. They could not achieve their goals unless they gained power, which they could not do except through the agency of one of the two major parties. Leaders high and low, and many voters as well, displayed a dedication to party that bordered on zealotry. Even so level-headed a politician as Treasury Secretary John Sherman once confessed to a friend that the idea of the opposing party coming to power "haunts me like a nightmare."

Parties were nearly as old as the Republic. The emergence of mass politics earlier in the nineteenth century had led to the creation of partisan structures and methods that were well established by the beginning of the Gilded Age. In a general sense, party organizations served as the essential link between leaders, who formulated policy and governed, and the voters, who, with their own beliefs and notions, sought guidance and inspiration. In an age when politicians had no independent means for reaching masses of voters (such as television in the late twentieth century), the party constituted the essential vehicle for communicating with the electorate. . . .

The traditional interpretation of Gilded Age politics held that in conducting their campaigns, politicians relied mostly on organizational techniques and machine management to win elections. Indeed, one important study labeled the era's political culture as "the triumph of organizational politics." Certainly, party managers perfected remarkably accurate advance polling schemes and created elaborate get-out-the-vote mechanisms, but close examination of politicians' behavior reveals that, in fact, they also placed great stress on the discussion of issues. The late nineteenth century saw a decline in the significance of parades, picnics, bonfires, rallies, and similar devices to ignite the emotions of the party faithful. More and more, political leaders turned to what they called the "campaign of education," appealing to voters on questions of government policy, especially those that affected citizens' economic well-being in an industrializing society. In the words of one campaign official in 1868, who was sending out tens of thousands of pamphlets to voters each day. "The people are intelligent and want something different from 'horrible caricatures and sensational trash.'"

Successful politicians came to realize that winning or retaining power rested largely on the flow of information to the electorate. Because communications technology had advanced little beyond the telegraph, they could reach voters only through public speeches or in print. Hence, in the months before elections, hundreds of state and national party leaders took to the hustings, speaking to audiences day after day for weeks on end, laying out their party's doctrines and appealing for support. For these men, the campaign season was a punishing time, filled with poorly ventilated halls or huge outdoor crowds, endless miles in jostling, dirty railroad cars, sleep deprivation, and indigestion. One campaigner reported to the Republican national committee in 1872 that "breathing railroad dust every day and speaking in the open air every night has played havoc with my voice. I am very hoarse and must lay up a day or two for repairs." By midcampaign that year the seemingly tireless James G. Blaine confessed that eight weeks of speechmaking had left him "completely worn out." Still, he and others returned to the task year after year, because they were convinced of the continuing need to appeal to what Blaine called the "will of the Sovereign People."

The closeness of elections heightened the possibility that vote buying or other forms of corruption could influence the outcome. It was a rare election that did not bring a barrage of allegations of fraud leveled by the two major parties against each other or by self-styled reformers and third-party losers against one or both major parties. Substantiating the myriad charges is difficult, however, and modern scholars disagree about the amount or the impact of election corruption in the period. According to one study, citizens who took money for their votes were relatively few in number and selected candidates from their own party anyway; those who sold their vote to the party that paid them more for it were an even smaller minority of purchased voters. Of course, in a close election even a small number of purchased "floating" votes could contribute to the result, but it is equally true that all the unpurchased votes—usually the vast majority—influenced the result as well. "The majority of voters," this study asserts, "were not bribed but, rather, voted for their party out of deep and long-standing loyalty."

Much more than bribery, legitimate campaign outlays represented a consistent and pervasive drain on party resources. Such expenses included the salaries of paid party officials and workers, travel expenses for campaigners, polling, outfitting headquarters rooms and public lecture halls, advertising, office supplies, postage, printing and distributing documents and textbooks, financial support for party newspapers, and on and on. In 1888, *Irish World* editor Patrick Ford itemized his expenses for organizing the Irish-American voters in New York City for the Republican party. Most of the funds went for salaries (district organizers, assistant directors, clerks, messenger boys, and so forth), but his list also included "Fitting Up 30 Ward Rooms" with such items as three thousand chairs at 35 cents each, banners and signs for each room at $25.00, and gaslight for each room at $3.00 per week for fourteen weeks. The total came to $73,465, and this was for only one portion of the population in a city usually carried by the opposing party. . . .

As the period progressed, parties looked increasingly to other sources of revenue, including economic interests that stood to benefit from the enactment of party policies. Traditional historians have referred to this sort of fund-raising as "frying the fat" from large capitalists who, in turn, expected subservience from the politicians, especially on issues affecting their businesses. In reality, the relationship was more complex. For one thing, there was no certainty that such contributions would be forthcoming. After narrowly losing his race for the presidency in 1884, Blaine complained, "I was beaten in New York simply for the lack of $25,000 which I tried in vain to raise in New York in the last week of the campaign. With all the immense interests of the tariff at stake, I don't think a single manufacturer gave $20,000. I doubt if one gave $10,000." . . .

Raising funds from business sources thus met with erratic success, and even when the party received such contributions, they did not automatically lead to businessmen getting what they wanted. James M. Swank, general manager of the American Iron and Steel Association, a strong backer of the protective tariff and always a big contributor to the Republican party, complained about the party's poor performance in the passage of the Tariff of 1883. "It is unfortunate," he wrote the chairman of the Senate Finance Committee, "that your Committee, in considering the Tariff Commission's schedules, did not invite a few leading representatives of the most important industries of the country to appear before it. The new tariff does not give satisfaction in many quarters." Swank and the iron and steel interests had to wait seven years, until the McKinley Act, for a tariff they found fully satisfactory.

Swank had been on hand in Washington for the hectic final days of congressional debate on the 1883 tariff, only to return home to Philadelphia disappointed and suffering from a severe cold and "physical prostration." His experience was not unusual and belies the stereotype of the overbearing lobbyist whipping politicians into line. The negative reputation of lobbyists notwithstanding, there was nothing inherently corrupt or even unreasonable in a legislator's listening to the recommendations of constituents and others affected by legislation. It was not unusual for a congressman to turn to such individuals as the only available source of information about a particular industry or interest. Moreover, politicians and business lobbyists frequently subscribed to the same basic views anyway. Senate Finance Committee leaders such as Justin Morrill, John Sherman, and Nelson Aldrich did not need Swank to convince them of the importance of tariff protection to further the nation's industrial development, although circumstances did not always permit them to enact their ideas.

More problematic were those instances in which congressmen came under pressure from conflicting interests. What was a senator to do, for instance, when woolen manufacturers urged a decrease in import duties on raw wool and sheep farmers demanded an increase? Consider the case of New York Senator William M. Evarts who, while Congress was considering the Interstate Commerce Act, received pleas from a Buffalo coal wholesaler "to render all the aid you possibly can to the passage of the Reagan Bill," and from a Seneca Falls pump manufacturer to "use your very best endeavors in killing this suicidal bill." American business interests, or "capitalists," were not a monolith, and a congressman obviously could not have a "sweetheart relationship" with both sides of diametrically opposed interests. . . .

In assessing the Gilded Age political universe as a whole, one might well ask: Was it wrong for citizens to have faith in their leaders? If not, why did not government accomplish more, especially at the federal level? In one sense, Americans got the government they asked for. With the major-party electorate evenly divided between Republicans and Democrats—leading to divided party control of the national government—stalemate often resulted. Yet, it would be wrong to dismiss the era as a whole as one of little accomplishment. The decades after the Civil War saw a shift in political concern away from the dominance of sectional issues toward questions of economic policymaking, with important implications for the evolution of government's role in the following century. When Gilded Age politicians tried to cope with the vexing and divisive currency issue, for example, they implicitly recognized that the government had a part to play in determining the country's money supply and, hence, the level of economic activity, a role that would be the essence of twentieth-century fiscal and monetary policy. The tariff issue had the power to touch people all across economic lines, and Congress's grappling with it was at its core a debate over what the government should do to promote prosperity— a question that continues to dominate policy debate to this day. Subsidies to railroads or other enterprises, often criticized as the quintessence of Gilded Age misfeasance, could be seen as an innovative approach to government/business cooperation in creating and modernizing the infrastructure of an industrializing nation. The late nineteenth century also witnessed the beginning of serious government regulation of business with the foundations laid down by the Interstate Commerce Act and the Sherman Antitrust Act, and the government began to police itself with the Pendleton Civil Service Act. Some scholars even see the government's pension program for Union veterans as an important antecedent for twentieth-century welfare policies.

Among the most important developments in the late nineteenth century was the growing strength and importance of the office of president. Having recovered from the blows struck by the attempted impeachment of Andrew Jackson and the scandals of the Grant administration, the presidency, by the end of the century, had become the center of the national political system. Historically, policymaking had been the province of Congress, but, more and more, presidents went beyond their traditional administrative role to act as legislative leaders on behalf of their policy objectives. By the end of the century, much legislation was being originally drafted in the executive branch. As with much else in American life, the 1890s brought an extraordinary transformation in presidential activism. At the beginning of the decade, Harrison employed a variety of means to achieve his ends: veto threats to influence the shape of legislation, well-timed messages and public statements to garner support, and informal dinners and other consultations with congressmen at the White House to push them in the right direction. Harrison's successor, Grover Cleveland, was in many ways a strong executive, but his ham-handed efforts to pressure Democrats in Congress frequently backfired and left him isolated from much of his party. McKinley picked up where Harrison left off. As a smoother, more skillful politician who saw the importance of cultivating good press relations, McKinley proved so effective as an administrator and legislative leader that recent scholars consider him the first modern president.

A strong national executive, with the president voicing citizens' concerns from the "bully pulpit," emerged as a defining feature of the Progressive Era that followed. In other ways as well the Gilded Age foreshadowed the Progressive Era, including the increasing emphasis on government activism to address economic problems and other issues and in the impulse toward reform. Progressivism was not merely the discovery of new purposes for government; it also represented the release of government activism from the restraining effect of the previous era's two decades of political equilibrium. One of the main reasons the Progressive Era started when it did was that the stalemate had been broken. Because the Republicans had established themselves as the majority party in the mid-1890s, President Theodore Roosevelt was freer than his predecessors of worries about perpetuating his party in power. Less fearful of frustration at the hands of historically obstructionist Democrats (many of whom were now taking on progressive ways of thinking), Roosevelt could move toward governing much more boldly.

The late nineteenth century witnessed profound changes in the United States. Scholars once treated its political life almost as an historical embarrassment, in Henry Adam's words, "poor in purpose and barren in result." Most historians now realize how inadequate that judgment was to describe this complex and portentous time, bridging the age of Abraham Lincoln and that of Theodore Roosevelt. In a rapidly evolving society, political leaders confronted problems of unprecedented intricacy and scope. That they were locked in partisan stalemate much of the time and frequently hamstrung by one of the major parties, the Democrats, who believed that Americans wanted less government, not more, often prevented vigorous action. Yet, they were able to post some modest success in reaching solutions to the society's problems. More important, leaders of a more activist inclination, including Republicans such as John Sherman, Benjamin Harrison, and William McKinley, glimpsed, if they did not fully appreciate, the broader possibilities for energetic government. In important ways they helped lay the groundwork for the twentieth-century American polity.

WEEK 7

DOCUMENTS

1. Haymarket Anarchist Michael Schwab
Fights for Freedom, 1886

Talk about a gigantic conspiracy! A movement is not a conspiracy. All we did

WAS DONE IN OPEN DAYLIGHT.

There were no secrets. We prophesied in word and writing the coming of a great revolution, a change in the system of production in all industrial countries of the globe. And the change will come, and must come. Is it not absurd, as the State's Attorney and his associates have done, to suppose that this social revolution—a change of such immense proportions—was to be inaugurated on or about the first of May in the city of Chicago by making war on the police! The organizer Furthman searched hundreds of numbers of the *Arbeiter-Zeitung* and the *Alarm,* and so the prosecution must have known very well what we understood when we talked about the coming revolution. But the prosecuting attorneys preferred to ignore these explanatory articles.

The articles in evidence were carefully selected and paraded as samples of violent language, but the language used in them was just the same as newspapers used in general against us and their enemies. Even against the police and their practices they used words

OF THE SAME KIND AS WE DID.

The president of the Citizens' Association. Edwin Lee Brown, after the last election of Mayor Harrison, made a speech in North Side Turner Hall in which he called on all good citizens to take possession of the courthouse by force, even if they had to wade in blood. It seems to me that the most violent speakers are not to be found in the ranks of the Anarchists.

It is not violence in word or action the attorneys of the State and their urgers-on are waging war against; it is our doctrine—Anarchy.

We contend for communism and Anarchy—why? If we had kept silent, stones would have cried out. Murder was committed day by day. Children were slain, women worked to death, men killed inch by inch, and these crimes are never punished by law. The great principle underlying the present system is

UNPAID LABOR.

Those who amass fortunes, build palaces, and live in luxury, are doing that by virtue of unpaid labor. Being directly or indirectly the possessors of land and machinery, they dictate their terms to the workingman. He is compelled to sell his labor cheap, or to starve. The price paid him is always far below the real value. He acts under compulsion, and they call it a free contract. This infernal state of affairs keeps him poor and ignorant; an easy prey for exploitation. . . .

. . . When I came to the United States, I found that there were classes of workingmen who were better paid than the European workmen, but I perceived that the state

From *The Accused and the Accusers: The Famous Speeches of the Eight Chicago Anarchists in Court* (New York: Arno, 1969), 24–28.

of things in a great number of industries was even worse, and that the so-called better paid skilled laborers were degrading rapidly into mere automatic parts of machinery. I found that the proletariat of the great industrial cities was in a condition that could not be worse. Thousands of laborers in the city of Chicago live in rooms without sufficient protection from the weather, without proper ventilation, where never a stream of sunlight flows in. There are hovels where two, three and four families live in one room. How these conditions influence the health and the morals of these unfortunate sufferers, it is needless to say. And how *do* they live? From the ash-barrels

THEY GATHER HALF-ROTTEN VEGETABLES,

in the butcher shops they buy for some cents offal of meat, and these precious morsels they carry home to prepare from them their meals. The delapidated houses in which this class of laborers live need repairs very badly, but the greedy landlord waits in most cases till he is compelled by the city to have them done. Is it a wonder that disease of all kinds kill men, women and children in such places by wholesale, especially children? Is this not horrible in a so-called civilized land where there is plenty of food and riches? Some years ago a committee of the Citizen's Association, or League, made an investigation of these matters, and I was one of the reporters that went with them. What these common laborers are today,

THE SKILLED LABORERS WILL BE TOMORROW.

Improved machinery that ought to be a blessing for the workingman, under the existing conditions turns for him to a curse. Machinery multiplies the army of unskilled laborers, makes the laborer more dependent upon the men who own the land and the machines. And that is the reason that Socialism and Communism got a foothold in this country. The outcry that Socialism, Communism and Anarchism are the creed of foreigners, is a big mistake. There are more Socialists of American birth in this country than foreigners, and that is much, if we consider that nearly half of all industrial workingmen are not native Americans. There are Socialistic papers in a great many States edited by Americans for Americans. The capitalistic newspapers conceal that fact very carefully.

Socialism, as we understand it, means that land and machinery shall be held in common by the people. The production of goods shall be carried on by producing groups which shall supply the demands of the people. Under such a system every human being would have an opportunity to do useful work, and no doubt would work. Some hours' work every day would suffice to produce all that, according to statistics, is necessary for a comfortable living. Time would be left

TO CULTIVATE THE MIND,

and to further science and art.

That is what the Socialist propose. Some say it is un-American! Well, then, is it American to let people starve and die in ignorance? Is exploitation and robbery of the poor, American? What have the great political parties done for the poor? Promised much; done nothing, except corrupting them by buying their votes on election day. A poverty-stricken man has no interest in the welfare of the community. It is only natural that in a society where women are driven to sell their honor, men should sell their votes.

But we "were not only Socialists and Communists: we were Anarchists."

What is Anarchy? . . . Anarchy is a dream, but only in the present. It will be realized.

REASON WILL GROW

in spite of all obstacles. Who is the man that has the cheek to tell us that human development has already reached its culminating point? I know that our ideal will not be accomplished, this or next year, but I know that it will be accomplished as near as possible, some day, in the future. It is entirely wrong to use the word Anarchy as synonymous with violence. Violence is one thing and Anarchy another. In the present state of society violence is used on all sides, and, therefore, we advocated the use of violence against violence, but against violence only, as a necessary means of defense.

2. "Freedom," Poem by Haymarket Anarchist Albert R. Parsons, 1886

Toil and pray! The world cries cold;
Speed thy prayer, for time is gold
At thy door Need's subtle tread:
Pray in haste! for time is bread.

And thou plow'st and thou hew'st,
And thou rivet'st and sewest,
And thou harvestest in vain;
Speak! O, man; what is thy gain?

Fly'st the shuttle day and night.
Heav'st the ores of earth to light.
Fill'st with treasures plenty's horn;
Brim'st it o'er with wine and corn.

But who hath thy meal prepared,
Festive garments with thee shared;
And where is thy cheerful hearth,
Thy good shield in battle dearth?

Thy creations round thee see
All thy work, but naught for thee!
Yea, of all the chains alone thy hand forged,
These are thine own.

Chains that round the body cling.
Chains that lame the spirits wing.

From *The Accused and the Accusers: The Famous Speeches of the Eight Chicago Anarchists in Court* (New York: Arno, 1969), 90–91.

Chains that infants' feet, indeed
Clog! O, workman! Lo! Thy meed.

What you rear and bring to light.
Profits by the idle wight,
What ye weave of diverse hue,
'Tis a curse—your only due.

What ye build, no room insures,
Not a sheltering roof to yours,
And by haughty ones are trod—
Ye, whose toil their feet hath shod.

Human bees! Has nature's thrift
Given thee naught but honey's gift?
See! the drones are on the wing.
Have you lost the will to sting?

Man of labor, up, arise!
Know the might that in thee lies,
Wheel and shaft are set at rest
At thy powerful arm's behest.

Thine oppressor's hand recoils
When thou, weary of thy toil.
Shun'st thy plough thy task begun.
When thou speak'st: Enough is done!

Break this two-fold yoke in twain;
Break thy want's enslaving chain;
Break thy slavery's want and dread;
Bread is freedom, freedom bread.

3. "Labor's Great Army," 1889

An army, with banners flying and music sounding, on its march to the battlefield, is a grand and inspiring spectacle. . . . An army in days of peace, with its pomp of ordered motion and its glowing colors and glitter of weapons, is always an attractive sight, charming the gazers, young and old, for a little while, away from the commonplaces of the everyday struggle for bread and wealth. . . . But an industrial army, such as Boston witnessed yesterday parading its historic streets, with a record of invincible patience, an ever widening purpose of righteous achievement, is a sight more attractive, a spectacle more impressive. It means more for the future than all the battlefields that have been drenched with human blood. It is a celebration of the partial reign of the common people.

So excellent were the exhibitions of all the different crafts that it would be almost invidious to particularize any as the chief ornaments. Yet, perhaps to most

From *The Boston Herald*, September 3, 1889.

people, the "floats" of the carpenters, by their striking contrast of the old log cabin of the fathers with a modern building caused the greatest impression and suggested, in addition, the immense strides in quality of work made by the workers in the last few years, just as the procession suggests in a larger way the immense strides made by the workers themselves in securing the recognition of their important position in the body politic. The industrial army of yesterday seemed to feel that the workers are the base of the heaven-seeking pyramid of civilization, and that, if that is not well founded and secure, the top must topple. . . .

Union 33 of Boston was most profuse in its exhibition of mottoes. . . . One was a huge saw made of wood and painted quite realistically. On one side was the inscription, "We are organized to elevate," and on the reverse, "Set on eight hours." Another device was a carpenter's square enlarged to a fairly heroic size. The inscription was: "We are all square union men; non-union men are not square."

Other mottoes which attracted especial attention were these: "Honest labor never rusts: up with wages, down with trusts." "Nine hours a day has paved the way: eight hours a day has come to stay." "Less work, more recreation." "We build the cities." "Those who build palaces should not dwell in hovels."

The Operative Tailors' Union gave some very sharp raps. They were accompanied by two large open wagons, trimmed and decorated, one drawn by four horses, and bearing a representation of a tailor shop in active operation with men engaged in cutting, sewing and pressing. The other wagon was fitted to resemble the interior of a room in a tenement house, with all its squalor and misery. The first wagon bore a large sign inscribed: "Away with the filthy scab tenement house labor. We will investigate a few tenement houses for $20." The second bore simply the pregnant remark: "Twenty coats a day's work."

4. Samuel Gompers Defends the Right to Strike, 1899

The working people find that improvements in the methods of production and distribution are constantly being made, and unless they occasionally strike, or have the power to enter upon a strike, the improvements will all go to the employer and all the injuries to the employees. A strike is an effort on the part of the workers to obtain some of the improvements that have occurred resultant from bygone and present genius of our intelligence, of our mental progress. We are producing wealth today at a greater ratio than ever in the history of mankind, and a strike on the part of workers is, first, against deterioration in their condition, and, second, to be participants in some of the improvements. Strikes are caused from various reasons. The employer desires to reduce wages and lengthen hours of labor, while the desire on the part of employees is to obtain shorter hours of labor and better wages, and better surroundings. Strikes establish or maintain the rights of unionism; that is, to establish and maintain the organization by which the rights of the workers can be the better protected and advanced against the little forms of oppression,

From testimony of Samuel Gompers, November 20, 1899, U.S. Congress, House of Representatives, *Report of the Industrial Commission on the Relations and Conditions of Capital and Labor,* 56th Congress, 2d Session, House Document 495, Part 7, 605–606.

sometimes economical, sometimes political—the effort on the part of employers to influence and intimidate workmen's political preferences; strikes against victimization; activity in the cause of the workers against the blacklist. . . .

It required 40,000 people in the city of New York in my own trade in 1877 to demonstrate to the employers that we had a right to be heard in our own defense of our trade, and an opportunity to be heard in our own interests. It cost the miners of the country, in 1897, sixteen weeks of suffering to secure a national conference and a national agreement. It cost the railroad brotherhoods long months of suffering, many of them sacrificing their positions, in the railroad strike of 1877, and in the Chicago, Burlington, and Quincy strike, of the same year, to secure from the employers the right to be heard through committees, their representatives. . . . Workmen have had to stand the brunt of the suffering. The American Republic was not established without some suffering, without some sacrifice, and no tangible right has yet been achieved in the interest of the people unless it has been secured by sacrifices and persistency. After a while we become a little more tolerant to each other and recognize all have rights; get around the table and chaff each other; all recognize that they were not so reasonable in the beginning. Now we propose to meet and discuss our interests, and if we can not agree we propose in a more reasonable way to conduct our contests, each to decide how to hold out and bring the other one to terms. A strike, too, is to industry as the right that the British people contended for in placing in the House of Commons the power to close the purse strings to the Government. The rights of the British people were secured in two centuries— between 1500 and 1700—more than ever before, by the securing of that power to withhold the supplies; tied up the purse strings and compelled the Crown to yield. A strike on the part of workmen is to close production and compel better terms and more rights to be acceded to the producers. The economic results of strikes to workers have been advantageous. Without strikes their rights would not have been considered. It is not that workmen or organized labor desires the strike, but it will tenaciously hold to the right to strike. We recognize that peaceful industry is necessary to successful civilized life, but the right to strike and the preparation to strike is the greatest preventive to strikes. If the workmen were to make up their minds tomorrow that they would under no circumstances strike, the employers would do all the striking for them in the way of lesser wagers and longer hours of labor.

5. Preamble of the Industrial Workers of the World, 1905

The working class and the employing class have nothing in common. There can be no peace so long as hunger and want are found among millions of working people and the few, who make up the employing class, have all the good things of life.

Between these two classes a struggle must go on until the workers of the world organize as a class, take possession of the earth and the machinery of production, and abolish the wage system.

From Industrial Workers of the World, *Preamble and Constitution of the Industrial Workers of the World, Organized July 7, 1905* (Chicago: Industrial Workers of the World, 1916).

We find that the centering of management of the industries into fewer and fewer hands makes the trade unions unable to cope with the ever growing power of the employing class. The trade unions foster a state of affairs which allows one set of workers to be pitted against another set of workers in the same industry, thereby helping defeat one another in wage wars. Moreover, the trade unions aid the employing class to mislead the workers into the belief that the working class have interests in common with their employers.

These conditions can be changed and the interest of the working class upheld only by an organization formed in such a way that all its members in any one industry, or in all industries if necessary, cease work whenever a strike or lockout is on in any department thereof, thus making an injury to one an injury to all.

Instead of the conservative motto, "A fair day's wage for a fair day's work," we must inscribe on our banner the revolutionary watchword, "Abolition of the wage system."

It is the historic mission of the working class to do away with capitalism. The army of production must be organized, not only for the every day struggle with capitalists, but also to carry on production when capitalism shall have been overthrown. By organizing industrially we are forming the structure of the new society within the shell of the old.

6. Fitz John Porter Explains How to Quell Mobs, 1885

Riots generally originate in crowded cities or in districts where the population is principally composed of operatives. They are due to two causes. First: the restlessness or peevish discontent of the working-classes, who imagine that others are reaping large gains from their labor. Second: the plotting of demagogues and designing men, too indolent to earn their bread by their own exertions, who hope to receive power and profit, or perhaps notoriety. A third cause may be mentioned: the desire of honest but misguided men to obtain a better position for themselves and their families, who, brooding over real or fancied wrongs, finally resort to unlawful measures for redress.

The actors in the first movements which finally lead to a riot rarely, if ever, imagine that they are inaugurating one of these ebullitions of popular fury.

A combination of workmen, who have banded together presumably for proper purposes, believing themselves to be imposed upon by their employers, take measures to secure what they consider their rights. Sometimes one, sometimes another method is adopted, either one of which finally leads to a breach between employers and employed. Then comes a strike. Perhaps the strikers are in the employ of a railroad company, which, with its connections, reaches across the continent: all operations are suspended upon the railroad; passenger and freight cars are stopped upon the tracks; each individual striker has a little circle which he influences; the circumferences of these circles touch each other, and thus commotion is spread through the land. Human sympathy always goes out to the oppressed; the strikers represent

From Fitz John Porter, "How to Quell Mobs," *North American Review* 141 (October 1885): 351–360.

themselves as oppressed by the monopolizing corporations, and the sympathy of the community for the weaker unites with its natural prejudices against the stronger in the contest; disorder begins; confusion becomes worse confounded. Now appear the baser elements of society—the tramp, the thief, the rogue, the burglar—and these elements, which before were the outcasts of society, now become the rulers of the hour. The quarrel, before confined to the railroad and its employés, now enlarges its field, and the bad is arrayed against the general good. Pillagers at first despoil the railroad company, and then seek the property of others, no matter whom, to satisfy their greed. The community awakes to the danger of the situation, but it is too late; anarchy has the upper hand, and vice and lawlessness reign supreme. . . .

"How shall the future riot be suppressed? Upon whom lies the duty of suppression—upon the general government, the State, or the municipality?"

These are the practical questions to be discussed.

The general government has no power, except such as is derived by cession from the States. It is the creature of the State governments, and in its relations with the States is governed by organic law, beyond which it cannot step. Like all general rules, there is an exception to this rule; for there is a law, not to be found in any written constitution, which must from necessity control the general government, and that is the law of self-preservation. While it cannot interfere in any of the municipal regulations of the States, still there may be an exigency when it is not only its right, but its duty to interfere. Whenever the property of the government is endangered by an unlawful assemblage of persons, the government should protect its property, even with the sacrifice of life. It can make no difference where that property is situated. It is not subject to the laws of the States; no taxes are paid to the State for its protection. . . .

It is very difficult to draw the line where forbearance shall cease to be a virtue, and where stern duty compels the authorities to use coercion. All this must be left to their good sense, alert judgment, and proper appreciation of each individual case. There should be no dallying with a mob. It is hydra-headed, many-sided, and, at the outset, undecided as to its future movements; but if, without the use of decided measures for prevention, it be suffered to take its own way, a leader will soon be found of sufficient capacity to direct and control these movements. Let this period once be passed, and let a master-mind be placed in command, with subservience on the part of his followers, and the control of the mob in the right direction is forever lost. . . .

The qualities most needed, in those who are charged with the duty of preventing riots, are coolness, decision, alertness, and courage. Let the mob once ascertain that any of these qualities are wanting in those who seek to suppress, and the opportunity for suppression is lost. It would have been more merciful in the end to those composing many mobs, certainly to those who suffered from their excesses, if instead of firing blank cartridges a few bullets had found their way into the muskets. One determined man, with fearless front and undaunted courage, has been of more service in preventing a riot than scores of dilly-dallying mayors and governors who read the riot act and begged and besought the rioters to disperse, and called them by endearing names.

In 1877 riots broke out all over the land. The history of these riots reveals strange inconsistencies and many shameful derelictions of duty. In the city of Pittsburg, with the police of the city at his back, and a large number of State troops at his command, the mayor of that great town, with an indecision which was indefensible and unaccountable (except upon the supposition that by so doing he hoped to preserve his popularity), suffered anarchy and pillage and murder to rule for days. He strove to stem a torrent of turbulence and violence with soft speeches, by reading the riot act, by kind words. But it was too late. The time for such formalities had passed. The sacrifice of a few lives by charges of fixed bayonets, or by salvos of musketry charged with bullets, would have scattered the howling, demoniac mob back to the holes and dreary retreats from which so many of them had come.

At Harrisburg, the same policy at first placed the troops of the great State of Pennsylvania, sent to relieve its capital from the depredations of the mob, prisoners in the hands of that very mob that they were sent to suppress. The militiamen were marched up and down the streets amid the jeers and howls of the rioters. But a different state of affairs was soon inaugurated, through the exertions of one determined man, the mayor of the city. He selected some of the best citizens, and with the sheriff of the county marched at their head, and almost in an instant dispelled the mob while in the very act of pillaging.

All along the line of the railroads extending west from Buffalo the employés were in commotion. Mobs of several thousand people had gathered at different points, but only at one place was the mob beyond the control of the authorities. This was at the city of Buffalo. At East Buffalo, where a mob which was estimated at more than three thousand persons was hooting, howling, and threatening vengeance, a captain of police, with the aid of the baton forcibly brought in contact with the heads of the rioters, in a very few moments dispelled the mob, so that, in the words of the historian who records this incident, "the East Buffalo grounds were as clear and quiet as a country field on a Sunday afternoon." . . .

Mobs are cowards at first. Crime always enervates. They only gain courage as they find that those whose duty it is to suppress them are themselves cowards. A mob is not to be feared when it is first aroused. It is only as its passion for carnage is whetted by the taste of blood, or its greed for pillage is gratified, that it becomes dangerous.

Upon whomsoever devolves the duty of suppression, let this be his first effort: check at the very beginning; allow no tumultuous gatherings; permit no delay; a few stern, resolute words; if these be not heeded, then strike resolutely, boldly; let there be no hesitation; if necessary, take life at the outset. It will be more merciful to take one life then than to suffer the mob to take the lives of many, or to be compelled to sacrifice the innocent with the guilty at the point of the bayonet, or in the discharge of musketry or cannon. But the necessity to take life will not arise unless there be inactivity and indecision at the outset on the part of the authorities.

Before the time shall come when it will be necessary to use musket-ball or bayonet, the opportunity will be afforded to suppress the riot; perhaps at the sacrifice of a few broken heads, or by the imprisonment of some of its leaders.

In every large city, in fact in every city where a police force is employed, a perfect drill should prepare policemen to meet the exigencies arising from any tumultuous assemblage of the people; so that, at a moment's warning, these conservators of the peace will be ready to act, and to act understandingly and promptly. It will be found that a few determined policemen, placed in the field at a moment's notice, will prove one of the best and most direct methods of quelling a mob. These, by skillful maneuvers, can take a mob in flank, or in rear, or in front, if necessary, and so employ themselves and their clubs that almost before the mob would know what was impelling them they would be driven from the field of action. . . .

The most fertile cause of all riots is the peevish discontent of wage-workers—too often ignorant of the true relations between themselves and their employers. This peevish discontent may perhaps be confined to a few, but those few will be able to avail themselves of the restlessness which may pervade the whole body of operatives. This discontent arises not so much from any real oppression, or from any wrong, but simply from the natural jealousy which every man feels, more or less, when he sees others living more luxuriously than himself, and especially when that luxury appears to be the result of his labor. Now this discontent may be dispelled, perhaps not in the present generation, though it may be greatly moderated; but, certainly, means can be taken to prevent it in the future. The employer and employé may surely be brought together in more intimate relations than those they at present sustain. Where lies the fault in the present system? Who is justly chargeable with the origin of this discontent? That question cannot be settled in this discussion. But so much may be said: the working-classes can be educated up to a higher tone of feeling, a better appreciation of their duty to their employers, a higher standard of morals, and a nobler level of thought and action. May not the employers find something in the present condition of things for which they are responsible; and which they, in the exercise of the duty they owe to common humanity, may be able to better?

There is a factory, in one of the large manufacturing towns of the country, where one of the employers, imbued with true Christian philanthropy, brings himself, in a measure, down to a level with his hundreds of employés. He mingles with their families; finds out the social status and wants of all; gives a word of advice to one; imparts counsel to another; sympathizes with the mourner; puts his strong arm round the weak; and employs all of his ability to raise his workingmen in the scale of human existence. He provides a reading-room for them, furnishes them with reading matter, and gives them lectures. Let this example be emulated by every employer in the land, and riots would be impossible.

1. John W. Holway, a Pinkerton Guard, Views the Battle of Homestead, 1892

JOHN W. HOLWAY sworn and examined.

By the CHAIRMAN:

Q. Please state your name, age, residence, and occupation.—*A.* John W. Holway; 23½ years old; 1008 Twelfth street, Chicago; occupation, chiefly that of student. . . .

Q. Were you a member of the company that was sent by the Pinkertons to Homestead during the recent strike?—*A.* Yes, sir.

Q. What kind of a contract did you enter into at that time?—*A.* The contract was stated about this way, that in case we were injured we would not sue the company for damages, and that in case we deserted their employ at any time without asking their leave we would forfeit the wages which were then due us.

U.S. Congress, Senate, Report No. 1280. 52d Session (Washington, D.C.: Government Printing Office, 1893), 68–73.

Q. And on the other hand, what were they to do for you; what rate of wages was to be paid?—*A.* We were to be paid $15 a week and expenses.

Q. How many men accompanied you from Chicago to Homestead?—*A.* I judge there was 125. . . .

Q. Did you understand, when you left here, that you were to bear arms when you reached your destination?—*A.* No, sir.

Q. Did you anticipate it?—*A.* From nothing that they had told us. I read the newspapers, and I formed that private opinion, but we received no such information from them.

Q. Were you given any arms of any kind when you left here?—*A.* No, sir.

Q. Were you transported rather quietly and secretly from this point to Homestead?—*A.* The trip was rather a quiet one, and very quickly and secretly planned.

Q. Describe it, and give us the route you took?—*A.* We started out from the office on Fifth avenue and we went along the street to the Lake Shore depot, where we entered the rear entrance on the platform. Instead of going up to the regular passenger entrance we took the one the employés take, so we went into the rear cars of the train very quickly. Directly we entered the rear of the cars, men who seemed to be detectives and not patrolmen, stationed themselves at the doors, and they prevented our exit, and they prevented the entrance of any outside parties who might wish to enter. We then, on this regular midnight train, went to Toledo, reaching there about 9 o'clock next morning. At Toledo a special engine was hitched on to our three special cars, and we went by way of Sandusky, not through Elyria, and around to Cleveland. We did what was called "running wild." We ran rather slowly—it was not a scheduled train—on to Cleveland, and there they gave us some lunches, and we went as fast as 40 or 50 miles an hour through Painesville, down to Ashtabula. There we waited for an hour. . . . We then, the whole train, went rapidly on through Jefferson County to Youngstown, and from Youngstown to Bellview, where we landed rapidly. We were told to prepare to land—to leave the cars. During our trip we were not allowed to leave the cars at all, we were kind of prisoners. We did not have any rights. That might have been because they were afraid of union men, perhaps spies, who would telegraph ahead to Homestead. They wanted to get inside the works without bloodshed, but we had no rights whatever. Then we entered the boats, some 300 of us. There was two covered barges, like these Mississippi covered boats. One was fitted up with bunks that reached to the ceiling on the sides. I entered that and we supposed that we would be allowed to sleep, but we did not sleep for twenty-four hours, but Capt. Nordrum, the man in charge, told us to leave the boat with bunks in and go to the other boat, and we did so. We were told to fall in, and the roll of our names was called, and we were told to secure our uniforms, which consisted of coat, hat, vest, and pair of trowsers. When we had secured our uniforms we were some distance down the river, and we were told to keep quiet, and the lights were turned out, and everything kept very quiet until we were given orders softly to arise. I was lying down about an hour when the order was sent around the boat for all the men to get ready to land. Then the captain called out for men who could handle rifles. I did not want to handle a rifle, and then he said we want two or three men here to guard the door with clubs, so I said I would do that, and I got over the table and got a club like a policeman's club to guard the side door—that was to prevent men from coming in boats and jumping on to our barge from the river. I stayed there while the men who could handle rifles were marched down to the open end of the boat, and I did not see anything more of them until the firing commenced.

Q. Tell what further occurred as a matter of knowledge on your part?—*A.* I had a curiosity to see what was going on on the bank. I was stationed inside the boat at the side door, and as there were three or four other men afraid to carry rifles, they took upon themselves the duty of watching the door, and so I was told to go down to the other end of the boat to see what was going on, and I saw what appeared to be a lot of young men and boys on the bank, swearing and cursing and having large sticks. I did not see a gun or anything. They were swearing at our men. I did not see any more, but came back and resumed my position at the door. I had not been back more than two minutes when I heard a sharp pistol shot, and then there were 30, 40, or 100 of them, and our men came running and stampeding back as fast as they could and they got in the shelter of the door, and then they turned around and blazed away. It was so dark I could see the flames from the rifles easily. They fired about 50 shots—I was surprised to see them stand up, because the strikers were shooting also, but they did not seem to be afraid of being hit. They had some shelter from the door. They fired in rather a professional manner I thought. The men inside the Chicago boat were rather afraid at hearing the rifles, and we all jumped for rifles that were laying on a table ready, and some one, I think a sergeant, opened a box of revolvers, and said, "all get revolvers," so I had now a Winchester rifle and a revolver. I called out to see if anybody had been hurt, and I saw a man there apparently strangling. He had been shot through the head and he died sometime afterwards, I think. His name was Kline, I believe. Of course it rather made us incensed to be shot at that way, but I kept out of danger as much as possible.

I was standing there when Nordrum came up, and he said to follow him, and I crossed over to the New York boat, where there were 40 men with rifles standing on the edge of the boat watching what was going on on shore. Nordrum spoke to the men on shore. He spoke in rather a loud manner—say a commanding manner. He said: "We are coming up that hill anyway, and we don't want any more trouble from you men." The men were in the mill windows. The mill is ironclad. There were a few boys in sight, but the men were under shelter, all of them. I supposed I should have to go up the hill, and I didn't like the idea very well, because it was pretty nearly certain death, as I supposed. I thought it over in what little time I had, and I thought I would have to go anyway. While I was standing there, waiting for Nordrum to charge up the hill and we follow him, he went away, and he was gone quite a few minutes. I took advantage of that to look around the New York men's boat to see what was going on, and I saw about 150 of the New York men hiding in the aisle furthest from the shore. It was divided into bunks. They were hiding in the bunks—they were hiding under the mattresses; they didn't want to be told to shoulder a rifle and charge up the hill; they were naturally afraid of it. They were watchmen, and not detectives. Now the men who had the rifles were mostly detectives. There were 40 of the detectives, who I afterwards learned were regular employés of Pinkerton, but these other men were simply watchmen, and hired as watchmen, and told so, and nothing else. Seeing these men so afraid and cowering rather dispirited the rest of us, and those who had rifles—I noticed there seemed to be a fear among them all. I went to the end of the boat, and there I saw crowds on the bank, waving their hands, and all looking at the boat and appearing to be very frantic.

I judged we were going to have trouble and went back to the end where I had been placed and waited for Nordrum to come, but he did not turn up, and after I stood there about half an hour I concluded, as there was no one there to order us to do anything and as it was stated that the steam tug had pulled out, taking all those who had charge of us—I concluded I would look out for my life, and if anything was said about my leaving and not staying there I would say I did not intend to work for them any more; so I returned to the door I was told to guard, and in that place I stayed for the remainder of the day, during all the shooting and firing. I concluded if the boat was burned—we expected a thousand men would charge down the embankment and put us to massacre; that was what we expected all throughout the day—I concluded if the boat was burned I would defend my life with the other men. . . .

At about 3 o'clock we heard something; we thought was a cannon, but it was dynamite. Afterwards I learned it was worse than a cannon; sounded like a very large cannon. It partially wrecked the other boat. A stick of it fell near me. It broke open the door of the aisles, and it smashed open the door, and the sharpshooters were firing directly at any man in sight. That was about 3 o'clock. Most of the men were for surrender at this time, but the old detectives held out and said, "If you surrender you will be shot down like dogs; the best thing is to stay here." We could not cut our barges loose because there was a fall below, where we would be sunk. We were deserted by our captains and by our tug, and left there to be shot. We felt as though we had been betrayed and we did not understand it, and we did not know why the tug had pulled off and didn't know it had come back. About 4 o'clock some one or other authorized a surrender, effected by means of a medical student, who studies at the eclectic college over here, the most intelligent man on board for that matter, a Freemason. He secured a surrender. I don't know how he secured it—by waving a flag. We secured a surrender. What he wanted was that our steam tug pull us away, but instead of that the strikers held that we should depart by way of the depot.

That surrender was effected, and I started up the embankment with the men who went out, and we were glad to get away and did not expect trouble; but I looked up the hill and there were our men being struck as they went up, and it looked rather disheartening. . . . I ran down a side street and ran through a yard. I ran about half a mile I suppose, but was rather weak and had had nothing to eat or drink and my legs gave out, could not run any further, and some man got hold of me by the back of my coat, and about 20 or 30 men came up and kicked me and pounded me with stones. I had no control of myself then. I thought I was about going and commenced to scream, and there were 2 or 3 strikers with rifles rushed up then and kept off the crowd and rushed me forward to a theater, and I was put in the theater and found about 150 of the Pinkerton men there, and that was the last violence offered me.

2. Eugene V. Debs Denounces the Role of Corporations and the Courts in the Pullman Strike, 1895

*Proclamation to American Railway Union**

TERRE HAUTE, IND., June 1, 1895.

Sirs and Brothers—A cruel wrong against our great order, perpetrated by Wm. A. Woods, United States Circuit Judge, has been approved by the United States Supreme Court, and from under its shadow I address this communication to you; but though prison walls frown upon myself and others whom you chose as officials, I assure you that neither despondency nor despair has taken the place of the courage which has characterized our order since the storms of persecution first began to beat upon us. Hope has not deserted us. Our faith in the future of our great order is as strong as when our banners waved triumphantly over the Great Northern from St. Paul to the coast. Our order is still the undaunted friend of the toiling masses and our battle-cry now, as ever, is the emancipation of labor from degrading, starving and enslaving conditions. We have not lost faith in the ultimate triumph of truth over perjury, of justice over wrong, however exalted may be the stations of those who perpetrate the outrages.

The Storm and the Battle

I need not remind you, comrades of the American Railway Union, that our order in the pursuit of the right was confronted with a storm of opposition such as never beat upon a labor organization in all time. Its brilliant victory on the Great Northern and its gallant championship of the unorganized employes of the Union Pacific had aroused the opposition of every railroad corporation in the land.

To crush the American Railway Union was the one tie that united them all in the bonds of vengeance; it solidified the enemies of labor into one great association, one organization which, by its fabulous wealth, enabled it to bring into action resources aggregating billions of money and every appliance that money could purchase. But in this supreme hour the American Railway Union, undaunted, put forth its efforts to rescue Pullman's famine-cursed wage slaves from the grasp of an employer as heartless as a stone, as remorseless as a savage and as unpitying as an incarnate fiend. The battle fought in the interest of starving men, women and children stands forth in the history of Labor's struggles as the great "Pullman Strike." It was a battle on the part of the American Railway Union fought for a cause as holy as ever aroused the courage of brave men; it was a battle in which upon one side were men thrice armed because their cause was just, but they fought against the combined power of corporations which by the use of money could debauch justice, and, by playing the part of incendiary, bring to their aid the military power of the government, and this solidified mass of venality, venom and vengeance constituted the foe against which the American Railway Union fought Labor's greatest battle for humanity.

---

*Issued when Debs' jail sentence for having participated in the Pullman strike was affirmed by the Supreme Court of the United States.

Writings and Speeches of Eugene V. Debs (New York: Hermitage Press, 1948), 1–2.

1. Unionized Workers in the Knights of Labor Demand a Fair Share of American Wealth, 1878

The recent alarming development and aggression of aggregated wealth, which, unless checked, will invariably lead to the pauperization and hopeless degradation of the toiling masses, render it imperative, if we desire to enjoy the blessings of life, that a check should be placed upon its power and upon unjust accumulation, and a system adopted which will secure to the laborer the fruits of his toil; and as this much desired object can only be accomplished by the thorough unification of labor, and the united effort of those who obey the divine injunction that "In the sweat of thy brow shalt thou eat bread," we have formed the * * * * * with a view of securing the organization and direction, by co-operative effort, of the power of the industrial classes; and we submit to the world the object sought to be accomplished by our organization, calling upon all who believe in securing "the greatest good to the greatest number" to aid and assist us:—

Preamble to the constitution of the Knights of Labor, 1878, in Timothy Patrick McCarthy and John McMillan, eds., *The Radical Reader: A Documentary History of the American Radical Tradition* (New York: Free Press, 2003), pp. 244–245.

I. To bring within the folds of organization every department of productive industry, making knowledge a standpoint for action, and industrial and moral worth, not wealth, the true standard of individual and national greatness.

II. To secure to the toilers a proper share of the wealth that they create; more of the leisure that rightfully belongs to them; more societary advantages; more of the benefits, privileges, and emoluments of the world, all those rights and privileges necessary to make them capable of enjoying, appreciating, defending, and perpetuating the blessings of good government.

III. To arrive at the true condition of the producing masses in their educational, moral, and financial condition, by demanding from the various governments the establishment of bureaus of Labor Statistics.

IV. The establishment of co-operative institutions, productive and distributive.

V. The reserving of the public lands—the heritage of the people—for the actual settler;—not another acre for railroads or settlers.

VI. The abrogation of all laws that do not bear equally upon capital and labor, the removal of unjust technicalities, delays, and discriminations in the administration of justice, and the adopting of measures providing for the health and safety of those engaged in mining, manufacturing, or building pursuits.

VII. The enactment of laws to compel chartered corporations to pay their employes weekly, in full, for labor performed during the preceding week, in the lawful money of the country.

VIII. The enactment of laws giving mechanics and laborers a first lien on their work for full wages.

IX. The abolishment of the contract system on national, state, and municipal work.

X. The substitution of arbitration for strikes, whenever and wherever employers and employes are willing to meet on equitable grounds.

XI. The prohibition of the employment of children in workshops, mines, and factories before attaining their fourteenth year.

XII. To abolish the system of letting out by contract the labor of convicts in our prisons and reformatory institutions.

XIII. To secure for both sexes equal pay for equal work.

XIV. The reduction of the hours of labor to eight per day, so that the laborers may have more time for social enjoyment and intellectual improvement, and be enabled to reap the advantages conferred by the labor-saving machinery which their brains have created.

XV. To prevail upon governments to establish a purely national circulating medium, based upon the faith and resources of the nation, and issued directly to the people, without the intervention of any system of banking corporations, which money shall be a legal tender in payment of all debts, public or private.

3. Sweatshop Conditions Horrify a Factory Inspector, 1893

[T]he sweating industry is carried on principally in the south-east part of Philadelphia; . . . at least 90 per cent. of the whole of this work in the sewing line is done right here; a close count shows from 3,500 to 4,000 people engaged, with a few exceptions, at work in tenement houses or a combination if you choose; the living apartments, cooking, eating and sleeping are on the first, and part second floors, the remaining part second and all of the third is used for work rooms. The nationalities represented are Russian Jews, Poles, Huns, Slavs and Italians, and their general temperament is of a most avaricious kind.

The matter of hours seemingly do not count. It is simply this; If a contractor wants a coat, pants, or vest as the case may be, the person who sub-contracts for the work has no choice of hours or aught else, but hastens to accomplish the task, being sure to get back at the given time or forfeit his chance for getting more work, so that after all the whole system is the effort of an industrial evil, which is being fostered by our American people through their very indifference to actual surroundings, and the sooner the whole people get on their thinking cap the better, and adopt such means (radical though they may seem) as will prohibit entirely, work of this kind being done in the home. Then and then only, will contractors provide proper work rooms subject to proper shop discipline, and regulated by a full enforcement of the Factory Law. For the conditions that surround this class of people is outrivaled by no other. Actual filth contributing largely to their immediate surroundings, and any attempt on my part to describe my actual findings, would mean a shock to the pride of our much boasted prosperity in this, our city of homes.

Speaking to a sub-contractor recently of the condition of trade, he said in answer to my query, "Why, the coat I used to get $3 for making two years ago, I now get $1.50 for. Then I was treated with some consideration, some respect, but since the invasion . . . of the tenement house workers I am glad to take just what I can get without making a remark, lest I be subject to insult and deprived of all work. It is a tremendous odds to be competing against, and the few of us who strive to keep shops would gladly hail the enactment of a law compelling all to do likewise." I will cite just a few instances that you may get a faint idea of some of the prevailing conditions.

In visiting what I can only describe as an old tinder box a few days since, I found three different contractors with men, women and boys amounting in the aggregate upwards of sixty. The drinking water was drawn in buckets and filled into a tin boiler, each day's sediment going to the bottom (for it was never cleaned,) only to be rolled

---

Fourth Annual Report of the Factory Inspector of the Commonwealth of Pennsylvania. For the Year 1893 (n.p.: Clarence M. Busch, 1894), pp. 38–39.

and raised by each day's filling. Cigarettes were being smoked at such a rate as to make the air blue; confusion reigned supreme; coal ashes were strewn all over the floor; this coupled with scraps of basting threads, clippings of cloth, etc., went to make up a most trying picture. In the midst of it all sat a young man who was temporarily disengaged from his work, eating a dark colored piece of bread with mustard. Out of the rooms and in the hallway was one water closet in a vile condition, and the stairway gave evidence of mistaken use too disgusting to mention.

Another was a building three stories high in which rag sorting was the main occupation. On the ground floor I discovered the wife of the proprietor and three of her children, aged 3, 5 and 8 respectively, the mother was acting as purchaser and sorter in the absence of the man. The children naturally were close beside her; when she sorted, they tried to help her; when she weighed they stood around the scales looking worldly wise. On I went to the second story and there discovered a number of old women working, who, from all appearances, were closing in on their three score years, they were surrounded by rags of the filthiest kind. After a general survey of this room I ascended still higher only to find more old women on the third floor, occupied in like manner as those on the floor below. The odor that pervaded this room was vile in the extreme. I immediately set to work to fathom the cause, when, lo and behold, there in a corner was a bin which was used as a receptacle for dog manure. I could scarcely believe my eyes, but there it was, and there it had been for the best part of the summer months, so the women told me. This is but a brief account of much more that could be enumerated by me, for this is the dark side of our darkest Philadelphia, and when I discover the reckless spirit manifest among those people, their total disregard for any law, only that which (as they themselves tell me) will bring them dollars and cents, I fear for the future.

4. Industrialist George M. Pullman Explains the Strike at Pullman Palace Car Works, 1894

The depression in the car-building business, which began in 1893, manifested itself not only in a falling off in the prices for cars, averaging in all classes 24%, but in such stagnation that the force in the Pullman shops on November 1st, 1893, was less than 1,100, while the average number employed in the fiscal year ending July 31st, 1893, was 4,497. In the months of August and September, 1893, we had an opportunity of making only six bids for work, of which but three were accepted.

In order to procure car-building contracts a reduction of the wages of April, 1893, of the car shop employes, averaging 19% was made, to make them correspond with those paid by other car manufacturers, and by making bids at shop cost and less, we secured work aggregating about $1,500,000, and were underbid on bids for nearly the same amount. On the accepted bids our net loss was over $50,000. By taking this course we had been able by last May to secure work enough to raise the number having employment to nearly 3,300.

"President Pullman's Statement at the Stockholders' Annual Meeting, October 18, 1894," in *The Strike at Pullman* (Pullman, Ill.: Pullman Company, 1894), pp. 39–42.

Although these conditions were carefully explained to a large committee of the shop employes, three-fourths of them were persuaded to enter upon the strike, because the company declined to restore wages to the scale of the prosperous times of the early part of 1893. Several suggestions were made to the company that it should consent to arbitration as a means of ending the strike, but it declined to do so upon the ground that it being an ascertained fact that even at the existing rates of wages, car building contracts could only be procured for execution at actual and serious losses, the company could not possibly submit to the discretion of any person, not responsible to its shareholders, the question whether or not it should increase its manufacturing losses by any increase of wages, or even whether or not it should continue the manufacturing of cars at current prices, at the wages complained of. . . .

There has been no substantial change in the condition of the car building business, and the contracts taken by us before the strike, and those taken since the strike, are being executed at prices which give no profit, and such contracts are taken because the shops are being kept in operation for the repairing of the company's own cars, and to give as much employment as is possible in the present condition of business.

I have learned in various ways that a good many persons during the strike lost sight of its true origin, and gained the impression that it was influenced by the house rents at Pullman not being lowered when wages were reduced from the high scale of the spring of 1893. That this is not true is shown by the fact that more than two-thirds of the employes who began the strike, were not tenants of the company; indeed, between 500 and 600 of them owned their own homes. . . .

The real cause of complaint during the autumn of 1893 and the succeeding winter was not altogether on account of the scale of wages, but largely because there was not enough work to give an opportunity for anything like full earnings by all the men. . . .

I may observe also, that there have been indications of a feeling in some quarters that this company ought to have maintained the scale of wages existing in the car manufacturing department in April, 1893, without regard to the current selling prices for cars, paying the consequent increased losses in the car-building business out of the company's earnings in the independent business of operating sleeping cars. . . . At what point did a principle take effect that the latter business must be kept going by the former, regardless of their independence or of the discrepancy between the cost and selling price of cars? At the time of the strike 227 of the shop employes had been in the employment of the company for less than a year, and more than half the entire force had been with the company less than five years. Had all of them earned a guaranty of uninterrupted, undiminished wages? . . .

Of the present force at the car shops only about 300 are new employes, and the remainder have returned to their former work with, I believe, a widely prevailing feeling, that they have learned by experience that this company was earnest in befriending them in seeking work for them when little was to be had, and in giving them work at wages which the selling prices of their product did not justify, and that the genuineness of the interest of this company in their welfare is far more to be trusted than the promises of the agitators who misled them.

ESSAYS

The Great Upheaval

JEREMY BRECHER

In the centers of many American cities are positioned huge armories, grim nineteenth-century edifices of brick or stone. They are fortresses, complete with massive walls and loopholes for guns. You may have wondered why they are there, but it has probably never occurred to you that they were built to protect America not against invasion from abroad but against popular revolt at home. Their erection was a monument to the Great Upheaval of 1877.

July 1877 does not appear in many history books as a memorable date, yet it marks the first great American mass strike, a movement that was viewed at the time as a violent rebellion. Strikers seized and closed the nation's most important industry, the railroads, and crowds defeated or won over first the police, then the state militias, and in some cases even the federal troops. General strikes brought work to a standstill in a dozen major cities and strikers took over authority in communities across the nation.

It all began on Monday, July 16, 1877, in the little railroad town of Martinsburg, West Virginia. On that day, the Baltimore and Ohio Railroad cut wages 10 percent, the second cut in eight months. Men gathered around the Martinsburg railroad yards, talking, waiting through the day. Toward evening the crew of a cattle train, fed up, abandoned the train, and other workers refused to replace them.

As a crowd gathered, the strikers uncoupled the engines, ran them into the roundhouse, and announced to B&O officials that no trains would leave Martinsburg until the pay cut was rescinded. The mayor arrived and conferred with railroad officials. He tried to soothe the crowd and was booed. When he ordered the arrest of the strike leaders they just laughed at him, backed up in their resistance by the angry crowd. The mayor's police were helpless against the population of the town. No railroad workers could be found willing to take out a train, so the police withdrew and by midnight the yard was occupied only by a guard of strikers left to enforce the blockade.

That night, B&O officials in Wheeling went to see Governor Henry Matthews, took him to their company telegraph office, and waited while he wired Col. Charles Faulkner, Jr., at Martinsburg. Matthews instructed Faulkner to have his Berkeley Light Guards "prevent any interference by rioters with the men at work, and also prevent the obstruction of the trains."

The next morning, when the Martinsburg master of transportation ordered the cattle train out again, the strikers' guard swooped down on it and ordered the engineer to stop or to be killed. He stopped. By now, hundreds of strikers and townspeople had gathered, and the next train out hardly moved before it was boarded, uncoupled, and run into the roundhouse.

About 9 a.m., the Berkeley Light Guards arrived to the sound of a fife and drum; the crowd cheered them. Most of the militiamen were themselves railroaders. Now the cattle train came out once more, this time covered with militiamen, their rifles

Jeremy Brecher, "The Great Upheaval," in *Strike!* (Boston: South End Press, 1997), pp. 13–37. Reprinted by permission of South End Press.

loaded with ball cartridges. As the train pulled through the yelling crowd, a striker named William Vandergriff turned a switch to derail the train and guarded it with a pistol. A soldier jumped off the train to reset the switch. Vandergriff shot him and in turn was fatally shot himself.

At this, the attempt to break the blockade at Martinsburg was abandoned. The strikebreaking engineer and fireman climbed down from the engine and departed. Col. Faulkner called in vain for volunteers to run the train, announced that the governor's orders had been fulfilled, dismissed his men, and telegraphed the governor that he was helpless to control the situation.

With this confrontation began the Great Upheaval of 1877, a spontaneous, nationwide, virtually general strike. The pattern of Martinsburg—a railroad strike in response to a pay cut, an attempt by the companies to run trains with the support of military forces, and the defeat or dissolution of those forces by amassed crowds representing general popular support—became the pattern for the nation.

With news of success at Martinsburg, the strike spread to all divisions of the B&O, with engineers, brakemen, and conductors joining with the firemen who provided the initial impetus. Freight traffic was stopped all along the line, while the workers continued to run passenger and mail cars without interference. Seventy engines and six hundred freight cars were soon piled up in the Martinsburg yards.

Governor Matthews, resolved to break the strike, promised to send a company "in which there are no men unwilling to suppress the riots and execute the law." He sent his only available military force, sixty Light Guards from Wheeling. But the Guards were hardly reliable, for the sentiment in Wheeling was strongly in favor of the strike.

The Guards marched out of town surrounded by an excited crowd, who, a reporter noted, "all expressed sympathy with the strikers." Box-makers and can-makers in Wheeling were already on strike and soon people were discussing a general strike of all labor. When the Guards' train arrived in Martinsburg, it was met by a large, orderly crowd. The militia's commander conferred with railroad and town officials, but dared not use the troops, lest they "further exasperate the strikers." Instead, he marched the Guards away to the courthouse. . . .

This "insurrection" was spontaneous and unplanned, but it grew out of the social conditions of the time and the recent experience of railway workers. The tactics of the railroad strikers had been developed in a series of local strikes, mostly without trade union support, that occurred in 1873 and 1874. In December 1873, for example, engineers and firemen on the Pennsylvania Railroad system struck in Chicago, Pittsburgh, Cincinnati, Louisville, Columbus, Indianapolis, and various smaller towns, in what Ohio's *Portsmouth Tribune* called "the greatest railroad strike" in the nation's history.

Huge crowds gathered in depot yards and supported the strikers against attempts to run the trains. State troops were sent into Dennison, Ohio, and Logansport, Indiana, to break strike strongholds. At Susquehanna Depot, Pennsylvania, three months later, shop and repair workers struck. After electing a "Workingmen's Committee," they seized control of the repair shops; within twenty minutes the entire works was "under complete control of the men." The strike was finally broken when 1,800 Philadelphia soldiers with thirty pieces of cannon established martial law in the town of 8,000.

The railroad strikes of 1873 and 1874 were generally unsuccessful; but, as historian Herbert Gutman wrote, they "revealed the power of the railroad workers to disrupt traffic on many roads." The employers learned that "they had a rather tenuous hold on the loyalties of their men. Something was radically wrong if workers could successfully stop trains for from two or three days to as much as a week, destroy property, and even 'manage' it as if it were their own." . . .

The more immediate background of the 1877 railroad strike also helps explain why it took the form of virtual insurrection, for this struggle grew out of the failure of other, less violent forms of action. The wage cut on the B&O was part of a pattern initiated June 1 by the Pennsylvania Railroad. When the leaders of the Brotherhoods of Engineers, Conductors, and Firemen made no effort to combat the cut, railroad workers on the Pennsylvania system took action themselves. A week before the cut went into effect, the Newark, New Jersey, division of the Engineers held an angry protest meeting against the cut. The Jersey City lodge met the next day, voted for a strike, and contacted other workers; by the day the cut took effect, engineers' and firemen's locals throughout the Pennsylvania system had chosen delegates to a joint grievance committee, ignoring the leadership of their national unions.

The wage cut was not the workers' only concern; the committee proposed what amounted to a complete reorganization of work. They opposed the system of assigning trains in which the first crew into town was the first crew out, leaving them no time to rest or see their families; they wanted regular runs to stabilize pay and work schedules; they wanted passes home in case of long layovers; and they wanted the system of "classification" of workers by length of service and efficiency—used to keep wages down—abolished.

But the grievance committee delegates were easily intimated and cajoled by Tom Scott, the masterful ruler of the Pennsylvania Railroad, who talked them into accepting the cut without consulting those who elected them. A majority of brakemen, many conductors, and some engineers wanted to repudiate the committee's action; but, their unit broken, the locals decided not to strike.

Since the railroad brotherhoods had clearly failed, the workers' next step was to create a new, secret organization, the Trainmen's Union. It was started by workers on the Pittsburgh, Fort Wayne and Chicago line. Within three weeks, lodges had sprung up from Baltimore to Chicago, with thousands of members on many different lines. The Trainmen's Union recognized that the privileged engineers "generally patched things up for themselves," so it included conductors, firemen, brakemen, switchmen, and others as well as engineers. The union also realized that the various railroad managements were cooperating against the workers, one railroad after another imitating the Pennsylvania with a 10 percent wage cut. The union's strategy was to organize at least three-quarters of the trainmen on each trunk line, then strike against the cuts and other grievances. When a strike came, firemen would not take engineers' jobs and workers on nonstriking roads would not handle struck equipment.

But the union was full of spies. On one railroad the firing of members began only four days after the union was formed, and other railroads followed suit. "Determined to stamp it out," as one railroad official put it, the company issued orders to discharge all men belonging to "the Brotherhood or Union." Nonetheless, on June 24 forty men fanned out over the railroads to call a general railroad strike for the following week. The railroads learned about the strike through their spies, fired the strike committee in a body, and thus panicked part of the leadership into spreading false word that the strike was off. Local lodges, unprepared to act on their own, flooded the union headquarters with telegrams asking what to do. Union officials were denied use of railroad telegraphs to reply, the companies ran their trains, and the strike failed utterly.

Thus the Martinsburg strike broke out because the B&O workers had discovered that they had no alternative but to act on their own initiative. Not only were their wages being cut, but, as one newspaper reported, the men felt they were "treated just as the rolling stock or locomotives"—squeezed for every drop of profit. Reduced crews were forced to handle extra cars, with lowered pay classifications and no extra pay for overtime. . . .

On July 19, four days into the strike, 300 federal troops arrived in Martinsburg to quell the "insurrection" and bivouacked in the roundhouse. With militiamen and U.S. soldiers guarding the yards, the company was able to move a few trains loaded with U.S. regulars through the town. When 100 armed strikers tried to stop a train, the sheriff and the militia marched to the scene and arrested the leader. No one in Martinsburg would take out another train, but with the military in control, strikebreakers from Baltimore were able to run freights unimpeded. The strike seemed broken.

But the population of the surrounding area also now rallied behind the railroad workers. Hundreds of unemployed and striking boatmen on the Chesapeake and Ohio Canal lay in ambush at Sir John's Run, where they stoned the freight train that had broken the Martinsburg blockade, forced it to stop, and then hid when the U.S. regulars attacked. The movement soon spread into Maryland, where a crowd of boatmen, railroaders, and others swarmed around the train at Cumberland and uncoupled the cars. When the train finally got away, a mob at Keyser, West Virginia, ran it onto a side track and took the crew off by force—while the U.S. troops stood by helplessly. Just before midnight, the miners of the area met at Piedmont, four miles from Keyser, and resolved to go to Keyser in the morning and help stop trains. Coal miners and others—"a motley crowd, white and black"—halted a train guarded by fifty U.S. regulars after it pulled out of Martinsburg. At Piedmont a handbill was printed warning the B&O that 15,000 miners, the united citizenry of local communities, and "the working classes of every state in the Union" would support the strikers. "Therefore let the clashing of arms be heard . . . in view of the rights and in the defense of our families we shall conquer, or we shall die." . . .

Faced with the spread of the strike through Maryland, the president of the B&O now persuaded Governor John Carroll of Maryland to call up the National Guard in Baltimore and send it to Cumberland. They did not expect, however, the reaction of Baltimore to the strike. "The working people everywhere are with us," said a leader of the railroad strikers in Baltimore. "They know what it is to bring up a family on ninety cents a day, to live on beans and corn meal week in and week out, to run in debt at the stores until you cannot get trusted any longer, to see the wife breaking down under privation and distress, and the children growing up sharp and fierce like wolves day after day because they don't get enough to eat."

The bells rang in Baltimore for the militia to assemble just as the factories were letting out for the evening, and a vast crowd assembled as well. At first they cheered the troops, but then severely stoned them as they started to march. The crowd was described as "a rough element eager for disturbance; a proportion of mechanics [workers] either out of work or upon inadequate pay, whose sullen hearts rankled; and muttering and murmuring gangs of boys, almost outlaws, and ripe for any sort of disturbance." As the 250 men of the first regiment marched out, 25 of them were injured by the stoning of the crowd, but this was only a love-tap. The second regiment was unable even to leave its own armory for a time. Then, when the order was given to march anyway, the crowd stoned them so severely that the troops panicked and opened fire. In the bloody march that followed, the militia killed ten and seriously wounded more than twenty of the crowd, but the crowd continued to resist, and one by one the troops dropped out, went home, and changed into civilian clothing. By the time they reached the Baltimore train station, only 59 of the original 120 men remained in line. Even after they reached the depot, the remaining troops were unable to leave for Cumberland, for a crowd of about 200 drove away the engineer and firemen of the waiting train and beat back a squad of policemen who tried to restore control.

The militia charged the growing crowd, but were driven back by brickbats and pistol fire. It was at that stage that Governor Carroll, himself bottled up in the depot by the crowd of 15,000 desperately wired President Hayes to send the U.S. Army.

Like the railroad workers, others joined the "insurrection" out of frustration with other means of struggle. Over the previous years they had experimented with one means of resistance after another, each more radical than the last.

The first to prove their failure had been the trade unions. Craft unions had grown rapidly during and after the Civil War and had organized nationally. The number of national unions grew from six in 1864 to about thirty-three in 1870, enrolling perhaps 5 percent of nonfarm workers. Railroad workers formed the Brotherhoods of Locomotive Engineers, Railway Conductors, and Firemen. But the depression devastated the unions. By 1877 only about nine of these unions survived. Total membership plummeted from 300,000 in 1870 to 50,000 in 1876.

Under depression conditions, the unions were simply unable to withstand the organized attack levied by lockouts and blacklisting. Unemployment demonstrations in New York had been ruthlessly broken up by police. Then the first major industrial union in the United States, the Workingmen's Benevolent Association of the anthracite miners, led a strike that was finally broken by the companies, one of which claimed the conflict had cost it $4 million. Next the Molly Maguires—a secret organization Irish miners developed to fight the coal operators through terrorist methods—were infiltrated and destroyed by agents from the Pinkerton Detective Agency, which specialized in providing spies, agents provocateurs, and private armed forces for employers combating labor organizations. Thus, by the summer of 1877 it had become clear that no single group of workers—whether through peaceful demonstration, tightly-knit trade unions, armed terrorism, or surprise strikes—could stand against the power of the companies, their armed guards, the Pinkertons, and the armed forces of the government.

Indeed, the Great Upheaval had been preceded by a seeming quiescence on the part of workers. The general manager of one railroad wrote on June 21: "The experiment of reducing the salaries has been successfully carried out by all the Roads that have tried it of late, and I have no fear of any trouble with our employees if it is done with a proper show of firmness on our part and they see that they must accept it cheerfully or leave." The very day the strike was breaking out at Martinsburg, Governor John Hartranft of Pennsylvania was agreeing with his adjutant general that the state was enjoying a calm it had not known for several years. In less than a week, it would be the center of the insurrection.

Three days after Governor Hartranft's assessment, the Pennsylvania Railroad ordered that all freights eastward from Pittsburgh be run as "double-headers"— with two engines and twice as many cars. This meant in effect a speed-up—more work and increased danger of accidents and layoffs. Pennsylvania trainmen were sitting in the Pittsburgh roundhouse listening to a fireman read them news of the strike elsewhere when the order came to take out a "double-header." At the last minute a flagman named Augustus Harris, acting on his own initiative, refused to obey the order. The conductor appealed to the rest of the crew, but they too said no. When the company sent for replacements, twenty-five brakemen and conductors refused to take out the train and were fired on the spot. When the dispatcher finally found three yard brakemen to take out the train, a crowd of twenty angry strikers would not let the train go through. One of them threw a link at a strikebreaker, whereupon the volunteer yardmen gave up and went away. Said flagman Andrew Hice, "It's a question of bread or blood, and we're going to resist."

Freight crews joined the strike as their trains came in and were stopped, and a crowd of mill workers, tramps, and boys began to gather at the crossings, preventing freight trains from running while letting passenger trains go through. The company asked the mayor for police, but since the city was nearly bankrupt the force had been cut in half, and only eight men were available. Further, the mayor had been elected by the strong working-class vote of the city, and shared with the city's upper crust a hatred for the Pennsylvania Railroad and its rate discrimination against Pittsburgh. The railroad was given no more than seventeen police, whom it had to pay itself.

As elsewhere, the Trainmen's Union had nothing to do with the start of the strike. Its top leader, Robert Ammon, had left Pittsburgh to take a job elsewhere, and the president of the Pittsburgh Division didn't even know that trouble was at hand; he slept late that morning, didn't hear about the strike until nearly noon—his first comment was "Impossible!"—and then busied himself persuading his colleagues to go home and keep out of trouble.

The Trainmen's Union did, however, provide a nucleus for a meeting of the strikers and representatives of such groups as the rolling-mill workers. "We're with you," said one rolling-mill man, pledging the railroaders support from the rest of Pittsburgh labor. "We're in the same boat. I heard a reduction of ten percent hinted at in our mill this morning. I won't call employers despots, I won't call them tyrants, but the term capitalists is sort of synonymous and will do as well." The meeting called on "all workingmen to make common cause with their brethren on the railroad."

In Pittsburgh, railroad officials picked up the ailing sheriff, waited while he gave the crowd a *pro forma* order to disperse, and then persuaded him to appeal for state troops. That night state officials ordered the militia to be called up in Pittsburgh, but only some of the troops arrived. Some were held up by the strikers, while others simply failed to show up. Two-thirds of one regiment made it; in another regiment not one man appeared. Nor were the troops reliable. As one officer reported to his superior, "You can place little dependence on the troops of your division; some have thrown down their arms, and others have left, and I fear the situation very much."

Another officer explained why the troops were unreliable.

Meeting an enemy on the field of battle, you go there to kill. The more you kill, and the quicker you do it, the better. But here you had men with fathers and brothers and relatives mingled in the crowd of rioters. The sympathy of the people, the sympathy of the troops, my own sympathy, was with the strikers proper. We all felt that those men were not receiving enough wages.

Indeed, by Saturday morning the militiamen had stacked their arms and were chatting with the crowd, eating hardtack with them, and walking up and down the streets with them, behaving, as a regular army lieutenant put it, "as though they were going to have a party." "You may be called upon to clear the tracks down there," said a lawyer to a soldier. "They may call on me," the soldier replied, "and they may call pretty damn loud before they will clear the tracks." . . .

All day Friday, the crowds controlled the switches, and the officer commanding the Pittsburgh militia refused to clear the crossing with artillery because of the slaughter that would result. People swarmed aboard passenger trains and rode through the city free of charge. The sheriff warned the woman and children to leave lest they be hurt when the army came, but the women replied that they were there to urge the men on. "Why are you acting this way, and why is this crowd here?" the sheriff asked one young man who had come to Pittsburgh from Eastern Pennsylvania for the strike. "The Pennsylvania [Road] has two ends," he replied, "one in Philadelphia and one in Pittsburgh. In Philadelphia they have a strong police force, and they're with the railroad. But in Pittsburgh they have a weak force, and it's a mining and manufacturing district, and we can get all the help we want from the laboring elements, and we've determined to make the strike here."

"Are you a railroader?" the sheriff asked.

"No, I'm a laboring man," he replied.

Railroad and National Guard officials, realizing that the local Pittsburgh militia units were completely unreliable, sent for 600 fresh troops from its commercial rival, Philadelphia. A Pittsburgh steel manufacturer came to warn railroad officials not to send the troops out until workingmen were back in their factories. "I think I know the temper of our men pretty well, and you would be wise not to do anything until Monday. . . . If there's going to be firing, you ought to have at least ten thousand men, and I doubt if even that many could quell the mob that would be brought down on us."

These words were prophetic. But, remembering the 2,000 freight cars and locomotives lying idle in the yards, and the still effective blockade, the railroad official replied, "We must have our property." He looked at his watch and said,

"We have now lost an hour and a half's time." He had confidently predicted that "the Philadelphia regiment won't fire over the heads of the mob." Now the massacre he counted on—and the city's retaliation—was at hand.

As the imported troops marched toward the 28th Street railroad crossing, a crowd of 6,000 gathered, mostly spectators. The troops began clearing the tracks with fixed bayonets and the crowd replied with a furious barrage of stones, bricks, coal, and possibly revolver fire. Without orders, the Philadelphia militia began firing as fast as it could, killing twenty people in five minutes as the crowd scattered. Meanwhile, the local Pittsburgh militia members stood on the hillside and ran for cover when they saw the Philadelphia regiment's Gatling gun come forward. Soon most militia members went home or joined the mob.

With the crossing cleared, the railroad fired up a dozen doubleheaders, but even trainmen who had previously declined to join the strike now refused to run the trains, and the strike remained unbroken. Their efforts in vain, the remaining members of the Philadelphia militia retired to the roundhouse.

Meanwhile, the entire city mobilized in a fury against the troops who had conducted the massacre and against the Pennsylvania Railroad. Workers rushed home from their factories for pistols, muskets, and butcher knives. A delegation of 600 workingmen from nearby Temperanceville marched in with a full band and colors. In some cases the crowd organized itself into crude armed military units, marching together with drums. Civil authority collapsed in the face of the crowd; they mayor refused to send police or even to try to quiet the crowd himself.

The crowd peppered the troops in the roundhouse with pistol and musket fire, but finally decided, as one member put it, "We'll have them out if we have to roast them out." Oil, coke, and whiskey cars were set alight and pushed downhill toward the roundhouse. A few men began systematically to burn the yards, despite rifle fire from the soldiers, while the crowd held off fire trucks at gunpoint. The roundhouse caught fire and the Philadelphia militia was forced to evacuate. As it marched along the street it was peppered with fire by the crowd and, according to the troops' own testimony, by Pittsburgh policemen as well. Most of the troops were marched out of town and found refuge a dozen miles away. The few left to guard ammunition found civilian clothes, sneaked away, and hid until the crisis was over. By Saturday night, the last remaining regiment of the Pittsburgh militia was disbanded. The crowd had completely routed the army.

On Sunday morning, hundreds of people broke into the freight cars in the yards and distributed goods they contained to the crowds below—on occasion with assistance from police. Burning of cars continued. (According to first U.S. Commissioner of Labor Carroll D. Wright, "A great many old freight cars which must soon have been replaced by new, were pushed into the fire by agents of the railroad company," to be added to the damages they hoped to collect from Allegheny County.) The crowd prevented firemen from saving a grain elevator, though it was not owned by the railroad, saying, "It's a monopoly, and we're tired of it," but workers pitched in to prevent the spread of the fire to nearby tenements. By Monday, 104 locomotives, more than 2,000 cars, and all of the railroad buildings had been destroyed.

Across the river from Pittsburgh, in the railroad town of Allegheny, a remarkable transfer of authority took place. Using the pretext that the governor was out of the state, the strikers maintained that the state militia was without legal authority, and therefore proposed to treat them as no more than a mob. According to the mayor, the strikers armed themselves by breaking into the local armory, dug rifle pits and trenches outside the Allegheny depot, set up patrols, and warned civilians away from the probable line of fire. The strikers took possession of the telegraph and sent messages up and down the railway. They took over management of the railroad, running passenger trains smoothly, moving the freight cars out of the yards, and posting regular armed guards to watch over them. Economic management and political power had in effect been taken over by the strikers. Of course, this kind of transfer of power was not universally understood or supported, even by those who approved of the strike. For example, a meeting of rolling-mill workers in Columbus, Ohio, endorsed the railroad strikers, urged labor to combine politically and legislate justice, but rejected "mobbism" as apt to destroy "the best form of republican government."

The strike spread almost as fast as word of it, and with it came conflict with the military. In the Pennsylvania towns of Columbia, Meadville, and Chenago, strikers seized the railroads, occupied the roundhouses, and stopped troop trains. In Buffalo, New York, the militia was stoned on Sunday but scattered the crowd by threatening to shoot. The next morning a crowd armed with knives and cudgels stormed into the railroad shops, brushed aside militia guards, and forced shopmen to quit work. They seized the Erie roundhouse and barricaded it. When a militia company marched out to recapture the property, a thousand people blocked it and drove it back. By Monday evening, all the major railroads had given up trying to move anything but local passenger trains out of Buffalo. . . .

. . . [T]he movement was no longer simply a railroad strike. With the battles between soldiers and crowds drawn from all sectors of the working population, it was increasingly perceived as a struggle between workers as a whole and employers as a whole. This was now reflected in the rapid development of general strikes. After the burning of the railroad yards in Pittsburgh, a general strike movement swept through the area. At nearby McKeesport, workers of the National Tube Works gathered and marched all over town to martial music, calling fellow workers from their houses. From the tube works the strike spread first to a rolling mill, then a car works, and then a planing mill. In mid-morning, 1,000 McKeesport strikers marched with a brass band to Andrew Carnegie's great steel works, calling out planing-mill and tin-mill workers as they went. By mid-afternoon, the Carnegie workers and the Braddocks car workers joined the strike. At Castle Shannon, 500 miners struck. On the South Side, laborers struck at Jones and Laughlin and at the Evans, Dalzell and Co. pipe works. . . .

In San Francisco, 7,000 attended a rally called by the Workingmen's Party, a national organization that had been formed the year before by predominantly immigrant followers of Karl Marx and Ferdinand Lassalle. The speakers demanded the eight-hour day and government operation of the struck railroads. But the movement soon was swamped by burgeoning hostility to the 50,000 Chinese workers who had been brought to California to build the railroads, many of whom had then been abandoned by the railroad companies and were finding their way into other occupations. At the Workingmen's Party rally someone in the crowd proposed the appointment of a committee to demand the discharge of Chinese workers from the

Central Pacific, but the chair refused to entertain the motion. The rally ended peacefully, but in its wake gangs began attacking Chinese laundries and residences. Several nights of anti-Chinese rioting were finally brought to an end by police and a Committee of Safety.

In Chicago, the Workingmen's Party called a series of mass rallies. At the same time, forty switchmen struck on the Michigan Central Railroad. The switchmen roamed through the railroad property with a crowd of 500 others, including strikers from the East who had ridden in to spread the strike, calling out other workers and closing down those railroads that were still running. Next the crowd called out the workers at the stockyards and several packinghouses. Smaller crowds spread out to broaden the strike; one group, for example, called out 500 planing-mill workers, and with them marched down Canal Street and Blue Island Avenue closing down factories. Crews on several lake vessels struck. With transportation dead, the North Chicago rolling mill and many other industries closed for lack of coke and other supplies.

The next day the strike spread still further: streetcars, wagons, and buggies were stopped; tanneries, stoneworks, clothing factories, lumberyards, brickyards, furniture factories, and a large distillery were closed in response to roving crowds. A day later the crowds forced officials at the stockyards and gasworks to sign promises to raise wages to $2 a day, while more dock and lumberyard workers struck. In the midst of this burgeoning activity, the Workingmen's Party proclaimed: "Fellow Workers . . . Under any circumstances keep quiet until we have given the present crisis a due consideration." . . .

. . . "This insurrection," said General Winfield Hancock, the commander in charge of all federal troops used in the strike, must be stifled "by all possible means." Not that the federal troops were strong and reliable. The Army was largely tied down by the rebellion of Nez Perce Indians, led by Chief Joseph. In the words of Lieutenant Philip Sheridan, "The troubles on the Rio Grande border, the Indian outbreak on the western frontier of New Mexico, and the Indian war in the Departments of the Platte and Dakota, have kept the small and inadequate forces in this division in a constant state of activity, almost without rest, night and day." Most of the enlisted men had not been paid for months, because Congress had refused to pass the Army Appropriations Bill to force the withdrawal of Reconstruction troops from the South. Finally, the Army included many workers driven into military service by unemployment. As one union iron molder in the Army wrote, "It does not follow that a change of dress involves a change of principle." No mutinies occurred, however, as the 3,000 available federal troops were rushed under direction of the War Department from city to city, wherever the movement seemed to grow out of control. "The strikers," President Hayes noted emphatically in his diary, "have been put down by *force*." More than 100 of them were killed in the process.

The Great Upheaval was an expression of the new economic and social system in America, just as surely as the cities, railroads, and factories from which it had sprung. The enormous expansion of industry after the Civil War had transformed millions of people who had grown up as farmers, self-employed artisans, and entrepreneurs into employees, growing thousands of whom were concentrated within each of the new corporate empires. Their work was no longer individual, but collective; they no longer directed their own work, but worked under control of a boss; they no longer controlled the property on which they worked or its fruits, and therefore could not find gainful employment unless someone with property agreed to hire them. The Great Upheaval grew out of workers' intuitive sense that they needed each other, had each other's support, and together were powerful.

This sense of unity was not embodied in any centralized plan or leadership, but in the feelings and action of each participant. "There was no concert of action at the start," the editor of *The Labor Standard* pointed out. "It spread because the workmen of Pittsburgh felt the same oppression that was felt by the workmen of West Virginia and so with the workmen of Chicago and St. Louis." In Pittsburgh, concludes historian Robert Bruce, "Men like Andrew Hice or Gus Harris or David Davis assumed the lead briefly at one point or another, but only because they happened to be foremost in nerve or vehemence." In Newark, Ohio, "no single individual seemed to command the . . . strikers. They followed the sense of the meeting, as Quakers might say, on such proposals as one or another of them . . . put forward. Yet they proceeded with notable coherence, as though fused by their common adversity."

The Great Upheaval was in the end thoroughly defeated, but the struggle was by no means a total loss. Insofar as it aimed at preventing the continued decline of workers' living standards, it won wage concessions in a number of cases and undoubtedly gave pause to would-be wage-cutters to come. Insofar as it aimed at a workers' seizure of power, its goal was illusory, for workers as yet formed only a minority in a predominantly agrarian and middle-class society. But the power of workers to virtually stop society, to counter the forces of repression, and to organize cooperative action on a vast scale was revealed in the most dramatic form.

It was not only workers who drew lessons from the Great Upheaval. Their opponents began building up their power as well, symbolized by the National Guard armories whose construction began the following year, to contain upheavals yet to come.

Certain periods, wrote historian Irving Bernstein, bear a special quality in American labor history. "There occurred at these times strikes and social upheavals of extraordinary importance, drama, and violence which ripped the cloak of civilized decorum from society, leaving exposed naked class conflict." Such periods were analyzed before World War I by Rosa Luxemburg and others under the concept of mass strikes. The mass strike, Luxemburg wrote, signifies not just a single act but a whole period of class struggle:

> Its use, its effects, its reasons for coming about are in a constant state of flux. . . . [P]olitical and economic strikes, united and partial strikes, defensive strikes and combat strikes, general strikes of individual sections of industry and general strikes of entire cities, peaceful wages strikes and street battles, uprisings with barricades—all run together and run alongside each other, get in each other's way, overlap each other; a perpetually moving and changing sea of phenomena.

The Great Upheaval was the first—but by no means the last—mass strike in American history.

Remembering Haymarket: Chicago's Labor Martyrs and Their Legacy

JAMES GREEN

On a rainy day in May 1886, as a squad of police marched to disperse a protest rally in Chicago's Haymarket Square, a ferocious explosion cut through the uniformed ranks. The bomb blast of May 4 that killed several policemen, the wild gun fire from police revolvers that took the lives of fifty or more workers, the sensational trial of the anarchists accused of the bombing, the public hanging of the four anarchist martyrs on Black Friday 11 November 1887, and the controversial pardon of the remaining defendants—all these dramatic events were remembered by workers engaged in the labor and radical movements for the next fifty years. During that time movement people were deeply divided about how to remember the Haymarket martyrs: as innocent victims of the grand struggle for the eight-hour day or as irresponsible anarchists who provoked a "red scare" that crippled the whole labor movement. . . .

The City

The "milieu de mémoire" in this story is the booming city of Chicago in the 1870s and 1880s, "hog butcher, steel maker to the world," a city segmented along class lines after the Civil War as militant immigrant workers confronted aggressive entrepreneurs; it was the site of the first May Day general strike in 1867 when ten thousand workingmen, led by the molders at the McCormick Reaper works, took direct action for the eight-hour day. Social revolutionaries like Albert Parsons, a Confederate soldier later radicalized by Reconstruction politics in Texas, gained a following among Chicago workers in the years after the brutal repression of the 1877 railroad strike by the police, state militia, and federal troops. One historian even describes a "socialist hegemony over the local labor movement" in these years. Immigrant socialists were far more visible in public than the secretive Knights of Labor and their largely English-speaking leaders. Chicago's vast immigrant working class (76 percent foreign born in 1884) included many newcomers who responded to socialist ideas, especially when articulated by trade union organizers.

After joining the Marxist International Working People's Association (IWPA), Albert Parsons and other social revolutionaries affiliated with Michael Bakunin's breakaway Black International in 1883. While remaining loyal to the teachings of Karl Marx and the principles of communism, they broke with the Second Socialist International because of its emphasis on electoral politics. The Chicago revolutionaries agreed with Johann Most, the bombastic German anarchist, on the need for armed insurrection to overthrow the capitalist state. They also shared his enthusiasm for dynamite as the great equalizer, but unlike Most they believed in the revolutionary potential of the labor movement. The "Chicago idea" placed "the union at the

From James Green, "Remembering Haymarket: Chicago's Labor Martyrs and Their Legacy," in *Taking History to Heart: The Power of the Past in Building Social Movements* (Amherst: University of Massachusetts Press, 2000), pp. 121–144. Reprinted by permission.

center of revolutionary strategy and the nucleus of the future society," writes Paul Avrich, the historian of anarchism.

Socialists and communists of the IWPA influenced Chicago's German and Bohemian immigrants, who constituted many of the forty thousand members of the Central Labor Union (CLU), a dual union formed in 1884 by revolutionaries disaffected with the moderate leadership of the Knights of Labor and the craft unionism of the new Federation of organized Trades and Labor Unions led by pragmatic men. These social revolutionaries, who would later be called anarchists, looked back for inspiration to the Paris Commune, the anniversary of which they celebrated each year in March with remarkably popular ceremonies. In 1879 a "monster" rally attracted 100,000 people to the lake front where a surviving Communard spoke. Nourished by a rich social and cultural life, which included armed self-defense groups (the workers militias), countless picnics and dances, and a vibrant proletarian theater, these ceremonies took place annually for thirty-seven years and "became more elaborate every year," an example of how radical workers created an enduring memorial tradition.

The groundswell of enthusiasm for the eight-hour day among Chicago's un-skilled and unorganized surprised even the revolutionaries. Though the shorter work-day seemed like a mild reform to them, the radicals in the Central Labor Union took leadership of the new movement. In 1884 the Federation of Organized Trades made 1 May 1886 the date for a nationwide general strike, but its leaders acted reluctantly, as did the Knights of Labor. The social revolutionaries filled the void. IWPA women such as Lucy Parsons and Lizzie Swank-Holmes organized in the needle trades, while Albert Parsons, Michael Schwab, and other socialists spread the eight-hour fever to other trades. Skilled organizers and passionate orators, they injected drama into movement culture with daring actions that showed "a flair for the theatrical."

The socialist Central Labor Union caught the rising wave of eight-hour mili-tancy and organized a demonstration on Easter Sunday 1886 in defiance of Chris-tian values. A few days later on that first May Day, eighty thousand striking workers marched down Michigan Avenue demanding "eight hours for work, eight hours for rest and eight hours for play." On May 3 Chicago police shot and killed three pickets at the McCormick works, and that night Albert Parsons and his anarchist comrades met to plan a protest rally in Haymarket Square. That meeting, on the evening of May 4, attracted a smaller crowd than expected—perhaps three thousand—to hear Parsons and other radicals. The city's mayor, concerned about the violence that erupted at McCormick's, had ordered a large squad of police to preserve order. He attended the rally and left, believing the crowd to be calm and orderly. After Parsons spoke and departed, rain threatened to fall and the crowd began to disperse. Only three hundred people remained in the large square as the anarchist Samuel Fielden finished his remarks denouncing the law as being "framed for your enslavers." Sud-denly, alarmed at Fielden's inflammatory language, two detectives hurried to the local police station where 176 police had been ordered to stand ready.

The Event

Soon a squad of 130 police marched out on the square in a military formation. The police captain asked Fielden to disperse the crowd and he agreed. Just as he stepped down from the hay wagon he used as a speakers' platform, someone (a perpetrator was never identified) threw an explosive device into the police ranks. The officers drew their pistols and began firing wildly, shooting blindly for five minutes. Seven police and an unknown number of rally participants and bystanders fell dead or wounded. One reporter estimated fifty civilian deaths. Sixty law officers were wounded and one of them died later. One policemen was killed by the bomb—six others died in the frenzied gunfire from their fellows' revolvers.

The Haymarket police riot lasted only a few minutes, but the explosion and what followed created the most powerful memory in U.S. labor history. And, unlike any other incident in nineteenth-century working-class history, except the Paris Commune, the Haymarket tragedy made an enduring international impact and became part of an oppositional memory constructed by workers outside of the United States where the official memory sought to criminalize the martyrs.

The chaos in the square provoked the first serious "red scare" in America. The *New York Times* editorial was typical: it called for a Gatling gun solution to the outbreak of anarchy and for the use of "hemp" in "judicious doses." In Chicago, where a state of martial law existed for two months, hundreds of men and women, mostly immigrants, were rounded up and interrogated. Employers and their allies seized on the bombing to discredit the eight-hour movement and the Knights of Labor, whose leaders failed to escape blame by denouncing the anarchists. Chicago's law officers and its press constructed a narration of what happened in the square to absolve the police of responsibility. They manufactured evidence of a horrible dynamite plot aimed at the complete destruction of Chicago.

The official interpretation of the Haymarket "riot" justified a massive assault on labor and radical movements in Chicago and elsewhere. As John Higham wrote in *Strangers in the Land:* "For years, the memory of Haymarket and the dread of imported anarchy haunted the American consciousness. No image prevailed more widely than that of the immigrant as a lawless creature, given over to violence and disorder." The bombing provoked a wave of anti-immigrant and anti-radical repression, including an Illinois "criminal syndicalism law" denying free speech to anarchists.

The memory of Haymarket caused awful problems for mainstream labor and socialist party leaders. The conservative Knights of Labor head Terence Powderly refused to plead clemency for the anarchists—a plea made from many foreign quarters, including a group from the French Chamber of Deputies. The German American leaders of the Socialist Labor Party denounced the Chicago anarchists and drew a lesson: given the "overwhelming superior strength" of the employers and their allies, any appeal "to physical force could only incur blood defeats" and retard the growth of socialism. American Socialists, even those like Joseph Buchanan who ardently defended the Haymarket "boys," reached similar conclusions. "The Chicago bomb" convinced Buchanan that until a working-class majority voted and was cheated out of the results, revolutionary action could not be justified. "Men who will not vote right," he used to say, "will not shoot right."

Samuel Gompers, president of the new American Federation of Labor, also condemned the anarchists' methods and blamed them for killing the eight-hour movement and for causing all unions to suffer. But Gompers also appealed for the convicts' lives on the grounds, he later wrote, that "labor must do its best to maintain justice for radicals or find itself denied the rights of freemen." In his clemency plea, Gompers warned the governor of Illinois not to create a memory that would be of use to the "revolutionary movement." Executing the Chicago anarchists would cause "thousands and thousands of labor men all over the world" to look upon the radicals "as martyrs," "executed because they were standing up for free speech and free press." This is exactly what happened as "labor men" invented a memorial tradition out of Haymarket, against the wishes of official leaders who wanted to forget the "catastrophe."

The Hangings

However, trade union and socialist party leaders who disassociated themselves from the Haymarket martyrs discovered that memories of the Chicago anarchists and their travails were widely shared and deeply held among workers in many nations. Protests "swept the European continent" on 11 November 1887, the date when Albert Parsons and three anarchist comrades went to the gallows. Peter Kropotkin, the well-known Russian anarchist, reported no city in Spain and Italy worth naming "where the bloody anniversary was not commemorated by enthusiastic crowds of workers." In these places, he said, "The commemoration of the Chicago martyrs has almost acquired the same importance as the commemoration of the Paris Commune." When Gompers visited European cities in 1895 he noticed "in nearly every labor hall there were pictures of Parsons, Spies, Lingg, etc., and with an inscription: 'Labor's Martyrs to American Capitalism.'" On later visits, he saw "the same pictures still there."

Why did the memory of the Haymarket martyrs endure? The events themselves provide a starting point. The bombing was the most sensational news story of the era: The hunt for suspects also attracted intense press coverage. The spectacularly publicized trial of the eight anarchists accused of the "bombing" created a remarkable drama of its own, including a jailhouse romance between defendant August Spies and the daughter of a prominent Chicago businessman. Faced with the overwhelming power of the state in determining their fate and their memory, the defendants and their supporters plotted a narrative of their own, reversing everything the prosecution charged. "In their narrative interpretation [which became central to the working-class memory of Haymarket] . . . their persecution and even their execution were paradoxically empowering acts . . . that proved all their ideas to be true," Carl Smith writes. In the oppositional memory of Haymarket, the condemned men were recalled as martyrs who died for democracy and freedom while the state relied upon "lies, force and violence to hold it together."

The trial and the hangings of Albert Parsons, August Spies, George Engel, and Adolph Fischer, along with the suicide of Louis Lingg (who killed himself by exploding a dynamite cap in his mouth), produced a "drama without end," because, Smith explains, even those who condemned the anarchists had adopted their view that "urban industrial society [w]as a ticking bomb." After the hangings a prominent Chicago minister said no event since the Civil War had produced "such profound and long continued interest and excitement." These events attracted attention because they occurred in a "free America and [in] a time of peace" and because they evoked "an apprehensive concern"—a fear that they were but a first phase "of a widespread discontent upon the part of millions of poor people of this and other countries."

The press was obsessed with the anarchists, and some journalists, like the cartoonist Thomas Nast, portrayed them sensationally as demonic bomb throwers. But at the same time, the publicity generated curiosity about the anarchists and what they looked like. Some of the many drawings in the newspapers depicted them as normal human beings. In this melodrama the anarchists themselves played compelling theatrical roles, particularly Albert Parsons, who acted with power and passion in ways that many found unforgettable. Joseph Buchanan, whose rich life as a labor agitator involved many important events, vividly remembered Parsons's boldness many years after his execution. "Every man who has passed the half century mile post has stored away in his memory cabinets pictures which illustrate important events—mayhap crises—in his past life," he observed. "Sometimes they steal out from their hiding-places unbidden, and they lead the thought procession back to other days." In that "small cabinet" where Buchanan "stored the few pictures" he called "my tragedies," one often stole out: the scene recreated his audience with the governor of Illinois when Buchanan made one of the last clemency please for "the Haymarket boys." First, he read a letter from Spies, who offered to die in place of the others and appealed only to "the judgement of history." Buchanan then turned to a short note from Parsons that he had not yet seen in which the condemned man asked that if he was to die, he be granted a reprieve only so that his wife and two children could die with him. Everyone in the room gasped and Buchanan nearly broke down. Partly through such dramatic gestures, Parsons and his comrades found their way into "the memory cabinets" of many labor activists.

The Haymarket story reached a sensational climax on 11 November 1887 with the hanging of the four anarchists—the "Black Friday" long remembered in labor and radical movements. Perhaps the intensive media coverage of the executions (especially the graphic on the cover of *Leslie's Weekly*) perpetuated the event's memory. Public hangings were intended to dramatize punishment and memorialize pain. . . . [But in the] Haymarket case the defendants were presumed innocent even after "proven guilty"—an innocence proclaimed by important public figures like Congressman Robert Ingersoll, Senator Lyman Trumbull, William Dean Howells, Henry Demarest Lloyd, and Illinois governor John Peter Altgeld.

The Martyrs

The innocence of the Haymarket martyrs seemed to make them especially tragic victims. Their heroism and stoicism added to their allure. Seeking to explain why the Haymarket episode "made such a powerful and lasting impression," one historian turned to Peter Kropotkin's observation that while others had died for labor's cause, none had been "so enthusiastically adopted by the workers as their martyrs." The moral qualities of the defendants appealed to workmen who believed the victims to be "thoroughly honest" as well as innocent. They "had no ambition," said Kropotkin, and "sought no power over others." Dedicated to their fellow workers and to their principles, they refused to plead for clemency on their own behalf during the entire year they awaited death. Even on the scaffold, "they hailed the day on which they died for those principles." As Kropotkin wrote one year after their execution: "Such men can inspire the generations to come with the noblest feelings."

But the anarchist movement did not depend solely upon inspiration to keep memories of Haymarket alive. The martyrs' families and supporters ritualized the act of remembering and began to do so immediately with a funeral many witnesses would never forget. After struggling with city officials who prohibited red flags and banned revolutionary songs, the anarchists led a large parade silently through Chicago's working-class neighborhoods on the long walk to Chicago's Waldheim Cemetery, a burial place for many of the city's German Jews. On Sunday 13 November 1887 thousands of workers marched in a funeral procession behind the bodies of the anarchists, past a half-million people who lined the streets to watch. Only when they reached the cemetery outside the city limits did they begin to sing "the Marseillaise"—the tune Parsons sang before his execution.

The mourners made Waldheim a "monumental memory site" partly because they were barred from access to the real "milieu de mémoire"—Haymarket Square. In his guide to the area for the Illinois Labor History Society, William Adelman describes the tempestuous history of this Square—a quintessential urban public space that like most markets, was a common gathering place for farmers, small traders, and plebeians of all sorts. It was so large that the Chicago anarchists chose it for the May 4 protest because they actually believed twenty thousand people would attend their rally. Nearby stood union halls so filled with eight-hour strike meetings the evening of May 3 that the anarchists planning the protest rally had to gather in the basement.

Soon after the Haymarket riot, the conservative *Chicago Tribune* started a fund drive to erect a statue in the square to memorialize the fallen police officers. The paper was owned by Cyrus McCormick, whose militant workers spearheaded the eight-hour movement. Many industrialists contributed and a statue of a policeman with an upraised arm was dedicated on Memorial Day 1889. The statue, which symbolized the authoritative memory of the bombing would experience a troubled history. In 1903 part of the inscription was stolen and later a streetcar operator ran his train off the track and knocked the statuary policeman off its base. The driver said he was tired of seeing that policeman with his arm raised in the air.

The police status symbolized an important activity for the forces of law and order: restricting urban public spaces from use by an insurgent working class. The labor movement could not reclaim the square itself for a memorial to mourn the workers who died there. But those who sought to preserve the memory of the martyrs could challenge official apportionments of "ceremonial space and time" by commemorating the anarchists' death every November 11 at Waldheim Cemetery.

The Monument

In the years that followed the executions, the official story of the riot was tarnished when the very same Chicago police who led the charge on the square were discredited by charges of corruption. In 1893 the AFL's Chicago Trades and Labor Assembly joined radicals and progressives, including the famous defense attorney Clarence Darrow, in asserting that the defendants had been denied a fair trail and in demanding a pardon for the three anarchists who remained in prison. On 25 June 1893 thousands of unionists again converged on Waldheim to dedicate a statue at the gravesite. Many foreign visitors from the Columbian Exposition boarded special trains to attend the ceremony nine miles from Haymarket. The statue, inspired by a lyric in the "Marseillaise," was forged in bronze in the form of a hooded woman laying a laurel wreath on the brow of a dying worker. It resembled earlier art in the French republican tradition in which strong female figures symbolized liberty and justice. The martyrs' followers created a place of memory with a monument at Waldheim in order to advance the work of remembering.

The day after the dedication, the new populist governor of Illinois, John Peter Altgeld—himself a German immigrant—pardoned the three other Haymarket defendants and ensured his own political demise. The governor's statement—a remarkably radical one for a public official—blamed repressive police action for the bombing tragedy, claimed evidence had been fabricated, and accused the trial judge of "malicious ferocity." This courageous statement added enormous power to the memory of the Haymarket defendants as innocent victims of a "judicial hanging." Altgeld himself, "the forgotten eagle" in Vachel Lindsay's poem, was in fact remembered, perhaps longer than any other governor, as a politician who put truth and honesty above ambition.

These events heightened the significance of the Haymarket martyrs' grave as a site of memory. "Waldheim, with its hauntingly beautiful monument, became a revolutionary shrine, a place of pilgrimage for anarchists and socialists from all over the world," writes historian Paul Avrich. For decades, it drew more visitors than the statue of Illinois's favorite son, the martyred President Lincoln. Always ready to repress radicalism, the Chicago police drew more attention to the site by placing "restrictions on the annual memorial ceremonies" and threatening to ban them entirely—a sign of things to come. . . .

The martyrs' lives and deaths provided a redemptive narrative for a whole generation of radicals who told the anarchists' story repeatedly in speeches and writings that appeared in many languages. After the Chicago trial Emma Goldman "devoured every line on anarchism I could get, every word I could get about the men, their lives their work." Their execution "crushed her spirits" at first but then caused her "spiritual rebirth," giving her a "burning faith, a determination to dedicate myself to the memory of my martyred comrades, to make their cause my own." . . . Eugene V. Debs, who became a socialist after being imprisoned for leading the great Pullman rail strike of 1894, prayed at the martyrs' graves after his release from jail, just before he went to downtown Chicago to be greeted by a quarter-of-a-million workers. . . .

No one in that remarkable "traveling community of radicals" worked harder to keep the dead alive in memory than Albert Parsons's widow. Lucy Parsons dedicated her life to preserving the legacy of her martyred husband and his comrades. She became a cause célèbre in Chicago when the police chief vowed to prevent her from speaking in public. Her fame grew outside of Chicago when in 1889 she published *The Life of Albert Parsons,* a remarkable book that held a "weird fascination" for one reviewer who wrote that "few stories in our literature hold such dramatic power as this . . . a tale of chivalry so exalted, with an ending so tragic and pathetic," that it seemed like a classic romance. Throughout the grim nineties Lucy Parsons continued memorializing the martyrs during her speaking tours, especially on November 11 when the hanging was remembered in many cities. . . .

The First Day of May

The memory of the martyrs also endured because many workers associated their deaths with the celebration of May Day and with the struggle for the eight-hour day—the issue that led to the choice of May 1 as a workers holiday by the 1889 International Socialist Congress in Paris. The Marxist champions of May Day had been active in the protests against the Haymarket executions and were well aware that the martyrs' memory was linked to the May 1 general strike of 1886. Many Italian immigrants in the United States observed May Day as "la pasgua dei lavoratori" (The Easter of the workers). Some of them learned of the Chicago martyrs for the first time in picnic songs and in speeches by charismatic anarchists like Luigi Galleani who often referred to the incident as an example of how American democracy could be as oppressive as European tyranny. Radicals recalled that all the Haymarket defendants were immigrants, except Parsons, and predicted that their fate awaited others in this so-called land of liberty.

The remembrance of the Haymarket martyrs on May 1 was more than ceremonial. Their martyrdom became a keystone in constructing a homily of supreme sacrifice for workers' movements on the ascendancy in many capitalists nations during the 1880s. Confronting aggressive employers, hostile churches and newspapers, and militarized police forces, these movements needed issues like the eight-hour day, tactics like the mass strike, and heroes like the Haymarket martyrs. Movement builders found all these things in the tragic Chicago story.

More than at any time in the subsequent century, radical movements identified across national boundaries—sharing common issues like the eight-hour day, fighting common struggles for trade union legality, and using similar tactics like the militant strike. The Chicago martyrs became their common heroes. Revolutionaries excited by the worker insurgencies of the 1870s and 1880s exerted a remarkable influence on labor movements around the world; and among them, the anarchists of the Black International exercised an outsized influence. . . .

In the United States labor radicals found it more difficult to perpetuate Haymarket rituals. During the early 1900s anarchists maintained November 11 as a memorial day, but the occasion lost its power to attract pilgrims even before World War I. After 1890 anarchists and socialists failed to revive May Day as an occasion for remembering the martyrs—that is, until another sensational murder trial in 1906 promised to send three more labor radicals to the gallows. Pinkertons and law officers kidnapped [the prominent radical] Bill Haywood and took him with two other union militants to stand trial in Idaho for the dynamite murder of that state's former governor. The labor and socialist movements roused themselves in furious protest. They revived May Day in 1907 as an occasion of mammoth demonstrations, especially in New York where over 100,000 immigrants marched all day, and even in Boston, hardly a radical labor town, where nearly as many rallied on the common.

The "spectacular show trial" in Idaho not only allowed the socialist movement to resurrect May Day, it provided a powerful occasion for remembering Haymarket. The events of 1886 and 1887 were invoked in the Haywood trial by Clarence Darrow, the defense attorney who had helped win a pardon for the surviving "Haymarket boys," and by Eugene Debs, author of the inflammatory tract "Arouse Ye Slaves," who recalled Haymarket in a threat that infuriated President Theodore Roosevelt. "Nearly twenty years ago," Debs wrote in the *Appeal to Reason,* "the capitalist tyrants put some innocent men to death for standing up for labor. They are now going to try to do it again. Let them dare! There have been twenty years of revolutionary education, agitation, and organization since the Haymarket tragedy, and if an attempt is made to repeat it, there will be a revolution and I will do all in my power to precipitate it."

Haywood and his comrades were acquitted, May Day was recreated as a memory day, and in 1908 Lucy Parsons, carrying copies of the martyrs' *Famous Speeches,* made such a successful tour of eleven western cities that she decided to reprint the collection. Her tours became even more popular as the IWW preached the Chicago idea of direct-action unionism and reclaimed through dramatic free speech fights the public space closed down to radical labor after Haymarket. But Lucy Parsons also spoke to mainstream union members—for example in New York City where early in 1911 the Central Federated Union endorsed her talks before AFL locals. Then in two cross-country tours she sold ten thousand copies of the new edition of the Haymarket anarchists' *Famous Speeches.* In November, after her return to New York, she and Bill Haywood "spoke to packed November 11th meetings." At a time when many unions fought desperate struggles with the courts and the police and when the AFL adopted a "strong anti-statist outlook" and a posture of "semi-outlawry," trade unionists remembered the Haymarket tragedy as part of a state assault on the labor and eight-hour movements. . . .

A few years later, when anarchists, socialists, and Wobblies faced extinction amid the furies of war, there were other trials to remember—the McNamaras, Mooney and Billings, Carlo Tresca—and other victims to mourn, the women and children murdered at Ludlow, along with the Wobbly martyrs Joe Hill and Frank Little and their comrades massacred in Everett, Washington. The IWW began a new campaign to "remember" these victims in "Black November," but in the next decade, after the destruction of the labor left, few occasions survived in which movement heroes and heroines could be honored.

May Day celebrations were targets of state repression during World War I. Some laws actually banned the flying of the red flag that used to appear at the head of May 1 parades. During the red scare just after the war, May Day marches were violently attacked in several cities. In any case, this holiday had little hope for a revival in the patriotic fervor of the time, a time when the official culture created a very different holiday in May. Memorial Day, at the end of the month, created for the Civil War dead, now became an occasion for honoring soldiers killed in France and for recalling memories of World War I. May Day, as a time of remembering the Haymarket affair, suffered from outright suppression, while November 11, the memorial day of the hangings, faced a different fate in the court of official remembrance. After 1918 this day in November would be celebrated as Armistice Day, a major creation of "patriotic culture"—a veneration of the very state the martyrs had violently opposed and of the soldiers who had died for that nation-state.

The History

Haymarket faded from working-class memory in the deeply repressive era of 1920s. Only private memories of Haymarket survived in individual "memory cabinets." "The act of remembering" Haymarket became an individual one, as is all the real work of remembrance. The memory of 1886–87 events now passed into recorded history. The Haymarket affair became a parable for the conservative interpretation of American history. In his influential six-volume history James Ford Rhodes concluded "that the punishment meted out to the anarchists was legally just." Another prominent historian concurred and added that the "wretches" who assumed "an impudent front" during the trial were found guilty and "merited" their "punishment." Thus did authoritative, academic history seek to negate the radical, proletarian memory of Haymarket.

But one historian unlocked the cabinets of private memory and made old movement recollections of Haymarket part of recorded history. In 1936, during a revival of progressive U.S. historiography, a young historian named Henry David published the first scholarly work on Haymarket that dismissed previous historians' judgments as "historically false." He demonstrated that the seven defendants could not have been guilty of murder given the evidence offered. He even questioned the possibility that the bomb could have been thrown by some other anarchist. The historian went on to challenge the interpretation of labor officials who blamed the anarchists for the failure of the Knights and the eight-hour movement. A scholar who studied at Columbia University, David absorbed the popular memory of Haymarket from Lucy Parsons; from George Schilling, the brilliant Chicago labor leader; and from his own immigrant father, who had an extensive personal knowledge of the American and European revolutionary movement; they passed their memory of the Haymarket directly to the historian. . . .

In 1937, a year after David's book appeared, a revived labor movement, with a historically conscious left wing, recalled the memory of 1887. In November union activists and leftists celebrated the fiftieth anniversary of the Haymarket executions in the Amalgamated Hall in Chicago. It was a year during which the cycle of conflict in the city turned again to anti-union violence. History seemed to be repeating itself. Lucy Parsons and others related to the martyrs spoke at the anniversary and at Waldheim. . . . Parsons referred to the newest tragedy in Chicago labor history. Just a few months before, the same city police who killed three strikers at the McCormick Works on 1 May 1886 shot down ten pickets at the Republic Steel Works on 31 May 1937—Memorial Day. For a short time, the memory of Haymarket became useful to the new industrial unions of the Committee of Industrial Organizations and to the Communists who led some of them.

The press and the authorities blamed the blood shed on Memorial Day 1937 on a "Communist riot," just as they had done after the Haymarket riot. But after a congressional committee viewed a suppressed newsreel of the shooting, the police were accused of killing peaceful strikers. Once again, a battle ensured over the memory of working-class martyrs in Chicago, and once again, influential voices sought absolution for innocent workers accused of being red rioters by the shapers of public opinion. Unexpectedly, the public response to the Memorial Day massacre helped create more protection for workers' rights and civil liberties. As a result, the memory of working-class martyrdom took on a different, less potent meaning. Cognizant of labor's violent past, and the effect of police actions at Haymarket and after, Chicago union leaders came to believe that workers' interests could only be protected by controlling or influencing the government. The Democratic mayor of Chicago repented for his decision to send police to guard Republic Steel's South

Chicago mill on Memorial Day and offered labor so much support that one of the strikers wounded by the police supported the Mayor's reelection campaign in 1939. As Democrats and as citizens, workers began to invest in "the state" because the government seemed to be standing by them in industry and in society as a whole.

The Cemetery

When Lucy Parsons was buried with her husband, her son, and her beloved comrades at Waldheim in 1942, so was one of the last carriers of the "Chicago idea" of revolutionary unionism—an idea based on anarchist and syndicalist hostility to the capitalist state. A few years before her death, Lucy had joined the Communist Party, which now became the principal interpreter of Haymarket and its place of memory, Waldheim Cemetery—this despite the party's hostility to anarchism. During the popular front, Albert Parsons and the "anarchosyndicalists" of 1886 fit into the pantheon of Communist Party heroes as "martyrs of class struggle who gave their all for the emancipation of the working class"—heroes that included some who traced their political lives to Haymarket, notably "Big Bill" Haywood, who before he died in Moscow, asked that half of his ashes be buried in the Kremlin Wall and the other half "scattered at the site of the Martyrs Monument." In 1942 Jack Johnstone, a prominent Chicago Communist and respected labor organizer, asked to be buried with the Haymarket anarchists; so would other party leaders in later years, including William Z. Foster and Elizabeth Gurley Flynn, who as a teenager had been inspired by Lucy Parsons at the IWW founding convention. By sharing sacred ground and by writing labor history that linked anarchists, Wobblies and Communists in a kind of popular front, party intellectuals attempted to absorb the memory of Haymarket within their own tradition.

But during World War II, when the Communist Party disbanded, Waldheim faded as a site memory. It now embodied a "memorial consciousness" that barely survived because "the intimate fund of memory" had disappeared. . . . The Haymarket anarchists no longer served as heroes for a labor movement whose leaders had abandoned old anti-statist traditions. Many union officials, especially the immigrants who rose to power in the new unions, had decided to forget the bloody past of police and military repression, to regret their ancestors' militant radicalism, to block out memories of their rejection as immigrants—all in order to embrace a new version of "working-class Americanism" in which unions (with their ethnic membership) would take their place as a legitimate interest group in a pluralistic society.

By this time those who had experienced Haymarket had died. The oral tradition through which stories of Haymarket had been transmitted barely survived in Cold War America. It was a time when, Marianne Debouzy says, memories of working-class radicalism sank into oblivion as individuals were silenced and as left organizations were dismantled or outlawed, making it difficult for people to share oppositional memories. During the 1950s the grandson of Oscar Neebe, one of the Haymarket defendants pardoned in 1893, traveled to Mexico where he was shocked to learn that his grandfather was a revered proletarian hero. The memory of Oscar Neebe had been suppressed within his own family, which had suffered "many persecutions for Haymarket." Neebe's grandson inherited only his grandfather's name with no knowledge of his famous role in labor history. . . .

The Reclamation

The memory of Haymarket was reclaimed in the 1960s by a new movement whose antiauthoritarian ideas were quite compatible with the beliefs of the Chicago martyrs. Like the anarchists of 1886, some antiwar radicals of the late 1960s believed in the propaganda of the deed; they declared war on a state that made war on Vietnamese insurgents and their supporters. On 4 May 1968, as antiwar demonstrators prepared for militant protests at the Democratic convention in Chicago, someone defaced the police monument in Haymarket Square. On 6 October 1969 the statue was blown up. The Weatherman faction of the Students for a Democratic Society took credit. An enraged Mayor Richard J. Daley promised to replace the edifice. On 4 May 1970— the anniversary of the 1886 bombing—a new statue was dedicated to the police.

While this violent struggle to memorialize the Haymarket victims pitted 1960s anarchists and the forces of law and order, the old voice of the labor movement arose taking its own stand on this site of conflict. The Illinois Labor History Society was formed in 1968 by union progressives like Les Orear, who worked for the Packinghouse Workers, and by labor historians like Bill Adelman, a labor educator. When the Teamsters and a few other unions contributed funds to rebuild the police statue blown up during the 1968 "days of rage," the Society was contacted by Bill Garvey, who edited the Steel Workers' union newspaper. He was dismayed that the scores of workers killed by the police in the 1886 riot had been totally forgotten in the controversy about the memory of the lawmen who died there. In 1969 he joined Labor History Society members in forming a Haymarket Workers' Committee to plan a memorial event in the Square to the innocent union members who lost their lives there simply by coming out to protest the shooting of fellow workers striking for the eight hour day. Garvey rented a hay wagon as a speakers' stand and asked radio personality Studs Terkel to keynote the memorial. The Labor History Society did not oppose the reconstruction of the police statue, but it demanded a compensatory place in Haymarket Square to mark the death of the workers who had gathered there for a peaceful protest in 1886. In 1970 Les Orear joined the Illinois State Historical Commission and persuaded its members to erect a memorial plaque in the square to honor the union dead. It was dedicated on May 4 of that year, but it was soon ripped down by vandals and never restored.

The struggle over Haymarket's divided memory escalated even further. On 6 October [1970] the newly dedicated police statue was bombed again.

Mayor Daley ordered round-the-clock security at the cost of $67,000 a year. Such protection became too costly, so city officials moved the official Haymarket icon indoors to police headquarters. On 4 May 1972 local anarchists and members of the IWW demonstrated at the site and attempted to erect on the empty pedestal of the police statue a paier-mâché bust of Louis Lingg, the anarchist who had cheated the hangman in 1887 by committing suicide in his jail cell. Once again, the Chicago police appeared to clear the square. . . .

Unable to mark the actual place where the workers died in the square, the Labor History Society acquired the deed to the Waldheim monument from the Pioneer Aid and Support Association of friends and family, which had had it constructed in 1893. It then maintained the site, which still attracted visitors from around the world. When the History Society organized a centennial event at the Cemetery in 1986, it even persuaded the Chicago Federation of Labor to endorse the commemoration. As Les Orear recalled, a younger generation now led the labor movement. These union officials were more open to the idea of honoring anarchists as innocent victims and less worried about identifying themselves with the memory of radical martyrs. But this was much too tame for a small band of anarchists who remained active in Chicago; they picketed the event because it was not organized to honor the martyrs as anarchists. Instead, it recalled the sacrifice of worker activists in the popular struggle for the eight-hour-day. Indeed, Chicago Mayor Harold Washington used the occasion to proclaim May Labor History Month, following the precedent of Black History Month in February. Rather than referring to the anarchists as men who died for their beliefs, he spoke to commemorate "the movement towards the eight-hour day, union rights, civil rights, human rights" and to the remembrance of the "tragic miscarriage of justice which claimed the lives of four labor activists."

Finally, . . . the monument at Waldheim gained official memorial status as a national landmark, but only after the directors of the labor-history theme study persuaded the park service to lift its ban on marking cemeteries and graves. . . . The long, patient work of the Illinois Labor History Society reached a successful climax as more than a thousand people came to Waldheim on 4 May 1998 for the official ceremony. The AFL-CIO presence was noticeable. Eight trade union leaders spoke—representative of a younger generation that had not inherited the criminalized memory of Haymarket.

However, unlike Waldheim Cemetery, Haymarket Square itself would remain unmarked, like many other sites of violence in American history. After the explosive events of the 1960s the site was neglected and forgotten, except by the Illinois Labor History Society. In 1982 Harold Washington became the first black mayor of Chicago after running against the old patronage system and its abuses, including police brutality. As part of the centennial anniversary in 1986, the Labor History Society proposed to Mayor Washington that the city recognize the martyrs of 1887 with a memorial park in the square. When Mayor Washington died in office, hopes for a Haymarket Square memorial faded, but not for Mollie West, a Chicago radical and survivor of the 1937 Memorial Day massacre, who clung to her belief that labor history sites, like Haymarket, can provide meaning for working people with no memory of struggles for social justice. She continued to advocate for a Haymarket Square memorial, but she could only imagine its construction through an act of resurrection: "We're waiting for Mayor Washington to come back," she said in 1993. "If he was here, this would've been done by now."

"Memory implies a certain act of redemption," writes John Berger. "What is forgotten has been abandoned . . . [and] with the loss of memory the continuities of meaning and judgment are also lost." More than any story told in American labor history, the Haymarket story preserved a memory of workers innocently victimized, of martyrs whose death gave meaning to the sacrifices made for labor rights and working-class empowerment, and of visionaries who created a labor movement to radically change capitalist society. Those who retold the story in this way rendered a harsh judgment on a city ruled by fear, a judiciary controlled by tyrants, a democracy defined by property.

The Depression of the 1890s

NELL IRVIN PAINTER

The showpiece of American progress, the American steel industry in the valleys of the Monongahela, Mahoning, and Ohio rivers of western Pennsylvania, northeastern Ohio, and northern West Virginia, was technologically sophisticated and efficient. Millions of tons of steel and steel products—rails, armor for railroad cars and locomotives, machines and the machines that made machines (the crucial capital goods sector of the economy)—poured out of the steel region in quantities that rivaled Europe's total output. For Americans who prized progress, this industry offered a splendid symbol of modernity.

The plants of Andrew Carnegie turned out a quarter of the nation's steel production in the mid-1890s, but the industry was still competitive, divided among three or four large companies and several small ones. But labor conditions in the steel industry were exceedingly harsh. For less than subsistence wages, workers put in twelve-hour days and seven-day weeks. In 1892 wage cuts, the early manifestation of hard times, struck the heart of the steel region. A sensational strike at Homestead, Pennsylvania, in 1892 pitted the nation's largest steel producer against the nation's strongest trade union. The bloody struggle ended in military occupation.

Writer Hamlin Garland found the steel town of Homestead "squalid and unlovely," a place whose people seemed "discouraged and sullen." The hot, onerous, dangerous work of attending the gigantic furnaces of the Carnegie mills struck him as downright inhuman. Once every two weeks steelworkers switched shifts and worked a long shift of twenty-four hours, then had twenty-four hours off. Considering the hours and the extremes of heat and cold, Garland wondered after a tour of the open-hearth works how steelworkers survived.

A factory town on the Monongahela River a few miles upstream from Pittsburgh, Homestead was the site of the most modern steelworks in the country. Andrew

Nell Irvin Painter, *Standing at Armageddon: United States, 1877–1919* (New York: W. W. Norton, 1987), 110–140. Copyright © 1987 by Nell Irvin Painter. Used by permission of W. W. Norton & Company, Inc.

Carnegie—the "star-spangled Scotchman"—had bought the mill from Henry Clay Frick in 1882. Carnegie also owned twelve neighboring plants, at Beaver Falls, Duquesne, Braddock, Pittsburgh, and other nearby locations. The Carnegie Steel Company owned every facet of the business, from ore mining to steel distribution, a vertically integrated trust. Thanks to efficient management and the scope of operations, Carnegie's industrial empire made more than $40,000,000 in profits per year in the early 1890s.

During the 1870s and 1880s Carnegie had written about labor sympathetically, insisting that manufacturers should "meet the men *more than half way*" and that "the right of the workingmen to combine and form trade-unions is not less sacred than the right of the manufacturer to enter into association and conferences with his fellows." He said experience had taught him that in general at least, unions were beneficial to both capital and labor, which were natural allies. An apostle of identity of interest, Carnegie preached that cooperative effort served the interests of capital and labor simultaneously. During strikes in the 1880s he had advised Henry Clay Frick, now his plant manager, to bargain with strikers. But in the 1890s Carnegie strengthened his position in the industry and took a harder line.

Carnegie and Frick's adversary at Homestead was the Amalgamated Association of Iron, Steel, and Tin Workers, formed in 1876. At its largest—in 1891—the Amalgamated Association had more than 24,000 members. The best organized and strongest union in the American Federation of Labor, the Amalgamated Association had won a strike at Homestead in 1889. But in 1892 Frick decided to break the union. According to the Homestead managers, the union undermined efficiency by objecting to workers' being fired when laborsaving equipment was installed and by demanding that workers receive higher wages when productivity increased. The union "placed a tax on improvement," a Carnegie partner concluded, "therefore the Amalgamated had to go."

When the contract between the Amalgamated Association and the Homestead mill expired in June 1892, Carnegie was at his castle in Scotland, and he gave Frick a free hand. Carnegie remained in Europe, while Frick broke the strike and the union, using wage cuts as an entering wedge. Instead of bargaining when the union rejected his terms, Frick locked workers out and erected a fence that was eight feet high and three miles long, surrounding the whole property of the Carnegie mill from the railroad to the river. Topped with barbed wire, the fence had a series of holes in it that appeared to have been designed for sharpshooters. At the ends of the mill buildings, twelve-foot-high platforms supported electric searchlights. As much as the wage cut, Frick's fortifications angered the workers, who interpreted his refusal to bargain as arrogance. They saw his barricading the plant, which they called Fort Frick, as warlike provocation, which it was.

The lockout began on June 28. The workers immediately established an advisory committee and began patrolling the town and the riverfront. On July 2 the company discharged all workers, with the intention of bringing in 300 Pinkerton agents, a private police force, to protect the new, nonunion workers from attack as they came into the plant.

The Pinkerton National Detective Agency had served in similar circumstances since the railroad strike of 1877. For working people, Pinkertons had come to symbolize the tyranny of corporate power and strikebreaking. A mercenary army independent of local police and beyond the reach of local politics, Pinkertons protected strikebreakers (scabs) from strikers, a role in which workers found the agents careless and trigger-happy. In 1890 Pinkertons had killed five people in a railroad strike.

When the Pinkertons appeared the morning of July 6 on two covered barges, the discharged workers understood the plan and stormed down to the river to prevent the Pinkertons from landing at the mill. . . .

Throughout the day Pinkertons traded gunfire with workers, who had hastily erected barricades of pig and scrap iron. Workers fired upon the barges with rifles and a cannon and attempted twice to set the barges afire with a burning barge and a flaming oil-doused handcart. They threw stones, metal, bricks, and lighted dynamite at the barges, injuring several Pinkertons, some fatally. The Pinkertons continued to return the fire. As it became clear that the workers could neither burn up nor kill off the Pinkertons and that the Pinkertons could neither return to Pittsburgh nor land, a committee of union men arranged an armistice. The Pinkertons were allowed to land, but they had to run a 600-yard-long gauntlet of workers, beating and kicking them.

When hostilities ceased, nearly 150 of the 300 Pinkertons were injured; 9 steelworkers and 7 Pinkertons were dead. Most Americans, shocked at the bloodshed and the passion displayed by the workers, blamed the Carnegie management for provocation through wage cuts and the fortification of the mill. But this was not the end of the chaos at Homestead.

Governor William Stone of Pennsylvania sent 8,000 militiamen to the town in the middle of July to maintain order. Thanks to a tightening of discipline after the 1877 railroad strike, the Pennsylvania militia was the best drilled in the country at a time when state militia routinely served to protect strikebreakers and company property in labor disturbances. Once the militia occupied Homestead, new workers began to come to the mill, which resumed operations, department by department, on July 15.

The regular work force, convinced that Frick would not be able to find enough skilled workers to run a nonunion plant, continued to strike. They gained support when workers at the Carnegie plants at Beaver Falls and Pittsburgh struck in sympathy. But the Homestead mill's schedule grew more normal every day. Even an assassination attempt failed to remedy the deterioration of the strikers' position. On July 23 Alexander Berkman, an anarchist. . . , shot Henry Clay Frick, thereby creating the first sympathy for Frick in the whole affair. Berkman was quickly sentenced to twenty-two years' imprisonment, and Frick recovered speedily.

In September affairs in Homestead took a new turn. Scores of striking workers were indicted on 167 counts of murder, rioting, and conspiracy. Some charges were dropped, and workers were acquitted of others; but as soon as the first round of trials ended, thirty-five of the leading union men were charged with treason under a hitherto unused 1860 Pennsylvania law that transformed what has been assaults against an employer into crimes against the state.

Unable to make their bail, the union men languished in jail until the middle of October, when the jury found them all not guilty. By then the Amalgamated leaders had been immobilized and isolated from their men for three weeks while their legal costs mounted. Meanwhile, the leaderless steelworkers of Homestead watched with resentment as new workers, many black, took their jobs. The Amalgamated Association barred blacks, and strikebreaking was one of the few avenues through which black workers could secure what were, for them, well-paid jobs in industry.

The last of the soldiers left Homestead in the middle of October, leaving a legacy of intense bitterness and a demoralized work force. the Homestead tragedy, where sixteen men lost their lives and thousands lost their jobs, was the first of the tremendous labor upheavals of the 1890s, and it showed that a strong employer could break a union that was strong if the company could hire a mercenary police force and could count on the cooperation of the courts. A company wealthy enough to shut down operations for a time could eventually starve its employees back to work on its terms. . . .

. . . [H]ard times scarred every part of the nation. In the fall of 1893, as the depression made jobs scarce, groups of unemployed workers in the Far West who had taken to the road looking for work had organized themselves along military lines, calling themselves industrial armies or industrials. Numbering from 50 to 300 each, these tramp armies overpowered railroad guards and rode about on trains for free. They personified the problem of joblessness as well as their hope that a political democracy would provide economic democracy, which they saw as the chance to get paid for a day's work.

Jacob S. Coxey led the best known of the industrial armies. Coxey's Army, also known as the "Commonweal of Christ," set out from Coxey's hometown of Massillon, Ohio (20 miles south of Akron), on Easter Sunday, March 25, 1894, intending to reach Washington on May Day. Forty years old and by no means unemployed, Coxey was a self-made businessman worth $200,000 who wore costly, hand-tailored suits and bred horses. Despite his prosperous appearance, he had been a currency reformer for years, having left the Democratic party for the Independent-Greenback party and the Greenbackers for the People's party.

Coxey's remedy for unemployment was a pair of bills that he had had introduced in Congress in 1892 and 1894 and that had won AFL backing in 1893. The non-interest-bearing bond bill, recalling the Greenbackers, interconvertible bond of the 1860s and 1870s, never gained congressional support because bonds that paid no interest were a contradiction in terms. Coxey's good roads bill, intended to put the unemployed to work, attracted wider support, particularly from labor, Populists, and the unemployed. According to Coxey's proposal, Congress would issue $500,000,000 in paper currency (greenbacks) at the rate of $20,000,000 per month, which would pay the unemployed $1.50 per day for eight-hour days, building good roads throughout the country, and would provide work for all who applied. To lobby Congress on the good roads bill, Coxey led his Commonweal of Christ to Washington, calling his army "a petition in boots." . . .

The Commonweal of Christ, about 100 strong and led by a young black man carrying an American flag, set out in snow flurries on Easter Sunday. . . . Behind a trumpeter Jacob Coxey, his wife, and baby son—named Legal Tender Coxey— rode in their coach. From time to time the army sang songs such as "Coxey's Army Song," written by Commonweal member George Nixon, to the air of the Union army song "Marching Through Georgia":

Come, we'll tell a story, boys, we'll sing another song,
As we go trudging with sore feet,
    The road to Washington!
We never shall forget this tramp,
    Which sounds the nation's gong.
As we go marching to Congress.

CHORUS
Hurrah, hurrah, we'll sound the jubilee;
Hurrah, hurrah for the flag that makes you free;
    So we'll sing the chorus now,
    Wherever we may be,
While we go marching to Congress.

All along the way the army received generous contributions of food and shelter from working-class settlements hard hit by the depression, a fact that impressed even skeptical observers. In labor and populist strongholds the welcome was especially enthusiastic, and the marchers received assistance from the WCTU at several points. Greeting committees, bands, and hundreds of volunteers met the Commonweal at Homestead and Beaver Falls, Pennsylvania, where workers had confronted the Carnegie Steel Company in 1892. At Homestead the Commonweal reached its greatest strength of 600 men.

When Coxey's Army reached Washington at the end of April, it was only one of several industrial armies converging on the capital from every part of the country except the South. A small but extremely radical army had left Boston on April 22, and several armies had left midwestern cities like St. Louis and Chicago (which contributed a Polish army). The biggest and most troublesome armies for the authorities and the railroads came from the West. . . . Industrial armies left from Los Angeles, Tacoma, Seattle, Spokane, and Portland. But all the western armies faced difficulties securing provisions and crossing the great distances between the West Coast and Washington, D.C. Industrial armies from Montana, Colorado, and Utah commandeered trains and waged pitched battles with sheriffs' deputies, winning the fights but losing volunteers for lack of food. By the time the remnants of these western armies reached Washington, Coxey had long since attempted to present his views.

Coxey's Army had marched through the city, 500 strong, accompanied by Annie L. Diggs, a Populist organizer and lecturer from Kansas. On a splendid white horse Jacob Coxey's seventeen-year-old daughter represented the goddess of peace. . . . Coxey, his wife, and baby Legal Tender rode in their carriage. The parade had stopped at the Capitol, where Coxey had mounted the steps and removed his hat to speak. Before he could begin his address, two policemen had grabbed him. . . . Mayhem broke loose, and police began clubbing spectators. As their supporters had expected, Coxey and his lieutenants were charged with walking on the grass.

Various industrial armies continued to arrive at the Coxey campground during the late spring and summer, swelling the numbers to 800 in mid-May and to more than 1,000 in July. The demonstration ended on August 10, after authorities had broken up all the camps and scattered 1,200 men.

Jacob Coxey died in 1951 at the age of ninety-seven, still believing in his good roads scheme and feeling vindicated by the federal government's adoption of much of his program in the Civilian Conservation Corps and the Works Progress

Administration in the 1930s. By then few remembered Coxey, but in the 1890s his movement had alerted many who belonged to the middle and upper classes to the magnitude of unemployment and the desperation of the jobless. . . .

As catastrophic incidents succeeded one another without pause, the spring of 1894 permitted little leisurely reflection on the larger meaning of recent events for the evolution of industrial society in the United States. No sooner had the Commonweal of Christ marched into Washington than labor unrest flared up in Chicago, throttling rail traffic throughout the central section of the country. The Pullman strike precipitated such chaos that it was called the Debs rebellion, after the Indianan Eugene Debs, who led a union of railroad employees.

The pullman strike in Chicago shared four characteristics with other labor disturbances of the 1890s: A cut in wages during a depression precipitated a strike sharpened by long-standing conflicts; George Pullman and the Pullman company management dealt with workers arrogantly; government entered the struggle on the employers' side; and the strikers and the unemployed attacked railroad property with an angry ferocity. But in this hostile exchange the government in question was not the state of Illinois. The Democratic administration in Washington initiated governmental support of the Pullman company and other railroads in Chicago against the American Railway Union (ARU), led by Eugene V. Debs, who had served his apprenticeship with the Brotherhood of Locomotive Engineers. What began as a strike against one company ended as a war between workers and the combined forces of the U.S. Army and the General [Railroad] Managers' Association.

In the wake of the railroad strike of 1877—which in Chicago had pitted strikers and supporters against police in a four-day battle that killed 13 and injured hundreds—George Pullman had conceived his own remedy for unrest and built a model town for his workers near his Pullman Palace Car Company. Carefully planned, Pullman village was clean, orderly, rationally arranged, carefully maintained, expensive, and dry (no liquor allowed). Pullman's purpose was to inculcate what he called "habits of respectability," and he predicted that housing workers in uplifting surroundings would initiate "a new era for labor" free from strikes and unrest. The town of Pullman epitomized the hierarchical ideal.

But workers rarely remained in Pullman for more than a few years. They preferred living beyond the village limits, where rents were lower and they could do as they pleased, including taking a drink at a favorite saloon, unobserved by informers. Workers complained that foremen pressured them to live in Pullman and that when workers were rehired after layoffs, the residents of Pullman came back first. Resisting such pressures, Pullman workers stayed as briefly as possible in a town in which they constantly felt spied upon.

At the outset of the Panic of 1893 the Pullman company had cut wages an average of 28 percent, without cutting rents in Pullman village. As rents were ordinarily deducted from pay, workers sometimes received pay envelopes containing $1 or $2 for two weeks' work, even less than $1 on occasion. In May 1894 a delegation of Pullman employees had petitioned for the restoration of wages to their 1892 level, but as at Homestead, the company refused to bargain; within a week three members of the committee had been laid off. The Pullman workers called a strike and asked the American Railway Union to represent them. Led by Eugene Debs and organized by industry instead of by craft, the ARU failed to persuade the Pullman workers not to go out during hard times. When the Pullman workers steadfastly refused to call off their strike, the 150,000 ARU members supported them and stopped handling Pullman sleeping cars. The strike began on May 12, 1894. By the end of June rail traffic through Chicago had stopped, shipping was tied up from California to Ohio, and the shortages that resulted sent food prices soaring in Chicago.

The General Managers' Association, formed in 1886 by managers of twenty-four railroads centered or terminating in Chicago, backed the Pullman company fully. However, the association's most powerful ally, Richard Olney, the attorney general of the United States, formerly a railroad officer and lawyer, was not in Chicago. After he had authorized the deputizing of U.S. marshals, railroad companies deputized their own personnel, making company men into law enforcement officers of the United States government. On July 2 Olney obtained a blanket injunction ordering strikers back to work for having blocked the U.S. mails. Strikers denied that they were interfering with the passage of mail and continued the strike.

Seeing Debs as a demagogic leader of the ignorant and lawless and the strike as a prelude to class war, President Cleveland ordered U.S. troops into Chicago on July 3 to disperse the crowds that he contended were obstructing the mails. (They had scrupulously avoided obstructing the passage of mail.) Troops arrived on the Fourth of July, over the strenuous objections of the governor of Illinois, John P. Altgeld. At that point violence began in earnest. Crowds stoned, burned, and wrecked trains and fought in the streets with police, state militia, and the U.S. Army numbering 14,000.

The combined military forces brought the strike to an end on July 8, after it had spread to several states and cost 34 lives. Debs was convicted for contempt of court (ignoring the blanket injunction), and he served six months in a federal penitentiary.

What came to be called the labor injunction made striking, an activity that had not previously been defined as illegal, a crime—contempt of court. The use of labor injunctions triggered a torrent of criticism, not only from Populists and organized labor but also from liberals in the legal field. The injunction served on Debs and the ARU leadership was the best publicized early such response, but it was not the first. During earlier strikes in 1893 judges had enjoined "all persons generally" from striking, notably in Milwaukee in December, on the ground that strikes that threatened to hinder the operations of the corporation in question (a railroad) might damage company property and intimidate strikebreakers. In the Pullman strike the injunction effectively rendered all strike activity illegal. After Pullman, courts used the labor injunction widely to declare strikes conspiracies to interfere with commerce and thereby within the purview of the Sherman Antitrust Act of 1890.

Like the labor injunction, President Cleveland's dispatch of federal troops to Chicago over the governor's protests also proved controversial. On the one hand, college men joined militia companies, sharing the belief of one Harvard alumnus "that it was a necessary police force. Like almost everyone else I was totally in the dark as to the merits of the Pullman strike of 1894 which led me to enlist. I approved President Cleveland's intervention in that strike and for many years considered Governor Altgeld a very dangerous person."

On the other hand, others criticized the President if only for his flagrant overriding of states' rights. Henry George, who had voted for Cleveland in 1888 and had attended the Democratic National Convention in 1892, now sided with Governor

Altgeld. Accusing the General Managers' Association of conspiring to block the mails expressly to bring the federal government into the struggle, George blamed capitalists for seeking to increase the standing army for use against the masses "because the millionaire monopolists are becoming afraid of the armies of poverty-stricken people which their oppressive trusts and combinations are creating."

Eugene Debs saw federal intervention as decisive. The American Railway Union had challenged corporate power as never before, and the union would have won but for the managers' enlistment of federal courts and armies, he said in a speech following his release from the penitentiary. Debs termed this an "exhibition of the debauching power of money," which Americans were seeing more often than ever before.

Quickly realizing that the Pullman strike had effectively destroyed the 150,000-member American Railway Union, Debs concluded, as Terence Powderly had eight years earlier, that strikes were self-defeating. Strikers were economically vulnerable, particularly in the hard times that caused so many strikes, and unions could not control the crowds (many of whom were not union members but people angry at the rich) that furnished a rationale for military intervention....

The 1890s had been a period of hard, hard times, political instability, and popular explosions that seemed to be harbingers of revolution. But as serious as the crises of the nineties had been, power relationships did not change radically. In part this was due to the removal of some of the unemployed who were so volatile a part of the masses. Europeans and Canadians who lacked work—their motive for coming here in the first place—simply went home. And in cases of labor unrest, like the Pullman strike of 1894, the federal government stepped in to undermine the bargaining power of organized labor and thereby curb serious challenges to the economic status quo. The army and courts of the United States attempted with considerable success to control strikes and related disorders through the use of labor injunctions and National Guards.

The Righteous Commonwealth of the Late Nineteenth Century

MICHAEL KAZIN

Jesus was only possible in a barefoot world, and he was crucified by the few who wore shoes.

—Ignatius Donnelly

On Washington's Birthday in 1892, hundreds of grassroots activists from all over the nation came to St. Louis to participate in a four-day Industrial Conference that concluded by launching a new political party.

This was not a unique occurrence. Third parties were common if not entirely respectable features of the frenzied political landscape of the late nineteenth century,

groups and political organizations with clashing priorities. Small farmers anxious about their debts wanted to inflate the money supply; while urban workers feared a hike in the prices they paid for food and rent. Prohibitionists and currency reformers both opposed the big money but differed over which of its sins was primary—the peddling of drink or the constriction of credit. And socialist voices in all their variety—Christian, Marxian, and Bellamyite—were at odds with most unionists and agrarian rebels, who affirmed their faith in private property and the malleability of the class structure. Factionalism was a perennial feature of reform politics in these years; not until 1892 did most groups cease pitching their panaceas long enough to unite behind the same third-party ticket.

But, over the preceding two decades, these disparate bands agreed about two vital matters: what had gone wrong in America since Lee's surrender at Appomattox and why; and the urgent need for a messianic awakening to bring about the sweeping changes required. These commonalities made a grand coalition seem possible.

Ignatius Donnelly was speaking to every segment of the dissident throng when he evoked the misery of working Americans and blamed it on immoral men at the top. . . . The unprecedented size, market dominance, union-busting and price-gouging behavior of such corporations as Standard Oil, Carnegie Steel, and Southern Pacific Railroad led many late-nineteenth-century reformers to question the laissez-faire views which had previously seemed the best assurance that hard work would receive its just reward. Power was no longer married to principle.

All the movements that rose after the Civil War used a similar vocabulary of self-defense, of urgent fortification against elitist foes. Their different constituencies and programs aside, Greenbackers and Knights of Labor, Prohibitionists and Socialists, members of the Farmers' Alliance, and disciples of Bellamy and Henry George agreed that a national crisis was at hand, comparable to the one that had led to the Civil War. Their beloved America had been wrenched from the path of righteousness and the control of the majority. Only the courageous, strenuous action of ordinary citizens could win it back. . . .

The sharp disillusionment that followed the war bred a bumper crop of anger. . . . Reform activists typically believed that they, or at least their parents, had fought a ruinous war to repel an assault on their freedom and way of life. But the war had solved nothing. Worse, in its aftermath, a new group of oppressors had captured power—armed with wealth, technology, and foreign allies far more extensive than those the antebellum lords of either lash or loom had been able to muster.

In their wrath, Gilded Age insurgents made no mean contribution to the era's reputation for extravagant rhetoric. Erstwhile Republicans, whose old party had led the nation when the betrayal began, were particularly immoderate. Ignatius Donnelly came to Washington during the war as a Radical Republican congressman but left several years later, denouncing "the waste, extravagance, idleness and corruption" of the federal government and observing that "the great men of the nation dwindle into pygmies as you draw near them." The suffragist Elizabeth Cady Stanton, the prohibitionist Frances Willard, the financial reformer James Weaver, and the labor journalist Andrew C. Cameron had also been dedicated Republicans. They broke with the party of Lincoln because they believed it had deserted its founding principles of free labor and moral government in the rush to court wealthy industrialists—in Donnelly's words, "the cruelest of all aristocracies, a moneyed aristocracy." These reformers dedicated (or, in Stanton's case, rededicated) themselves to causes that required the same missionary zeal and certainty that a momentous choice was at hand that had earlier motivated their actions as abolitionists and/or Radical Republicans. In contrast, former Democrats . . . were restrained and ironic; they had never expected the party of Northern factory owners to serve the public interest.

For all grassroots reformers, the contemporary enemy bore many of the same names Jacksonians had employed—especially "the money power" and "monopoly." To these was added "plutocrat," a neologism all but unknown in the antebellum era. By any name, central banks and investment houses were still the main culprits. But now they were perceived as intertwined with large manufacturing concerns; men like J. P. Morgan and Andrew Carnegie had . . . assembled a malignant force of unprecedented strength and unity of purpose. . . . The "money power" now signified a nonproductive, immeasurably wealthy octopus whose long, slimy tentacles reached from private firms on both sides of the Atlantic to grasp every household, business, and seat of government. "The money monopoly is the parent of all monopolies—the very root and essence of slavery," asserted labor's Andrew Cameron, underlining a dread of bondage older than the republic itself.

It was the unsung Greenbackers, who, starting in the late 1860s, first made elaborate arguments about the links between plutocrats and the low wages and lost chances of many Americans. Then, amid the severe depression of the mid-1870s, "the money power" trope was sprinkled generously throughout the speeches, articles, and letters of millions of people who were seeking a way to stigmatize the unseen, faraway forces that had such influence over their lives. When the term *capitalist* was used, it normally referred to the men who controlled investment markets rather than, as in the Marxist sense, to the employers of wage labor.

Curiously, such attacks never explained why "the money power" had shifted from the advocacy of paper currency that had drawn Old Hickory's fire to a "hard money" position that sanctified the gold standard. Clearly, what mattered, in each case, was the monster's theft of honest labor and hard-won property, not the particular brand of financial fire it spouted.

The continuity from the age of Jackson is obvious. Like that earlier generation of rhetorical democrats, Gilded Age reformers could disagree about which particular elite represented the greatest evil but were in accord on the immorality of parasitic wealth itself and the need to educate all citizens to its dangers. Neither Henry George's speculative landlords, the WCTU's liquor traffickers, nor Terence Powderly's "industrial oligarchs" had amassed their fortunes through honest toil—unless conspiracies to corner a market, to buy cheap and sell dear, or to debauch tired laborers were to be considered honest.

This attack on the most successful men in American society could be crude, as in Greenback oratory about "thieves" and "frauds," or brilliant, as in *Progress and Poverty* (1879), Henry George's clear, passionate dissection of the woeful intricacies of land tenure and industrial development. In fact, long, learned arguments like George's against reigning economic orthodoxy were surprisingly popular. *Progress and Poverty* sold well over a million copies. The traveling lecturers and local editors of the Populist crusade delivered briefer but similar messages to audiences of small farmers and wage earners across the South and West. These political circuit rides assumed "the plain people" would comprehend their sermons, which were larded with metaphors drawn from European history and ancient philosophy as well as the Bible, simply because it was in their self-interest to do so.

At the same time, insurgents often predicted that deliverance would have to come from a higher Power than the people themselves. "Revolution of some sort is not far off," warned Reverend George Herron, a Christian socialist, in 1895. "Either a religious movement, producing a revival such as the prophets dimly or never dreamed of, or blood such as never flowed will remit the sins of the existing order." In a plainer style, Jacob Coxey told his band of angry, unemployed followers before they set out on their small but well-publicized 1894 march on Washington, "This movement will either mark the second coming of Christ or be a total failure."

Christian language was ubiquitous among those who tried to knit together an insurgent coalition. Secular arguments alone could neither evoke the scale of the problem nor incite the upheaval needed to set it right. A new surge of Christian revivalism—the third Great Awakening in American history—provided the context. In the 1870s and 1880s, hundreds of thousands of Americans flocked to tent meetings featuring the enormously popular sermons of Dwight L. Moody and the music of Ira Sankey; missionary societies sprouted from nearly every Protestant denomination. A growing number of urban ministers argued that the Lord's Prayer and the life of Jesus taught the collective nature of sin; these social gospelers— whose most prolific figures included Washington Gladden, Walter Rauschenbusch, and George Herron—aimed to create a new community of altruistic souls and rejected the conservative image of the individual miscreant left alone to face divine wrath. Mass movements had the potential to realize a solidarity that would turn America away from the worship of Mammon. Purifying society mattered more than did personal piety. . . .

. . . Most insurgents used a Christian vocabulary because it was the only way they knew to speak with great emotion about ultimate social concerns. Few activists called bluntly for the "application of Christian principles to politics," as did the Prohibition Party of Maine. But the contrast with prominent elite thinkers at the time is striking. In the late nineteenth century, appeals to "science" and "reason" came far more frequently from social Darwinist intellectuals like William Graham Sumner than from the ranks of trade unionists, discontented farmers, and temperance advocates.

Thus, Gilded Age insurgents wailed that Mammon and hypocrisy reigned over God, man, and principle in every major institution from the church to the factory to the once hallowed places where laws were debated and passed. Their prescription for change was, in a sense, a reactionary one. Edward Bellamy, the railroad union leader Eugene Debs, and the journalist Henry Demarest Lloyd all called for a "counterrevolution of the people" to dismantle this alarmingly radical new system that had fastened on the American republic.

But defining "the people" created something of a problem. It was not enough to say that the majority of Americans belonged to what a Greenback propagandist called "the wealth-producing classes" and leave it at that. . . . [B]y the late nineteenth century, the nation's social demography had become fearfully complex.

Freed slaves and new immigrants from Eastern and Southern Europe and East Asia competed in the cities and on the land for work, property, and profits with those who had come earlier. How would the emerging producer coalition bridge gaps that were as much cultural as economic?

The path taken was a contradictory one, viable for a few election campaigns but ill suited to a movement seeking a long-term constituency and a secure niche in the political landscape. On the one hand, activists tended to inflate their definitions of producer and labor into a grand abstraction that ignored most differences of income and occupation. In so doing, they negated, ironically, their own impassioned charge that a yawning social gulf had made America resemble the "two nations" that had always existed in places like Britain, France, and Russia. Insurgents denounced the misery caused by unemployment, low wages, and tight money. But the humanitarian impulse led few to criticize employers or property owners as a class. To envision a political force parallel to that which Jackson or Lincoln had once commanded, it was necessary to deny that unequal economic rewards for various "producers" might hinder the search for a just, permanent solution to America's troubles.

Therefore, the most compelling definition of class standing became one's politics. Any sincere fighter against monopoly and plutocracy, regardless of occupation or social status, was, in effect, a producer. Among the "platforms of labor societies" printed in a widely circulated 1886 book about grassroots activism were statements from a variety of third parties, organizations of self-employed farmers, and groups composed mainly of wage earners. Nearly every platform—whether from the Knights of Labor, Agricultural Wheel, or Anti-Monopoly Party—hailed the "industrial masses" or "working classes" of both field and factory and cursed their "plundering" enemies.

Under construction here was a moral community of self-governing citizens, not a conflict of economic classes. In fact, sympathetic local businessmen and professionals joined many local organizations of producers and sometimes served as their spokesmen. The Knights of Labor rarely allowed people other than wage earners to lead their local assemblies. But the Knights underlined the ethical core of their identity by barring only five groups from membership: bankers, land speculators, lawyers, liquor dealers, and gamblers. Such men (the gender was assumed) either preyed on human weaknesses or made a lucrative income without having to work very hard for it. Certainly, no sweat begrimed their well-fed countenances.

Divisions on moral rather than class lines did inspire short-lived displays of social unity against "monopolistic" foes. The entire towns that rose up against railroad corporations during the mass strike of 1877, the explosive creation of independent parties in the 1880s, and the regional successes of the People's Party in the early 1890s all demonstrated the potential that support for a class-inclusive producer ethic had to throw a scare into local and national elites.

However, there was a danger in such an appeal that had not been evident upon its creation earlier in the nineteenth century. First, its fuzziness and hortatory style were fairly simple to imitate; Democratic and Republican competitors—who shared ideological roots and ancestral icons with the reformers—could and did co-opt it, plucking the chords of antimonopoly while rejecting enforceable measures to break up or discipline big corporations. The very suppleness of their rhetoric prevented Gilded Age reformers from blocking the political competitors who wanted to put them out of business.

Second, the romance of producerism had a cultural blind spot; it left unchallenged strong prejudices toward not just African-Americans but also toward recent immigrants who had not learned or would not employ the language and rituals of this variant of the civic religion. Many insurgents who lauded the producer also stated or hinted that certain groups of people lacked the capacity to take on the monopolists in a sustained, ideologically stalwart way. This belief was clearest among unionists who asserted that "Slavs and 'Tally Annes' . . . Hungarians and Chinamen" were ignorant "black sheep" whom industrialists could easily manipulate and use to break strikes. "The republic cannot afford to have such ignorant animals within its borders," wrote one labor editor from Pittsburgh. . . .

. . . By the 1880s, sharp, derogatory references to "Asiatics" and "Mongolians" were commonplace in the literature of the Knights of Labor and Farmers' Alliances, which aimed to attract working-class support. *Breaking the Chains,* a serialized 1887 novel by T. Fulton Gantt that championed the Knights, featured one Chinese character, the clever and unscrupulous cook for an opium-smoking land speculator and army officer. "He was among the most intelligent of the Chinamen immigrating to this country when Asia first turned loose upon us her horde of filthy, festering degradation," wrote Gantt. "He was a slave Coolie. . . . Upon getting his freedom he determined to seek employment as a body servant to the wealthiest debauchee he could find."

That image of the scheming, amoral "Chinaman" starkly outlined the cultural limits of Gilded Age producerism. The regular performance of manual work was not enough to qualify one as a member of the laboring classes. As in Jackson's time, one also had to demonstrate a manly self-reliance, a refusal to defer to unjust authorities that was considered to be at the heart of Christian and American principles. Even a "most intelligent" immigrant from East Asia was still judged to be thinking and acting like a slave.

African-Americans recently freed from bondage could conceivably meet the test. But they had to eschew black nationalist sentiments, join white-dominated movements of workers and farmers, and avoid demanding a halt to the brutal regimen of Jim Crow instituted in the wake of Reconstruction. It also helped if blacks echoed the view that "Chinamen" naturally preferred submission to freedom, thus shifting the onus of dependency away from themselves. In 1879, a black coal miner wrote to a Greenback-Labor paper about "how divided the miners on the North and South railroad of Alabama are as regards a uniform price for mining coal. One would suppose that all emigrated from China or some other heathen country, to see the way they conduct themselves."

For two decades before the founding of the People's Party, then, insurgents were nurturing a language of bitterness and betrayal. Sentimental about the mythic, lost world of smallholders and artisans, they demanded that elites cease their financial manipulation and political corruption and allow the people to rule once again. Millions of Americans were drawn to this critique—as the great popularity of *Progress and Poverty* and *Looking Backward* testified.

As politics, however, it fell woefully short. In no national election from 1872 to 1888 did the combined votes of all alternative parties top 4 percent of the total. The People's Party offered the best and perhaps the last chance to convert antimonopoly sentiment into a winning strategy.

Leading Populists understood that collective anger, no matter how well articulated, was not enough. To transcend despair, champions of the producing classes had to appeal to the majority of citizens whose interests they were so fond of invoking. Social differences had to be submerged, controversial moral issues played down, and regional divisions overcome in order to build a truly national organization.

A concept of Americanism unsullied by Civil War rancor could help. Opening the 1892 St. Louis conference, Benjamin Terrell of Texas counseled delegates that "the eyes of the toiling masses are upon you and they are expecting a second declaration of independence." Leonidas Polk of North Carolina, a favorite for the new party's presidential nomination, received a standing ovation when he declared: "This meeting represents those men who are loyal to duty and loyal to country." And Polk, a former Confederate colonel (but never an apologist for slavery) took part in a ceremony that symbolically healed the sectional wound. Before the entire assemblage, he clasped hands with former Union Navy Commodore Van De Voort of Nebraska. A group of delegates then unfurled a huge American flag and waved it as the crowd cheered. Similar ceremonies of reconciliation were taking place elsewhere in the country as the nineteenth century neared its end—just as racial segregation was, not coincidentally, being written into law.

Also needed was a broad definition of "the people" that did not dull the term's producerist edge. Polk called on "the great Northwest, great South, and great West" to take over the government and right the economic balance upset by the financial powers of the Northeast. Orator after orator hailed "the toilers," "the industrial classes," and "farmers and laborers of the entire country" in a manner simultaneously vague and imbued with a muscular pride in manual production that men who worked for a living and were accustomed to voting for one of the two major parties could appreciate.

There were occasional hints of a more restrictive meaning. Terence Powderly of the Knights of Labor, himself an Irish Catholic, scorned new immigrants as "unfortunate" creatures whom good Americans "must educate year after year to prevent them from using bombs instead of ballots." But this narrowing of "the people" to earlier arrivals and the American-born apparently brought no protest. Few Populists were flagrant nativists. But all could applaud Powderly's implication that they were defending vital national interests "plutocrats" and their pawns in government were betraying. . . .

The Populists put forth a platform intended to satisfy a range of constituencies, only a few of which were already safely inside its fold. For debt-ridden agrarians, they promised an increase in the money supply, a ban on alien land ownership, and a state takeover of the railroads that so often made small farmers pay whatever they could bear. For wage earners, they endorsed the ongoing push for a shorter working day, called for the abolition of the strike-breaking Pinkerton Agency, and declared that "the interests of rural and civil labor are the same." For currency reformers and residents of Western mining states, they demanded the unlimited coinage of both silver and gold. Appended to the platform were such "supplementary resolutions" as a "pledge" to continue the healthy pensions already being granted to Union veterans and support for a boycott of a Rochester clothing manufacturer being struck by the Knights of Labor.

Except for the pensions (a Republican standby), this was an agenda neither of the major parties would support. But it clearly showed a desire to move away from the monistic nostrums that had gripped the competing battalions of reform for a generation. The defeat of planks for prohibition and woman suffrage at the St. Louis conference signaled there would be no open attack on cultural attitudes that separated Northern men from Southern men, and most Catholics from most Protestants. The Populists didn't just want to be heard, they wanted to win. Through a network of over 150 local newspapers (most in the South and West) and scores of skilled itinerant lecturers attached to the movement, the Populists articulated a shrewd synthesis of beliefs grassroots reformers and radicals had been writing, orating, and praying about for the past twenty years.

They first attempted to reconcile the contradictory truths inherited from antebellum and more recent champions of the common man. To keep faith with a proud (and consensual) lineage, Populist writers and orators repeatedly quoted one or more of the deceased icons of democracy. Perhaps the best practitioner of this was the popular Texas lecturer James "Cyclone" Davis. As he spoke around the nation, Davis kept the complete works of Thomas Jefferson—"the sainted sire of American liberty"—close to him on the podium. He often searched through them, as if they were scripture, for answers to audience questions about such issues as free silver and government ownership of the railroads. In a few Southern states, reformers called their new political organization Jeffersonian Democrats before adhering to the People's Party; similarly, in Kansas, the Abraham Lincoln Republicans provided one route out of the GOP. In such ways did insurgents express their hope that, with God's assistance, "the simplicity, the purity and the prosperity of the early days" might return.

To this end, classical liberal cries for individual freedom and against "artificial" restraints on economic competition were combined with a classical republican emphasis on the need to enhance public virtue and oppose corporate assaults on industrious communities. The interests of the self-aggrandizing property owner could thus coexist, rhetorically, with a nostalgic evocation of a past in which champions of the people had ruled for the good of the vast majority. As one perceptive historian comments, the Populists "tried to make use of their heritage without allowing themselves to be limited by it, to recreate with new policies a society of equal right for all and special privileges to none."

While not mentioned in the Omaha Platform, the traditional Protestant concern with upright behavior was woven throughout the language of most committed Populists. A party based among evangelical, rural churchgoers could not help speaking about vanquishing all agents of corruption—saloon keepers as well as plutocrats, secular urban sophisticates as well as dishonest public officials, and occasionally "English Jew bankers" as well as more generic financiers at home and abroad—on the way to the promised commonwealth. "The party was known as the party of righteousness, and such groups as the Germans feared for their Sunday cards and beer," writes one scholar.

Opponents of Populism were quick to criticize this tendency. Republican Senator John Ingalls of Kansas complained, baroquely, to a New York reporter: "The decalogue and the Golden Rule have no place in a political camp. . . . This modern cant about the corruption of politics is fatiguing in the extreme. It proceeds from the tea-custard and syllabub dilettantism of the frivolous and desultory sentimentalism of epicenes." But the fact that this interview helped the new party make Ingalls one of its first electoral victims testifies to the power of Christian moralism to motivate critics of an unethical status quo.

The senator's charge of effeminacy also indicated something more than his view (common among major-party stalwarts) that politics was just another form of war. Women played a role in Populism far beyond the incidental status accorded them in Democratic or Republican circles, before or after the Civil War. They organized revivalistic camp meetings on the prairies, spoke in public and wrote articles for movement newspapers, and extended female networks already established in the WCTU and local farmers' alliances. Most Populist women spoke of their actions as extensions of the domestic ideology and evangelical fervor that had propelled them and other female activists through decades of collective struggles since the 1820s. Swore one woman: "I am going to work for prohibition, the Alliance, and for Jesus as long as I live." A male journalist from the North Carolina Farmers' Alliance viewed that stance as a political necessity: "The ladies are and always have been the great moral element in society; therefore *it is impossible to succeed without calling to our aid the greatest moral element in the country.*" To battle the manifest corruption of the old parties, the tough, manly aspect of the producer ethic was thus temporarily suspended.

Morality, for Populists, meant the tacit (if not active) encouragement of state temperance legislation and even the eventual abolition of the "liquor traffic." It meant forcing nominally Christian candidates and officeholders to stop compromising with big business and urban machines and to stand up for policies that favored the meek and the exploited. The notion that a democratic politics must concern itself with the enforcement of ethical standards, both public and private, was integral to the appeal of Populism. Near the end of another century, we know how explosive that conviction can be, how difficult to confine its targets to one end of the ideological spectrum.

Unlike the call for a new moral order, the issue of race posed an acute dilemma for white Populists, particularly those in the powerful detachments of the cotton-growing South. Black farmers and tenants, over 90 percent of whom lived in Dixie, shared many of the economic grievances of white yeomen and suffered to a greater degree from mounting debts to furnishing merchants and landlords. It would have been foolish for the People's Party to neglect black voters, many of whom were unhappy with a Republican Party that no longer said or did much about racial inequity. Yet, the Populists had no chance to win statewide contests or presidential electors unless they also won over a plurality of white Democrats. And not a few of the latter, the majority constituency, would certainly have agreed with the sentiments of the upcountry Alabama farmer depicted in a later novel, who grumbled: "Them black bastards is takin' the food out 'n our mouths. . . . They're down there sharin' the good things with the rich while good white folks in the hills have to starve."

That almost all white Populists (Northern and Southern) shared the era's dogma about the desirability of Caucasian supremacy made the dilemma even more agonizing. How could they promise blacks enough to get their votes without unleashing fears of "nigger equality" that would send whites fleeing back to the "party of the fathers"?

The Southern Populists' solution was to appeal to blacks exclusively on matters of shared economic concern while assuring fellow whites that nothing resembling a biracial order was being contemplated. Thus, the segregated Colored Farmers' Alliance, led by the white Baptist minister Richard Manning Humphrey, grew when it attacked the crop-lien system but fell apart in 1891 after some of its members who were tenants waged an unsuccessful strike against white landowners, some of whom were Populists (which did not stop the lynching of fifteen strikers). Thus, Tom Watson risked the ire of Democratic mobs when he shared speaking platforms with black Populists and derided his opponents' manipulation of race: "The argument against the independent political movement in the South may be boiled down into one word—NIGGER!" But Watson also opposed any federal intervention to protect black voters, endorsed the Jim Crow laws that Populist and Democratic legislators alike were then passing in Georgia and other states, and hotly denied allegations that he had broken bread with a black ally.

Certainly, as many historians have argued, even a limited, tactical alliance with black Southerners was a dangerous, even heroic step at the time. But such an alliance did not represent a break with white Americans' racial beliefs or the social hierarchy they justified. By themselves, the Populists could not have transformed the color consciousness of the Southern electorate even if that had been one of their primary aims—which it never was. Black farmers and laborers, for their party, had to be extremely courageous to join a rebellion against the Bourbon Democrats who controlled the land, businesses, and local governments on which the very survival of African-Americans depended. But the Populists continued to assume, as had their Jeffersonian and Jacksonian forebears, that "the plain people" meant those with white skin and a tradition of owning property on the land or in a craft. Not surprisingly, most blacks did not accept the Populists' circumscribed offer and instead cast their ballots, where they were still allowed to do so, either for the party of Lincoln or for that of their ancestral overlords.

Of course, Populist speakers in every region devoted most of their energy to waging a zealous and skillful assault on corporate wealth. "Old-party debaters," wrote the historian John Hicks, "did not tackle their Populist antagonists lightly, for as frequently as not the bewhiskered rustic, turned orator, could present, in support of his arguments, an array of carefully sorted information that left his better-groomed opponent in a daze." Movement publicists were pioneers of the investigative morality plays Theodore Roosevelt would later disparage as muckraking. They gathered thousands of damning details, large and small, about trusts that secretly conspired to bilk the public and bribe politicians. In the mode of alternative economists like Henry George, Populist writers educated their audiences about securities and commodities markets, business organization, and international trade while never neglecting to draw a taut battle line. "The most distressing feature of this war of the Trusts," wrote the antimonopoly reformer James B. Weaver, in a 1892 tract entitled *A Call to Action,* "is the fact that they control the articles which the plain people consume in their daily life. It cuts off their accumulations and deprives them of the staff upon which they fain would lean in their old age."

As a counterbalance, the Populists argued that a stronger state could, if the electoral ground shifted their way, be the plain people's best ally—an enhancer of democracy instead of the servant of plutocracy. Weaver advocated "stringent penal statutes" against corporations that broke the law and a tax of up to 40 percent on any business controlled by a trust. The Omaha Platform called for "the powers of government" to "be expanded" and, in a revealing aside, named the postal service as a model because of its tradition of cheap, efficient, and absolutely egalitarian delivery. Party activists made clear they were not advocating socialism. In fact, they maintained that their reforms would improve not lower the status of the millions of Americans who owned small amounts of property.

At the same time, the Populists remained ambivalent about a more powerful state. The American icons the Populists worshiped had left no clear guidance on the limits of federal power. Jefferson and Jackson preached the virtues of a small, nonintrusive government and insisted on a literal interpretation of the Constitution. Yet the Louisiana Purchase and the Cherokee Removal demonstrated how elastic such pronouncements could be. Even Lincoln, who vastly expanded the federal purview to defeat the Confederacy, had never advocated a nationalized rail system or laws to end land speculation.

The Populists resolved their doubts in a pragmatic way. They spoke about the state as the creation and property of people like themselves. Greedy, tyrannical men had usurped that birthright; government power itself was not the problem. Everything depended on what kind of men with what ideas and ethics sat in the statehouse, the Capitol, and the White House.

In the elections of 1892 and 1894, the Populists thrust their well-crafted message into the cauldron of national politics. At first glance, the results seemed encouraging. In 1892, the presidential nominee James Weaver, a former Union officer from Iowa (Leonidas Polk, the Southern favorite, had died that June) gained over a million votes, 8.5 percent of the total. Weaver . . . won a majority in three states (Colorado, Idaho, and Nevada) and pluralities in two others (North Dakota and Kansas). Two Populist governors were also elected. In 1894, the party did even better. Its candidates won over 1.5 million votes; seven nominees for the House and six for the Senate were victorious, along with hundreds of state legislators. At the state level, the insurgents were not averse to tactical alliances; some of their victories were the result of a fusion with the weaker of the major parties—Republicans in the South, Democrats in the North. Nevertheless, the "producing classes" seemed, at last, to have found their national voice and to be striding forward to reshape American society.

But the image of mounting strength was an illusion. The People's Party scored all its wins in two underdeveloped regions—the Deep South and the trans-Mississippi West—whose white residents had long nursed an anger against the urban, moneyed East. Aside from knots of radical unionists in such cities as Chicago and San Francisco, the Populists had failed to reach the craft and industrial workers they hoped would be responsive to their message of producer redemption. Pleasing words alone could not bridge the gap between rural evangelicals and American-born city dwellers, a great many of whom were neither American born nor Protestant.

Agrarian "organizers looked at urban workers and simply did not know what to say to them—other than to repeat the language of the Omaha Platform," observes the historian Lawrence Goodwyn. Only radical workers who thought in strategic terms were willing to ignore the cultural gap, and they had little more success with the Populist standard than with earlier alternative tickets.

To break out of their electoral confinement, the Populists took a fatal leap into compromise. After the 1894 campaign, a large faction in the party began to downplay the more radical planks in the Omaha Platform (like state-run railroads) and to emphasize the inflationary demand for the free coinage of silver, which appealed to underemployed and indebted citizens in several regions of the country. Meanwhile, national Democrats, severely weakened by a serious depression that began in 1893, were reborn as Jacksonian scourges of "parasites" and "privilege." In 1896, the flagging party came out for free silver and nominated for president William Jennings Bryan, a former Nebraska congressman who had built his short political career on the foundation of monetary reform and cooperation with local Populists (Republicans being the majority party in his state).

In their own national convention that year, the Populists argued long and heatedly about whether to support Bryan or to keep to the independent road. But the outcome was never really in doubt. A majority of delegates chose the hope of partnership in a governing coalition of producers over the fear that their party was being seduced and destroyed. They asked only that the Democrats accept Tom Watson as their candidate for vice president instead of Arthur Sewall, the Maine shipping magnate who'd already been nominated. The request was curtly declined.

During the presidential campaign, the major parties fought, more pointedly than ever before, to control the symbols and definitions of patriotism. The Republicans . . . distributed millions of American flags, many of them at "flag days" organized to honor nominee William McKinley as the nation's protector of order and, amid a depression, its "advance agent of prosperity." The fusion ticket was likened to a Confederacy controlled by Socialists. As in 1861, traitors were gathering strength, "plotting a social revolution and the subversion of the American Republic," in Theodore Roosevelt's overwrought opinion. In the Midwest, where the election would be close, Union Army veterans, calling themselves "Patriotic Heroes," perched on a flatcar filled with battlefield regalia and rode against the rebellion one last time. "So pervasive was the Republican campaign," writes Lawrence Goodwyn, "that frustrated Democrats found it difficult to show proper respect for the national emblem without participating in some kind of public endorsement of McKinley." The most expensive campaign ever waged to that date was undertaken to save the nation from those who would destroy it in the name of reform.

Against this onslaught, the only response the underfinanced effort led by William Jennings Bryan could make was to protest that the Republicans did not represent the *real* America of farms and workshops. But the message had to be conveyed almost entirely through the spoken word; almost every urban newspaper outside the South backed McKinley. And Democratic cartoons displaying the flag with a field of moneybags instead of stars only confirmed that the opposition was setting the terms of the iconographic debate.

Bryan, with the help of a few Populist surrogates like the stalwart Tom Watson, did his best to redefine the electoral contest. It *was* a struggle to defend America, he said. But the assault was not coming from a half-crazed rabble but from the wealthiest men in the land—"goldbugs," "the idle rich," and the lawyers and politicians who did their bidding. Campaign buttons proclaiming free silver to be, unlike the Anglophiles' gold standard, "American Money for Americans" played a nativist variation on the same class-conscious theme.

The most radical Populists never supported Bryan; they correctly, if futilely, argued that fusion for free silver would condemn the third party's broad platform to irrelevance. "The Democracy raped our convention while our own leaders held the struggling victim," Ignatius Donnelly contended in characteristically, purple language. Yet even he could not miss the brilliant way the 36-year-old Bryan gathered under the rhetorical umbrella of the money issue both the Populists' cherished ideals and their favorite modes of expressing them: evangelical fervor; a broad, moralistic definition of producerism; continuity with the icons of democracy; the equation of Americanism with the interests of the common people; and the need for a popular uprising to cleanse the nation.

That synthetic skill is what made the "Cross of Gold" speech, first given at the Democratic nominating convention and paraphrased by Bryan hundreds of times in his 18,000 miles of barnstorming that summer and fall, such a powerful document—inspiring to many yet threatening to more. "Bryan . . . said nothing new," one historian points out; "he had made no profound argument which men would remember and cite later. He had said, however, what hundreds of delegates, inarticulate and mute, felt and believed."

Bryan's great speech framed the campaign in pietistic terms ("With a zeal approaching the zeal which inspired the Crusaders who followed Peter the Hermit" and with his final, unforgettable crucifixion image itself). He challenged the Republican claim to being the party of business—proclaiming that "the farmer who goes forth in the morning and toils all day" and "the miners who go down a thousand feet into the earth" were "businessmen" equal to "the few financial magnates who, in a back room, corner the money of the world." He declared, echoing Jefferson, that agrarian pursuits were more vital than urban ones: "Burn down your cities and leave our farms, and your cities will spring up again as if by magic; but destroy our farms and the grass will grow in the streets of every city in the country." He cited Jackson and Jefferson on the right of the people, through the government, to regulate the currency; and flayed those who allowed "foreign potentates and powers" to violate American sovereignty. Speaking to and for loyal citizens who once believed in the system, Bryan raged: "We have petitioned, and our petitions have been scorned; we have entreated, and our entreaties have been disregarded; we have begged, and they have mocked when our calamity came. We beg no longer; we entreat no more; we petition no more. We defy them!"

The barrier such eloquence could never surmount was that Bryan was, despite his leadership of the nation's oldest political party, a protest candidate. Voters who did not agree that America was gripped by crisis (or who defined "crisis" as the breakdown of social and political norms) tended to view the fusionists as advocates of an unpredictable, perhaps dangerous future, in which those who had organized Coxey's Army, waged the 1894 national railway strike, and talked, like Kansas Populist Mary Lease, about "raising less corn and more hell" might actually run the government. Moreover, Bryan's pietistic rigor and his criticisms of urban life chilled many Catholic workers and other city dwellers in the East and Midwest who usually voted Democratic. Thousands heard the Republicans promise not to disturb the nation's ethnic and religious heterogeneity and marked their ballots for McKinley. Bryan drew more votes than any Populist could have, but he had cast his lot on the same side of the cultural divide.

So the man who became known as the Great Commoner went down to the first of three national defeats, and the People's Party rapidly shrank from the spearhead of a social movement into an insignificant sect (before expiring in 1908). In the decades to come, many Bryan supporters—and their scholarly defenders—would speak of the election of 1896 as a negative millennium. It was, they believed, the pivotal defeat for the grand coalition of the industrial classes and a decisive victory for corporate America, an event that had never been revenged or redeemed.

In 1896, Vachel Lindsay was a teenager living in rural Illinois. In 1919, after the disillusioning struggle of World War I, he wrote "Bryan, Bryan, Bryan, Bryan," a long (and once widely read) poem that captures the blend of cultural resentment, regional pique, and producer antagonism that helped stoke the Populist revolt. Lindsay, chanted, in part:

> Election night at midnight:
> Boy Bryan's defeat.
> Defeat of western silver.
> Defeat of the wheat.
> Victory of letterfiles
> And plutocrats in miles
> With dollar signs upon their coats,
> Diamond watchchains on their vests
> And spats on their feet.
> Victory of custodians,
> Plymouth Rock,
> And all that inbred landlord stock.
> Victory of the neat.
> Defeat of the aspen groves of Colorado valleys,
> The blue bells of the Rockies,
> And blue bonnets of old Texas,
> By the Pittsburg alleys.
> Defeat of the alfalfa and the Mariposa lily.
> Defeat of the Pacific and the long Mississippi.
> Defeat of the young by the old and silly.
> Defeat of tornadoes by the poison vats supreme.
> Defeat of my boyhood, defeat of my dream.

Lindsay was not wrong to eulogize the insurgent agrarians whose spirit he had imbibed at the end of the nineteenth century. Small farmers would never again possess the numbers, the confidence, or the leadership to mount a national crusade capable of drawing in reform-minded Americans from other classes and fusing with a major party. But the significance of the People's Party transcended its own demographic and electoral fate. Through Populism coursed a rich, sometimes contradictory amalgam of dreams, demands, and prejudices whose expression, since the founding of the United States, had been indispensable to the making of democratic politics.

The People's Party stood at a point of transition for that language. On the one hand, it spoke out in pride and anger for the lost commonwealth of agrarians and artisans, the moral center of a society that had spun away from its once noble orbit. Wordsmiths like Ignatius Donnelly, Tom Watson, and Frances Willard may have been looking backward in order to vault ahead. But one cannot escape their yearning for a social harmony that could be glimpsed again only in Heaven. On the other hand, the Populists were forerunners of a more pragmatic style of expressing discontent. Blending the many hues of reform and radicalism into a single national organization, however short-lived, and maneuvering, however fatally, to take advantage of an opening at the political top demonstrated the zeal of missionaries armed with a sensible method. In the Populists' wake, activists from narrower but more durable movements would deny there was any contradiction between a faith in social progress and a defense of the hardworking people.

WEEK 8

DOCUMENTS

1. Haymarket Anarchist Michael Schwab
Fights for Freedom, 1886

Talk about a gigantic conspiracy! A movement is not a conspiracy. All we did

WAS DONE IN OPEN DAYLIGHT.

There were no secrets. We prophesied in word and writing the coming of a great revolution, a change in the system of production in all industrial countries of the globe. And the change will come, and must come. Is it not absurd, as the State's Attorney and his associates have done, to suppose that this social revolution—a change of such immense proportions—was to be inaugurated on or about the first of May in the city of Chicago by making war on the police! The organizer Furthman searched hundreds of numbers of the *Arbeiter-Zeitung* and the *Alarm,* and so the prosecution must have known very well what we understood when we talked about the coming revolution. But the prosecuting attorneys preferred to ignore these explanatory articles.

The articles in evidence were carefully selected and paraded as samples of violent language, but the language used in them was just the same as newspapers used in general against us and their enemies. Even against the police and their practices they used words

OF THE SAME KIND AS WE DID.

The president of the Citizens' Association. Edwin Lee Brown, after the last election of Mayor Harrison, made a speech in North Side Turner Hall in which he called on all good citizens to take possession of the courthouse by force, even if they had to wade in blood. It seems to me that the most violent speakers are not to be found in the ranks of the Anarchists.

It is not violence in word or action the attorneys of the State and their urgers-on are waging war against; it is our doctrine—Anarchy.

We contend for communism and Anarchy—why? If we had kept silent, stones would have cried out. Murder was committed day by day. Children were slain, women worked to death, men killed inch by inch, and these crimes are never punished by law. The great principle underlying the present system is

UNPAID LABOR.

Those who amass fortunes, build palaces, and live in luxury, are doing that by virtue of unpaid labor. Being directly or indirectly the possessors of land and machinery, they dictate their terms to the workingman. He is compelled to sell his labor cheap, or to starve. The price paid him is always far below the real value. He acts under compulsion, and they call it a free contract. This infernal state of affairs keeps him poor and ignorant; an easy prey for exploitation. . . .

. . . When I came to the United States, I found that there were classes of working-men who were better paid than the European workmen, but I perceived that the state

From *The Accused and the Accusers: The Famous Speeches of the Eight Chicago Anarchists in Court* (New York: Arno, 1969), 24–28.

of things in a great number of industries was even worse, and that the so-called better paid skilled laborers were degrading rapidly into mere automatic parts of machinery. I found that the proletariat of the great industrial cities was in a condition that could not be worse. Thousands of laborers in the city of Chicago live in rooms without sufficient protection from the weather, without proper ventilation, where never a stream of sunlight flows in. There are hovels where two, three and four families live in one room. How these conditions influence the health and the morals of these unfortunate sufferers, it is needless to say. And how *do* they live? From the ash-barrels

THEY GATHER HALF-ROTTEN VEGETABLES,

in the butcher shops they buy for some cents offal of meat, and these precious morsels they carry home to prepare from them their meals. The delapidated houses in which this class of laborers live need repairs very badly, but the greedy landlord waits in most cases till he is compelled by the city to have them done. Is it a wonder that disease of all kinds kill men, women and children in such places by wholesale, especially children? Is this not horrible in a so-called civilized land where there is plenty of food and riches? Some years ago a committee of the Citizen's Association, or League, made an investigation of these matters, and I was one of the reporters that went with them. What these common laborers are today,

THE SKILLED LABORERS WILL BE TOMORROW.

Improved machinery that ought to be a blessing for the workingman, under the existing conditions turns for him to a curse. Machinery multiplies the army of unskilled laborers, makes the laborer more dependent upon the men who own the land and the machines. And that is the reason that Socialism and Communism got a foothold in this country. The outcry that Socialism, Communism and Anarchism are the creed of foreigners, is a big mistake. There are more Socialists of American birth in this country than foreigners, and that is much, if we consider that nearly half of all industrial workingmen are not native Americans. There are Socialistic papers in a great many States edited by Americans for Americans. The capitalistic newspapers conceal that fact very carefully.

Socialism, as we understand it, means that land and machinery shall be held in common by the people. The production of goods shall be carried on by producing groups which shall supply the demands of the people. Under such a system every human being would have an opportunity to do useful work, and no doubt would work. Some hours' work every day would suffice to produce all that, according to statistics, is necessary for a comfortable living. Time would be left

TO CULTIVATE THE MIND,

and to further science and art.

That is what the Socialist propose. Some say it is un-American! Well, then, is it American to let people starve and die in ignorance? Is exploitation and robbery of the poor, American? What have the great political parties done for the poor? Promised much; done nothing, except corrupting them by buying their votes on election day. A poverty-stricken man has no interest in the welfare of the community. It is only natural that in a society where women are driven to sell their honor, men should sell their votes.

But we "were not only Socialists and Communists: we were Anarchists."

What is Anarchy? . . . Anarchy is a dream, but only in the present. It will be realized.

REASON WILL GROW

in spite of all obstacles. Who is the man that has the cheek to tell us that human development has already reached its culminating point? I know that our ideal will not be accomplished, this or next year, but I know that it will be accomplished as near as possible, some day, in the future. It is entirely wrong to use the word Anarchy as synonymous with violence. Violence is one thing and Anarchy another. In the present state of society violence is used on all sides, and, therefore, we advocated the use of violence against violence, but against violence only, as a necessary means of defense.

2. "Freedom," Poem by Haymarket Anarchist Albert R. Parsons, 1886

Toil and pray! The world cries cold;
Speed thy prayer, for time is gold
At thy door Need's subtle tread:
Pray in haste! for time is bread.

And thou plow'st and thou hew'st,
And thou rivet'st and sewest,
And thou harvestest in vain;
Speak! O, man; what is thy gain?

Fly'st the shuttle day and night.
Heav'st the ores of earth to light.
Fill'st with treasures plenty's horn;
Brim'st it o'er with wine and corn.

But who hath thy meal prepared,
Festive garments with thee shared;
And where is thy cheerful hearth,
Thy good shield in battle dearth?

Thy creations round thee see
All thy work, but naught for thee!
Yea, of all the chains alone thy hand forged,
These are thine own.

Chains that round the body cling.
Chains that lame the spirits wing.

From *The Accused and the Accusers: The Famous Speeches of the Eight Chicago Anarchists in Court* (New York: Arno, 1969), 90–91.

Chains that infants' feet, indeed
Clog! O, workman! Lo! Thy meed.

What you rear and bring to light.
Profits by the idle wight,
What ye weave of diverse hue,
'Tis a curse—your only due.

What ye build, no room insures,
Not a sheltering roof to yours,
And by haughty ones are trod—
Ye, whose toil their feet hath shod.

Human bees! Has nature's thrift
Given thee naught but honey's gift?
See! the drones are on the wing.
Have you lost the will to sting?

Man of labor, up, arise!
Know the might that in thee lies,
Wheel and shaft are set at rest
At thy powerful arm's behest.

Thine oppressor's hand recoils
When thou, weary of thy toil.
Shun'st thy plough thy task begun.
When thou speak'st: Enough is done!

Break this two-fold yoke in twain;
Break thy want's enslaving chain;
Break thy slavery's want and dread;
Bread is freedom, freedom bread.

3. "Labor's Great Army," 1889

An army, with banners flying and music sounding, on its march to the battlefield, is a grand and inspiring spectacle. . . . An army in days of peace, with its pomp of ordered motion and its glowing colors and glitter of weapons, is always an attractive sight, charming the gazers, young and old, for a little while, away from the commonplaces of the everyday struggle for bread and wealth. . . . But an industrial army, such as Boston witnessed yesterday parading its historic streets, with a record of invincible patience, an ever widening purpose of righteous achievement, is a sight more attractive, a spectacle more impressive. It means more for the future than all the battlefields that have been drenched with human blood. It is a celebration of the partial reign of the common people.

So excellent were the exhibitions of all the different crafts that it would be almost invidious to particularize any as the chief ornaments. Yet, perhaps to most

From *The Boston Herald,* September 3, 1889.

people, the "floats" of the carpenters, by their striking contrast of the old log cabin of the fathers with a modern building caused the greatest impression and suggested, in addition, the immense strides in quality of work made by the workers in the last few years, just as the procession suggests in a larger way the immense strides made by the workers themselves in securing the recognition of their important position in the body politic. The industrial army of yesterday seemed to feel that the workers are the base of the heaven-seeking pyramid of civilization, and that, if that is not well founded and secure, the top must topple. . . .

Union 33 of Boston was most profuse in its exhibition of mottoes. . . . One was a huge saw made of wood and painted quite realistically. On one side was the inscription, "We are organized to elevate," and on the reverse, "Set on eight hours." Another device was a carpenter's square enlarged to a fairly heroic size. The inscription was: "We are all square union men; non-union men are not square."

Other mottoes which attracted especial attention were these: "Honest labor never rusts: up with wages, down with trusts." "Nine hours a day has paved the way: eight hours a day has come to stay." "Less work, more recreation." "We build the cities." "Those who build palaces should not dwell in hovels."

The Operative Tailors' Union gave some very sharp raps. They were accompanied by two large open wagons, trimmed and decorated, one drawn by four horses, and bearing a representation of a tailor shop in active operation with men engaged in cutting, sewing and pressing. The other wagon was fitted to resemble the interior of a room in a tenement house, with all its squalor and misery. The first wagon bore a large sign inscribed: "Away with the filthy scab tenement house labor. We will investigate a few tenement houses for $20." The second bore simply the pregnant remark: "Twenty coats a day's work."

4. Samuel Gompers Defends the Right to Strike, 1899

The working people find that improvements in the methods of production and distribution are constantly being made, and unless they occasionally strike, or have the power to enter upon a strike, the improvements will all go to the employer and all the injuries to the employees. A strike is an effort on the part of the workers to obtain some of the improvements that have occurred resultant from bygone and present genius of our intelligence, of our mental progress. We are producing wealth today at a greater ratio than ever in the history of mankind, and a strike on the part of workers is, first, against deterioration in their condition, and, second, to be participants in some of the improvements. Strikes are caused from various reasons. The employer desires to reduce wages and lengthen hours of labor, while the desire on the part of employees is to obtain shorter hours of labor and better wages, and better surroundings. Strikes establish or maintain the rights of unionism; that is, to establish and maintain the organization by which the rights of the workers can be the better protected and advanced against the little forms of oppression,

From testimony of Samuel Gompers, November 20, 1899, U.S. Congress, House of Representatives, *Report of the Industrial Commission on the Relations and Conditions of Capital and Labor,* 56th Congress, 2d Session, House Document 495, Part 7, 605–606.

sometimes economical, sometimes political—the effort on the part of employers to influence and intimidate workmen's political preferences; strikes against victimization; activity in the cause of the workers against the blacklist. . . .

It required 40,000 people in the city of New York in my own trade in 1877 to demonstrate to the employers that we had a right to be heard in our own defense of our trade, and an opportunity to be heard in our own interests. It cost the miners of the country, in 1897, sixteen weeks of suffering to secure a national conference and a national agreement. It cost the railroad brotherhoods long months of suffering, many of them sacrificing their positions, in the railroad strike of 1877, and in the Chicago, Burlington, and Quincy strike, of the same year, to secure from the employers the right to be heard through committees, their representatives. . . . Workmen have had to stand the brunt of the suffering. The American Republic was not established without some suffering, without some sacrifice, and no tangible right has yet been achieved in the interest of the people unless it has been secured by sacrifices and persistency. After a while we become a little more tolerant to each other and recognize all have rights; get around the table and chaff each other; all recognize that they were not so reasonable in the beginning. Now we propose to meet and discuss our interests, and if we can not agree we propose in a more reasonable way to conduct our contests, each to decide how to hold out and bring the other one to terms. A strike, too, is to industry as the right that the British people contended for in placing in the House of Commons the power to close the purse strings to the Government. The rights of the British people were secured in two centuries— between 1500 and 1700—more than ever before, by the securing of that power to withhold the supplies; tied up the purse strings and compelled the Crown to yield. A strike on the part of workmen is to close production and compel better terms and more rights to be acceded to the producers. The economic results of strikes to workers have been advantageous. Without strikes their rights would not have been considered. It is not that workmen or organized labor desires the strike, but it will tenaciously hold to the right to strike. We recognize that peaceful industry is necessary to successful civilized life, but the right to strike and the preparation to strike is the greatest preventive to strikes. If the workmen were to make up their minds tomorrow that they would under no circumstances strike, the employers would do all the striking for them in the way of lesser wagers and longer hours of labor.

From Industrial Workers of the World, *Preamble and Constitution of the Industrial Workers of the World, Organized July 7, 1905* (Chicago: Industrial Workers of the World, 1916).

6. Fitz John Porter Explains How to Quell Mobs, 1885

Riots generally originate in crowded cities or in districts where the population is principally composed of operatives. They are due to two causes. First: the restlessness or peevish discontent of the working-classes, who imagine that others are reaping large gains from their labor. Second: the plotting of demagogues and designing men, too indolent to earn their bread by their own exertions, who hope to receive power and profit, or perhaps notoriety. A third cause may be mentioned: the desire of honest but misguided men to obtain a better position for themselves and their families, who, brooding over real or fancied wrongs, finally resort to unlawful measures for redress.

The actors in the first movements which finally lead to a riot rarely, if ever, imagine that they are inaugurating one of these ebullitions of popular fury.

A combination of workmen, who have banded together presumably for proper purposes, believing themselves to be imposed upon by their employers, take measures to secure what they consider their rights. Sometimes one, sometimes another method is adopted, either one of which finally leads to a breach between employers and employed. Then comes a strike. Perhaps the strikers are in the employ of a railroad company, which, with its connections, reaches across the continent: all operations are suspended upon the railroad; passenger and freight cars are stopped upon the tracks; each individual striker has a little circle which he influences; the circumferences of these circles touch each other, and thus commotion is spread through the land. Human sympathy always goes out to the oppressed; the strikers represent

From Fitz John Porter, "How to Quell Mobs," *North American Review* 141 (October 1885): 351–360.

themselves as oppressed by the monopolizing corporations, and the sympathy of the community for the weaker unites with its natural prejudices against the stronger in the contest; disorder begins; confusion becomes worse confounded. Now appear the baser elements of society—the tramp, the thief, the rogue, the burglar—and these elements, which before were the outcasts of society, now become the rulers of the hour. The quarrel, before confined to the railroad and its employés, now enlarges its field, and the bad is arrayed against the general good. Pillagers at first despoil the railroad company, and then seek the property of others, no matter whom, to satisfy their greed. The community awakes to the danger of the situation, but it is too late; anarchy has the upper hand, and vice and lawlessness reign supreme. . . .

"How shall the future riot be suppressed? Upon whom lies the duty of suppression—upon the general government, the State, or the municipality?"

These are the practical questions to be discussed.

The general government has no power, except such as is derived by cession from the States. It is the creature of the State governments, and in its relations with the States is governed by organic law, beyond which it cannot step. Like all general rules, there is an exception to this rule; for there is a law, not to be found in any written constitution, which must from necessity control the general government, and that is the law of self-preservation. While it cannot interfere in any of the municipal regulations of the States, still there may be an exigency when it is not only its right, but its duty to interfere. Whenever the property of the government is endangered by an unlawful assemblage of persons, the government should protect its property, even with the sacrifice of life. It can make no difference where that property is situated. It is not subject to the laws of the States; no taxes are paid to the State for its protection. . . .

It is very difficult to draw the line where forbearance shall cease to be a virtue, and where stern duty compels the authorities to use coercion. All this must be left to their good sense, alert judgment, and proper appreciation of each individual case. There should be no dallying with a mob. It is hydra-headed, many-sided, and, at the outset, undecided as to its future movements; but if, without the use of decided measures for prevention, it be suffered to take its own way, a leader will soon be found of sufficient capacity to direct and control these movements. Let this period once be passed, and let a master-mind be placed in command, with subservience on the part of his followers, and the control of the mob in the right direction is forever lost. . . .

The qualities most needed, in those who are charged with the duty of preventing riots, are coolness, decision, alertness, and courage. Let the mob once ascertain that any of these qualities are wanting in those who seek to suppress, and the opportunity for suppression is lost. It would have been more merciful in the end to those composing many mobs, certainly to those who suffered from their excesses, if instead of firing blank cartridges a few bullets had found their way into the muskets. One determined man, with fearless front and undaunted courage, has been of more service in preventing a riot than scores of dilly-dallying mayors and governors who read the riot act and begged and besought the rioters to disperse, and called them by endearing names.

In 1877 riots broke out all over the land. The history of these riots reveals strange inconsistencies and many shameful derelictions of duty. In the city of Pittsburg, with the police of the city at his back, and a large number of State troops at his command, the mayor of that great town, with an indecision which was indefensible and unaccountable (except upon the supposition that by so doing he hoped to preserve his popularity), suffered anarchy and pillage and murder to rule for days. He strove to stem a torrent of turbulence and violence with soft speeches, by reading the riot act, by kind words. But it was too late. The time for such formalities had passed. The sacrifice of a few lives by charges of fixed bayonets, or by salvos of musketry charged with bullets, would have scattered the howling, demoniac mob back to the holes and dreary retreats from which so many of them had come.

At Harrisburg, the same policy at first placed the troops of the great State of Pennsylvania, sent to relieve its capital from the depredations of the mob, prisoners in the hands of that very mob that they were sent to suppress. The militiamen were marched up and down the streets amid the jeers and howls of the rioters. But a different state of affairs was soon inaugurated, through the exertions of one determined man, the mayor of the city. He selected some of the best citizens, and with the sheriff of the county marched at their head, and almost in an instant dispelled the mob while in the very act of pillaging.

All along the line of the railroads extending west from Buffalo the employés were in commotion. Mobs of several thousand people had gathered at different points, but only at one place was the mob beyond the control of the authorities. This was at the city of Buffalo. At East Buffalo, where a mob which was estimated at more than three thousand persons was hooting, howling, and threatening vengeance, a captain of police, with the aid of the baton forcibly brought in contact with the heads of the rioters, in a very few moments dispelled the mob, so that, in the words of the historian who records this incident, "the East Buffalo grounds were as clear and quiet as a country field on a Sunday afternoon." . . .

Mobs are cowards at first. Crime always enervates. They only gain courage as they find that those whose duty it is to suppress them are themselves cowards. A mob is not to be feared when it is first aroused. It is only as its passion for carnage is whetted by the taste of blood, or its greed for pillage is gratified, that it becomes dangerous.

Upon whomsoever devolves the duty of suppression, let this be his first effort: check at the very beginning; allow no tumultuous gatherings; permit no delay; a few stern, resolute words; if these be not heeded, then strike resolutely, boldly; let there be no hesitation; if necessary, take life at the outset. It will be more merciful to take one life then than to suffer the mob to take the lives of many, or to be compelled to sacrifice the innocent with the guilty at the point of the bayonet, or in the discharge of musketry or cannon. But the necessity to take life will not arise unless there be inactivity and indecision at the outset on the part of the authorities.

Before the time shall come when it will be necessary to use musket-ball or bayonet, the opportunity will be afforded to suppress the riot; perhaps at the sacrifice of a few broken heads, or by the imprisonment of some of its leaders.

In every large city, in fact in every city where a police force is employed, a perfect drill should prepare policemen to meet the exigencies arising from any tumultuous assemblage of the people; so that, at a moment's warning, these conservators of the peace will be ready to act, and to act understandingly and promptly. It will be found that a few determined policemen, placed in the field at a moment's notice, will prove one of the best and most direct methods of quelling a mob. These, by skillful maneuvers, can take a mob in flank, or in rear, or in front, if necessary, and so employ themselves and their clubs that almost before the mob would know what was impelling them they would be driven from the field of action. . . .

The most fertile cause of all riots is the peevish discontent of wage-workers—too often ignorant of the true relations between themselves and their employers. This peevish discontent may perhaps be confined to a few, but those few will be able to avail themselves of the restlessness which may pervade the whole body of operatives. This discontent arises not so much from any real oppression, or from any wrong, but simply from the natural jealousy which every man feels, more or less, when he sees others living more luxuriously than himself, and especially when that luxury appears to be the result of his labor. Now this discontent may be dispelled, perhaps not in the present generation, though it may be greatly moderated; but, certainly, means can be taken to prevent it in the future. The employer and employé may surely be brought together in more intimate relations than those they at present sustain. Where lies the fault in the present system? Who is justly chargeable with the origin of this discontent? That question cannot be settled in this discussion. But so much may be said: the working-classes can be educated up to a higher tone of feeling, a better appreciation of their duty to their employers, a higher standard of morals, and a nobler level of thought and action. May not the employers find something in the present condition of things for which they are responsible; and which they, in the exercise of the duty they owe to common humanity, may be able to better?

There is a factory, in one of the large manufacturing towns of the country, where one of the employers, imbued with true Christian philanthropy, brings himself, in a measure, down to a level with his hundreds of employés. He mingles with their families; finds out the social status and wants of all; gives a word of advice to one; imparts counsel to another; sympathizes with the mourner; puts his strong arm round the weak; and employs all of his ability to raise his workingmen in the scale of human existence. He provides a reading-room for them, furnishes them with reading matter, and gives them lectures. Let this example be emulated by every employer in the land, and riots would be impossible.

1. John W. Holway, a Pinkerton Guard, Views the Battle of Homestead, 1892

JOHN W. HOLWAY sworn and examined.

By the CHAIRMAN:

Q. Please state your name, age, residence, and occupation.—*A.* John W. Holway; 23½ years old; 1008 Twelfth street, Chicago; occupation, chiefly that of student. . . .

Q. Were you a member of the company that was sent by the Pinkertons to Homestead during the recent strike?—*A.* Yes, sir.

Q. What kind of a contract did you enter into at that time?—*A.* The contract was stated about this way, that in case we were injured we would not sue the company for damages, and that in case we deserted their employ at any time without asking their leave we would forfeit the wages which were then due us.

U.S. Congress, Senate, Report No. 1280. 52d Session (Washington, D.C.: Government Printing Office, 1893), 68–73.

Q. And on the other hand, what were they to do for you; what rate of wages was to be paid?—*A.* We were to be paid $15 a week and expenses.

Q. How many men accompanied you from Chicago to Homestead?—*A.* I judge there was 125. . . .

Q. Did you understand, when you left here, that you were to bear arms when you reached your destination?—*A.* No, sir.

Q. Did you anticipate it?—*A.* From nothing that they had told us. I read the newspapers, and I formed that private opinion, but we received no such information from them.

Q. Were you given any arms of any kind when you left here?—*A.* No, sir.

Q. Were you transported rather quietly and secretly from this point to Homestead?—*A.* The trip was rather a quiet one, and very quickly and secretly planned.

Q. Describe it, and give us the route you took?—*A.* We started out from the office on Fifth avenue and we went along the street to the Lake Shore depot, where we entered the rear entrance on the platform. Instead of going up to the regular passenger entrance we took the one the employés take, so we went into the rear cars of the train very quickly. Directly we entered the rear of the cars, men who seemed to be detectives and not patrolmen, stationed themselves at the doors, and they prevented our exit, and they prevented the entrance of any outside parties who might wish to enter. We then, on this regular midnight train, went to Toledo, reaching there about 9 o'clock next morning. At Toledo a special engine was hitched on to our three special cars, and we went by way of Sandusky, not through Elyria, and around to Cleveland. We did what was called "running wild." We ran rather slowly—it was not a scheduled train—on to Cleveland, and there they gave us some lunches, and we went as fast as 40 or 50 miles an hour through Painesville, down to Ashtabula. There we waited for an hour. . . . We then, the whole train, went rapidly on through Jefferson County to Youngstown, and from Youngstown to Bellview, where we landed rapidly. We were told to prepare to land—to leave the cars. During our trip we were not allowed to leave the cars at all, we were kind of prisoners. We did not have any rights. That might have been because they were afraid of union men, perhaps spies, who would telegraph ahead to Homestead. They wanted to get inside the works without bloodshed, but we had no rights whatever. Then we entered the boats, some 300 of us. There was two covered barges, like these Mississippi covered boats. One was fitted up with bunks that reached to the ceiling on the sides. I entered that and we supposed that we would be allowed to sleep, but we did not sleep for twenty-four hours, but Capt. Nordrum, the man in charge, told us to leave the boat with bunks in and go to the other boat, and we did so. We were told to fall in, and the roll of our names was called, and we were told to secure our uniforms, which consisted of coat, hat, vest, and pair of trowsers. When we had secured our uniforms we were some distance down the river, and we were told to keep quiet, and the lights were turned out, and everything kept very quiet until we were given orders softly to arise. I was lying down about an hour when the order was sent around the boat for all the men to get ready to land. Then the captain called out for men who could handle rifles. I did not want to handle a rifle, and then he said we want two or three men here to guard the door with clubs, so I said I would do that, and I got over the table and got a club like a policeman's club to guard the side door—that was to prevent men from coming in boats and jumping on to our barge from the river. I stayed there while the men who could handle rifles were marched down to the open end of the boat, and I did not see anything more of them until the firing commenced.

Q. Tell what further occurred as a matter of knowledge on your part?—*A.* I had a curiosity to see what was going on on the bank. I was stationed inside the boat at the side door, and as there were three or four other men afraid to carry rifles, they took upon themselves the duty of watching the door, and so I was told to go down to the other end of the boat to see what was going on, and I saw what appeared to be a lot of young men and boys on the bank, swearing and cursing and having large sticks. I did not see a gun or anything. They were swearing at our men. I did not see any more, but came back and resumed my position at the door. I had not been back more than two minutes when I heard a sharp pistol shot, and then there were 30, 40, or 100 of them, and our men came running and stampeding back as fast as they could and they got in the shelter of the door, and then they turned around and blazed away. It was so dark I could see the flames from the rifles easily. They fired about 50 shots—I was surprised to see them stand up, because the strikers were shooting also, but they did not seem to be afraid of being hit. They had some shelter from the door. They fired in rather a professional manner I thought. The men inside the Chicago boat were rather afraid at hearing the rifles, and we all jumped for rifles that were laying on a table ready, and some one, I think a sergeant, opened a box of revolvers, and said, "all get revolvers," so I had now a Winchester rifle and a revolver. I called out to see if anybody had been hurt, and I saw a man there apparently strangling. He had been shot through the head and he died sometime afterwards, I think. His name was Kline, I believe. Of course it rather made us incensed to be shot at that way, but I kept out of danger as much as possible.

I was standing there when Nordrum came up, and he said to follow him, and I crossed over to the New York boat, where there were 40 men with rifles standing on the edge of the boat watching what was going on on shore. Nordrum spoke to the men on shore. He spoke in rather a loud manner—say a commanding manner. He said: "We are coming up that hill anyway, and we don't want any more trouble from you men." The men were in the mill windows. The mill is ironclad. There were a few boys in sight, but the men were under shelter, all of them. I supposed I should have to go up the hill, and I didn't like the idea very well, because it was pretty nearly certain death, as I supposed. I thought it over in what little time I had, and I thought I would have to go anyway. While I was standing there, waiting for Nordrum to charge up the hill and we follow him, he went away, and he was gone quite a few minutes. I took advantage of that to look around the New York men's boat to see what was going on, and I saw about 150 of the New York men hiding in the aisle furthest from the shore. It was divided into bunks. They were hiding in the bunks—they were hiding under the mattresses; they didn't want to be told to shoulder a rifle and charge up the hill; they were naturally afraid of it. They were watchmen, and not detectives. Now the men who had the rifles were mostly detectives. There were 40 of the detectives, who I afterwards learned were regular employés of Pinkerton, but these other men were simply watchmen, and hired as watchmen, and told so, and nothing else. Seeing these men so afraid and cowering rather dispirited the rest of us, and those who had rifles—I noticed there seemed to be a fear among them all. I went to the end of the boat, and there I saw crowds on the bank, waving their hands, and all looking at the boat and appearing to be very frantic.

I judged we were going to have trouble and went back to the end where I had been placed and waited for Nordrum to come, but he did not turn up, and after I stood there about half an hour I concluded, as there was no one there to order us to do anything and as it was stated that the steam tug had pulled out, taking all those who had charge of us—I concluded I would look out for my life, and if anything was said about my leaving and not staying there I would say I did not intend to work for them any more; so I returned to the door I was told to guard, and in that place I stayed for the remainder of the day, during all the shooting and firing. I concluded if the boat was burned—we expected a thousand men would charge down the embankment and put us to massacre; that was what we expected all throughout the day—I concluded if the boat was burned I would defend my life with the other men. . . .

At about 3 o'clock we heard something; we thought was a cannon, but it was dynamite. Afterwards I learned it was worse than a cannon; sounded like a very large cannon. It partially wrecked the other boat. A stick of it fell near me. It broke open the door of the aisles, and it smashed open the door, and the sharpshooters were firing directly at any man in sight. That was about 3 o'clock. Most of the men were for surrender at this time, but the old detectives held out and said, "If you surrender you will be shot down like dogs; the best thing is to stay here." We could not cut our barges loose because there was a fall below, where we would be sunk. We were deserted by our captains and by our tug, and left there to be shot. We felt as though we had been betrayed and we did not understand it, and we did not know why the tug had pulled off and didn't know it had come back. About 4 o'clock some one or other authorized a surrender, effected by means of a medical student, who studies at the eclectic college over here, the most intelligent man on board for that matter, a Freemason. He secured a surrender. I don't know how he secured it— by waving a flag. We secured a surrender. What he wanted was that our steam tug pull us away, but instead of that the strikers held that we should depart by way of the depot.

That surrender was effected, and I started up the embankment with the men who went out, and we were glad to get away and did not expect trouble; but I looked up the hill and there were our men being struck as they went up, and it looked rather disheartening. . . . I ran down a side street and ran through a yard. I ran about half a mile I suppose, but was rather weak and had had nothing to eat or drink and my legs gave out, could not run any further, and some man got hold of me by the back of my coat, and about 20 or 30 men came up and kicked me and pounded me with stones. I had no control of myself then. I thought I was about going and commenced to scream, and there were 2 or 3 strikers with rifles rushed up then and kept off the crowd and rushed me forward to a theater, and I was put in the theater and found about 150 of the Pinkerton men there, and that was the last violence offered me.

2. Eugene V. Debs Denounces the Role of Corporations and the Courts in the Pullman Strike, 1895

*Proclamation to American Railway Union**

TERRE HAUTE, IND., June 1, 1895.

Sirs and Brothers—A cruel wrong against our great order, perpetrated by Wm. A. Woods, United States Circuit Judge, has been approved by the United States Supreme Court, and from under its shadow I address this communication to you; but though prison walls frown upon myself and others whom you chose as officials, I assure you that neither despondency nor despair has taken the place of the courage which has characterized our order since the storms of persecution first began to beat upon us. Hope has not deserted us. Our faith in the future of our great order is as strong as when our banners waved triumphantly over the Great Northern from St. Paul to the coast. Our order is still the undaunted friend of the toiling masses and our battle-cry now, as ever, is the emancipation of labor from degrading, starving and enslaving conditions. We have not lost faith in the ultimate triumph of truth over perjury, of justice over wrong, however exalted may be the stations of those who perpetrate the outrages.

The Storm and the Battle

I need not remind you, comrades of the American Railway Union, that our order in the pursuit of the right was confronted with a storm of opposition such as never beat upon a labor organization in all time. Its brilliant victory on the Great Northern and its gallant championship of the unorganized employes of the Union Pacific had aroused the opposition of every railroad corporation in the land.

To crush the American Railway Union was the one tie that united them all in the bonds of vengeance; it solidified the enemies of labor into one great association, one organization which, by its fabulous wealth, enabled it to bring into action resources aggregating billions of money and every appliance that money could purchase. But in this supreme hour the American Railway Union, undaunted, put forth its efforts to rescue Pullman's famine-cursed wage slaves from the grasp of an employer as heartless as a stone, as remorseless as a savage and as unpitying as an incarnate fiend. The battle fought in the interest of starving men, women and children stands forth in the history of Labor's struggles as the great "Pullman Strike." It was a battle on the part of the American Railway Union fought for a cause as holy as ever aroused the courage of brave men; it was a battle in which upon one side were men thrice armed because their cause was just, but they fought against the combined power of corporations which by the use of money could debauch justice, and, by playing the part of incendiary, bring to their aid the military power of the government, and this solidified mass of venality, venom and vengeance constituted the foe against which the American Railway Union fought Labor's greatest battle for humanity.

---

*Issued when Debs' jail sentence for having participated in the Pullman strike was affirmed by the Supreme Court of the United States.

Writings and Speeches of Eugene V. Debs (New York: Hermitage Press, 1948), 1–2.

1. Unionized Workers in the Knights of Labor Demand a Fair Share of American Wealth, 1878

The recent alarming development and aggression of aggregated wealth, which, unless checked, will invariably lead to the pauperization and hopeless degradation of the toiling masses, render it imperative, if we desire to enjoy the blessings of life, that a check should be placed upon its power and upon unjust accumulation, and a system adopted which will secure to the laborer the fruits of his toil; and as this much desired object can only be accomplished by the thorough unification of labor, and the united effort of those who obey the divine injunction that "In the sweat of thy brow shalt thou eat bread," we have formed the * * * * * with a view of securing the organization and direction, by co-operative effort, of the power of the industrial classes; and we submit to the world the object sought to be accomplished by our organization, calling upon all who believe in securing "the greatest good to the greatest number" to aid and assist us:—

Preamble to the constitution of the Knights of Labor, 1878, in Timothy Patrick McCarthy and John McMillan, eds., *The Radical Reader: A Documentary History of the American Radical Tradition* (New York: Free Press, 2003), pp. 244–245.

I. To bring within the folds of organization every department of productive industry, making knowledge a standpoint for action, and industrial and moral worth, not wealth, the true standard of individual and national greatness.

II. To secure to the toilers a proper share of the wealth that they create; more of the leisure that rightfully belongs to them; more societary advantages; more of the benefits, privileges, and emoluments of the world, all those rights and privileges necessary to make them capable of enjoying, appreciating, defending, and perpetuating the blessings of good government.

III. To arrive at the true condition of the producing masses in their educational, moral, and financial condition, by demanding from the various governments the establishment of bureaus of Labor Statistics.

IV. The establishment of co-operative institutions, productive and distributive.

V. The reserving of the public lands—the heritage of the people—for the actual settler;—not another acre for railroads or settlers.

VI. The abrogation of all laws that do not bear equally upon capital and labor, the removal of unjust technicalities, delays, and discriminations in the administration of justice, and the adopting of measures providing for the health and safety of those engaged in mining, manufacturing, or building pursuits.

VII. The enactment of laws to compel chartered corporations to pay their employes weekly, in full, for labor performed during the preceding week, in the lawful money of the country.

VIII. The enactment of laws giving mechanics and laborers a first lien on their work for full wages.

IX. The abolishment of the contract system on national, state, and municipal work.

X. The substitution of arbitration for strikes, whenever and wherever employers and employes are willing to meet on equitable grounds.

XI. The prohibition of the employment of children in workshops, mines, and factories before attaining their fourteenth year.

XII. To abolish the system of letting out by contract the labor of convicts in our prisons and reformatory institutions.

XIII. To secure for both sexes equal pay for equal work.

XIV. The reduction of the hours of labor to eight per day, so that the laborers may have more time for social enjoyment and intellectual improvement, and be enabled to reap the advantages conferred by the labor-saving machinery which their brains have created.

XV. To prevail upon governments to establish a purely national circulating medium, based upon the faith and resources of the nation, and issued directly to the people, without the intervention of any system of banking corporations, which money shall be a legal tender in payment of all debts, public or private.

2. Journalist Henry Demarest Lloyd Exposes the Standard Oil Monopoly, 1881

Kerosene has become, by its cheapness, the people's light the world over. In the United States we used 220,000,000 gallons of petroleum last year. It has come into such demand abroad that our exports of its increased from 79,458,888 gallons in 1868, to 417,648,544 in 1879. It goes all over Europe, and to the far East. . . . After articles of food, this country has but one export, cotton, more valuable than petroleum. It was worth $61,789,438 in our foreign trade in 1877; $46,574,974 in 1878; and $18,546,642 in the five months ending November 30, 1879. In the United States, in the cities as well as the country, petroleum is the general illuminator. We use more kerosene lamps than Bibles.

The raw material of this world's light is produced in a territory beginning with Cattaraugus County in New York, and extending southwesterly through eight or nine counties of Pennsylvania, making a belt about one hundred and fifty miles long, and twelve or fifteen miles wide, and then, with an interval, running into West Virginia, Kentucky, and Tennessee, where the yield is unimportant. The bulk of the oil comes from two counties, Cattaraugus in New York, and McKean in Pennsylvania. . . .

Very few of the forty millions of people in the United States who burn kerosene know that its production, manufacture, and export, its price at home and abroad, have been controlled for years by a single corporation,—the Standard Oil Company. This company began in a partnership, in the early years of the civil war, between Samuel Andrews and John Rockefeller in Cleveland. Rockefeller had been a book-keeper in some interior town in Ohio, and had afterwards made a few thousand dollars by keeping a flour store in Cleveland. Andrews had been a day laborer in refineries, and so poor that his wife took in sewing. He found a way of refining by which more kerosene could be got out of a barrel of petroleum than by any other method, and set up for himself a ten-barrel still in Cleveland, by which he cleared $500 in six months.

Andrews' still and Rockefeller's savings have grown into the Standard Oil Company. It has a capital, nominally $3,500,000, but really much more, on which it divides among it stockholders every year millions of dollars of profits. It has refineries at Cleveland, Baltimore, and New York. Its own acid works, glue factories, hardware stores, and barrel shops supply it with all the accessories it needs in its business. It has bought land at Indianapolis on which to erect the largest barrel factory in the country. . . . It buys 30,000 to 40,000 barrels of crude oil a day, at a price fixed by itself, and makes special contracts with the railroads for the transportation of 13,000,000 to 14,000,000 barrels of oil a year. . . .

The Standard produces only one fiftieth or sixtieth of our petroleum, but dictates the price of all, and refines nine tenths. Circulars are issued at intervals by which the price of oil is fixed for all the cities of the country, except New York, where a little competition survives. . . . There is not to-day a merchant in Chicago, or in any other

Henry Demarest Lloyd, "Story of a Great Monopoly," *Atlantic Monthly* 47 (March 1881): 320–323, 327–330.

city in the New England, Western, or Southern States, dealing in kerosene, whose prices are not fixed for him by the Standard. . . .

This corporation has driven into bankruptcy, or out of business, or into union with itself, all the petroleum refineries of the country except five in New York, and a few of little consequence in Western Pennsylvania. . . .

Their great business capacity would have insured the managers of the Standard success, but the means by which they achieved monopoly was by conspiracy with the railroads. . . . The Standard killed its rivals, in brief, by getting the great trunk lines to refuse to give them transportation. Commodore Vanderbilt is reported to have said that there was but one man—Rockefeller—who could dictate to him. . . .

. . . [T]he Pennsylvania Railroad agreed with the Standard, under the name of the South Improvement Company, to double the freights on oil to everybody, but to repay the Standard one dollar for every barrel of oil it shipped, and one dollar for every barrel any of its competitors shipped. . . . Ostensibly this contract was given up, in deference to the whirlwind of indignation it excited. But Rockefeller, the manager of the Standard, was a man who could learn from defeat. He made no more tell-tale contracts that could be printed. He effected secret arrangements with the Pennsylvania, the New York Central, the Erie, and the Atlantic and Great Western. . . . The Standard succeeded in getting from Mr. Vanderbilt [of the New York Central Railroad] free transportation for its crude oil from the wells in Pennsylvania, one hundred and fifty miles, to the refineries at Cleveland, and back. This stamped out competing refineries at Pittsburg, and created much of the raw material of the riots of July, 1877. Vanderbilt signed an agreement, March 25, 1872, that "all agreements for the transportation of oil after this date shall be upon a basis of perfect equality," and ever since has given the Standard special rates and privileges. He has paid it back in rebates millions of dollars, which have enabled it to crush out all competitors. . . . He united with the Erie [Railroad] in a war on the Pennsylvania Railroad, to force it to sell to the Standard all its refineries, and the great pipe lines by which the oil . . . was carried from the wells to the railroads. He then joined with the Erie and the Pennsylvania in a similar attack on the Baltimore and Ohio, which had to sell out to the Standard. So the Standard obtained the control of all the pipe lines and of the transportation, of everything. . . . Mr. Vanderbilt began, as did the Erie and Pennsylvania railroad kings, with paying back to the Standard, but to no other shipper, ten per cent of its freight bills. He continued making one concession after another, till when he was doing the business for other shippers at $1.40 and $1.25 a barrel, he charged the Standard only eighty and eighty-one cents, and this was afterwards reduced to sixty cents a barrel. During the war against the Pennsylvania road to make it sell out to the Standard, the New York Central carried oil for less than nothing. Besides the other allowances, Mr. Vanderbilt paid the Standard through its alias, the American Transfer Company, a rebate of thirty-five cents a barrel on all the crude oil shipped by it or its competitors. . . .

So closely had the Standard octopus gripped itself about Mr. Vanderbilt that . . . its competitors could not get transportation from him. He allowed the Standard to become the owner of all the oil cars run over his road, and of all his terminal facilities for oil. As the Standard owned all but 200 of the oil cars run on the Erie, and leased all that road's terminal facilities, it could charge its rivals anything it pleased for the privileges of New York harbor. . . .

If we turn to the experience of the refiners we find they fared as badly as the producers. The handful of New York refiners who survived the conspiracy against them . . . had to keep their capacity limited and to do as little as they could. They did not dare to build large refineries, because they would not be able to get oil enough carried to them to keep them going. Mr. Alexander, of Cleveland, tells how he was informed by Rockefeller, of the Standard, that if he would not sell out he should be crushed out. . . . Refiner after refiner in Pittsburg, buying his crude oil in the open market, manufacturing it at his works, shipping it to the seaboard, met with a continued succession of losses, and was forced into bankruptcy or a sale of his works to the Standard, who always had a buyer on the spot at the right time. The great majority of these refineries, when bought by the Standard, were dismantled. . . .

Its genius for monopoly has given the Standard control of more than the product of oil and its manufacture. Wholesale merchants in all the cities of the country, except New York, have to buy and sell at the prices it makes. Merchants who buy oil of the Standard are not allowed to sell to dealers who buy of its few competitors. Some who have done so have been warned not to repeat the offense, and have been informed that, if they did so, the Standard, though under contract to supply them with oil, would cut them off, and would fight any suit they might bring through all the courts without regard to expense. . . .

To-day, in every part of the United States, people who burn kerosene are paying the Standard Oil Company a tax on every gallon amounting to several times its original cost to that concern. The average price of crude oil at the wells or at Cleveland, as the railroads carry the crude free to the Standard's refineries, was in December last about three cents a gallon. The price of refined at Cleveland was seventeen cents a gallon. Oil that the Standard sells in New York at a profit, at ten and one half cents a gallon, they charge nineteen and three fourths cents for in Chicago. The average cost, last December, of the one and a third barrels of petroleum needed to make a barrel of kerosene was $2.05 at Cleveland. The cost of refining, barreling, and all expenses, including a refiner's profit of half a dollar a barrel, is . . . $2.75 a barrel. To bring it by rail to Chicago costs seventy cents, making the total cost $5.50 for a barrel of fifty gallons, or eleven cents a gallon. The price the Standard charges in Chicago is nineteen and three fourths cents a gallon, in which, as the difference between eleven and nineteen and three fourths cents, there is a tax on the public of eight and three fourths cents. This tax is transmitted by the middle-men, jobbers, and retailers to the consumer. When at twenty-five cents a gallon the workingman buys kerosene because it is cheaper than gas, or the student because it is better, each pays the Standard this tax of eight and three fourths cents a gallon. A family that uses a gallon of kerosene a day pays a yearly tribute to the Standard of $32, the income from $800 in the four per cents. . . .

[T]he Standard pays dividends of $1,000,000 a month. It can do this, and have millions left to pay the suits of refineries it has leased and keeps idle, its backsheesh [payback] to railroad men, the bribes it has had to give judges, state legislatures, and state inspectors, and its salaries of hundreds of thousands of dollars a month to men whom it has turned out of the business, and who are acting as its paid agents. To-day the only visible hope of cheap light for the people of this country is the discovery, announced by the Atlantic cable on January 28th, that in the Hanover petroleum district in Germany a basin has been found, which is thought by experts to be, beyond doubt, as large and rich as the one in Pennsylvania. In Europe, such alliances between the railroads and the refiners as created the Standard monopoly are impossible. German oil wells, German refineries, and the Canadian canals may yet give the people of the interior of this continent what the American Standard and the American railroads have denied them,—cheap light.

3. Sweatshop Conditions Horrify a Factory Inspector, 1893

[T]he sweating industry is carried on principally in the south-east part of Philadelphia; . . . at least 90 per cent. of the whole of this work in the sewing line is done right here; a close count shows from 3,500 to 4,000 people engaged, with a few exceptions, at work in tenement houses or a combination if you choose; the living apartments, cooking, eating and sleeping are on the first, and part second floors, the remaining part second and all of the third is used for work rooms. The nationalities represented are Russian Jews, Poles, Huns, Slavs and Italians, and their general temperament is of a most avaricious kind.

The matter of hours seemingly do not count. It is simply this; If a contractor wants a coat, pants, or vest as the case may be, the person who sub-contracts for the work has no choice of hours or aught else, but hastens to accomplish the task, being sure to get back at the given time or forfeit his chance for getting more work, so that after all the whole system is the effort of an industrial evil, which is being fostered by our American people through their very indifference to actual surroundings, and the sooner the whole people get on their thinking cap the better, and adopt such means (radical though they may seem) as will prohibit entirely, work of this kind being done in the home. Then and then only, will contractors provide proper work rooms subject to proper shop discipline, and regulated by a full enforcement of the Factory Law. For the conditions that surround this class of people is outrivaled by no other. Actual filth contributing largely to their immediate surroundings, and any attempt on my part to describe my actual findings, would mean a shock to the pride of our much boasted prosperity in this, our city of homes.

Speaking to a sub-contractor recently of the condition of trade, he said in answer to my query, "Why, the coat I used to get $3 for making two years ago, I now get $1.50 for. Then I was treated with some consideration, some respect, but since the invasion . . . of the tenement house workers I am glad to take just what I can get without making a remark, lest I be subject to insult and deprived of all work. It is a tremendous odds to be competing against, and the few of us who strive to keep shops would gladly hail the enactment of a law compelling all to do likewise." I will cite just a few instances that you may get a faint idea of some of the prevailing conditions.

In visiting what I can only describe as an old tinder box a few days since, I found three different contractors with men, women and boys amounting in the aggregate upwards of sixty. The drinking water was drawn in buckets and filled into a tin boiler, each day's sediment going to the bottom (for it was never cleaned,) only to be rolled

---

Fourth Annual Report of the Factory Inspector of the Commonwealth of Pennsylvania. For the Year 1893 (n.p.: Clarence M. Busch, 1894), pp. 38–39.

and raised by each day's filling. Cigarettes were being smoked at such a rate as to make the air blue; confusion reigned supreme; coal ashes were strewn all over the floor; this coupled with scraps of basting threads, clippings of cloth, etc., went to make up a most trying picture. In the midst of it all sat a young man who was temporarily disengaged from his work, eating a dark colored piece of bread with mustard. Out of the rooms and in the hallway was one water closet in a vile condition, and the stairway gave evidence of mistaken use too disgusting to mention.

Another was a building three stories high in which rag sorting was the main occupation. On the ground floor I discovered the wife of the proprietor and three of her children, aged 3, 5 and 8 respectively, the mother was acting as purchaser and sorter in the absence of the man. The children naturally were close beside her; when she sorted, they tried to help her; when she weighed they stood around the scales looking worldly wise. On I went to the second story and there discovered a number of old women working, who, from all appearances, were closing in on their three score years, they were surrounded by rags of the filthiest kind. After a general survey of this room I ascended still higher only to find more old women on the third floor, occupied in like manner as those on the floor below. The odor that pervaded this room was vile in the extreme. I immediately set to work to fathom the cause, when, lo and behold, there in a corner was a bin which was used as a receptacle for dog manure. I could scarcely believe my eyes, but there it was, and there it had been for the best part of the summer months, so the women told me. This is but a brief account of much more that could be enumerated by me, for this is the dark side of our darkest Philadelphia, and when I discover the reckless spirit manifest among those people, their total disregard for any law, only that which (as they themselves tell me) will bring them dollars and cents, I fear for the future.

4. Industrialist George M. Pullman Explains the Strike at Pullman Palace Car Works, 1894

The depression in the car-building business, which began in 1893, manifested itself not only in a falling off in the prices for cars, averaging in all classes 24%, but in such stagnation that the force in the Pullman shops on November 1st, 1893, was less than 1,100, while the average number employed in the fiscal year ending July 31st, 1893, was 4,497. In the months of August and September, 1893, we had an opportunity of making only six bids for work, of which but three were accepted.

In order to procure car-building contracts a reduction of the wages of April, 1893, of the car shop employes, averaging 19% was made, to make them correspond with those paid by other car manufacturers, and by making bids at shop cost and less, we secured work aggregating about $1,500,000, and were underbid on bids for nearly the same amount. On the accepted bids our net loss was over $50,000. By taking this course we had been able by last May to secure work enough to raise the number having employment to nearly 3,300.

"President Pullman's Statement at the Stockholders' Annual Meeting, October 18, 1894," in *The Strike at Pullman* (Pullman, Ill.: Pullman Company, 1894), pp. 39–42.

Although these conditions were carefully explained to a large committee of the shop employes, three-fourths of them were persuaded to enter upon the strike, because the company declined to restore wages to the scale of the prosperous times of the early part of 1893. Several suggestions were made to the company that it should consent to arbitration as a means of ending the strike, but it declined to do so upon the ground that it being an ascertained fact that even at the existing rates of wages, car building contracts could only be procured for execution at actual and serious losses, the company could not possibly submit to the discretion of any person, not responsible to its shareholders, the question whether or not it should increase its manufacturing losses by any increase of wages, or even whether or not it should continue the manufacturing of cars at current prices, at the wages complained of. . . .

There has been no substantial change in the condition of the car building business, and the contracts taken by us before the strike, and those taken since the strike, are being executed at prices which give no profit, and such contracts are taken because the shops are being kept in operation for the repairing of the company's own cars, and to give as much employment as is possible in the present condition of business.

I have learned in various ways that a good many persons during the strike lost sight of its true origin, and gained the impression that it was influenced by the house rents at Pullman not being lowered when wages were reduced from the high scale of the spring of 1893. That this is not true is shown by the fact that more than two-thirds of the employes who began the strike, were not tenants of the company; indeed, between 500 and 600 of them owned their own homes. . . .

The real cause of complaint during the autumn of 1893 and the succeeding winter was not altogether on account of the scale of wages, but largely because there was not enough work to give an opportunity for anything like full earnings by all the men. . . .

I may observe also, that there have been indications of a feeling in some quarters that this company ought to have maintained the scale of wages existing in the car manufacturing department in April, 1893, without regard to the current selling prices for cars, paying the consequent increased losses in the car-building business out of the company's earnings in the independent business of operating sleeping cars. . . . At what point did a principle take effect that the latter business must be kept going by the former, regardless of their independence or of the discrepancy between the cost and selling price of cars? At the time of the strike 227 of the shop employes had been in the employment of the company for less than a year, and more than half the entire force had been with the company less than five years. Had all of them earned a guaranty of uninterrupted, undiminished wages? . . .

Of the present force at the car shops only about 300 are new employes, and the remainder have returned to their former work with, I believe, a widely prevailing feeling, that they have learned by experience that this company was earnest in befriending them in seeking work for them when little was to be had, and in giving them work at wages which the selling prices of their product did not justify, and that the genuineness of the interest of this company in their welfare is far more to be trusted than the promises of the agitators who misled them.

6. President Theodore Roosevelt Advocates Regulation, 1901

The tremendous and highly complex industrial development which went on with ever accelerated rapidity during the latter half of the nineteenth century brings us face to face, at the beginning of the twentieth, with very serious social problems. The old laws, and the old customs which had almost the binding force of law, were once quite sufficient to regulate the accumulation and distribution of wealth. Since the industrial changes which have so enormously increased the productive power of mankind, they are no longer sufficient.

The growth of cities has gone on beyond comparison faster than the growth of the country, and the upbuilding of the great industrial centers has meant a startling increase, not merely in the aggregate of wealth, but in the number of very large individual, and especially of very large corporate, fortunes. The creation of these great corporate fortunes has not been due to the tariff nor to any other governmental action, but to natural causes in the business world, operating in other countries as they operate in our own.

The process has aroused much antagonism, a great part of which is wholly without warrant. . . . The captains of industry who have driven the railway systems across this continent, who have built up our commerce, who have developed our manufactures, have on the whole done great good to our people. Without them the material development of which we are so justly proud could never have taken place. . . . The slightest study of business conditions will satisfy anyone capable of forming a judgment that the personal equation is the most important factor in a business operation; that the business ability of the man at the head of any business,

Theodore Roosevelt, First annual address to Congress, December 3, 1901, in James D. Richardson, ed., *A Compilation of the Messages and Papers of the Presidents,* vol. 16 (New York: Bureau of National Literature, 1897–1914), pp. 6643–6647. This document can also be found in Richard Hofstadter, ed., *The Progressive Movement, 1900–1915* (Englewood Cliffs, N.J.: Prentice-Hall, 1963), pp. 141–144.

big or little, is usually the factor which fixes the gulf between striking success and hopeless failure.

An additional reason for caution in dealing with corporations is to be found in the international commercial conditions of today. . . . Business concerns which have the largest means at their disposal and are managed by the ablest men are naturally those which take the lead in the strife for commercial supremacy among the nations of the world. America has only just begun to assume the commanding position in the international business world which we believe will more and more be hers. It is of the utmost importance that this position be not jeoparded, especially at a time when the overflowing abundance of our own natural resources and the skill, business energy, and mechanical aptitude of our people make foreign markets essential. Under such conditions it would be most unwise to cramp or to fetter the youthful strength of our Nation.

Moreover, it cannot too often be pointed out that to strike with ignorant violence at the interests of one set of men almost inevitably endangers the interests of all. The fundamental rule in our national life—the rule which underlies all others—is that, on the whole, and in the long run, we shall go up or down together. . . .

The mechanism of modern business is so delicate that extreme care must be taken not to interfere with it in a spirit of rashness or ignorance. Many of those who have made it their vocation to denounce the great industrial combinations which are popularly, although with technical inaccuracy, known as "trusts," appeal especially to hatred and fear. These are precisely the two emotions, particularly when combined with ignorance, which unfit men for the exercise of cool and steady judgment. In facing new industrial conditions, the whole history of the world shows that legislation will generally be both unwise and ineffective unless undertaken after calm inquiry. . . .

All this is true; and yet it is also true that there are real and grave evils, one of the chief being over-capitalization, because of its many baleful consequences; and a resolute and practical effort must be made to correct these evils.

There is a widespread conviction . . . that the great corporations known as trusts are in certain of their features and tendencies hurtful to the general welfare. This . . . is based upon sincere conviction that combination and concentration should be, not prohibited, but supervised and within reasonable limits controlled; and in my judgment this conviction is right.

It is no limitation upon property rights or freedom of contract to require that when men receive from government the privilege of doing business under corporate form, which frees them from individual responsibility, and enables them to call into their enterprises the capital of the public, they shall do so upon absolutely truthful representations as to the value of the property in which the capital is to be invested. Corporations engaged in interstate commerce should be regulated if they are found to exercise a license working to the public injury. It should be as much the aim of those who seek for social betterment to rid the business world of crimes of cunning as to rid the entire body politic of crimes of violence. Great corporations exist only because they are created and safe-guarded by our institutions; and it is therefore our right and our duty to see that they work in harmony with these institutions.

The first essential in determining how to deal with the great industrial combinations is knowledge of the facts—publicity. In the interest of the public, the

Government should have the right to inspect and examine the workings of the great corporations engaged in interstate business. Publicity is the only sure remedy which we can now invoke. What further remedies are needed in the way of governmental regulation, or taxation, can only be determined after publicity has been obtained. . . . The first requisite is knowledge, full and complete. . . .

The large corporations, commonly called trusts, though organized in one State, always do business in many States, often doing very little business in the State where they are incorporated. There is utter lack of uniformity in the State laws about them; and as no State has any exclusive interest in or power over their acts, it has in practice proved impossible to get adequate regulation through State action. Therefore, in the interest of the whole people, the Nation should, without interfering with the power of the States in the matter itself, also assume power of supervision and regulation over all corporations doing an interstate business. This is especially true where the corporation derives a portion of its wealth from the existence of some monopolistic element or tendency in its business. There would be no hardship in such supervision; banks are subject to it, and in their case it is now accepted as a simple matter of course. Indeed, it is now probable that supervision of corporations by the National Government need not go so far as is now the case with the supervision exercised over them by so conservative a State as Massachusetts, in order to produce excellent results.

When the Constitution was adopted . . . no human wisdom could foretell the sweeping changes, alike in industrial and political conditions, which were to take place by the beginning of the twentieth century. At that time it was accepted as a matter of course that the several States were the proper authorities to regulate, so far as it was then necessary, the comparatively insignificant and strictly localized corporate bodies of the day. The conditions are now wholly different and wholly different action is called for. I believe that a law can be framed which will enable the National Government to exercise control along the lines above indicated; profiting by the experience gained through the passage and administration of the Interstate Commerce Act. If, however, the judgment of the Congress is that it lacks the constitutional power to pass such an act, then a constitutional amendment should be submitted to confer this power.

5. Jane Addams Explains the Need for Social Settlements, 1892

In a thousand voices singing the Hallelujah Chorus in Handel's "Messiah," it is possible to distinguish the leading voices, but the differences of training and cultivation between them and the voices of the chorus, are lost in the unity of purpose and in the fact that they are all human voices lifted by a high motive. This is a weak illustration of what a Settlement attempts to do. It aims, in a measure, to develop whatever of social life its neighborhood may afford, to focus and give form to that life, to bring to bear upon it the results of cultivation and training; but it receives in exchange for the music of isolated voices the volume and strength of the chorus. It is quite impossible for me to say in what proportion or degree the subjective necessity which led to the opening of Hull-House combined the three trends: first, the desire to interpret democracy in social terms; secondly, the impulse beating at the very source of our lives, urging us to aid in the race progress; and, thirdly, the Christian movement toward humanitarianism. It is difficult to analyze a living thing; the analysis is at best imperfect. Many more motives may blend with the three trends; possibly the desire for a new form of social success due to the nicety of imagination, which refuses worldly pleasures unmixed with the joys of self-sacrifice; possibly a love of approbation, so vast that it is not content with the treble clapping of delicate hands, but wishes also to hear the bass notes from toughened palms, may mingle with these.

"The Subjective Necessity for Social Settlements," in Jane Addams, *Twenty Years at Hull House* (New York: Macmillan, 1910), 97–100.

The Settlement, then, is an experimental effort to aid in the solution of the social and industrial problems which are engendered by the modern conditions of life in a great city. It insists that these problems are not confined to any one portion of a city. It is an attempt to relieve, at the same time, the overaccumulation at one end of society and the destitution at the other; but it assumes that this over-accumulation and destitution is most sorely felt in the things that pertain to social and educational advantages. From its very nature it can stand for no political or social propaganda. It must, in a sense, give the warm welcome of an inn to all such propaganda, if perchance one of them be found an angel. The one thing to be dreaded in the Settlement is that it lose its flexibility, its power of quick adaptation, its readiness to change its methods as its environment may demand. It must be open to conviction and must have a deep and abiding sense of tolerance. It must be hospitable and ready for experiment. It should demand from its residents a scientific patience in the accumulation of facts and the steady holding of their sympathies as one of the best instruments for that accumulation. It must be grounded in a philosophy whose foundation is on the solidarity of the human race, a philosophy which will not waver when the race happens to be represented by a drunken woman or an idiot boy. Its residents must be emptied of all conceit of opinion and all self-assertion, and ready to arouse and interpret the public opinion of their neighborhood. They must be content to live quietly side by side with their neighbors, until they grow into a sense of relationship and mutual interests. Their neighbors are held apart by differences of race and language which the residents can more easily overcome. They are bound to see the needs of their neighborhood as a whole, to furnish data for legislation, and to use their influence to secure it. In short, residents are pledged to devote themselves to the duties of good citizenship and to the arousing of the social energies which too largely lie dormant in every neighborhood given over to industrialism. They are bound to regard the entire life of their city as organic, to make an effort to unify it, and to protest against its over-differentiation.

It is always easy to make all philosophy point one particular moral and all history adorn one particular tale; but I may be forgiven the reminder that the best speculative philosophy sets forth the solidarity of the human race; that the highest moralists have taught that without the advance and improvement of the whole, no man can hope for any lasting improvement in his own moral or material individual condition; and that the subjective necessity for Social Settlements is therefore identical with that necessity, which urges us on toward social and individual salvation.

2. William Graham Sumner Elaborates the Principles of Social Darwinism, 1885

The competition of life has taken the form, historically, of a struggle for the possession of the soil. In the simpler states of society the possession of the soil is tribal, and the struggles take place between groups, producing the wars and feuds which constitute almost the whole of early history. On the agricultural stage the tribal or communal possession of land exists as a survival, but it gives way to private property in land whenever the community advances and the institutions are free to model themselves. The agricultural stage breaks up tribal relations and encourages individualization. This is one of the reasons why it is such an immeasurable advance over the lower forms of civilization. It sets free individual energy, and while the social bond gains in scope and variety, it also gains in elasticity, for the solidarity of the group is broken up and the individual may work out his own ends by his own means, subject only to the social ties which lie in the natural conditions of human life. It is only on the agricultural stage that liberty as civilized men understand it exists at all. The poets and sentimentalists, untaught to recognize the grand and world-wide cooperation which is secured by the free play of individual energy under the great laws of the social order, bewail the decay of early communal relations and exalt the liberty of the primitive stages of civilization. These notions all perish at the first touch of actual investigation. The whole retrospect of human history runs downwards towards beast-like misery and slavery to the destructive forces of nature. The whole history has been one series of toilsome, painful, and bloody struggles, first to find out where we were and what were the conditions of greater ease, and then to devise means to get relief. Most of the way the motives of advance have been experience of suffering and instinct. It is only in the most recent years that science has undertaken to teach without and in advance of suffering, and as yet science has to fight so hard against tradition that its authority is only slowly winning recognition. The institutions whose growth constitutes the advance of civilization have their guarantee in the very fact that they grew and became established. They suited man's purpose better than what went before. They are all imperfect, and all carry with them incidental ills, but each came to be because it was better than what went before, and each of which has perished, perished because a better one supplanted it.

It follows once and for all that to turn back to any defunct institution or organization because existing institutions are imperfect is to turn away from advance and is to retrograde. The path of improvement lies forwards. Private property in land, for instance, is an institution which has been developed in the most direct and legitimate manner. It may give way at a future time to some other institution which will grow up by imperceptible stages out of the efforts of men to contend successfully with existing evils, but the grounds for private property in land are easily perceived, and it is safe to say that no *a priori* scheme of state ownership or other tenure invented *en bloc* by any

Albert Galloway Keller, ed., *War and Other Essays by William Graham Sumner* (New Haven: Yale University Press, 1911), 167–192.

philosopher and adopted by legislative act will ever supplant it. To talk of any such thing is to manifest a total misconception of the facts and laws which it is the province of sociology to investigate. The case is less in magnitude but scarcely less out of joint with all correct principle when it is proposed to adopt a unique tax on land, in a country where the rent of land is so low that any important tax on land exceeds it, and therefore becomes indirect, and where also political power is in the hands of small landowners, who hold, without ever having formulated it, a doctrine of absolute property in the soil such as is not held by any other landowners in the world. . . .

We have seen that if we should try by any measures of arbitrary interference and assistance to relieve the victims of social pressure from the calamity of their position we should only offer premiums to folly and vice and extend them further. We have also seen that we must go forward and meet our problems. We cannot escape them by running away. If then it be asked what the wit and effort of man can do to struggle with the problems offered by social pressure, the answer is that he can do only what his instinct has correctly and surely led him to do without any artificial social organization of any kind, and that is, by improvements in the arts, in science, in morals, in political institutions, to widen and strengthen the power of man over nature. The task of dealing with social ills is not a new task. People set about it and discuss it as if the human race had hitherto neglected it, and as if the solution of the problem was to be something new in form and substance, different from the solution of all problems which have hitherto engaged human effort. In truth, the human race has never done anything else but struggle with the problem of social welfare. That struggle constitutes history, or the life of the human race on earth. That struggle embraces all minor problems which occupy attention here, save those of religion, which reaches beyond this world and finds its objects beyond this life. Every successful effort to widen the power of man over nature is a real victory over poverty, vice, and misery, taking things in general and in the long run. It would be hard to find a single instance of a direct assault by positive effort upon poverty, vice, and misery which has not either failed or, if it has not failed directly and entirely, has not entailed other evils greater than the one which it removed. The only two things which really tell on the welfare of man on earth are hard work and self-denial (in technical language, labor and capital), and these tell most when they are brought to bear directly upon the effort to earn an honest living, to accumulate capital, and to bring up a family of children to be industrious and self-denying in their turn. I repeat that this is the way to work for the welfare of man on earth; and what I mean to say is that the common notion that when we are going to work for the social welfare of man we must adopt a great dogma, organize for the realization of some great scheme, have before us an abstract ideal, or otherwise do anything but live honest and industrious lives, is a great mistake. From the standpoint of the sociologist pessimism and optimism are alike impertinent. To be an optimist one must forget the frightful sanctions which are attached to the laws of right living. To be a pessimist one must overlook the education and growth which are the product of effort and self-denial. In either case one is passing judgment on what is inevitably fixed, and on which the approval or condemnation of man can produce no effect. The facts and laws are, once and for all, so, and for us men that is the end of the matter. The only persons for whom there would be any sense in the question whether life is worth living are primarily the yet unborn children, and secondarily the persons who are proposing to found families. For these latter the question would take a somewhat modified form: Will life be worth living for children born of me? This question is, unfortunately, not put to themselves by the appropriate persons as it would be if they had been taught sociology. The sociologist is often asked if he wants to kill off certain classes of troublesome and burdensome persons. No such inference follows from any sound sociological doctrine, but it is allowed to infer, as to a great many persons and classes, that it would have been better for society, and would have involved no pain to them, if they had never been born.

ESSAYS

Social Darwinism: Adapting Evolution to Society

EDWARD CAUDILL

For a concept that seems so familiar to so many historians, the meaning of the term "social Darwinism" is strangely elusive. Despite the familiarity of the term, it is a misnomer. That social Darwinism could be derived from *On the Origin of Species* is obvious, but it is debatable whether Darwin supported the idea. Although he never endorsed the idea, Darwin did not protest the application of his biological theory to society, and passages from his writings even suggest that Darwin himself made such applications. For example, in his *Descent of Man*, Darwin wrote:

> The wonderful progress of the United States, as well as the character of the people, are [*sic*] the results of natural selection; for the more energetic, restless, and courageous men from all parts of Europe have emigrated . . . and have there succeeded best.
>
> With savages, the weak in body or mind are soon eliminated; and those that survive commonly exhibit a vigorous state of health. We civilized men, on the other hand, do our utmost to check the process of elimination; we build asylums for the imbecile, the maimed, and the sick; we institute poor-laws; and our medical men exert their utmost skill to save the life of everyone to the last moment. . . . Thus, the weak members of civilized societies propagate their kind. No one who has attended to the breeding of domestic animals will doubt that this must be highly injurious to the race of man.

Nevertheless, social Darwinism's relationship to Darwin himself is problematic for several reasons. First, the philosophy was attributed to the wrong person. Second, it was a *social* philosophy, based on the writings of the English philosopher Herbert Spencer, rather than a scientific theory. This distinction often was lost in popular accounts and, in later decades, in the work of eugenicists. Third, the ideas that eventually grew up around it, particularly in the field of eugenics, went far beyond even Spencerian ideas about evolution and human society.

Darwin responded to Spencer with a lack of enthusiasm, his remarks about the philosopher ranging from snide to befuddled. Darwin wrote to [botanist Joseph] Hooker that he was sorry pangenesis, Darwin's theory of heredity, perplexed Hooker, confessing "that it is abominably wildly horridly speculative (worthy even of Herbert Spencer)." On another occasion, Darwin admitted that he enjoyed his talk with Spencer, "though he does use awesomely long words." Darwin, with his habits of observation and inductive reasoning, confessed his exasperation in reading Spencer: "I am quite delighted with what you [Hooker] say about Herbert Spencer's

Edward Caudill, *Darwinian Myths: The Legends and Misuses of a Theory* (Knoxville: University of Tennessee Press, 1997), 64–68, 71–78. Copyright © 1997. Used with permission of the University of Tennessee Press.

book; when I finish each number I say to myself what an awfully clever fellow he is, but when I ask myself what I have learnt, it is just nothing."

Social Darwinism was not merely the adaptation of Darwinism to economics. Originally it was a social philosophy that applied evolution to human society. In this respect, the philosophy coincided with Darwin's insistence on seeking material and not supernatural explanations of phenomena. Social Darwinism gained its "tooth-and-claw" reputation because, too often, people explained competition in Darwinian terms but forgot about the role of cooperation in his theory of natural selection. In its popular origins, social Darwinism was not a rationale for eliminating the weak. For example, many social Darwinists noted the inevitability of suffering in society. This was not, however, a proclamation of the necessity of suffering; it was an empirical observation about the state of society. Social Darwinism also pushed evolution far beyond the evidence presented by Darwin, who worked largely in natural science rather than in the emerging social sciences. For the two individuals who are the focus of this reassessment of social Darwinism, improving society was the goal, not eradicating unfit people. Those two were the most prominent social Darwinists of America in the late nineteenth and early twentieth centuries: Spencer, the philosopher of evolution, and William Graham Sumner, a Yale professor of sociology. Spencer enjoyed greater fame and notoriety in America than in his native England, and his concept of survival of the fittest in society was the primary inspiration for Sumner's social philosophy. . . .

Social Darwinism and the Problem of Definition

Social Darwinism seems a very straightforward proposition: applying natural selection, Darwin's explanation of how evolution works, to human society. However, defining the idea has been difficult. It has been used to defend both socialism and capitalism, to explain the need for cooperation and for competition, and to justify both social harmony and conflict. The rise of eugenics in the early twentieth century added another layer of meaning to the term, incorporating Mendel's theories of heredity and Francis Galton's genetics. The ultimate consequence of eugenics—Nazi Germany's attempt to purify the "Aryan" race in the 1930s—gave social Darwinism an especially evil cast and destroyed whatever intellectual integrity it may have had.

Social Darwinism has encompassed concepts that are broadly evolutionary, as well as those that apply to society only the narrower theory of natural selection. A number of scholars in the twentieth century have written about the subject, with Hofstadter remaining the one cited most frequently. However, Hofstadter's very broad definition of the term blurs distinctions among important thinkers, especially between Darwin and Spencer, and is so expansive that just about anyone can be classified as a social Darwinist, merely by accepting the idea that life has evolved. Barzun, in *Darwin, Marx, Wagner,* notes the confusion surrounding the idea. Darwin's *Descent of Man,* Barzun says, "wobbled between keeping man under the regime of natural selection and putting him under the modified regime of cooperation, reason, and love." That work also wobbled between asserting the primacy of the individual and reserving primacy for the group. Was the fittest individual to survive, or the fittest group?

In addition, there has been debate over the extent of the influence of the movement. Hofstadter, Curti, and others assign it great power, while Wyllie and Russett believe that it was appropriated by the few, not the many. LaVergata points out that social Darwinism has been used to defend capitalism, socialism, and even anarchism. Interpretation, he says, ranges from seeing the idea as a merely reactionary phenomenon to seeing it as part of a larger movement of "biologism." Bannister, studying the "myth" of social Darwinism, does an excellent job of exploring this definitional morass, stating that social Darwinism "consistently derived its sting from the implication that the struggle and selection of the animal realm were also agents of change (and progress) in human society—the governing assumption being that men shared natural laws with the rest of Creation." So social Darwinism has been many things, including contradictory.

Spencer and Sumner: The Heart of Social Darwinism

Spencer, not Darwin, was the original and foremost social Darwinist. And in America, Sumner was the most eminent, visible, and vocale disciple of Spencer. Part of the strength of the idea of social Darwinism lay in its "scientific" foundation, which was extremely important to both Spencer and Sumner and greatly affected the meaning they attached to the concept. Spencer was a self-taught Englishman with an ambition to explain everything in the universe. Over the course of a dozen volumes of philosophy, he argued for an evolutionary philosophy of the universe, encompassing the inorganic and organic worlds, including human society.

Spencer was a social determinist who believed that society gradually would move toward its potential in a uniform manner. The progress of society would be accelerated by favorable conditions or slowed by neglecting or impeding those conditions, although social evolution could not be diverted from its general direction. He was a defender of free enterprise and was extremely critical of government intervention in the economy. Free competition, he argued, was a natural law of economics and the best guarantor of a community's well-being. Government interference with the natural law of competition would hinder social progress and ultimately would result in economic misfortune. From the end of the Civil War through the 1880s, Spencer influenced thinkers in virtually all intellectual fields and had a particularly strong impact upon the founders of American sociology. One of those founders was Sumner.

Sumner, who was most prominent in the 1880s and 1890s, always was oriented toward the practical consequences of his work. He taught the first sociology course in the United States (perhaps in the world) and offered the first methodology course in the subject. Sumner believed that state interference in any economic matter betrayed the individualism that was so highly valued in the nation and so firmly fixed in the laws of nature. For Sumner, competition was as much a natural law as gravity, and regulation of competition ultimately was as futile as attempting to regulate gravity. Sumner used Spencer's social determinism to battle reformers, who he believed were operating under the illusions that there were no natural laws of society and that society could be remade with legislation. Sumner attacked socialists, sentimentalists, and metaphysicians as well, as he advocated free trade and laissez-faire economic policies. He believed that Spencer's science would explode socialist and reformer fantasies. . . .

Spencer's "Survival of the Fittest"

It was Spencer, not Darwin, who coined the term "survival of the fittest," but Darwin incorporated it into later editions of *On the Origin of Species*. Spencer was not pleased with Darwin's preeminence in evolutionary thought. On several occasions, Spencer criticized Darwin and pointed out that he had preceded Darwin in publishing work on evolution. It did not escape Spencer, as it sometimes did other writers in popular periodicals, that Darwin's chief contribution was the idea not of evolution, but of natural selection, the mechanism by which evolution worked. A bit of jealousy was in the air at times, as Spencer and other writers for *Popular Science Monthly* found it necessary to show readers that Spencer had been publishing books and essays on evolution well before Darwin published *The Origin* in 1859.

Spencer's and his allies' struggles to establish his primacy in evolutionary thinking reveals a problem in studying social Darwinism—Spencer's criticism of Darwin. Struggling to differentiate himself from Darwin, Spencer said that the concept of natural selection was an "untenable hypothesis," basically because of what he called the assumption that it could "pick out and select any small advantageous trait; while it can, in fact, pick out no traits, but can only further the development of traits which, *in marked ways,* [emphasis in original] increase the general fitness for the conditions of existence." Spencer argued that it was not shown how the slight variations posited by Darwin actually were providing an advantage. Spencer subtly rejected an important part of Darwin's argument, and at the same time assimilated parts of Darwin's thinking into his system of synthetic philosophy. In discussing the evolution of society, Spencer said that it was "impossible for artificial molding to do that which natural molding does," apparently denying the relevance of Darwin's argument from artificial selection in domesticated animals. But, he stated, "in the absence of variety, life would never have evolved at all." Variation was, of course, a critical part of Darwin's explanation of evolution.

Spencer's attempts to distinguish himself from Darwin often were labored and his points unclear. Both men clearly saw "survival of the fittest" as being cooperative as well as competitive, but they differed on the significance of natural selection as an explanation of biological evolution. This latter point was the problem for Spencer because Darwin increasingly became preeminent in the realm of biological evolution, so much so that he appeared to be gaining credit in the public mind for all of evolutionary thinking. Darwin was a scientist, Spencer a philosopher. The theory of natural selection was of limited use to a philosopher but invaluable to a biologist.

Popular Science Monthly correctly considered Spencer a philosopher first and a scientist second. The philosopher's social Darwinism was far more complex than economic survival of the fittest, as Spencer attempted to embrace physical and intellectual vitality, along with individual and social progress. Most significant for Spencer and the popular concept of "survival of the fittest," however, is the fact that he was not endorsing a vicious, tooth-and-claw social order. Subsequent interpretations of social Darwinism often ignored the role of cooperation in evolution and dwelled upon competition, particularly when it was manifested as conflict. Spencer's brand of social evolution allowed for "sentiments and institutions both relaxing" from a predatory atmosphere. He attacked government welfare and embraced private charity.

Like Darwin, Spencer accommodated cooperation as well as competition in evolution. He did not want the less fit, "the feeble, the unhealthy, the deformed, the stupid" to be eradicated, but he suggested some "private industrial institution" to discourage their marriage and breeding. He conceded that suffering might be necessary to decrease government welfare, which encouraged a stratum of "worthless people." However, he believed that the movement from "state-beneficence to a healthy condition of self-help and private beneficence, must be like the transition from an opium-eating life to a normal life—painful but remedial."

Spencer opposed government but not private help. He believed that programs to aid the poor should promote self-help, in order that the poor might elevate themselves. His endorsement of self-help revealed a positive side of Spencer's social Darwinism. He was a critic of what he called the "pleasure-hunting life," which he believed would result in an unfit individual and, ultimately, an unfit society. Self-assertion and self-preservation, he said, benefited society by keeping the divisions of society strong, or "more fit." In numerous instances, Spencer's survival of the fittest was rather benign, notably lacking in tooth-and-claw logic. Spencer denied that he wished the principle to operate identically among people as among "brutes": "The survival of the fittest, as I construe it in its social applications, is the survival of the industrially superior and those who are fittest for the requirements of social life. . . . aggression of every kind is hateful to me; . . . I have urged the change of all laws which either inflict injustice or fail to remedy injustice."

Spencer explained that two "sets of conditions" were necessary in order for people living together to achieve the greatest happiness: justice and generosity. The closest that *Popular Science Monthly* came to espousing a brutal kind of social Darwinism was in an editor's column that criticized socialism's condemnation of economic competition. The problem, the editor said, was not "survival of the fittest," but human nature: "We have only to think for one moment of what the world would be in the complete absence of competition—in other words, in the absence of all means for selecting the fit and rejecting the unfit or the less fit—in order to see that competition in itself is not and cannot be evil. That evils attach themselves to it signifies nothing more than that human society is as yet imperfect." Most of the article was devoted to the "golden rule": Do unto others as you would have them do unto you. The editor argued that competition served that rule by promoting the general welfare of society via orderly and *fair* competition.

Spencer, in the pages of *Popular Science Monthly*, fit evolution to society. Contrary to popular interpretations, however, Spencer was not a Darwinian, and he actually disavowed natural selection. Riding the crest of popular interest that *The Origin* generated, Spencer agreed with Darwin that both competition and cooperation were critical to social, as well as biologic, evolution. This point was lost on later eugenicists.

Sumner: Putting Spencer into Practice

Sumner was a prolific writer and lecturer, but in some respects he contrasted strongly with Spencer. The latter man outlined fairly early in his career a twenty-year agenda for completing the multitude of volumes that would comprise his synthetic philosophy. He then set about writing the intellectually weighty tomes. Sumner, who praised Spencer as the man "who has opened the way" to sociology, was not so disciplined in publishing or so subservient to an agenda as his mentor. Much of his writing has survived as lecture notes, drafts of chapters, and essays that were never published, as well as in the form of wide-ranging articles for, and letters to, various newspapers and magazines. From 1869 to 1896, he wrote approximately 125 articles and letters for popular publications, including daily newspapers in New York and Chicago, and magazines such as *Collier's Harper's Monthly, Cosmopolitan, London Economist,* and *The Independent.* The specialty publications for which he wrote included the *New York Mercantile Journal,* the *Northwestern Lumberman, Rand McNally's Banker's Monthly,* and the *Bond Review.* His debates, too, were public matters. In 1883, in New York and New Haven newspapers, nearly twenty letters were exchanged, with Sumner opposing protective tariffs and a local linen manufacturer strongly favoring them.

Both Sumner and Spencer tended to publish in the upscale literary magazines most likely to have an educated audience interested in social, economic, and political issues. In *Collier's,* for example, one would find a literary orientation that attempted to rival *Harper's. Collier's,* founded in 1888, published the work of such writers as Rudyard Kipling and Frank Norris, the poetry of James Whitcomb Riley, and Henry James's serialized *The Turn of the Screw.* The magazine's content was a bit lighter than that of *Harper's,* which was viewed as both a model and a competitor, but the circulation of *Collier's* rose to three hundred thousand shortly after the turn of the century. Similarly, *Cosmopolitan,* founded in 1886, was a general literary magazine, not quite on the level of *Harper's* or the *Atlantic,* but comparing favorably to them. It was oriented more toward public affairs and by the 1890s was one of the leading illustrated magazines in the nation, noted for its coverage of current events as well as its fiction, which included work by William Dean Howells and Jack London. Compared to its competitors, *Cosmopolitan* carried more features on economic, political, and social issues, and here Sumner's writing fit very well.

Like Spencer's, Sumner's popular writings were concerned with large social issues, and "survival of the fittest" constituted only a part of his arguments. A character sketch in *Popular Science Monthly* very accurately and succinctly provided the context for studying Sumner, to whom the magazine attributed a philosophy that "denies anything arbitrary or accidental in social phenomena, or that there is any field in them for the arbitrary intervention of man. He therefore allows but very limited field for legislation. He holds that men must do with social laws what they do with physical laws—learn them, obey them, and conform to them." Sumner followed Spencer's thinking in believing that society, like nature, was subject to laws, and people were obligated to follow them, and should not attempt to tamper with them. The basic law, of course, was evolution. Furthering this philosophy was a major theme in Sumner's popular writing. For Sumner, the role of government was narrow. He stated, in his widely read *What Social Classes Owe to Each Other,* that government had to deal only with two primary things: "They are the property of men and honor of women. These it has to defend against crime."

Folkways (1907) was the book upon which Sumner's reputation came to rest. Sociologist Charles Horton Cooley compared *Folkways,* which was the first book to become a sociological classic in America, to *The Origin* in significance. Sumner's primary contribution to sociology was the introduction of general concepts that were based upon methodical observation and collection of evidence. His sociology was descriptive and based on facts, in contrast to Spencer's abstract philosophizing.

Sumner and "Natural Law"

Sumner paralleled Darwin in relying upon natural law, not metaphysics or theology, for answers to questions about the workings of the world. But where Darwin disciplined himself to stay within the confines of empirical science, Sumner did not, putting his energy into economic policy, immigration, tariffs, and any number of legislative initiatives that he saw as naïvely defying the law of evolution. This was Sumner's distortion of Darwinian evolutionary theory, as well as the way in which he applied the Spencerian philosophy to everyday political and social issues.

Sumner's intellectual relationship to Spencer is most apparent in the idea of an "organic" society. Like Spencer, Sumner declared that customs, including laws and regulations, had to evolve slowly in order to be effective: "Legislation and state action are stiff, rigid, inelastic, incapable of adaptation to cases. . . . Hence, the higher the organization of society, the more mischievous legislative regulation is sure to be." In the same essay, Sumner asserted that people were limited in their power and by their antecedents. The answer was "in ourselves," and there was no escaping the "struggle for existence."

Sumner believed that legislative meddling in the economy usually started with legislators and their backers, who worked in ignorance of the nature of society and economics. Typically they only made matters worse by attempting to change natural law. For example, he cautioned that regulating railroads should begin with knowledge gained by "experience and observation," and he even conceded that a regulatory commission might be a good idea—a concession that would not have been made by one espousing a merely antagonistic survival of the fittest. But Sumner warned that "blundering experiments in legislation cannot be simply abandoned if they do not work well; . . . they leave their effects behind." Sumner extended Spencer's "organic society" concept by making each component of a more complex society, like the organs of more highly evolved life forms, highly sensitive to changes in any other "organ" of the society.

This highlights one of the points of confusion about social Darwinism, as it was presented to the public: the "unit of analysis" problem. What was being studied, society as a whole or the individuals within society? Both Sumner and Spencer compared "organic society" to a biological organism, implying that society was the object of analysis; but they also spoke of individual fitness as being critical to the progress of society, suggesting that the essential concern was with the individual. This ambiguity invited conflicting applications of Darwinism. If the law acted upon society generally, then one easily could interpret it as advocating cooperation and regulation. If, however, the individual was preeminent, then competition and minimal government were the engines of progress.

Sumner drew not only from Darwin and Spencer but also from Malthus, who articulated the idea that a very real law affecting humanity was the ratio of population to available land. Populations would grow geometrically (2, 4, 8, 16), Malthus hypothesized, while resources grew only arithmetically (2, 4, 6, 8). Sumner called this one of the "facts of the social order . . . which control the fate of the human race." Ignoring these laws meant being unable to understand the workings of society. In the laws of nature, he said, "It will be found that men are subject to supply and demand, . . . and that any correct comprehension of the existing industrial system must proceed from supply and demand."

It was in this broader conception of laws that Sumner found a place for the idea of "survival of the fittest" in society. For both Sumner and Spencer, the concept of natural selection, or survival of the fittest, was actually an idea of secondary importance in understanding humanity. Unlike Spencer, who was working out a whole philosophical system, Sumner was dealing only with the sociological impact of Darwin's theory. The struggle for existence was necessary, according to Sumner, because it was dictated by natural law and could not be abolished. But for Sumner, to posit a struggle for existence was not to glorify men grinding one another out in bloody struggle. In fact, he condemned strife: "It is legitimate to think of Nature as a hard mistress against whom we are maintaining the struggle for existence. All our science and art are victories over her, but when we quarrel amongst ourselves we lose the fruits of our victory just as certainly as we should if she were a human opponent. All plunder and robbery squander the fund which has been produced by society for the support of society. It makes no difference whether the plunder and robbery are legal or illegal in form." He did not deny that "weaker" societies had perished at the hands of stronger ones, a pattern that he saw in history when civilized and uncivilized societies clashed, with the former usually emerging as victors. Europeans dominated the world, he believed, because they had been the most enterprising people in the fifteenth and sixteenth centuries.

Economic competition was, for Sumner, a law that forced individuals to develop "all powers that exist according to their measure and degree. . . . Liberty of development and equality of result are therefore diametrically opposed to each other." Individuals varied according to inherited powers, advantages of training, and personal attributes such as courage and perseverance; the results of their efforts varied accordingly. Millionaires, he said, "are a product of natural selection, acting on the whole body of men to pick out those who can meet the requirement of certain work to be done." Society benefited by imposing discipline on the economic system, as competitors studied the victor's winning ways, and by insuring that those talented in special areas eventually would find their way to those areas. In this fashion he reconciled a "ceaseless war of interests" with the betterment of the whole society.

The struggle for existence, Sumner said, was a struggle with nature. Moreover, "Competition . . . is a law of nature." He abhorred socialism, which he saw as a system making some people pay for the self-indulgence, idleness, and ignorance of others: "We shall favor the survival of the unfittest, and we shall accomplish this by destroying liberty. Let it be understood that we cannot go outside of this alternative: liberty, inequality, survival of the fittest; not-liberty, equality, survival of the unfittest. The former carries society forward and favors all its best members; the latter carries society downward and favors all its worst members." Socialism was mere sentimentalism that ignored the reality of society's fixed laws, "precisely analogous to those [laws] of the physical order." The socialist or philanthropist who saved victims of poverty was accused of "only cultivating the distress which he pretends to cure." Sumner believed that hardships were the products of thousands of years of evolution of human society and that poverty was part of the whole system. "This is a world in which the rule is, 'Root, hog, or die,' . . . It is the popular experience which has formulated these sayings. How can we make them untrue?"

Socialism's antithesis was individualism. Sumner called socialism a scheme to defraud an individual of liberty, "robbing him of his best chance of improving his position." The complaint against socialism was the same as the complaint against undue state interference in the economy—it would impede the natural progress of society by stifling the advancement of the fittest members. The "observation of facts will show that men are unequal through a very wide range of variation," he asserted, setting up the proposition that survival of the fittest was a scientific concept based upon observable fact. Even the idea that monopolies should be controlled by the state was a "sort of current dogma" that had not been adequately studied with attention to observable facts. Sumner's disdain for sentimental socialism, misguided reformers, and whimsical regulation was based upon his insistence on the necessity of looking at the "facts," of treating the study of society like a physical science, with observation, analysis, and verification at the core of the search for knowledge. Any other path, he believed, was mere speculation.

Sumner was willing to peel back the assumptions (which he felt commonly were paraded as facts) of human existence to a core of discomforting propositions: "Our assumption is that we should all be here, under any circumstances whatever, and that the provision for us here is, or ought to be, somewhere on hand. Unfortunately none of these ideas can be verified by an examination of the facts. We are not needed here at all; the world existed no one knows how long without any men on it."

Natural Law, Natural Selection

Sumner and Spencer stressed the results of a long evolutionary process on society. They offered social reality as evidence—the existence of the poor, the existence of weaker and stronger nations, and the economic progress of the U.S. under capitalism—and in doing so borrowed the prestige of Darwin and of science. They used the language of Darwin—employing such terms as "selection" and "organism"—but not his painstaking, tedious attention to collecting data in support of a theory.

As popularizers, . . . Spencer and Sumner were prominent at a time when science and social science were increasingly important in the academy and for the public. Social Darwinism justified a number of Victorian ideals: the divisions of society, the rewards of industry, the goal of "the good life," the virtues of civility and civilization. Hofstadter depicts social Darwinism as basically a defense of unregulated capitalism, a system of ideas that fit easily into the American mythology of the rugged individualist. Hofstadter recognizes the contradictory applications of social Darwinism, such as defending both socialism and capitalism, but he asserts that the American middle class's ideology of achievement made tooth-and-claw Darwinism the accepted version of the philosophy's many permutations. However, Spencer's and Sumner's writing in periodicals, which were aimed at middle- and upper-class audiences, reveal far greater complexity in the tenets of the movement. Although the robber barons might seize upon social Darwinism, such an application was only one act in the grander mission of uplifting all of society. This use of social Darwinism may have reached its zenith in Andrew Carnegie's 1889 article of social Darwinism, in which the author linked individualism, social divisions, and economic competition. But Sumner and Spencer reached a conclusion unlike Carnegie's, because their goal was to elaborate a coherent world view which might both explain society and establish an agenda for further sociological inquiry. Carnegie, as well as others who eschewed his simplistic view, were only defending the status quo.

Social Darwinism itself was well suited to popularization. Its core idea was rather simple: the survival of the fittest in human society. Although it had its complexities and contradictions, its essence was, and is, quite easy to convey in nontechnical language. The idea gained power and attention because it offered a good explanation of social problems, such as poverty and disease. At the same time, it provided a good defense of one's relative wealth and health. Thus, inequality could be seen not as a political or social problem but merely as the working out of natural law.

However, an incongruity arose in the association of Darwin with nonbiological social Darwinism. The nonbiological nature of the ideas espoused by Sumner and Spencer is shown in their attempts to divorce themselves from, and at times to criticize, the central tenet of Darwinism—natural selection. The social Darwinists could not divorce themselves from the Darwin name, nor would they have wanted to lose the credibility that association with his empirical science entailed. To the chagrin of Spencer, Darwin's name became a vehicle for popularizing an evolutionary philosophy. Through its association with Darwin and natural selection, the philosophy took on the aura of a science. For both Sumner and Spencer, so-called "social Darwinism" (neither of them used the term) was a secondary idea, not a primary one. Both derived their social laws from the broader concept of natural law, to which humanity, as well as the rest of the universe, was subject. Both Spencer and Sumner gave minimal credit to Darwin but were strongly identified with him. Charles Darwin was not central to the philosophy of social Darwinism in its popular origins.

Why Did Some American Businesses
Get So Big?

COLLEEN A. DUNLAVY

Why did big business in the United States become so big that in the late nineteenth century Americans came to demand antitrust legislation? Historians, by and large, have agreed that pure economic forces brought on concentration. But in taking this view they have neglected a strikingly different explanation that was widely propounded at the time it was all happening. This alternative view saw the bigness of some American business as the result of government policies—in particular, protectionism in the form of high tariffs. Because they believed that protective tariffs had encouraged excessive concentration, a number of them viewed free trade as one of the best remedies against the trusts.

The accepted view among business historians, strongly influenced by the work of Alfred D. Chandler, Jr., is that the extraordinary bigness of American business grew naturally from the workings of the market and the demands of modern, capital-intensive technology. The United States, already world-renowned for giant enterprise by the turn of the century, possessed both the world's largest domestic market and entrepreneurs capable of perceiving, exploiting, and expanding that market. In doing so, some built mass production enterprises of impressive proportions and then went on to integrate forward and backward, producing even larger firms, while others joined forces with their competitors, combining horizontally during the great merger movement (1895–1904). The two paths often intertwined, but the result in every case was enterprises of truly enormous proportions. U.S. Steel, formed in 1901, epitomized the process of concentration.

Colleen A. Dunlavy, "Why Did American Business Get So Big?" *Audacity, The Magazine of Business Experience* 2 (Spring 1994): 43, 45–47, 49. Reprinted by permission of American Heritage.

In 1898 Congress created the United States Industrial Commission. It immediately began investigating the trusts, and from April 1899 through early January 1900 it heard testimony from a broad array of public figures. Among the witnesses was the New York attorney John R. Dos Passos.

In testimony that filled nearly forty pages, Dos Passos defended economic concentration as a natural development that legislation should not—and could not—inhibit. History makes abundantly clear, he declared, the futility of legislation to block combinations, whether of manufacturers, distributors, or labor. "And the simple reason," he maintained, "is that the laws of trade, the natural laws of commercial relations, defy human legislation; and that is all there is in it. Wherever the two clash the statute law must go down before the operations of those natural laws."

John D. Rockefeller, the head of what was popularly termed the Standard Oil Trust, echoed this view in a written response to the commission in 1899. "It is too late to argue about advantages of industrial combinations," he flatly asserted. "They are a necessity."

Halfway across the country, Chicago's Civic Federation convened the Chicago Conference on Trusts in September 1899. "Some months since," the federation president, Franklin H. Head, explained, "no topic seemed so widely discussed as what was designated by the general title of 'Trusts,'—and . . . upon no current topic was there so widespread and general an ignorance and confusion of ideas." So the federation invited hundreds of men to Chicago for "a conference in search of truth and light." They included governors, attorneys general, state delegates, academics, congressmen, state and federal officials, representatives of chambers of commerce and boards of trade, and delegates from a large number of associations that represented agricultural, labor, and other interests.

Many speakers at the Chicago conference also concurred with the economic view. "Consolidations are the outgrowth and the symptom of the advancing civilization of to-day, and the inevitable tendency of its complex trade conditions," maintained a Pennsylvania lawyer, A. Leo Weil. David Ross of the Illinois Bureau of Labor Statistics observed, "Men talk of destroying such combinations by legal enactment, on the supposition, presumably, that it is possible and desirable to return to the simpler systems of the past." But it would do no good, he thought: "Our development as an industrial state is the result of trade conditions and opportunities which no legislative power could anticipate or control." Even the labor leader Samuel Gompers adhered to the economic view. "For our part, we are convinced," he explained, "that the state is not capable of preventing the legitimate development or natural concentration of industry." Instead Gompers merely wanted the right for his men to organize on a scale comparable to the level of organization achieved in industry.

Two years later a Chicago lawyer and the author of a two-volume tract on the law of combinations put the economic view succinctly. The legal world had not yet come to grips with combinations, Arthur J. Eddy observed; "the lack of harmony is only too apparent." But eventually the law would be brought in line: "Combination as an economic factor in the industrial and commercial world is a fact with which courts and legislatures may struggle, and struggle in vain, until they frankly recognize that, like all other conditions, it is a result of evolution to be conserved, regulated and made use of, but not suppressed."

The economic interpretation of the concentration movement then under way thrived in business circles in the ensuing years. "The business world generally," Francis Walker reported in 1912, "regards great combinations . . . as the natural and necessary development of trade, and declares in picturesque metaphor that 'natural laws can not be repealed by statute.'"

This is the view that has come down to us as a consensus, but it was nothing of the kind. On the contrary, out of the diversity of views expressed before the Industrial Commission, at the Chicago Conference on Trusts, and in print, a broadly opposing view emerged, one that saw dangerous economic concentration as a political phenomenon. The Industrial Commission recognized this broad dichotomy of views on the trust problem, and it concluded its hearings with testimony from both camps. Two men were called to speak on "general aspects" of the problem. One was Dos Passos; the other was the St. Louis lawyer Charles Claflin Allen, whose testimony filled another thirty pages and who took issue with Dos Passos on nearly every point.

Allen did not deny that *some* consolidations in the merger movement then under way "followed a natural normal tendency under economic laws," as the economic view maintained, but like others who endorsed a political view of trusts, he saw the bigness of American business as a product of the nation's industrial policy.

We usually associate the term *industrial policy* with direct intervention or "industrial targeting" of specific industries. But Chalmers Johnson, much acclaimed for his 1982 study of Japan's Ministry of International Trade and Industry (MITI) and Japanese policy, sees this as only one kind of industrial policy—what he terms *microindustrial policy.* More broadly, he argues, "industrial policy" also encompasses "all government measures [that] . . . have a significant impact on the well-being or ill-health of whole sectors, industries, and enterprises in a market economy." Thus what he terms *macroindustrial policy* comprises the array of policies (e.g., fiscal, monetary, trade, or labor policies) that subtly shape the broad environment in which business operates. Macroindustrial policies, in effect, create what Germans call the *Wirtschaftsordnung* (economic order).

Adherents of the political view of big business did not like the direction in which the American economic order was moving at the turn of the century, but it would be wrong to assume (as their contemporaries often did and as historians frequently do) that these critics opposed economic development or did not understand the value of large-scale enterprise. Their quarrel was with the form that economic change was taking. Those who saw economic change as fundamentally political in origin, as the historian Victoria Hattam suggests in *Labor, Visions, and State Power,* preferred a decentralized pattern of growth that would be devoid of concentrations of power. Seeing government policies at the root of the problem, they sought to revamp those policies to promote economic development along more decentralized lines. Therefore, they drew special attention to two aspects of late-nineteenth-century industrial policy: tariffs and railroad-rate regulation.

"The mother of all trusts is the customs tariff bill," Henry O. Havemeyer, the president of the American Sugar Refining Company, declared before the Industrial Commission in June 1899. Since he headed what was popularly known as the Sugar Trust, Havemeyer's statement generated a good deal of excitement. The potential benefits of horizontal combination, he argued, "bear a very insignificant proportion to the advantages granted in the way of protection under the customs tariff." He at first testified that tariff protection had helped the leaders of the iron and steel industries; but under questioning he admitted that his own sugar industry was affected too, conceding, as the commission's summary of evidence noted, "that had it not been for the high protective tariff existing at the time the original Sugar Trust was formed he would probably not have taken the risk of putting his refineries into the trust."

At the Chicago Conference on Trusts three months later, Havemeyer's opinions stirred considerable interest. Byron W. Holt, of the New England Free Trade League, applauded his comments. Havemeyer's views had "startled the country," Holt reported, but they ought not to have: "That the tariff, by shielding our manufacturers from foreign competition, makes it easy for them to combine, to restrict production, and to fix prices—up to the tariff limit—ought to be evident to every intelligent man." Among protected industries, he named "glass, furniture, leather, iron and steel, paper, coal, woolen goods, and silk goods"—not to mention Havemeyer's refined sugar—and he singled out for lengthy discussion the tinplate industry. "The heart of the trust problem is in our tariff system of plunder," Holt concluded. "The quickest and most certain way of reaching the evils of trusts is not by direct legislation against them, or by constitutional amendment, but by the abolition of tariff duties."

In *The Tariff and the Trusts,* a book published in 1907, the New York lawyer Franklin Pierce also laid the problem at the feet of Congress: "Our protective tariff is the genesis of the trust. The trust comes out of it as naturally as fruit from blossom. Obviously the control of a market by a combination or trust is facilitated where the field of competition is artificially limited to one country since it is easier to combine the producers of one country than those of all countries, and to that extent all must concede that the tariff encourages trusts."

The McKinley tariff of 1890 had raised rates to levels not seen since the Civil War, and the Dingley tariff of 1897 had pushed them even higher. Events in the business world since then, Pierce maintained, left little doubt about how the process worked.

But in one sense Pierce endorsed the economic view of American "bigness." He too saw the nation's large domestic market as essential to the rise of the trusts: "When the trust is established the very largeness of our country results in the largeness and success of the trust." But only market size and tariff protection working in tandem produced giant enterprise: "So vast a field secured to them from outside competition is tempting enough to invoke the energies of immense capital for its exploitation, and as a result gigantic trusts protected by the tariff come into existence with a power for evil in trade and politics which would be impossible in a small country, however high might be the tariff sheltering them from competition."

Although pessimistic, Pierce knew what should be done: "The true remedy against our trusts is to seek out the cause of a trust and remove that cause." He meant lower tariff levels: "Throw down the tariff wall which encircles every trust . . . and let the trust contend with the full stream of international commerce. If it continues to exist, it will be because it sells its products at home for cheaper prices than the cost of the imported foreign product."

But the necessary political action, Pierce thought, would demand "a rebirth of patriotism." His words sound oddly contemporary to the late-twentieth-century ear: "Let the people come together, not as Republicans nor as Democrats but as Americans loving their country and ready to join battle against the interests which corruptly rule it. There is no other question of importance before the country. It is simply a fight at close quarters between the people and this mighty system of wrong and corruption." In the late twentieth century his words would have rallied support for NAFTA—provided, of course, that *it* would not be surrounded by a new wall of protection.

Turn-of-the-century proponents of the political view also perceived another kind of tacit industrial policy promoting combination: railroad rate regulation, or more precisely the failure of regulation to eliminate discriminatory rates. "Numerous witnesses," according to the Industrial Commission's summary of evidence, "attribute the growth of combinations primarily to discriminating rates or other advantages given by railways."

Independent oil producers, for example, argued before the Commission that Standard Oil's market control depended on the special low rail rates that it enjoyed, even after creation of the Interstate Commerce Commission. M. L. Lockwood, the president of the American Anti-Trust League and an oil producer in Pennsylvania since 1865, maintained that the roots of the problem extended back to his first years in business: "Away back in the latter part of the sixties some of the refinery men in the oil regions who did not have the ear of the railway managers were unable to get a freight rate over the railroads that would enable them to sell their oil in New York and the export cities at a profit. They were obliged to sell the refined oil to the men who afterwards helped to create the Standard Oil Company, for these men even at that early date seemed to have an advantage in freight rates that enabled them to market oil at a profit when no one else could." He wanted it understood that his testimony was directed not at the Standard Oil men themselves but "against an accursed system of railway discriminations which has made this great curse, the Standard Oil Trust monopoly, a possibility. . . ."

Lockwood proposed three measures to combat monopoly: government ownership of the railroads, a policy of equal rates, and "a law forcing the great trusts and monopolistic combinations to fix a price upon their goods which, freights considered, will be the same in every township and hamlet of the land." Lockwood, like others at the time, saw capital-intensive industry in a class with natural monopolies and wanted to see pro rata principles applied to the mass production industries as well as to the railroads. A committee member interrupted to clarify Lockwood's views: Did he consider rate discrimination "the mother of all the great trusts of this country?"

Lockwood replied: "I do, largely, yes; that is really the foundation; a trust must be protected in some way; the brains of the country are not in the heads of a few men. The protection which has created the Standard Oil Company, the Big Four Beef Combine, and trusts and monopolies of that class, is that of discrimination in freights."

In these views Lockwood had the support not only of other independent oil producers but also of men outside the industry. Charles Claflin Allen concurred with and elaborated on Lockwood's views. "It is in the railroad companies that the greatest danger lies," he declared, for their discriminatory rates, contrary to law, formed the basis on which "the large trusts or combinations" accumulated "their wealth and power." At the Chicago conference testimony ran along similar lines, although with interesting variations. S. H. Greeley, of the National Grain Growers' Association, viewed railroads as "the very mainspring of many of the combinations and trusts, which are now crushing out the middle class in the United States." The "skillfully managed combinations" that controlled the grain trade of the Mississippi Valley, he said, had been "created by secret rates and special privileges, granted them by railroads." His solution was government ownership of the railroads.

Others at the Chicago conference went further, however, stressing the interplay of tariffs and discriminatory railroad rates. J. G. Schonfarber, a member of the Executive Committee of the Knights of Labor, neatly tied trusts to railroads [and] to tariffs, and he advocated political action to cut the knots that bound them: "Corporate ownership of railroads is the backbone of the trust and a protective tariff its right arm. It is within the limit of possibilities for the government, by the right of eminent domain, to come into the ownership and control of the railroad, and also to repeal the tariff tax upon every article controlled by a trust. Do both these things, and it is scarcely probable that trusts could exist at all." Implicitly, his words denied that concentration was a natural economic process. In his view, a trust problem created by government policy could be cured by government policy.

But not all those who adhered to the political view of big business agreed. The Democratic presidential candidate William Jennings Bryan also spoke to the Chicago conference, creating a great stir among the public. Although Bryan maintained "that the primary cause of monopoly is the love of money and the desire to secure the fruits of monopoly," he also allowed that high tariffs and discriminatory rates were contributing factors. "No question about it," he said of rate discrimination. But he did not think that lowering tariffs and equalizing rates would suffice. "The great trouble has been," he noted, "that, while our platforms denounce corporations, corporations control the elections and place the men who are elected to enforce the law under obligations to them." Thus he proposed that antitrust law be made uniform at the state and national levels and that it be made "a penal offense for any corporation to contribute to the campaign fund of any political party."

Such differences in strategy aside, these men clearly brought to bear a broader analysis than business historians and economists have employed in understanding how American business became so big. Viewing the world through the lens of a different political economy, they saw a de facto industrial policy at the root of the trust problem—and at least a partial remedy in free trade.